The Hudson Fourth Edition
Volume 2 Table of Cases
A Reprint

AUSTRALIA
Law Book Co.
Sydney

CANADA and U.S.A.
Carswell
Toronto

HONG KONG
Sweet & Maxwell Asia

NEW ZEALAND
Brookers
Auckland

SINGAPORE and MALAYSIA
Sweet & Maxwell Asia
Singapore and Kuala Lumpur

THE LAW

OF

BUILDING, ENGINEERING, AND SHIP BUILDING CONTRACTS

AND OF THE

DUTIES AND LIABILITIES OF ENGINEERS, ARCHITECTS, SURVEYORS, AND VALUERS;

WITH

Reports of Cases and Precedents.

BY

ALFRED A. HUDSON,

OF THE INNER TEMPLE AND THE WESTERN CIRCUIT; ONE OF HIS MAJESTY'S COUNSEL;

Author of "The Law of Compensation"; Contributor to "The Laws of England";
Joint Author of "The Law of Light and Air";
President of the Tribunal of Appeal under the London Building Acts, 1894 to 1908;
Commissioner under the Boiler Explosions Acts, 1882 and 1890;
Chairman of the Joint District Board for South Derbyshire under the
Coal Mines (Minimum Wage) Act, 1912;
One of the Panel of Chairmen of the Railway Conciliation Boards; and
One of the Panel of Chairmen of the Court of Arbitration for the Settlement of
Trade Disputes.

ASSISTED BY

C. S. REWCASTLE, B.A., LL.B.,

OF THE INNER TEMPLE AND THE NORTH-EASTERN CIRCUIT; BARRISTER-AT-LAW.

FOURTH EDITION.

VOL. II.

LONDON:

SWEET AND MAXWELL, LIMITED,

3, CHANCERY LANE,

Law Publishers.

1914.

[This is a copy of the original title page from the Fourth Edition published in 1914]

Fourth Edition 1914

Abridged and reprinted 2001

Published by Sweet & Maxwell Limited of
100 Avenue Road, Swiss Cottage, London, NW3 3PF
(http://www.sweetandmaxwell.co.uk)

Typeset by YHT Ltd, London
Printed and bound in Great Britain by Athenaeum Press, Gateshead, U.K.

No natural forests were destroyed to make this product:
only farmed timber was used and replanted.

A CIP catalogue record for this book is available from the British Library

ISBN 0 421 82730 0

Foreword © Ian Duncan Wallace QC

ISBN 0-421-82730-0

9 780421 827301

FOREWORD

Sweet & Maxwell are, in my opinion, to be commended for deciding to publish a reprint of Part I of Volume 2 of the Fourth Edition of Hudson, which was originally published in 1914. Parts II and III have not been reprinted. Part II consisted of a number of precedents, including the then RIBA form of contract and no less than 289 model forms of clauses for construction contracts and 65 forms of clauses for Specifications, as well as other miscellaneous forms such as bonds, guarantees and assignments of retention money. The model clauses principally serve to illustrate the extreme and repetitive prolixity (fee per folio driven?) of much nineteenth century legal draftsmanship, but are otherwise today of only incidental historical importance. Part III contained the then current scales of fees for architects and surveyors respectively. The decision not to reprint these two quite lengthy Parts of Volume 2 is in my view justified as having little relevance for modern practitioners or for a better understanding of construction contracts.

The cases reported by Alfred Hudson himself in the 478 pages of Part I are a different matter altogether. To understand their importance, it should be explained that, prior to the ubiquitous and perhaps excessive electronic retrieval of all High Court cases at the present day, barristers and judges have traditionally used a primary mixed database of official and unofficial law reports. Apart from the very early private reports in England known by the reporters' initials and later accorded semi-official status via the English Law Reports, the more important unofficial reports in 1914 would have included the Times Law Reports (T.L.R.); Law Times Reports (L.T.); Law Journal Reports (L.J.); and the Justice of the Peace Reports (J.P.). By 1948, when the writer was called to the Bar, the All England Reports, Lloyds' Reports and the much shorter Estates Gazette (E.G.) and Solicitors' Journal (Sol. Jo.) reports needed to be added and later Knight's Local Government Reports (L.G.R.). The novice practitioner's first task as a pupil at the Bar in 1948 was to learn to search this expanded database, supplemented by the English and Empire Digest, to extract reported material relevant to clients' problems in England and overseas.

However, particularly in specialist chambers, there was a further secondary (and sometimes crucially important) source of judicial material—namely the transcripts of judgments in unreported cases, only likely to be available on a "beg-borrow-or-steal" basis from the immediately involved litigants or their legal advisers. In most chambers individual barristers, or more rarely chambers collectively, would keep copies of unreported transcripts and notes of judgments in their own or colleagues' cases, or obtained from other chambers in the same field on a word-of-mouth basis or from the solicitors involved, if deemed valuable for future use. It seems a fair inference that nearly all the Hudson Volume 2 cases fall into this "privately collected" category of cases thought to be useful. Thus in relation to one of the most important cases in Volume 2 (on conduct short of fraud invalidating a certificate) which ultimately reached the House of Lords (and so became officially reported as *Hickman v. Roberts* [1913] A.C. 229), Hudson himself noted (Volume 2, pp. 425-6):

> "The history of the publication of the report in the following case will not be without interest. The case was decided in 1911, and *the author had prepared a report of the case for the purpose of his practice* as well as for publication in this edition of this work, because, though important to the highest degree, it had not apparently been thought worthy of report by any of the regular law reporters. In the course of an arbitration in which the author was engaged, however, he had occasion, while the report was still in manuscript, to cite it in the course of argument, and in that way it became known. (My emphasis)
>
> "Later, the manuscript was borrowed from the author by the Court of Appeal for use during the case of *Aird v. Bristol Corporation*, and the author was then requested to publish it, which he did in a Supplement to the third edition of this work. In that form it was used in the case before referred to in the House of Lords. After that judgment of the House of Lords had been delivered, a report of *Roberts v. Hickman* appeared in the Law Reports, [1913] A.C. 229.
>
> "The author has, however, thought it well to preserve the original report in this edition, as it is the only report, so far as he is aware, which contains the judgments in the Divisional Court and in the Court of Appeal. The report has been supplemented, as it now appears, by copies of the material portions of the correspondence".

Again, in relation to a very short summary of a case in 1860, decided by Blackburn J. sitting with a jury, a note is added as to its authenticity (Volume 2, p.6):

> The above was stated to be correct by Chambers QC [counsel in the 1860 case] in *Scrivener v. Pask*, 18 C.B.N.S. 785, 791, 792; L.R. 1 C.P. 715 718".

Sweet & Maxwell published Hudson's first three editions in 1891, 1895 and 1906. He himself begins to appear in the reports (as junior counsel and later as a junior leading a junior) in a very few of the Volume 2 cases from about 1900. By 1914, however, he had taken silk, was the author of three works in other areas of the law, as well as President, Chairman, Commissioner or member of no less than six statutory boards or bodies connected with mining, engineering or building. Furthermore, notwithstanding that Volume 1 of the Fourth Edition contained a list of *some hundreds* of named sets of reports (many relating to U.S. law) in its "List of Abbreviations" at pp. xxix to xl of its Introduction, it seems reasonable to assume that he had made so much use of his own "private collection" of unreported cases in the text of his book that he now felt the need to regularise their position more formally, which he then proceeded to do by recording them in Volume 2 of the 1914 edition. Incidentally, contrary to what has sometimes been unfairly suggested, there are only a very few cases reported in Volume 2 where Hudson himself was counsel. The impression from his selections is one of very great industry and of a pioneering and disinterested enthusiasm and concern for his chosen subject.

Volume 2 contains a total of 58 cases in chronological order, dating from 1853 to 1912. So far as I have been able to ascertain, no less than 45 of these have never been reported elsewhere. Only four of the original 58 cases no longer receive any mention in the latest 11th Edition of Hudson, and, perhaps rather surprisingly, no less than 41 are still dealt with by way of illustration, sometimes more than once. Even in those cases which have been reported elsewhere, the exceptional authority and experience which underlie Hudson's concise and vigorous headnotes, together with his industry in obtaining additional contractual information for some of the cases, and his occasional decisions to report first instances as well as appellate judgments, can make the Volume 2 reports a uniquely valuable and rewarding supplementary source of material.

All the cases reported in Volume 2 are of High Court or superior appellate status. Some of the earlier first instance judgments, particularly where the judge was sitting with a jury, could be very short due to the need in such cases for studiously concise directions identifying the nub of the point at issue for the jury's benefit, but lose little or nothing in the process. Referees' judgments are sometimes mentioned but not reported, while the first instance judgments are in many cases those of distinguished commercial judges who later became household names and to whom it can be inferred that construction cases were at that time being allocated. No doubt reflecting contemporary judicial attitudes, together with the lower importance then attached to construction cases, many of the reported judgments, whether appellate or not, can be seen from their wording to have been fairly obviously delivered *ex tempore*, again with little or no loss. There is also a degree of independence of view in the judgments and a less obvious desire than today to search for and comply closely with earlier authority, again not perhaps surprising in the light of the relatively cumbrous and informal reporting systems of the time and the comparative novelty and unimportance of construction contract disputes in the then thinking. This in turn leads to some inconsistencies in the cases in Volume 2 which, together with the need to take account of later case law or legislation and differently worded standard forms, may mean that the relevance of these cases at the present day needs to be modified or explained, as it is hoped the current illustrations and text in Hudson succeed in doing where this is necessary.

The six decades of cases covered by Volume 2 saw the Courts having to grapple for the first time with provisions involving the satisfaction or certificate of the owner's A/E (Architect/Engineer) entering into the forms of contract in use, with the need to distinguish and reconcile the role and powers of certifiers and arbitrators and to resolve difficult problems of interpretation as to the precise binding effect of A/Es' certificates, as well as to define the exact nature of any duty or responsibility owed to contractors by owners and A/Es alike in such situations, all in the face of highly obscure contract draftsmanship (probably due to the contemporary draftsman's lack of practical experience of site realities and of the typical disputes likely to arise in construction projects). This early case law, properly understood, remains of great value when interpreting certification provisions and, as is well known, this particular part of construction contract interpretation has continued to trouble modern judiciaries (often afforded equally little assistance by modern draftsmen in indicating their precise practical intentions). Many cases in Volume 2 thus serve to explain the modern principles and treatment of these provisions. Less relevant to the modern reader, though extremely interesting historically, are a number of cases dealing with problems arising from the very odd early practice of engaging quantity surveyors for the benefit of lump sum tenderers at the pre-tender stage, as well as the comparatively late emergence of the full remeasurement concept based on bills of quantities. Others more important at the present day include the early cases on clerks of works and resident engineers, on contractors' risks, on extension of time, and on indiscreet conduct by owners or A/Es invalidating or dispensing with the need for binding certificates.

It would be misleading to suggest that this Reprint can by itself be a textbook for newcomers to construction law. On the other hand, particularly in the context of the substantive interpretation of construction contracts, where Courts in all jurisdictions can and do go astray, no really serious student of the subject and no library of construction law, whether in practitioners' offices or elsewhere, should be without access to this first and earliest example of specialist construction law reporting. Volume 2 of the 1914 Edition remains a very important source of material which, in its present form, has become a rarity and difficult to acquire. Its new availability in the form of this reprint will be a considerable advantage for purposes of citation as well as research, and not least in enabling some of the current Hudson reasoning and explanations in disputed areas of substantive interpretation to be re-examined and if necessary debated more effectively.

I.N. Duncan Wallace Q.C.

TABLE OF CONTENTS

OF

VOLUME II.

PART I.

CASES REPORTED IN THIS VOLUME

TABLE OF CASES

CITED IN

VOLUME II.*

[* Publishers' Note: Please note, this is an abridged reprint of Vol II and that cases cited as appearing at pages 479 and beyond do not apear in this version.]

𝔍𝔫 𝔱𝔥𝔢 𝔠𝔬𝔲𝔯𝔱 𝔬𝔣 𝔔𝔲𝔢𝔢𝔫'𝔰 𝔅𝔢𝔫𝔠𝔥.

(*Before* Mr. JUSTICE ERLE and a Jury.)

TURNER *v.* GARLAND AND CHRISTOPHER.

Architect's Negligence—Novel Invention.

The plaintiff employed the defendant, an architect, to prepare plans for and superintend the erection of model lodging-houses after the latest improvements, and the plaintiff further instructed the defendant to put in a new patent concrete roofing, which cost only a quarter of what a lead or slate roof would have cost. The concrete roof proved a failure, let in water, and had to be removed and replaced, and the plaintiff sued the architect for negligence.

ERLE, J., charged the jury that though failure in an ordinary building was evidence of want of competent skill, but if out of ordinary course an architect is employed in some novel thing in which he has not experience, failure is consistent with skill; and the defendant had a verdict.

The plaintiff was Mr. John Turner, of North Brook, a gentleman eighty years of age; and the defendants are architects, in the Adelphi. Mr. Christopher had been for some years professionally employed by plaintiff. In 1848 he purchased for him the premises of Mr. Biers, the builder, in Dorset Place and New Street Mews, Marylebone. The plaintiff determined to erect a model dwelling house in the Mews, in place of the workshops; had a great variety of designs prepared, and took twelve months to determine. The architect was restricted as to the height of the building; it was to have a flat roof, and lead was too expensive; it was to be economical, to return 7*l.* per cent on outlay, and it was desirable that it should be fireproof, and include the latest improvements in buildings of this description.

In the autumn of 1848, Mr. C. being at Bristol, had his attention called to the principle, now known as Fox and Barrett's patent, at Northwoods; he was much struck with its apparent merits; he wrote on his return a letter, describing what he had seen, to the *Builder*, which was subsequently republished by the patentees, and sent to Mr. Turner, accompanied by a note of recommendation. It was not until August, 1849, that it was decided to adopt this mode of construction; then a contract was entered into with Messrs. Birds, builders, of Hammersmith, for the works generally, the iron girders being reserved for a special contract with Messrs. Grissell, the London founders, under the direction of Fox and Barrett, who furnished a detailed specification for the construction of the floors, roofs, and ceilings, on their patent principle, and sent the founders plans and sections of the cast-iron girders, with the proof weights to which they were to be tested; they also laid down upon the plans the position of each girder used.

The building was erected during the autumn and winter of 1849, and in April, 1850, possession was given up to the plaintiff, and it was immediately occupied. The roof, with ceilings, had cost 74*l.*, while an ordinary slated roof and ceiling would have cost 232*l.*, three times as much; and a lead roof would have cost 300*l*. The roof for a considerable time was considered a specimen of workmanship, and was seen and admired by many.

The builders' account was settled in November, 1850, and the architect's in, March, 1851. It was not until the summer of 1851 that anything of importance occurred to the roof, when it showed some serious cracks, through which the rain gained admission.

During June and July the defendant, by the desire of the plaintiff, surveyed the roof and reported the cracks were entirely superficial—not caused by any settlement or unsoundness of concrete—and suggested several effectual modes of making it watertight at a cost of from 20*l./ to 30l.*

In February, 1852, the roof was in part demolished, and a new roof of ordinary construction placed on it at a cost of 230*l.*

Mr. Bramwell and Mr. Unthank were counsel for plaintiff, and Mr. Bovill and Mr. Aspland for defendants.

ERLE, J., in the course of summing up, said: The plaintiff will merit your verdict, if the defendant was found to be wanting in the competent skill of an ordinary architect. If he possesses competent skill, and was guilty of gross negligence, although of competent skill, he might become liable. If of competent skill, and had paid careful attention to what he undertook, he would not be liable. You should bear in mind that if the building is of an ordinary description, in which he had had abundance of experience, and it proved a failure, this is an evidence of want of skill or attention. But if out of ordinary course, and you employ him about a novel thing, about which he has had little experience, if it has not had the test of experience, failure may be consistent with skill. The history of all great improvements shows failure of those who embark in them; this may account for the defect of roof.

The charge in the plaintiff's case is "the deflection and insufficiency of girders." The case was brought into Court on the insufficiency of the girders, and I am not aware of any other case on the part of the plaintiff. As the plaintiff's counsel declined putting it on any other ground, this was his case. Christopher is called on to give his evidence. His answer was, "the girders were sufficient." Grissell and Barrett, from their experience, are clearly of opinion that they are "quite adequate." Testimony to this is borne by the other witnesses, who severely tested the strength of the roof, and one of whom says it was strong enough "to bear a crowd of people to witness a passing show." Christopher had introduced it as a novelty, and if a novelty, I do not know how he could have taken better care than putting it into the hands of the Messrs. Birds, to whose high respectability testimony is borne by the plaintiff's counsel, and Messrs. Grissell, known to us all, and securing the co-operation of the patentees, and going down and consulting the architect of North-woods, and then getting plans (sections of the girders) from Barrett.

One thing dwelt upon was the omission of the tar-paper covering specified in the patent, but the Building Act prevents that being used, and something else had to be substituted, but it would not be a want of skill, for the moment not remembering the provisions of the Building Act. The plaintiff's counsel, after his admission as to the Building Act, would not contend this. It appears to me the defendant brought an earnest mind and careful attention to the work he had undertaken; and if he brought also competent skill, he ought not to be called upon to rectify any partial failure of the work. The new roof seems to me prematurely put on.

The jury brought in "Verdict for the plaintiff—damages, 30*l.*," with this written statement:— "The jury are of opinion that the novelty of the experiment is a sufficient excuse for the leakage, but consider the defendant was bound to make the roof watertight."

The judge held this was substantively a verdict for the defendants (on seeing it next morning), and the parties agreed to withdraw and stop proceedings.

1853
June 3.

Court of
Queen's
Bench.

𝕺𝖝𝖋𝖔𝖗𝖉 𝕮𝖎𝖗𝖈𝖚𝖎𝖙 (𝕸𝖔𝖓𝖒𝖔𝖚𝖙𝖍).

(*Before* BYLES, J., and a Special Jury.)

BOLT *v.* THOMAS.

Inaccurate Quantities—Quantity Surveyor's Liability.

The defendant, an architect, took out quantities which were appended to the tenders, and it was stipulated that the successful tenderer should pay the defendant:— Held, that the plaintiff, who was the successful tenderer, could sue the defendant for negligence in furnishing inaccurate quantities.

The plaintiff, H. P. Bolt, was a builder at Newport, and he sued the defendant, R. G. Thomas, who was an architect in the same town, to recover damages for supplying to the plaintiff an inaccurate statement of the quantities of work and materials required for the erection of a building which the plaintiff contracted to erect. The defendant advertised for tenders for the erection of a Baptist chapel, stating that the plans and specifications could be seen and that the quantities of work and materials would be furnished. The plaintiff obtained

1859
August 8.

Oxford
Circuit
(Monmouth).

1859
August 8.

Oxford
Circuit
(Monmouth).

from the office a table of such quantities, headed by a statement that it was to be paid for by the successful competitor. From this table the plaintiff calculated his tender, which was accepted, and according to the plaintiff's evidence, but contradicted by the defendant, the latter expressly stated to the plaintiff that he was responsible to him for the quantities. The defendant, however, admitted that in the plaintiff's absence he (the defendant) on one occasion assured the committee that the quantities were correct, and that he guaranteed them. There was a second claim made by the plaintiff in respect of a contract for building a gentleman's villa, the bill of quantities being headed "2 per cent. for quantities."

Huddleston, Q.C., and Smythies appeared for the plaintiff.

Whately, Q.C., and Phipson for the defendant.

Huddleston, for the plaintiff, contended that, independently of the computations, there was an implied undertaking in law that the bill of quantities paid for by the plaintiff should be reasonably correct.

Whately, for the defendant, contended that there was no contract between the architect and the builder; that the committee had stipulated with the plaintiff that he should pay the architect, and the architect was not liable to the builder for any inaccuracy in the quantities.

Byles, J., in summing up the evidence, directed the jury that the defendant had stipulated that the plaintiff should pay him for the calculation of the quantities, and having been paid for them by him, was liable to compensate him if the bill were not reasonably correct.

The jury thereupon found for the plaintiff, it being agreed that the amount of the damages should be ascertained by Mr. Barrett, a barrister.

Op. *Priestley* v. *Stone, post,* p. 134.

In the Court of Queen's Bench.

1860
February 7.

Court of
Queen's
Bench.

(*Before* BLACKBURN, J., and a Special Jury.)

SHERREN *v.* HARRISON (a).

Erroneous Quantities—Extras without Written Orders—Building Contract—Misleading Estimates—Extras.

Held, that a builder is bound by his special contract, however improvidently entered into, and cannot, in the absence of fraud or waiver, sue for extra work on the ground that the quantities are grossly erroneous and misled him.

The plaintiff, a builder, sued the defendant, a clergyman, to recover a balance of 1,483*l*. 17*s*. 9*d*. for extra work done beyond that specified in the contract and specification. The defendant paid into Court 209*l*. 15*s*., and said that that sum was sufficient to satisfy the plaintiff's claim.

M. Chambers, Day, and Martin for the plaintiff; Hawkins and Archibald for the defendant.

The defendant was a clergyman of the Church of England, and was desirous of building a small church at Northumberland Park, Tottenham, Middlesex, and in January, 1858, inserted an advertisement accordingly for plans, &c. in the *Builder* for a small church, to cost 2,000*l*. Mr. Mumford became the architect, and, as the plaintiff stated, induced him to become the builder and sign the building contract. The working drawings and estimated quantities were supplied by Mr. Mumford to the plaintiff, and there was sufficient evidence given to establish that he was acting as agent on behalf of the defendant. But the plaintiff's case was that the estimates and quantities so supplied by Mr. Mumford were so incorrect and false that they amounted to a species of fraud upon him, inasmuch as he was induced by means of them to sign the contract to do the work for 1,998*l*., whereas, when the work was subsequently done and quantities calculated, the cost was found to amount to 3,600*l*.

The miscalculations were proved by Mr. Eppy, of Lincoln's Inn Fields, and his statement was corroborated by Mr. Lewis and Mr. Lee, of the Adelphi. Mr. Mumford's estimates were said by the plaintiff's witnesses to be such as were very likely to mislead the plaintiff, who had been chiefly engaged in building public-houses, and had never previously built a church, and moreover that in them the quantities were quite incorrect. The written contract contained a stipulation that no extras were to be done or charged for without a written order from the defendant, and signed by Mr. Mumford. For the extra work done in this case there were no such written orders.

Hawkins, at the close of the plaintiff's evidence, submitted that there was no case, and that the plaintiff was bound by the written contract, however improvident the bargain he had made might be, and that, as there was no

(*a*) See also *Bottoms* v. *Mayor, & c. of York, post,* p. 208; *Macdonald* v. *Mayor, &c. of Workington, post,* p. 228.

SHERREN v. *HARRISON.*

1860
February 7.

Court of
Queen's
Bench.

written order for the extras by the defendant and no certificate by the architect, the plaintiff was not entitled to recover.

Chambers contended that the plaintiff was entitled to recover on this ground, that Mr. Mumford's drawings and estimates amounted to a fraud practised on the plaintiff, and that the defendant, having employed Mr. Mumford as his agent, was bound by his acts, and that in fact the case was the same as if the defendant himself had prepared and submitted the drawings and estimates to the plaintiff; and further, that the contract not being one under seal of the parties, it was competent to them to waive it by parol, and that there was evidence that the stipulation as to requiring a written order for extras had been waived.

BLACKBURN, J., ruled that there was no evidence to go to the jury on the question of fraud, and that, as to the extras, the written contract was binding, and that there was no evidence of waiver. He then directed the plaintiff to be non-suited, reserving leave to the plaintiff to move the Court above to set aside the non-suit on the grounds taken as above by Mr. Chambers.

The above was stated to be correct by Chambers, Q.C., in *Scrivener* v. *Pask*, 18 C. B. N. S. 785, 791, 792; L. R. 1 C. P. 715, 718.

1869

Court
of Exchequer
(Ireland).

In the Court of Exchequer (Ireland).

(*Before* BARON FITZGERALD.)

ARMSTRONG *v.* JONES.

Building Contract—Architect—Negligence in Superintendence.

The plaintiff had engaged B. to build a house for the plaintiff in accordance with certain plans. B. was to be paid on certificates by the defendant, the plaintiff's architect, to the effect that the house was properly built in accordance with the plans. The defendant certified and B. received payment from the plaintiff. The plaintiff sued, alleging that the house was not properly built in accordance with the contract, and that the defendant was guilty of negligence in superintendence.

FITZGERALD, B. (subsequently Lord Fitzgerald), charged the jury that the defendant would be responsible if they should find that the giving of the certificates arose from his negligence and want of caution in his duty of superintending the works, and that there was incumbent on the defendant the duty of skilled superintendence, and the plaintiff had a verdict.

This was an action to recover from the defendant, an architect and civil engineer, damages for alleged negligence in preparing plans, specifications, and working drawings for, and in superintending the erection of, a dwelling-house and premises for the plaintiff at Temple Road, Upper Rathmines. The case was at hearing for several days.

1869

Court
of Exchequer
(Ireland).

Baron FITZGERALD (the late Lord Fitzgerald), in the course of his charge to the jury, said that in substance the action was a complaint that the defendant had been guilty of a breach of duty. The defendant was employed by the plaintiff as an architect to prepare plans and specifications, and to superintend the execution of those plans and specifications, for the dwelling-house of the plaintiff. It appeared to him that when the defendant accepted this employment he came immediately under the obligation to exercise, both in the making of the plans and specifications and in the superintendence of the work, reasonable care, diligence, attention and skill; and if there had been any default on his part in that superintendence, from which actual damage had arisen to the plaintiff, then the defendant was responsible.

A very serious question arose upon the contract. It appeared that for the completion of the whole contract Mr. Bolton was to be paid 3,224*l.* 9*s.* 9*d.* The mode of payment was to be by instalments, but the right to receive any instalment could only be conferred on Mr. Bolton by the defendant's certificate, given under his hand, certifying that work had been done to the amount of 250*l.* at least. Then he was to be paid seven-eighths of the amount so certified. It was also provided by the contract that none of the certificates should be given unless the work was done to the satisfaction of the defendant, and in conformity with the contract. There was to be a final certificate, however, which would be conclusively binding on both parties–that was on Mr. Bolton and the plaintiff. The allegation of the plaintiff was that the defendant was responsible for want of due care, attention, and caution in the giving of these certificates. That allegation was the subject of the other three counts which they had to consider.

The contention of the defendant was, that he was only to be held responsible for an honest and *bonâ fide* performance of his superintendence, independent of care and skill. That appeared to him to be a question deserving of much consideration; but for the purpose of determining between the parties in the shortest and most inexpensive mode, he should ask them to treat it as that the defendant was responsible for the want of care, skill, and attention in the performance of his duty. If he was wrong in that, he would be set right; but, in the meantime, he would ask them so to treat it.

1869

Court
of Exchequer
(Ireland).

If they found that there had been want of reasonable skill, care, and attention in the superintendence of the works, then would arise the question of what actual damage arose to the plaintiff from this default of the defendant in his duty of superintendence.

The measure of damages could not by any possibility be what would be necessary to put the work in the condition required by the contract—that would be as against the party who was paid for the performance of the work; but now the damages should be measured as to what loss the plaintiff had suffered by reason of the negligent performance of his duty of superintendence.

It appeared six certificates had been given—1st, 27th April, 1867, for 500*l.*; paid 437*l.* 10*s.* 2nd, 31st December, 1867, 500*l.*; paid 437*l.* 10*s.* 3rd, 1st February, 1868, 500*l.*; paid 437*l.* 10*s.* 4th, 5th March, 1868, 1,000*l.*; paid 875*l.* 5th, 11th April, 1868, 500*l.*; paid 437*l.* 10*s.* There were certified in all 3,000*l.*, out of which had been paid 2,625*l.* On the 9th of July, 1868, the sixth certificate was given for 500*l.* on the contract; and 300*l.* for extras, together 800*l.*, out of which the sum payable was 700*l.* Now, as to the giving of the sixth certificate, it was given *ultra vires*, and the plaintiff could have refused to pay it— he was not compelled by the powers of the contract to pay it. It would be almost impossible to say that the giving of the certificate was not a gross want of caution, and very negligent, to say the least of it.

Now, the plea of the defendant was that this certificate was given by the leave of the plaintiff. It was a question whether this plea ought to have been allowed, but for the purposes of the present trial it was not necessary to consider it. It would be impossible to say that he did not pay this with full knowledge that 2,625*l.* had been already paid, and he or his attorney had the actual possession of the draught of the contract by which he was apprised that he was not compelled to pay, and yet he (Mr. Armstrong) made no complaint until February, 1869. He had now gone through the questions they had to try, and as they were as familiar with the evidence as he was, it was unnecessary for him to review it.

His lordship then left the following questions to the jury:—

> 1st. Were the houses and premises in Temple Road in any respect built of inferior or insufficient materials, or erected in an unskilful or unworkmanlike manner, or permanently injured or diminished in value, or were any deviations or omissions from the plans and specifications made?
> 2nd. Were they, or any of them, made or done by the authority or per-

mission, or by reason of want of reasonable skill, care and attention of the defendant in his superintendence of the works?

3rd. The damage arising to the plaintiff from such default of the defendant in said superintendence.

4th. Whether the certificates, or any of them, were given to the builder in respect of works which were not done to the satisfaction of the defendant, or according to the contract.

5th. Whether the certificates, or any of them, were given to the builder without taking into consideration deviations and omissions made by the builder in the work, and without making any deductions in respect thereof from the unit mentioned in such certificate or certificates.

6th. Whether the giving of such certificate was by reason of the negligence and want of caution of the defendant in his duty of superintending the works.

7th. The damage thence arising.

8th. Whether the 6th certificate was given through negligence and want of due caution on the part of the defendant in superintending the work.

9th. Whether the plaintiff, with full means of knowing the default of the said 6th certificate, acquiesced in and adopted the same.

The jury, after an absence of an hour and a half, returned, handed in a verdict, with an answer in the affirmative to each question, and assessing the damages on the 2nd and 3rd questions at 75*l.*, and on the 5th, 6th, and 7th questions at 5*l.*

1869

Court of Exchequer (Ireland).

𝔍𝔫 𝔱𝔥𝔢 𝔠𝔬𝔲𝔯𝔱 𝔬𝔣 𝔈𝔵𝔠𝔥𝔢𝔮𝔲𝔢𝔯.

(*Before* KELLY, Lord Chief Baron, and BRAMWELL and PIGOTT, BB.)

1870
Nov. 16.

Court of Exchequer.

EBDY *v.* M'GOWAN.

Architect's right to keep his Plans.

The plaintiff was an architect, who had been employed by the defendant to prepare plans and get tenders for a vicarage. The payment was to be 5 per cent. on money expended if the vicarage was completed; if tenders were obtained and work not commenced, 3 per cent. on the estimated cost; if no invitations for tenders issued, $2\frac{1}{2}$ per cent. The plans were prepared, but defendant then changed his mind and declined to proceed, and wrote to the plaintiff offering to pay, and asking for the plans. The plaintiff declined to give up the plans, but sued for payment, and set up a custom among architects to retain their plans if the work was not proceeded with:—Held, that such custom, even if proved, would be unreasonable, and that the defendant need not pay for the plans unless he got them.

This case was tried in London before the Lord Chief Baron. The defendant

1870
Nov. 16.

Court of
Exchequer.

paid into Court a sum of 101*l.* 5*s.*, and the plaintiff obtained a verdict for 97*l.* 12*s.* beyond that sum, the defendant having leave reserved to move to reduce the verdict by a sum of 60*l.* The case involved the vexed question whether the plans executed by the architect, and for which he is to be paid, are to be retained by him as his property. The plaintiff was an architect, and the defendant a clergyman at Homesdale, and the former was asked by the latter to prepare plans and specifications and get tenders for the erection of a church and vicarage house. About the work done for the church there was no dispute, although the question was stoutly fought at the trial, and the sole matter now before the Court related to the vicarage house.

The contract between the parties was that if the vicarage was completed, the plaintiff was to receive 5 per cent. on the money expended. If the tenders were given and the work not commenced he was to receive 3 per cent. on the estimated cost, but if the plans only were drawn, and tenders not issued, he was to have $2\frac{1}{2}$ per cent. on the estimated cost of the building. The plans were prepared, but the defendant, for reasons of his own, did not wish the work to proceed, and wrote to the plaintiff asking for his account, which he said he would settle, at the same time requesting that the plans might be sent to him. The plaintiff sent in his claim for the work and labour of preparing the plans, but declined to let the defendant have them, saying that they belonged to him. The defendant declined to pay without having the plans, and hence the action.

Aspinall, Q.C., in pursuance of leave reserved, moved to reduce the verdict by a sum of 97*l.* 12*s.*, or such sum as the Court should determine, on the ground that the plaintiff was not entitled to recover in respect of the parsonage house, without delivering or being ready to deliver to the defendant the plans, estimates, and other papers which were the result of his employment by the defendant.

Digby Seymour, Q.C., and Gainsford Bruce, showed cause for the plaintiff; Aspinall, Q.C., and John Edge, for the defendant, argued in support of the motion.

The plaintiff at the trial set up the usage or custom of the Royal Institute of British Architects not to deliver up plans, and called evidence in support of it. The defendant called a very eminent architect, Mr. Smirke, who swore that there was no such usage or custom, but the jury found in favour of the plaintiff. At the close of the arguments, their lordships said that the leave to move related only to a sum of 60*l.*, and in the interests of the parties suggested that some arrangements had better be arrived at between them as to the difference between that sum and the sum of 97*l.* 12*s.*, and eventually it was agreed that the 37*l.* 12*s.* should be reduced to 21*l.*, and the Court deal with the motion in accordance with the terms of the leave reserved.

The Lord Chief Baron KELLY, in the course of his judgment, said that the defendant had employed the plaintiff as an architect to build a vicarage house, and he was to act as such in relation to that building, and do the necessary work included in such employment. The plaintiff accepted the employment, and prepared plans and specifications, and solicited tenders for the work. While the work was proceeding

1870
Nov. 16.

Court of
Exchequer.

the defendant put an end to the plaintiff's employment of architect, and requested him to send in his account, and required that the plans and specifications might also be sent to him. The plaintiff wrote to say that he would send in his account, but would not deliver the plans, as he intended keeping them. Looking at the original contract between the parties, there was no stipulation either one way or the other as to the plans, either that the defendant was to have them, or that the plaintiff should retain them. Nothing was stated about them at all, except an objection to hand them over to the defendant.

The only question between the parties seemed to be whether, though not expressed, it was a provision of the contract that in the event of the employment of the plaintiff being stopped by the defendant, the plaintiff was entitled to retain the plans. If there was no such provision, the plaintiff had no right to retain them; if there was such a provision or stipulation, then he would have. The plaintiff gave evidence of a custom or usage among architects that, in the event of the employment of an architect being stopped, he was entitled to be paid for the plans and retain them.

Then came the question of fact, was there any such usage as the evidence for the plaintiff said existed? His lordship was not prepared to express an opinion on the evidence as it stood; but, supposing such a custom or usage to exist, then came the question, was it a reasonable one? He thought it was not. No such right as that set up by the plaintiff, viz., to retain the plans, existed, unless there was an express stipulation in the contract between the parties to that effect, and he could not accept the suggestion which had been urged upon the Court on the behalf of the plaintiff that such a stipulation was, by implication a part of the contract. It appeared contrary to reason, good sense, and justice that, in the event of a contract being put an end to, the architect should retain the plan for which he was entitled to be paid; it would require at least a clearly expressed stipulation in the contract to enable him to do so. The defendant was perfectly justified in refusing to pay until he had the plans. The execution of and the plans themselves formed the work and labour for which the architect charged the defendant, who was entitled to them if he had to pay for them. The rule, therefore, to reduce the verdict by the sum of 60*l.* would be made absolute.

Baron BRAMWELL agreed with the Lord Chief Baron, and stated that the question could not be said to be one governing the future, because parties to contracts might make their own bargains. The real contract between the parties was that the plaintiff was to receive $2\frac{1}{2}$ per cent. for the preparation of the plans upon the estimated cost

EBDY v. *M'GOWAN.*

1870
Nov. 16.
Court of
Exchequer.

of the building, and the 3 per cent. and 5 per cent. were contingent engagements after the preparation of the plans. The defendant had a right to say that he discontinued the plaintiff's employment or would stop it at the preparation of the plans. The defendant had a right to the benefit of the plaintiff's work before he paid for it. His lordship continued that he entertained a very high opinion of architects as a body; they were a very intelligent, high-minded, and useful body of men, and he wished to say nothing in disparagement of them, but was there such a usage as had been set up by the plaintiff, and which some architects had sworn existed? In his lordship's judgment the usage contended for was impossible; he could not help saying that it was perfectly suicidal; so soon as it was brought into being, it cut its throat with its own absurdity. Suppose an attorney to be employed to conduct a suit, and his client deemed it expedient to put an end to the suit and his attorney's employment at the same time, and paid the attorney his costs whatever they were, had the attorney a right to say that he would not deliver up the pleas, as they might be demurred to, and he would lose the costs of opposing the demurrer? If the work be carried on to a certain point, and not further, in all common sense a man is entitled to what he is compelled to pay for. Before usage could be insisted upon it must be proved to be one well known to prevail. It required the most rigid proof that it actually existed. It was very well for some two or three gentlemen to say there was such a usage, but he (the learned Baron) would like to see the public in the box, and hear what they had to say about it. Mr. Smirke, the architect, had stated there was no such usage as the plaintiff had set up. His lordship concluded by saying that he was clearly of opinion that there was no such usage, and that the defendant was entitled to the plans. If the defendant did not get them, he was paying for no benefit whatever.

Baron Pigott concurred with their lordships, saying that, looking at the contract between the parties, the question was free from all doubt.

The rule was made absolute to reduce the verdict by a sum of 60*l.*, the form of the rule to be drawn up to be settled by the Court.

𝕴𝔫 𝔱𝔥𝔢 𝔈𝔵𝔠𝔥𝔢𝔮𝔲𝔢𝔯 𝔠𝔥𝔞𝔪𝔟𝔢𝔯.

(In Error from the Court of Exchequer, 27th of November, 1874.)

1874
Nov. 27.

Exchequer
Chamber.

(*Before* Lord Coleridge, Chief Justice, Mr. Justice Lush, Mr. Justice Grove, Mr. Justice Quain, and Mr. Justice Archibald.)

LAIDLAW *v.* THE HASTINGS PIER COMPANY.

Building Contract—Waiver of Penalties by Payment—Implied Extension of Time by Engineer's Certificates—Countersigning of Orders for Extras dispensed with by Engineer's Certificate— Engineer's Certificate a Decision as to Differences.

The plaintiffs contracted to erect a pier for the defendants. Payments were to be made on production of the engineer's certificates. Penalties of 20*l.* a week were to be retained by the defendants if the work was not completed by the 16th of March, 1871; payments were made by the defendants after that date, without retaining any sum for penalties.

Held, that by so doing the defendants had, by their conduct, disentitled themselves to insist upon the penalties.

By the contract the engineer had power to extend the time for the completion of the work. He sent in certificates from time to time after the 16th of March, 1871, and in his final certificate no account was taken of the penalties.

Held, that this afforded evidence that the engineer had extended the time.

By the contract it was provided that no extra work should be paid for unless the contractors should produce special and positive written instructions for it, signed by the engineer, and countersigned by the chairman of the company. The engineer was to furnish monthly certificates of the value of the work executed, including extra work, and the contractors were to be paid 85 per cent. of the amount forthwith, and the balance at the expiration of three calendar months after the certificate of the engineer of the satisfactory completion of the work should have been given, provided that within three months after the giving of such certificate the contractors should have delivered to the engineer a full account of all claims which they might have upon the company, and he should have given a certificate of the correctness of such account. Any disputes or differences arising upon any matter connected with the contract were to be referred to the engineer, whose decision was to be conclusive.

The engineer certified for, as extra, work which had not in fact been done

1874
Nov. 27.

Exchequer
Chamber.

at all, and work which, although extra, had not been done on signed and countersigned orders.

Held (Mr. Justice Grove and Mr. Justice Quain dissenting), that the last certificate of the engineer precluded the defendants from raising the question whether extras had been done, or done without countersigned orders.

Held also (Mr. Justice Grove and Mr. Justice Quain dissenting), that the facts stated in the case showed that differences had arisen, and that the certificate of the engineer was a decision upon them within the meaning of the contract.

This was an appeal from a judgment of the Court of Exchequer in favour of the plaintiffs.

Mr. Watkin Williams, Q.C., and Mr. A. L. Smith appeared for the plaintiffs; Mr. Prentice, Q.C., and Mr. Holl for the defendants.

The questions which were raised, and the parts of the contract which are material, appear from the judgments.

LORD COLERIDGE, Chief Justice: This is an appeal from the decision of the Court of Exchequer. That Court decided that the plaintiffs were entitled to recover. Now, the plaintiffs are contractors who entered into a contract with the Hastings Pier Company to erect a pier. The stipulations of that contract, so far as they are material, I will allude to in a moment; but generally speaking the work was to be executed under an engineer, according to plans, drawings, and specifications, and there were to be from time to time payments of money on account, to the amount of 85 per cent. on work done under the contract, and on work done extra to the plans, drawings, and specifications of the contract, but provided for as extras within the terms of the contract itself. The work was done, and large payments were made from time to time, in point of fact, both for work done according to the plans, drawings, and specifications, and also for the work done extra to them. Considerable sums of money were paid upon monthly certificates by the engineer upon both heads of work. Now, the pier was completed, and has been taken-to by the defendants, and I do not understand that any complaint has been made as to the goodness of the work done. A large sum of money, between 15,000*l.* and 20,000*l.*, has been paid. The action is brought for a sum of between 5,000*l.* and 6,000*l.*, the balance said to be due upon the works specified for, and works extra those specified for. The sum of 2,000*l.* is paid into Court, and the action is brought for the remainder. A good many questions have been raised and argued before us, but substantially the objections taken by the defendants to the payment of the money plus the money paid into Court resolve themselves into but a few. First of all, they say these works were done extra to the contract. They were done extra to the contract, but in the contract itself are to be found provisions requiring them to be done in a particular way, and after certain conditions precedent have been fulfilled. The conditions precedent have not been fulfilled. They say the engineer who has certified for these works, which by the contract he must do before the plaintiffs could bring their action, exceeded his jurisdiction in so certifying; and we have a right to examine into the matter just as if he had not given those certificates; at all events, to the extent to which his jurisdiction was exceeded; and to that extent we decline to pay. We say that there are mistakes in these accounts, that the engineer has certified on mistaken grounds, that as to some matters, whether they have been done or not, in point of fact they have not been done according to the conditions precedent in the contract, and therefore we refuse to pay. Further, they say: "We have never led the plaintiffs to believe we did not intend to act on the terms of the contract; we have done nothing to change their position, or to disentitle us to insist upon the contract, and we insist upon it." Then, further, they say: "The contract stipulates for the payment by the plaintiffs of certain penalties in the event of the non-completion of the works within the terms of the contract within a specified time; that time has been exceeded, those penalties have been incurred, and we desire to set off those penalties against the sum of money claimed by the plaintiffs in this action."

Now, I will deal with the last question first, because it really has not been seriously argued before us. I am of opinion that the contention in respect of the penalties is not well founded. The Court of Exchequer decided against the defendants upon the question of whether they had a right to set off the penalties, and I am of opinion that the Court of Exchequer decided rightly. It appears to me that they have by their conduct disentitled themselves to insist upon the penalties, because the penalties, as I understand, are to be reserved*

1874
Nov. 27.

Exchequer
Chamber.

---

* The following is the clause in the deed referred to:—"The whole of the works . . . . shall be completed and handed over to the company by the contractors within fifteen calendar months after the date of the engineer's order to commence the work, and in case the said works are not completed within the said period of fifteen calendar months, or within such extended period as hereinafter mentioned (any delay that may arise from loss of vessels surveying the materials, or damage by storm, or other the act of God accepted), the said contractors shall forfeit and pay to the company 20*l.* a perk to be paid to, and retained by the company as ascertained and liquidated images; and not by way of penalty, for each and every week during which much work shall remain unfinished, after the expiration of the period above mentioned; and the engineer shall have power to delay the execution of the works on account of stormy weather or for any other cause which in his dis-

1874
Nov. 27.

Exchequer
Chamber.

or retained by them the moment they accrue from time to time; and they have not been so retained by them. They have paid money for fourteen months subsequently to the first accruing of the penalties (if they were entitled to act upon the penalty clause), and I am of opinion that they must be considered to have put an end to that clause of the deed. But, independent of that, I am of opinion that the clause of the deed giving the engineer power to extend the time for the completion of the contract puts them out of Court; that there is overwhelming evidence that the engineer did so extend the time. He sent in his certificates from time to time for work done after the time stipulated by the contract had long elapsed. His final certificate was sent in, taking no account of the penalties; and as no particular form is set out in this deed in which the engineer must exercise the power undoubtedly given to him, I am of opinion that he has exercised that power, and that on both those grounds our judgment should be against the defendants on this point.

Then there comes by far the most important question whether the provisions of the deed are so clear and the position of the engineer is so ascertained that the defendants are not entitled to take advantage of certain mistakes which from the case it is admitted might be discovered if it were possible to reopen the accounts certified by the engineer.* It is found that those mistakes amount to a considerable sum, it is not said what, but they are classed under various heads, into the details of which heads it is not necessary to go, but it is

cretion he may deem proper and sufficient, and shall also have power to grant such extension of time for completing the whole of such works as he may consider to be required in respect of any such delay or of any additions or alterations made to the works which may render an extended time necessary for their due execution."

* It was stated in paragraph 42 of the case that: "amongst the itemscharged for as extras in the plaintiffs' account, and included in the certificates given by the company's engineer, are claims made by the plaintiffs for work as extras which has never in fact been done. Also, among the items charged as extras in the said account and included in the said certificates are claims made for work and materials as extras which are in fact included in the drawings and specifications which formed part of the contract. Also, amongst the items charged for as extras and included in the said certificates are claims in respect of works and materials which have been substituted in lieu and instead of other works and other materials which were included in the contract, but which have not been executed; and although the plaintiffs in their said account for extras and the engineer in his said certificates have included the full value of such substituted works and materials, they have made no deduction therefrom or allowance in respect of the works and materials so included in the contract, but left unexecuted."

1874
Nov. 27.

Exchequer
Chamber.

enough to say in general that it is ascertained by the case that there have been mistakes. The sums awarded are certified by the engineer, and the important question in the case is whether the defendants are entitled to discredit his certificates, to go behind them and to reopen the accounts he has so certified. Now, I think they are not, and I agree with the Court of Exchequer that on this point, too, judgment should be entered for the plaintiffs.

Now, this deed is a deed in some respects of a peculiar kind. It does not appear to have been drawn according to the exact precedent of any other deed which, at least in the decided cases I have looked at, has been brought under discussion in a court of law, and there has been a great deal of argument in discussing the particular provisions of the deed in order to ascertain what is the exact position of the engineer of the company under it. Now, the points which it is alone material to state for this purpose are these: there is a claim by the plaintiffs; there is a resistance by the company; and there are certificates which, if they are final and cannot be examined, are conclusive that the sum of money sued for in this action is due to the plaintiffs. The questions upon this matter are simply: is the final certificate, and are the other certificates, of the engineer conclusive as to the facts ascertained in them, so that the defendants must pay, even if there have been errors in those certificates, which, for the purpose of discussing the question, I will assume to be the fact. Now, the matter has been argued upon several grounds, distinguishable in idea and distinguishable in point of fact. It has been said, first of all, that the engineer is placed in a position under the deed to exercise particular functions, and that the case has arisen for the exercise of those functions, that he has exercised them in fact, and that his exercise is therefore conclusive upon the parties. It has also been put, not exactly that he fills the position of agent to the defendants, clothed with peculiar functions as between the plaintiffs and the defendants, but that he is by the terms of the deed–I do not like to use the word *quasi*-arbitrator, because the moment you introduce the word *quasi* you introduce indefiniteness into legal decisions–but I take it that it must be understood he is made by the deed an arbitrator, and if there has been a reference to him of matters in dispute between the plaintiffs and the defendants, he is made arbitrator by the deed, and his decision is final.

Now, I think, speaking for myself, that the true view of the engineer's position under the deed is not the latter, but the former view. I do not think that he is an arbitrator under the deed. I do not think that a submission of differences in the ordinary sense of the

1874
Nov. 27.

Exchequer
Chamber.

word, and a decision thereupon as an arbitrator's decision, was
necessary under the provisions of the deed. He appears to me, from
the beginning to the end of the deed, out of the four corners of which
his position and authority are to be collected, to have been treated as
agent to the defendants, but agent to the defendants clothed with
peculiar functions, and those are to be exercised in certain cases
provided for by the deed; and when he exercises those functions, they
are to be conclusive, or otherwise, according as the deed provides.
Now, let us see what are those provisions. I do not propose to read the
whole of the deed, but to take merely one or two provisions which
have to do with the matter now in dispute. The deed, after a recital
that the plaintiffs have agreed to execute certain works and to
complete them, the completion to be certified as hereinbefore
mentioned, goes on to provide that the drawings and specifications
contained in the schedule hereto annexed, and the provisions of these
presents, shall be taken together to explain each other, and that if in
the execution of the work it should be found that anything has been
omitted or any discrepancy exists between the drawings and
specifications, or between the different portions of the drawings
themselves, or if any doubt should arise as to the intent or meaning of
any part of them, reference shall be made to the engineer, whose
decision shall be conclusive. I apprehend, therefore, without discussing what the earlier part of these words may mean, that if a doubt
arose as to the drawings and specifications, to the extent of its being
disputed whether a particular amount of work or a particular kind of
work was or was not within the fair construction of the contract, or
was an extra outside the contract, that was a matter of which
reference should be made to the engineer, and that upon that fact the
engineer's decision should be conclusive. I quite agree that the
provision, stopping there, says nothing about payment, and therefore
it would be quite true that so far the deed would only provide that in
the event of the question arising, extra or no extra, the decision of the
engineer upon that fact would be final and conclusive, leaving the
other matters as to payment and so forth unprovided for. Then it goes
on to say shortly afterwards that the execution of the works shall be
carried out under the entire control and superintendence, and
according to the directions of the engineer, or of a superintendent
approved by him, and that the contractors shall attend to and execute
without delay all orders and directions in respect of the execution of
the contract given to them by the engineer or superintendent. Here,
therefore, is a provision subordinating the plaintiffs in the execution
of the works entirely to the engineer, or to a deputy to be appointed

by him, and at once and without delay they are to execute all orders and directions in respect of the execution of the contract given them by him. That must include, not only in its very terms, but in any reasonable construction of it, extras. I should think in its very terms it must include extras, because the contract provides for extras and contemplates extras. In a contract of this kind, almost of necessity, something not specified for will arise in the execution of the works, and when it does arise, and the engineer orders it to be done, the contract makes it an absolute and unqualified duty on the part of the plaintiffs to execute it without delay. That is important as showing the position in relation to the plaintiffs which the engineer, the agent of the defendants, occupies. I agree, further, that there is no stipulation here as to the payment, and it is left entirely at large so far. It is important as showing the great control taken by the defendants into their own hands through their engineer.

1874
Nov. 27.

Exchequer
Chamber.

Then we come to the question of what may be called extras; and upon the question of direct extras the provision is this: "In case the engineer shall consider it desirable to order additional work, or to increase, alter, or diminish the quantities, or the dimensions, or alter the character of the works described in the contract, drawings, and specifications, such additions, diminutions, or alterations shall not in any way vitiate this contract, but shall be performed by the said contractors under all the conditions, stipulations, and responsibilities therein contained, in like manner as if they had been expressly described and included in the specifications and drawings." Now, that makes all extras and additional work ordered by the engineer as if it had been included in the contract. It brings the execution of such extras within the provision I have just read, and subordinates the plaintiffs in their execution to the absolute and uncontrolled authority of the engineer, who can order them to be executed without delay. They are to be executed in every respect as if they had been included in the contract, "save and except that the value of such additions, diminutions, and alterations shall be estimated according to the schedule of prices hereto annexed, and the value so ascertained shall, as the case may require, be added to or deducted from the money payable to the said contractors under these presents." Then these distinct extras are made part of the contract, are subordinated to all the rules of the contract, are put under the authority of the engineer, and when done they are to be paid for according to the schedule of prices, and are to be paid for as if they had been performed under the direct stipulations of the contract, that is, by

1874
Nov. 27.

Exchequer
Chamber.

monthly instalments up to 85 per cent. upon certificates to be given by the engineer.

Now, so far as to the power of the engineer and the duty of the plaintiffs, up to this point there is nothing said as to payment. Then comes the provision on which reliance has been placed by the defendants: "And the contractors shall not be allowed to plead any acts, orders, or directions of the engineer or any person acting on his behalf in justification of any departure from the requirements of the contract, unless they shall produce special and positive written instructions to such effect, signed by the engineer, and countersigned by the chairman of the company." That particular provision is not material, because it is not said there has been any departure from the requirements of the contract. But it goes on to say that no additional or extra work, that is to say, the additional or extra work that is described in the paragraph to which I have been referring, "shall be paid for, unless it has been executed under the authority of such signed and countersigned instructions."

Now, therefore, it is in effect said, you must do it, but before you do it you must have signed and countersigned instructions, or you will not be paid. If that stood alone and nothing further was to be found in the contract, that no doubt would be a very strong passage in favour of the defendants, and it is upon that passage I conceive that the argument for the defendants must mainly rest, and on which the difference of opinion, which I regret to have arisen on the Bench, I believe is founded. That says, they shall not be paid for unless they are done upon orders signed by the engineer and countersigned by the chairman of the company. Then it goes on to say how they shall be paid, and some way on in the contract this passage occurs, and as the whole of it is important, it must be taken together, and upon the construction of it I, for my part, base this portion of my judgment: "The engineer shall furnish monthly certificates of the value of the work executed and materials delivered, which certificates shall also include any extra or additional work, according to the terms of this contract, and 85 per cent. of the amount thus certified shall be forthwith paid to the contractors, and the balance shall be paid at the expiration of three calendar months after the certificate of the engineer of the satisfactory completion of the works shall have been given, provided that within three calendar months after such certificate the contractors shall have delivered to the engineer a full account in detail of all claims they have on the company, and the engineer shall have given a certificate in writing of the correctness of such claims; and if at any time during the progress or after the completion

1874
Nov. 27.

Exchequer
Chamber.

of the contract any disputes or differences shall arise between the company and the contractors as to the manner of executing the works, or as to the quality and quantities of the materials employed, or as to any charge, or as to any other account or thing arising out of or connected with the contract, the disputes or differences shall be referred to and settled by the engineer, whose decision shall be binding and conclusive on both parties; and that in case of non-performance by the contractors of any of the stipulations contained in these presents, the engineer shall be at liberty to withhold all or any of the certificates until such stipulations are complied with, and the decision of the engineer shall be final in respect of every question concerning the construction of the works to be done by the contractors, and the plans, sections, and drawings, and the nature of the materials, and the completion and condition of the work."

I say that even if those provisions ended with that which states that the monthly certificates were to be given, and that 85 per cent. was to be paid at once, and the remaining 15 per cent. within three months after the completion of the whole work to the engineer's satisfaction, I think it would be difficult to say that the defendants could go behind the final certificate of the engineer, and could claim to reopen all the questions with regard to the extras, which had been done to the satisfaction of the engineer, done upon the orders of the engineer, which the contractors could not upon the terms of the contract refuse to perform at once and without delay, upon the ground that some of them or the majority of them had not been done in point of fact on signed and countersigned orders, and that the defendants could resist payment on that ground. The signature and counter-signature is no doubt a condition precedent to the right of payment, but so is the completion of the work; so is the completion of the work to the satisfaction of the engineer; but so are a variety of other matters all conditions precedent. But all those matters are to be taken into account, as it seems to me, by the engineer, the agent of the defendants, to protect them; and when a request is made for the sending in of an account, the right to which is to be ascertained by certificate, the engineer is to go into all those matters, is to satisfy himself that the conditions precedent to a right to payment have been fulfilled; and he would have neglected his duty if he had certified for any work if any of the stipulations of the contract which he, as the agent of the defendants, was to enforce had not been complied with by the plaintiffs. But when the engineer has once ascertained, and has once given his decision, that the right to those payments has arisen, a condition precedent to their arising being this, that and the

1874
Nov.
27.

Exchequer
Chamber.

other circumstances having occurred, it does not lie in the mouth of the defendants, it seems to me, who have placed their own agent in the position of absolute control over the plaintiffs to see that the work is done, and not to certify unless it is done according to the contract, to say, You have neglected your duty to us, and therefore we will not pay according to your certificates. If it were not for the difference which exists on the Bench, I should have said it was a clear enough thing that, even if it stood alone, these certificates would be conclusive, and the defendants would be bound by them; but it does not stop there, for it goes on to say, in words which I have read once, and which I will not repeat, but which I will only say appear to refer to every kind of dispute or difference that could arise upon the contract, that if any dispute about those works, or any charge or account whatever should arise between the plaintiffs and the defendants, the engineer of the defendants is to decide, and his decision is to be binding on both parties. It seems to me, therefore, that upon that ground, too, which requires little further explanation, it is plain that the plaintiffs must succeed in this action, because, as I think, differences and disputes did arise between the plaintiffs and defendants—differences and disputes contemplated in this very section of the contract; they were submitted, within the meaning of the contract, to the engineer of the defendants, and he decided thereupon, and his decision is therefore binding. He decided as he was bound to do in the discharge of his duty. Therefore, whether I look at the matter as a matter of certificates *simpliciter*, or whether I look at it as a dispute and difference decided in the form of a certificate, in either case it appears to me that on the true construction of this contract these certificates are conclusive, and that the defendants must pay.

Now, I think that differences did arise, and that there was a submission and a decision within the meaning of this contract. (His lordship then examined the evidence bearing upon this question, and continued:)

Now, it appears to me that there was a claim made for a certain sum in respect of certain extras, that those extras were matters the payment of which the defendants intended to dispute, that the matter was referred in the fair ordinary sense and meaning of that word to the engineer, because he was asked to look to it, and to take this and that into account before he decided, that he did look through it, and did ascertain that certain things were, in his opinion, due, and that certain things were not due, and that he certified for the balance which he thought was due, and in my opinion that was a decision within the meaning of the contract. It seems to me that a technical

1874
Nov. 27.

Exchequer
Chamber.

submission and a regular formal reference were not required by this deed. (His lordship then stated that he thought that the case of *Goodyear* v. *The Mayor of Weymouth** was rightly decided, and that the principle of that case was applicable to the present, and said that in his opinion the plaintiffs were entitled to judgment, and that the judgment of the Court of Exchequer should be affirmed.)

Mr. Justice Lush: I do not think that it is necessary that I should add anything to the judgment which has just been delivered by my Lord, and I simply desire to state that I agree with him in all that he has said.

Mr. Justice Grove: Upon the two main points the balance of my mind is against the judgment of the Court of Exchequer. Upon the question of penalties I agree with my Lord and my brother Lush. The difference of opinion which I am now expressing does not arise upon any legal principle, but I cannot see that the facts make out such a case as, it seems to me, ought to be made out before an explicit provision in the deed is entirely abrogated. Now, that provision is. "In case the engineer shall consider it desirable to order additional work, or to increase, alter, or diminish the quantities or the dimensions, or alter the character of the works described in the contract, drawings, and specifications, such additions, diminutions, or alterations shall not in any way vitiate this contract, but shall be performed by the said contractors." I do not read the rest of it, but I give every force which can be given to the remaining words, and I quite admit that if that clause stood alone, and if that portion of the deed had ended with the words "under these presents," that that would have given the engineer power to order any extras, and to insist on their being performed, and that the company would be liable to pay for them. But then the deed goes on thus, and it follows so immediately that it must be taken as part of the same provision: "And the said contractors shall not be allowed to plead any acts, orders, or directions of the engineer, or of any person acting on his behalf, in justification of any departure from the requirements of the contract, unless they shall produce special and positive written instructions to such effect, signed by the engineer, and countersigned by the chairman of the said company, and no additional or extra work of any kind or description whatsoever shall be paid for unless it has been executed under the authority of such signed and countersigned instructions." The meaning of that appears to me to be this: the engineer, when extras are wanted, is to draw up instructions, and before those in-

---

* *Goodyear* v. *The Mayor of Weymouth*, 35 L. J. C. P. 12.

1874
Nov. 27.

Exchequer
Chamber.

structions have the force of an order, they must be countersigned. If I rightly read the word "order" as an order consistent with the contract, unless that is either dispensed with by a waiver or overridden in some way, it appears to me that the defendants are entitled to the benefit of that clause which they have inserted for their own protection, and without which they would be at the mercy of their engineer. The object of the clause seems to me to be extremely plain. The question is not what is the meaning of the clause, but has it been dispensed with or overruled by the conduct of the parties, or by the authority vested in the engineer by another provision of the deed. (His lordship then referred to those parts of the case and of the correspondence which bore upon the question of waiver, and proceeded:) I cannot see that there is any satisfactory proof that the defendants, either by the correspondence or by their conduct coupled with the correspondence, waived that provision.

Now, I come to the only other point upon which I have the misfortune to differ from other members of the Court. I am bound to give the result of my judgment on the matter, and that is, that the last certificate does not amount to a decision within the meaning of the reference clause. It does not amount to a decision of the arbitrator, and therefore is not so final and binding as to excise from the deed the provision as to counter-signatures by the defendants. Now, the provisions of the deed are as follows. (His lordship then read the arbitration clause.)

Now, it seems to me that here the position of the engineer is changed. Up to this time, in all parts of the deed the engineer is supposed to be a representative, to a great extent, of the defendants; but here he is invested with a new character, because here, when a dispute has arisen between the contractors and the company, it is to be referred to and settled by the engineer. I admit that extras would come within this clause. I quite concede that no particular form of reference is necessary, but I think that it should be substantially understood between the parties that there is a dispute which the engineer is to decide in the capacity of judge, and not as the defendants' representative. I do not think that the correspondence shows that he has decided as judge, having heard the representations of both parties. My Lord has read the correspondence. It amounts to this: A certificate is sent in for 2,000*l.* beyond the contract price. The defendants wrote and complained of this to the engineer. But the engineer, although frequently written to by the order of the directors, never sent an account with observations as requested by them. The engineer never appears to have entered into the matter in the capacity

1874
Nov. 27.

Exchequer
Chamber.

of judge. He first sends in a certificate that 1,500*l*. is due on account of
the contract and extras, and says that he will decide the balance as
soon as possible, and communicate the result. Does "decide" then
mean, "I will decide the matter as judge," or does it mean, "I will look
into the matter, and see whether the work has been done"? It admits
of both interpretations. But then they request to have a copy of the
account with his observations, which seems to me to mean this: "We
will not dispute about any extras which we think necessary or
desirable, but we have retained a voice as to extras within the
contract; let us look into them before you decide." He does not
furnish them with the materials they ask for, but he ultimately gives a
certificate, not as the decision of a judge, but a certificate stating that
the plaintiffs have done work to the amount of 570*l*. That is the last
certificate, and it appears to be in the form of the previous certificates.
Therefore, it does not appear to me that here the engineer really did
take upon himself the functions which he had a right to take upon
himself, or which the parties might invest him with under the deed,
but that he absolutely does not adopt the character of being a judge,
instead of the representative of the defendants, and actually sends in
his account without listening to them or telling them, "I am going to
give judgment against you; have you anything to say on the subject?"
If the engineer had, as in the case of *Goodyear* v. *The Mayor of
Weymouth*,* been an absolute judge of the matters, quite irrespective
of any control which the defendants might exercise, the case would
be different. Chief Justice Erle there says: "The architect was the
supreme judge as to extras and additions. This undefined claim as to
work said to be independent of the contract would be within the
words 'contracted for and connected therewith.' " Mr. Justice
Keating says: "The contract gives the architect jurisdiction over all
extras and additions," which, I venture to say, the contract here does
not, "and all the items resolve themselves into these." Therefore it
does not appear to me that the facts of this case bring it within the
case of *Goodyear* v. *The Mayor of Weymouth*, because here the
engineer has two functions to fulfil, the one as engineer, in which he
would come within that case, having arbitrary powers as to what he
should compel to be done, and how he should compel it to be done
by the plaintiffs, and also to give certificates which are compulsory
as to payment by the defendants; but when it comes to a dispute as to
extras, I do not think that they are within that arbitrary power. If
he has to decide as a judge, he changes his functions, and he could

* 35 L. J. C. P. 12.

1874
Nov. 27.

Exchequer
Chamber.

not then decide as if they were going on with the work over which he had arbitrary power. He should, at all events, perform the first function of a judge, which is to hear both sides before he decides. At all events, he should have let the parties know that he intended to act under this clause as a judge. It appears to me that he has not done so, and therefore I cannot say that I am satisfied that he did act under that clause. If he did, I should agree with the majority of the Court that his decision was final. As the majority of the Court are in favour of the respondents, it is unnecessary for me to enter into the other parts of the case.

Mr. JUSTICE QUAIN: In this case I agree with my brother Grove, and think that the judgment of the Court of Exchequer should be reversed. I have, therefore, the misfortune with him of differing from the judgment of this Court, and from the judgment of the Court of Exchequer; but having considered this case according to the best of my judgment for two days, I am unable to agree with the conclusion at which the majority of the Court have arrived. I might probably have contented myself with saying that I agree with my brother Grove, for the reasons he has given, and in which reasons I entirely concur; but seeing the importance of the case and the great weight of authority against us, I feel it right to state my own views for coming to this conclusion.

Now, the first question we are asked is, are the certificates of the engineer conclusive of the amount to be paid by the defendants to the plaintiffs, so as to preclude the defendants from going in any way behind the certificates, or making any deduction in respect either of unfounded charges or for penalties? And I find that in paragraph 30 of the case the same contention is stated on behalf of the defendants. They contend that the certificates, without mentioning any particular certificate, are conclusive. I confess I was at first rather astonished that those certificates, which were given from time to time, and which, as the recital of the deed states, are given merely for the purpose of enabling the contractor to get instalments from time to time to put him in funds, as it were, for carrying on the work, and which are given from month to month hastily, and in which there are often mistakes by the contractor's agent on the one hand, and by the engineer on the other, should be considered conclusive, either as to the work having been done, or as to the value of it. These certificates are merely provisional and temporary. I am now speaking of what are called "progress certificates," given from time to time solely with the view of enabling the contractor to get the 85 per cent., and

1874
Nov. 27.

Exchequer
Chamber.

I have never heard, until the contention in this case, that in any sense of the word they could be considered conclusive.

Now, I think I am right in saying that it is not contended now that these certificates given from time to time are conclusive if you could show that the work contained in them was never done. But I believe it is now contended that these certificates, taken together with the document of October 19, are conclusive of this case, and that they shut out all inquiry even as to whether the work was ever done to which they relate, or whether those extras were executed under proper authority. That is a very strong proposition, and it appears to me that it lies upon the plaintiffs to make it out to the fullest extent.

Now, let us see what the certificates are. They are described in the way in which certificates are generally described, and it is recited, "And whereas the company have agreed to advance to the contractors from time to time during the progress of the works so contracted to be done by them, sums of money by way of instalments upon account of and in part payment of the works then actually done and executed by them, such executions to be certified by the engineer of the company." Therefore they are for the purpose of paying in advance during the progress of the works sums of money by instalments. I do not really understand on what principle any such certificates, really for the purpose of calculating the amount of the instalments to be paid on account, can be conclusive as to the work that was done, or whether there was any work done, or whether there were extras or not. It strikes my mind as obvious that this kind of provision is intended merely as temporary and provisional, leaving a considerable margin, so that when the parties come to the end of the contract, they shall consider what and how much is to be paid.

This is what is called a lump sum contract; it is not a contract to be paid for by measure and value. It has a schedule of prices to regulate the extra work. Where are there any words in the case that make these certificates in the slightest degree conclusive, or that state that you shall not go behind them to show that there were mistakes in them? I should say that the strongest possible words were necessary to make it conclusive. I find no such words here, and the very nature of it appears to me to be in direct opposition to such a view.

The progress certificates went in from time to time, and finally a certificate is given on the 14th of October for 1,500*l.*, and a further and final certificate for 570*l.* is given on the 29th of October, being the last progress certificate given by the engineer, and on that day he sent in a detailed account—he does not call it a certificate—at the bottom of which he wrote these words: "The above account as altered

1874
Nov. 27.

Exchequer
Chamber.

in red ink is approved by me." Now, that is not a certificate for the 570*l.*, because he had no authority to give it. That did not become due until three months after he had given his certificate that the works had been satisfactorily completed, which he did on the 14th of October. That document was sent in under the express provision of the contract which provides, "And the balance shall be paid at the expiration of three calendar months after the certificate of the engineer of the satisfactory completion of the works shall be given, provided that within three calendar months after the giving of such certificate the said contractors shall have given to the engineer a full account in detail of all claims they have on the company, and the engineer shall have given a certificate in writing of the correctness of such account." In order, therefore, to entitle them to the balance within the three months, upon the 14th of October a full account must be sent in to the engineer, which this is, and be approved and corrected by him. That explains what is the meaning of that document, and shows, in my judgment, if anything else is wanted, that that document is not a decision under the arbitration clause, but that it is merely sending in a detailed account and approving of its correctness in compliance with the proviso of the deed. If the certificates, therefore, as certificates, are not conclusive, the only thing that can make them conclusive is a decision under the arbitration clause of the deed; and really the struggle in the case is, and the difference of opinion in the Court arises, as to whether these certificates, and that last document which I say is not a certificate, amount to a decision. If they do, then I agree that if there has been a decision of the arbitrator, however erroneous it may be, the company are bound by it. Even if there had been such a decision, I have some doubt whether this question of the extras could be so submitted to the arbitrator as to justify him in dispensing with the express provision of the deed, because it seems that by the deed the company determined to keep the control over that provision, and therefore the arbitrator could not take upon himself to decide it. It is unnecessary to decide that, because I am of opinion that there was no decision under the arbitration clause which was binding and conclusive upon the parties.

The wording of the deed with reference to the extra works is so special, and so unusual in its stringency, that it is well to direct attention to it again. (His lordship then read the provision as to extras.) Therefore, they say, in effect, this is a matter they will not trust entirely to the engineer; they will not be bound even by his written order; but they will keep their own control over it, and they

1874
Nov. 27.

Exchequer
Chamber.

will take care not to be liable for extras, unless there is the order of the engineer countersigned by the chairman. It is said the certificates are conclusive—you cannot go behind them. But how can it be presumed that because the engineer has given a certificate the chairman had countersigned the orders?

With regard to the question of waiver, it is an elementary principle that you cannot waive that which you do not know of. Now, it cannot be argued that up to the 16th of January, 1871, the directors had any knowledge that for the last twelve months any extra work had been done. The certificates do not ascertain the extras, and they never saw the accounts which were sent in by the contractors to the engineer. On that day they receive a letter, which shows that the contractors had a dispute with the engineer in reference to an undoubted extra–screwing the piles deeper than was shown in the drawings. There is no doubt, therefore, that that is a letter relating to extras, and calling the attention of the company to a dispute with their engineer. To that letter all that the company said was that they could not enter into a correspondence on the matter, and that copies of the contractors' letter had been sent to their engineer, and to their solicitors, who would reply to it if necessary. Now, as I have said, to get rid of such a stringent clause as that, strong and unambiguous language is essentially necessary. Now, I do not think it is likely that the company, having no knowledge of what extras had been done up to that time, would give a general authority to their engineer to dispense with this special provision of the contract; and, accordingly, their solicitors, to whom they have referred the plaintiffs' letter of the 16th, write to the plaintiffs, and say that the directors will require them to carry the contract into effect in all respects, and that as regards all matters of detail they must refer them to the engineer. I do not think that this was dispensing with the countersigned order, or that, by referring the contractors as to matters of detail to the engineer, the directors intended to put themselves entirely into his hands, and to give him the power of dispensing with this provision in the deed, by which, up to that time, they had for their own protection kept from the engineer the power of ordering extras without their express authority.

The only remaining question is whether the certificates amount to a decision of the arbitrator. The clause in the deed is, in my opinion, a strict arbitration clause. It is not like a case where a man buys property or agrees to do work at a price to be fixed by a third person. (His lordship then read the arbitration clause, and the paragraphs in the case showing that the directors repeatedly requested the engineer

1874
Nov. 27.

Exchequer
Chamber.

for his observations on the account which included the extras.) Now, I do not think that the note of the engineer, "Approved by me," at the foot of the account was, or was intended to be, a decision under the arbitration clause; but if it was so intended, I consider the decision null and void, inasmuch as the engineer had express notice that the defendants wished to be heard. For these reasons I agree with my brother Grove in thinking that the judgment of the Court below is wrong.

Mr. Justice Archibald: I agree in the opinion taken by my Lord and my brother Lush, and I concur in the reasons given by my Lord. We are all agreed as to the claim for penalties. In my judgment the defendants are not entitled to succeed upon that claim. In the first place, they were in default; and in the next place, I agree that there is abundant evidence of the extension of the time.

With regard to the certificates, I think that they are made conclusive by the terms of the deed; but, if not, I agree that they have been made conclusive and binding by what has taken place.

In my experience, contracts of this description have been repeatedly altered and added to, with a view of making them more stringent upon the contractor, and the mode in which that has been done is by giving the engineer or architect supreme control over the contract. But if his authority is binding as against the contractor, it must, of course, be equally so in those cases in which he is made absolute judge against the parties with whom he contracts. And, in looking at the terms of this contract with regard to extras, it appears to me that we must not only endeavour to harmonise the two portions of the deed to which allusion has been made by my brother Grove, but there is another portion which must be harmonised. In the first place, we find a stringent clause binding the contractor to obey the orders of the engineer, and then we come to the part which relates to extras. There is a provision that the engineer may, without in any way invalidating the contract, give directions for the performance of extra work. And then follows this clause. (His lordship read the clause referring to extras.) It is said that the meaning of those two clauses taken together is that the engineer may give orders for extra works, but that those orders must be signed by him and counter-signed by the chairman of the company. But then there is another part of the deed to which we must give effect, which is the provision with regard to certificates. (His lordship read the clause with regard to certificates.) Now, it is upon those certificates that the contractors are entitled to receive payment of the 85 per cent. The duty of preparing those certificates, and of ascertaining how much is to be

1874
Nov. 27.

Exchequer
Chamber.

certified for, what amount of extra work has been actually done, and whether that extra work has been done in accordance with the terms of the contract, devolves upon the engineer, and before he can give his certificate he must of necessity form a judgment as to whether extra work has been done, and whether orders have been given to do the extra work within the terms of the contract. He may make a mistake, he may come to a wrong determination, as to whether the orders are sufficiently within the terms of the contract; but I think it is clear that he is to form an opinion on that point; and that it necessarily precedes the granting of a certificate, and without it he is not in a position to grant a certificate within the terms of the deed. Therefore, harmonising these together, although it may be that the order must be signed and countersigned, yet, when it comes to the giving the certificate, the engineer must have decided that point before he gives it. That appears to be the *ratio decidendi* of the case of *Goodyear* v.*The Mayor of Weymouth*,* and the Court there decided on the ground that those were matters within the competency of the engineer to deal with, and that unless he had dealt with them no certificate could be granted, and that having dealt with them, his decision was final.

But I also think that those certificates are conclusive on the defendants, on the ground that this dispute having arisen about the extras, the engineer has decided and settled the matter. It is said that, with regard to that description of questions, he was in the position of an arbitrator. It appears to me that there is some misapprehension on that point. I say it with respect, but it appears to me that the engineer stands in the position of a valuer. I do not think it can be supposed that he was to decide upon the question of extras otherwise than upon the grounds of his own skill, observation, and knowledge in those matters. It seems apart from the intention of the parties that he should summon the contractors on the one hand, and the directors on the other, and go into a regular inquiry, receiving observations from one and the other as to any dispute that might arise. Clearly, if a dispute were to arise during the progress of the work as to whether certain things were extras, he would decide it then.

When we come to the other part of the deed, spoken of as the arbitration clause, I can see no difference, because when carefully looked at it relates to precisely the same description of questions: "If at any time during the progress or after the completion of the con-

* 35 L. J. C. P. 12.

1874
Nov. 27.

Exchequer
Chamber.

tract any disputes or differences shall arise between the company and the contractors as to the manner of executing the works, or as to the quality or quantities of the materials employed." How did they intend that the engineer was to decide as to the quality of the work? Is he to decide as a skilled man, or is he to have a regular argument with the contractors on one side and the directors on the other? It seems to me that the latter construction cannot be put upon the clause—"or as to any charge or account, or as to any other account or thing arising out of or connected with the contract, the said disputes and differences shall be referred to and be settled by the engineer, whose decision shall be final and binding on both parties." There, again, the engineer would have all the matters before him, not to enter upon a regular arbitration, but to form a judgment upon the matter when there is a dispute, and to settle it according to his own skill and judgment. It seems to me that this is not a case in which the contract provides for anything in the shape of a formal arbitration, or for a formal decision. If the decision were given in effect and in substance, it would be in accordance with this part of the deed.

Then, what do we find when we turn to the case to see whether there was any such decision? As long back as January, 1871, the directors had notice that extra works were designed and contemplated, that the working drawings did include extra works, and they must have been aware that the works were carried out in accordance with the working drawings. I do not dwell upon the correspondence which followed. I pass on to the two certificates for the 1,500*l.* and the 570*l.* When we look at that part of the case and pay attention to the dates, it seems clear there was a difference precisely of the kind that falls within the meaning of that clause which, merely for the sake of description, I call the arbitration clause; and this letter is written on the 17th of September, with a full account of all the work, amounting to more than 25,000*l.*, including extras—"Those we hope you will find correct, or if you wish them charged in any other form, we shall be glad to do so on hearing from you. We shall be much obliged if you can conveniently look into this matter as early as possible and certify for the extras." Then the case proceeds to state that the engineer communicated to the defendants the amount of the plaintiffs' account for extras. That may be ambiguous as to whether it was more than the actual sum, but the remainder of the paragraph puts it beyond doubt, for the secretary states that he has received the bill of extras amounting to upwards of 2,000*l.* So that the inference I should draw is that he had the items composing those extras, and that the directors had an opportunity of seeing what was the nature

1874
Nov. 27.

Exchequer
Chamber.

of the claim. It is then ordered that a letter be written to the engineer expressing the surprise of the directors at the amount of the extras, and asking for a copy of the account with his observations. I do not take that to mean that they had no copy of the account, but that he should make one, and append his observations to it on each item, to enable the directors to make their observations before he decides. Now, it is suggested that, this being a regular arbitration clause, the engineer did not follow out the terms of the provision, because he did not comply with that request, and did not give the directors an opportunity of making their observations. But the engineer took a correct view of his duty in the matter, which was to act on his own knowledge and skill. Probably, it would have been more satisfactory to the directors if he had allowed them to make their observations, but I do not think that the fact that he proceeded without this can in any way invalidate the certificate. Then, on the 14th of October, comes a certificate that work has been done to the amount of 1,500*l*. I understand that certificate to have been precisely in the same form as the specimen certificate in the case, which was that the contractors are entitled to be paid that amount; and that was a decision given by him. He settles the amount in dispute, and then he gives a certificate that he has found that the contractors have completed the work satisfactorily; and the letter including the whole of their claim and a detailed account is sent in afterwards, which he goes through, alters, and returns as the final account, which, of purse governs the 15 per cent. remaining, and he gives on the 29th of October a certificate that the balance due is the 570*l*.

Now, it appears to me that the only effect we can attribute to that is that there having been dissatisfaction on the part of the directors, and a question having arisen at the conclusion of the work, or during the progress of it, the engineer decides it in the way which is pointed at to him to decide it in the contract between the parties, that is, that he should act on his own knowledge and upon the materials which were in his hands.

With regard to whether that was a waiver, I do not think it necessary to add anything to what has been said by my Lord. I concur in a view taken by my Lord and my brother Lush of the effect of the correspondence. I think that it appears from it that the directors referred the contractors to the engineer, and that they (the contractors) afterwards asked him to give them properly signed orders though they were referred to the engineer, they might say— "Let have the signed orders in accordance with the contract, but in any payment if you do not do that, allow us to be assured that at the

termination of the work our claims shall be taken into account"; and
if the engineer then said, "Do not be anxious about written orders,
you shall have all that you are fairly entitled to when the time
comes," I think that in effect would be a waiver of these signatures
and countersignatures. For these reasons I agree with my Lord and
my brother Lush that the judgment of the Court of Exchequer should
be affirmed.

Solicitors for the plaintiffs, Gregory, Rowcliffes & Co.; solicitors for the
defendants, Van Sandau and Cumming.

[NOTE.—The author is indebted to Mr. Edward Jenkins and Mr. John
Raymond for their kind permission to publish the above report.]

𝔍𝔫 𝔱𝔥𝔢 𝕮𝔬𝔲𝔯𝔱 𝔬𝔣 𝕼𝔲𝔢𝔢𝔫'𝔰 𝔅𝔢𝔫𝔠𝔥.

(*Before* QUAIN, J., and a Common Jury.)

GWYTHER *v.* GAZE.

Quantity Surveyors—Employers' Liability to Pay—Rate of Remuneration.

The defendant, intending to erect a warehouse, employed S., an architect, to prepare
plans, and S. employed the plaintiff to take out quantities. Tenders were sent in, but
none accepted, and no building erected. The plaintiff sued the defendant for $2\frac{1}{2}$ per
cent. on the lowest tender. The defendant set up that the architect had only a limited
authority.

QUAIN, J., left it to the jury to say whether the architect's authority was so limited,
and, if not, charged them that the defendant was liable to pay the plaintiff reasonable
remuneration, but ruled that a $2\frac{1}{2}$ per cent. on the lowest tender set up as customary
was unreasonable. The plaintiff had a verdict, and the damages being left to the judge,
he assessed them at $1\frac{1}{2}$ per cent.

This case raised a question of considerable interest to architects and
surveyors, and to those who may employ them.

Thesiger, Q.C., and Willis for the plaintiff; Talfourd Salter, Q.C., and W. A.
Lewis for the defendant.

In 1873 the defendant was anxious to build a warehouse, dwelling-house,
and shop in Finsbury, and he instructed the late Mr. Thomas Staward, jun.,
an architect, to prepare plans and specifications. Mr. Staward instructed the
plaintiff, a surveyor, to take out the quantities. In October, 1873, three
tenders were sent in by the builder to Mr. Staward. None of the tenders
were accepted. It was proved that it was usual for an architect who prepares
plans to employ a surveyor for taking out the quantities, and that when a

1875
February 6.

Court of
Queen's
Bench.

tender is accepted the builder pays the surveyor for taking out the quantities, but that if no tender is accepted the building owner pays him. In the beginning of July of last year the building was proceeded with on Mr. Staward's plans, with the exception that the height of the building was one storey less than those in the plans. The builder employed had not any contract, but was paid as the work proceeded. Mr. Staward died in July of last year. In September the plaintiff sent in his account to the defendant. The builder employed to do the work was not one of those who had tendered, and he had not seen the plaintiff's quantities. The plaintiff contended that, according to the custom, as no tender had been accepted he was entitled to be paid by the defendant, the building owner. He claimed 158*l.* 5*s.*, being $2\frac{1}{2}$ per cent. on the amount of the lowest of the tenders sent in. It was stated that this was a customary charge.

QUAIN, J., said he thought that a custom that the surveyor should be paid $2\frac{1}{2}$ per cent. on the lowest tender, when no tender had been accepted, would be unreasonable, and that the plaintiff would be entitled, if to anything, to what the jury might think a reasonable remuneration.

Mr. Peebles and Mr. Cooke, the former a Member and the latter a Fellow of the Royal Institute of British Architects, were called, and stated that they thought that $2\frac{1}{2}$ per cent. on the lowest tender was, in the present case, a reasonable charge. They said that from 2 to $2\frac{1}{2}$ per cent. on the amount of the accepted tender was the charge usually made by the quantity surveyor, and that such a charge was reasonable; that sometimes $1\frac{1}{2}$ per cent. was charged, but this was done by special agreement. On this point the builder at present employed on the work was called for the defendant, and stated that $1\frac{1}{2}$ per cent. was the charge invariably made for taking the quantities for such a building as that in the present case.

The plaintiff's claim included a sum of twelve guineas which he had paid for lithographing the drawings.

The case for the defendant was that the architect in the present instance had only a limited authority, and that he was told that the defendant had engaged a builder, so that there would be no necessity to take out the quantities to enable the builders to tender.

QUAIN, J., left it to the jury to say whether the architect's authority was limited in the way stated by the defendant, and told them that, if it was not limited, the defendant was liable to pay the plaintiff a reasonable remuneration for taking out the quantities.

The jury returned a verdict for the plaintiff.

It was agreed that Quain, J., should assess the damages, and he assessed them at 83*l.* 10*s.*

The basis of his lordship's assessment would seem to have been $1\frac{1}{2}$ per cent. on the actual cost of the building, as estimated in the lowest tender.

LORD BATEMAN v. *THOMPSON.*

1875
Nov. 18.

Common
Pleas
Division.

𝔍n the Common Pleas Division

(Lord Coleridge, C.J., and Grove and Archbold, JJ.)

𝔍n the Court of Appeal.

LORD BATEMAN *v.* THOMPSON.

Building Contract under Seal—Construction—Provision as to Certificate of Completion and Satisfaction by Architect and as to Right of Action for Bad Materials for Twelve Months after Certificate—Limitation of Right to Sue.

Where a certificate of completion and satisfaction by the employer's architect is made conclusive and is given, the employer has no right of action against the builder for defects subsequently discovered, except within the time and upon the terms specially stipulated by the contract.

This was an action brought to recover damages for improper workmanship, and the use of improper materials in the execution by the defendant for the plaintiff, of certain works, alterations, and additions to the mansion and buildings at Shobdon Court, the plaintiff's residence in Herefordshire.

The writ was issued on the 28th July, 1871.

1873
Aug. 5.

Hereford
Assizes.

The case came on for trial at Hereford Assizes, on the 5th day of August, 1873, when by consent a verdict was taken for the plaintiff subject to a special case to be stated by Mr. J. O. Griffiths, who on 1st May, 1875, stated and signed the following case: —

Case.

1. In the year 1856 the plaintiff was desirous of having extensive works, alterations, and additions executed at Shobdon Court, his residence in Herefordshire.

2. The defendant was then in partnership as a builder and contractor with Mr. Francis Ruddle.

3. The defendant's firm tendered for the work to be done at Shobdon Court, and their tender was accepted.

4. On the 30th of July, 1856, a deed was executed by the plaintiff and the defendant and his partner, Francis Ruddle, therein called the contractors, by which the defendant and Ruddle undertook to do the work at Shobdon Court for 12,250*l.*, one Alexander Milne being named in the said deed, and acting as the plaintiff's architect in the matter.

5. The following are the most material parts of the deed:—

A recital as follows:—

(*A.*) "And whereas the contractors have accordingly agreed with the said Lord Bateman to execute and complete the said alterations, additions, improvements, buildings, and works as particularized or mentioned in the general specifications and drawings prepared for the purpose by the said Alexander Milne (who and also

1875
Nov. 18.

Common
Pleas
Division.

every other the architect for the time being of the said Lord Bateman, his heirs, executors, or administrators is hereinafter referred to as the architect), and all such other works of what sort soever as may be implied herefrom or from these presents according to the said specification and drawings, and also to such further or other plans, designs, and instructions as shall or may from time to time be furnished to the contractors by the architect, and upon and subject to the terms and conditions in the said specification and these presents contained mentioned or referred to."

A joint and separate covenant by the defendant and Francis Ruddle, the contractors, as follows:—

(*B.*) "That the contractors, their executors, and administrators will, on or before the 25th day of May, which will be in the year 1858, in a good, substantial, and workmanlike manner, and with the best materials of their several kinds (in the case of all such materials as by the terms of the said specification are to be provided or purchased by the contractors), and with such material as shall be supplied by the said Lord Bateman, his heirs, executors, or administrators (in the case of all such materials as by the said specification are to be supplied by the said Lord Bateman, his heirs, executors, or administrators), but in every event and particular to the satisfaction in all respects of the architect and of the said Lord Bateman, his heirs, executors, or administrators, make, execute, and complete the said alterations, additions, improvements, buildings, and works described or mentioned or referred to in the said specification and drawings, and likewise such other works as are necessarily implied therein, or may be reasonably inferred therefrom, or from these presents although not expressly mentioned or described therein respectively, and will execute and complete the same (and every of them) and every part thereof in conformity with such general instructions of the architect, and with such working or explanatory or further or other drawings, plans and designs, as shall or may hereafter from time to time or at any time be respectively given and provided by the architect.

(*C.*) "That if the said Lord Bateman, his heirs, executors, or administrators shall at any time before the said works are completed be desirous that any alterations, additions, or omissions should be made to, or in, or about the same, and written instructions signed by the architect for such alterations, additions, or omissions shall be given to the contractors, their executors or administrators, they shall execute and complete the said works as varied by such instructions in the same manner and upon and subject to the same or the like terms and conditions in all respects as if such altered, substituted, or additional work by or by force of such instructions directed had been originally described in the said specification.

(*D.*) "That whenever any works, matters, or things requisite to the proper and substantial and workmanlike completion of the several works shall happen to be not described in the said specification, or in such written instructions as last aforesaid, or the scantlings or sizes shall happen not to be specified therein respectively, such works, matters, or things shall not by reason thereof be omitted or not executed by the contractors, but they shall be considered and taken as if they had been respectively described and specified as of, and shall be accordingly executed and supplied by the contractors, their executors or administrators, of the respective sizes, qualities, and kinds usual or proper for the respective purposes, and shall correspond in all respects with the remaining portions of the said alterations, additions, improvements and works."

A provision in the following terms:—

(*E.*) "It is hereby further agreed between and by the parties to these presents that the decision of the architect with respect as well to the state and condition

1875
Nov. 18.

Common
Pleas
Division.

from time to time as to the completion of the said works or of any portion thereof respectively and also with respect to every question which may arise concerning the construction or effect of the said specification, drawings, plans, designs and instructions, or any of them, shall at all times be final and conclusive on the contractors, their heirs, executors, and administrators."

A provision in the following terms:—

(*F.*) "That if at any time or times during the progress of the said works, or within twelve calendar months after the completion thereof, the architect (not-withstanding any certificate or report which may have been then previously given or made by him as to the due execution of the works or any part thereof) shall consider part of the said works unsound, or to have been insufficient or improperly executed, the contractors, their executors, or administrators will, upon like notice in writing, without making any extra charge whatsoever, immediately, at the cost of the contractors, take down such unsound or improperly-executed part or parts of the said works and replace the same by sound and properly-executed work and material, and effectually make good all such parts (if any) of the said works or of the said mansion-house as shall have been in anywise injured or affected by such taking down or replacement, and that in case the contractors, their executors or administrators shall fail within seven days after the delivery of such notice, to commence taking down and re-executing such unsound or improperly-executed work or works, or if the contractors, their executors, or administrators shall not duly proceed therein to the satisfaction of the architect, then and in every such case the architect shall have full power to cause such unsound or improperly-executed work or works to be taken down and removed, and properly re-executed by such workmen and other persons as he may choose to employ, and the said Lord Bateman, his heirs, executors, and administrators shall be entitled to repay himself and themselves all monies which the architect shall report in writing to have been so expended out of the monies (if any) which shall then be or hereafter become due to the contractors, their executors, or administrators under this present contract, and if no such monies shall be or become due, or the amount thereof shall be insufficient, the monies so reported to be expended shall be repaid by and may be recovered from the contractors, their executors, or administrators as liquidated damages."

And a provision in the following terms:—

(*G.*) "Provided always, and it is hereby agreed and declared that if at any time within a period of twelve months from the date of the final certificate of the architect, that all the said works have been well and duly performed to his satis-faction, after the said works or any part thereof shall have been certified by the architect to have been duly completed, and either before or after the contractors, their executors, or administrators shall have received from the said Lord Bateman, his heirs, executors, or administrators all or any of the sums of money hereinbefore contracted to be paid to the contractors, their executors, or administrators for the performance thereof, it shall appear that the contractors, their executors, or administrators have used any unsound materials in any part of the said works, or have in any other way not performed the said works according to the stipulation and true intent and meaning of these presents in a substantial, workmanlike, and proper manner, then and in such case it shall be lawful for the said Lord Bateman, his heirs, executors, or administrators, notwithstanding anything in these presents contained or any certificate which may have been given by the architect of the due completion of the said works or any part thereof, to institute any action or suit or take any proceeding which the said Lord Bateman, his heirs, executors, or

1875
Nov. 18.

Common
Pleas
Division.

administrators shall think fit against the contractors, their executors, or administrators for the damage which shall have been sustained in consequence of the use of any unsound materials by the contractors, their executors, or administrators in the said works, or in consequence of the same or any part thereof not having been performed in a substantial, workmanlike, or proper manner, and in all other respects according to these presents, or for the recovery of any liquidated damages by these presents made payable. And it is hereby agreed that any certificate which shall have been given by the architect as aforesaid shall not in any manner bar or prejudice any such action, suit, or other proceedings."

6. The specification referred to in the deed was at the time signed by the plaintiff and the contractors.

[Those parts of the specification which relate to the matters in respect of which the claim was made in the action were set out at length in the Appendix, and the case gave liberty to refer to them: but the material portions have been already set out.]

7. By the general remarks applying to the whole of the works set forth in this specification, it was provided that all the stone except the paving stone should be quarried on the estate, the steps to be out of the Northfield Pit, the rest of the work out of the Honeyhole Pit or any other quarry which might be opened near it of the same stone.

And that the new brick would be furnished by the plaintiff at 18*s.* 6*d.* per thousand, the dressed and moulded ones for the chimney heads and gauged arches at 1*l.* 15*s.* per thousand.

And also that the whole of the works should be done with the best materials of the kind specified and executed in a workmanlike manner, and to the entire and perfect satisfaction of Lord Bateman's architect for the time being.

8. The specification provided for a new external cornice to the main building, to be of Portland cement, with plinth, balusters, pedestals, and finials, and a new 4-lb. lead flashing of the required width. Also for several flights of steps, with pedestals, cornices, and balusters.

9. By the specification and drawings, and the architect's written instructions varying the works, a considerable amount of brickwork was to be done by the contractors.

10. Shortly after the execution of the contract, the contractors commenced the work. Alterations in the work were made by the plaintiff's said architect's directions, and on the 25th October, 1856, the plaintiff's said architect wrote the letter of that date, which appears in the Appendix, with the view of making four open areas on the east and west fronts of the main building. The defendant, with reference to this work, wrote the letter of 31st December, 1856, and this was answered by the letter of the 6th of January, 1857. Copies of these letters are in the Appendix.

11. Early in 1857, the plaintiff found that he should have a difficulty in supplying from his estate a sufficient quantity of stone, of a description suitable for the work, and the plaintiff's said architect accordingly asked the defendant to estimate the cost of supplying Bath stone, to be used instead of the native stone. And the defendant, on behalf of his firm, offered to supply the Bath stone required for 550*l.*, and this offer was ultimately accepted by the plaintiff through his said architect.

12. In one of the letters from the plaintiff's said architect, the stone to be supplied is termed "Ground Bath Stone," but there is no stone known by this

name in the building trade. It is to be taken that Bath stone was meant, and there is Bath stone known by the respective names of "Box Ground" and "Corsham," of different degrees of hardness.

13. No clerk of the works was employed by the plaintiff, but the plaintiff's said architect himself, from time to time, supervised the works in progress.

14. In the execution of that part of the work in which Bath stone was to be used, the contractors used a large quantity of Bath stone of a kind unsuitable for the purpose to which it was applied, and from this cause considerable damage arose. This stone, though unsuitable for the purpose for which it was used, was otherwise of a good class, the best of its kind, and free from objections.

15. The plaintiff's said architect, from time to time, saw the Bath stone that was used, and where the same was used, and made no objection.

16. The workmen employed by the contractors also treated some of the Bath stone that was used in an improper manner, part of it by and under the said architect's instructions, and part not, and from this cause some damage arose.

17. In the construction of the plinth and cornice above mentioned, materials different from those mentioned in the specifications were used by and under the said architect's verbal instructions, and in the construction of the soffit for this plinth and cornice materials different from those mentioned in the specification were used without the architect's instruction, and in such a manner as to prevent such materials being seen by the architect. These materials in each of these cases were unfit for the purpose, and from these causes damage arose.

18. Drawings and instructions given by the said architect for the lead flashing, to be put up by the contractors, were faulty, and damage arose from these drawings and instructions being followed.

19. The damage was caused by the use of too scanty an amount of material in the construction of this flashing.

20. The said architect was of opinion that too little material was not used for this flashing, and he approved of the way in which this work had been done by the contractors.

21. The bricks for the whole of the brickwork to be done under the contract were supplied by the plaintiff as prescribed in the specification, and for these bricks the plaintiff was duly paid by the defendants at the rates prescribed by the said specification, but the contractors selected from the bricks supplied, those which should be and were used in the different parts of the work.

22. The bricks used in some parts of the works were not fit for the purpose to which they were applied, and some danger arose from this cause.

23. The plaintiff's said architect from time to time saw the bricks which were being used, and where the same were being used, and on some occasion he made objections to some qualities of them, and the bricks so objected to were thereupon removed, but he made no objection to the particular bricks which were ultimately used, and from which the damage above mentioned arose.

24. During the execution of the works, certificates that amounts were due to the contractors for work done were given from time to time by the said architect, and the amounts so certified were paid. The form of these certificates and of the receipts given is shown in the Appendix hereto.

25. The work was completed, and afterwards in the month of September, 1861, the plaintiff's said architect wrote a letter to the plaintiff passing the

1875
Nov. 18.

Common
Pleas
Division.

work, and also a letter to the defendant, dated the 18th of that month, saying: "I have written to Lord Bateman passing the Court and Uphamton excepting this square of glass to the former and the slates to the latter." The square of glass was shortly afterwards made satisfactory. The plaintiff accepted the certificate of his said architect at the time as sufficient and satisfactory.

26. A correspondence ensued, and meetings took place between the parties to adjust the accounts between them, but no complaint was made by the plaintiff or his said architect about the works during this time. The account was finally adjusted between the parties—this account is set out in the Appendix. On the 19th day of March, 1864, the plaintiff paid to the defendant 562*l.* 7*s.* 3*d.*, the balance agreed to be due according to the said account, and a receipt was given for the said balance.

27. Much more than six years having elapsed from the completion of the work before the commencement of this action, no claim is to be made or allowed against the defendant for breach of a simple contract with regard to any part of the work.

28. The Court is to have power to draw inferences of fact.

29. The question for the opinion of the Court is whether the plaintiff is entitled to recover in the action, in respect of the damage arising from any, and if so, which of the following causes: —

A. The use of an unsuitable description of Bath stone.

B. The improper treatment of the Bath stone.

1. Under the architect's instructions; and 2, not under his instructions.

C. The use of improper materials under the architect's verbal instructions in the construction of the plinth and cornice.

D. The construction of the soffit with different materials without the architect's instructions or knowledge.

E. The faultiness of construction of the lead flashing prescribed by the said architect's drawings and instructions.

F. The selection and use by the contractors of improper bricks for part of the work.

If the Court shall be of opinion that the plaintiff is not entitled to recover in respect of any of these matters, the verdict entered for the plaintiff is to be set aside, and a verdict and judgment are to be entered for the defendant.

If the Court shall be of opinion that the plaintiff is entitled to recover in respect of all or any of these matters, the verdict for the plaintiff is to stand, and judgment is to be entered thereupon.

The judgment in either case is to be entered in conformity with the order made herein, dated the 20th day of January, 1875.

November 18, 1875, the special case came on for hearing. Henry Matthews, Q.C., and Jeune for plaintiff; W. Graham and Percival for defendant.

Lord COLERIDGE, C.J.: In this case I am of opinion that our judgment ought to be for the defendant.

Lord Bateman wished to have very considerable works done to his place in the country, and a specification was provided by an architect of the name of Milne, and that was submitted to the defendant on the signing of the contract, and it is upon the terms of that contract

1875
Nov. 18.

Common
Pleas
Division.

and certain findings in the case before us that I base my judgment.

The contract provides that by a certain time the contractors will do the work in a "good, substantial, and workmanlike manner, but in every event and particular," that is to say, whether supplied by the contractor or by Lord Bateman, "to the satisfaction in all respects of the architect described, or mentioned, or referred to in the said specification and drawings." That is what the contractor contracts to do, and the contract goes on to provide various things with regard to which the architect is to be—(I avoid the word final and conclusive) but it is to be authoritative and is to have despotic authority over the contractor, at all events, as to the performance of certain works. If work is badly done in his judgment, he is to order the work to be done again to his satisfaction.

There is a provision in the contract for the appointment, either by the architect or by Lord Bateman, of a clerk of the works; there is provision that that clerk of the works "shall and will from time to time and at all times that he thinks fit go into the works and see that the orders of the architect and the provisions of the contract are being complied with," and the certificates of the architect and the decisions of the architect are in some cases made in terms final and conclusive; but I think, as far as I have observed, always in cases where in truth they are decisions against the contractor. They would be decisions upon the work of the contractor, and therefore necessarily binding upon him, and then there is a provision to which so much attention has been directed. [The learned judge then read proviso F and continued.] Those appear to me to be the important provisions of the deed, and under that deed the work was completed.

Now, it is found in the case that there were from time to time (and specimens of them are set out) payments made upon account in accordance with the provisions of the deed upon the various certificates given from time to time by the architect. The architect certified that the contractors were entitled to such a sum on account of their contract, and Lord Bateman paid the sum so certified from time to time upon the certificate of the architect. It is found in the case that the whole work was completed.

It is found that the whole sum of money was paid, and it is found that after the work was completed the architect wrote a letter to the plaintiff, to use the words of the statement of the case, "passing the work," and also a letter to the contractor, saying, "I have written to Lord Bateman passing the work." "The plaintiff," that is, Lord Bateman, "accepted the certificate of his said architect at the time as sufficient and satisfactory." Therefore, it is found that the work was completed, and we have powers of drawing inferences of fact. I come to the conclusion that, as a matter of fact, the architect certified to Lord Bateman, because no particular form of certificate is set out as requisite, that all the works specified for had been done, further; that it had been done to his satisfaction, that Lord Bateman accepted that certificate and paid what was then due upon that certificate, clearing off the account as far as money went between himself and the contractor.

1875
Nov. 18.

Common
Pleas
Division.

I find, further, as a fact, that by so doing Lord Bateman himself expressed his satisfaction with the work, and, indeed, Mr. Matthews very properly and candidly, when the question was put to him, not making any false point about it, was obliged to say and did say frankly that at that time Lord Bateman was satisfied with the work. Lord Bateman would clearly not have paid for it if he had not been satisfied, and Lord Bateman being, I will not say deceived—I do not wish to use an expression that would bear hardly upon an absent man, because it may have been in consequence of a mistake in point of fact, but he being, nevertheless, in a state of satisfaction with his architect, having accepted the work as satisfactory, he paid for it as done according to the contract.

Then, further, I will not go into detail, but I quite admit that it is found in the case, that there have been improper materials used, and the photographs which have been laid before us (if one is at liberty to refer to them) show plainly that Lord Bateman has had put upon him an amount of work utterly bad and such as ought not to have been certified as satisfactory, and that certainly so far from being good work, is extremely bad work: and it not only has cost him great expense in money, but I should think must have occasioned him very just indignation and great annoyance of mind.

The question is whether there was any breach of this contract. I am of opinion that even without the proviso, upon the true construction of this contract no action lies. The contractor is to perform the work in a good, substantial, and workmanlike manner, and with the best materials of their several kinds, and to the satisfaction of the architect and Lord Bateman. That, I think, is the true construction of that contract. They are to be good, substantial, and workmanlike, and to his satisfaction—that is to say, he is to be satisfied that they are good, substantial, and workmanlike materials and work. He was so satisfied, and within the terms of this contract both he and his architect, the architect by his certificate and Lord Bateman by his conduct, as a matter of fact, were satisfied within the words of the contract, and, accordingly, the covenant in this deed was in its term

1875
Nov. 18.

Common
Pleas
Division.

performed by the defendant, and having been performed by the defendant clearly no action lies upon it. I must say the matter is clear to my own mind upon the construction of the contract irrespective altogether of the proviso.

If there could be any doubt about it, it appears to me that it is taken away altogether by the proviso, because the proviso says if in spite of the certificate of the architect of the works having been well and duly performed, which I already assume has been given, and in spite of the works having been certified as having been completed, which I have already said has been certified as having been done, if in spite of that Lord Bateman, within a year after the giving of the certificate, finds out such a thing as has been suggested by Mr. Matthews, although I do not find it stated in this case that there has been a conspiracy between the architect and the builder, he may set the certificate aside, and that if he finds there is a gross defect disclosed twelve months after the certificate has been given, that he may then bring his action. [The learned judge then again read the proviso F and continued.] What is the meaning of the proviso? Mr. Matthews was pressed in vain—I do not wonder at it, even with all his ingenuity he was pressed in vain—to give any reasonable construction to it consistent with the maintenance of this action. He was obliged to say that it meant nothing. It meant nothing in fact; because he said it was satisfied by saying that during the twelve months Lord Bateman was at liberty to say that there was no certificate, or that the certificate did not express satisfaction, but that after the twelve months Lord Bateman was restrained from saying that the certificate did not express satisfaction, but he contended that it did not bind Lord Bateman, and that he might take any other course that he might think fit consistently with admitting that as a matter of fact the architect had expressed his satisfaction. I must say that it appears to me to read it so would give an utterly inadequate construction of the proviso. Read as a matter of common sense and common knowledge, the true intention of it is what has been suggested by the Court. "As I put myself into the hands of the architect the architect is to certify that the work is completed, the architect is to certify that the work is done to his satisfaction. If he does so, I must pay the contractor, but if within a year I find out that he has done that wrongly, in spite of his certificate and in spite of my payment I may bring my action for any damage I have suffered from the non-compliance of the contractors with the proper sense of the contract."

I do not think really any question arises of *res judicata* or whether the architect is an arbitrator or not. When that arises we are bound

1875
Nov. 18.

Common
Pleas
Division.

by the authorities to which Mr. Matthews referred. This is the ordinary case, not of an arbitration, but of the employer having made the certificate of the architect binding in certain cases against himself, and still more of his having made his own expression of satisfaction binding against himself. And having received the one and having expressed the other he cannot now say that he did not receive the one and did not express the other. It may seem a hard thing to say, but the answer is the answer which Mr. Justice Willes gave in the case of *Goodyear* v. *Mayor of Weymouth (a)*, that if you employ an architect who does not know his business, and who certifies that he is satisfied when he ought not to express satisfaction, you must be bound by his mistake. It is not in the least an answer to say that you have employed an architect who does not know his work, and if people employ architects who do not know their work, and who lead them into mistakes, and place contractors bound hand and foot into the hands of such persons, and such persons either pass bad work, or, as it appears in this case, actually direct bad work, they cannot afterwards in any equity or fairness turn round on the contractor, whom they have delivered hand and foot into the hands of an incompetent person, and say, "Now, I will bring an action for damage that I have sustained," as in many cases here, "because you have fulfilled the direct instructions of a man whose authority I made binding upon you, but as he did not know what he was about, and because I suffered damage from an authority which I myself made despotic over you, I now turn round upon you to make you liable for the damage I have sustained." Now, it may be very hard and very disagreeable to the plaintiff in this case, but a man must submit to the consequence of employing a person who seems to have allowed the use of improper materials in some cases, and to have directed the employment of improper materials in others, and I am of opinion that the plaintiff in this case is not entitled to succeed, and the defendant is entitled to our judgment.

GROVE, J.: I am of the same opinion. The two questions— possibly one might call them three in this case—are, first of all, whether the covenant that the contractors will on or before a certain date do certain work in a good, substantial, and workmanlike manner, and with the best materials of their several kinds (in the case of all such materials as by the terms of the said specification are to be provided or purchased by the contractors), and with such materials as shall be supplied by the said Lord Bateman, his heirs, executors, or

(a) 35 L. J. C. P. 12.

1875
Nov. 18.

Common
Pleas
Division.

administrators (in the case of all such materials as by the said specification are to be supplied by the said Lord Bateman, his heirs, executors, or administrators), but in every event and particular to the satisfaction in all respects of the architect and of the said Lord Bateman. The second question is whether that is in fact a double covenant, a covenant for two things to be done on the behalf of the defendants or a covenant in which the former part is subject to the latter, in other words, whether the covenant independently and quite irrespective of any such certificate of the architect, or any such satisfaction of Lord Bateman, is that they will do it in a good, substantial and workmanlike manner, and with the best materials as to such materials that they have to supply, or whether it is also to apply to the materials to be supplied by Lord Bateman, which are to be the best materials, provided such supplying of materials be sufficiently good to satisfy the architect and Lord Bateman.

Now, I am strongly inclined to the latter construction, namely, that the supply of the best materials on their part is to be subordinated to the satisfaction of the architect and of Lord Bateman, and that if after proper inspection and examination by the architect and Lord Bateman of those materials they are satisfied, that this covenant is to be taken as complied with. And even if I were to take it otherwise, to take it as a covenant for two things, and not an absolute covenant, but a covenant that they will supply good materials, and also that whatever they supply shall be to the satisfaction of the architect and Lord Bateman, still, I think the proviso which subsequently follows, when read with the covenant, shows that these parties by this deed intended to limit any right against them to twelve months after the final certificate of the architect that the works had been duly performed to his satisfaction, and that the works had been duly completed. What appears to me in favour of the first construction of the first covenant is that in addition to the words "but in every event and particular to the satisfaction of the architect and of Lord Bateman," I find in the deed that there is a proviso giving very considerable power of interference both to the architect and to Lord Bateman. [The learned judge then read provisoes C and F of the deed set out in the case and continued.]

It certainly would be a very strong thing to say that if the contractors have employed, whether really good, substantial, and proper materials, or improper materials, and if the architect and Lord Bateman have a power of ordering them to make alterations, to remove those materials and to substitute others, and after the architect expresses his satisfaction and gives his certificate, which I will

1875
Nov. 18.

Common
Pleas
Division.

presently refer to, which is called final and conclusive, that notwithstanding that those alterations are actually not only suggested, but enforced by Lord Bateman or by his architect, still, if those things are unsound or improper, although they have been actually found and furnished by the architect and approved by Lord Bateman, and the contractors are obliged at the instance of Lord Bateman to put in those materials instead of those previously placed in by them, they shall be held at any time within twenty years to have broken this covenant if those materials should be found to be unsound. I think the argument must be pushed that length because they are the materials placed by the contractors under the covenant, and if the materials are unsound, and if the breach of covenant merely depends on the unsoundness of the materials, they would be liable. That, I say, would certainly be a very strong thing.

But I think it is more important in another point of view as showing, as it appears to me to show, what was the intention of those parties as gathered from the language they have used in these deeds. Now, if you read the covenant in this way the whole seems to be perfectly consistent. The object of the proviso on which the decision of this case mainly depends is perfectly clear as far as the reason of the thing goes. I speak only of the deed itself; of course, we know nothing *aliunde* the deed.

We know nothing about the negotiations or determinations of these parties, but from the deed itself the object and meaning of the proviso is perfectly clear if you read the covenant in this way. That Lord Bateman says it may be there are certain things which are not discovered by the architect, it may be that there are certain materials put in which may turn out to be unsound, notwithstanding the certificate. of the architect. I still wish to have twelve months to see how the materials stand, that I am at all events not to be debarred from bringing an action until twelve months after the certificate of the architect of the completion of the house.

The words seem to import that "if at any time within a period of twelve months from the date of the final certificate of the architect that all the said works have been well and duly performed to his satisfaction, after the said works or any part thereof shall have been certified by the architect to have been duly completed, and either before or after the contractors, their administrators, or executors shall have received from the said Lord Bateman, his heirs, executors, or administrators, all or any of the sums of money hereinafter con- tracted to be paid to the contractors, their executors, or administrators for the performance thereof, it shall appear that the contractors, their

1875
Nov. 18.

Common
Pleas
Division.

executors, or administrators have used any unsound materials in any part of the said works." It may be said that that would not therefore apply to this proviso, that he used materials indicated by the architect, but if it should appear that the contractors have used any unsound materials, then in such case it shall be lawful for the said Lord Bateman, notwithstanding anything in those presents contained or any certificate which may have been given by the architect of the due completion of the said works, or any part thereof, to institute any action or suit or take any proceedings which the said Lord Bateman, his heirs, executors, or administrators, shall think fit against the contractors, I cannot read them in any other sense than that the parties who executed this deed say, although we might otherwise be estopped, or if the word estopped be importing too much, we might be unable to bring an action after the architect has certified, and after Lord Bateman has expressed his satisfaction, yet, notwithstanding that the architect has certified and Lord Bateman has expressed his satisfaction, that is, notwithstanding anything in the presents contained or any certificate of the architect my right shall not be stopped, for that is the obvious meaning of the whole covenant as it appears to my mind.

The universal principle is that all the parts of a deed must be taken together in order to ascertain its construction. And even if Mr. Matthews were right in its construction the proviso would qualify the covenant; and if my Lord is right, and if the opinion to which I strongly incline be right, that the covenant does not import that the certificate shall not be decisive upon these matters, then it is an absolutely clear explanation, the whole of the document is perfectly consistent, the reason for it is clear and apparent: and in order to depart from that we must be driven to niceties of conjecture as to what the parties possibly mean by such a proviso. If the construction of the covenant which Mr. Matthews contends for is the right one, Lord Bateman has a perfectly clear right of action for twenty years, and we ought to construe a very stringent covenant in his favour, and besides that he should have a right of action if the work is not well done for twenty years. But if the other construction is the proper one, as it seems to me it is, and the only reasonable construction of the agreement, the power of inspection and the power of removal are all perfectly consistent with it, upon that view, notwithstanding all that the certificate of the architect is to be final; that is to say, subject to a year's inspection it shall be conclusive—it shall be subject to a year's inspection by Lord Bateman and his architect, and subject to that year's inspection it shall be final and conclusive

1875
Nov. 18.

Common
Pleas
Division.

The deed also says "that the decision of the architect with respect to the state and condition from time to time as to the completion of the said works or of any portion thereof respectively, and also with respect to every question which may arise concerning the construction or effect of the said specifications, drawings, plans, designs, and instructions, or any of them, shall at all times be final and conclusive of the contractors, their heirs, executors, administrators." That, again, is quite consistent, and gives a strong reason for this proviso being inserted.

But for the proviso it may be contended that as against Lord Bateman a certificate would be final and conclusive, so that if you find out when the work is all done it is all rotten and improperly done, you are debarred from complaining. It seems to me the construction we put upon it is the reasonable one, and makes the whole of the deed consistent, and to construe it in any other way appears to me to make the deed a very inconsistent one, and the proviso would be made with no object at all, and it would be inconsistent with the words, "notwithstanding anything in these presents contained or any certificate which may have been given by the architect." It seems to me that that cannot be the construction of the deed. Therefore I agree with my Lord, although I do not think it is absolutely necessary to the decision of the case that the question of soundness or unsoundness is to be decided by the certificate of the architect, and that if it were not for this proviso there would not be an action for breach of covenant. I think on the true construction of the deed, taking it altogether, the plaintiff's right of action continues up to the end of the twelve months after the certificate of the architect has been given of the completion of the works, but that after that time the certificate is final and conclusive, therefore I think our judgment should be for the defendant.

ARCHIBALD, J.: I also agree that our judgment must be for the defendant, and I also agree in that for the reasons given by my Lord and my brother Grove, and it is scarcely necessary for me to add anything to what they have said. I need scarcely observe that the right of Lord Bateman under which he maintains this action depends entirely on the construction to be put on this deed. Now, the covenant, of which the important part provides that the work is to be done in a good, substantial, and workmanlike manner, and with the best materials, goes on to specify that there are some materials to be provided by Lord Bateman and some to be provided by the contractor, but in every event and particular to the satisfaction in all respects of the architect and of the said Lord Bateman. I read that as meaning that this work is to be done in a good and workmanlike manner so as to satisfy Lord Bateman and the architect, and that is what the contractors have stipulated to do, and upon the covenant alone I confess and incline very strongly to the opinion that if that is done, and if that satisfaction is expressed in the way provided, that that is a performance of the covenant on the part of the contractor, and that except for the proviso which comes afterwards with regard to the year, no action would be maintainable against him, but if there were any doubt as to whether that was the true construction, it would be entirely disposed of, it seems to me, when we look at the other portion of the deed, and, as my brother Grove has already pointed out, the true mode of construing a document of this kind is to look at all the provisions of it and see how they bear upon each other, and to see what light each part reflects upon the rest.

Now, with regard to the certificate of the architect, I think it is clear from the passage to which I have already referred in the deed that the architect is to give a certificate not only as to the completion of the works, that is to say, when the work is finished, but he is made a judge of the soundness and sufficiency of the materials, for he has great powers conferred upon him by the clause which my brother Grove has read, and which I need not read again, to order the work which is unsound and improper and insufficient, and so found by him or a clerk of the works or a foreman, to be removed and other works substituted, subject, nevertheless, to such reference to a decision of the architect as hereinafter is provided. That is to say, if done by the clerk of the works or by the foreman, it is still to be subject to the decision of the architect. I think there can be little doubt that the meaning of this covenant must be that if the work is done to his satisfaction and that of Lord Bateman, that the satisfaction is expressed both with regard to the character of the materials, the workmanship, the nature of the work, and the fact that it has been finished and duly completed, and that, therefore, the true view of the covenant in my own mind is that when that is once done by the contractor and there is no fraud, which is not imputed here, that that is a performance of the covenant.

Then, there come by way of proviso certain parts of the deed which strongly support that view of it. In addition to what I have already pointed out there is the clause (E) which provides that the decision of the architect with respect as well to the state and condition from time to time as to the completion of the said works, or of any portion thereof respectively, and also with respect to every question which may arise concerning the construction or effect of the said specifica-

1875
Nov. 18.

Common
Pleas
Division.

tion, drawings, plans, designs, and instructions, or any of them, shall at all times be final and conclusive on the contractors. This is to be done to the satisfaction of Lord Bateman himself and to the satisfaction of the architect, but the contractors are not at liberty to dispute or to question the certificate of the architect when it is given. In that view of the case, if the covenant is performed, upon this work being done and certified by the architect, and once accepted by Lord Bateman, there would be an end to every remedy at once against the contractors if it were not that the parties have made a further stipulation by the proviso which says, "It is agreed that if at any time within a period of twelve months from the date of the final certificate of the architect that all the said works have been well and duly performed to his satisfaction," and I agree with what has already fallen from my Lord that we must assume from this case there has been a final certificate. That is the inference I draw from the statement in the case, and that that matter is disposed of—"That if at any time within twelve months from the date of the final certificate of the architect that all the said works have been duly performed to his satisfaction, after the said works or any part thereof shall have been certified by the architect to have been duly completed, and either before or after the contractors, their executors, or administrators shall have received from the said Lord Bateman, his heirs, executors, or administrators all or any of the sums of money herein-before contracted to the contractors, their executors, or administrators for the performance thereof, it shall appear that the contractors, their executors, or administrators have used any unsound materials in any part of the said works, or have in any other way not performed the said works according to the stipulation and true intent and meaning of these presents in a substantial, workmanlike and proper manner," without reading the proviso in detail, if anything of that kind is discovered in the year, although but for this there would have been no remedy against the contractor, still, the covenant is qualified to that extent, that Lord Bateman is entitled to maintain an action against him in respect of that, and the certificate is not to operate as a bar.

Now, I draw another conclusion from this proviso. It reflects light upon the covenant. The object certainly must be to give that right of action which otherwise would not have been given. When Mr. Matthews was asked what was the meaning of it he said it was put in *ex majori cautela*, but it would have been idle and it might be cut out. One cannot conceive why a clause of this kind should be put in if it was not the intention of the parties, taken with the other

1875
Nov. 18.

Common
Pleas
Division.

portions of the deed, that but for this all the rights of the parties as to an action should be at an end. Taking that view, therefore, I think that it is not open to Lord Bateman, except in case of fraud, which is not here alleged, to bring an action after the twelve months. Of course, that does not interfere with his remedy against the contractor, and if it were possible in any other case to show that there was fraud, which is not the case here, his rights and remedies would be entirely different, but taken as it stands here, and there being no fraud suggested, I think there is no right of action against the contractor, and therefore that our judgment should be for the contractor.

Judgment for defendants.

The plaintiff appealed to the Court of Appeal. The appeal was heard in the Hilary Sittings, 1876, and dismissed with costs.

Solicitors for the plaintiff: Norton, Rose, Norton and Brewe. Solicitors for the defendant: Clarke, Rawlins and Clarke, agents for Percival and Son, Peterborough.

1877
June 3.

Queen's
Bench
Division.

𝕳𝖎𝖌𝖍 𝕮𝖔𝖚𝖗𝖙 𝖔𝖋 𝕵𝖚𝖘𝖙𝖎𝖈𝖊 (𝕼𝖚𝖊𝖊𝖓'𝖘 𝕭𝖊𝖓𝖈𝖍 𝕯𝖎𝖛𝖎𝖘𝖎𝖔𝖓)

(*Before* MANISTY, J., and a Common Jury.)

WAGHORN v. THE WIMBLEDON LOCAL BOARD (a).

Building Contract—Payment of Quantity Surveyor—Employer's Inability.

The defendants, a Burial Board, by resolution, instructed R., their architect, to prepare plans and get tenders for a cemetery chapel. R. employed the plaintiff, a quantity surveyor, to take out quantities; the work went to tender, but none being accepted the plaintiff sued the defendants, who set up that they never authorised R. to employ the plaintiff, and that as a corporation they must contract under seal.

MANISTY, J., ruled, that as the defendants had instructed R. to get tenders, they impliedly authorised him to get quantities taken out, and overruled the objection as to the necessity of sealing; the plaintiff had judgment.

The plaintiff, Mr. Joseph Waghorn, is a "quantity surveyor." The defendants are, by statute, the Burial Board, as well as the Local Board, for the district of Wimbledon. In 1875 they instructed their salaried surveyor,

(a) *See,* however, *Young* v. *Mayor, & c. of Leamington,* 8 App. Cas. 517.

1877
June 3.

Queen's
Bench
Division.

Mr. Rowell, to prepare plans and specifications, and to procure tenders for the erection of a cemetery chapel. These instructions were embodied in a resolution passed at a meeting of the Board. When Mr. Rowell had prepared the plans, he instructed the plaintiff to take out the "quantities," and he advertised for tenders in the *Builder*. Several builders sent in tenders, having used the quantities taken out by the plaintiff in arriving at their estimates. The defendants did not accept any of the tenders, the amount of the lowest being higher than the sum which they intended to expend.

The case for the defendants was that they never authorised Mr. Rowell to employ the plaintiff to take out the quantities. Several architects and surveyors were called for the plaintiff, who stated that the business of a quantity surveyor was quite distinct from that of an architect, and that it was necessary that the quantities should be taken out to enable the builders to tender. They also stated that the custom was for the builder, when sending in a tender, to add the charges of the quantity surveyor to his estimate, and that if the tender was accepted he paid the quantity surveyor. If, however, none of the tenders were accepted, the building owner was liable to pay the quantity surveyor's charges.

Mellor, Q.C., Graham and Raymond, for the plaintiff; Day, Q.C., and William Patterson, for the defendants.

At the end of the plaintiff's case, it was submitted that there was no evidence that the defendants had authorised Mr. Rowell to employ the plaintiff to take out the quantities.

MANISTY, J., ruled, that as they had instructed him to procure tenders, and as tenders could not be made without quantities, they had impliedly authorised him to get the quantities taken out.

It was then submitted that the defendants, being a corporation, could only contract under seal, and there being no contract under seal here, the plaintiff could not recover.

MANISTY, J., ruled, that as the defendants had by resolution impliedly authorised Mr. Rowell to get the quantities taken out, and had the benefit of the work which had been done, their objection was not tenable.

Judgment was accordingly entered for the plaintiff for the amount claimed (170*l.* 19*s.* 10*d.*).

1879
July 22.
—
1880
February 25.

Common
Pleas
Division.

𝔍n t𝔥e 𝔥ig𝔥 Court of 𝔍ustice (Common 𝔓leas 𝔇ibision).

Lord Coleridge, L.C.J.

On Appeal:

Lord Coleridge, L.C.J.; Grove and Lindley, JJ.

CLEMENCE *v.* CLARKE.

Building Contract—Bill of Quantities—Certificate of Architect— Acceptance by Architect of Quantity Surveyor's Measurements.

An architect's certificate as to the builder's rights to payment is conclusive, even if on its face it is based on measurements made by another person for the certifying architect, provided that it is not shown that the architect has acted corruptly or abdicated his duty. Where, in a building contract, it is stipulated that the certificate of the architect *or an award of the referee* is to be conclusive, a certificate, if given, cannot be the subject of reference to the referee. Construction of Clauses 17, 18, and 19 of the then existing conditions cf contract agreed upon between the Royal Institute of British Architects and the Builders' Society.

Plans for a building in King Street, Covent Garden, were prepared by Mr. Cross, surveyor to the Duke of Bedford, and the quantities were taken out by Mr. Waghorn, a surveyor. The first tenders proved too high; but Mr. Clemence, the plaintiff, in March, 1878, sent in a revised tender by which he undertook to execute the whole of the works required to be done for the erection and completion of the warehouse, according to drawings and specification signed by him, and general condition of contract, and revised bills of quantities for the sum of 6,765l. In order to provide for the prospect of alterations or reductions in the work it was agreed that the contract should not be a lump sum contract, but that the reduced bills of quantities should be sealed up and made part of the contract to regulate the charges for extras or alterations, and that the contract price should be settled by reference to them. In pursuance of this agreement a contract was drawn up which was in accordance with the agreement between the Royal Institute of British Architects and the Builders' Society and adopted by the Central Association of the master builders of London. The clauses material to the case are the following:—

(6.) The contractor is not to vary or deviate from the drawings or specification or execute any extra work of any kind whatsoever, unless the same be required to comply with any of the provisions of any of the Acts of Parliament by clause or regulations hereinbefore mentioned, or unless upon the authority of the architect to be sufficiently shown by any order in writing or by any plan or drawing given and signed by him or an extra or variation or by any subsequently-written approval signed or initialled by him.

1879
July 22.

Common
Pleas
Division.

(11.) Any defects, shrinkage, and other faults which may appear within months from the completion of the building and arising out of defective or improper materials or workmanship or upon the direction of the architect to be amended and made good by the contractors at their own costs, unless the architect shall decide that they ought to be paid for the same, and in case of default the employer may recover from the contractors the cost of making good the works.

(17.) When the value of the works executed and not included in any former certificate shall from time to time amount to the sum of *l.*, or otherwise, at the architect's reasonable discretion, the contractors are to be entitled to receive payment at the rate of 80 per cent upon such value until the difference between the percentage and the value of the works executed shall amount to per cent. upon the amount of the contract, after which time the contractors are to be entitled to receive payment of the full value of all works executed and not included in any former payment, and the architect is to give to the contractors certificates accordingly, and when the works shall be completed, or possession of the building shall be given up to the employer, the contractors are entitled to receive one moiety of the amount remaining due according to the best estimate of the same that can then be made, and the architect is to give to the contractors certificates accordingly within three months from the completion of the works, except 50*l.*, which is to be retained for six months. The contractors are to be entitled to receive any sum reserved for painting and papering, or otherwise, on the completion thereof. Provided always that no final or other certificate is to cover or relieve the contractors from their liability under the provisions of clause No. 11, whether or not the same be notified by the architect at the time, or subsequently to granting any such certificate.

(18.) A certificate of the architect or an award of the referee hereinafter referred to, as the case may be, showing the final balance due or payable to the contractors, is to be conclusive evidence of the works having been duly completed and that the contractors are entitled to receive payment of the final balance, but without prejudice to the liability of the contractors under the provisions of clause No. 11.

(20.) Provided always that in case any question, dispute, or difference shall arise between the employer, or the architect on his behalf, and the contractors as to what additions, if any, ought in fairness to be made to the amount of the contract: (a) by reason of the work being delayed through no fault of the contractors; or (b) by reason, or on account of any directions, or requisitions of the architect, involving increased cost to the contractors beyond the cost properly attending the carrying out the contract according to the true intent and meaning of the signed drawings and specifications; or (c) as to the works having been duly completed; or (d) as to the construction of these presents; or (e) as to any other matter or thing arising under, or out of, this contract, except as to matters left during the progress of the works to the sole decision, or requisition, of the architect under clauses No. 1, 9 and 10; or (f) in case the contractors shall be dissatisfied with any certificate of the architect under clause No. 7, or under the proviso in clause No. 15; or (g) in case he shall withhold, or not give, any certificate to which they may be entitled; then such question, dispute, or difference, or such certificate (h), or the value or matter which should be certified, as the case may be, is to be from time to time referred to the arbitration and final decision of , architect, or in the event of his death, or unwillingness to act, then of , architect, being a Fellow of the Royal Institute of British Architects, or, in the event of his death, or unwillingness to act, then of an architect to be appointed, on the request of either party, by the President, for the time being, of such Institute, and the award of such referee is to be equivalent to a certificate of the architect, and the contractors are to be paid accordingly.

CLEMENCE v. *CLARKE*.

1879
July 22.

Common
Pless
Division.

Mr. Hayward was appointed architect instead of Mr. Cross, and supervised the execution of the works and gave successive certificates. Nos. 1–7 were paid without demur. Nos. 8 and 9, the last two, were as follows:—

(No. 8.)

London, August 2nd, 1878.

I hereby certify that Mr. John Clemence, of No. 32, Villiers Street, W.C., is entitled to receive the sum of one thousand five hundred pounds on account of works executed by him at Warehouses in Hart Street, Covent Garden, W.C.

C. F. HAYWARD (Architect).

To Allen H. Clarke, Esqre.,
39, King Street, Covent Garden.

	£	s.	d.	
Previous certificates, Nos. 1 to 7...	6,600	0	0	up to February 27th, 1878.
Present certificate, No. 8	1,500	0	0	
Total amount certified	£8,100	0	0	up to August 2nd, 1878.

Fo. 13, p. 40.
(No. 9.)

London, September 19th, 1878.

I hereby certify that Mr. John Clemence, Builder, of 32, Villiers Street, Strand, is entitled to receive the sum of five hundred and eighty-five pounds twelve and tenpence to balance account of works as certified by the measuring surveyors to be the final amount due thereon executed by him at Warehouses at Hart Street, Covent Garden, and to Premises 39, King Street, Covent Garden.

C. F. HAYWARD (Architect).

To Allen H. Clarke, Esqre.,
39, King Street.

	£	s.	d.	
Previous certificates, Nos. 1 to 8...	8,100	0	0	up to August 2nd, 1878.
Present certificate, No. 9................	585	12	10	up to September 19th, 1878.
	£8,685	12	10	

For the purpose of making out certificate No. 9, Mr. Hayward had the sealed bill of quantities opened, and employed a quantity surveyor to survey and measure the work in accordance with the bill on 15th November, 1878. The plaintiff sued the defendants for work and labour done and materials provided as per the final certificate of Mr. Hayward, claiming 2,085*l*. 12*s*. 10*d*., the unpaid balance, or certificates 8 and 9 with interest. The defendant pleaded that the certificates were bad, and counter-claimed for 500*l*. money had and received and 1,000*l*. damages for breach of contract.

The action came on for trial before Lord Coleridge, L.C.J., and a special jury.

Webster, Q.C., and E. Pollock, for plaintiff; W. G. Harrison, Q.C., and Crispe, for defendant.

The plaintiff put in the contracts and certificates, and relied on them and clause 18 of the contract.

For the defence it was contended that the reference in certificate 9 to the measuring surveyor made the certificate bad, as not being an exercise of the skill and judgment of the architect, and also that no written order had been given for the extras included in the certificate, and that this defect was not cured by the certificate itself.

1879
July 22.

Common
Pleas
Division.

Lord Coleridge ruled that as no allegation of corruption was made against the architect the contract and certificates were conclusive against the defendant, and directed a verdict and judgment for the amount claimed, with costs.

4th November, 1879, W. G. Harrison, Q.C., moved for and obtained a rule *nisi* for Groves and Lopes, JJ., to set aside the verdict and judgment, on the grounds of misdirection and rejection of evidence.

25th February, 1880. Cause was shown against the rule before Lord Coleridge, L.C.J., and Grove and Lindley, JJ. The arguments were confined to the effect of certificate No. 9.

Grove, J.: I am of opinion that this rule should be discharged. There were two broad points upon which the rule was granted—the main one being that the certificate under clause 18 was not final, and that if the clause were final, the certificate of the architect showed upon the face of it that he had not properly exercised the duties which he was supposed to have undertaken, of certifying to the work being done and the balance being due—that he had not properly exercised those duties—because in the certificate, after stating that the contractor was entitled to receive the sum of 585*l.*, &c., to balance account of works, he used these words, "as certified by the measuring surveyors to be the final amount due thereon."

Now, a strong contest was made before myself and my brother Lopes when this rule was moved that the certificate of the architect showed upon the face of it that he had not exercised his own judgment, because he used the words "as certified by the measuring surveyors to be the final amount due thereon." I do not mean at all that the words "as certified" applied to the amount of money, but to the works—I quite mean that; and if I expressed myself otherwise I did not express what I intended to express. I read the words thus, "as certified by the measuring surveyors": perhaps I ought to have paused there: those words are in a parenthesis: and upon the face of it I think, putting it as clearly as I can, the certificate in regard to this point would have been good if he had said, "I certify that Mr. Clemence is entitled to receive the sum of 585*l.*, the final amount due thereon for the works executed by him to balance account of the works as certified by the measuring surveyor."

I take the objection to be not that the architect does not pledge himself to the proper balance due, but that he takes the measuring surveyor's certificate of the measurement, and it may possibly be of other matters connected with the work—that is to say, as to whether certain details, such as certain extras, ought to be paid for, are or are

1880
February 25.

Common
Pless
Division.

not included in the measurement which the measuring surveyor has made—that it is further objected that he has delegated his authority to the measuring surveyors, and that the certificate shows that upon the face of it, which is not a legal document nor drawn up with all the care which a lawyer would apply to it. Now, all that appears to me necessarily to arise upon the certificate, reasonably read, is that the measuring surveyor has gone over the measurements of the work for the architect, and that upon that measurement the architect missed nothing, because he must be assumed, I think, to have the contract before him in which the prices are named, to *reduce* from that the balance due, but I will assume not himself to have either measured or gone over the work done by the measuring surveyors. That I take to be the fair construction of this document, and to give it all the force which the document in this case can fairly claim to have given to it. Now, I do not think that avoids this certificate.

It appears to me that if an architect is entrusted with the general direction and superintendence of work, it is not reasonable that he should be expected to go over every matter in detail; and, indeed, practically his duties could not be performed if he were expected to go over individually every matter in detail, and if his certificate were to be held bad by a Court of law because he has not himself gone into every detail throughout. The architect in this case evidently, by the history of the case, must have known the general character of the work. He must have seen what was done. It is not contended that he did not know the contract—that he did not know the specification, or that he did not know the general nature of the work, or that he did not know of certain extra work and of certain omissions which had taken place in the course of the work, because we have it admitted that he gave certain certificates anterior to this final certificate and that he attended as architect to the work.

Then, I will assume that the taking out the quantities and the measuring up was done by a surveyor. I do not see how any architect could ever discharge such a duty if he were required to personally go in detail into all the work (*a*). It may be that the measuring up and the quality of the material in some classes of work could be properly got at by skilled persons who might be employed under the architect. The architect, though in certain parts of the document he is treated as an agent of the party, is for the purpose of this certificate a judge; and if he were bound to do all the details of various kinds of work himself, in all probability he would be incompetent to do them:

(*a*) Hereon see also *Kirkwood v. Morrison* (1877), 5 Ct. Sess. Cas. (4th series) 79.

1880
February 25.

Common
Pleas
Division.

because although he is skilled as an architect—skilled as a person generally in surveying work—he may not be skilled in the particular details of all this general work. I do not think, therefore—it being admitted that the architect has behaved with perfect honesty in the matter and that there is nothing in the shape of corruption or improper conduct attributed to him—that this certificate is the less final because he has taken the measurement of the works from another person, namely, the surveyor, who has gone through the work and made a report of the measurements to him.

I do not know that I am not, in saying what I now do, going further than the certificate, upon the face of it, may necessarily indicate; because, as I observed in the course of Mr. Harrison's motion, and have observed since during the course of the argument here, the certificate does not upon the face of it absolutely negative his having gone over them, because it says "to balance account of works as certified by the measuring surveyor." Now, he might have gone over them as well as the measuring surveyor. It does not exclude him. But I would rather put it upon the other ground, because without assuming the other ground the question of rejection of evidence would become much stronger in favour of the present rule.

Then, I am of opinion that where such a function is by both parties agreed to be conferred upon an architect as that mentioned in clause 18 of this contract, it would be virtually to put an end to the whole value of the clause if Courts of law were to reopen the case (where there is no misconduct, either legal or moral, in the architect), merely because he has not investigated every measurement and every item of the work himself. I think all that you can infer under those circumstances is that the parties, both of them, relied upon the judgment of the person whom they appoint, and agreed, in the absence of misconduct, to accept the decision.

I do not mean to say that if the architect had delegated the whole of his duty to another person, if he had taken another architect and paid him a smaller sum of money than probably he would be entitled to, taken another architect of inferior station and had appointed him to supervise and look over all the work instead of him, and had abdicated his whole functions and delegated them wholly to another person—that there would not have been a ground for setting aside the certificate, because in that case it would have amounted in my mind to misconduct—it might not amount to fraud, because, though he might not think that he was doing an utterly wrong thing, it would in my mind amount to that which the law would call misconduct, since it would be delegating his own duties, upon the performance of which

1880
February 25.

Common
Pleas
Division.

the parties rely, to another person. But it does not appear to me that that is the case here; it certainly is not this case from anything one can judge looking at the face of the certificate.

Then, I go to the question of the rejection of evidence. If I were satisfied either by the shorthand notes or by anything the learned counsel said—the shorthand notes would be the better test, because that is what took place before my Lord—that evidence had been tendered which showed that the architect had so abdicated his functions—had employed another person to do what I will call architect's work, or to do a large part of the architect's work instead of him—I should have been disposed to make this rule absolute for a new trial. But I have attended carefully to everything Mr. Moulton has said upon the subject and read over the shorthand notes, and it appears to me that what was really tendered was this. Supposing the certificate does not sufficiently, upon the face of it, show that he devolved the measurement upon the measuring surveyors, it is said that Mr. Harrison was prepared to give evidence to show that what he contended to be implied by the words of the certificate was really in fact what was done by the architect. I will assume that he had evidence to that effect. I will assume that he had evidence that the measurements were in fact left to the measuring surveyors and not gone over by the architect himself, and possibly some other matters of detail, such as the question of adding up the extras and the omissions, though I find nothing in what Mr. Harrison said at the trial—he certainly did say so to me when moving for the rule, but I find nothing in what he said at the trial referring to extras and omissions. But he presented to my Lord presiding at the trial his objection to this certificate upon the face of it, and then he went on to say that he has correspondence, and in particular he read one letter showing that he could substantiate his objection *aliunde* to the document itself by evidence to that effect. I therefore assume that he did tender evidence to show that the architect had taken the measurements from the measuring surveyor, and possibly, though he does not mention it, something beyond mere measurements—that is to say, the quantity of extra work done and of certain work omitted. To my mind that does not avoid the decision of the architect or affect the force of the final certificate under clause 18. I think the fair and the legal view of the matter is, that where parties determine to put the matter into the hands of a third party for this purpose, he is not supposed to be a partisan of either party. Where each party agrees that they shall be bound by his decision they are bound by that decision, unless something which amounts practically to misconduct be shown.

1880
February 25.

Common
Pleas
Division.

Now, then, that brings me to the terms of the clause making the certificate final. In section 17, which I will not read in full, there is a proviso that, when the work shall be completed, "the contractor is entitled to receive one moiety of the amount remaining due" (after deducting any sum for works delayed by order of the architect, which are to be paid for within four weeks after the same shall have been executed) "according to the best estimate of the same that can then be made, and the architect is to give the contractor certificates accordingly, and the contractor is to be entitled to receive the balance of all moneys due or payable to them under or by virtue of the contract within three months from the completion of the works."

I do not think it necessary to pronounce an opinion as to whether the plural word "certificates" includes or excludes the final certificate. Reading it most in favour of the defendant here I will assume that it includes all certificates, both intermediate and final. That is a proviso that the money shall be paid in a certain time, and it is followed by this proviso— "Provided that no final or other certificate"—showing that this clause applied to both classes, and, therefore, perhaps in favour of the contention that the final certificate is included in it for certain purposes only—"that no final or other certificate is to cover or relieve the contractor from his liability under the provisions of clause 11"—[the learned judge read the clause to the words "such certificate"]. Now, it is clear at all events that that proviso includes the final certificate, whether the word "certificates" before do or not. Now, that proviso does not at all touch the question before the Court here. That proviso is that certain defects, such as shrinking and other faults that may appear after the completion of the building, shall be amended and made good by the contractor, and that the employers may recover from the contractors the cost of them. That does not apply to anything here.

Now comes the clause in question, No. 18, "The certificate of the architect, or award of the referee hereinafter referred to, as the case may be" [the learned judge read down to the words "the liability of the contractor under the provisions of clause 11"], that is the same clause which I have referred to before.

The words of that clause are as clear, and to my mind as un-ambiguous, as any words in the English language can be; but it is contended that that certificate, which they call a certificate showing the final balance, but which has been previously called a final certifi-cate in the previous clause—which shows that it is to be conclusive evidence—is not a final certificate, that it does not show the final balance, and is not conclusive evidence of the works having been done,

1880
February 25.

Common
Pleas
Division.

but that the whole may be under certain circumstances reopened. Well, it seems to me you cannot meet the argument, because the mind does not see the force of it. It seems to me that the words are so clear and expressive that I can add nothing to them to make them more absolute and more distinct.

But it is said in aid of the argument that this does not mean finality—that there is an arbitration clause. But the arbitration clause is that "in case any question or dispute" [the learned judge read clause 20 to the words "or as to the works having been duly completed"], then there may be a reference. It appears to me that mainly applies to intermediate work, but it may also apply, and does undoubtedly in form apply, to the question of the matter being completed. But to what does this refer? To my mind to disputes, not between the employer and his architect, but between the employer and the architect on the one hand and the contractor on the other hand. And who is the person who is likely to dispute the question of the works having been completed? Why, I should think the architect. The contractor would be anxious to get something. The contractor might allege that the works were completed when the architect might say they were not; and in case of a dispute like that between the contractor on the one hand and the architect on the other, the architect is not to act as a judge. That would be the reason of the arbitration clause. Where he enters into a dispute with a contractor, then he is not to be allowed to be a judge in his own case. Then a reference should be had.

In such a dispute as that the arbitrator is put in the place of the architect, and then his certificate or his award is to be final, and that is obviously provided for by clause 18 in question, because it is the "certificate of the architect or an award of the referee hereinafter referred to," showing that the final balance is to be conclusive evidence.

Now, if the argument is that the certificate of the arbitrator is not to be conclusive, and does not show the final balance, precisely the same argument must apply to the award of the referee, and therefore the award of the referee to whom the parties have referred any difference is not final and can be reopened in a Court of law, so that virtually both clause 18 and clause 20 become practical nullities, only provisional, and the whole matter can be reopened and referred to a Court of law. I cannot adopt that construction of the contract. I read it in this way, speaking generally, and without going into further detail. If there be a dispute between the architect and the contractor, that shall be referred to an arbitrator. If, on the other hand, there be no such dispute, and the certificate of the architect be given, then that certificate is to be final: and here it appears that there was an endeavour to refer the case, but the order was discharged by the learned judge.

1880
February 25.

Common
Pleas
Division.

I take it, therefore, the matter stands thus. The parties have agreed that in certain circumstances, which have occurred here, there shall be a certificate of the architect showing a final balance, which certificate shall be conclusive evidence of the amount of that final balance. That certificate has been given here; that certificate is not bad *ex facie*, because, construing it most favourably to the defendant, that some portion of the measuring work or detail has been done by a measuring surveyor, there is nothing to show that the architect has deputed his judicial position as architect to another person or has acted, not upon his own judgment, but upon the judgment of another person. There is nothing to show to my mind that the architect was obliged to go through all the details of the measurements, and the other details to which I have referred, himself, and that therefore the certificate of the architect, who is arbitrator in some sense, is good.

And then as to the evidence: I cannot gather from the shorthand notes that any evidence was tendered to show further than what I have already said; not that the architect devolved his general judgment to another person, but only that he accepted from other persons measurements and details which I think the architect could not well have done or as well done himself as the person whom he got to do them for him.

I am, therefore, of opinion that there was no evidence rejected which would have altered the matter, or which could have altered the matter so as to show anything like that which in fact is denied, and not put forward on the part of the defendants anything like either legal or moral misconduct on the part of the architect—and that therefore the architect's certificate within clause 18 is final, and that the money upon that is due, and the verdict ought to stand.

LINDLEY, J.: I am of the same opinion. The questions which have been discussed really may be considered under two heads. First of all, the true construction of the deed and of what is called "the final certificate," and, secondly, the alleged error in rejecting evidence to impeach the certificate.

They are totally different matters, and I will consider them, therefore, separately. With respect to the true construction of the deed, *primâ facie* this certificate, which purports to be a final certificate, appears to be binding under clause 18 of the conditions. Mr. Moulton, however, says that this is not a final certificate such as is

1880
February 25.

Common
Pleas
Division.

contemplated by these conditions, and that he is not bound by it—that the final certificate which was contemplated by the conditions was to be made by the architect upon the completion of the works, and he relies for that construction upon the language in clause 17. Now, I have looked at clause 17 with some care, and it provides for the granting by the architect of what may be called interim certificates, and then says what is to be done when the work is completed; and when the work is completed it appears the general scheme of it is this—that an estimate is to be made of what remains due under the contract, and half of that estimate is to be paid at once; then, the ultimate balance is left for future determination. Of course, the ultimate balance will not be an estimate. It will be a careful calculation. It will not be the ultimate balance of the estimate: it will be the ultimate balance of what is due according to the contract, and clause 17 is a little imperfectly worded, because it does not show in so many terms that the architect is to settle that by a final certificate.

But, although it does not say so in so many words, it is impossible to construe clauses 17 and 18 without seeing that he is the person to do it in the first place, if he is not there is no other machinery for finding out what this final balance is, and when we look at the language of clause 17, after providing for the payment of half the estimate, it runs thus—"and the contractor is to be entitled to receive the balance of all moneys due or payable to him under or by virtue of the contract within three months from the completion of the works, except 50*l*., which is to be retained for six months, provided always that no final or other certificate is to cover or relieve the contractor from his liability under clause 11 whether or not the same is notified by the architect at the time or subsequent to granting any such certificate." That language shows plainly enough that a final certificate was to be granted, and the only thing final is the ultimate balance of what was due under the contract. It appears to me to be quite impossible to construe 17 in any other way than this—that the person who is to ascertain and settle what the final balance is is the architect. And that is more plain still when you come to clause 18; because, pursuing the same idea, clause 18 says: "A certificate of the architect or an award of the referee hereinbefore referred to, as the case may be, showing the final balance due or payable to the contractor is to be conclusive evidence of the work having been duly completed and that the contractor is entitled to receive payment of the final balance, but without prejudice to the liability of the contractor under clause 11."

Now, I confess I cannot follow Mr. Moulton's argument to the

1880
February 25.

Common
Pleas
Division.

extent that he desires that we should go—that is, to hold that the final balance here is not the final balance at all, but that rough casting which is to be made on the completion of the works, and upon which the payment on account is to proceed. It strikes me that the final balance is the thing to be ultimately calculated, the final balance in fact as expressed; and although it does not say so in so many words that the architect is to make that, it appears to me quite impossible to construe clauses 17 and 18 except in the sense that he is the person to make it, and that when made it is conclusive as provided by section 18.

Then, it is argued it is not to be conclusive, because it is open to submission to arbitration under clause 20. I confess I doubt very much whether it is. But, assuming that it is, the case will stand thus. There will be two clauses in this provision. One says that the final certificate is to be final; the other says it may be referred. Assuming that to be so, what does that mean? What interpretation is to be put upon two such clauses? I apprehend—and you must give them both effect—it would stand in this way; that if it is capable of being made the subject of a reference it is not to be conclusive for the purpose of that reference, but it is to be conclusive for every other purpose. That would be the construction I should put upon it, assuming that the certificate is a proper subject-matter of reference, which I doubt very much indeed, particularly because of the language of the body of the clause, and more particularly because of the language at the end, where it says that the award of the referee is to be equivalent to the certificate of the architect. Therefore, either it is not open to refer under clause 20, or, at all events, if it is, it is final for every purpose except the purpose of reference, and in every view the construction put upon it by Mr. Moulton would in my judgment be erroneous. It appears to me, therefore, that so far as the construction of the contract goes the case must be decided adversely to him, and that there is no misdirection at all, but the proper view was taken of the true construction of that document.

The next question is whether evidence which ought to have been received for the purpose of impeaching this certificate was rejected. A certificate, of course, can be impeached for fraud: it may be impeached for collusion: on the other hand, it cannot be impeached for mere negligence, or mere mistake, or mere idleness on the part of the architect. I have read the shorthand notes of what took place at the trial with some care, and I have come to the conclusion that what was meant was that evidence would have been forthcoming to prove some such matters as these—namely, to prove, for example, that the

1880
February 25.

Common
Pleas
Division.

architect had never given signed orders for extras—that evidence would have been given that he trusted to the measurement of the quantity surveyors. That last point is apparent upon the face of this final certificate, and I have looked through the shorthand notes with a view to see whether Mr. Harrison did in substance suggest that he had any evidence at all to show that the certificate was not in point of law the architect's certificate—that is to say, to show such an abdication of his functions as to render the certificate not his or anything of the kind.

I cannot come to the conclusion that any such evidence as that was tendered or that Mr. Harrison suggested that he had anything going to anything like that extent. But it appears to me that nothing short of that, or, of course, fraud or collusion—which was not suggested—would have been of any avail, and upon the whole of the shorthand notes of what took place, which I have read with care, it appears to me that there was no evidence rejected which would have availed the defendant. It was said that evidence might have been brought to show such matters as I have alluded to, and in particular to show an abdication of function on the part of the architect—but I can discover nothing further—nothing amounting at all to evidence to show that there was such an abdication by the architect of his functions as to render the certificate bad, or that any such evidence was ever really tendered or suggested to be producible at the trial.

Upon these grounds, therefore, I am of opinion that the rule ought to be discharged.

LORD COLERIDGE, L.C.J.: I concur in the judgment of my learned brothers upon the whole, though for some reasons, which I will indicate in a moment, I should have been myself disposed to let Mr. Clarke have a new trial. I say so for this reason—that it is always better, if there is any real belief upon the part of a party to a cause or his advisers that anything has been excluded from the hearing—that he has not had an opportunity of placing before the jury or before the Court anything which might have really tended to alter the state of facts of which he complains—it is, in my opinion, always better, if there is anything like a feeling of that sort, to yield to it, and to allow everything that a party desires to place before a jury to be placed before them.

In this case I must say that I concede at once that if evidence in support of anything like such a case as has been suggested to-day had been really tendered, most undoubtedly it ought to have been received. If it had been suggested that evidence was forthcoming which could have shown that upon points really of taste or skill or

1880
February 25.

Common
Pleas
Division.

scientific judgment, the arbitrator appointed under this contract had abdicated his functions to somebody else, and had allowed really judicial functions to be exercised by somebody other than himself whose conclusions, without consideration, he had adopted as his own, without saying that it would ultimately have led to a different conclusion, about which, till I had heard the case, I should pause, I certainly should have received that evidence. I say, further—though I think it would be hard upon counsel to expect, in the way in which cases are habitually managed *at nisi prius*—that there should be a formality of statement and that a mention to the presiding judge of every particular head of evidence or every class of evidence that is intended to be put forward should be made.

I think it would be very hard upon counsel—business could not probably be conducted in that way, and I do not in the least for myself desire to exact any such fulness of statement in this case, or any other, but at the same time I do think that if heads of evidence differing widely in their nature are intended afterwards to be relied upon, there should be some distinct indication to the presiding judge that those heads of evidence are tendered to him for acceptance or rejection; and what I think in the present case is—and I have now had the opportunity of carefully reading through the shorthand notes of the motion for a new trial—there was no contention made that evidence intending to impute such conduct to the arbitrator as I have suggested was tendered or was intended to be tendered at the trial.

To-day, unless I have misunderstood—and if I have, I sincerely regret any strong expressions I have made use of—it has been suggested that evidence was distinctly tendered to me at the trial to show, not merely that the statement in the certificate was correct— namely, that quantity surveyors had been allowed to do their work, and that the architect, without enquiry possibly, had adopted the conclusions of those quantity surveyors upon the work which no doubt was tendered, and which rightly or wrongly was rejected, and which rightly or wrongly would be rejected again—it has been suggested to-day, and, indeed, more than suggested, as I have understood, that evidence was tendered to me to show that certain definite and very important questions of taste and skill and scientific judgment were relegated by the architect to persons certainly unfit to express judgments upon them, and that the judgment of those quantity surveyors upon matters altogether beyond their province were gone into by them, and that their conclusions were adopted by the architect and made the foundation of certificates—that questions

5 (2)

1880
February 25.

Common
Pleas
Division.

of whether things should be under the contract treated as day work or as piece work were dealt with by them.

I should say that even upon such a question the certificate would be conclusive; but it is said that important questions of whether things were to be treated as day work or as piece work were brought to my attention, and that evidence to show that questions of that kind were handed over to quantity surveyors was tendered to me and rejected by me, and, further, that questions of what I call skill and taste and judgment as to whether this was an extra within the meaning of the contract and that was an addition within the meaning of the contract, that questions of that sort were handed over by the architect to these quantity surveyors, and that evidence showing that that had been done was distinctly tendered to me and was distinctly rejected.

Now, if I have misunderstood that contention, I desire to say that any heat that I have shown, or any strength of expression I have used, I am very sorry for; but if I have rightly understood that suggestion, now, upon looking at the shorthand notes, and somewhat confirmed by the view my learned brother has taken, I must say that I think no such suggestions ought to have been made—that they are wholly contrary to the facts which took place at the trial, and that suggestions of that kind being made (if they have been made) are fatal to the confidence and the perfect good faith that ought to exist between the Bar and the Bench, when evidence is not formally tendered and formally rejected, but when general expressions are used on one side and met by general expressions on the other, and business is conducted, as I say, upon the footing of perfect good faith, which could not be if the course which I understand to-day to have been pursued were commonly pursued.

But at the same time, though I say that, and I must say it strongly, I am aware that counsel and judges, too, may take erroneous views of what passes between them, and that understanding which one person may think very clear may not be at all so clear to the mind of another person, and that there may be honest misunderstandings as to what takes place on such an occasion as this; and to that extent, and so far as there has been an honest misunderstanding of what took place at the trial, of course, any observations which I have made before or now do not apply. But, as I say, upon grounds of that sort—feeling that if there is a chance of a misunderstanding, it is always better that the person who insists that something has been rejected which he understands himself or believes himself to have been tendered, or instructs his counsel to say has been tendered, has been rejected—on such grounds as that I should myself have been willing that there should have been a new trial; but only upon those grounds, because upon the law of the case I entirely agree with the judgment that my learned friends have pronounced. I think this certificate was conclusive.

1880
February 25.

Common
Pleas
Division.

I think as soon as the contract was read and the certificates were produced there was practically an end of the case—that if there had been—which I observe Mr. Harrison most carefully and emphatically and in the strongest and handsomest terms repudiates—if there was anything like a suggestion of real moral misconduct on the part of the architect—if there had been anything like fraud on his part, the case would have been very different. I think, as things stand, as soon as the contract was produced and the certificates were put in there was really an end of the case.

Collusion on the part of the architect with the plaintiff was not so much as suggested—indeed, was pointedly disavowed—collusion, of course, of the architect with the plaintiff would in my judgment have affected the validity of the certificate. I desire to say, as far as my present impression goes, that nothing short of collusion with the architect on the part of the plaintiff would have rendered these certificates invalid as regards the plaintiff. The plaintiff, as it appears to me, having got them in good faith and without any suggestion of collusion or fraud, has the right to rely upon them, and the defendant's remedy, if he has one, would be by proceeding against his architect for misconduct.

If his architect had been guilty of anything like misconduct the defendant would not be without remedy, because I think I pointed out at the trial, and I should say it over again, if the architect, by gross misconduct in his office, although not by collusion with the plaintiff—still, by gross misconduct in his office, had inflicted damage upon the defendant in the action, I strongly think that the defendant would have had an action against his architect to recover damages from the architect, and, amongst those damages, any sum that he had improperly to pay to a contractor in consequence of his architect's misconduct. The defendant would therefore be by no means without remedy even if his architect had misconducted himself. However, that is not suggested here; indeed, as I say, it is most handsomely disavowed by Mr. Harrison, and, therefore, I only mention it for the purpose of guarding myself from being supposed to think that under all circumstances such a certificate as this would be conclusive, or that if conclusive as between these parties, the person against whom it had been improperly obtained would be without a remedy.

1880
February 25.

Common
Pleas
Division.

On these grounds I concur in the judgment of the Court and think this rule should be discharged. If I have misunderstood what has been said to-day I regret it, and I regret anything that I have said in consequence of that misunderstanding; but if I have not misunderstood it I must say that what has been suggested to-day is totally different from anything that at least I understood to have been suggested to me at the trial of the case.

Rule discharged with costs.

––––––––––––

1879
December 4.

1880
May 27.

Court of
Appeal.

𝕴𝖓 𝖙𝖍𝖊 𝕳𝖎𝖌𝖍 𝕮𝖔𝖚𝖗𝖙 𝖔𝖋 𝕵𝖚𝖘𝖙𝖎𝖈𝖊 (𝕼𝖚𝖊𝖊𝖓'𝖘 𝕭𝖊𝖓𝖈𝖍 𝕯𝖎𝖛𝖎𝖘𝖎𝖔𝖓).

(*Before* FIELD, J.)

AND

𝕴𝖓 𝖙𝖍𝖊 𝕮𝖔𝖚𝖗𝖙 𝖔𝖋 𝕬𝖕𝖕𝖊𝖆𝖑.

(*Before* BRAMWELL, BAGGALLAY and BRETT, L.JJ.)

YOUNG *v.* SMITH (*a*).

Payment of Quantity Surveyor—Custom.

The plaintiff, a quantity surveyor, was employed by A., the architect of the defendant, S., who wished to erect a house at L., to take out quantities, which he did in consideration of a payment calculated at $2\frac{1}{2}$ per cent. on the accepted tender and 18*l.* 15*s.* 6*d.* for lithography. The work went to tender and C.'s tender was accepted, the plaintiff's charges being expressly included in it. The work was commenced, but when it was partly finished and partly paid for, C., the builder, became embarrassed and then bankrupt, and S. took the work out of his hands. The plaintiff sued S. for his charges:—
Held, that as there was an accepted tender and S. had found a builder, the plaintiff had no cause of action against the defendant.

The facts of the case are as follows:—

Mr. Young, the plaintiff, is a quantity surveyor, Mr. Alexander is an architect, Dr. Smith is a gentleman practising as a surgeon at Lewisham, and Mr. Cook is a builder.

In 1877 Dr. Smith instructed Mr. Alexander to prepare drawings and a specification and to obtain tenders for a house for him at Lewisham. And in August, 1877, Mr. Alexander (having prepared the drawings and specification) instructed Mr. Young to take out the quantities, which he did accordingly, and the summary which formed one of the bills of quantities contained

(*a*) This case was cited and approved in *Bassett* v. *North*, [1892] 1 Q. B. 333.

an item of $2\frac{1}{2}$ per cent. upon the amount of the tender and another item of 18*l.* 15*s.* 6*d.* for lithography, these two items being what is usually called "Surveyor's charges."

The bills of quantities were sent to certain builders (a copy to each one) and the 19th September was appointed to receive the tenders. The tender of Mr. Cook was the lowest, and was 2,700*l.*, but when arrangements were being made for the contract to be signed, Mr. Cook discovered that in sending in his tender he had omitted to include the surveyor's charges, and thereupon Dr. Smith himself added them (86*l.* about) to the tender, and brought the tender as revised up to 2,786*l.* 15*s.* 6*d.*, which sum was made the contract sum, and the works were thereupon commenced and about 1,400*l.* worth of work was executed. The architect gave to the builder certificates as the work went on (these certificates amounting in the whole to about 1,100*l.*), and these certificates were given entirely for work done, and none of them included anything for or on account of surveyor's charges.

The builder (Cook) became unable, from want of funds, to carry on the work, and the contract was determined. Dr. Smith thereupon ceased to consult his architect and employed other builders to complete the work.

Mr. Young, during the time Cook was carrying on the work, applied to him twice for payment of his (the surveyor's) charges, being under the impression that the architect had certified them, and that Cook had thereupon become possessed of them, and would hand them over in usual course. But Cook took no notice of these applications, and thereupon Mr. Young applied to Mr. Alexander for an explanation, when he was informed that the surveyor's charges had not been certified for or paid by Dr. Smith to Cook, and that they would not then be likely to be paid over, as Dr. Smith and Mr. Cook were at issue as to the completion of the contract, and that in all probability Dr. Smith would take the work out of Cook's hands. Some correspondence then ensued, in which Mr. Young applied to Dr. Smith for payment of the quantities, which Dr. Smith declined to make.

Judgment.

FIELD, J.: I am very clearly of opinion that this case fails. I thought so yesterday, and I think so still more to-day.

This is an action to recover the sum of 86*l.*, which the plaintiff alleges is the fair value of his work and services as a quantity surveyor, and he brings the action, not against the builder, but against Dr. Smith, whom I will call, shortly, the employer. In order to prove that contract, he must prove in the ordinary way that he was employed by Dr. Smith, either personally or by means of some authorised agent, to do the work in question, upon the terms that Dr. Smith would pay him the fair value of his work. He has got to make out that contract, otherwise he fails.

Now, what does he prove? He proves that Dr. Smith was about to build a house, and that he had adopted a course very common in those cases. First of all, I presume, he called in his architect, Mr.

1879
December 4.

1880
May 27.

Court of
Appeal.

1879
December 4.

1879
December 4.
───
1880
May 27.
───
Court of
Appeal.

Alexander, and, I presume, that having told Mr. Alexander what sort of a house he wanted, the number of rooms, and size, and particularly, I have no doubt, what the amount was that he was prepared to spend, Mr. Alexander prepared what is called a specification. That informs any person who wants to build what the work is which the architect says he wants done. There are plans and the specification, and they point out together exactly what the house is to be, and what the character of the work is to be as to bricks, timber, and everything else.

The employer and the architect in that state of mind have now got to get someone to build the house. How shall they do it? There are various modes. By employing a builder himself sometimes, and sometimes he then loses a great deal of money by it. Perhaps he says, "I will not do that, I will employ an architect." "How will you have it done?" says the architect. "Well, what do you recommend?" he says. "I do not want to spend more than a certain sum of money." The architect says, "If you are particular about the amount, and if that is more important than the character of the work, my advice to you is, put it up for tender. If you like me to go to William Cubitt, or any man of that sort, I think I can tell them enough of it for them to give you an estimate, and you will get the work done very well. You will pay ten per cent. more than anybody else would charge, but you will have ten per cent. in value on the work done. If you do not like that, let all the builders come in and say what they will do it for." Of course, you say, "How are the builders to know what they are to do? Looking at the plans will not tell them. Then there must be somebody to take out the quantities, that is to say, how much wood and timber and excavation, and everything else are required, and then those quantities and the specification will indicate to anybody's mind what the price they can afford to do it for is." Upon that, the plans and specifications are placed in the hands of the quantity surveyor. They are very able gentlemen and they do a very large business, and I hope make very large profits when they are successful, but sometimes, like every other profession, I suppose they have losses.

What is the contract made with the quantity surveyor? I take it to be very clear that the contract is this. "I am going to build a house," says Dr. Smith, "and I am going to put it up for tender, that is, I am going to let the trade tender, or certain named people" (because, generally speaking, the tenders are invited from certain builders selected by the architect). He says, "I am going to ask if they will tender upon your quantities, and what sum they will ask to

1879
December 4.

1880
May 27.

Court of
Appeal.

have this work done for." If it is put up for tender, and if there is a successful competitor who enters into a contract, what happens? "It is not intended that I shall pay you, but that the successful person shall pay you" (the builder, I will call him). That is the contract made with the employer. I am putting it as the employer now, irrespective of the case that was cited in the course of the argument; the contract is not a contract for payment, it is a contract that "I will go on regularly in course to obtain a contractor, who, by his contract, shall not only contract that he will build the house, but shall also enter into an implied contract with you (the quantity surveyor) that if I will add to the sum mentioned in the contract the sum due to you, he (the builder) will pay you."

That is the conditional contract. Therefore, if things take their ordinary course, that contract becomes completed by the course of conduct. What was the course here? Mr. Young did his work, and I have no doubt that he did it very well, and it went to tender. On the first occasion none of the offers were within the limit which the employer had fixed; at least, I presume so. At all events, none of them were accepted, for some reason or other which I do not know. After that Mr. Cook, a builder, makes a tender, and thereupon the contract is made. I forget the exact date of it; and Mr. Cook adding as he does the amount due to Mr. Young in respect of his quantities to the amount, a contract under seal is executed; at least, I suppose it was under seal, it does not matter whether it was or not.

At any rate, a contract is entered into by which, with the knowledge of Mr. Young, and upon the custom or usage of the case, the employer, instead of paying Mr. Young or making any engagement with Mr. Young to pay him for his services, engages and contracts with the builder that he will pay the builder for these services. Thereupon, according to the usage as proved to-day, there is a new contract made, an A. B. C. contract which entirely gets rid of and destroys the old contract. No doubt that is what happened in this case. Mr. Cook did make that contract, and the sum was added to the tender and added to the contract price, and there was a contract to pay by instalments all but 25 per cent. until the matter should be completed, the 25 per cent. being kept for caution money until the final completion, and until the building should be certified by the architect.

In this case everything went on in the ordinary way. The contract was made. The architect certified up to a certain sum, but in the month of May, or earlier—at all events, April or May—the builder became embarrassed—sometimes builders do get embarrassed. I

1879
December 4.

1880
May 27.

Court of
Appeal.

observe upon the facts of the case that Smith asked, apparently with good intention, the architect, Mr. Alexander, to advance money for wages which the builder was not able to find himself. Therefore, in the months of May and June the state of things was that there was a considerable sum certified for, 1,100*l.*, and there was also work still left undone. On the 18th June, Mr. Smith had not, as Mr. Turner said, determined or rescinded the contract, but under the powers and provisions of the contract he took the work out of the hands of Cook and completed the work himself.

The evidence shows, I think, that up to this time Mr. Young had never made any application whatever to the defendant Smith, but had applied to the builder for payment, and the builder had said, "I cannot pay you as Mr. Alexander has not included any sums for quantities in my certificate." Thereupon Mr. Young waited, perhaps in accordance with the usage; I do not know. He thought he could not sue the builder, perhaps. It will be for me to decide that point when the question arises. At present I shall hesitate before I say that the builder should have any advance under these circumstances. That is a matter I do not dispose of to-day.

The question to-day is whether he has any right of action against Dr. Smith. I say that there has been no contract here by Dr. Smith to pay. I do not adopt the language we heard of yesterday about shifting liability. There was never any contract here which Dr. Smith has broken. His contract was, "I will go on and will employ a contractor to build this house at such sum as I think reasonable." He did employ a contractor for the sum which he thought reasonable, and the contractor went on, and ultimately made default. Then, Mr. Turner grounds himself upon the authority, or the supposed authority, of the case of *Moon* v. *Witney Union (a)*. But that case does not carry him any distance at all. In that case the employer had failed in his own conditional contract. He had not got a builder at all. He had got no one at all. Therefore, the true view, I think, of *Moon* v. *Witney Union (ubi supra)*, so far as it does not depend upon the particular facts of the case, so far as it is a principle at all, is in accordance with the conclusion at which I have arrived in regard to this case.

Mr. Turner says, the question arises upon the defaults of Dr. Smith. I know of no default of Dr. Smith at present, none whatever. He gave him a builder, and, as far as I know, he has performed his engagement with the builder. There is no evidence that he has

(*a*) 3 Bing. N. C. 814.

not. There is not the smallest evidence that he has done other than
perform his contract with the builder. He has not paid the builder,
and for aught I know the builder does not deserve to be paid. I do not
want to make any reflection upon Mr. Cook, but he seems to have
gone into liquidation very soon afterwards, and for aught I know, Dr.
Smith has paid all that he has to pay. The misfortune of Mr. Young, no
doubt, is that the architect did not think it right to include in the
certificate anything for quantities. That is not the affair of Dr. Smith. I
am sure a gentleman like Mr. Alexander knows well the high position
which an architect holds between the employer, the building
surveyor, and the contractor. He is a judge, and is bound to do his
duty to them all three, and in the exercise of that duty it is for him to
consider whether his certificate should or should not include
anything on account of quantities. According to Mr. Young's very
fair and good evidence, he exercised that discretion according to his
best judgment, and Dr. Smith is not liable for that in any shape or
way. The architect is not the agent of Dr. Smith, he is the judge
between the three parties, and I hope and believe that all good and
honest men know that duty and thoroughly exercise it between man
and man. There is no liability whatever on Dr. Smith for any act of
that kind, nor is it any default whatever of Dr. Smith.

I have therefore not the slightest hesitation in saying (although I
regret it for Mr. Young's sake, because he cannot make Dr. Smith
liable) that I must non-suit him.

In the Court of Appeal, the Lords Justices, after hearing counsel for
the plaintiff, but without calling on the other side or stating reasons,
dismissed the appeal, with costs.

1879
December 4.

1880
May 27.

Court of
Appeal.

1881
April 13.

Queen's
Bench
Division.

In the High Court of Justice (Queen's Bench Division).

(*Before* MANISTY, J., and a Special Jury.)

BIRDSEYE

v.

COMMISSIONERS OF DOVER HARBOUR BOARD (*a*).

Quantity Surveyor's Charges for Measuring Up—Customs.

Custom of the building trade for an architect to call in a quantity surveyor at the employer's expense.

This was an action brought by a quantity surveyor against the defendants to recover the sum of 76*l.* 5*s.* for fees. The plaintiff relied on an employment by the defendants' architect and on a custom in the building trade that when a builder or contractor did work, the architect had a right to call in the assistance of a quantity surveyor, to be paid by his employer. The defendants denied any contract and employment, denied the custom, and said it did not apply to this case.

It appeared that in April, 1878, a Mr. Adcock had agreed to take certain land of the defendants at Granville Gardens, Dover, and to build there certain waiting-rooms, refreshment-rooms, and baths. He was to lay out the residue in gardens and pleasure-grounds.

By June it became necessary, as the buildings and gardens were nearly completed, that they should be measured up and the amount ascertained. Thereupon the plaintiff was employed, and rendered the services sued for in the present action. Mr. Adcock was to be paid for any expenditure he was put to beyond 350*l.* by the Board, and the large sum of 4,150*l.* was alleged to have become due to him. The greater part was paid off, but there remained a balance of 1,005*l.*, and this was reduced, by a compromise made by Mr. Adcock with Mr. Finnis, a member of the Board, to 700*l.* on November 4th, 1878. Mr. Adcock stated he was induced to accept the lower sum on the condition of the Board's paying the professional charges, *i.e.*, the solicitor, the arbitrator, and the surveyor.

The plaintiff sent in his account to the Board on January 13th, 1879, but Mr. Stilwell, the solicitor and registrar, replied the next day that the Board knew nothing about it, and had never authorised the employment of the plaintiff. The following day the plaintiff again wrote: "Mr. Adcock informed me that the Board had agreed to pay my account direct, or I should not have sent it to you." The matter thus slumbered till October, when Mr. Adcock wrote to the chairman: "May I ask you to pay Mr. Birdseye's account, as it was

(*a*) See *Young* v. *Smith*, *post*; and *North* v. *Bassett*, [1892] 1 Q. B. 333.

1881
April 13.

Queen's
Bench
Division.

agreed by Mr. Finnis with me, when the compromise was effected, that the Board should pay the surveyor." To this Mr. Stilwell answered: "The Board know nothing about it, and the plaintiff was so informed as far back as January of this year (1879)." Nearly a year elapsed after this before the plaintiff issued his writ.

For the plaintiff, several architects and surveyors were called, who spoke to the custom of the building trade, that in any large matter, say over 2,000*l.*, the architect was entitled to call in a quantity surveyor, to be paid by the employer.

For the defendants there were called Mr. Stilwell, Mr. Finnis, Mr. Humphreys, Mr. Pearce, and Mr. Court, member of the Harbour Board, who were present at the meeting of February 5th, 1878, when Mr. Williams, one of the plaintiff's witnesses, was there. The plaintiff's name was not mentioned as a man to be employed. Mr. Finnis said he had told Mr. Adcock the Board would pay the architect, but he did not see why the architect should not pay his own surveyor. He was only advising Mr. Adcock to accept the compromise of the 700*l.*; he had always denied that he promised to pay the plaintiff.

Murphy, Q.C., A. L. Smith, and R. M. Bray, for the plaintiff; M'Intyre, Q.C., and Finlay for the defendants.

MANISTY, J., in summing up, said the evidence of a direct contract to employ the plaintiff was not so satisfactory as, perhaps, the jury might desire. But the great question was whether they thought the custom set up had been proved, viz., whether in a work of this magnitude the architect or contractor had a right to call in to his assistance a quantity surveyor, whose services the employers were to pay for. Mr. Adcock appeared to fill the double part here of contractor and tenant under the defendant board, and that, perhaps, accounted for the plaintiff being left out in the cold when payment was made. And the second question would be, had Mr. Adcock accepted the 700*l.* on the assurance that he would not have to pay the surveyor, but the board would do so.

The jury promptly returned a verdict for the plaintiff for the amount claimed.

1881
May 4, 27.

Queen's
Bench
Division.

𝕳igh 𝕮ourt of 𝕵ustice (𝕼ueen's 𝕭ench 𝕯ibision).

(*Before* Lord Coleridge, C.J., and Manisty and Bowen, JJ.)

EVANS AND ANOTHER *v.* CARTE.

Building Contract—Liability of Employer to pay for Reduced Quantities—Custom.

An architect was employed to make plans for a theatre. The employer objected to the cost of the theatre as planned, and the architect employed a quantity surveyor to reduce the quantities; but the employer ultimately decided not to build. Held, that the quantity surveyor could recover his charges against the employer only upon evidence of actual instructions, and not by virtue of any custom.

This action was brought by a firm of quantity surveyors against Mr. D'Oyly Carte, the well-known theatrical manager, in respect of work done for the theatre now being built for him on the site of Beaufort Buildings, Strand.

Mr. Carte employed as his architect, a Mr. Emden, and the quantities were taken out on his original plans by the plaintiffs, for which work they had claimed 344*l.* This sum had been paid to them by Mr. Carte, who refused to set up any defence as to his legal liability, seeing that he thought himself clearly morally liable for that sum.

Mr. Emden, as Mr. Carte said, had led him to suppose that the theatre on his original plans could be built for about 12,000*l.*

On his return from the United States, where he had gone in October, 1879, for a six months' tour with an operatic company, Mr. Carte was shown some tenders for the building of the theatre by Mr. Emden, which had been obtained by the latter in his absence, and the lowest of which amounted to over 18,000*l.*

At an interview between them on June 2nd, 1880, Mr. Emden showed Mr. Carte that the total cost would be about 21,000*l.*, but said that it might be fairly expected that this amount might be reduced by some 3,000*l.* As to what had happened as the consequence of this interview, there was a conflict of evidence.

Delays arose, and on the 20th May, 1880, Mr. Carte wrote a letter to the *Times,* in which he stated that the plans were perfectly approved, but that he was delayed by the "red-tapeism of the Board of Works."

Mr. Carte said that he had then told Mr. Emden that nothing more was to be done in the matter until he had himself carefully looked over the estimates and considered the matter more fully. This Mr. Emden denied. On June 8th, Mr. Carte gave the latter notice that he refused to allow him any longer to act as his architect.

The claim now made by the plaintiffs was for work done "in preparing quantities on reductions, and 1 per cent. on omissions," between June 3rd and 9th. This work, as Mr. Carte said, had not been done for him at his request, and indeed, if ordered by Mr. Emden, the latter in doing so had acted contrary to his express instructions not to proceed in the matter after June 2nd.

1881
May 4, 27.

Queen's
Bench
Division.

The action was tried before Mr. Justice Bowen, and resulted in a verdict in favour of the plaintiffs for 132*l.* Bowen, J., told the jury that the question was whether there had been an actual authority from Mr. Carte to get the quantities reduced.

W. Y. Clare moved in this case for a rule *nisi* for a new trial, on the ground that the verdict was against the weight of evidence.

The Court granted a rule *nisi* for a new trial, and cause was shown on May 27th, 1881.

In the course of the argument, Lord COLERIDGE said that (apart from actual contract) it was quite monstrous that the employer should pay for the "quantities"—that is, that he should pay for what it is the duty of the architect to do. The builders are to make their tenders upon the plans, but before they do so they must know the "quantities" they represent. Why should the architect's employer pay for them? In the actions I have tried, it has been urged that if the building goes on the employer actually pays for the "quantities," as the builder adds them to his prices; but it has never been suggested that the employer is directly liable to pay for them, except upon the ground of some custom or contract. No doubt, architects have been called to prove that it is reasonable and customary; but so I have heard architects state that where, years after their plans are furnished, buildings are erected on other plans, the original architect is entitled to his commission on the sum expended on works he did not execute. In the present case, however—the claim having been put upon the ground of actual authority—the general question of law does not arise, and it becomes a question as to the alleged authority.

This question was accordingly argued, but it, indirectly, a good deal involved the other, which arose with reference to the probabilities on the one side and the other as to the alleged authority. On the part of the plaintiffs, strong reliance was placed on Mr. Carte's letter in the *Times*, as showing that the real cause of the delay was not any difficulty about the plans and the estimates. On the other side it was urged that it was the business of the architect, who had made plans the execution of which would prove far too expensive, to cut them down.

Lord COLERIDGE, C.J., observed that, probably, the original plans would be too ornamental, and the architect had to cut out superfluous ornaments and make his designs more simple, and then the employer is to pay the surveyor the architect employs to simplify his own designs and reduce his own estimates.

1881
May 4, 27.

Queen's
Bench
Division.

After hearing the whole case argued at some length Lord COLERIDGE, after conferring with his brethren, said: I suppose this is more a matter of feeling than of mere money. I mean that the costs of another trial would probably exceed the sum at stake. There are, indeed, probably, few such cases in which the costs will not exceed the sum at stake. In this case, certainly, the cost of a second trial would exceed 132*l.*, the amount of the sum at stake. Is it worth pursuing?

However, the counsel for the defendant pressed for a new trial, and at the close of the argument, Lord Coleridge, after conferring with his brethren on the bench, said, so far as he was concerned, he should himself have given a different verdict, as he did not believe that Mr. Carte had really given the authority for these "reduced quantities." But he did not think it was a case in which the Court ought to set aside the verdict of a jury who had seen and heard the witnesses. The action was for the cost of "reducing the quantities" upon designs of the architect, which had been found too ornamental and expensive. The recollection of the parties was at variance as to the fact of the alleged authority, but Mr. Carte did not positively deny that he knew the "quantities" were being "reduced," and ratification or tacit assent would be equivalent to precedent authority. And, therefore, though with some hesitation, the conclusion to which the jury have arrived having been one at which they might not unreasonably have arrived, he thought it best not to disturb the verdict.

Mr. Justice MANISTY concurred in the conclusion. Though not quite agreeing with his lordship's view in favour of the defendant, he thought, he said, that to set aside this verdict would be to usurp the functions of the jury. A verdict ought not to be set aside unless the Court was satisfied that it was wrong, and that he was not satisfied of in this case.

Mr. Justice BOWEN concurred. The case, he said, was tried, not by himself as judge without a jury, but with a jury, and it was not a sufficient ground for setting aside the verdict that perhaps the judge, had he tried it himself, might have come to a different conclusion.

Judgment for the plaintiffs.

𝔍n the Court of Appeal.

(Lord Esher, M.R., Cotton and Lindley, L.JJ.)

𝔍n the House of Lords.

(Present: Earl of Selborne, Lords Watson, Bramwell, Fitzgerald, Halsbury, and Ashbourne.)

JACKSON (Appellant)

v.

EASTBOURNE LOCAL BOARD (Respondents).

1885
February 18.

Court of
Appeal.

1886
March 2.

House of
Lords.

Construction of Sea-Wall—Special Act—Respective Liabilities of Contractor and Employer on its Destruction by the Seas and Winds.

Where a contract is entered into to construct a sea-wall, the contractor, and not the employer, takes the risks of interference with the work while in progress by the action of the winds and seas, which, in the ordinary contemplation of all, are risks incidental to the complete performance of the contract; and there is no implied contract by the employer that the seashore on which the proposed works are to be executed, shall remain in the same condition as at the date of the contract. The fact that the employer is by a special Act of Parliament bound to protect the adjacent shore from the action of the winds and seas does not create any obligation on their part in favour of the contractor, or exonerate him from the special terms of his own contract.

In this case the Eastbourne Local Board sued John Jackson, the contractor, and Robert Preston and William Edwin Jackson, his sureties, for alleged breaches of contract to build a sea-wall at Eastbourne. Clause 9 of the contract was as follows:—

The said contractor shall take upon himself and be answerable for all accidents and damages from or by seas, winds, drift of craft, fire, or any cause whatsoever which may occur during the construction of the works under this contract, and, in case of such accidents or damages arising, shall repair and make good the same as soon as possible at his own costs and charges.

The other material terms of the contract and the facts are sufficiently stated in the special case and judgments. Before the issue of the writ the defendant, John Jackson, had appointed an arbitrator under the arbitration clause of the contract, and on the issue of the writ he took out a summons to stay the action under the Common Law Procedure Act, 1854, upon which the master ordered a stay. This was appealed from, and ultimately an order was made by consent on 31st January, 1883, referring the action and all matters in difference to Mr. Harrison Hayter, C.E., with Mr. A. M. Channell as legal assessor; and with liberty to state a special case.

The arbitrator made his award on 12th August, 1884, in the form of a special case, which, omitting immaterial portions, was as follows:—

(1.) This is an action brought by the Eastbourne Local Board against John Jackson, as contractor, and against Robert Preston and William Edwin Jackson, as sureties to the extent of 1,000*l.* for John Jackson, as such contractor, for damages for alleged breaches of a contract to build a sea-wall at Eastbourne.

(2.) The said contract contained an arbitration clause, under which, prior to the issuing of the writ, the said John Jackson had given to the Local Board notice that he required an arbitration in respect of certain claims which, he alleged, he had against them, and upon the action being commenced the defendants therein took out a summons to stay the action under the Common Law Procedure Act, 1854, *s.* 11.

(3.) Thereupon, by order of the Honourable Sir H. Hawkins, dated 31st January, 1883, it was, by consent, ordered that the action and all matters in difference should be referred to the award of Harrison Hayter, Esquire, Member of the Council of the Institution of Civil Engineers, who should have as his legal assessor Arthur Moseley Channell, Esq., such legal assessor being, at his discretion, at liberty to state a case on any question of law, or the legal effect of any evidence, for the opinion of the Court, and that the arbitrator should make a separate award as to the matters on which the assessor should not think fit to state a special case. No proceedings to be taken to enforce that separate award until the decision of the special case, and the sums awarded by the separate award and those found due by the decision of the Court to be set off against each other in such manner as the Court should direct.

(4.) It was, by the said order, further ordered that the defendants in the action should have the conduct of the reference, and that the costs of the cause and of the reference and award should be in the discretion of the arbitrator.

(5.) The evidence adduced by the respective parties having been heard before us, the said Harrison Hayter and Arthur Moseley Channell as legal assessor, and I, the said Arthur Moseley Channell, having, in the exercise of the discretion given to me by the said order, decided, on the application of the parties, that a case should be stated for the opinion of the Court on the question of law hereinafter raised, and on the legal effect of the evidence hereinafter stated, we state the following—

Case.

(6.) By the Eastbourne Improvement Act, 1879 (42 & 43 Vict. cap. xevii.), a local and personal Act passed on the 3rd July, 1879, the Eastbourne Local Board acquired power (amongst other things) to make a sea-wall about 1,800 feet in length. A print of the Act may be referred to by either party on the argument, and the Act is to be taken to form part of this case. The most material part of it is the 16th section, which is as follows:—

> Subject to the provisions of this Act, and to the powers of deviation hereby given, the Board may, in the lines and situation and upon the lands in that behalf delineated on the deposited plans, and described in the deposited book of reference, and according to the levels in that behalf shown on the deposited sections, make and maintain the works following (that is to say), a sea-wall or embankment, commencing at or near the eastern end of the Grand Parade at a point called or known as Splash Point, thence continuing in an easterly direction and terminating on the foreshore at or near the paved glacis of the Government Fort known as the Grand or Circular Redoubt.
>
> The widening and improving on the south side thereof of the street called or

known as South Street, such widening to commence at or near the junction of Gildridge Road with the said South Street, and to terminate at or near the junction of South Street with Grange Road, and all necessary and proper roads, approaches, sluices, openings, groynes, and other works and conveniences connected therewith or incidental thereto respectively. But nothing in this Act contained shall authorise the Board to construct the breakwater shown upon the deposited plans. Provided that the Board shall make and complete the sea-wall or embankment within the period by this Act limited for the completion thereof and for ever after maintain the same, and shall take all reasonable precautions for preventing encroachments by the sea during the construction thereof. Provided also that in the event of the Board failing to complete the sea-wall or embankment within the said period, all lands shown on the deposited plan relating thereto, which shall have been purchased by the Board, shall thereupon vest in and become the property of the owners of the lands adjoining thereto, in proportion to the extent of their lands respectively adjoining the same.

(7.) After the passing of the said Act the Local Board invited tenders for the sea-wall according to certain drawings, bills of quantities, and specification, and general conditions and stipulations which they had prepared.

(8.) John Jackson, who is a contractor for public works, having considerable experience in works of a similar character, sent in a tender for the sum of 16,923*l.* 2*s.* 4*d.*, which, though not the lowest tender, was accepted by the Board under the advice of their consulting engineer.

(9.) Thereupon a contract under seal, bearing date the 5th April, 1880, was entered into between John Jackson and the Local Board. The first clause of the contract incorporated the drawings, bill of quantities and specification. The general conditions and stipulations formed part of the specification. A complete copy of the said contract, and of the specification and general conditions and stipulations, is contained in the appendix. A tracing of the principal contract plan or drawing, and sections, is also hereunto annexed and forms part of the case. The bill of quantities may be referred to on the argument by either party if desired.

(10.) By bond, dated the ————, Robert Preston and William Edwin Jackson became bound to the Local Board as sureties to the extent of 1,000*l.* for the due performance of the contract by John Jackson.

(11.) The wall designed and contracted for was to be built on a shingle beach at a point between high and low water mark. There were in the beach, at and before the time of the invitation of tenders, certain groynes which had been erected some time previously (without any reference to the intended wall) for the purpose of preserving the shingle beach as it then was as a protection against the inroads of the sea. The level of the beach on the line of the proposed wall at the time of the making of the plan is shown thereon by a line edged with burnt sienna, and the position of the then groynes is also indicated on the plan.

(12.) The documents forming the contract contain no express provision for the making of groynes by either party. The only express reference to groynes is a clause in the specification that "all the old timber in groynes" and other old material are to remain the property of the Local Board, and "are not to be removed from their present position without the special instructions of the surveyor."

(13.) The documents forming the contract contain the following indications, which would show to any person understanding such matters that the wall shown to be thirty feet high was designed on the assumption of the preservation of the beach at a height not materially less than that of the existing beach shown in the contract drawings. The contract sections of the wall show a battered face (that is a face sloping inwards) for a depth of fifteen feet from the coping, the remaining fifteen feet being vertical. Of this, latter vertical fifteen feet, eleven feet six inches is shown to be in the beach, and the galt being then reached the remaining three feet six inches is shown as founded in the galt. The upper fifteen feet below the coping was specified to "be rendered on the face with Portland cement" for the purpose of improving the appearance of the part which it was assumed might be exposed. The wall designed, though of sufficient strength to answer its purpose as long as the beach remained at or about its then level, was not of sufficient strength to stand if the height of the beach was reduced below a level of about fifteen feet from the coping.

(14.) The natural consequence of building a wall in the beach below high-water mark would be to increase the effect of the sea in washing away the shingle at and about the foot of the wall. The scour of the shingle along the face of the wall, caused by the wash of the sea, would cut into a concrete wall, and weaken, and in time destroy it. Proper groynes are the only engineering means resorted to to stop such action. Assuming some groynes to be required before the wall was erected to preserve the shingle, further groynes, longer, stronger, and raised to a higher level, would be required when the wall was built, and this might have been and ought to have been foreseen, even if it was not, in fact, foreseen. The groynes which would be required would be structures of a permanent character, to serve a permanent purpose, and not temporary expedients such as a contractor is called upon to execute in order to carry on operations.

(15.) Before the contractor, John Jackson, sent in his tender, he had a conversation, in which groynes were mentioned, with Mr. Tomes, the surveyor to the Local Board, who had (under the superintendence of Mr. Stileman, the consulting engineer) prepared the drawings and specification, and under whose supervision the wall was to be built. It was objected on the part of the Local Board that this conversation was not admissible in evidence, and it was received and is here stated subject to that objection, which is referred by us to the Court.

(16.) The purport of this conversation was that Mr. Jackson asked Mr. Tomes, "What about groynes?" or some such general question, and that Mr. Tomes replied that the Local Board had not definitely decided whether to keep the old groynes or put in new ones, but "you (Mr. Jackson) will not have anything to do with that—it will not be in the 'contract,' " or words to that effect.

(17.) Soon after the contract was signed some work was commenced by the contractor, but difficulties arose with fishermen who had been in the habit of beaching their boats and drying their nets on the ground. From this cause there was great delay, for which the contractor was not responsible, but his claims for such delay are not included in this special case.

(18.) During the year 1880 some part of the wall had been erected, notwithstanding the interruptions caused by the fishermen, and after the 12th May, 1881, more rapid progress was made. By the 22nd October, 1881, when a large part of the wall was washed down, the state of the wall was as follows: Foundations in for a length of 940 feet or thereabouts; wall finished and backed up for a length of 450 feet or thereabouts; wall finished but not backed up for a length of 375 feet or thereabouts.

(19.) As the wall was built the shingle diminished. Considerable injury was done from time to time to the face of the wall by the scour of the shingle along it, and before the 22nd October, 1881, the face of the wall had become exposed in many places to a considerable depth below the battered face.

(20.) Mr. Jackson and his local manager from time to time mentioned the subject of groynes to Mr. Tomes, and suggested the advisability of their being put in to protect he wall. They got no definite reply as to what would be done, being usually told that no decision had been come to; but Mr. Tomes, when pressed, repudiated there being any obligation on the Board to put in groynes. There was a correspondence going on between the parties and their solicitors on other subjects, and in several of these letters groynes are mentioned. Copies of the letters or extracts from the letters in which groynes are referred to are in appendix.

(21.) On the 5th July, 1881, the Board informed Mr. Jackson that they had decided to erect groynes, at the same time repudiating liability for damage to the wall by reason of there being no groynes. (See letter of 5th July, 1881, copied in the appendix.)

(22.) On the 15th July, 1881, drawings, specifications and bills of quantities for the intended groynes were forwarded by the Board to Mr. Jackson with a view to his tendering, and on the 29th July, 1881, he sent in a tender for the work substantially in accordance with the invitation of the Local Board, but suggested a small alteration as to the depth at which the land ties were to be secured. (See letters in the appendix.) The tender was within a few shillings of the lowest tender. After some correspondence the Board (on the 13th September, 1881) refused to depart from the specifications and plans of their surveyor, and they postponed the consideration of any tender for the groynes. I, the arbitrator, am of opinion that the departure from the specifications and plans, suggested by Mr. Jackson, was a reasonable suggestion which might with advantage have been adopted by the Local Board. The reason Mr. Jackson's suggestion was not adopted, and that a contract for the erection of groynes was not then made, appears to have been the disinclination of the surveyor of the Board to pay any attention to criticisms of his plans by Mr. Jackson.

(23.) On the 21st October, 1881, Mr. Jackson wrote another letter (see appendix), in which he alluded to the grave consequences to the Board which might occur from the want of groynes. On the same day Mr. Jackson's manager at the works, having his attention called to the extent to which the face of the wall was exposed by the diminution of the shingle, took measurements at various places, and found the wall exposed in many places to a depth twenty-two feet below the coping, thus leaving only eight feet to the bottom of the wall, instead of there being fifteen feet maximum exposed and fifteen feet minimum to the bottom of the wall, as shown in the contract section.

(24.) On the next day, the 22nd October, 1881, a severe storm occurred, and a large part of the completed wall was washed down. A length of between 400 and 500 feet altogether fell. The cause of the wall falling was that the beach had not been kept up to the level shown in the contract drawings by efficient groynes.

(25.) Portions of the old groynes had remained to this time. They had been allowed to get out of repair to such an extent that they had ceased to act as groynes. If the old groynes had been in a proper state, and had been raised in height, lengthened and strengthened, so as to become in effect new groynes, similar to those proposed and ultimately constructed by the Local Board, they might have been effectual in preserving the shingle. Effective groynes, to be provided either by the reconstruction of the old ones, or by making entirely new ones, were necessary adjuncts to the carrying out and completion of the sea-wall as designed. The storm which destroyed it, though a heavy one, was not a very exceptional storm, but was such a storm as might be expected to occur once or oftener every year, and during the progress of the works or before their completion.

(26.) After the fall of the wall further correspondence took place, which will be found in the appendix, and some interviews took place between Mr. Jackson and the Board; and ultimately, on or about the 30th March, 1882, the Local Board took possession of Mr. Jackson's plant, or the greater part of it, with a view of finishing the contract themselves, claiming to be entitled to do so under clause 13 of the contract. The Board rely on the letters dated the 8th November, 1881, and 7th February, 1882, as being notices in writing within the said clause, which were not complied with within seven days. No work had been done between the fall of the wall and the taking possession by the Local Board.

(27.) At the interview, and during the correspondence which resulted in the Local Board taking the works out of the contractor's hands, the Board held the opinion (which they expressed to Mr. Jackson) that the wall as designed could be built and would stand without groynes, while Mr. Jackson held the opinion (which he expressed to the Board) that the wall as designed would certainly not stand without groynes, and that it was very doubtful whether it would stand with groynes. The ground of Mr. Jackson's refusal to continue the work was expressed in his letter to the Board dated February 13th, 1882, and was that, under the then present conditions of the altered level of the shingle, the wall was not fit to withstand the seas, and that it had become impracticable to build the wall.

(28.) In fact it was, in the then state of the shingle, impracticable to build the wall as designed, and so that it would stand. The only way in which it was practicable to execute the work as designed, and with any probability of it standing, was in the manner ultimately carried out by the Board, viz., by making groynes, and thereby causing the shingle gradually to accumulate, and carrying up the wall simultaneously. At the time of Mr. Jackson's refusal to continue the Board had made no contract for groynes, and although they had proposed to do so in the previous year they had declined Mr. Jackson's tender for the work on grounds which he, with some reason, considered frivolous. The Board never gave him any express undertaking to make groynes if he would continue the work, and consequently he never expressly refused to continue the work on the basis of groynes being made by the Local Board. On the other hand, it does not appear that after the wall fell he expressly offered to resume and continue the contract work if the Board would simultaneously erect groynes, and thereby bring back the shingle to the height which was necessary to make the wall safe. I find that Mr. Jackson had, to the date of the storm, used every exertion to complete the wall in spite of difficulties arising from non-possession of the land and from interruptions over which he had no control, and that he at last gave in because it was impracticable to complete the wall unless groynes were erected.

(29.) On or about the 30th March, 1882, the Local Board took possession of the greater part of Mr. Jackson's plant. After doing so it was reported to the Board that the contractor (Mr. Gansden) who had in the previous years tendered for the groynes at about the same price as Mr. Jackson, was willing to stand by his tender with a small addition for clearing away the débris of the fallen wall, and on the 22nd April a contract was entered into by the Board with Mr. Gansden for the erection by him of the groynes.

(30.) Work was begun on the groynes in May, 1882, but no work was then done to the wall. The opinion of the consulting engineer of the Board, Mr. F. C. Stileman, and of Mr. James Abernethy, member and formerly President of the Institution of Civil Engineers, was taken by the Board, and they advised that the failure of the wall was mainly due to the removal of the shingle beach by the action of the sea in front of it, the wall being, in their opinion, obviously designed on the supposition of the conservation of the beach as shown in the contract drawings, and they advised that on the completion of the groynes then in progress the shingle would undoubtedly accumulate, and the new wall might then be erected on the foundation of the fallen portion with some minor modifications. (See their opinions dated 26th June, 1882, and 5th July, 1882, in appendix.)

(31.) In the month of September, 1882, the Local Board commenced to rebuild the wall. They have continued the work, and it has now been recently completed. It has been built in accordance with the original designs, though with some slight modifications. There have been some severe storms in which it has sustained no

injury. The new groynes continued to accumulate shingle in most places which Court of Appeal.
afforded the desired protection as the wall was carried up.

(32.) On the facts it was contended before us, on behalf of Mr. Jackson (who, by reason of his having made his claim for arbitration before the Board began their action, and by reason of the order of reference giving him the conduct of the proceedings, was treated as plaintiff in the reference), that he was entitled to damages against the Board for their not having made the groynes and thereby preserved the shingle at or about the level shown in the contract drawings, and so rendered it possible for Mr. Jackson to carry out his contract. It was also contended that even if there was no positive obligation on the Board to make the groynes, yet the contract was based on the assumption of the beach being preserved, and, therefore, Mr. Jackson was not to suffer the loss from the wall falling, and was entitled to recover for the work done. It was further contended that the circumstances did not justify the seizure of Mr. Jackson's plant, and that he was entitled to recover the value of it.

(33.) On the part of the Board it was contended that, the contract being silent as to groynes, the Board were not bound to make them; that if they were necessary to enable the contractor to execute the work he should have made them himself; that the contract bound Mr. Jackson to repair the damage done to the wall; that Mr. Jackson broke the contract by refusing to continue the work, and that the Board were entitled to exercise the power of clause 13.

(34.) The claims made by Mr. Jackson against the Local Board on the arbitration as to which any questions arise for the opinion of the Court are as follows:—

(1st) His claim for the value at contract prices for the work actually done by him before the fall of the wall over and above what he had been paid on account. The amount payable to him on this claim, if he is entitled to maintain it, is assessed at the sum of 1,683*l.*

(2nd) His claim for damage by reason of his plant lying idle from 22nd October, 1881, when the wall fell, to the 30th March, 1882, when the Board took possession of it. He alleges that this damage was occasioned to him by the default of the Board in not making the groynes. The amount payable to him on this claim, if he is entitled to maintain it, is assessed at the sum of 888*l.*

(3rd) His claim for the value of his plant and materials seized by the Local Board. The amount payable to him on this claim, if he is entitled to maintain it, is assessed at the sum of 3,894*l.* This is for plant and materials included in an inventory taken by Mr. Slade, and for certain water-pipes, all of which plant, if Mr. Jackson recovers the 3,894*l.*, will be the property of the Local Board.

(35.) The claims of the Local Board in respect of which any question arises for the opinion of the Court are as follows:—

(1st) Their claim to be paid by Mr. Jackson the cost of rebuilding the portion of wall which fell. The amount payable to them on this claim, if they are entitled to maintain it, is assessed at the sum of 2,500*l.*

(2nd) Their claim to be paid by Mr. Jackson, under clause 13, the excess of the cost of their completing the work over and above what they would have had to pay Mr. Jackson for completing it under the contract. The amount payable to them on this claim, if they are entitled to maintain it, is assessed at the sum of 800*l.* This sum is arrived at by deducting from the sum which I, the arbitrator, assess as the cost to the Board of the work done by them (other than the rebuilding of the fallen portion) the whole sum remaining unpaid of the contract price, including the sum of 1,683*l.* mentioned in paragraph 34 of this case as due in respect of work actually done, and if the Local Board are entitled to recover on this head they are to have the said sum of 800*l.* without the sum of 1,683*l.* being set off against it.

(36.) Mr. Jackson also claimed interest on the amount of his claims. Subject to the opinion of the Court as to whether interest ought to be allowed on such claims I, the arbitrator, allow interest on such of the said sums as he may be entitled to recover at all, at the rate of 5 per cent. per annum from the 31st January, 1883, the date of the order of reference.

(37.) Other claims of the respective parties were made on the arbitration as to which no question arises for the Court, and on which I have made a separate award pursuant to the order of reference.

(38.) The appendix hereto is to be taken to be part of this case.

(39.) The questions for the opinion of the Court are whether, on the facts herein stated, Mr. Jackson is entitled to all or any, and which, of the said sums of 1,683*l.*, 888*l.*, and 3,894*l.* And whether the Local Board is entitled to both or either, and which, of the sums of 2,500*l.* and 800*l.*

Judgment is to be entered as to the above-mentioned sums in such manner as the Court may direct, and together with such interest as the Court may direct, and in case, by the judgment of the Court or by the separate award, any sums are found in favour of opposite parties, such sums are to be set off in such manner as the Court may direct.

If the Court find that the Local Board are entitled to damages against John Jackson for breach of the said contract, they are also to have judgment against the said Robert Preston and William Edwin Jackson for such damages or for 1,000*l.*, whichever may be the least.

The costs of the argument of the special case are to be in the discretion of the Court, and the costs of stating the special case and of the reference and award are, by agreement between the parties, reserved for the decision of the arbitrator after the decision on the special case.

(Signed)   Harrison Hayter.

The special case was argued before Mathew and Day, JJ., who directed judgment to be entered for the contractor.

The Local Board appealed.

Webster, Q.C., and Edwyn Jones for the Local Board; Sir F. Herschell, S.-G., and H. Sutton for Mr. Jackson.

The appeal was allowed with costs, but execution was stayed by consent, and the contractor appealed to the House of Lords.

For the appellant it was argued—

(1.) That upon the facts there was an implied contract by the respondents to maintain the beach at the level shown in the plans and drawings.

(2.) That the premises of the respondents were not in a fit state to receive the plaintiff's work, by reason of default in complying with such implied contract.

(3.) That the events which had happened excused the appellant from further performance of the original contract, and entitled him to be paid on a *quantum meruit* (a).

(a) Hereon see *M'Donald* v. *Mayor, &c. of Workington, post; Bottoms* v. *Lord Mayor, &c. of York, post*; and *Bush* v. *Trustees of Port and Town of Whitehaven, post.*

1886
March 2.

House of
Lords.

For the respondents it was contended that—

(1.) There was no express or implied contract to construct or maintain the groynes.

(2.) The only obligation undertaken by the respondents under the contract was to pay the contract price for the construction and maintenance of the sea-wall.

(3.) The damage or destruction of parts of the sea-wall arose from no act or default of the respondents, but wholly from the acts of the appellant and his mode of building the wall.

(4.) The appellant expressly contracted to do all works connected with, or required for, forming, erecting and completing the sea-wall, and for upholding the work for six months after completion.

(5.) The appellant expressly took on himself the risk of all accidents and damage from seas or winds during the construction of the works, and undertook to repair and make good the same at his own cost; and the damage and destruction of part of the wall arose from the action of the seas and winds.

EARL OF SELBORNE: My Lords,—It is impossible not to feel sympathy with the appellant in this case, who probably has sustained a very great pecuniary loss by the misfortune which has happened to him in the execution of his contract; but, in deciding the law between the appellant and the respondents, we cannot be influenced by any feelings of that kind. The case has been argued with the usual ability of the learned counsel who have been entrusted with it, but I believe that the full discussion which it has undergone has only confirmed all your lordships in the view that the decision of the Court of Appeal was right.

It is a mere question, as I view it, of contract between these parties, and the only parts of the contract to which I shall think it necessary to make any reference at all are those which are found at pages 46, 50 and 59. At page 46 the contractor undertakes:

> In a good, substantial, and workmanlike manner, and with sufficient and proper materials of the description and quality set forth in detail in the bill of quantities and specifications hereunto annexed, to execute, perform, and complete, all and singular, the several works connected with or required for the formation, erection, and completion of a sea-wall at Eastbourne according to the specification and the drawings.

He undertakes to do that, and, as it appears to me, it is for him, undertaking that obligation, which he is the only judge of before he undertakes it, to satisfy himself that he can fulfil and perform it. Whatever is possible and necessary for the fulfilment and performance of it by him, he must do. If it be a specified work, of course, then, it is part of the contract to do that specified work. If it is

1886
March 2.

House of
Lords.

required as an additional work, he will get paid for it; but if it is neither a specified work nor an additional work, yet if it be a *sine quâ non* to the performance by him of the contract, as he binds himself absolutely to perform the contract he must use, for his own protection and on his own account, and not as a specific obligation due to the other party, the proper means, whatever they are, of enabling him to perform the contract. That is the obvious effect of that particular obligation, which is the general obligation which he undertakes. But when we come to particulars we find, as it appears to me, that he has expressly, and in terms, undertaken the very risks from which he now seeks to be relieved; because, at page 50, the next passage to which I propose to refer, this is expressly agreed:

> The said contractor shall take upon himself the risk of, and be answerable for, all accidents and damages from or by seas, winds, drift of craft, fire, or any other cause whatsoever, which may occur during the construction of the works under this contract, and in case of such accidents or damages arising, shall make good and repair the same as soon as possible at his own costs and charges.

The question is whether this particular accident did not fall within the terms of that stipulation. My Lords, what is the accident? At page 16, in the 24th paragraph of the special case, this is what is stated:

> A severe storm occurred [on the 22nd October, 1881] and a large part of the completed wall was washed down.

The length which fell is mentioned, and then something, which I shall advert to afterwards, is stated as to the cause. But it is quite manifest that the cause was the severe storm, the impact of the waves, and whatever was carried with the waves, against the wall; and nothing can be more clear, I imagine, than that that was an accident and damage from or by seas or winds, one or both. Therefore, he had expressly undertaken that risk, unless there be something else to qualify or to displace it. The other passage to which I propose to refer, at page 59, wholly confirms that conclusion. It is in the specification, in the 14th paragraph:

> The tender must include every expense necessary for completing and upholding the works for six months after their completion, subject to all the contingencies, conditions and stipulations herein contained or referred to. No additional allowance or payment whatever will be made over and above the contract sum for any work described, or comprised, or shown

in the specification or the drawings, or which may be fairly inferred therefrom respectively, or which may become necessary in the execution of the works.

1886
March 2.

House of
Lords.

Therefore, on the very face of the agreement, besides the specified works, besides the additional works required, he is to be answerable for anything else which may become necessary in the execution of the works, and is not to be paid for it. Such is the contract. Now, the principle of *Thorn's case* (*a*) determines this, that even if the specification does contemplate means which turn out to be insufficient or impracticable, and which, in consequence, require him to go to an expense which was not contemplated when the specification was prepared, he is not guaranteed against that expense; he undertakes to do the work; and if the particular means contemplated turn out not to be as available as it was thought they would be, that is his risk. Now, I go on to consider the next point. Is there anything in this contract which qualifies those obligations? If there be not, I apprehend it to be quite clear that the judgment below is right. It is said that this plan, taken in connection with some findings in the special case to which I will presently refer, does qualify them. What is the plan? A plan exhibiting the actual state of the ground—the beach on which the work was to be executed—at the date of the contract, and also exhibiting the height, and so on, of the intended wall. The plan of the actual state of the ground shows certain existing groynes of a certain irregular outline and varying levels, and the beach between the different groynes as it then existed.

The argument is that that amounts to an implied agreement between the parties that during the progress of the work all that shall remain exactly as it is without alteration. I must say, my Lords, it seems to me the most extraordinary and the most startling suggestion possible, even upon the first view of the matter, and having regard only to the nature of the subject-matter, and the case; because, even if nothing had been found about it in the special case, everybody who enters into a contract of this sort must know the natural conditions of the matter with which he has to deal—the sea, the action of the sea upon a moveable beach or shingle, the nature of every such beach; not a fixed quantity, or a fixed thing, but a thing which, according to the mechanical forces brought to bear upon it, is subject to change. In its then state, and without the wall, in order to arrest or modify, or more or less control, the operation of the natural causes producing those changes, these groynes here shown are used, but everybody

(*a*) 1 App. Cas. 120; 45 L. J. Ex. 487.

1886
March 2.

House of
Lords.

must have known—at least, every contractor must have know—that when the wall began to be built the very building of the wall would vary the operation of those natural causes, and that the existing groynes might, without some work being done to them, become insufficient for the purpose of preventing a change in the surface, the nature, the height, and the other circumstances of this beach.

But not only is there the knowledge which, even in the absence of any special finding, we must have attributed to every such contractor, but the passages in the special case which relate to the matter are, to my mind, perfectly clear. I pass over the 13th paragraph, on page 14, that is to say, I will not read it all through; it contains a statement that the documents forming the contract contain certain indications to a man of intelligence that the wall, shown as being thirty feet high, was designed on the assumption of the preservation of the beach at a height materially less, and so on. I will not refer to the particular parts of the contract that are said to contain those indications—but I will assume that they do—although if it were a question of construction it is not for the arbitrator, but it would be for your lordships to construe the contract. But I take that passage, in connection with the 14th paragraph, which says:

> The natural consequence of building a wall in the beach below high-water mark would be to increase the effect of the sea in washing away the shingle at and about the foot of the wall. The scour of the shingle along the face of the wall, caused by the wash of the sea, would cut into a concrete wall, and weaken, and in time destroy it.

Therefore, the special case finds that these would be the natural consequences of building the wall; and, assuming it to be the fact that it was designed upon the assumption of the preservation of the beach at a height sufficient to prevent that, is there anything there to alter the obligation of the person who undertakes to build the wall? If the wall cannot be built without preserving the beach at that height during its progress, both parties must be taken to have known— certainly the contractor as much as the Local Board—what the natural consequence of building the wall on such a beach would be.

It is impossible that the contract can have taken place between them on the footing of no change taking place by the scour of the tides during the operations on the beach; it is impossible that they could have supposed that this beach was to be a fixed quantity, undergoing no change at all; and if it was necessary to preserve it for the purpose of the work, on whom was that obligation? Upon the man who contracted to do the work, unless it can be shown that

1886
March 2.

House of
Lords.

the Local Board had contracted to do it. Nothing of the kind is shown. What is the argument? That the proper means or the usual means of doing it would be by groynes. Well, supposing it were; it is admitted that the contract contains no provision that the Local Board shall make groynes, and no provision that the Local Board shall maintain the existing groynes.

It is not alleged that either the Local Board or the Board of Trade have thrown any impediment or difficulty whatever in the contractor's way as to doing those things which, in the special case, are suggested as things which, being done, might have prevented the mischief which arose. The existing groynes, it is said in one place, have got out of repair. If they had been in a proper state and raised in height, lengthened, and strengthened, and so on, they might have been effectual in preserving the shingle. If those means could have been used, the Local Board have not said that they would use them; and the fact that they have not required that to be done by the contractor does not, in the least degree, exonerate him from fulfilling his contract, and, if those means were necessary, using those means. The 14th paragraph seems to suggest that that would not have been necessary; that some groynes of a character less solid, less firm, than what would be necessary eventually, after the work was done, might have been sufficient.

But it is not, in my judgment, at all necessary to go into the question what works would have been sufficient, what degree of strength of groynes, what character of permanence of groynes—it is enough to say that there is nothing whatever in any of these facts to exonerate the contractor from the obligation which he has undertaken, or to throw on the Local Board the obligation of doing these or any other particular works. As to the Act of Parliament, I own I have the greatest possible difficulty in following the argument founded upon it. The Act of Parliament is antecedent to the contract; it rules nothing whatever between the contractor and the Local Board; it imposes certain obligations upon the Local Board, and it gives them some powers, amongst other things, powers to make groynes. It does not say that they must make groynes—still less that they must make groynes for the protection of the works of the contractor. And as to the obligation to prevent, or to take reasonable precautions to prevent, encroachments by the sea during the construction, I do not at all hold the appellant to the view of one of his learned and able counsel rather than the others; but my own view distinctly agrees with that of Mr. Rigby, namely, that that relates to such an encroachment of the sea upon the land as carries away part of the

1886
March 2.
_____
House of
Lords.

land which is ordinarily unaffected by the wash and the operations of the sea. That event has not happened; and, therefore, that part of the Act of Parliament seems to me to be entirely immaterial.

I come back, therefore, my Lords, to the positive stipulations of the contract, and, if there be nothing to qualify them, it seems quite clear that the appellant, unfortunately, did not execute the work, and not having executed the work, and being in default, the Local Board were entitled to take possession, as they have done, and to finish it, and to charge him with those sums which the arbitrator has found.

The conclusion is that I must move your lordships to dismiss the appeal, and to affirm the order appealed from.

Lord WATSON: My Lords, I concur in the judgment which has been proposed. Whether a contractor remains bound to complete his contract when he meets with serious impediments which necessarily alter the character of the work which he has to perform, and are due to causes which were not and could not reasonably be held to have been in the contemplation of either party at the time of making the contract, is a question which does not arise upon this appeal, and upon which, therefore, I offer no opinion (*a*). It is admitted that the plan which is incorporated with this contract does indicate that a wall, or bank of shingle, was necessary in order to protect the sea-wall which the appellant had contracted to erect, and that the maintenance of that beach shown upon the plan was necessary for that purpose.

I think it is matter of plain inference from the contract that any person whose attention was directed and who applied his mind to it must have seen that the action of the sea was to be continuous during the period of eighteen months embraced within the contract, and that it might have the effect, possibly, of increasing the deposit of shingle along the face of the wall, or, more probably, of diminishing it. Be that as it may, it was a matter which was within the contemplation of the parties, or, at least, ought to have been, because we must not construe the contract of parties according to what they actually applied their minds to, but we must construe the contracts of parties upon the footing that a man of ordinary intelligence must have had regard to the terms of the contract, and what was exhibited upon the face of the plan. Now, that being so, I think the legal inference, if there were nothing more in this contract bearing upon the respective liabilities of the parties, would have been that the man who had contracted to build the wall had also contracted to do everything that

(*a*) *Bush* v. *Trustees of Port and Town of Whitehaven, post.*

1886
March 2.

House of
Lords.

was reasonably necessary for the purpose of protecting the wall during its construction. That was his work, not the work which he had contracted to give to the Local Board; it was no part of the contract work which they desired, it was a precaution which he was obliged to resort to, and which it was his duty to resort to, for the purpose of enabling himself to execute his contract.

But, my Lords, in this case the question of liability is not, I think, left to be matter of legal inference; I think it is matter of express contract between the appellant and the respondents. When I read together (I am not going to repeat them, because the noble and learned Earl has already read them) the 14th article of the general conditions which are embodied in the specification, and the 9th head of the agreement of the parties, they appear to me substantially to amount to an undertaking, on the part of this appellant, that he will execute, without receiving payment for them, all works which become at any time necessary in and for the execution of the works in consequence of the action of the sea.

That being the view which I take of the stipulations of this contract, though I agree with my noble and learned friend who has already spoken that this obligation will bear hardly upon the appellant, all that that amounts to is that he has made an improvident contract, from which neither your lordships nor any other Court of law can relieve him.

Lord BRAMWELL: My Lords, I am entirely of the same opinion. I own that this case appears to me to be so plain that it is impossible to be long in giving reasons for the conclusion to which I have come. Just let me say this: it is hard upon the appellant, no doubt, but it is a hardship for which the Local Board is not responsible; I cannot blame them in any way. It is a misfortune which has happened, I believe, owing to neither of the parties foreseeing what would be the consequence of proceedings such as the appellant took. Now, I understand his case to be this: The works could not be done without groynes. Somebody, therefore, was bound to erect groynes. Nobody could be so bound but you, the Board, or I, the contractor. I was not, therefore you were. I think that is a logical statement of the position of the appellant.

The statute was relied upon. I entirely agree with everything that was said by the noble and learned Earl on the Woolsack, that it creates no duty between these parties which should influence their contract at all. I am further of opinion that there was no encroachment within the meaning of it. Therefore, that being out of the case, we must now look at the contract.

1886
March 2.

House of
Lords.

Now, I will assume that groynes were a practical necessity. There might possibly be, by some excessive expense, some other mode of keeping the shingle up, or protecting the new walls from it, but I will assume that, practically, groynes would be the right thing to have recourse to. Now, I agree (and, again, I quote the noble and learned Earl on the Woolsack) that there was no duty to the Board lying upon the appellant to erect groynes if he could have done his work by any other contrivance, or if, by good fortune, there had been no turbulent water until his contract had expired. But if it was practically a necessity, for the doing of his work, that groynes should be erected, then he ought to have erected them, and was bound to erect them, for the purpose of doing that work. In that sense there was a necessity for his doing it—not as a duty towards anyone in particular, but as an obligation necessarily incidental to the performance of the contract.

The case, therefore, to my mind, is not at all like any of those which were put; for instance, the suggestion of a toll-house to be built upon a bridge which was washed away—it is nothing like that. There would there be a physical impossibility of doing the agreed work; here there was not. Had the contractor been minded to erect these groynes he could have done so; and inasmuch as there was a practical necessity for his so doing, I am clearly of opinion that he had the power by law to interfere with the foreshore and put his groynes down for the purpose, upon the general principle that whenever anything is conceded, or granted to, or imposed upon a person, all the necessary powers for the doing of it are practically conceded, or granted to, or imposed upon him.

I am, therefore, very clearly of opinion that this judgment should be affirmed.

Lord FITZGERALD: My Lords, I am also of opinion that the judgment of the Court of Appeal should be affirmed, and very much for the same reasons as have been given by the noble and learned Earl. My Lords, I may also, before dealing with the case, express some regret that we are not able to adopt either the reasons given in the Queen's Bench Division or the result at which that Division has arrived, although, possibly, it would have worked out a nearer approach to justice in the abstract if it could have been adopted. But Lord Justice Cotton, in the Court of Appeal, puts, I think, the true and real question, after discussing the much controverted matter of fact who was bound to erect groynes, or whether groynes were to be erected by anybody. It is clear upon the contract that the contractor was not bound to erect groynes in the sense of such permanent structures as would have protected the work and made it in a measure perpetual. But it is equally clear to my mind that he was bound to protect the work which he was doing until he had completed the sea-wall and handed it over to the Local Board. But Lord Justice Cotton says, and says truly, that is not the question at all in the case who was to erect these groynes.

1886
March 2.

House of
Lords.

> The question is whether there is anything to relieve the contractor from the obligation which he undertook, to bear all risks of sea and wind, and to build this wall, to repair what might come down, and to maintain it for six months.

I shall drop "to maintain it for six months" for the present, but, at any rate, to maintain it and protect it until he had given it over into the hands of the Local Board. The Lord Justice says:

> Of course, there is no contract on his part to put up groynes, and that is not the real question, therefore, talking about groynes permanent or temporary.

My Lords, assuming that that is the question, I can have no doubt whatever, upon the contract, not only that the contractor bound himself to erect this sea-wall according to the specification and the plans, but that he was equally under an obligation, in some manner, it matters not how, to protect the work which he was doing, so as to be able, at the end of the twelve months within which he was to complete the sea-wall, to hand it over to the Local Board in a complete form. And I may say, in addition to what the noble and learned Earl has read from the contract, there is this provision in clause 3, that "in case any portion of the works shall become damaged or injured in the execution thereof, the contractor" shall make it good.

My Lords, there are also clauses 8 and 9, both leading to the same conclusion, that the contractor, not foreseeing, as he ought to have done, or might have done, that, in the course of events, storms might arise which would injure the work, and not providing for that by any term of the contract, but undertaking to complete this wall and deliver it over in a completed state, that necessarily imports that he was to take on his own part those precautions which might be requisite for his own protection. After having completed the wall and handed it over in a completed state to the Local Board, there is an obligation that he will repair any damages that may arise for six months afterwards; but it is subject to this condition, by clause 10,

1886
March 2.

House of
Lords.

that he shall not, within that period of six months, be bound "to repair or make good any damage or injury done or caused by any act or default of the Local Board." A very different question, indeed, might have arisen in the case had that been the clause which we had to deal with.

Then, as to an obligation arising from implied contract on the part of the Local Board to keep the surface of the beach in the same condition, at the same level, as at the time when the specification and plans were drawn, that appeared to me all through the case to be somewhat absurd. I have no doubt that the drawing or plan represents the state of things which existed at the time when that plan was made. It is not suggested that there was any default on the part of the Local Board in making that plan. It is not suggested that it could mislead anyone or did mislead anyone; and the contractor, having regard to the very nature of the thing which he was dealing with, a beach that was ever changing, ought to have foreseen the casualties to which his work was likely to be subject, and if he intended to guard himself against those casualties, he ought to have insisted upon there being a provision in the contract for that purpose. I may illustrate what I mean very well by this: it is possible that the surface level shown upon that plan, taken I know not when, represented the beach as much higher than it may have been at ordinary tides; it may have been the result of the operations of nature, that is to say, the operations of the sea, some time previously, which increased the height of the beach; or it may even have been represented to be lower than it was; but was ever changing, and subject to fluctuation at almost every tide; and to say that this was a contract to keep it in its present condition (I mean by "present condition" the condition in which it was when the plan was drawn) appears to me to be utterly unfounded.

I therefore agree that the judgment of the Court of Appeal should be affirmed.

Lord HALSBURY: My Lords, I must confess that I look upon this case as a particularly plain case. Unless we are to imply a contract which the parties manifestly never entered into, the appellant cannot succeed. Here, it appears to me that there is an express contract by the appellant to remedy a mischief which has, in fact, taken place; so that the argument amounts to this, that we must imply against the Local Board a contract which they did not make, and exempt the contractor from an obligation which he expressly entered into. It appears to me that that would be a very serious infringement of the rule upon which contracts are construed; and, therefore, upon these

1886
March 2.

House of
Loards.

very short grounds, I agree with the judgment that has been proposed.

Lord ASHBOURNE: My Lords, I also entirely concur in the opinions which have been pronounced, and in the reasons upon which those opinions have been based. I also concur in the statement which has just been made by my noble and learned friend, that this is a case which, when it is looked at, is tolerably plain.

The contractor here entered into a contract which is, on the face of it, perfectly plain, namely, that he would erect a sea-wall, within a certain time, in a certain method; and he says himself in his argument, now, at the Bar of your Lordships' House, that it was essential to the performance of his contract, and to the stability and protection of his work, that the shingle should be kept at the height at which it was when the work was commenced, and he indicates the method by which the shingle was so to be kept up at the requisite height, by the making of certain works called groynes.

My Lords, Mr. Rigby, in his clear and full argument, used a remarkable expression; he said that the Local Board had taken this obligation upon themselves. I asked the question, "And how did they take this obligation upon themselves?" This is a question of contract; the question of the construction of a contract. That obligation, which they are said to have taken upon themselves, is certainly not to be found in express terms anywhere in the contract, and I can find nothing anywhere to indicate a single circumstance from which we should imply such a grave and serious obligation.

My Lords, it was suggested also, I think, in the course of the argument, that it might be held to be a mutual understanding between the parties. That is a rather vague and elastic expression; it is not a satisfactory way of construing a contract which is put in writing and in plain terms. But I see nothing to indicate anything from which we can arrive at that conclusion. The contractor himself is bound to inquire whether the performance of the work is possible or requires to be safeguarded by certain conditions; and if he has omitted to perform those obligations which lie upon him, the loss, if any is incurred, must fall upon himself. Here, my Lords, there is a clear contract to build a sea-wall and to maintain it for six months; and, as has been pointed out by all your lordships, one of the plain conditions of the contract, that in clause 9, is that he is to bear all the risks of sea, wind, drift, and certain other circumstances. My Lords, the onus of showing that he is relieved from any of these conditions clearly rests upon the contractor, and I see nothing whatever to

1886
March 2.

House of
Lords.

indicate that he is in any way relieved from a single one of the obligations which he has undertaken.

Order appealed from affirmed, and appeal dismissed with costs.

Solicitors for the contractor: Tahourdin and Hargreaves.
Solicitors for the Local Board: Coles and Carr.

1886
February 4.

Queen's
Bench
Division.
——
March 30.

Court of
Appeal.

In the High Court of Justice (Queen's Bench Division).

(Denman and Mathew, JJ.)

And in the Court of Appeal.

(Lord Esher, M.R., Lindley and Lopes, L.JJ.)

In the matter of an Arbitration between the HOHENZOLLERN ACTIEN GESELLSCHAFT FÜR LOCOMOTIVBAU *and the* CITY OF LONDON CONTRACT CORPORATION, LTD.

Contract—Construction—Arbitration Clause—Certificate Clause— Refusal to Certify—Certificate not Condition Precedent.

A contract for the supply of locomotives for a tramway company contained provisions that the locomotives should be built according to plans, to be made to the satisfaction of an engineer named, and under his inspection and to his satisfaction, and that payment should be made on his certificate, and also contained an arbitration clause. clause. The engineer declined to certify, and the contractor demanded arbitration. Held, that the absence of a certificate was not conclusive against the contractor's right to payment, and that a dispute as to the certificate was a dispute within the arbitration clause, and that the award made was valid.

Murphy, Q.C., and Aspland for the plaintiffs, the German manufacturers. They cited *Clemence* v. *Clarke* (1880), reported *ante*, p. 54, and *Goodyear* v. *Mayor of Weymouth* (1865), 35 L. J. C. P. 12.

Willis, Q.C., and Bradford (with them G. S. Bower) for the City of London Corporation. They cited in the Court of Appeal *Sharpe* v. *San Paulo Rail. Co.* (1873), L. R. 8 Ch. App. 597; 29 L. T. 9; and *Piercy* v. *Young* (1879), 14 Ch. D. 200.

The material parts of the contract and the judgments in the Court below and in the Court of Appeal are here set out in full.

Memorandum of Agreement made this 18th day of July, 1883, between the City of London Contract Corporation, Ltd., hereinafter called the purchasers, of the one part, and the Actien Gesellschaft fÅr Locomotivbau Hohenzollern, Dusseldorf, Germany, hereinafter called the vendors, of the other part, whereby it is agreed as follows:—

1886
February 4.

Queen's
Bench
Division.

The said purchasers will buy and the said vendors will sell six locomotive tramway engines and two boilers, with necessary fittings, at the price hereinafter named, and subject to the conditions hereinafter mentioned.

1. The locomotives and boilers shall be delivered at the purchaser's option at one of the railway stations, in the parish of Croydon, on the trucks, at the risk and expense of the vendors, six months from the date hereof. They shall be of the very best materials and workmanship, and the locomotives shall be adapted to the curves and gradients of the Croydon and Norwood tramway system.

2. The price of the locomotives shall be 750*l.* each, with all the appurtenances, and of the boilers and appurtenances, 700*l.* each.

3. The boilers shall have 540 square feet heating surface, and shall be made according to the plans, to be signed by Mr. Floyd, so far as the same are applicable to boilers of the capacity herein mentioned, and with such modification as may be necessary on account of the Board of Trade requirements or any other statutory or legal requirements with reference thereto. . . . The testing shall be at the expense of the vendors and shall take place in the presence of the engineer of the purchasers. . . . Here follows description of boilers, &c.

4. The locomotives are to be in all respects according to specifications and plans, and to coloured working drawings, to be signed by Mr. Floyd, with the implements therein mentioned, and all the conditions in such specification are to apply as if the same were specifically contained therein.

5. The purchasers shall pay the vendors one-half of the contract price upon the certificate (*a*) of Mr. Floyd, or other their engineer, that the locomotives and boilers are in perfect working order at Croydon, one quarter thereof two months after the date of such certificate, and the remainder thereof four months after the date of such certificate.

6. The vendors shall, at their own expense, provide a competent engineer to superintend the erection of the locomotives and boilers, and for the period of two weeks after the erection of the boilers and the delivery of the last engine, to instruct the engineer, stokers and drivers of the purchasers in the proper use and direction of the locomotives and boilers, and for such longer period, at the rate of fifteen shillings per day, as the vendors may elect.

7. If the vendors shall fail to deliver the locomotives and boilers within the specified time, they shall (unless such default is caused by *force majeure*) forfeit a sum of $\frac{1}{2}$ per cent. in respect of each week they shall be so in default, provided that none of the locomotives shall be considered as delivered within the time unless and until one of the boilers has been delivered.

8. The locomotives and boilers are to be built under the inspection of and to the satisfaction and approval of the engineer of the purchasers, and shall pass the inspection of the Board of Trade, and they may be inspected during their construction at all reasonable times by the engineer or his representatives.

(*a*) It must be observed that the certificate was not required to be in writing.

1886
February 4.

Queen's
Bench
Division.

9. The vendors guarantee to make good any failure of the locomotives or boilers, as regards each locomotive or boiler, for a space of six months after the date of the delivery of the same, if arising from bad material, faulty workmanship, or from the system of construction of the engines.

10. All disputes are to be settled by the engineer of the purchasers and the engineer to be appointed by the vendors, or their umpire in case of difference, such arbitration to be conducted in conformity with the Common Law Procedure Act, and any existing statutory modification of the same.

In witness whereof the said parties have caused their common seals to be hereunto affixed the day and year first above written.

Judgment.

DENMAN, J.: This is an application to set aside an award, that is to say, to prevent all further proceedings upon that award, to prevent, for instance, an action ever being brought upon it, or any other advantage being taken of it, and the Court is not in the habit of adopting that course unless the case is very very clear indeed. Looking at the present agreement under which this arbitration arose, so far from thinking it clear that this award is without jurisdiction, I must confess that upon the whole I have a somewhat strong opinion that the award is a good one, and that it is made upon a matter which, in the circumstances of this particular case, was within the jurisdiction of the arbitrators.

Several objections were taken to the award, one of which was that the umpire who ultimately gave his decision sat with the arbitrators, and that he expressed an opinion in the matter upon which the arbitrators ought to have expressed an independent opinion in the course of the case. I do not find that there is anything in the affidavits to show that he then and there decided that point. He sat with the arbitrators, and the arbitrators being unable to agree, he ultimately, upon what he had heard upon the inquiry before the arbitrators, gave his own independent judgment. There is nothing in that to cause the award to be bad. On the contrary, it is the proper and usual course, where an umpire is appointed, for the umpire to sit with the arbitrators, and to hear the evidence, and ultimately to give his decision upon what he hears. There is nothing to preclude him from asking questions or making observations for his own enlightenment in the course of the case. That point therefore fails.

The main question, however, is, whether here the umpire did, in making his award, act beyond his jurisdiction in this one respect. The agreement between the parties says, in its fifth clause, that the purchasers shall pay the vendors one-half of the contract price upon the certificate of Mr. Floyd or other their engineer that the locomotives and boilers are in perfect working order at Croydon, one quarter two months after the date of the certificate, and the remainder four months after the date of the certificate.

1886
February 4.

Queen's
Bench
Division.

It is contended, in the first place, that Mr. Floyd gave no certificate at all, and that that not having been done it is impossible for the umpire to have had any jurisdiction in the matter, for no payment can have become due without that certificate. The answer is three-fold: first, that upon the facts that took place, Mr. Floyd did sufficiently, though not in writing, which is unnecessary, certify to the parties that the locomotives and boilers were in sufficiently perfect order; secondly, that if there were a question as to the certificate of Mr. Floyd being sufficient, there was a fair question for the umpire to decide, and therefore a matter within his jurisdiction; and, thirdly, that looking at this agreement as a whole, there might be a case, and not only one, but several cases might arise, in which, notwithstanding the refusal of the engineer to give his certificate, there might, nevertheless, be a dispute between the parties fit to be settled by an umpire within the meaning of the agreement.

Now, upon the first question, whether there was or was not here a certificate of Mr. Floyd that the locomotives and boilers were in perfect working order at Croydon, the great difficulty in the way of holding that there was a certificate is, in my judgment, that at the time at which the thing contended for as equivalent to a proper certificate of Mr. Floyd's, given at Croydon, was given, was a time when only one of the engines had actually arrived at Croydon and shown itself to be in perfect working order there. It is true that Mr. Floyd had seen the engines, and seen them working, before they came over to this country, and there is in the report that he made a notification that he saw them, in what, I think, is equivalent to saying they were in perfect working order as locomotives and boilers. But the fact not having been that all of them, but only one of them, was at Croydon at the time he stated his satisfaction with them there, it is difficult to contend that that was a certificate that they were in perfect working order at Croydon. But even upon that question, looking at the whole of the contract—not only at this clause, but at other clauses—I am not at all sure that we ought (and I certainly think that we ought not, upon the question of setting aside the award) at once finally to conclude that there was not a fair question to be decided by the arbitrators upon that point of whether there was or was not within the meaning of the whole contract a certificate of Mr. Floyd, given at Croydon on that occasion on which those parties

1886
February 4.

Queen's
Bench
Division.

were present, that the locomotives and boilers were in perfect working order at Croydon. The question was a question for his decision, even though it might be a strong decision if he took that particular view in the affirmative.

But upon that point I do not feel so strongly as I do upon the other points of the case. It is to be observed that this clause 5 is only an affirmative clause. It would give the purchaser a right to have payment of one-half of the contract price immediately upon the obtaining of Mr. Floyd's certificate to that effect. Mr. Willis admits that you cannot construe that so nicely as to hold that if Mr. Floyd had given a certificate that they were in working order at Croydon it would not be a fair question for the umpire to say whether that was not equivalent to a certificate that they were in perfect working order at Croydon. It is not to be construed so nicely as that. On the other hand, if Mr. Floyd did give his certificate that they were in perfect working order at Croydon, and it turned out afterwards that they were not in perfect working order at Croydon at all, and that Mr. Floyd had never seen them at all, but yet chose to give that certificate, I am not at all prepared to say that that would have given a right to payment on the part of the plaintiffs, the persons who were supplying the engines, and I say that because I think you are not to look at this clause alone, but you are to look at it in connection with other clauses, especially clause 8 of the agreement.

I say at once that I think this question is to be decided, not by general propositions laid down in other cases in which the words may be different, but upon this contract, looking at it as a whole, and looking at every clause as bearing upon every other clause, as you ought to do in the construction of all agreements. Paragraph 8 of the agreement is this—"The locomotives and boilers are to be built under the inspection of, and to the satisfaction and approval of, the engineer of the purchaser." Then it goes on to say that they shall pass the inspection of the Board of Trade, and they may be inspected during their construction at all reasonable times by the engineer. The substance of the thing is, that the locomotives and boilers are to be built under the inspection of (and, in fact, they were, as we hear) and to the satisfaction and approval (and there is very good evidence here that they were) of the engineer of the purchasers.

But, then, it is said they did not pass the inspection of the Board of Trade. Now, that arose in this way. They could not pass the inspection of the Board of Trade unless upon the application of the persons who received them—the purchasers—and the purchasers not choosing to apply to the Board of Trade for an inspection, or for a certificate of having passed, they did not in fact pass the inspection of the Board of Trade. That being the other clause bearing upon clause 5, and to be construed with it as part of the same agreement, then comes clause 10, and that clause is as large as possible. It is not "all disputes as to this, that, or the other part of the agreement," but "all disputes are to be settled by the engineer of the purchasers and the engineer to be appointed by the vendors, or their umpire in case of difference." That shows an intention on the part of the contracting parties that the engineer of the purchasers is not to be the final judge in favour of the persons employing him, but that there is to be an arbitration in case of dispute. Now, what dispute is more likely to arise under an agreement such as this than whether the engineer of the purchasers has acted reasonably, has performed his duty of inspection properly, has sufficiently shown his satisfaction and approval of the locomotives to make the payment due? It appears to me that nothing is more likely to have been in the contemplation of the parties, and that unless the words are so limited as to prevent a dispute of this kind being before the umpire, then it was a dispute before the umpire, and the dispute which has arisen in this case is the very sort of dispute which, under this agreement, probably was, and, at all events, ought to be construed to have been, within the decision of the umpire.

Now, the cases which have been cited are every one of them cases upon agreements from which the inference was to be drawn that the clause relating to the certificate should be conclusive upon both parties, or upon one or the other parties, or upon one or other party, with reference to that clause itself, and to the other clauses of the agreements which were then in dispute. I have not looked at them all, but I do not think it would be found, if you went through every one of them, that there was any agreement which was exactly in the same terms as this, and which would prevent us having the duty of considering what this particular agreement means.

I have observed that the two first leading cases upon this subject, which were referred to in all the books—*Morgan* v. *Birnie* (*a*) and *Milner* v. *Field* (*b*)—were beyond all question, because in *Morgan* v. *Birnie* (*a*), in the first instance, prices were to be settled and so on by the surveyor and architect, who was to be sole arbitrator in settling such a price, and then the payment was to be upon his certificate in writing. Obviously, therefore, without his decision there could not be anything due. And in *Milner* v. *Field* (*b*), which is the basis of

(*a*) (1833), 3 M. & Scott, 76; 9 Bing. 672.
(*b*) (1850), 5 Ex. 829; 20 L. J. Ex. 68.

1886
February 4.

Queen's
Bench
Division.

1886
February 4.

Queen's
Bench
Division.

all these decisions, there was a provision that none of the instalments should be payable unless the plaintiffs should deliver to the defendant a certificate signed. I think it will be found that in every one of the cases there are words upon which arguments were founded. In one of them Lord Justice Mellish held that the point was whether it was a condition precedent or not. They all turned upon their own words, and none of them are cases in which the words are so similar to the words in this contract as to dispense with the necessity on our part of looking at this contract and saying what the parties really meant.

Now, looking at it in that way, and looking at all the clauses together, clause 9 (to which I dare say my brother Mathew will call attention, he called my attention to it just now) is another clause bearing on the question. Looking at it as a whole, I think the words "all disputes" are large enough to include the very dispute which has arisen in this case, and that that being so, the umpire had jurisdiction, and that we ought not to set aside this award. If we are wrong, there may be an appeal, I suppose, and, at all events, an action may be brought upon it, in which any question which can now be raised may be raised, and it is not a case in which we ought to exercise the summary jurisdiction of this Court to set aside an award which, for aught that appears, is very honestly made, and made according to justice.

Mr. MURPHY: I ought to mention to your lordship that there is a motion here to enforce the award.

MATHEW, J.: In this case I am of the same opinion. The doubts that I had as to what the parties meant by this agreement enable me to pronounce an opinion upon this motion which is altogether free from doubt. We ought not to set aside this award unless we are perfectly clear that the arbitrators have decided without jurisdiction. Now, ordinarily, in contracts of this sort, where the rights of the contractors depend upon the certificate of the engineer, there is no question that he is appointed and intended to be appointed sole arbitrator between the parties as to matters to be dealt with by his certificate, and his certificate is final and binding upon both parties. It is impossible for either to get behind it.

Now, was the certificate mentioned here a certificate of that character? Clearly not; because, if you turn to clause 9, you find a condition of things in which the certificate would not be binding upon the parties, because by clause 9 the vendor guaranteed to make good any failure of the locomotives or boilers for a space of six months after the date of the delivery of the same-not always, but, as the clause goes on to show, if arising from bad material, faulty workmanship, or from the system of the construction of the engines. That would be bad material, faulty workmanship or defective construction of the engines at the very time when the certificate of the engineer was given. So that the persons to whom the engines were to be delivered can get behind the certificate in that way, and can show that the grounds upon which the certificate was granted are open to dispute, and can refer that matter to arbitration. Then, may they not refer the grounds upon which the certificate is refused exactly in the same way, or is it an unreasonable construction of the contract to say that that is such a matter of dispute as was intended to be referred to arbitration? I come to the conclusion that there is too much doubt about the meaning of this contract to justify setting the award aside, and I can see very good reasons for contending that the arbitrators were right in the view they appear to have taken, and that they were justified here in considering the grounds upon which the certificate was refused in setting those grounds aside.

Motion to set aside the award was dismissed with costs, and an order was made absolute for enforcing the award.

This decision was appealed against, and on the 30th March, 1886, was affirmed by the Court of Appeal.

Lord ESHER, M.R.: I really cannot entertain any doubt in this case. The question is whether the arbitrators had jurisdiction to try the matter which was submitted to them. If they had jurisdiction to try the matter submitted to them, their decision upon that matter cannot be reviewed. The parties have done what, to my mind, in contracts of such magnitude as this, is wonderful, but, nevertheless, it is the fashion. People who have a tribunal of the highest order, with power of revision over that tribunal, prefer to go to a tribunal which they are persuaded to think is far better, without any appeal, and when they get a wrong decision, as they think, by that tribunal which they have chosen, they seek to get such decision set aside.

The case here must depend upon what is the true construction of the submission, and not upon an examination of what the dispute was—that is the question which the parties wish to try between them, and we have to see whether that question is one which was within the submission. The submission here is contained in the contract. The contract is a contract of purchase and sale, the vendors being, besides sellers, manufacturers, and there are many intricate stipulations with regard to the things to be manufactured and sold. The payment is made to depend upon whether the certificate of a certain engineer is

*1886
February 4.*

Queen's
Bench
Division.

*1886
March 30.*

Court of
Appeal.

1886
March 30.

Court of
Appeal.

given. That being the contract, with all those intricate stipulations in it, you have a stipulation as to what is to happen if there is a dispute. That is the tenth clause, which is in the largest terms, and which says all disputes are to be settled by the engineer for the purchaser, and an engineer to be appointed by the seller, or an umpire. Of course, "all disputes" may mean a dispute as to anything, not referring to this contract at all, but the words are so large that they would seem to me to include all disputes that may arise between the parties in consequence of this contract having been made. I think what my brother Mathew has pointed out goes very strongly to show how large the clause is. The clause, in effect, is this, there being these complicated stipulations in this contract, and it being foreseen that disputes will very likely arise in regard to them, it is agreed that all disputes are to be settled by arbitration. I must say I agree with what my brother Lopes said; amongst other things, there might be a dispute as to what is the true construction of the contract, and that, amongst other disputes, would come within the tenth clause.

That being the large submission, because that is really the submission carried out by the appointment of the arbitrators afterwards to settle the dispute, then comes the question whether the dispute that arose was a dispute that arose in consequence of this contract having been made. What was the evidence? The engines were made, and some of them, or all of them, were sent to Croydon, but the engineer declined to give a certificate, and he declined to give his reasons for refusing a certificate, but, nevertheless, the vendors, the manufacturers, said: "We are entitled to the price stipulated by this contract." Now, how could that dispute have arisen except in consequence of this contract having been made? It could not. It is not a dispute with reference to something else at the other end of the world, but it is a dispute arising in consequence of this contract having been made. It is obvious the contention on the part of the vendors would be, "Notwithstanding the engineer having refused his certificate, either upon the true construction of the contract, or by reason of something else, by reason of his not having given his reasons, and so being unreasonable, we assert and maintain that we are entitled to the price mentioned in the contract." The contention on the other side would be, "Whatever his reasons were, whether good, bad, or indifferent, you are not entitled to the price unless he has given his certificate." That is a dispute raised which only could have been raised in consequence of this contract of purchase and sale having been made, and it seems to me it was a dispute within the

1886
March 30.

Court of
Appeal.

tenth clause, and therefore that the arbitrators appointed were appointed under the submission contained in that tenth clause, and they were therefore entitled to decide the question that they have decided.

Under those circumstances it is not material to consider whether they have decided rightly or wrongly. I have my own suspicions about what has happened, but that is immaterial. The parties have elected their own tribunal, and they have the great satisfaction of coming to that which is the fashionable proposition, that it is far better to have a decision against you than to have an appeal; they have got that, and much good may it do them, but it is the result of their own choice. They have got that and must abide by it. It seems to me there was ample jurisdiction and perfect jurisdiction in these arbitrators to decide what they have, and it follows from that that the Court ought not to leave the vendors to bring their action, and that the decision of the Court below was quite right, and under those circumstances the appeal must be dismissed.

LINDLEY, L.J.: I am of opinion that the arbitrators here have not exceeded their jurisdiction. The truth is that these agreements, without an arbitration clause, are very often extremely onerous, and extremely harsh in their operation. The payment of the price is made to depend upon the certificate of an engineer, who for any reason, good, bad, or indifferent, will not give a certificate, and it is to mitigate that state of things that they put in the tenth clause in this case, which is to the effect that all disputes are to be settled by arbitration. We are asked to say that that language does not mean what it says. We are asked to say "all disputes" does not mean a particular kind of dispute, the dispute being this, whether the purchase-money is payable or not under the contract. It appears to me so to construe the contract would be very much to cut down and discount the very meaning of the language of the tenth clause, and I see no reason for it. It appears to me that we must construe clauses 5 and 10 together, and when we do that it appears to me that it is precisely one of the disputes the parties contemplated referring to arbitration. Under those circumstances I think that the appeal must be dismissed, and with costs.

LOPES, L.J.: In this case we have not got to consider the question as to whether the arbitrators have rightly decided, but we have to consider whether or not they have acted within their jurisdiction. However wrong their decision may be, provided they have acted *intra vires*, their decision is final. The question, therefore, that arises is with regard to the true construction of this contract, especially with

1886
March 30.

Court of
Appeal.

regard to the true construction of clauses 5 and 10 of the contract. In point of fact, it comes to this: is the dispute that has arisen a dispute within the submission—is it a dispute within clause 10? Now, first, I will call attention to clause 5, which is in these words: "Tho purchasers shall pay the vendors one-half of the contract price," &c. (reads the clause). The engineer refused to give his certificate, and also refused to give his reasons, and in consequence a dispute has arisen under this clause as to whether or not the contract money is payable, or whether, in point of fact, the engineer has unreasonably withheld his certificate. That being so, we now come to clause 10, and it must be borne in mind that there are other clauses besides under which disputes may arise. Clause 10 is in these words: "All disputes are to be settled by the engineers of the purchasers," &c. (reads clause). I read the words "all disputes " in this way, that it means all disputes respecting the contract or its construction. If that is the true construction, there can be no doubt the dispute about which I have spoken, which has arisen under clause 5, must come within the words "all disputes." I think, therefore, the decision of the Court below was right, and that the appeal must be dismissed.

E. Dean, Solicitor for the City of London Contract Corporation.
Woodard, Hood and Wells, solicitors for the Hohenzollern Co.

1887
November
12, 21, 22.

Queen's
Bench
Division.

𝕳𝖎𝖌𝖍 𝕮𝖔𝖚𝖗𝖙 𝖔𝖋 𝕵𝖚𝖘𝖙𝖎𝖈𝖊 (𝕼𝖚𝖊𝖊𝖓'𝖘 𝕭𝖊𝖓𝖈𝖍 𝕯𝖎𝖛𝖎𝖘𝖎𝖔𝖓).

(Before Mr. Justice Denman.)

YOUNG v. BLAKE and ANOTHER.

Building Contract—Liability of Employer and Architect in respect of Errors in Bills of Quantities.

A firm of architects took out quantities and supplied them to the builders, and were paid by them. In an action by the builder against the employer and his architect for damages occasioned to the builder by alleged errors in the bills of Quantities—Held, (1) That there was no warranty by employer or architect of the accuracy of the quantities; (2) that no action lay for negligence in taking quantities; (3) that the quantities were not made the basis of the contract: *Scrivener v. Pask* (1866), L. R. 1 C. P. 715 (Ex. Ch.); and *Stevenson v. Watson* (1879), 4 C. P. D. 148, considered.

The facts of the case appear in the judgement appended. The case arose out of errors in a bill of quantities. The plaintiffs, a firm of builders, sued

Mr. Blake, the employer, and Messrs. Farrell and Edmonds, the architects of the building owner. The architects had taken out the quantities, and had been paid by the builders.

1887
November
12, 21, 22.

Queen's
Bench
Division.

Lumley Smith, Q.C., and Macaskie for plaintiffs; Alderson Foote for defendants Farrell and Edmonds; Pitt Lewis, Q.C., and Fossett Lock for defendant Blake.

The plaintiffs by their statement of claim said that:—

1. The defendant Blake warranted the accuracy of the quantities.

2. By the contract it was agreed that the bill of quantities should be treated as the basis of the contract, and that in case of error in the quantities the plaintiffs should be paid for the work and materials in excess thereof.

3. They alternatively claim as for work and labour done.

As against the defendants Farrell and Edmonds they alternatively said that:—

1. They employed them for reward, and claim the loss occasioned by the errors in quantities on the ground of negligence.

2. And alternatively they warranted the accuracy of the quantities.

The defendant Blake denied the allegations in the statement of claim, and said that:—

1. They sent in a final account which plaintiff paid in settlement.

2. There were no errors in the quantities, and that the architects never measured the work and adjusted the same in accordance with the quantities as required by the contract.

3. The architect never awarded or decided in favour of the plaintiffs' claim.

By way of counterclaim the defendant Blake said that:—

1. The plaintiffs had not performed their contract, and that the work was badly done.

2. The plaintiffs contracted for reward, with the defendants Farrell and Edmonds, to take out the quantities.

3. The plaintiffs, without authority from this defendant, included the cost of the quantities in their tender and concealed it from this defendant, who was induced to believe that the whole contract price was the price of the buildings, and claimed damages, penalties for delay, and repayment of the sum paid for quantities.

The defendants Farrell and Edmonds by their defence said that:—

1. They denied they were employed for reward to take out the quantities, or that they did so negligently.

2. They deny that they warranted the correctness thereof.

The plaintiffs in their reply said that:—

1. The contract does not require the work to be measured or adjusted.

2. The architects have wrongfully refused to measure and adjust the work.

3. The architects at the time the plaintiffs entered into the contract did not and do not possess unbiassed minds necessary for the discharge of their duties.

As to the counterclaim of the defendant Blake, the plaintiffs denied that they broke the contract, and said that:—

1. The delay was due to extra work.

2. The penalties were compromised by payment of a certain sum.

3. The architects' certificate of satisfaction was by the contract made conclusive of due performance of the work, and they have certified.

1887
November
12, 21, 22.
———————
Queen's
Bench
Division.

4. The architects, if they contracted at all, contracted as to the quantities as agents of the defendant Blake.

5. The plaintiffs did not conceal the charge for quantities.

6. The agreement for payment of the charge for quantities was a term of the contract.

In the alternative the plaintiffs included the charge for quantities in their tender according to a custom of the trade.

The case cannot be followed without reference to the contract, the principal part of the clauses of which are set out. The parts to which special attention was directed are printed in italics.

Memorandum of agreement made and entered into the 23rd day of January, 1885, between hereinafter called "the said contractors," of the one part, and William Heitland Blake, of Sherborne, in the county of Dorset, gentleman, of the other part, as follows:—

Whereas the said William Heitland Blake is desirous that a messuage or dwelling-house shall be erected on a certain piece or parcel of ground, portion of a close of land called Chapel Field, belonging to him, situate near a street called Acreman Street, in Sherborne, oforesaid, and has appointed Messrs. Farrell and Edmonds, of Sherborne, aforesaid, architects and *surveyors*, and hereinafter called "the said architects," to be the architects for that purpose:

And *whereas plans, sections, and elevations of the said intended messuage* or dwelling-house and premises, and a *specification* of the works to be done and of the materials to be provided in and for the erection of the same have been prepared by the said architects and approved of by the said William Heitland Blake:

And whereas the said contractors are willing to contract for the execution of the said works for the sum of 3,800*l.*:

And whereas the said plans, sections, elevations, and specifications have been signed by the contractors, and also by the said architects and the said William Heitland Blake: Now, therefore, the said contractors . . . . will in all respects comply with and abide by the *true intent and meaning of the said specifications, plans, sections and elevations*, and also of this agreement.

2. The said contractors . . . . shall complete and finish the said messuage or dwelling-house and premises on or before the 1st day of November, 1885, and in case the said messuage and premises shall not be completely finished on that day the said contractors shall forfeit . . . . the sum of *1.* for every day which shall elapse after the said 1st day of November, 1885, until the said messuage and premises shall be so completely finished. Provided always, that in case the said contractors shall be prevented by strike, bad weather, &c.

3. The said contractors . . . . shall provide everything necessary for the performing and completing the said work according to the true intent and meaning of the said *plans, sections, elevations, and specifications* . . . . and in case the architect shall at any time consider any portion of the said work to be executed in an unsound or improper manner, the said contractors shall cause the same to be taken down and executed to the satisfaction of the architect.

4. In case the said contractors or either of them shall become bankrupt or make any arrangement, &c. . . . . .

5. In case the architects, or such other architect as aforesaid, should by their

order in writing, or the said William Heitland Blake should at any time think proper to make any addition to, omission from, or other alteration in, the said works as detailed in the said *plans, sections, and specification,* no such alteration, or addition, or omission shall vacate the present contract, but the same shall be duly made, performed, or omitted by the said contractors, and the value thereof, whether an addition or deduction, shall be ascertained by a measurement to be made by the said architects, or such other architect as aforesaid, and such value shall be either added to or deducted from the sum then due to the said contractors, as the case may be, *according to the priced bills of quantities whereon the tender of the said contractors was based,* and the work undertaken by them, and the award or decision of the said architects shall in every such case of admeasurement or valuation be final, binding and conclusive.

6. The bills of quantities supplied by the said architects are believed to be correct, but should any error or misstatement be found therein either in favour of or against the said contractors, *it shall be lawful and in the power of the said architects to measure any or all the works contained and described in the said bills of quantities and to adjust the same* in accordance with the prices therein contained, and whereon the said tender was based and the work undertaken, and the said contractors shall for this purpose produce on demand to the said architects the said priced bills of quantities.

7. ——

8. ——

9. The said William Heitland Blake doth hereby contract . . . . that he will duly and regularly pay or cause to be paid to them the same sum of (the contract price) in manner following, that is to say, by instalments of 75*l.* per cent. upon the value of the works from time to time executed by them *upon the certificates of the said architects,* to be supplied by them from time to time, stating that work has been done and materials provided to a sufficient amount up to the date of giving such certificates respectively, and that the same has been executed, provided, and carried out by the said contractors to their complete satisfaction, and the balance of the said sum of (the contract price) shall be paid within three calendar months after the whole of the said works shall have been completed and finished to the satisfaction of the said architects.

10. ——

As witness the hands of the said parties the day and year first before written.

Signed by the said WALTER JOHN YOUNG and CHARLES SQUIRE YOUNG.

Signed by the said WILLIAM HEITLAND BLAKE.

DENMAN, J.: This was an action brought by Messrs. Young, builders, against Mr. Blake, the headmaster of the Sherborne Grammar School, and against Messrs. Farrell and Edmonds, architects and surveyors.

It was an action of a very peculiar description, and upon a basis which was somewhat unusual, very unusual I should say, and it was agreed, as I understand, between the parties that the question which was to be raised before me here—and, really it was the only question

1887
November
12, 21, 22.

Queen's
Bench
Division.

1987
November
12, 21, 22.

Queen's
Bench
Division.

which could be reasonably raised before me—should be the question of the respective liability of Mr. Blake, on the one hand, or the architects on the other.

The two actions, though mixed up in the sense of being with reference to the same transactions, are totally distinct and different causes of action. I think the best way of dealing with them will be first to deal with the action against Mr. Blake, and then to deal with the action against Messrs. Farrell and Edmonds. It is not necessary to state the facts in very great detail, but I will state the facts so far as I find them upon the evidence, and so far as they bear on the question which is for me, viz., the liability of the parties.

Young and Company were builders, residing and carrying on their business at Salisbury, and the work to be done was to be done at Sherborne, in Dorsetshire, about one hour and a quarter's journey by fast train from the one place to the other. Farrell and Edmonds are architects and also surveyors.

In 1884 Farrell and Edmonds had been employed by Mr. Blake to prepare plans at all events, and specifications probably, for a new house, and other matters connected with the school.

It appears from the evidence that Farrell and Edmonds had, in consequence of their employment by Mr. Blake, the other defendant, informed him that it would be necessary that quantities should be taken out. A conversation had taken place between him and them in which he showed very great ignorance of the usages of architects and surveyors; he asked them certain questions as to who would have to pay for it, and who would do it; he had heard of such persons as quantity surveyors, but they informed him that they were quantity surveyors as well as architects, and they did, for the purpose of getting a tender for the then contemplated school houses and buildings, take out certain quantities and prepare plans and specifications. At that time I find, in accordance with Mr. Blake's evidence, that they had somewhat led him to suppose that the building which was to be built, or he had rather intimated to them that the building which was to be erected, was not to be a building which would cost above 3,000*l.*, but it appears that they did, in their plans and specifications, or in their contemplated building upon which they drew up their quantities, devise a building which would cost a great deal more. The consequence was that he declined to have anything to do with that building, the tenders were not accepted, and the whole thing went off.

There is still a question pending between the parties as to whether in those circumstances the sum which it might be said to have cost

1887
November
12, 21, 22.

Queen's
Bench
Division.

Farrell and Edmonds to take out the quantities should be paid to them for the trouble they had in taking out quantities. I do not in any way intend by what I say to decide that question, it may be that the one or, the other side may be right in that contention. On the one hand, Mr. Blake contends that it was owing to their fault, with the instructions that they had, that they did not effectively bring about a tender for the thing that he intended, by reason of the devising of a very much more expensive thing, they, on the other hand, contending that as he did not choose to undertake the work, they acting for him in the matter, they would be entitled to remuneration for taking out those quantities.

The only importance, therefore, of that original transaction is with reference to what might be gathered as to the terms upon which those two parties dealt with one another, and what authority the one gave to the other upon a subsequent transaction which took place, and which is the one upon which the present dispute arises.

Now, the present dispute began at a later date, and the correspondence, I think, very clearly shows the course of events so far as it bears upon the present action. It would appear that on the 1st of December, 1884, after the other transaction had altogether gone off, Messrs. Farrell and Edmonds, being architects, and being, no doubt, at that time authorised by Mr. Blake to set to work to obtain tenders, did write to Messrs. Young & Co., the plaintiffs, and in fact to a good many other builders, a letter in which they asked them whether they would be willing to tender for the erection of so and so, "quantities to be supplied, an early answer will oblige." Then, on the next day Messrs. Young write to say that they would be quite willing to tender, and then at a time which is not exactly fixed, but between that date and the 18th (as clearly appears by a letter from the plaintiffs referring to the "bill of quantities"), the bill of quantities was sent which is impeached in the present action. Farrell and Edmonds say, "We have pleasure in sending you herewith a bill of quantities, tenders to be sent to us," and so on.

Now, the bill of quantities itself is an important document; it is headed, "Estimate for master's residence, boarding house, and preparatory school, to be built at Sherborne for W. Blake, Esq.— Farrell and Edmonds, Architects."

Then comes the quantities "excavation"—so many yards for this, so many yards for that; in fact, an ordinary bill of quantities. At that time, of course, it was not priced, that would have to be done by the persons before they tendered, and the bill as I now have it has in pencil the figures that were put in by the plaintiffs, Messrs. Young,

1887
November
12, 21, 22.

Queen's
Bench
Division.

and put in with a view of seeing what the cost at which they could do the building was to be.

On the 18th December there was a letter referring to that bill of quantities. On the 19th there was a small matter which the architects spoke about as being an overlooking of a certain sum, and certain arrangements were made between them and the builders. On the 23rd came the acceptance of the tender, and Messrs. Young, on the 23rd of December, wrote, "We will undertake to do the work comprised in the bill of quantities for the erection of master's residence, &c., at Sherborne, for W. Blake, Esq., for the sum of 3,800*l.*"

Now a question arises as to the exact date at which an interview, and the only interview, took place between the plaintiffs and Mr. Farrell before the contract was actually signed. I do not think it is necessary to determine (and I do not myself feel absolutely certain) what that date was; on the one hand, it is sworn by Messrs. Young that it was at some date before the estimate was actually accepted, before the tender was actually made for 3,800*l.*, that they had the bill of quantities before them. On the other hand, there was some doubt raised about that—as to the only time that they had seen the specification and the plan, because there is a letter from Mr. Farrell to Messrs. Young preparing for a meeting at a certain time, namely, half-past two on the Monday, which is after the 29th of December or the 27th of December, and as there was only one meeting, it would look as though that contemplated the meeting which actually took place, but I do not think it is very important in the view I take of the case. I only allude to it because it must not be taken that my decision depends on it in any way. Eventually the builders, the plaintiffs, set to work.

There is a good deal of correspondence which I have read, and which was referred to and read at length before me, as to small matters about which special arrangements had to be made; certain plans to be supplied are got by the architects themselves, and there was a question as to delay in beginning, and delay in the work, and so on, but all these matters seem to me to have been disposed of practically, and to have been wiped away by the fact (and it is really an admitted fact in the case upon the evidence) that at a certain date, namely, by September, 1886, at all events, there had been a payment in full for the work done, certain arrangements being made, and certain gives and takes having taken place, that there had been payment for all the work done, and all the matters arising upon the contract, subject only to the question which is raised in this case, that is to say, whether there is any liability on the part either of

1887
November
12, 21, 22.

Queen's
Bench
Division.

Mr. Blake or of Mr. Farrell in respect of deficient quantities, because that is the complaint.

Assuming the quantities to be correct, granted that there has been payment for all that has been done in the way of work and extras, the contention is that upon the events which have occurred and upon the discovery by the plaintiffs at a subsequent date, or rather by August, 1886, that does give the plaintiffs as against Mr. Blake, and, secondly, as against Mr. Farrell, a right of action.

First, as regards Mr. Blake, I must look at the claim against him. The claim against Mr. Blake is shaped in two or three different ways. First, it states that Mr. Blake, in or about December, 1884, warranted and represented to the plaintiff that the work to be done and the materials provided therein were fully and accurately stated in a certain bill of quantities, in writing, which he delivered to the plaintiffs.

It is necessary to observe that the relations between Mr. Blake and the plaintiffs are those contained in the agreement of a date subsequent to December, namely, some day in January, 1886, that is, the date of the actual contract between the parties, and it seems to me, upon the true construction of that contract, coupled with all the evidence that there is in the case as regards Blake, that it is quite clear that Mr. Blake never did at any moment warrant the accuracy of the quantities.

With regard to the contract, it is to this effect. It is between Messrs. Young and Blake—the architect is no party to the contract. It recites that he wishes to build, and that he has appointed Messrs. Farrell and Edmonds, architects and surveyors, and that they are hereinafter called "the said architects"—they are to be architects for the purpose. Then it recites that plans and sections, elevations and specifications, have been prepared and approved of; and then it recites the fact that, for the sum of 3,800*l.*, this building was to be erected. Then it recites that plans and specifications have been signed by the contractors and by the architects, and then in paragraph 6, which is the paragraph bearing most upon the bill of quantities, there is the following provision. (His lordship then read clause 6.)

Now the case, both against Mr. Blake and against Mr. Farrell, depends very much indeed, so far as the liability here is concerned, upon the real meaning of that clause, and I may at once therefore state what I understand it to be. It begins by the assertion that the bills of quantities supplied to the architects are believed to be correct. That certainly seems to me to dispose altogether of the statement that Blake warranted the quantities to be correct. The parties are parties

1887
November
12, 21, 22.

Queen's
Bench
Division.

to a contract which merely states that they are believed to be correct. Then it goes on to state, "*Should any error or misstatement be found therein in favour of or against the contractors, it shall be lawful and in the power of the architect to measure any or all of the works contained or described in the bill of quantities.*" There I will stop for the present.

Now, what is the meaning of that? It appears to me that it is a discretionary power given to the architects, making it lawful and in their power to measure any or all of the works—"any" during the progress of the works, or "all" as soon as they are finished—to measure any of the works in the bill of quantities if any error or misstatement is found therein.

Now, I do not think that that gives the power, upon the mere assertion of the builders themselves that there is an error or misstatement, to compel and to call upon the architect as a matter of right to re-measure the work. I think that would be too unreasonable a power to suppose to be given to the builder in a contract of this kind, because it really would involve a most expensive and a most damaging operation to the works at the mere option of a person who undertakes to do them properly, and undertakes by this agreement to do certain works. I think, therefore, that the meaning of that must be that the architect is to be left in his discretion to re-measure if he finds there is reasonable ground to think that there is an error or misstatement of the works, and that then he may re-measure them and he may adjust them, as the words follow on—"and to adjust the same in accordance with the prices therein contained"—then he may adjust them as between the parties, and the difference, of course, would be allowed to the party, and the gains would be allowed as against the party who loses by that re-measurement. The architect had a right in order that that may be efficiently done to ask for the priced bill of quantities from the builder, in order that he might do that work.

That being so, it appears to me that the architect stands in a *quasi*-judicial position between the parties; he is architect not merely as a person who is employed as the agent of the building owner for all purposes, nor is he a person who is employed by the builder in any sense so as to be liable to him as a person at his will and pleasure to be ordered to do anything because the builder is dissatisfied.

Now, if that be true, it seems to me to dispose of the case, not only as against Blake, but as against the architects themselves, because if that be the true position, then the architects here are made by the parties persons in a *quasi*-judicial position—they are persons who, unless they are guilty of fraud or misconduct of any kind beyond

1887
November
12, 21, 22.

Queen's
Bench
Division.

mere allegations of negligence, are not to be harassed with actions against themselves, nor are the people whose architects they are as well as the architects of the other party to be harassed with actions merely because the architect in his discretion may refuse, on the demand of the builders, to re-measure any of the works.

That principle seems to me to be the principle of a case which counsel called my attention to yesterday, *Stevenson* v. *Watson* (*a*), in which, when a tender was made upon a statement that the quantities had been negligently certified for a much less sum than was the net balance, an attempt was made to fix a liability in consequence of that, and the decision was, "*That the functions of the architect in ascertaining the amount due to the plaintiff were not merely ministerial, but such as required the exercise of professional judgment, opinion and skill, and that he, therefore, occupied the position of an arbitrator, against whom, no fraud or collusion being alleged, the action would not lie.*"

That was a decision of the Chief Justice and myself, and I do not see any reason to doubt that it was right. Several cases were relied upon for that principle. It was very well argued on the other side by the present Mr. Justice Cave. I do not think it went to any Court of Appeal, and therefore, at present, I must take it to be good law.

Another case cited, *Scrivener* v. *Pask* (*b*), though the facts are not identical with the present case, also seems to me to go to a considerable length in favour of the defendants in this case—both of them. *Scrivener* v. *Pask* seems to me only to amount to this, that where there is nothing more than the ordinary employment of a quantity surveyor, the quantity surveyor being paid out of the first receipts by the builder of a building owner who must have quantities taken out in one sense, that is to say, who will not get tenders unless the quantities are taken out—where there is that simple case, there is nothing in that case, merely from the fact that the building owner orders things which involve the probability of quantities being taken out, to fix him with a liability to pay for the quantities so taken out which are taken out by a quantity surveyor ordered by the architects, or by the architect himself. It appears to me that that case at least goes so far as this, that unless there is something binding the owner, some understanding between the parties to be gathered from correspondence or words making himself liable for the taking out of the quantities, that he is not so liable.

(*a*) (1879), 4 C. P. D. 148.
(*b*) (1866), L. R. 1 C. P. 715 (Ex. Ch.).

1887
November
12, 21, 22.

Queen's
Bench
Division.

Now, as regards Mr. Blake, I can see nothing. There is no agreement such as that which is set out in the second paragraph of the statement of claim—namely, that it was agreed that the bill of quantities should be treated as the basis of the contract, and that if they were found to be incorrect, the plaintiffs should be paid by the defendant for the work and materials done and provided.

The meaning of the contract is, that the architect is to be responsible for deciding between the parties, and if he decides honestly, that the parties should have no right to complain of anybody. That really disposes of the case as against Mr. Blake.

Now, then, as regards the architects themselves. I think the same observation almost entirely disposes of the case against them, because if the relations had been that which I have stated—I think it is between the architects and the parties—then I think that they were in the position of persons trusted with a judgment, and, unless it was a dishonest judgment, a mere inaccuracy would not render them liable.

They are not parties to the contract in any way: they do not sign the contract, and they are only sought to be made liable by the supposition—first, that there is a custom that they should be liable under such circumstances, which, I think, is entirely unavailing in this case, because the clause is a very peculiar one in its language and in its relations in every way. That will not avail them; and, next, it was alleged that they were liable upon a certain special undertaking on their part to be liable, which was to be gathered from language which was said to be used by them in an interview between them and Messrs. Young & Co.

Now, I have carefully considered the language which has been sworn to on both sides, and though I do not know that I can say that I disbelieve the statements on the part of Messrs. Young—the words "the quantities are full" may have been used, I think it is admitted almost by one of the defendants—Mr. Edmonds, I think, admits that those words may have been used—I do not think that that can be, looking at the relation between the parties and at the contract which they knew of, and which both parties were fully aware of, construed into a warranty. There is no evidence of warranty against them.

Then, is there evidence of a warranty independently of that? There may be such a thing, and if the plaintiffs' evidence is believed, there would be evidence, perhaps, to go to a jury of it, if it stood uncontradicted, but we have evidence on the other side, and the evidence on the other side is very distinct and positive to the effect

1887
November
12, 21, 22.

Queen's
Bench
Division.

that the question of guarantee was actually raised, and the question was put, "Do you guarantee the quantities?" And here I believe the evidence of those witnesses that when the expression "guarantee" was put, they positively repudiated any such notion. I forget the exact expression in which it was repudiated, but it was as strong as it could be—"nothing of the kind," or "certainly not."

I think that that is the probability of the case—they would have been very foolish, and it would have been very unlikely that they should have guaranteed the quantities, when they had the discretion in them by the contract itself, which said that the quantities were believed to be correct, but that if any error or misstatement should be found, then it was lawful for them and in their power to measure any or all of the works, and so on.

This is no action for not doing anything under the contract, it is an action founded upon, in the first instance, warranty, and in the next place, upon an allegation of negligence.

Now, the allegation of warranty is not made out, but disproved.

The allegation of negligence, to my mind, is one which does not give a cause of action upon such a contract as this. It puts the architect in the position of persons trusted by both parties, and if a man with his eyes open chooses to enter into such a contract giving the architect that power, he cannot turn round and by mere allegation of negligence say, "I have discovered that there was an error in the measurements, and I have asked you to act under the contract and you won't do it in your discretion, but I will now sue you because you negligently took out those quantities." I do not think that is the relation between the parties at all. The architect is not put in that position so as to be the servant of either party in that sense, but he is in a different position altogether; and, therefore, I think the action fails against Farrell and Edmonds as well as against Blake, and I must, therefore, give judgment for both defendants, with costs.

Solicitors for plaintiffs: Taylor, Hoare, Taylor and Box. For defendant Blake: Macarthurs, Charlton and Smith. For defendants Farrell and Edmonds: Gregory, Rowcliffes, Rawle and Johnstone.

1888
May 18.
𝕾𝖎𝖌𝖇 **Court of Justice (Queen's Bench Division).**

(Cave, J., and a Special Jury.)

Queen's
Bench
Division.

June 26.
On appeal to Divisional Court.

Court of
Appeal.
(Lord Coleridge, L.C.J., and Mathew, J.)

𝕵𝖓 𝖙𝖍𝖊 **Court of Appeal.**

(Lord Esher, M.R., Lindley and Lopes, L.JJ.)

BUSH

v.

TRUSTEES OF PORT AND TOWN OF WHITEHAVEN.

*Contract to Lay Water Mains—Delay in Providing Site—Alteration
of Conditions Contemplated by Contract—Recovery of Conse-
quential Increase of Cost of Executing Works.*

Where the circumstances contemplated by a building contract for works are so
changed as to make the special conditions of the contract inapplicable, the contractor
may treat the contract as at an end and recover upon a *quantum meruit.*

1888
May 18.

Queen's
Bench
Division.

The plaintiff entered into a contract with the defendants to construct a 15-
inch water main from Ennerdale Water towards Whitehaven for 1,335*l.*

The conditions of the contract material to the present report are the
following:—

GENERAL CONDITIONS upon which the Works . . . are to be performed.

(1) Interpretations.— . . . The word "engineer" shall be held to mean the town
surveyor and harbour engineer of Whitehaven for the time being . . .

(2) General Explanations.— This contract comprises the formation and completion of
the several works shown on the drawings hereinbefore referred to and described in the
foregoing specifications. . . . Should any misunderstanding arise as to the meaning or
import of the said specification or drawing, or about the quality or dimensions of the
materials, or the due or proper execution of the works, or as to the quality or valuation,
of the works executed under this contract, or as to extras thereupon, or as to any other
matter or thing whatsoever arising out of this contract, the same shall be explained by
the engineer, and this explanation shall be final and binding upon the contractor, and
the contractor shall execute the work according to such explanation, and without
charge or deduction to or from the contract sum.

(4) Extra Work to be Ordered in Writing Only.—No allowance shall be made to the
contractor for any alterations in, or additions to, the work specified, unless he can
produce a written order, signed by the engineer, for the same.

1888
May 18.

Queen's
Bench
Division.

(6) Contractor not to Occupy Premises until Authorized.—The contractor shall not commence any work in, upon, under, across, or through any area, roadway, or ground until he shall be authorized in writing by the engineer so to do.

(11) Commencement of Works.—The contractor shall commence the works and carry them on at whatever point or points, and in such portions as the engineer may direct; but none of the works are to be commenced without a written order signed by the engineer. The trustees will, with the engineer's written order to commence any section of the works, give to the contractor the use of so much of the site of works as may, in the opinion of the engineer, be required to enable the contractor to commence and continue the execution of the works, and will, from time to time, as the works proceed, give the contractor the use of such further portions as the engineer may from time to time consider proper in that behalf; *but the non-delivery in the manner aforesaid of the use of such site, or any part thereof, shall not vitiate or affect the contract, nor any provision therein or in this specification contained, nor entitle the contractor to any increased allowance in respect of money, time, or otherwise, unless the engineer may grant him any extension of time, and then only to that extent under the provisions for that purpose hereinafter contained.*

(22) Time of Completion.—The contractor shall complete and deliver up to the trustees the whole of the works within a period of, &c. . . . Provided always, that if by reason of the non-possession of the site required for the purposes of the work, or by reason of any additions to the work (which additions the engineer is hereby authorized to make), or in consequence of strikes or other unavoidable circumstances, the contractor shall, in the opinion of the engineer, have been unduly delayed, it shall be lawful for the engineer, if he shall so think fit, to extend the time, without thereby prejudicing or in any way affecting the validity of the contract or the sufficiency of the tender, or the adequacy of the sums or prices therein mentioned.

(23) Penalty for Non-completion.—That time shall especially be considered the essence of this contract on the part of the contractor, and in case the contractor shall fail in the due performance of the works to be executed under this contract by and at the times herein mentioned . . . he shall be liable to pay the trustees as and for liquidated damages the sum of 50*l.* for each and every week which may elapse between the appointed and actual time of completion and delivery herein-before mentioned or provided for.

The plaintiff's tender was sent in on 12th June, 1886, and he was given to understand that he was to begin at once, and to have four months in which to finish the work, and his calculations were based on that footing, as the cost of doing the work in the winter months would be at least 50 per cent, higher than the tender.

The contract was accepted on June 23rd, and plaintiff was then told that arrangements for immediate possession had been made with five out of eight owners and five out of ten occupiers of the land necessary for the works. The plaintiff began work on the 12th July, before the Corporation had sealed the contract; but the land was not all available until the 6th October. In consequence of this delay, the work was thrown into the winter months, and the contractor was put to heavy extra expense, for which he sued the defendants. The further facts involved in the case are sufficiently elucidated in the judgments.

The action was tried at the Liverpool Assizes before Cave, J., and a special jury.

1888
May 18.

Queen's
Bench
Division.

Henn Collins, Q.C., C. A. Russell, and Morris for plaintiff; Bigham, Q.C., and Joseph Walton for defendants.

The following were the questions left to the jury by Cave, J., and their answers:—

(1) Was it the duty of the defendants under the contract to be in a position at the commencement of and at all times during the contract to give the contractor the use of so much of the site of the works as might, in the opinion of the engineer, be required to enable the contractor to commence and continue the execution of the works in accordance with the contract?—Yes.

(2) Was the contract made upon the basis that the defendants would be in a position to act as aforesaid?—Yes.

(3) Were the defendants at the commencement of the contract in a position to act as aforesaid?—No.

(4) When first, if at all, were the defendants in a position to act as aforesaid?—On the 8th October, 1886.

(5) *Were the conditions of the contract so completely changed, in consequence of the defendants' inability to hand over the sites of the work as required, as to make the special provisions of the contract inapplicable?—Yes.*

(6) Was the plaintiff unduly delayed by reason of the defendants not giving him possession of the sites required for the purpose of the work?—Yes.

(7) Did the engineer grant the plaintiff an extension of time by reason of the plaintiff not getting possession of such sites?—Yes.

(8) What damage has the plaintiff suffered by reason of the inability of the defendants to hand over the sites required for the purposes of this work?—Answer: 600*l*. over and above the contract price.

(9) What amount is due to the defendants on their counterclaim?—Answer: 12*l*.

On these findings judgment was entered for the plaintiff for 600*l*.

The defendants appealed to a Divisional Court.

Lord COLERIDGE, L.C.J.: This is a case in which I feel that there is very considerable embarrassment owing to the very strong language of the 11th and 22nd clauses of this contract. It is an action brought by a contractor who has signed a contract, and who has undertaken to be bound by the terms of that contract, to recover not only the contract price, but to recover a sum of money either by way of *quantum meruit* or by way of damages against the defendants—it does not very much matter which view is taken—to recover a considerable sum of money beyond the contract price, on the ground that the circumstances under which he completed the contract were wholly different from those under which he entered into it, and that therefore he is set free from the terms of it and has a right to recover this sum of money.

Now, the contract is a contract substantially in the terms which are very common in cases of this sort, whereby the contractor is, if the

1888
May 18.

Queen's
Bench
Division.

literal terms of the contract be adhered to, handed over, bound hand and foot, to the other party to the contract, or to the engineer of that other party, and the argument for the plaintiffs in this case, as I shall explain in a moment, must be that if this plaintiff is not entitled to succeed, under no conceivable circumstance (I put *mala fides* out of the question), however arbitrary and however unreasonable, short of corrupt and unfair intention—however unreasonable may be the alteration of the term of time stipulated for in this contract made by the act of the defendants, nevertheless, the plaintiff is absolutely without his remedy.

Now, the 11th section, no doubt, must be construed with the 22nd, and the difficulty is, I feel, considerable upon the very stringent words of those sections in maintaining that under the contract, and maintaining this contract as an existing contract, the plaintiff is entitled to succeed. I admit the difficulty, but as at present advised I do not think the difficulty insuperable. The trustees contract that when the engineer gives a written order to the contractor to commence the works they will—I summarize it for the purpose of convenience—give him so much of the site upon which the works are to be constructed as may be necessary for their construction. That they undertake, and then the parties go on to stipulate that the non-delivery of the site, or any part, shall not vitiate or affect the contract or any of its provisions, or entitle the contractor to any increased allowance in respect of money, time, or otherwise, unless the engineer grants him an extension of time in the manner pointed out by the 22nd section—I give the substantial effect of the provisions— and the 22nd section stipulating that the work shall be done in four months from the date of the engineer's order, which it is admitted was to date from the middle of July—I think I am right—some time in July—they were to be delivered up in a perfect condition, and so on: "Provided that if by reason of the non-possession of the site required for the purpose of the works, or by reason of any addition to the work, which addition the engineer may make, or in consequence of strikes or other inevitable circumstances, the contractor shall have been unduly delayed, the engineer, if he thinks fit, may extend the time without thereby prejudicing or in any way affecting the validity of the contract." Now, the only thing under the 22nd section which he may do apparently is to extend the time, and the only effect of extending the time, as far as I see, is to relieve the contractor from the penalty of 50*l.* a week imposed by the 23rd section if he does not complete the works within the time specified in the 22nd section.

The sections read together then come to this. The defendants, a

1888
May 18.

Queen's
Bench
Division.

Corporation, undertake, on the written order of the engineer, when the written order of the engineer is given, to give the contractor so much of the site as may be necessary for the works. In the view of the defendants, if they do not the contractor shall not have any increased allowance in respect of money, time, or otherwise, except under the 22nd section. The 22nd section, as I have already pointed out, says nothing about allowance or anything else, but simply says time may be extended, and the only effect of extending time, as I have already said, is to relieve from penalties.

Now, first of all, it seems that the construction of the contract insisted upon by the defendants is in the highest degree oppressive. It seems to me, further, that it is very unreasonable, but I first of all say that it is extremely oppressive because it is manifest that if, howsoever produced, delay is occasioned, and however fatal to the interests of the contractor such delay may be—I put aside corruption and *mala fides*—the only power under this contract which the engineer has is to relieve him from the penalties for the non-completion of work which by hypothesis it was impossible for him to complete, or to begin. It seems to me that that is in itself an extremely oppressive contract, but, nevertheless, although it is oppressive, it may be so plain that if people with their eyes open will enter into contracts which may be used for their oppression they must be held to them. But one may struggle if one can fairly struggle—we must not do violence to good sense and to the English language; but one may struggle if one could do so consistently with good sense, and within the rules of language, against a construction so manifestly unjust and oppressive as that would be.

First of all, it should seem that it is not unreasonable to adopt the view that Mr. Collins has presented to us, that as a substratum and as a basis of this contract it was implied between the parties that the defendants should, within a reasonable time for the completion of the works, give to the contractor the possession of the site without which he could not even begin them. Next, it seems not unreasonable to contend that the words, "That he shall not be entitled to any increased allowance in respect of money, time, or otherwise, unless the engineer grants him an extension of time," may fairly and reasonably be intended to mean that if he grants an extension of time, then as a consequence of that extension of time the contractor may have an increased allowance in respect of money or otherwise. Time, of course, is by hypothesis already given him by the authority of the engineer.

Therefore, it does not seem to me to be clear by any means that,

1888
May 18.

Queen's
Bench
Division.

even upon the true construction of this contract, the contractor is without remedy, because here it is admitted there has been a very long delay, and it is admitted that that very long delay has—and the finding of the jury in that respect is not complained of—very grievously added to the expense and cost to which the contractor has been put, and it may well be that if the time has been extended, as it seems to me, unless the words of the clauses are too strong for us, that the consequence follows that if the time is extended, allowance in point of money or otherwise may be within the terms of the contract.

Now, then, I have pointed out what seems to me to be the extreme difficulty of contending that the contractor and the defendants could have intended by the words which I have been dealing with to bind themselves to such a construction as that, although the whole incidence of the contract might be changed at the sole will of tho defendants and the whole onus of the contract altered, doubled, trebled, quadrupled, perhaps, upon the contractor, that, nevertheless, that was a contingency which they both contemplated, which the words necessitate one to suppose they did contemplate, and that, therefore, however heavy and however burdensome the result upon the contractor may be, a contract is a contract, and he must be bound by what he has signed. I think, therefore, that upon the true construction of this contract we are not bound to arrive at any such exceedingly oppressive and unreasonable construction, and that a reasonable time—the giving of these sites within a time that shall be reasonable for the completion of the work—either within four months or within such further extension of time as the engineer shall have given—must be taken to have been the true view of the parties, and, that view being consistent with the words, it must be taken to be the true construction of the words which the parties have used.

But, supposing that I should be wrong in the criticism that I have applied to the very words of the contract itself, there seems to me to be another principle now well established, a sensible and and a just principle, which may enable us to deal with this case after the findings of the jury, approved of as they are in terms in the report which my learned brother has furnished us with, at the end of the case, where he says, "The answers of the jury are such as I approve of." The answers of the jury to the questions which were put by the learned judge, at the request of the parties, enable us to apply the principle I have spoken of, and, therefore, to do what I think is justice in this case.

Now, what is that principle? I find it stated in very clear terms

1888
May 18.
———
Queen's
Bench
Division.

in the judgment of the majority of the Court in *Jackson v. The Union Marine Insurance Company* (*a*), in the 8th Law Reports, Common Pleas, at page 581, and after going through a variety of authorities, with which I need not now trouble myself, the result is stated in this way: "These authorities seem to support the proposition, which appears on principle to be very reasonable, that where a contract is made with reference to certain anticipated circumstances, and where, without any default of either party, it becomes wholly inapplicable to, or impossible of application to any such circumstances, it ceases to have any application; it cannot be applied to other circumstances which could not have been in the contemplation of the parties when the contract was made."

Now, what were the circumstances when the contract was made? It was a contract made in August to run from July. It was a contract to complete the work within four months from the 12th of July, I think—the particular day is immaterial. As a matter of fact, the contract could not be begun; no work could be done under the contract. A general order was given ordering the work to be done throughout the whole length of it—a length of many miles—from Ennerdale Lake to the town of Whitehaven. A general order was given to do the whole, and it has been suggested to us, and not denied, that it was important for the reasonable completion of this contract that the whole site should be put into the hands of the contractor at once. As a matter of fact, the order having been given early in August, a very important part of the site of the contracted works was not given until some time in October. It was, therefore, in the first place, a contract to be completed within four months from the 12th of July—what may be called, in the popular language which has been used, both from the Bench and at the Bar, a summer contract. It was turned into a winter contract—into a contract when wages were different, probably, or may have been; when days were short, instead of long; when weather was bad, instead of good; when rivers which had to be dealt with, and had to be crossed by the pipes, were full or empty; and when, in fact, I will not say every circumstance, but a great many most important circumstances under which the contract was to be executed, had wholly changed from those which, it is reasonable to suppose, were in the contemplation of both the parties when the contract was entered into.

The contract, nevertheless, was carried on, and was completed. It was carried on and was completed, of course, with the knowledge of

---

(*a*) L. R. 8 C. P. 572.

1888
May 18.
Queen's
Bench
Division.

the contractor, and equally of course, with the knowledge of the defendants. The defendants knew as well as the contractor that the work was being carried on under totally different circumstances to those contemplated in the contract. They knew that perfectly well, and although the plaintiff possibly or probably might at the expiration of the four months have thrown up the contract and refused to proceed, he had also a perfect right, if he had thought fit, with the knowledge and assent of the defendants, which in this case is to be presumed, and, indeed, was proved, to go on with the contract and to complete it under the altered conditions, or I will not say to complete the contract, but to complete the work under the totally altered conditions that had arisen.

Now, under those circumstances the jury are asked the question, "Were the conditions of the contract so completely changed, in consequence of the inability to hand over the sites of the work as required, as to make the special provisions of the contract inapplicable?" That is to say, I take for granted—there has been no technical dispute about that subject—to make sections 11 and 22 and 23 inapplicable. That is the meaning of the question, and the jury say "Yes" in answer to that question. Now, I said rather early in the argument, Could such a state of things occur under this contract? It seems to me the defendants are driven to say that they could not— that under no circumstances could any change in the conditions of the contract created by delay emancipate the plaintiff from the fulfilment of the contract—no circumstances. If they shrink from that, and if they say that such circumstances might arise, then the question arises, Did they arise in this case? The jury have found that they did, and the learned judge is satisfied with the finding of the jury in point of fact; and if the jury should find that, then we have the authority of *Jackson v. The Union Marine Insurance Company* (a), affirmed on appeal in the 10th Law Reports, Common Pleas—we have the principle laid down and always since accepted that if circumstances arise which alter the whole—not adventure, because this can hardly be called an adventure, but alter the whole work, or, as it is put in the question, entirely change the conditions of the contract, then the contract cannot be held applicable to those changed conditions, because those conditions could not have been in the contemplation of either party at the time when the contract was signed. I think, therefore, that there is plenty of evidence in this case to warrant that finding of the jury.

(a) L. R. 10 C. P. 125.

1888
May 18.

Queen's
Bench
Division.

Supposing the criticisms I have endeavoured to pass upon the language of the contract, which, if they are correct, give the plaintiff a right of recovery under the contract, upon further consideration and further enquiry by more astute minds should be found not to be correct, then, at any rate as at present advised, it appears to me that the finding of the jury is warranted by fact. If it is warranted by fact, the law says that under such circumstances the contract must be held to be inapplicable. Then, either in the way of *quantum meruit* or in the way of damages for not having done what they had undertaken to do, the plaintiff is entitled to succeed, and this rule must be refused.

MATHEW, J.: I am of the same opinion. The case appears to me to be one in which the literal interpretation of the contract would lead to manifest absurdity and injustice—absurdity, in fact, so gross that we cannot suppose the parties ever contemplated any such bargain, and the learned counsel for the defendants was driven to admit that under the provisions of this contract the defendants might postpone indefinitely the time for its performance, and that under no circumstances could the contractor treat the contract as at an end, so that if he were not put in possession of the site for a year, and made complaint and threatened to throw up the contract, the defendants would be entitled to say, under section 22, the time has not come for extending the period during which the contract is to be completed. We hold you to your bargain, and you have contracted yourself out of the right of terminating or getting rid of your liability. I cannot suppose for a moment that that was what either party meant. It appears to me there was abundant evidence to justify the conclusion of the jury that the plaintiff and the defendants permitted the works to go on upon the understanding that those works were being done, not under the original contract, but under a contract with altered conditions. I see no reason for disturbing the conclusion of the jury, and for those reasons, as well as the reasons given by my Lord, I think the motion for judgment and to enter the verdict for the plaintiff must succeed.

The defendants then appealed to the Court of Appeal.

(*Before* LORD ESHER, M.R., LINDLEY and LOPES, L.JJ.)

THE MASTER OF THE ROLLS: It seems to me, on the finding of the jury in answer to the 5th question, that the case is brought within the principle (of course, not within the circumstances) which was

1888
May 18.

Queen's
Bench
Division.

acted upon in *Jackson* v. *The Union Marine Insurance Co.* (*a*), which was not a new principle, but which, as it was shown in that case by long and arduous judgments, was a principle which had been established before that in many or several other cases. Now, the answer to the 5th question (if you take it to be a binding finding of the jury), in my opinion, comes to this, that the condition of things had so been altered after the making of the original contract (they had been so greatly altered) that it was not reasonable, or right, or fair, or just to hold that the original contract was made with regard to those circumstances. In other words you may put it thus, that the condition of things was so altered that if they had been supposed to be the things with regard to which the first contract was made, neither party acting as (I must use my favourite phrase) reasonable men of business could have made the original contract in the terms in which it was with regard to that state of circumstances. The result of that, if it is true, is this, that the original contract is made with regard to a different subject-matter from the subject-matter which was dealt with by the parties. If that finding stands, then the condition of things with which the parties dealt ultimately was so very different from the condition of things with regard to which the original contract was made, that the circumstances with regard to which the original contract is made have ceased to exist. The contract made with regard to those circumstances ceases to exist because those circumstances have ceased to exist. Then the contract is at an end, and there is no further application of it at all.

Then, with regard to the new circumstances, the parties are in the same position as if no contract at all had been made with reference to them. Now, what is the result? Why, that, with regard to the new circumstances, neither party is called upon to do anything. Either party or both parties may leave those circumstances alone. If they do not leave them alone, and undertake to deal with them, and do deal with them, the law applicable to what they then do with regard to those new circumstances is the law which would be applicable to those circumstances even though there had never been the former contract at all, which was made with regard to other circumstances.

Now, what is that? In that case, as I say, both parties might have left the thing alone, but they do not. The one party goes on to deal with the new state of circumstances and does work with regard to those. The other party knows that that party is dealing with that

(*a*) L. R. 8 C. P. 572; 10 C. P. 125.

1888
May 18.

Queen's
Bench
Division.

new state of circumstances and allows him to do so. Therefore, the one does work which he intends to be for the other. The other person allows him to do that work, knowing that it is intended to be done for him. It is work which he knows that the one party is doing upon the terms of being paid for it somehow, and he allows him to go on, with an understanding that he is to be paid for it somehow. What does that give rise to? It gives rise to a claim for a fair remuneration for that work done. That fair remuneration is called in legal language a payment according to a *quantum meruit*. If the first contract was gone, if the state of circumstances with regard to which it was made were really no longer in existence as between the parties, if the one did work for the other upon the new state of circumstances which the other accepted, knowing that it was being done on the terms of being paid for, that gives rise to a *quantum meruit*.

Now, all that depends upon whether the answer to the 5th question is a right answer, *i.e.*, whether we can now undertake to say that that was a finding contrary to the weight of the evidence. Now, everybody who has heard the arguments so ably put forward by Mr. Bigham and Mr. Walton must have observed that they both of them flinched from really and actually arguing that this was a verdict contrary to the weight of evidence; and I think they were right not to urge it. It is a verdict come to by the jury upon a direction which seems to me to be amply correct. It is a verdict come to by the jury upon that, and it is a verdict accepted by the judge who tried the case as satisfactory, and there is evidence which, in my mind, entitled the jury to say that the new state of circumstances was so different from the former that it is wholly unreasonable and unjust to suppose that either party, if they had known this state of circumstances, would have made the same contract with regard to them.

The matter was to lay a pipe in a peculiar country where the difference of work to be done in the summer and winter, to anybody who knows that country, is at once manifest—such work as this— work dealing with streams in Cumberland and in the neighbourhood of Whitehaven—to deal with those streams and to overcome them—to do work in them in summer and in winter. It is idle to tell anybody who knows the place that it is not of the most extreme difficulty— where you have to deal with one of these streams in five different places, and one of those places a very considerable place, and that one near the dam head—to tell one that the circumstances are not almost wholly different with regard to those streams in summer and winter is really to tell one things which one cannot believe. The jury, to

1888
May 18.

Queen's
Bench
Division.

my mind, were justified in taking that into account, and I believe it is the truth, and the difference, of course, to the man really shows how true it was and how enormous the difference was, in a mercantile sense, of what he was asked to do at first and what he did at last. I will not say whether I should have found the same verdict; that is not our business. I am not prepared to say that if you push this doctrine too far it may not give sympathetic juries a somewhat large power; but one cannot decide law upon such technical terms as that. The tribunal is one which is given by the country. As far as I know, it acts in almost all cases honestly and reasonably, and I am not prepared to say that it acted unreasonably in this case. I think, therefore, that, if that finding stands to the 5th question, the case is brought within the law, and that the verdict of the jury was right; that the judgment of the Divisional Court must be accepted, and I think, therefore, that this appeal must be dismissed.

LINDLEY, L. J.: I am of the same opinion. I think if I had tried the case without a jury, I should have had very great difficulty in coming to the conclusion which the jury did on the 5th finding; but I am not prepared to say it is wrong at all; and when both Mr. Bigham and Mr. Walton flinch from saying or contending that that verdict was against the weight of the evidence, I assume that the weight of the evidence supported it. Now, when once you get over that difficulty the serious problem solves itself, because the jury say practically (as we may now suppose) that the circumstances were such as to render this contract different—in other words, that a state of things was assumed by both parties which was never realised, and that the contract was based on the supposition that the state of things assumed would exist.

Now, the real difficulty in point of law arises from this, that the 11th and 22nd conditions of this contract show that the parties had before their minds the contingency of delay, and of delay on the part of the defendants, in getting possession and giving possession to the contractor of the lands or parts of the lands over which he had to put his pipes, and they provided for delay. There is no stipulation as to how long the delay should be. The words are loose and general, but at the same time it is quite obvious that there must be some limit, and the jury have found here that the delay was so great as not to be fairly within the terms of the contract at all; that is to say, that the delay was so great that the contract cannot apply to the state of things to which the contractor and the defendants had imagined that it did. I think that the case of *Jackson* v. *The Union Marine*

1888
May 18.
——
Queen's
Bench
Division.

Insurance Company (*a*) does apply, and that the decision of the Divisional Court must be affirmed.

LOPES, L.J.: It has not been contended before us that the finding of the jury, in their answer to the 5th question, is against the weight of the evidence. That being so, that finding stands. If that finding stands, it appears to me that this case is brought within the principle of *Jackson* v. *Union Marine Insurance Company* (*a*), which has been cited. I think the appeal should be dismissed.

Appeal dismissed.

Solicitors for the plaintiff: Yates and Johnson, Liverpool. Solicitors for the defendants: Lamb and Howton, Whitehaven.

———————————

1888
January 13.
——
Queen's
Bench
Division.
——
July 30.
——
Court of
Appeal.

𝔍n the 𝔔ueen's 𝔅ench 𝔇ivision.

(*Before* STEPHEN, J., without a Jury.)

𝔍n the 𝔠ourt of 𝔄ppeal.

(*Before* LORD ESHER, M.R., and LINDLEY and BOWEN, L.JJ.)

PRIESTLEY AND ANOTHER *v.* STONE (*b*).

Erroneous Quantities—Action against Quantity Surveyor employed by Building Owner and paid by Builder.

Held, that a quantity surveyor employed by the architect or employer is not liable to the accepted builder either by contract or representation for errors in the quantities. The custom was not satisfactorily proved.

This was an action brought by builders against a quantity surveyor. The Rev. Reginald Tuke, who was about to build a Roman Catholic Church at Chiswick, employed one Kelly as architect. Kelly prepared the plans and instructed the defendant, a quantity surveyor, to take out the quantities according to the plans. The defendant accordingly prepared a bill of quantities, had a number of copies lithographed, and handed them to Kelly. Kelly made alterations in the plans, and thereupon applied for tenders for the building of the church upon the original quantities supplied by the defendant,

(*a*) 8 C. P. 572; 10 C. P. 125.
(*b*) Also briefly reported, 4 T. L. R. 730; cp. *Lelièvre* v. *Gould*, [1893] 1 Q. B. 491; and, on the point as to usage, *North* v. *Bassett*, [1892] 1 Q. B. 333.

1888
January 13.

Queen's
Bench
Division.

unaltered to suit the altered plans, and the plaintiffs, among others, tendered and were accepted as contractors. The plaintiffs brought this action to recover damages for injury caused by inaccurate quantities.

The plaintiffs by their statement of claim said that they had suffered damage from the defendant's negligence and breach of duty as a quantity surveyor of and for the plaintiffs, and in the alternative said—

That the defendant, in consideration that the plaintiffs would agree to pay him $1\frac{1}{2}$ per cent. upon the amount of their tender, if accepted, supplied for the use of the plaintiffs a bill of quantities; and

That the defendant represented and warranted to the plaintiffs that the bill of quantities contained accurate and detailed particulars of the work and materials required for the building.

That the defendant did not use care and skill in the preparation of the bill of quantities, and that they were inaccurate.

The defendant by his defence generally denied all the allegations in the statement of claim, and said that he was not employed by the plaintiffs, and that there was no privity of contract between them and him, nor any agreement with them that they should pay defendant $1\frac{1}{2}$ per cent.

He further said that he was employed by Kelly, as architect for Tuke, to take out the quantities from plans only, and that no specification was supplied to him, and that after he delivered the bill of quantities to Kelly alterations were made in the plans.

And by counterclaim, the defendant said (1) that he was employed by Kelly as agent of Tuke to prepare bills of quantities; (2) that it was agreed between Kelly and defendant that he should be paid $1\frac{1}{2}$ per cent. on the amount of the accepted tender as well as the lithographer's charges; (3) that it was afterwards agreed between Tuke and the plaintiffs that Tuke should pay the plaintiffs the amount of the defendant's charges, viz., 80*l.* 14*s.* 4*d.*., and that the plaintiffs should pay that amount to the defendant; (4) that Tuke paid the said money to the plaintiffs for that express purpose, but the plaintiffs have only paid 52*l.* 10*s.*, a part of the said 80*l.* 14*s.* 4*d.*, and have failed to pay the balance, which the defendant now claimed.

The plaintiffs, as to the counterclaim, replied that they admitted the counterclaim, subject to their claim in the action.

At the trial, before Stephen, J., without a jury, the judge non-suited the plaintiff on the claim, and gave judgment for the defendant on the counterclaim.

STEPHEN, J.: I have considered this case very carefully, and I am of opinion that there must be a non-suit.

There are, substantially, two points raised. There is, first of all, raised the point that there is a contract, and the second point raised is that there was misrepresentation, or such misrepresentation as would render the quantity surveyor liable for what he has done. In the first place, I must remark that the case appears to me to be one which must be decided mainly on principle. I think the authorities that have been referred to are very far off indeed. The case which

1888
January 13.

Queen's
Bench
Division.

has most reference to it is the case of *Moon* v. *Witney Guardians* (*a*), but that is not a question either as to the responsibility of the quantity surveyor himself, or as to the employment of builders, but a question whether the architect had, according to the usual practice of the trade, a right to employ a quantity surveyor, and to be paid by his employer for the money that he had paid to that quantity surveyor, and it was held that he had. That is entirely different from this case, and has nothing to do with it, and it is the only case cited upon this matter, if worth going into, which I do not think it is. Then, there was the case of *Scrivener* v. *Pask* (*b*), which was not quoted from by Mr. White, who, in fact, referred to it as the only one that occurred to him like the present one. I do not think it is like it. I think, as far as it goes, to some extent it is unfavourable, although I do not rely upon it, and it does not influence my judgment at all. I will point out why it is more unfavourable than otherwise. Pask, in that case, employed an architect to prepare plans and specifications for a house, and to procure a builder to erect it. Then the architect took the quantities and represented to the plaintiff that they were correct. Thereupon a builder made a tender, which was accepted. The tender turned out less than it ought to have been, by reason of the misrepresentation of the architect; thereupon, says Lord Blackburn, "To entitle the plaintiff to recover" (that is, those who were in the position of the plaintiffs in this case) "they must make out three things—that Paice was the defendant's agent—that Paice was guilty of fraud or misrepresentation, and that the defendant knew of and sanctioned it. There is no evidence here of either of these things; if there has been misconduct on the part of Paice, the plaintiffs have their remedy against him." That appears to me to be rather like this, for if the plaintiffs are under a misrepresentation, or have anything to complain of in regard to the quantities which they have acted upon, they must go against either the building owner or the architect, who made those representations.

First of all, as to the question of contract. Now, as regards that, a great deal has been said as to the custom. I confess that the evidence about custom in the whole case appears to me extremely unsatisfactory, not only unsatisfactory and vague in itself, but as far as it went it was rather in favour of the defendant than in favour of the plaintiffs, as the witnesses certainly said, and with obvious truth, that either the architect, or, ultimately, the building owner, who had

(*a*) 3 Bing. N. C. 814.
(*b*) L. R. 1 C. P. 715.

1888
January 13.

Queen's
Bench
Division.

employed the architect, must pay the quantity surveyor in case he is not paid, and that the contract, really and substantially, was with the building owner or architect. And one of the witnesses said so, very completely, and acting the part of Balaam to the learned counsel who called him, he came to curse the other side and blessed them altogether, and that, to a certain extent, was the clear result of most of the witnesses. No doubt, the opinion is general amongst members of this profession that the quantity surveyor ought to be made liable, and ought to be accurate, and no doubt he is liable. There is no question, if he undertakes this distinct business, he is liable to the architect who employs him, but whether he is liable for that to the building owner, who employs the architect, I do not say at all.

Now, here is the contract, as they have called it. I cannot see anything of a contract in the matter with the exception of the written contract so called upon folio 41 of this paper. Now, folio 41 of the estimate or quantities contains this memorandum. There is a summary here of all the different estimates. Then, it says, "Add surveyor's charges for preparing the quantities $1\frac{1}{2}$ per cent. on the above amount 55*l.* 2*s.*; add also $1\frac{1}{2}$ per cent. on the amount of second estimate and third estimate, 3*l.* 6*s.* and 10*l.*; add for lithography 11*l.* 10*s.*" Then there is a marginal note: "To be paid out of the first instalment." Now, it was said by Mr. Meadows White that that constitutes a contract between the contractor and the quantity surveyor, and that the quantity surveyor, in consideration of the money being paid out of the first instalment, he, the quantity surveyor, would exercise due care and skill in preparing these quantities; and Mr. White went on to say, and I think I heard him make use of the term, "would guarantee with regard to this specification that his quantities were in accordance with the specification." But the contract is between the building owner and the contractor, and the contractor contracts, among other things, that the first charge he will pay will be a certain amount of money payable to the quantity surveyor by the building owner, and that he will pay that out of the first instalment. Therefore, as a matter of contract, I think there was no privity of contract between the quantity surveyor and the building owner. The only contract is between the quantity surveyor and the person who employed the quantity surveyor.

Then we come to the representation. There is no doubt that the architect and the building owner represent to the contractor—and it is very likely it is a representation—that these quantities are correct. In fact, they do represent, no doubt. They hand out the quantities, and you put your fingers upon them and ask if they are correct;

1888
January 13.

Queen's
Bench
Division.

whether or no the architect is responsible, or the building owner is responsible, or whether the architect is responsible to the building owner or not, is an issue upon which I need say nothing. The contract between the building owner and the contractor is one embodied in writing. It is not necessary to decide, for the purpose of my judgment, that this is a representation. If it is a representation at all, it is a representation by the building owner to the contractor. Then, that being so, there comes another consideration to which attention was called, in the course of the argument, which Mr. Meadows White passed over, and I can quite understand why he passes it over, because as he takes a different view that is not material; but I do not agree with him, because in my point of view it is extremely material, and that is clause 11, which is so much spoken of in the specification. The clause in question is intended obviously to put an end to this question. Suppose it were not there, the man who made the estimate would say, I know nothing about your quantity surveyor, you have represented to me that these quantities are correct, I made my estimate from those quantities; I have been deceived, you must pay me damages, because you induced me by false representation to make an imprudent tender. I do not say how that would work out or whether that would succeed or not; it is enough to say that it is very likely to be raised. In view of that happening, they put this clause in: "The contractor will be allowed the opportunity, and must, previously to signing the contract, examine the drawings and specifications and compare them (if requested upon the site) with his estimate, so as to satisfy himself that his price includes all the work and materials"; that is to say, "Mind, you have made your estimate, it goes on, all the work and materials shown or described in the specification and drawings which constitute the contract, as no departure or alteration will be allowed to be made from or in his tender in the event of any error therein being subsequently discovered, however arising." Several of the witnesses said, we never would have signed a contract which had that clause, and they gave their reasons, and I am not surprised at what they said.

Now, this clause being put in, however, shows really two things. First, that the building owner and his architect and more particularly the architect, were well aware that they might be liable for the estimate upon which the matter was based. Secondly, that they determined that they would not be liable, but would throw the liability upon the builder himself by the express terms of that clause 11. I can hardly conceive how there could be another contention than that, which appears to me to be plain commonsense in itself,

1888
January 13.

Queen's
Bench
Division.

that the contract is between the owner and the contractor, and that the owner will not be liable for any alteration, or for any want of correctness or any error, however arising, which has taken place in the early stages of the matter.

It does not, of course, follow, because the building owner has protected himself, that, therefore, the quantity surveyor is not liable. The quantity surveyor, if he did anything wrong, would be liable to his architect and the building owner for any damage he has caused to them. Apart from that, I cannot see that there is any further liability unless such liability can be proved. That brings me to the question of misrepresentation. It is said that he has made a misrepresentation for which he is liable; I cannot see that. The case which is referred to, *Heaven* v. *Pender* (a), and which comes near to this, is founded upon the language in *Langridge* v. *Levy* (b), and that class of cases. They are mere cases of physical bodily injury, either bodily injury to a man or a physical damage to a thing. That is a matter which stands upon quite a different kind of footing from being misled by a person's conduct. I feel, therefore, that there is no privity here either between the quantity surveyor and the person who ultimately has rendered an account, and who may be injured with regard to his estimate by what may be done by mistakes made by him, if such mistakes were made.

There is another matter in this case which I rather asked Mr. White to explain to me, and which, in my judgment, I am sorry to say he did not succeed in explaining; at all events, he did not make it clear to me. To what did this estimate apply? The estimate was made for the plaintiffs in this case. At present I assume that it is accurate, although not admitted to be accurate, and is not satisfactorily proved to be accurate, because Mr. Kelly's evidence was certainly not very minute about the transaction. I take it from him that some of the plans were before the quantity surveyor when he took out these quantities, and that the specification was not drawn up till afterwards. There is nothing to show, as far as I can see, that Mr. Stone had any real opportunity of making the specification correspond with the quantities. There is this, at all events, which is perfectly certain, which shows amongst other things that Mr. Kelly has fallen into some confusion, or rather mistake, in his evidence about what has taken place, because he was very confident that Mr. Stone had received that plan B., but it appears afterwards that he

(a) 11 Q. B. D. 503.
(b) 4 M. & W. 337.

1888
January 13.

Queen's
Bench
Division.

could not have seen plan B., because he worked on the basis of twelve columns, which are represented on the other plans, and not on the basis of ten columns, which are represented in plan B. Therefore, it is obvious that the design is altered in a material particular after the estimate was made and the quantities were taken out.

That alteration in respect of the plan would run through the whole estimate, and affect every one of them, A., C., D., E. and F.; but Mr. White stated over and over again, until I was almost tired of hearing him, "We do not charge him about that." No, but you stand by altering your plans, and then say that there is a misrepresentation sentation. If the architect had made serious alterations after the estimate is drawn up, it shows to my mind clearly that the representation made by it might very well be the representation of the architect and not the representation of the quantity surveyor, because they apply to different things.

He said he had to alter everything. It is impossible to say that the representation made to the contractor is the same representation which Mr. Stone authorised Mr. Kelly to make to anybody, and therefore I say it is Kelly's representation and not Stone's representation, and the only representation from Stone is a representation to Kelly, for which, if inaccurate, or if he is damaged by it, Kelly may take his remedy.

Then I have one other remark to make, and that is this: that one of the witnesses who came here on behalf of Mr. White certainly did again make an observation which struck me very much, although not much attention was paid to it by the learned counsel, and which was this: "If we do not think much of the quantity surveyor, and entertain any doubt about him, then we take care to have the quantities put into the contract." That is no doubt the proper course. If you like to leave the thing at large, why then you take your chance, and you take your remedy, whatever it may be, from the building owner, or from the architect, or from the building owner through the architect, but if you wish to be safe in the matter, and wish to have it clear that these quantities and no others are to be worked upon, then your remedy is to put it into the contract, and in that way you will be saved all trouble. If they do not choose to have that, then that is their own affair. If they choose, upon the other hand, not to compare their quantities, and put clause 11 in the specification, then they must take their chance, and lose their remedy for any estimated loss that may be afterwards discovered in the bill of quantities. At all events, it appears to me that there must be in this case judgment and non-suit with costs.

Mr. Bosanquet: Then there is the question as to the amount in the counterclaim, 28*l*.

1888
January 13.

Queen's
Bench
Division.

Mr. Justice Stephen: Yes, judgment on the counterclaim with costs.

The plaintiffs appealed, but the question of the counterclaim was not raised in the Court of Appeal.

Edwyn Jones for the plaintiff. Spokes, for the defendant, was not called upon.

The Court dismissed the appeal.

Judgment.

1888
July 30.

Court of
Appeal.

Lord Esher, M.R.: *Heaven* v. *Pender* (*a*) has no more to do with this case than it would have to do with an action for breach of promise of marriage, or a divorce suit. Let us get rid of that. First, this is an action by the builder against the person who takes out the quantities for the architect. That is a business which has been now known for sixty or seventy years. There have been ample disputes about the matter; and there is not a single one on which to found such an action as this upon this relation between the two parties. That is strong to show what the law is. Now, let us come a little closer to it. There is a contract between the architect and the man who takes out the quantities. The architect employs that man, and he has to pay that man. Therefore the contract, if any, is between the architect and that man, or between whoever is the principal of the architect, if there is a principal who is authorised to do such things, and that man; and that is the only contract.

Now, what is it that the man who is employed to take out the quantities is employed to do for the architect? He is employed to take out the quantities for the architect, and to give those quantities to the architect; and he has no control over what may be done with those quantities; he has no knowledge of anybody to whom those quantities will be shown. At the moment he has given the details to the architect, the architect and his employer may change their minds as to the plan, may reject those quantities, may never use them, and may never offer to anybody a contract based upon them at all. The man who takes out the quantities has no possible means of knowing whether those quantities will be shown by the architect to anybody, and certainly not to any particular person. Therefore those quantities are given to the architect. Now, do they make a representation to the architect that they are true in fact? Certainly not. The architect can check them just as much as when

(*a*) 11 Q. B. D. 503.

1888
July 30.

Court of
Appeal.

a tradesman gives you your bill over the counter. If you add it up yourself, you can see whether he has added it up correctly. It is nothing like such a representation as one upon which you can base an action for false representation. If what is done is wrong, it is only a representation to the architect. The architect can check this thing directly it is done; and what is more, notwithstanding what Mr. Jones says, in my opinion, if the architect were to accept quantities from the man he has employed which were grossly wrong as against his principal and employer, the architect would be guilty of negligence in not looking to the quantities—he would probably be guilty of negligence, and be liable to his employer. So that it is no representation even to the architect as one upon which you can found an action for misrepresentation. If it were fraudulently made, that is quite a different thing. Then not only the architect, but it is possible that the builder too—if it were a fraud—might have an action against the man for the fraud. In the absence of fraud there is no representation at all.

We will now come to the next point. Supposing there were a representation in this case, there is no evidence of negligence in the way of taking out the quantities. None whatever. Only that this is relied upon—that there were, it is stated, errors so gross that a jury-tribunal might infer negligence from them; and the negligence is met with and called "gross negligence." But that case was not presented, and the negligence never went. It is called not only "gross" but "reckless"; they put it "reckless negligence" in order to make out some supposed contact to fraud. It is true that negligence is evidence of fraud. That we are all agreed upon. Some people call it "fraud," and some "evidence of fraud"; but there was none here, because it was arranged that the question of how great the errors were, or what the errors were, was to be left until after the liability was determined by the judge. Then those who agreed to that, if they wanted to rely upon the amount of error as showing gross negligence and reckless statement, ought to have presented that, because that is the question upon which the liability depends. Instead of which it is now suggested that that being left to the arbitrator or the official referee, if he found a great quantity of error, they could revert back and say that that was evidence of reckless statement. That is impossible. That there was evidence of reckless error before the judge cannot be maintained. If evidence of the amount of error had been laid before him in order to induce him to come to such a conclusion as that, it is obvious that the other side have counter evidence to contradict it. Therefore that cannot be relied upon.

1888
July 30.

Court of
Appeal.

So that here there is no representation to anybody, not even to the architect. There is no representation to all the world. What has all the world got to do with taking out the quantities for an architect? As I have said, there is no evidence—there is nothing to show that the man who takes out the quantities is bound to contract that his quantities might be shown to anybody. They may or they may not be; and what I said in the course of the trial is equally true—that the architect has the sole control of these quantities; and if he does not like them when he has got them he can alter them. So that to say that the man who takes out the quantities is to assume that his quantities, without alteration, will be shown to anybody who may be asked to contract is not true in fact; and it is for all these reasons that such an action as this has never been maintained, and hardly ever proposed. This is an attempt to manufacture a new action, which, if the Court would entertain it, would be the precedent for about a hundred actions of the same kind per year. There is no evidence upon which the learned judge could be asked to find anything against the defendant.

LINDLEY, L.J.: I am of opinion that the judgment of the Court below in this case was correct. The action was brought upon two grounds. First, the one which has been argued—that there was some sort of contract between the plaintiff who was a builder, and the defendant who was a quantities surveyor. When one comes to examine that proposition it breaks down. In point of fact there is no contract between the two; and the alleged custom which was relied upon as establishing such a contract was not proved. If the custom had been proved, I do not know whether it would be good for anything. It appears to me in that respect this case is wholly analogous to the alleged custom which came before the Court in *Bradburn* v. *Foley* (*a*), where it was attempted to be made out that there was a custom by which the incoming tenant paid for something. This custom has not been established as a fact, and if it were that authority goes to show that the custom is nothing, and that there is no contract.

Then it is put upon the ground that Stone made a negligent representation to the plaintiff in order that the plaintiff might act upon it; and that, that being the case, the representation having been made, and the plaintiff having suffered damage, he is entitled to maintain an action in order to prove that suggestion. We must look a little more to the state of facts. The real truth is that the quantities surveyor is employed by the architect, and I suppose the architect in

(*a*) 3. C. P. D. 129.

1888
July 30.

Court of
Appeal.

that manner acts as the agent of the building owner. I dare say if the case were fought out the building owner would be responsible for this; but, at all events, a quantities surveyor is not employed by a builder, although it appears to be customary that the successful builder shall pay the quantities surveyor. Now, what is the custom when he has taken out the quantities according to the instructions of the parties? It may be true, and probably is true, that those quantities which are taken out by the quantity surveyor will be laid before a person who is desirous of attending to do so. But then this has to be considered. Those quantities are supposed to be made, and are in fact made, with reference to the instructions given at the time; and suppose this happens—as I understand the learned judge this did happen—that after the quantities were taken out they desired to change, and notwithstanding that, owing to some circumstances which I do not understand, the architect here laid the quantities before the builder with the design. How is that to be turned, by any possible ingenuity, into a representation by the unfortunate quantities surveyor to the builder that the quantities taken out by him are applicable to the changed state of things? The question has only to be asked to be answered. It appears to me there is absolutely no evidence whatever of anything fraudulent. It appears to me, under the circumstances, there is absolutely no proof of want of possible care, or anything that should make this action stand. The judgment will be that the appeal will be dismissed with costs.

Bowen, L.J.: I am of the same opinion. This action is without any precedent at all. I never recollect any similar action being suggested. None of the members of the Court, and none of the Bar, have been able to contribute from their own knowledge any similar experience of a similar action. That is, of course, very much against the idea of an action; and at the best, when you come to examine it upon reason it seems to me that there are two fatal difficulties. In the first place, there is no privity between the builder and the quantity surveyor; and in the second place, that there can be no duty out of which the supposed liability arises, because whatever duty there is must be a duty arising out of the relations between the two, and if there is no privity between the two there really is no responsibility, and how can this arise? However, it has been suggested that it can be supported upon the ground that the quantities surveyor, in handing the quantities to the architect by whose direction he took them out, makes a statement which is a misstatement. It is said that he makes that misstatement knowing it is to be handed on to a third person, and therefore he is liable to

1888
July 30.

Court of
Appeal.

the third person for such misstatement, provided the case is one which comes within the doctrine of false representation, as extended by the other Division of the Court in the case of *Peek* v. *Derry* (*a*).

I think whenever people have to cite the case of *Peek* v. *Derry*, they will find it extremely necessary to be careful in the interpretation they put upon the word "statement." A man makes a statement about many a matter in which he does not pledge anything except his own opinion, or his own estimate, or his own belief. You can hardly say with regard to a statement made by a man as to his own belief that if he has not got reasonable ground for believing it, that it would come within the cases of fraudulent misrepresentation, or that the case of *Peek* v. *Derry* could be extended to that. I do not see how it could be. Either he believes a thing, in which case it is true he has made a statement about his belief, or if not that it must be false, because he has not made a statement about his own belief. Outside the class of statements about your own mind or belief, there may be many statements as to which you pledge something thing more than your own belief; but you must distinguish carefully between the two classes of statement.

Now, to what class of statement is it that the quantities surveyor's representation belongs? Is it, so far, a representation that can be supposed to consist in handing a paper of quantities from the surveyor? It does not seem to me that he pledges anything. He is bound to take care, it is true, as between himself and the architect. Whether he be the employee or be the employer he is bound to take care; but that is because he is employed to take care. He does not make any representation that he has taken care. He leaves that to stand according to the view of his own character that the person who receives the paper has formed. All he does is to represent that those are his quantities. They are the quantities which he himself has taken out, and they therefore are the quantities which he believes to be accurate. As to that being a false representation, how can you say that any amount of negligence on his part in taking it out, unless it amounted to recklessness—any amount of negligence unless it was so gross as to raise a suspicion of fraud (in which case it would be evidence of fraud) makes it fraudulent? But mere evidence would not make the representation fraudulent.

It seems to me that the only representation that he makes is one as to his own belief. In this particular instance it does not rest there. I will assume that there was before the learned judge some evidence

(*a*) 37 Ch. D. 541; since reversed, 14 App. Cas. 337.

1888
July 30.

Court of
Appeal.

of negligence. What does that mean? Why, it means one of two things. Either that the quantity surveyor himself was not careful, or that some of the people he employed were not careful. In either case there might be a negligence which would be in the eye of the law gross negligence. The people employed were his own agents; but it does not suggest that from that there was such personal negligence as amounts to a displacement of all reasonable ground for the statement which the man has made.

Supposing, for a moment, his foreman had taken out all the figures inaccurately and carelessly, that may be evidence in an action of fraud against the man he employed for it; but it is not evidence that the person who employs the foreman has no reasonable grounds upon which he goes. He goes upon the statement; and it is obvious therefore that, even assuming that there may be evidence before the judge of negligence here (and I will take it so), there will be no evidence of fraudulent representation before him. If such a case had been put it ought to have been met; and I entirely agree with what the Master of the Rolls has said, that the very line upon which this case has run shows that the plaintiff did not make before the judge any case of fraud or fraudulent misrepresentation, or such misrepresentation as would be treated as fraudulent. But assume that taking some negligence, however slight, as proved, that would prove a liability towards the builder on the part of the quantities surveyor. But that will not do. Evidence of negligence in the quantities is not enough to render him liable towards the builder, because there is no privity—no duty between them; and in the absence of misrepresentation there is no liability. I think, therefore, that this appeal must be dismissed.

Solicitors for the plaintiffs: Loughborough & Co. Solicitor for the defendant: C. H. T. Wharton.

See report of the same case ((1888), 4 Times L. R. 730), which is incorrect in stating that the plaintiffs' tender was not accepted.

In the High Court of Justice (Queen's Bench Division).

1889
March 19.

(A. L. Smith, J.)

Queen's
Bench
Division.

LONDON SCHOOL BOARD

v.

NORTHCROFT, SON, AND NEIGHBOUR, AND OTHERS.

Quantity Surveyors—Measuring up.

The plaintiffs had employed the defendants, as quantity surveyors and measurers, on buildings of the value of 12,000*l.*, which had been completed and measured up. They now sued (1) in detinue for certain papers of calculations and memoranda; (2) for negligence in a clerical error in the calculation, whereby they had overpaid two sums of 118*l.* and 15*l.* 15*s.*; (3) for money had and received in respect of 74*l.* charged by the defendants for lithography. Held, (1) that the measuring up having been done, the plaintiffs had no right to the memoranda; (2) that the defendants, having employed a competent skilled clerk who had carried out hundreds of intricate calculations, were not liable for negligence in respect of these two clerical errors; (3)as to a sum of 15 per cent. by the lithographer to the quantity surveyor, that, although the defendants being the plaintiffs' agents, the payment of any commission to the defendants was illegal and improper, yet, as it was agreed in this case that the defendants should employ their own lithographer, they might retain this, which was really a discount for cash.

This was an action for detinue of certain bills of quantities, dimensions, and abstracts made by the defendants, and relating to certain property belonging to the London School Board. The plaintiffs also claimed damages for negligence in drawing up certain bills of quantities and the recovery of certain moneys received by the defendants to the use of the plaintiffs.

The defendants denied the plaintiffs' right to have the documents in question, as they alleged such documents were prepared by them solely for the purpose of making up their bills of quantities for the contractors, and further, on the ground that the plaintiffs did not ask for them for the purpose of verifying the measurements of the schools, but for the purposes of an inquiry into the conduct of certain persons connected with the building operations. With regard to the negligence, the defendants said that the mistakes were purely clerical, and quite unavoidable.

The further facts of the case will appear sufficiently from the judgment.

Murphy, Q. C., Douglas Walker, and Gore-Browne for the plaintiffs. Bosanquet, Q. C., and Wightman Wood for the defendants.

A. L. Smith, J.: This is an action brought by the School Board for London against Messrs. Northcrft & Co., upon five separate and distinct heads of action, and I shall have to deal with them shortly *seriatim* apart from each other. The controversy between the plain-

1889
March 19.

Queen's
Bench
Division.

tiffs and the defendants arises out of an agreement which was come
to somewhere about April, 1879, at which time the defendants undertook to take out bills of quantities for the London School Board. Prior
to that date the defendants had taken out bills of quantities for the
London School Board, but new terms were then arranged between
the parties. The reasons for those new terms appear in the
correspondence that took place. In 1879, it not being contemplated,
very naturally, that the Board would have such a large amount of
building on hand as they had theretofore had, negotiations thereupon
took place between the Board and Messrs. Northeroft as to the terms
upon which they would undertake to do the bills of quantities which
were wanted by the Board, and the ultimate agreement was that the
defendants agreed to do one-fourth of the Board's work in taking out
bills of quantities at 1 per cent. That was the agreement which was
come to in 1879. I pass now to the year 1885, when, as I understand,
new schools had to be added to, or rebuilt by, the School Board. One
school was in Henry Street, and the other school was in Pocock
Street. I will first deal with what took place in Henry Street, and leave
Pocock Street out for the moment, because, in reality, what rules as
to Henry Street rules as to Pocock Street.

The ordinary specifications and plans are made by an architect,
and Messrs. Northcroft were engaged to take out the bills of
quantities, and they took out the bills of quantities. Without going
into details now, they took out the bills of quantities in nine parts at
the instance of the Board, and they sent in their bills of quantities,
upon which of course, the builders were to tender, and at the end of
five out of the nine parts of the bill of quantities they had
lithographed in, what I may shortly state as "Moiety of charges for
lithography, postage, &c., &c., do., do." There is a large general item
at the end of five out of the nine parts of those bills of quantities.
Each item is not only in the same words (I think I read the largest),
but suffice it to say that it is a sort of general sweeping-up clause at
the end of five out of the nine parts of the bills of quantities.

Matters went on, and the contractor who tendered was a gentleman
named Wall, and he got the contract for 10,700*l.* There was, I have
been told, a further contract for about 1,000*l.*, and the upshot of it was
that the works were completed in June, 1887. The works were
measured up by Messrs. Northcroft, the defendants, and the whole
matter was settled between the Board and the builder, except as
regards retention money, which is kept in hand to the present day, but
for all practical purposes, as regards what Messrs. Northcroft had to
do upon this job, and as regards them and the Board, matters came

1889
March 19.

Queen's
Bench
Division.

to an end in June, 1887. I want to emphasize that date, because it is material upon a point which I will deal with in a moment. Shortly after this time, or about this time, according to the correspondence, it would appear that the School Board were not satisfied with the way in which their buildings had been executed.

It would seem from the correspondence that passed that they had an idea that something had not gone right somewhere, and they ordained that a committee of inspection or investigation should be appointed for the purpose of looking into the matter as regards their respective buildings. I have nothing whatever to do with any other buildings except the buildings in Henry Street and in Pocock Street. It is manifest to me that they very soon, indeed as early as August, 1887, began to attack (and I use the word advisedly) Messrs. Northcroft & Son. The solicitors wrote a letter demanding that they should deliver up to the Board all dimensions, memoranda, details, and so on, which they (that is to say, Messrs. Northcroft) had taken out. Messrs. Northcroft prepared the bills of quantities for the school-house in Henry Street. Messrs. Northcroft took their stand upon this:—"If you make a demand upon us in law, we say that in law you are not entitled to them; and we will not give them to you." That leads up to the first head of Claim No. 1, for which the present action is brought.

The first head of claim is a claim in detinue, and the plaintiffs allege that the defendants have detained the plaintiffs' goods, *per quod* they are damnified to the extent of 38*l.* And the way the damages are made out is this:—If the defendants had delivered up what the plaintiffs alleged to be their documents, these original dimensions, memoranda, and so on, Mr. Rickman, whom they employed to re-measure these buildings, would have been able to measure them quickly, more expeditiously, and at less cost than he did to the Board. Mr. Rickman's charge was 38*l.* Say the plaintiffs:—"You have detained our memoranda, and we have lost because we could not get them, our man whom we put on to remeasure, charged us 38*l.* more than he otherwise would have done, and we claim to recover that 38*l.* from Messrs. Northcroft in this action." Now, in my judgment, detinue clearly will not lie, and for this reason. To maintain detinue the plaintiff must make out that the defendant has detained the plaintiffs' goods. Now, I should like to know how it can be said that what I call the private memoranda, which were made by Messrs. Northcroft for the purpose of framing that which ultimately became the property of the plaintiffs, namely, the bill of quantities, ever became the property of the plain-

1889
March 19.

Queen's
Bench
Division.

tiffs. The paper belonged to Messrs. Northcroft, the ink belonged to Messrs. Northcroft, and the brains that put the calculations on paper belonged to Messrs. Northcroft, and I want to know how that document which came into existence ever became the property of the plaintiffs. In my judgment it never did, and therefore the demand which was made by Messrs. Gedge, Kirby & Millett, as early as August, 1887, for the return of this manuscript was ill founded in law, and Messrs. Northcroft were well founded in law when they say, "Your legal demand we will not comply with, and we will not give them to you."

But there is another aspect to this case. I think a declaration could be made against gentlemen in the position of Messrs. Northcroft upon a breach of duty in this form, and I should amend, because in these days we do not stickle about any form of pleadings. If the building owner wanted to measure up the work, and he made a demand from the quantity surveyor, "Give me those details which you have, because I want to measure up and finish this work which you have initiated by your quantities," I think it would be the duty then (assuming he had them) of the quantity surveyor to hand them over to his principal, because, in my judgment, his duty would be to do the best he could for his principal until the whole work had been finished, completed, measured up, and done with. In this case, as was pointed out by counsel, that is not what the plaintiffs want. The plaintiffs do not want, and never did want, these memoranda, details, and dimensions, to finish the measuring up of this building, because that ought to have been finished in June, 1887, but what they wanted were the documents to see whether they could not make out a case against Messrs. Northcroft, so that they might bring the matter into a court of law, and in my judgment, holding the scales as evenly as I can between the parties, at this time Messrs. Northcroft were perfectly right in saying, "You shall not have them."

Let a plaintiff, when he attacks a defendant, bring his action, and the law then allows him to have the documents which he is entitled to, that is, by the process of discovery. It therefore seems to me that the first head of claim which is put forward in this case, namely, 38*l*., by reason of the defendants not allowing the plaintiffs to have these memoranda and details, is ill founded in law, because that is not the way you frame your statement of claim, and that, therefore, the defendants are right upon that head.

I now come to No. 2, and that is a question as regards 118*l*. said to have been overpaid by the School Board to Mr. Wall, the builder, by reason of a blunder on the part of Messrs. Northcroft's clerk.

Now, in order to succeed upon this head, the plaintiffs must make out, to my satisfaction, that the defendants have been guilty of some omission of duty towards the plaintiffs, which, otherwise, a man of reasonable care could not have been guilty of, which, in other words, is called negligence. Upon that I wish to make this remark. There is a very large building, practically 12,000*l.* worth of bricks and mortar were put up at this place in Henry Street. It was a lumpsum contract for 10,700*l.*; there was also a contract for another thousand pounds. It seems to me, upon the figures according to what one gentleman stated, that the Board have had this work put up for somewhere about 300*l.* more than they contemplated it would cost originally, with the omissions and additions, taking one against the other. I do not think a building owner ought to complain if he never meets with a worse fate than that the work costs no more than 300*l.* above what was originally contemplated. They, however, say, "No, we have paid 118*l.* too much to the builder by reason of your (Messrs. Northcroft's) negligence."

1889
March 19.

Queen's
Bench
Division.

Now, what is the negligence? It is conceded how the blunder arose, or, if it is not conceded, it is proved by the witnesses who have been called by the plaintiffs, and I have not to rely upon anything that was stated by the defendants as regards this point. It was a pure clerical error on the part of the clerk of Messrs. Northcroft. Nobody suggests that the clerk is incompetent, and, what is more, if they did, it seems to me, if he is the man who carried out these hundreds of calculations which must have been carried out with regard to the works, it is not remarkable that there is a blunder in it, at any rate they have only been able to pick out of the whole account two blunders, and that is 118*l.* and the 15 guineas, which I will deal with in a moment. There is no evidence, therefore, before me that the clerk is incompetent, the evidence before me is that the clerk was competent, and I have only to turn to Mr. Theobald's own evidence, in re-examination by counsel, to get the statement that no one else could have found out the mistake except the person who took out the quantities. That error was made by the clerk, and it would not have attracted the defendants' attention unless there was a variation in the excavations, and they never would have had their attention called to it again unless that had happened. Can I find, upon that evidence, that the defendants have been guilty of actionable negligence? Counsel said, and it certainly pressed me hard, why did they do away with the book of measurements? Now, I am not satisfied about the doing away with that book at all; the blunder here is proved; and if we had this book

1889
March 19.

Queen's
Bench
Division.

of measurements here *qua* this item, I feel certain that nothing would
have been got out of it to the detriment of one side or to the benefit of
the other. Still, upon that point I must say I feel it is a most
suspicious circumstance, when litigation is going on, that any
document should be made away with, and I protest that it is a most
suspicious act, and I advise everybody who hears me, if he ever gets
into litigation, to take care to keep all the documents, whether they
are for him or against him, because getting rid of a document when
everybody suspects that something is in it, which perhaps is not,
does him much more harm than producing it, so that the parties may
be able to find out the facts. I weigh that circumstance, but I come to
the conclusion that in this case the plaintiffs have not made out a
case of negligence, which they must do in order to recover this 118*l.*
from the defendants. I should also add this. It has nothing to do with
my judgment, but it is in evidence before me, and it is quite clear that
the Board are not going to lose it, because Mr. Wall has written a
letter (it has nothing to do with the issue which I have to decide)
saying, "If I have been overpaid 118*l.*, I shall be only too glad to
return it to the Board." So much for No. 2.

I pass over the question about the lithography for one moment, and
I come now to No. 3. The Board say they are entitled to get 150*l.* out
of Messrs. Northcroft, because Messrs. Northcroft have certified that
150*l.* worth of work has been done, which was omitted to be done,
and that therefore they have paid 150*l.* for nothing. Now, counsel,
curiously enough, in opening this case, frankly told me that he could
not explain to me what the cause of action was until the facts were
ascertained, and he said he would address me further upon it, and I
can well see now why he took that course. It was because he had got
no facts at all to address me upon. His own witness, when in the box,
could give me no evidence that that 150*l.* worth of work suggested to
have been overcharged had been omitted. And, what is more, upon
that I said, "If you on the plaintiffs' side cannot say that there has
been an omission of 150*l.* worth of work, am I to say that the
plaintiffs are to put their hands into Messrs. Northcroft's pockets by
reason of negligence, inasmuch as they have allowed them to pay for
150*l.* worth of work which has not been done?" When Mr. Northcroft
came into the box he clearly satisfied me that upon that head the
plaintiffs cannot recover.

Then there is another item, and that is No. 4. The plaintiffs'
claim against the defendants is 94*l.* odd, and the case against them is
this. In the original tender, or bills of quantities, if you like,
which were tendered upon, it was put down that there was to be a

1889
March 19.

Queen's
Bench
Division.

stone coping, with an iron railing on the top, to the value of 94*l*. odd. It is said, "That has not been done; the Board, through your negligence, paid the builder 94*l*. odd, which you ought to have seen never had been done, and we have therefore paid 94*l*. too much." The plaintiffs say, "We want to get that out of you because you were negligent." I am bound to say that no intelligible evidence on that point was given on the plaintiffs' side. Counsel might well have left the case there, but he was not content, and he called Mr. Northcroft, and Mr. Northcroft entirely satisfied me that it was originally contemplated to be in two portions, namely, stone coping and railing, one at the south-east and the other at the south-west corner. I think that 41*l*., a component part of this 94*l*., was spent in a stone coping and an iron railing, and that as to the other part, instead of having a stone coping and an iron railing, it was subsequently decided that they would build a wall 7 ft. 6 in. high, with a coping on the top of it. That was done, and Mr. Northcroft tells me that 94*l*. worth of work was erected upon this site, although it was not spent altogether on iron railings and stone coping. There is no evidence on the other side as to that, and I therefore find that that point falls.

Now I come to what, to my mind, is certainly a more difficult point, and it is one upon which my mind has fluctuated during the hearing of this case, and that is, the question about the charge of 74*l*. 15*s*. 6*d*. for lithography, postage, &c., &c. It is quite true, as pointed out by counsel over and over again, that the Board demanded vouchers for what the defendants had paid the lithographer, and I cannot wholly accept the statements which were made by Mr. Northcroft, junr., that he did not know perfectly well that the Board wanted to get hold of the fact as to how much they had paid the lithographer. They would not, however, tell the Board. They were at arm's length before this, they had got at arm's length about dimensions before the question as to the lithography came upon the surface. The same position, however, was taken up by the defendants as regards the vouchers for lithography as was taken up as regards dimensions and memoranda for bills of quantities, and, although Mr. Northcroft suggested to me that he could not see it, I cannot read the correspondence which has been read, and which is before me, without seeing that the parties were at arm's length, and that, in reality, the Board were imputing misconduct, to put it shortly, to Messrs. Northcroft, and that Messrs. Northcroft were resisting that, and would not help the Board. And I am not surprised at it. If a man is having misconduct imputed to him, he has a right not to help the gentleman who is imputing it to him. At last interroga-

1889
March 19.

Queen's
Bench
Division.

tories were administered to Messrs. Northcroft as to this matter, and
as to how much they paid out of this 74*l.* 15*s.* 6*d.* for lithography, and
then they say, in answer to that interrogatory, that they charge 42*l.*
10*s.* for lithography, and 15 guineas, 5 guineas, 5*l.*, 3*l.* 2*s.* 6*d.*, and 3
guineas for the services which they rendered. At one time I certainly
was disposed to hold, and I had practically made up my mind upon
this point, that, as regards the 15 per cent. which had been allowed to
Messrs. Northcroft by the lithographers, that must go into the
pockets of the Board. Counsel has undoubtedly stated the law
correctly, and I wish to state it again, because it cannot be too often
repeated, considering what is going on. I know in every branch of
business, from your menial servant, from your outside servant, from
your agent, and from everyone, that cankerworm of taking
commission and discount pervades the whole system of business
from start to finish, and the result is the master is robbed, because, of
course, the master has to pay for it in the result.

Undoubtedly the law is that, if an agent goes for his principal to get
an article for his principal, that agent is only entitled to charge his
principal the price which he could have got that article for, and
which he would have had to pay for that article, and he is not, in law,
entitled to make a profit or to get a discount or a commission, or
whatever you like to call it, and put it into his own pocket; and the
law is, if an agent does that, and if it is found out, the principal is
entitled to bring an action against the agent to disgorge that and to
put it into the principal's pocket. There is no doubt upon the law on
that subject, and I certainly was strongly of opinion to hold this case
to the ordinary law, but there was a remarkable absence of evidence
on the plaintiffs' side. They leave it on the ordinary law, and they are
entitled to leave it on the ordinary law, but the bellwether witness, if
I may call him so, of the plaintiffs was Mr. Rickman. Counsel may
discount Mr. Rickman as much as he likes, but Mr. Rickman was the
man put on by the Board for the purpose, if possible, of seeing
whether the Board had not been imposed upon by the gentleman
whom they had employed in erecting these buildings, and Mr.
Rickman has made a written report to the Board.

Now, what is the view that Mr. Rickman puts forward to the Board
as being the proper way in which the Board should pay their quantity
surveyor? Mr. Rickman speaks of $1\frac{1}{2}$ per cent., but it is perfectly
immaterial whether it is $1\frac{1}{2}$ per cent., or 1 per cent., because, if it is
worth Messrs. Northcroft's while to do the Board's work at 1 per
cent., they doing a quarter of the work which the Board had to
do, that makes no difference, in my judgment, to the principle, Mr.

1889
March 19.

Queen's
Bench
Division.

Rickman says here, as to the case of lithography and the other necessary expenses, it is better for the surveyor to employ his own lithographer. Whom did Messrs. Northcroft employ? Did they employ the Board's lithographer or their own lithographer? That is the materiality of that evidence, because it is a very different thing whether the lithographer is the lithographer of Messrs. Northcroft, or whether he is the lithographer employed for the principal by the agent. Mr. Rickman says it is better for the surveyor to employ his own lithographer, and that the lithographer's account should be submitted, when there is a dispute, to the principal, and it is understood that such accounts are subject to a discount for cash. That is what the Board had in their pocket when they were attacking Messrs. Northcroft yesterday and to-day upon this system of discount.

We know that their own witness had reported to them in writing that the usual and proper way, and what he recommended, was that the quantity surveyor should employ his own lithographer, and that he would pay his own lithographer, subject to a discount for cash. That is exactly what Messrs. Northcroft have done, and I, sitting here, cannot come to the conclusion, and I do not come to the conclusion, that in this case they have done wrong, although I am bound to say that in ninety-nine cases out of one hundred, unless there is some such custom proved, I should say they had done wrong. Therefore, as regards this first point about the discount, although it is a matter small in amount, it is large in principle, because I think one came to 6*l.* odd and another to 5*l.* odd on the Pocock Street School, and I am of opinion that the plaintiffs have failed in making out that charge against Messrs. Northcroft.

As regards the 15 guineas, that is a question which arises from a blunder again. I am satisfied how it arises, and I am also satisfied that I should not hold Messrs. Northcroft responsible for that. The observation I made as regards the 118*l.* applies to the 15 guineas, and also the observation which has been already made that the builder, Mr. Wall, has already said he has been overpaid that 15 guineas, and he is quite willing to refund that to the Board.

As regards the other items, which are paltry in the extreme, 5 guineas, 5*l.*, 3*l.* 2*s.* 6*d.*, and 3*l.* 3*s.*, they are all small matters which Mr. Northcroft states he was retained to do by the architect as the work went on. They are trivial in the extreme, and they are very small sums when we are dealing with a contract for 12,000*l.* There is, therefore, the total of these small sums which it is now left for me to decide. As counsel says, the architect is not called to contradict it. But supposing that he did tell Mr. Northcroft. "You

1889
March 19.

Queen's
Bench
Division.

may do some of these items," that would not bind the Board. I suppose counsel's suggestion is that you should have it under the common seal of the Board before Messrs. Northcroft could sue for such a trivial sum as 3 guineas. I am sure I do not know how that is, but I am not going to act upon that to-day.

As regards all these items, I am of opinion that the Board have not made out their case, and I therefore give judgment for the defendants with costs.

1890
June 10.

Queen's
Bench
Division.

In the High Court of Justice (Queen's Bench Division).

(*Before* Vaughan Williams and Lawrance, JJ.)

GEORGE SMITH

v.

THE HOWDEN UNION RURAL SANITARY AUTHORITY, IN THE County OF York, AND ALFRED MOUNTAIN FOWLER.

Engineering Contracts—Certificate of Engineer withheld by Fraud without Collusion with the Employer—Extras.

The plaintiff, by agreement in writing dated August 5th, 1885, contracted to construct certain specified sewers for the defendant union for the price of 2,616*l.*, payable on certificates by the engineer of the union. There was also a clause providing that extras must be ordered in writing. The plaintiff commenced in August, 1885, and though the work was not a success, proceeded according to the specification and following the directions of the engineer, and was not in default when, on July 10th, 1886, the defendants took possession of the works and excluded the plaintiff. At that time 2,318*l.* only had been paid to the plaintiff.

The plaintiff sued for the balance of the contract price and for money due for extras, part of such extras not having been ordered in writing, and it was found by the referee that the engineer, F., had *malâ fide* and wrongfully refused to certify, but that the defendant union had not colluded with F.:—Held, that the plaintiff's remedy was damages for wrongfully preventing the plaintiff from completing the contract work by wrongfully taking possession, the measure of damages being the amount to which presumably the plaintiff would have been entitled if the work had been completed, and had the engineer thereupon issued such certificate as he ought to have issued. The plaintiff had judgment for the unpaid balance of the contract, 398*l.*; for extras under written orders, 119*l.* 6*s.* 8*d.*; for extras in respect of which no written orders were given, but which were allowed in certificates already given, 385*l.* 10*s.*; plant unduly seized, 25*l.*; total, 927*l.*, for which judgment was directed to be entered. *Semble*, wrongful behaviour or *mala fides* in the certifier gives no ground of action against the employer who has not actually colluded with such certifier.

1890
June 10.

Queen's
Bench
Division.

This was an action brought by George Smith, a contractor, against the Howden Union Sanitary Authority, in the county of York, and A. M. Fowler, their engineer, under a contract for constructing certain sewers and drainage work in the town of Howden.

To quote from the official referee's judgment: "The matter arises out of the contract that was entered into by the plaintiff for constructing particular specified sewers in the town of Howden; and without alluding at full length to the particular clauses of the contract, I may state, to put it briefly, that the sewers were to be carried out to the satisfaction of the union and of the engineer employed by them, and in accordance with the contract plans and specifications. The payments were to be monthly, to the extent of 90 per cent. of the work done, the engineer having power to withhold his certificate if he was not satisfied with the progress of the works; and there were also provisions that extras were not to be carried out or done without the written order of the engineer. I will not allude more at length to these clauses, because it would take time, but that is in effect the purport of the clauses in the agreement.

"Now, upon this agreement the work was carried out. It commenced in August, 1885, and it was finished more or less at the end of March, 1886, although the plaintiff remained on the work, and was carrying out work under the supervision of the engineer or his representative until later than that, and ultimately the union took possession on the 10th of July, 1886, which terminated the whole matter.

"Now, under the circumstances, the contractor having been paid 2,318*l.* only, and the contract having been for 2,616*l.*, besides a claim for extras, he brings his action for the balance which he says is due to him."

The dispute in the case shortly was as follows:—

The engineer designed sewers at a very slight fall of only two-thirds of an inch in 100 feet. He set them out very roughly by driving a peg in the ground, and he left the supervision of the work entirely to a clerk of the works whose reports he adopted, and certified thereon for payment during the progress of the works, and was satisfied with the completion thereof. Various works alleged to be extras were ordered, but not in writing.

Soon after the completion of the works, the drains being found out of level, he condemned the work and refused to certify. Hence the action.

The plaintiff claimed as against the defendant union:—

(1) The sum of 1,452*l.* 13*s.* 9*d.* as money due under a contract of the 8th August, 1889 (including extras and additions), and delivered particulars thereof.

(2) Alternatively, the same sum as damages under paragraph 4 of the statement of claim.

(3) A further sum of 300*l.* as damages for having taken possession of the works and determining the agreement.

Against the defendant Fowler:—

In a further alternative to the claim in paragraph 4 (mentioned below), the said sum of 1,452*l.* 13*s.* 9*d.* as damages against him in respect of paragraph 5 (also mentioned below).

1890
June 10.

Queen's
Bench
Division.

The paragraphs 4 and 5 were as follows:—

Para. (4) In the alternative to the second paragraph hereof, the plaintiff says that the defendant Fowler was the engineer of the defendant union, and was appointed by them to superintend and control the execution of the work under the said contract, and to ascertain from time to time the amount done thereunder and in pursuance of orders and directions given by the said defendant to the plaintiff, and to determine and certify to the defendant union the sums which were due to the plaintiff in respect of the said work. The said defendant undertook the said duty to the defendant union and to the plaintiff, but in breach thereof, and with a view to deprive the plaintiff of the sums due to him as aforesaid, and acting in collusion with and by the procurement of the defendant union, the defendant Fowler has from time to time wilfully refused and neglected, and still refuses and neglects to ascertain the work done under the said contract, and in pursuance of his orders and directions as aforesaid, and to determine and certify the sums which were and are payable to the plaintiff from the defendant union in respect thereof. There is now due to the plaintiff in respect of work executed by him the above mentioned sum of 1,452*l*. 13*s*. 9*d*., but owing to the wrongful refusal of the said defendant Alfred M. Fowler, and the collusion and procurement aforesaid, the plaintiff is without certificates relating to the said work, and without legal means of enforcing his claim against the defendant union in respect thereof.

Para. (5) In a further alternative the plaintiff says that the defendant Fowler having been employed, and being subject to the obligation and duty above mentioned, in order to deprive the plaintiff of his right to recover payment for the work done by him as aforesaid, and in order to conceal the defects committed by the said defendant in connection with the plans, levels, specifications, and quantities relating to the said contract work, and in connection with his supervision and direction thereof, wilfully and in breach of his said duty has neglected and refused, and still neglects and refuses to take the steps necessary to determining the amount of the certificates entitling the plaintiff to receive payment of the said sum of 1,452*l*. 13*s*. 9*d*., and has refused, and still refuses to issue the said certificates, whereby the plaintiff has lost and is unable to obtain payment from the defendant union of the said sum.

The defendant union pleaded that by the terms of the contract they were not liable for any extra or additional work unless the instructions for the same should have been given in writing by the engineer, or unless the same should have been claimed for by the plaintiff in writing within seven days after the week in which the same should have been executed in accordance with the terms of the contract.

That they had paid all sums certified for.

That the plaintiff had not carried out the work, nor done work extra or otherwise beyond the sum of 2,355*l*. which they had paid.

That the extra work claimed was not ordered in writing, nor claimed within the time specified.

That they had a right to take the work out of the plaintiff's hands, and in doing so had spent more than the sum then remaining due to the plaintiff.

They denied the allegations in paragraph 4, and they denied that the work was done to their satisfaction or that of the defendant Fowler, and they sought to set off penalties for delay.

1890
June 10.

Queen's
Bench
Division.

And the defendant union counterclaimed against the plaintiff and the parties to a bond for the due performance of the contract, viz., Westmacott, Murray and Edgar.

The defendant union by their counterclaim alleged that the work done by the plaintiff was not executed in accordance with the said agreement, the levels and fall of the drains were irregular, and not according to the plans, and the work defective, and the defendant union was put to additional expense in completing the same and making the same in accordance therewith, and with remedying the defects in the part of the works already executed. The following are the particulars thereof:—

	£	s.	d.
Paid for relaying part of the drains	119	9	11
Estimated cost of resighting and relaying other parts thereof	1,500	0	0
Estimated cost of repairing outfall works washed away by the tide owing to inefficient workmanship	200	0	0
Estimated cost of restoring streets to their original condition	200	0	0
	£2,019	9	11

Being a sum of 1,712*l.* 8*s.* 7*d.* in excess of what the defendant union would have paid if the plaintiff had carried out the said works according to the said agreement.

The defendant union also counterclaimed for the penalties, viz., 240*l.*

The defendant union also claimed the sum of 27*l.* 10*s.* which they had been obliged to pay for tenants' compensation for damage caused during the execution of the works, for which the plaintiff was bound to pay by the terms of the said agreement.

Alternatively, they claimed 2,600*l.* under the bond.

The defendant Fowler denied all the plaintiff's allegations, and alleged that the plaintiff did not carry out the works according to the contract, and that the plaintiff executed the said work with improper and imperfect materials, and not in the time and at the levels intended and prescribed in the said contract and the said plans, sections, and specifications, and in an unworkmanlike and unskilful manner.

The other defendants to the counterclaim also raised pleas not material to the issue.

The cause was referred to Mr. Edward Ridley, one of the official referees, who sat for several days and made a report.

Official Referee's Report.

In pursuance of an order herein dated March 22nd, 1889, I, Edward Ridley, Official Referee, having tried the issue in this action and counterclaim, do find as follows:—

The plaintiff, by an agreement in writing dated August 8th, 1885, contracted with the defendant union to execute certain works in

1890
June 10.

Queen's
Bench
Division.

accordance with the terms of such agreement, and Westmacott, Murray, and Edgar, defendants to the counterclaim, were parties to the said agreement as sureties for the due performance thereof by the plaintiff.

The plaintiff did carry out the works to the satisfaction of the defendant Fowler, and of his agent, William Lewis, the clerk of the works, but after the completion thereof the defendant Fowler refused to certify any further sums to be due to the plaintiff in respect thereof than the sum already paid, that is to say, 2,318*l.*

In refusing to certify as aforesaid, the defendant Fowler did not act honestly with the sole aim and intention of fulfilling his duty under the said agreement, but acted improperly and unfairly, and refused to exercise his honest judgment upon the question whether any further sum was due to the plaintiff.

The defendant Fowler's conduct, although unfair and improper as aforesaid, was not so to the knowledge of the defendant union, and was not procured by them, but the said union, without knowledge of such unfairness, adopted the acts of the defendant Fowler and made use of them to resist the plaintiff's claim in this action.

The works were done by the plaintiff in accordance with the terms of the agreement, and the plans, sections and specification annexed thereto, and in accordance with orders given by the defendant Fowler or his agents, and with proper materials, and the faults in the said work were due to errors in the said plans and sections and to the said orders.

The delay in executing the works was not due to any default of the plaintiff, but was caused by the action and conduct of the defendant union or their agent, the defendant Fowler.

The defendant union, on or about July 10th, 1886, took possession of plant relating to the works, and such taking possession was in breach of the said agreement and wrongful. The value of such plant was 25*l.*

Extra work was done under the said agreement without any written order of the defendant Fowler to the value of 385*l.* 10*s.* The defendant Fowler gave to the clerk of the works discretion to order such extra work and he did verbally order it; the said work was claimed for in writing by the plaintiff, it was approved and accepted by the defendant Fowler as necessary for the proper completion of the work, and allowed for by him in the certificates for payment which he granted to the plaintiff during the progress of the works. The defendant Fowler's reason for not giving written orders for such extra work was that it had been already ordered by the clerk of the works.

1890
June 10.

Queen's
Bench
Division.

Additional work was done by the plaintiff to the value of 429*l.* 16*s.* in relaying work already done, and in further work rendered necessary by the default of the defendant Fowler. This work was done by the order of the defendant Fowler or his agents, and the said sum is now due to the plaintiff.

The work alleged to have been done by the defendant union in the 13th paragraph of the counterclaim did not require to be done owing to any default of the plaintiff.

The sum of 37*l.* 10*s.* has been paid by the defendant union since they took possession of the plant, as stated in paragraph 7 hereof, for tenants' compensation for damage done in the execution of the works, but such sum was not paid at the request of the plaintiff.

There is due and owing in respect of the said works to the plaintiff the sum of 1,277*l.* 18*s.* 9*d.*, made up as follows:—

	£	s.	d.
Price under agreement	2,616	6	1
Extras under written order	119	6	8
Extras mentioned in paragraph 8 hereof .	385	10	0
Relaying mentioned in paragraph 9 hereof	429	16	0
Engineering expenses to which the plaintiff was put in consequence of the refusal of the defendant Fowler to grant further certificates	20	0	0
Plant mentioned in paragraph 7 hereof .	25	0	0
	3,595	18	9
Paid	2,318	0	0
	£1,277	18	9

And I direct judgment to be entered for the plaintiff against both defendants for 1,277*l.* 18*s.* 9*d.* with costs, including the costs of the counterclaim, and that the defendants do also pay the costs of George Frederick Westmacott, defendant to the counterclaim, but that James Murray and Edward Edgar, defendants to the counterclaim, do bear their own costs.

Some further directions as to costs, *&c. &c.*

EDWARD RIDLEY,
Official Referee.

Nov. 26th, 1899.

The Howden Union moved to set aside the above report, and asked for a new trial.

1890
June 10.
———
Queen's
Bench
Division.

Forbes, Q.C., and Yerburgh Anderson for the defendants, relied on *Clarke* v. *Watson* (a) and *Batterbury* v. *Vyse* (b) as showing that nothing short of collusion or prevention by the Howden Union would dispense with the condition precedent of the engineer's certificate.

Lawson Walton, Q.C., for the plaintiff, cited *Waring* v. *Manchester and Sheffield Railway* (c) and *McIntosh* v. *Great Western Railway* (d).

[Vaughan Williams, J.: "Whatever was expressed in the judgments in those cases they were both on demurrer. In the first case the bill alleged that the employer prevented the certificate being given, and in the latter case the bill, by alleging that what was done was under the authority of the employer, thus expressly included the acts of defendants or their agents."]

He also cited *Scott* v. *Liverpool Corporation* (e) and *Pawley* v. *Turnbull* (f).

There was the further claim for extras, 429*l.* 16*s.*, allowed by the Official Referee, as to which the Court intimated that the respondents had no claim within the case of *Thorn* v. *Mayor of London* (g).

The Court also intimated that the respondents could not claim the 20*l.* for engineering expenses, allowed by the Official Referee.

The Court reserved judgment.

Judgment.

The judgment of the Court was delivered by Vaughan Williams, J.: I do not think that the judgment of the learned Referee is right upon his own findings. It appears by these findings that the defendant Fowler, the engineer to the defendant union, has not certified any further sum to be due to the plaintiff than the sum already paid—that is to say, 2,318*l.* Now the certificate of the engineer seems by the contract to be a condition precedent to the right to payment of the price and every part of it, and I find no case in which it has ever been held, either at law or in equity, that where a contract provides that the contractor as a condition precedent

(a) 18 C. B. N. S. 278; 34 L. J. C. P. 148.
(b) 2 H. & C. 42; 32 L. J. Ex. 177; 8 L. T. N. S. 283.
(c) (1849), 7 Hare, 482.
(d) (1848), 2 De G. & Sm. 758; 2 Mac. & G. 74; 19 L. J. N. S. Ch. 374; 3 Sm. & G. 146; 24 L. J. N. S. Ch. 469.
(e) (1858), 3 De G. & J. 334; 28 L. J. Ch. 230.
(f) (1861), 3 Giff. 70.
(g) (1876), 1 App. Cas. 120; 45 L. J. Ex. 487.

1890
June 10.

Queen's
Bench
Division.

to the right to payment, whether of intermediate instalments or of the final balance, must obtain the engineer's or the architect's certificate in writing, the price can become payable as such without the production of such certificate. The case of refusal by the engineer in collusion with the building owner to grant certificates is spoken of as an exception. It is not, however, really an exception. In such a case, the building owner and engineer fraudulently prevent the contractor from doing that which is necessary to obtain the price—viz., from getting the certificates, and what is recoverable by the contractor in such a case is not really the price, but damages. That the performance of the condition precedent is necessary at law appears from the case of *Clarke* v. *Watson* (a).

The cases in equity which were cited to us in the argument of this case, and which were cited in the arguments of *Clarke* v. *Watson*, may contain observations seeming to show that misconduct or fraud of the architect or engineer, without collusion of the employer, will entitle the contractor to recover the price without obtaining the certificate required by the contract. But when these cases are looked at, nothing of the sort seems at all events involved in the decision. In both *McIntosh* v. *The Great Western Railway Company* (b) and *Waring* v. *The Manchester, Sheffield and Lincolnshire Railway Company* (c) the bills contained strong allegations of collusion and concert, and in each case it was a demurrer to bills containing such allegations which was overruled. The decree which was ordered at the hearing of *McIntosh* v. *The Great Western Railway Company* was not ordered on the ground of collusion, or even of misconduct of the engineer, but on the ground of the complication of the accounts being such that the questions between the parties could not be determined at law. The Master of the Rolls, Sir John Romilly, in *Bliss* v. *Smith* (d), says: "Courts of Equity will interfere in two cases—one, where there is collusive dealing between employer and the person whom he has appointed architect, for the purpose of defeating the contractor; secondly, where there are very long and complicated accounts, which cannot be conveniently taken at law." *Pawley* v. *Turnbull* (e), which looks like a case to the contrary, is not really so. There the architect had ousted the contractor, and his conduct was alleged to have been unfair, and what

(a) (1865), 18 C. B. N. S. 278.
(b) (1848), 3 Sm. & G. 146.
(c) (1849), 7 Hare, 482.
(d) (1865), 34 Beav. 508.
(e) (1861), 3 Giff. 70.

11 (2)

1890
June 10.

Queen's
Bench
Division.

was really assessed by the Court and ordered to be paid was, not the amounts for which the certificates would have been necessary, but damages for preventing the contractor from completing.

I think that, in the present case, what the plaintiff is entitled to recover is, not judgment for the amounts which the engineer ought to have certified, but damages for wrongfully preventing the plaintiff from completing the contract work by wrongfully taking possession of the works; and the measure of damages is the amount to which, presumably, the plaintiff would have been entitled if the work had been completed, and the engineer thereupon had issued such certificates as he ought to have issued.

The result will be, in measuring these damages, and the items will be—first, balance unpaid on contract price, 398*l.*; secondly, extras under written orders, 119*l.* 6*s.* 8*d.*; thirdly, extras in respect of which no written orders were given, but which were allowed in certificates already given, 385*l.* 10*s.*; plant mentioned in paragraph 7 of Referee's report, 25*l.*—927*l.* 16*s.* 8*d.*, for which we direct judgment to be entered for the plaintiff. We think that there ought to be no costs in this appeal.

1890
October 25.

Queen's
Bench
Division.

In the High Court of Justice (Queen's Bench Division).

(*Before* Mathew and Grantham, JJ.)

SAUNDERS AND COLLARD

v.

BROADSTAIRS LOCAL BOARD (*a*).

Engineering Contract—Negligence of Engineer—Measure of Damages.

Engineers in the employ of a local board were negligent in the design, construction and supervision of a drainage scheme entrusted to them, and in certifying its due and satisfactory completion, and in over-certifying the amount of work done:—Held, that they were liable in damages for their neglect for the sum necessary to make good the defects of the scheme and to repay the amount by which the contractor was overpaid on their certificates, and that their liability was not limited to the amount of their professional charges.

(*a*) See also *Rogers* v. *James, post,*

1890
October 25.

Queen's
Bench
Division.

Action for 521*l*. 12*s*. 6*d*. for work done as engineers and surveyors in preparing surveys, schemes and estimates, specifications, drawings, plans and sections for sewerage and drainage works for the urban sanitary authority at Broadstairs, and for obtaining tenders for and superintending the execution of the contract for the works. The plaintiffs alleged that the defendants had approved and accepted the drainage works.

The defendants admitted the employment of the plaintiffs, but denied acceptance or approval, and all liability for the engineers' charges, and counterclaimed against the plaintiffs for damages upon the ground that it was one of the terms of the plaintiffs' employment that they should exercise due and reasonable care and skill with respect to the works, and that the defendants had suffered damage by reason of the negligence of the plaintiffs and by reason of the breaches by them of their obligation to exercise due and reasonable care and skill, and they made the following specific charges of negligence and want of skill:—

(a) The plaintiffs, as engineers, prepared bills of quantities for the defendants, showing, or purporting to show, the amount of work required to be done, upon which bills of quantities one Charles Home made an estimate of the amount for which he would do the works and tendered for the works at the price so estimated. His tender was accepted, and a contract was entered into by which Home agreed to do the work mentioned in the bills of quantities at the price of 5,046*l*. 3*s*. 8*d*., payable upon the certificates of the plaintiffs. The bills of quantities were so unskilfully and negligently prepared that they showed a much larger quantity of work to be done than was in fact done or required to be done by Home, and the plaintiffs so negligently, improperly and unskilfully measured up the said work that they granted certificates for much larger sums than Home was entitled to be paid in respect of the work actually done by him, and the defendants were consequently obliged, under the contract with Home, to pay him much larger sums than he was in fact entitled to in respect of the work actually done by him.

(b) The plans were so unskilfully and negligently made and the work of making and superintending the sewers was so badly, improperly and negligently done by the plaintiffs, that a deflection was made in the said sewer by reason of which the said pipes always contained a quantity of sewage and water, and the said sewage and water does not freely pass through the pipes, and the defendants have been required by the Local Government Board and will be compelled to take up and relay the said pipes at a uniform gradient, and will be put to an expense of 200*l*. in so doing.

(c) The concrete specified by the plaintiffs in the bill of quantities to be used for the sewer was of so inferior and improper a description that it will have to be removed and replaced at great expense to the defendants. The plaintiffs were guilty of negligence in specifying such a concrete, and in ordering, suffering or allowing it to be used.

(d) The plaintiffs unskilfully and negligently omitted to make or cause to be made any means of escape for compressed air or gas from the pipes in the sewer, by reason of which several pipes have burst and been replaced and several more will have to be replaced, and the defendants have been and will be put to great expense in that behalf.

The plaintiffs replied that they at all times exercised due and reasonable care and skill with respect to the said works. They were employed to make plans for and superintend the said works, but not to make the said sewers. The defendants appointed a clerk of the works to superintend the levels of the sewers and for the other matters connected with the said works, and the plaintiffs remonstrated with the defendants as to the said appointment at the time of making the same. The plaintiffs are not responsible for any errors committed by reason of the defendants' selection of a clerk of the works. They prepared the bills of quantities, and measured up the work included therein with proper care and skill. They denied that they granted certificates to Home for any larger sums than he was entitled to be paid in respect of work done by him, or that the defendants had, in fact, paid Home any greater sums than he was entitled to receive in respect of the work done by him, and certified by the plaintiffs.

They also denied the want of skill and care imputed to them under head (b), and said that from time to time they set out bench marks, and showed the defendants' clerk of the works the depths the sewers should be laid in each section of the said works. They denied the alleged deflection, and the alleged result therefrom, and did not admit that the defendants had been injured, as alleged, or that they would be put to any expense by reason of the plaintiffs' alleged negligence. In the alternative, they said that if any deflection existed it had arisen entirely from the incompetence of the clerk of the works selected by the defendants, and from the interference of the defendants with the plaintiffs.

The concrete specified by the plaintiffs was of a proper description, and is effective, and its removal was not necessary.

They denied the whole of the allegations made under head (d), and said that they had provided means for the escape of gas, and made twenty holes or thereabouts for the flushing and inspection of the said sewers, but the defendants objected to the expense of flushing, and caused the said holes to be stopped up. The plaintiffs said they were not responsible for this or any other interference on the part of the defendant board with the said works. They also averred that the plans, prior to their acceptance by the defendants, were approved both by a civil engineer selected by the defendants and by the Local Government Board, and that defendants had accepted and approved all the said drainage works, and in answer to inquiries by the Local Government Board as to any complaints, had expressed themselves as completely satisfied with the works, and since the bringing of this action have stated to the said board that no complaint whatever had been received in relation thereto.

The counterclaim was referred to and tried before Mr. Ridley, the Official Referee, who gave judgment as follows:—

"This is a very extraordinary case. I at first expected evidence to be brought to rebut the evidence of extraordinary negligence. No such evidence is brought, and I am bound to find both Saunders and Collard guilty of gross negligence. For this I am sorry. I am not at all sure we have got at the bottom of this. These things must have been done on purpose. But I do not base my judgment on this. I will take facts as they stand. The scheme appears to have

1890
October 25.

Queen's
Bench
Division.

been approved by the Local Government Board, but seems to me bad. If they did approve, it was because the pipes were to be laid in concrete. The negligence of the engineers, in my opinion, consisted—

(1.) In preparing plans not showing properly the works to be executed;

(2.) In allowing the concrete to be composed of so small a proportion of cement as one of cement to nine of shingle, '1 in 10';

(3.) In over certifying the quantity of work done. It is not a small matter, but a huge sum, and there is a deficiency in every part of the work.

Collard says he left it all to Saunders, but that is no defence. He has not exercised reasonable skill or judgment. There is nothing whatever to protect him.

As to the *concrete*, it is suggested by Mr. Sankey that it has not given way in places; but it began to give way directly, and is still going on.

As to the want of proper *ventilation*, it does not necessarily follow from this one fact that all the damage would have accrued. But it is a part of a case showing negligence, and must not be left out of consideration.

(1.) If the engineers relied on the clerk of the works in this case, they were negligent, because (see letters in August, 1883) they knew he was not reliable. It was their business to see to the levels. This again was negligence.

(2.) If they did not trust to the clerk of the works it is worse still, and they were guilty of gross and culpable negligence, for which both are liable, and I must not shrink from making plaintiffs liable for what is due to their negligence.

The Official Referee assessed the damages upon the counterclaim at 4,686*l*. 12*s*. 6*d*., made up in the following manner:—

2,046*l*. 12*s*. 6*d*. amount overpaid to the contractor by reason of negligence of the engineers in over certifying the quantities.

2,400*l*. estimated cost of doing over again bad work.

240*l*. actual cost of repairs already done to defective work."

The plaintiff Collard moved to set aside the findings and judgment of the Official Referee.

Stuart Sankey for the plaintiff Collard. T. E. Crispe and H. F. Dickens for the defendants.

MATHEW, J.: This is a motion to set aside the verdict and judgment of the Official Referee on the ground that the verdict is against

1890
October 25.

Queen's
Bench
Division.

the weight of evidence, and that the damages are excessive. We have heard the matter fully discussed by the learned counsel on both sides, and I agree with the conclusion at which the learned Referee has arrived.

The first point made was a striking one, and it was this. The whole amount of the contract which these engineers were instructed to superintend, was a sum of about 5,000*l.*, and the damages against them are calculated at the large sum of 4,600*l.* That, of course, on the face of it, required explanation. There was first a counterclaim of 2,000*l.*, which the contractor had been paid in excess, and beyond the amount which the engineers ought to have certified for. Now, Mr. Sankey says that that 2,000*l.* ought to be displaced, because, in the first instance, the claim was confined to 900*l.*, but then the learned Referee was entitled to amend from the sum of 900*l.* to 2,000*l.*, and he practically did so. Mr. Sankey sought to make that a grievance by saying that he was not allowed an adjournment, which he said he was entitled to when this larger claim was put forward. But it appears his client had ample notice, when the case was opened at Maidstone, as to what was going to be said about it, and although elaborate measurements had been made by the Board, and those measurements were submitted to the Official Referee, upon which his award was made, the defendants never sought to have the work measured, or to bring forward evidence to contradict it.

Under these circumstances I am of opinion that we cannot interfere with the decision at which the Official Referee has arrived. Then comes another claim, in respect of which Mr. Sankey makes the same remark. It appears there was a grievous complaint of the way in which the sewers had been laid, and the claim made by the counterclaim in respect of that was 200*l.*, but there again the Official Referee was entitled to make any necessary amendment, and I do not think the amendment he made was excessive; indeed, I think the damages sustained by the Board will be far above that stated by the Official Referee. There was evidence before the Official Referee to show that by reason of the negligence of these engineers a material part of the work has had, or will have, to be done over again. No evidence was offered on behalf of the plaintiff as to this, except by one of the plaintiffs, and his evidence established such circumstances as lead me to think that there is no ground for interfering. On these grounds I am of opinion that this motion must be dismissed, and with costs.

GRANTHAM, J.: I am of the same opinion. It has been said, and said with a great deal of truth, that this at first sight appears to be a

1890
October 25.

Queen's
Bench
Division.

startling result. The cost of the works amounted to 5,000*l.*, and the defendants contend that they are entitled to recover from the engineers who had the superintendence of the works nearly the whole of that sum of money, on the ground of their improper conduct in reference to its supervision. I never remember, having had considerable experience of those matters when at the Bar and on the Bench, hearing such a case as this, but I am very glad it has arisen, because it will, I hope, show people in the position of the plaintiffs that they must be more careful in the future than they have been in the past. It is said it is very hard upon them, because their remuneration only amounted to 270*l.* as commission, that they should be made liable to the extent of nearly 5,000*l.*; but it is quite true that they can be made so liable, and I am very glad of it, because it will be not only a warning to them but to others, that they cannot allow works of this description to be done in any slip-shod way that the contractor chooses to do them, and allow the contractor to get any money he chooses. On reading the evidence of Mr. Collard himself, it seems that the supervision of the engineers was as disgraceful a piece of business as was ever brought forward in a Court of justice.

I will read one or two passages in the evidence of some of the witnesses. This, it must be remembered, is a question affecting the health of thousands, and the whole of this expenditure was undertaken for the benefit of the health of the people who live in and resort to Ramsgate and Broadstairs. People who desire to recruit their health resort to where they can obtain it, and instead of that, people seem to have gone there and become ill, or possibly died. One of the witnesses said, you must have ventilators; the pipe is nothing more than a long cesspool, with gas arising therefrom carefully laid on to the town in consequence of the way in which the work has been done. Then another witness says, the concrete would not stick to the earthenware glaze; and then I find in another place, "There was no ventilation, and the stench in the town was intolerable." That was after thousands of pounds had been spent in the way described. Then when I read the evidence of one of the plaintiffs, he, in cross-examination, admitted that which is certainly as startling a thing as I have ever heard. He says, "No man in his senses would call that sample concrete. Saunders thinks otherwise. I did not agree with Saunders at the time. The contract specified what the concrete was to be. I signed for the proportions. I am sorry I did. I never used my own judgment. I thought Saunders was more experienced than I was. I yielded my judgment to him in everything and everything else connected with the outfall sewer,

1890
October 25.

Queen's
Bench
Division.

taking the plan proposed as correct. The pipes were very badly laid indeed, and Saunders did not exercise proper superintendence. He must have been guilty of gross negligence."

Now, that is the evidence of one of the plaintiffs. "I know the contractor had not put the deflection right when he got the final certificate. I relied on Saunders' judgment. As to the concrete, there is something more than an error in judgment." After that evidence of one of the plaintiffs, can it be suggested that this verdict is against the weight of the evidence? The evidence is all one way—not only the evidence given on the part of the defendants, but the evidence of one of the plaintiffs, which is the best evidence to be obtained, and he confirms absolutely to the letter all the charges made by the defendants against his co-partner. I hope that this will be a warning, not only to contractors, but to engineers who profess to supervise works of this great importance, and if so the money which has been spent by the Local Board in this litigation, if they get the money refunded, will be very well spent indeed.

1891
November
13.

Queen's
Bench.
Division.

𝕳𝖎𝖌𝖍 𝕮𝖔𝖚𝖗𝖙 𝖔𝖋 𝕵𝖚𝖘𝖙𝖎𝖈𝖊 (𝕼𝖚𝖊𝖊𝖓'𝖘 𝕭𝖊𝖓𝖈𝖍 𝕯𝖎𝖛𝖎𝖘𝖎𝖔𝖓).

(Vaughan Williams, J.)

ELMES v. BURGH MARKET COMPANY.

Building Contract—Completion—Certificate—Surveyor for the time being—Maintenance.

A certificate of completion of a building contract may be given orally in the absence of specific provision to the contrary in the contract.

Action by a contractor for money alleged to be due to him under a contract made with the directors of the Burgh Market Co., Ltd., for the execution of certain works in the making and completion of a cattle market at Spilsby. Clause 2 of the contract provided that:—"The works shall be completed in all respects and cleared of all implements and tackle, &c., within three months from date hereof to the satisfaction of the (said) surveyor, to be testified by a certificate under his hand." ... Clause 3 provided that:—"The contractor shall receive payment for his contract at the rate of 80*l.* per centum for the works completed on the surveyor's certificate of completion, and the balance at the end of the term of maintenance, less deductions that may be made in accordance with the terms of the contract, and on the surveyor certifying that the whole of the works are in a complete and satisfactory state." The "maintenance" clause, contained in the specification, provided that "the contractor shall maintain the whole of the works in a complete state of repair for a period of three calendar months from the full completion of the works to be testified by a certificate from the surveyor." . . . The other material facts sufficiently appear from the judgment. The action was tried at the Lincoln Assizes before Vaughan Williams, J., and judgment was subsequently given at Nottingham during the same circuit. Lindsell for plaintiff. Appleton, for defendants, contended that no proper certificate had been given by the surveyor to satisfy the terms of the contract.

1891
November
13.

Queen's
Bench
Division.

VAUGHAN WILLIAMS, J.: This is an action brought by a contractor for the balance of money alleged to be due to him for works executed by him for the defendants. The first defence raised is that, under the contract, a certificate from the surveyor appointed under the contract is a condition precedent to the plaintiff's right of action, and that no such certificate has been obtained. The plaintiff relies upon a certificate dated the 22nd of November, 1890, which is in the following terms:—"Works at Burgh Market, Spilsby, 22nd November, 1890, J. W. Thimbleby, Esq. I, the undersigned, do certify that Thomas Elmes is entitled to receive the sum of 127*l.* in payment of final instalment of contract after maintenance of the above-named works. 127*l.*—(Signed) J. B. BUTCHER, Architect." Two objections are taken by the defendants to this certificate—first, it is said that it is not such a certificate as is required by the contract; that the whole of the works were in a complete and satisfactory state; and, secondly, it is said, that the person who gave the certificate was not at the time of giving it surveyor within the meaning of the contract. I am inclined to think that the first objection is on the authority of *Morgan* v. *Birnie* (*a*) a good objection; for the document of the 22nd of November seems to me to be a mere statement of account, and not the required certificate.

I further think it doubtful whether the person giving the certificate continued to be the surveyor for the purpose of certifying after his discharge, which occurred before the 22nd of November, although there are some grounds for saying that "surveyor" means the person who in fact was the surveyor when the work was executed. But neither of these points is of much importance, because the plaintiff also relies on the oral certificate of Mr. Butcher given to the chairman of the defendant company and to the directors; and I find that this certificate was, in fact, given; and, in my opinion, it was the giving of this oral certificate which really led to the dismissal

(*a*) 6 Bing. 672.

1891
November
13.

Queen's
Bench
Division.

of Mr. Butcher from his post of surveyor. I also hold that the certificate required by the third clause of the contract is not a certificate in writing; and I find that the plaintiff did in fact complete the whole of the works to the satisfaction of the surveyor, and that such works were in a complete and satisfactory state to his satisfaction at the end of the period of maintenance. Under these circumstances I give judgment for the plaintiff for the amount claimed with costs.

NOTE.—After the delivery of this judgment, Appleton, for the defendants, applied that the consideration of the case might be further reserved in order to enable the defendant to call certain witnesses, whose evidence had not been taken at the trial, to contradict the statement of the surveyor that he had given a verbal certificate of the satisfactory condition of the works to the secretary of the defendant company. The case was accordingly further adjourned to London, and that evidence was given; and on 22nd November, 1891, the learned judge confirmed his prior judgment, saying that he saw no reason to alter it.

Solicitors for plaintiff: Walker, Sons and Rainey. Solicitors for defendant: Thimbleby and Son, Spilsby.

1891
November
18.

Court of
Appeal.

𝔖upreme 𝔆ourt of 𝔍ubicature (𝔆ourt of 𝔄ppeal).

(*Before* LORD ESHER, M.R., and LOPES and KAY, L.JJ.)

ROGERS v. JAMES (a).

Architect—Liability for Negligence.

An architect was employed to design and superintend the erection of a house, and by the terms of the contract between the building owner and the builder the architect's decision in all matters between builder and building owner was to be final.

The architect gave a final certificate, and brought an action for his fees. The defendant (the building owner) counterclaimed for negligence by the architect in the supervision of the work. The architect in his defence to the counterclaim alleged that he had taken the defects into consideration in certifying the final amount due, and had allowed a sum in respect thereof.

The jury found a verdict for the plaintiff on the claim for 58*l*, and for the defendant on the counterclaim for 90*l*.

Held, that the final certificate or award of an architect in a dispute between the building owner and the builder is only a final decision as between the building

(a) See *Saunders* v. *Broadstairs Local Board, ante,* p. 164.

owner and the builder, and not as between the building owner and the architect, and that the building owner was entitled to recover damages for the negligence in supervision, notwithstanding the certificate.

Motion by plaintiff for new trial.

At the trial before Mathew, J., and a special jury at Maidstone, it appeared that the plaintiff was an architect and surveyor carrying on business at Bromley, in Kent, and that he was employed by the defendant to design and superintend the construction of a residence at that place.

After the plans were prepared and tenders received a contract was entered into between the defendant and a builder, Mr. Lay, the material conditions of which were as follows:—

(1) "The contractor shall in consideration of the sum of   at his own cost erect, build, and completely finish for habitation in a good, substantial and workmanlike manner, and with the best materials of their several kinds, a residence or dwelling-house, &c."

(2) "The said works shall be executed under the direction, and to the satisfaction in all respects, of the said Fred. Rogers (the architect), and the said architect shall have power to reject any materials or workmanship not in accordance with the said specification and drawings . . . . and on non-compliance . . . . the said architect shall have power to procure materials or workmanship from other parties. . . ."

(6) After providing for payment by instalments the balance was to be paid "within six months after the whole of the said works shall have been certified by the said architect to have been completed and furnished, and any defects that may have arisen during the time shall be made good and amended by the contractor at his own expense or at the expense or value thereof and retained and deducted by the employer out of the amount which shall be retained as aforesaid."

(7) "Provided always, that the said architect shall not give his certificate in respect of any works while the contractor is not using due diligence in the performance of the works or otherwise making default in the performance of this contract."

(10) "The employer shall be entitled to deduct any moneys which the contractor shall be liable to pay to the employer under this contract from any sum which may become payable to the contractor hereunder, and the said architect in making his certificate as aforesaid shall have regard to any sums so chargeable against the contractor. Provided always, that this provision shall not affect any other remedy by action at law or otherwise to which the employer may be entitled for the recovery of any such moneys."

(16) *"The decision of the said architect with respect to the amount, state and condition of the works actually executed, and also in respect of any and every question that may arise concerning the construction of this present contract or the said plans and specification, or the execution of the said works hereby contracted for or in any wise relating thereto, shall be final and without appeal except that the said architect may by any certificate make any correction or modification in any previous certificate which shall have been made by himself or by any predecessor in his office."*

The works were then proceeded with, but the builder did not do his work properly. Complaints were made by the architect to the builder of various defects and omissions and of improper work, and the employer (the defendant) also complained to the architect of his (the architect's) negligence in not pre-

1891
November
18.
—————
Court of
Appeal.

venting various deviations from the contract by the builder. Matters were, however, arranged for a time; but renewed complaints by the employer of the architect's negligence resulted in the employer placing the matter in his solicitor's hands, but not before the builder had placed his affairs also with a solicitor and brought an action against the owner for 700*l*. The architect eventually gave a final certificate allowing the builder a little more than 100*l*. instead of 700*l*. claimed by him, and upon that certificate the owner successfully defended the action brought against him.

The architect then brought the present action for his fees amounting to 123*l*. for services rendered in connection with the erection of the house.

The defendant counterclaimed for damages for negligence in not supervising the builder and in permitting or neglecting to prevent various deviations from the contract, specification and detail drawings. The plaintiff denied that he was negligent, and further stated that in giving his final certificate to the builder he deducted 82*l*. in respect of the omission now complained of from the amount certified to be due to the builder, and contended that his certificate, as it had been accepted and acted upon by the defendant, was binding upon him under clause 16 of the contract. The jury found that the plaintiff had been guilty of negligence and had certified for more than he ought to have done. They found a verdict for the plaintiff on the claim for 58*l*. and for the defendant on the counterclaim for 90*l*. The learned judge gave judgment accordingly. The plaintiff now moved for judgment on the counterclaim or for a new trial.

Willis, Q.C., and Cecil Chapman appeared for the plaintiff, and contended that the certificate of the plaintiff was binding upon the defendant, as it is not permissible to question the decision of an arbitrator, and the deduction of 82*l*. from the sum payable to the builder was conclusive as between the plaintiff and defendant, who must otherwise get twice over damages for the same wrong. They also contended that the verdict was against the weight of the evidence.

Channell, Q.C., and H. F. Dickens, for the defendant, were not called upon.

The Court dismissed the motion.

Lord ESHER, M.R.: This is an application for a new trial on the ground that the verdict of the jury was against the weight of evidence. We cannot find that. The jury found that the architect had been guilty of negligence. Then the only question is the point of law raised on the counterclaim. It is said that the certificate of the architect comes under sect. 16 of the original agreement, and that that is a final statement of the amount of the damage, and, therefore, that the amount cannot be questioned. The plaintiff has been paid that amount. It is said that that is final as between the building owner and the architect. That is not a correct view of the law. It is only a final decision as between the building owner and the builder, and the question as between the building owner and his architect is not in the least decided by that certificate. Therefore it was an open question to go to the jury—was the architect negligent, and, if he was, what is the amount of damage which the owner has suffered in consequence of that negligence? It is true that he himself has settled that amount as between himself and the builder. I admit he made that decision honestly; I cannot find fault with it as between him and the builder, but he did not deduct enough; he made a mistake. That question has been put to the jury, and the jury have found that the architect was negligent, and that the amount he settled as between the building owner and the builder was incorrect, and that he did not deduct enough. The jury have found that, and we cannot interfere with the verdict.

LOPES, L.J.: I am of the same opinion. It is said here that the architect himself, in a certain arbitration which took place, decided the question as to the amount of damage; if he did, he could only have done it under clause 16. That clause gave him no jurisdiction of any sort or kind to certify so as to bind the building owner as against himself in respect of any negligence. It left the building, owner at liberty to bring an action against him for negligence if he thought fit. The jury have had that before them, and have come to the conclusion that the sum of 80*l.* which was deducted by the architect was not sufficient, and that the building owner ought to receive a further sum from the architect, which they have given. I have had an opportunity of speaking with the learned judge who tried the case, and he said that he gave the architect every chance, and that he was perfectly satisfied with the verdict which the jury returned. In these circumstances we cannot interfere.

KAY, L.J.: I agree altogether. The building owner claims against the architect damages for negligence for the way in which he performed his duty. The defence of the architect in point of law is put by Mr. Chapman that the building owner is estopped; and he says: "I myself, the defendant to the action, in awarding under the arbitration clause of the contract between the builder and the building owner, determined that the damages were so much; whether that was right or wrong, whether the damages I gave were enough or not, I say that acts as an estoppel." I cannot see how it is possible that the award made by an architect himself, in a dispute between the building owner and another person, can possibly be an estoppel in an action by the building owner against the architect. In my opinion the point of law fails entirely. There is every reason in the world against it. In the first place, to all intents and purposes the argument is that there is a legal estoppel involved in it, that under the contract between the builder and building owner the architect had a right to make himself the judge in his own cause to this extent, that any award he made between the builder and the building owner he

1891
November
18.

Court of
Appeal.

1891
November
18.
_____
Court of
Appeal.

should be able to plead as an absolute defence in an action brought against himself for negligence although the award might be wrong but honestly made. It seems to me quite impossible.

Then the question comes as to whether the damages given were enough, but that was a question essentially for the jury. The building owner went to the jury saying, "My case is that the damages I have received were not enough, and I ask you to say they were not enough." The jury found they were not enough, and found a certain sum as additional damages, to be paid by the architect. The learned judge says he was entirely satisfied with the verdict, and I understand that the architect had every chance to have that question determined in his favour. On this motion for a new trial it is quite impossible that this Court can interfere with the verdict. On the whole question you must take it that the jury were right and that they had materials for coming to the conclusion that the amount was not enough, and that there was ground for giving additional damages against the architect.

Solicitor for plaintiff: George Weller. Solicitors for defendant: Collison, Prichard & Greene.

[This case is also reported in 8 T. L. R. 67.]

[NOTE.— This case lays down for England the law as to architects' liabilities enunciated in Canada: *Badgley* v. *Dickson* (1886), 13 Ont. App. 494, *ante*, vol. 1, ch. 2, architects' liabilities.]

1891
May 6.
October 31.
November
22.
_____
Queen's
Bench
Division.

𝕳𝖎𝖌𝖍 𝕮𝖔𝖚𝖗𝖙 𝖔𝖋 𝕵𝖚𝖘𝖙𝖎𝖈𝖊 (𝕼𝖚𝖊𝖊𝖓'𝖘 𝕭𝖊𝖓𝖈𝖍 𝕯𝖎𝖛𝖎𝖘𝖎𝖔𝖓).

(DENMAN, J.)

LONDON SCHOOL BOARD *v.* JOHNSON.

Building Contract—Condition as to Fraud or Wilful Deviation.

A building contract provided that "no final or other certificate shall, under any circumstances, cover or relieve the contractor from his liability for any fraud, default, or wilful deviation from this contract and the works described in the drawings and specification" until four years from completion had elapsed Held, that to prove breach of this condition, it was necessary to show that deliberate and substantial variations have been made with the object of benefiting the contractor or saving his pocket; that is, something in the nature of what is popularly known as "scamping the work."

The defendant contracted with the plaintiffs to erect school-houses for them by three contracts dated respectively 2nd January, 1885, 16th June, 1885, and 23rd June, 1885. All the contracts, except with reference to the place and position of the school-house to be erected, were in identical terms. The material conditions are the following:—

1891
November
22.
———
Queen's
Bench
Division.

(3) The whole of the works, as shown on the drawings or described in the specification, or reasonably to be inferred therefrom, or set forth in such drawings and instructions as may be from time to time during the progress of the works given by the architect to the contractor, shall be executed by the contractor with the best materials of their several kinds, and the most skilful workmanship, to the entire satisfaction of the architect.

(4) No additions, deductions, alterations or deviations made in the works shall annul or invalidate the contract, but the value of such additions, deductions, alterations and deviations (if any) shall be assessed by the architect and added to or deducted from the amount of the contract, as the case may be, subject only to the proviso in clause 5.

(5) The architect shall have full power and authority from time to time, and at all times, to make and issue such further drawings, and to give such further instructions and directions as may appear to him necessary for the guidance of the contractor and the good and proper execution of the works according to the specification, and the contractor shall receive, execute and obey, and be bound by the same as fully and effectually as though they had been mentioned and referred to in the specification; and the architect may also alter and vary, or only partially execute any of the works contemplated by the specification and contract, but the board shall not become liable to the payment of any charges in respect of any such additions, omissions, variations or deductions, unless the instructions for the same shall have been given and signed by the architect as an official order (on the recognized printed form) and countersigned by the clerk of the board (such counter-signature being necessary in the case of sums included in the contract amount), nor unless the same shall have been claimed for by the contractor in writing within seven days after the week in which the same shall have been executed, such claim to contain the description and the quality of such works so done, the labour employed and materials used therein, and to be accompanied by vouchers for all labour claimed for.

(9) The architect shall have at all times access to the works, which shall be entirely under his control, and he shall have full liberty from time to time, and at all times, to inspect the materials and workmanship employed in and about the works hereby contracted for, and he may at any time reject any of the materials or workmanship furnished by the contractor which may appear to him to be defective, unfit, or improper for the several purposes to which they have been or are intended to be applied, or which are not in accordance with the description mentioned in or intended by the specification, or the drawings, instructions and directions respectively, and the contractor shall forthwith remove all such materials and workmanship so rejected when required to do so by the architect, and shall remove and carry away the same from the works and lands of the board, and shall replace the same with such better and more sufficient quality and descriptions of materials and workmanship as shall be satisfactory to the architect, and in case the contractor shall neglect or refuse to comply with the foregoing conditions it shall be lawful for the architect, on behalf of the board, by his agents servants, and workmen, to remove the materials and workmanship so rejected, or any part thereof, and to replace the same with such other materials and workmanship as may be satisfactory to him; and the board may, on the certificate of the architect, deduct the expenses incurred thereby, or which the board may thereby be put to

1891
November
22.

Queen's
Bench
Division.

or be liable for, or which may be or become due to the contractor, or to recover the same by action at law from him as the board may determine.

(11) The contractor shall give all necessary personal superintendence during the execution of the works, and shall constantly employ thereon one good and competent foreman, careful and skilled in the trades and callings required by the specification, to manage and direct in the absence of the contractor, and such foreman shall, on behalf of the contractor, receive and have charge of such drawings, specifications and documents as may be furnished for the guidance and use of the contractor, and shall also receive and obey all such instructions as may be given by the architect, and shall not be changed without the consent of the architect, but may be objected to by him, and thereupon the contractor shall forthwith dismiss such foreman and employ another good and competent foreman in his stead, and so on from time to time, and as often as the architect may require.

(16) Any defects, shrinkage and other faults which may appear within four months from the completion of the works, and arising out of defective or improper materials or workmanship, are, upon the direction of the architect, to be amended and made good by the contractor at his own cost, unless the architect shall decide that he ought to be paid for the same, and in case of default the board may recover from the contractor the cost of making good the works.

(19) The contractor shall be entitled to payment for his work in manner following, that is to say, to an instalment every month equal in amount to four-fifths of the prime cost of the work executed in the preceding month, according to the value of the same as computed by the architect, and to the balance (whatever the amount of the same) at the end of four calendar months after the architect shall have given his certificate in writing to the board and to the contractor that the works have been completed according to the true intent and meaning of the specification and of these conditions, and have been delivered to the board. Provided, nevertheless, that no such certificate shall be given until the contractor shall have delivered to the architect a full and particular account in writing of all his claims upon the board in respect of the contract and everything therein and herein contained, including all claims for extras and additions.

(20) A certificate of the architect, or an award of the referee hereinafter mentioned, as the case may be, showing the final balance due to the contractor, is to be conclusive evidence of the works having been duly completed, and that such balance is payable to the contractor at the time under clauses 16 and 22, and until such certificate or award shall have been given the contractor shall have no claim whatever at law or in equity against the board for any balance alleged to be due to him in respect either of the works comprised in the contract or of any extras in addition thereto.

(22) Lastly.—It is expressly provided and agreed that no final nor other certificate shall, under any circumstances, cover or relieve the contractor from his liability for any fraud, default or wilful deviation from this contract and the works described in the drawings and specification, but he shall remain responsible for four years from the time of the completion of the works for such fraud, default or wilful deviation, and for the consequences thereof, whether the same be discovered or noted previously or subsequently to the granting of such final or other certificate.

After the work was completed and certified, the plaintiffs, on 24th March, 1890, brought an action against the defendant on the grounds (1) that he had been guilty of fraud, default and wilful deviation from the works described in the drawings and specification annexed to the contract, within the meaning of the 22nd condition; (2) that he had obtained the architect's certificate by false representations as to work and materials done and provided. The defendant denied these allegations, and pleaded that the works were carried out in pur-

1891
November
22.

Queen's
Bench
Division.

suance of the contracts, drawings, and specifications, and under the direction of the plaintiffs' architect.

The case came on to be heard before Denman, J., and a special jury, but after being opened was referred by consent to Mr. H. A. Hunt, architect and surveyor, for investigation and report to Denman, J., on the following questions:—

(1) Whether the defendant had been guilty of fraud in carrying out the three contracts.

(2) Whether the defendant had been guilty of scamping the work in his own interest.

(3) Whether the defendant had been guilty of wilful deviation from the contract in the sense of intentional and substantial departure from it with a view to his own interest.

(4) To what amounts the buildings were the worse by reason of the defects caused by the defendant being so guilty of any of the aforesaid three breaches.

(5) Whether any, and if so which, of the aforesaid breaches were discovered within four years.

Further consideration was adjourned until receipt of the report.

The action came on for further consideration on the report, the material parts of which are set out in the judgment.

Lockwood, Q.C., and Ram for the plaintiffs. Reid, Q.C., and Gore for the defendants.

DENMAN, J.: [After reading the various conditions of the contract and the plaintiffs' statement of claim, the learned judge continued.] The plaintiffs in this action sought to recover very large sums of money, amounting on the whole to 4,000*l.* odd, against the defendant in respect of work done or omitted to be done by him some years before action brought, on three Board schools which defendant undertook to erect for the plaintiffs under three contracts which, for all practical purposes, were identical in their provisions. The defendant had been paid soon after the completion of the several schools upon certificates of the architect, but it was contended that the Board was entitled to claim damages notwithstanding the lapse of time since the receipt of the sums paid, and notwithstanding the architect's certificates, by reason of the special provisions of the contracts between them and the defendant, and on the ground that the payments made to him had been obtained by fraud. The provisions of the contracts bearing upon the disputes between the parties were contained in the contracts themselves and in the specifications and conditions annexed thereto. The prices were respectively 11,600*l.*, 12,200*l.*, and 12,900*l.*; total, 36,700*l.* The main provisions constituting the relation between the parties were contained in the following conditions: Nos. 3, 4, 5, 9, 11, 16, 19, 20 and 22 (set out *supra*).

1891
November
22.

Queen's
Bench
Division.

The plaintiffs, on March 24, 1890, brought their action for alleged breaches of the three above-mentioned contracts, and it is important to observe the exact nature of these complaints as set out in their statement of claim. The defendant in his defence denied that he had been guilty of any fraud, default or wilful deviation, and in paragraph 4 set out the 20th condition of the contracts, which provided that a certificate of the architect showing the final balance due to him was to be conclusive evidence of the completion of the works, and that the balance was payable. The defendant alleged that he had received such certificates, and that the time provided by condition 16 (*i.e.*, four months) had long since elapsed. The plaintiffs delivered particulars at various times of defects which they alleged to have been discovered, and to be due to fraud, default or wilful deviation. I do not think it necessary to call attention to the mere question of the dates of the discovery of the several alleged defaults, for reasons which will be obvious presently.

The case came on to be heard before me and a special jury on May 5 last, when counsel for plaintiffs proceeded to open the case. It very soon became apparent that the case was one wholly unfitted for investigation by a jury, as it consisted of three claims for sums respectively of 2,130*l.*, 1,000*l.* and 880*l.*, made up of numerous kinds of alleged deficiencies in multitudinous matters, said to have been improperly dealt with by the defendant, and requiring a protracted examination of plans and documents by a person having such knowledge as only architects and surveyors possess.

The parties having desired my opinion as to the construction to be put upon clause 22 of the conditions, I intimated that I thought the plaintiffs, in order to recover, would have to make out something in the nature of what is popularly known as "scamping the work" in order to entitle them to go behind the certificates given three or four years before action, and after some discussion the counsel agreed that it should be referred for inquiry and report to an architect to be chosen by me, who should investigate and report to me on the claims in the action, and that upon his report I should direct judgment from which there should be no appeal, and deal with all costs; and an order was drawn up by consent to that effect.

I appointed Mr. Henry Arthur Hunt, of 45, Parliament Street, architect and surveyor, to hear the case and report upon the questions raised by consent of the parties, which were as follows: (1) Was the defendant guilty of fraud in carrying out the contract? (2) Was the defendant guilty of scamping the work, with a view to his own interest? (3) Was the defendant guilty of wilful deviation from

1891
November
22.

Queen's
Bench
Division.

the contract in the sense of intentional and substantial departure from the contract, with a view to his own interest? (4) To what amount, if any, are the buildings the worse for the defects consequent on the defendant so being guilty of each of the previously-named breaches (if any), and (if not necessary to replace) what the defendant has saved by such breaches? Mr. Hunt, in pursuance of this order, held an inquiry, which lasted upwards of twenty days, and inspected the schools in question, so far as he deemed necessary, and heard counsel and witnesses for both sides, and eventually, on August 10 last, reported to me as will appear presently. The case was put in the paper for judgment on the last day of the sittings before the Long Vacation, but it was then agreed by both parties that the report raised questions which would require more discussion than the parties had contemplated, and that it would be better that it should stand over for discussion until after the Long Vacation.

Accordingly, on October 31, the case came before me again, and after some further discussion it was agreed that I should, after going through the shorthand notes of all the proceedings before Mr. Hunt (which I have since done), and ascertaining from him his intentions as to the ambiguous expressions in his report, give judgment without further argument, unless I saw any reason for requiring further discussion. Having now had the opportunity of seeing Mr. Hunt and obtaining his view of the case, I see no reason for abstaining from giving judgment; but before stating the result at which I have arrived it will be right that I should state *seriatim* the result of the inquiries I addressed to Mr. Hunt as to the exact intentions of his mind in all cases in which the language of his report is at all ambiguous; and I may add that, having carefully gone through the shorthand notes of all the proceedings before him, I can see no reason to doubt that the conclusions he has arrived at, as now more fully reported to me, are the correct conclusions to be drawn from the evidence upon a correct view of the questions upon which the case turns.

The first finding is as follows: "The defendant was not personally guilty of fraud, but to a small extent a plumber was guilty in laying light lead in the gutters to the amount of 7 cwt. of the value of 5*l*. 5*s*." Mr. Hunt informs me that he was clearly of opinion, and indeed the learned counsel who conducted the case before him was obliged to admit, that in no single case was there any reason to suppose that the defendant had any fraudulent intent. The finding with regard to the plumber's conduct was inserted by him in consequence of an argument that nevertheless the defendant might be

1891
November
22.

Queen's
Bench
Division.

responsible because the plumber who laid light lead to the extent of
5*l.* 5*s.* in the gutters was an agent for the defendant, and so the
defendant was responsible for his fraud. He informs me, however,
that this act of the plumber was known to no one else. I am not of
opinion that it was the intention of clause 22 of the conditions that in
such a case as this the Board should be entitled to go behind the
architect's certificate at any time within the four years, as contended
for the plaintiffs. I do not think that the cases relating to liability for
fraud of an agent apply to such a case, or that defendant, in the
absence of personal fraud, can be rendered responsible, however
fraudulent the conduct of the plumber may have been.

The second finding was as follows: "I say that generally the work
has been well done, notably the lead work, the joiners' work, the
plasterers' work, the brick and stone work, and that although there
are serious failures in the drainage work of at least one school, I do
not consider that, as a whole, the work has been 'scamped.='" It is
obvious that this finding is open to the objection that it does not
answer the question put; but after reading the shorthand notes and
making full inquiry of the referee, he informs me that he considers
the fair result of his minute inquiry to be this—(1) that, looking at the
work done under the three contracts as a whole, he is of opinion that
it was well and conscientiously done; (2) that as regards the drainage
there were serious defects; but (3) that these defects were not due to
any desire on the part of the defendant to obtain any advantage for
himself, nor on the part of any foreman employed upon the works to
make the contract a more advantageous one for the defendant, but
that such defects were due to the slovenly work of the persons
actually engaged upon the work, which ought to have been objected
to at the time by the plaintiffs' clerks of the works, who were not
called as witnesses, and who seemed to him to have done their part
in the most perfunctory manner. I may say that upon this part of the
case there was a serious conflict of evidence between a witness
named Keech and a foreman of defendant's named Spicer, as to
which the referee felt himself unable to accept the version given by
Keech, who was the plaintiffs' witness, as against that of Spicer, who
was called by the defendant. But even assuming that there was some
blame to be attached to the defendant's foreman in respect of the
work done and the deviations from the contract, so far as the drains
were concerned, I think the referee is right in the view he takes of the
case—viz., that the defects in the drains cannot be ascribed to any
desire on the part of the defendant, or any one responsible to him, to
put money into his pockets, but rather to a loose surveillance on the

part of the plaintiffs' clerks of the works and to an erroneous notion thereby entertained by the defendant's workmen that what was being done was being done in exact accordance with the contract, or at most to a still more erroneous notion that it would be pleasing to the defendant if they did the work at less expense to him than if it were done in strict accordance with the contract.

1891
November
22.

Queen's
Bench
Division.

As to the third question, I have had considerable difficulty in appreciating any distinction between its meaning and that of the second question, but it is not necessary to discuss this question in the view I take of the findings, which were as follows: "I say there have been substantial departures from the contract—(1) with the full cognizance of or to comply with the wishes or orders of the clerks of the works—which have doubtless put money in defendant's pocket, but should have been adjusted by the measuring surveyors in the usual way; (2) there has been a departure in the width of the wall gutters. Although it is difficult to ascertain from the drawings what the width should be, and the specification does not explicitly state the *minimum* width of a wall gutter, still I am of opinion that about 20 cwt. of lead has been saved in two of the schools and 3 cwt. additional put into the third." Here, again, it was necessary that I should ascertain from the referee the full meaning of his findings, and upon inquiry as to these I find that what he intends to report—and I can see no reason for dissenting from his conclusions—is as follows: (1) That there are several cases in which work has been done in a way substantially different from that provided for in the contract and specification, and that in some of such cases the effect has been to put money into the pocket of the defendant, but that the work as actually done was either expressly sanctioned by the clerks of the works of the plaintiffs or done with their full cognizance, and that in other cases of such departure the defendant might have claimed an addition to the contract price, which on adjustment, after measuring the work, might have been set off against the cases in which defendant had been the gainer by other departures, and that no such adjustment had taken place. (2) That in the case of the wall gutters the contract had been departed from, but that, owing to the ambiguity of the specification, and drawings applicable to each work, there was no reason to impute any unfair intention either to defendant or his foremen in consequence of such departure. The referee, on inquiry, reports to me that he did not intend to report that in either of the above cases there was, in his judgment, any intentional departure from the contract either by defendant or his men, with a view to either his or their own interests.

1891
November
22.

Queen's
Bench
Division.

The answer to the fourth question put to the referee was as follows: "I beg to state that with the exception of the drainage I do not consider that it is necessary to replace or take up and restore any of the work, but I am of opinion that the defendant has saved by the above-named breaches the sum of 240*l.*, and to make good defects which have manifested themselves the sum of 175*l.* should be allowed." The answer of the referee to this question at first sight seems inconsistent with the last statement in relation to the answer to question (3), because it seems to be an answer which assumes a liability under one or other of the former answers; but he informs me that he did not intend by the use of the words "by the above-mentioned breaches" to adopt the words of the question, "so being guilty of the three previously-named breaches," so as to find that there had been any breaches amounting to fraud, or scamping, or wilful deviation with a view to defendant's own interest, but only to assess the damages for deviation and defects in case the defendant should be held liable, in spite of the admission that he was not guilty of any personal misconduct, of himself or by others for whom he was responsible, on the ground of such deviation having been established.

The last finding of the referee as to the time of discovery of defects becomes immaterial in the view I take of the whole case, but he has added two paragraphs to his report which are not in answer to any specific question. They are as follows: "I have not especially reported on many of the claims in the particulars which I have not considered proved, neither do I mention the amount of work which the defendant did over and above the contract, and for which he has not been paid, as I am of opinion that, as the defendant has not made any counter-claim, he is not entitled to any set-off.

"In conclusion, I would beg leave to remark that the defects that have manifested themselves in the buildings could not have existed without the contributory negligence of the School Board and its agents." In order to avoid misunderstanding, I may as well state that I think he was fully entitled to take into consideration, when deciding such questions as the first three submitted to him, the fact that there were cases in which the defendant had done work beyond the requirements of the contract and made no claim for it, only as bearing upon the question whether he was actuated by a desire to put money into his pocket beyond what he was fairly entitled to, though he was right in not considering the liability of the defendant (if he was liable at all) as being entitled to be diminished by the amount of extra expense incurred by him in respect of such work beyond the requirements of the contract, no counter-claim having been pleaded. The last paragraph of the report might have been omitted, but it was inserted in consequence of the importance naturally attributed to a fact which is amply proved by the evidence which I have read through—viz., that throughout the work there was so much laxity in the attendance and surveillance of the work by the Board's clerks of the works that the workmen of the defendant were not controlled from committing errors, the very object of appointing clerks of the works being to prevent errors and rectify them during the progress of the works. On the whole, I have no hesitation in giving judgment for the defendant with costs.

Solicitors for the plaintiffs: Messrs. Gedge, Kirby & Millett. Solicitor for the defendant: Mr. W. Eley.

In the High Court of Justice (Queen's Bench Division).

(Lord Coleridge, L.C.J., and Mathew, J.)

In the Court of Appeal.

(Lord Esher, M.R., and Fry, L.J.)

In the Matter of an Arbitration Between DE MORGAN, SNELL & Co., and THE RIO DE JANEIRO FLOUR MILLS AND GRANARIES, LTD. (*a*).

Building Contract—Resident Engineer—Independent Position— Effect of his Mistakes.

A resident engineer was appointed to superintend the execution in Brazil of a works contract:—Held, that he was not a mere servant or agent of the employers, but in an independent position, and that the employers were not liable for any damage or delay caused to the contractors by any honest error made by him in the exercise of his duties, without any interference on the part of the employers.

By an indenture dated the 13th day of December, 1886, and made between the Rio de Janeiro Flour Mills and Granaries, Ltd. (thereinafter called the company), and De Morgan, Snell & Co. (thereinafter called the contractor), the contractor agreed to construct and equip for the company the flour mills,

(*a*) Also reported 8 T. L. R. 108, 272.

1891 November 22.
Queen's Bench Division.

1891 November 30.
Queen's Bench Division.

1892 February 2.
Court of Appeal.

1891 November 30.
Queen's Bench Division.

1891
November
30.

Queen's
Bench
Division.

granaries and other works enumerated or referred to in a specification annexed to the contract.

The portions of the contract and specification material for the purposes of this report are the following:—

(1) The contractor will, at his own expense, within three months from the commencement of the works, provide and cause to be vested in the company, with a good title, free from all incumbrances, all such lands, buildings and rights as shall be required for the purposes of the works or in connection therewith, and shall also duly pay and satisfy all claims for damage done to buildings or lands, whether temporary or permanent, in the construction of the said works, and all other cases of compensation arising out of the same; and shall build and equip the works so that upon completion the same shall be capable of grinding nine tons of wheat per hour and producing 35 per cent. of the best quality flour and about $37\frac{1}{2}$ per cent. second quality flour, with offals and bran, and of landing and storing 60 tons of grain per hour, and so as in all respects to conform to the preliminary plans, elevations and designs deposited with the chief engineer of the company in the manner and with the materials, buildings, machinery, plant, equipment and other conveniences prescribed in the specification hereunto annexed so far as the same are therein prescribed. All the provisions, conditions and stipulations of the said specification (hereinafter called the specification) not including therein the schedule of prices annexed thereto are adopted and incorporated with this contract, and shall have the same force and effect as if they had been actual stipulations in the body of this contract, but if and whenever the terms of this contract and of the specification are inconsistent the terms of this contract shall prevail. The work to be done hereunder shall be done to the reasonable satisfaction and approval of the consulting engineer of the company (hereinafter called the chief engineer), to be duly certified by him when completed.

(3) The contractor shall, at his own expense, prepare or cause to be prepared all detailed drawings necessary for the construction of the mills, stores, sea wall, wharves, buildings and any other edifices, and also those required for machinery, plant, equipment, and other conveniences, and shall at least one month before commencing the work submit the same for approval to the chief engineer, or, with his consent, to the company's resident engineer; and if at the end of such one month the decision of the chief engineer (or resident engineer, as the case may be), approving or requiring modifications in such plans and other detailed drawings, have not been given and communicated to the contractor, the same shall as between the parties hereto be considered approved. The contractor shall commence the said works before the close of this present year, 1886, and shall continuously proceed with the execution of the works, and in so doing he agrees that he will supply materials and execute works pursuant to this contract at a rate which, in the opinion of the chief engineer, shall be sufficient to cause the due completion of the works before the 30th November, 1888, but in case the contractor is delayed by *vis major* or by reason of the loss of materials by shipwreck, or by failure of the company to perform on their part any of the covenants and conditions of this contract, the term for completing the works shall be prolonged for an equivalent period, to be fixed by the chief engineer of the company, but if the delay shall arise from the failure of the company as aforesaid, the contractor shall be entitled to compensation from the company for any damage he may have sustained thereby, the amount thereof to be settled by arbitration in the manner hereinafter specified,

1891
November
30.

Queen's
Bench
Division.

and the extension of the time (if any) in manner aforesaid shall not prejudice the said claim. If the said works shall not be completed as aforesaid, owing to the default of the contractor, within the time or extended time aforesaid, the contractor shall pay to the company the sum of 250*l.* for every month after the expiration of such time or extended time until the said works are complete, so as to be fit to be open for use, by way of liquidated damages for the non-completion as aforesaid, within the time aforesaid, but without prejudice to any further payments to be made by the contractor to the company for administration expenses or otherwise under any of the terms of these presents, or to any of the other remedies of the company hereunder, or to any claim the company may have for damage or compensation for the breach of any other clause of this contract; such liquidated damages applying only to a breach as to time.

(4) The contractor shall be paid by the company, as the contract price for the execution of the works, and for providing the necessary land and the buildings, machinery, materials and other things, and for all other acts and payments of the contractor required by the terms of this contract, the sum of 250,000*l.*, which as to 3,070*l.* shall be paid in cash, and as to 246,930*l.* shall, subject as hereinafter appears, be paid and satisfied by the allotment to the contractor, or his nominees, of shares in the capital of the company to that nominal amount, credited as fully paid up, and being the shares numbered from 308 to 25,000, both inclusive, and no extras or additions whatsoever shall be payable by the company.

(5) Subject as hereinafter appears, the whole of the said shares representing the contract price (except only a portion thereof amounting in nominal value to 10,000*l.* to form a retention fund) shall be issued to the contractor, or his nominees, upon production to the company of a certificate by the chief engineer that the works have been completed in accordance with the terms of these presents; and the said shares to the nominal value of 10,000*l.*, forming the retention fund, shall also be issued to the contractor or his nominees upon production to the company of a certificate by the chief engineer that the contractor has fulfilled the obligation respecting the maintenance of the works hereinafter undertaken by him.

(9) The contractor shall pay or allow by way of discount to the company, in respect of every cash payment made by them to him under the foregoing provisions, a percentage upon all sums so paid to him from time to time, as from the date of payment to the date when the works shall be handed over to the company, at such rate or rates as shall be equivalent to 6 per cent. per annum upon the amount for the time being credited as paid up upon the issued share capital of the company.

(11) In the event of the company being called upon to make payments in cash such payments shall, subject to all deductions for discount, or otherwise, be made as follows:—

(c) The said retention fund and the interest thereof shall be invested from time to time by the company at the request of the contractor in such securities as shall be agreed upon between them for the benefit and at the risk of the contractor, and shall, together with any interest thereon, be transferred or paid, as the case may be, to the contractor, one-half upon the final certificate of the chief engineer of completion of the works, and the remaining half at the expiration of the period during which the contractor shall be liable to maintain the works as hereinafter provided.

(12) For the purpose of regulating the payments to be made to the contractor on

1891
November
30.
———
Queen's
Bench
Division.

account of the said contract price the chief engineer shall give his certificates as follows, that is to say:—

(e) The chief engineer shall, on the completion of the works in accordance herewith, give his final certificate to that effect, which shall be a complete discharge to the contractor from all liabilities in respect of the matters herein agreed to be done by him except for the maintenance of the works as hereinafter provided.

(14) The contractor will provide or pay to the company the sum of 10,000*l.* in cash for its administration expenses during construction, including therein all engineering and other charges, and the same shall be paid by the contractor to the company as to one moiety thereof within thirty days, and as to the other moiety within ten months from the date of these presents. Provided always, that if from any cause whatever, other than default on the part of the company, the works shall not have been completed before the 30th November, 1888, the contractor shall pay in cash to the company for its administration expenses the further sums of 400*l.* for each calendar month or a proportionate part for each part of a calendar month until the said works shall be completed. The contractor will also provide or pay to the company, three months before the completion of the works, the sum of 27,500*l.* for working capital. The provisions of this article shall apply whether the contractor shall or shall not require payment of the contract price in cash as aforesaid.

(16) The contractor shall insure all such materials, machinery, plant and equipment to the full value thereof, and all shipments shall be made to the resident engineer on behalf, and as agent, of the company, or otherwise as the company from time to time direct, and in such time that the same may be transmitted to the port of unloading in time that the same may be received by the agent of the company and the unloading may be proceeded with without delay; and the company, on receipt of same, will forthwith and without delay, and by next mail, forward the same to Brazil for the above purpose.

(19) A resident engineer [herein called by that name] shall at all times during the continuance of this contract be employed at the works, and he shall be subordinate to the chief engineer, and it shall be his duty to measure up or cause to be measured up the works duly executed, and materials duly approved and delivered on the ground, and without delay to communicate, in manner hereinbefore mentioned, to the chief engineer to enable him to give certificates to the contractor as aforesaid, and should the resident engineer fail to measure up the work, the chief engineer may give a certificate on account upon the statement of the contractor, if satisfied therewith, and should the chief engineer fail to give any certificate claimed for fourteen days after being claimed, he shall, if the contractor shall have required payment of the contract price in cash as aforesaid, within seven days after being required by the contractor, give the contractor notice in writing of what he requires to be done to entitle the contractor to such certificate, and if the contractor do not comply therewith, or if he consider such requirements unnecessary, or if, the same having been satisfied, such certificate is still refused, the matter shall be referred to the arbitrator, and if the decision is against the contractor he shall conform thereto, and if in his favour the chief engineer shall, within three days after notice of such decision, give such certificate, or, in default thereof, such award shall be deemed equivalent to such certificate.

(23) The contractor shall give delivery of the works, and the company shall take over the same upon completion as aforesaid; and upon the satisfaction and handing

to the contractor of any amount due to him, except such retention fund as herein mentioned, and contemporaneously with such delivery and taking over, the contractor shall procure and place at the disposal of the company, for employment by the company in the mill and stores, an efficient staff capable of working the same so as to attain the result stipulated by article 1 of these presents; and the contractor shall, during the period of maintenance next hereinafter mentioned, be entitled to select and nominate persons to fill casual vacancies in such working staff. And provided that the company employ such working staff as may from time to time, as hereinbefore mentioned, be selected and nominated or otherwise approved by the contractor, the contractor shall, until and for a period of six months after the whole of the said works shall have been handed over to the company, maintain the same in good and sufficient repair at his own expense, ordinary wear and tear by working the same and damage by fire only excepted. Upon the due completion of the maintenance of the works the chief engineer shall certify the same.

(25) Mr. Charles Neate, of 4, Victoria Street, Westminster, shall be the first chief engineer of the company, and, in the event of his death, resignation, or removal, from the position of the chief engineer of the company, his successor shall be appointed by consent between the company and the contractor, or, failing agreement, shall be nominated by the President, for the time being, of the Institute of Civil Engineers.

(26) If at any time, or times, the works, or any part thereof, are not, in the judgment of the chief engineer, or resident engineer, executed in a workmanlike manner, and with due diligence in conformity with this contract, and at such rate as herein mentioned, the same shall be intimated in writing to the contractor by the resident engineer, and, if for one month after such intimation the contractor shall neglect to alter and duly execute the same, or if the contractor shall after one calendar month's notice from the said resident engineer continue unduly to delay the works, or if the contractor shall be declared bankrupt, or compound with his creditors, or have his affairs liquidated by arrangement, the chief engineer of the company, or his delegate, may take the works out of the hands of the contractor and take possession of all plant, materials, stores, and articles of all kinds upon the works, and may use the same, and the company may proceed to complete the works in such manner by the employment of other contractors or otherwise, as they may think proper, and at the expense of the contractor, and the company shall be entitled to recover from the contractor any expense that they may incur in so completing the works over and above the contract price, and to retain and to apply in and towards the satisfaction thereof any capital or moneys, which the contractor may be entitled to for work previously completed by the contractor, and may also sell and apply for the same purpose the proceeds of all plant, stores, materials, or other articles.

(30) Every difference or dispute between the company and the contractor as to the meaning or effect of the present contract, including in that term the specification and schedule hereunto annexed, or in any way arising out of this contract, or relating thereto from time to time as it arises, including therein any act or decision of the chief engineer, shall be referred to arbitration; and every arbitration under this contract shall, unless a sole arbitrator shall be agreed upon, be determined by the award of two arbitrators, one to be named by the company and the other by the contractor, and, in case they, do not agree, by an umpire named by the two arbitrators, or, failing agreement, by the President of the Institute of Civil

1891
November
30.

Queen's
Bench
Division.

1891
November
30.

Queen's
Bench
Division.

Engineers in London, who shall give the final decision. Every such arbitration, unless otherwise agreed, shall be held in London.

By clause 1 of specification—

The term "engineer" in the specification shall mean the chief engineer, and the term " resident engineer" shall signify any person appointed by the engineer to superintend the execution of the work in Brazil.

By clause 19 of the specification it was provided that—

If at any time during the progress of the work the engineer or resident engineer shall disapprove of any of the materials employed, the contractor shall be bound forthwith to remove such objectionable materials from the works, and to substitute for them others of an approved quality, and in case any portion of the work executed shall, in the judgment of the engineer or resident engineer, be considered imperfect, defective or not in accordance with the terms of the contract, such portion shall forthwith be removed, and the work re-executed in an approved manner.

Under clause 19 of the contract a resident engineer was appointed by the chief engineer to superintend the execution of the work in Brazil.

By a supplemental indenture dated the 17th day of May, 1888, and made between the same parties, the contractor agreed to execute certain other works in substitution for a part of those specified in the original contract.

The supplemental indenture incorporated by reference the arbitration clause (30) in the original contract.

The only other parts of the supplemental indenture material for this report are clauses 9, 10, 11:—

(9) The company shall be at liberty, if they so desire, before completion of the works to enter upon and take possession of such part thereof as may be fit for occupation, and use and work the same at their own expense, and in such case the company shall pay over to the contractor the net profit, if any, derived from such working up to the 30th November, 1888, or up to the date when the whole of the works shall be completed, whichever shall first happen. In ascertaining such net profit, the additional premium payable in respect of the insurance of such portion of the said work as may be put into use under the provisions of this clause, together with all revenue charges incurred by the company, are to be included in working expenses, excepting only directors' fees, London office rent, secretary's salary, passages of employees and wages until arrived at Rio de Janeiro, the amount of such net profit to be certified by the company's auditor.

(10) In the event of the works not being finally completed by the 30th November, 1883, and the company continuing to occupy and work the premises after that date, the net profits shall be retained by the company for its own use.

(11) Nothing herein contained shall prejudice or release the contractor's obligations under the principal indenture in respect of final completion and guarantee of the works and payment of interest until completion. Provided, however, that should any loss by fire during the intermediate possession or use of the said works

by the company, as provided by clause 9 hereof, occasion rebuilding or reconstruction of any portion of such works, the contractor shall not be liable to pay interest during the time of such rebuilding or reconstruction.

1891
November
30.
___
Queen's
Bench
Division.

In consequence of the disapproval by the resident engineer of part of the materials supplied by the contractor, disputes arose between contractor and company, which were submitted to the arbitration of Edward Woods, Esq., by an agreement dated the 7th day of January, 1890.

In the arbitration the contractor claimed—

(1) Transfer of the securities on which the retention fund was invested or of their market value at the date of the award, and the difference, if any, between the market value at that date and 1st June, 1889, and damages for detention of the securities after that date.

(2) 34,080*l.*; made up of—

(a) Unpaid balance of contract price.

(b) Charges for extras.

(c) Damages for delay caused by the engineer and for wrongful refusal by him to give his certificate.

The company counter-claimed—

(1) For work not executed.

(2) For work executed and paid for as an extra subject to the question whether it was not part of the contract.

(3) Damages for imperfect execution and failure to maintain under cl. 23.

(4) Damages for non-completion.

(5) Administration expenses under cl. 14.

(6) Discount under cl. 9.

The award was made on the 17th day of March, 1891. The material portions are as follows:—

(1) "I find that the works were completed and handed over to the company within the meaning of clauses 3, 14 and 19 of the contract upon the 30th day of June, 1889.

(2) "I award and find that the chief engineer should have given his final certificate that the works were completed upon the said 30th day of June, 1889.

(3) "I award and find that no extension of the time for the completion of the said works was applied for by or granted to the contractor.

(4) "I award and find that the delay in the completion of the works, though partly due to default of the contractor, was to a very material extent caused by wrongful and unreasonable interference during the construction of the works by the company's resident engineer.

(5) "I award and find that the company's resident engineer, apart from the special powers conferred upon him by the contract, was, by virtue of his appointment as the company's resident engineer (according to the invariable practice in the execution of contracts of this description) invested with general authority from the company to interfere with the execution of the works as and when he did.

(6) "I award and find that, of the total delay in the execution of the works, which amounted in all to seven calendar months, five months of such delay was caused by the wrongful interference of the company's resident engineer aforesaid, and two months by the default of the contractor, and that, but for the wrongful interference aforesaid, the contractor would have completed and handed over the

works to the company within the meaning of clauses 3, 14 and 19 of the contract aforesaid by the 31st day of January, 1889."

A motion was made to set aside the award. The award was referred back to the arbitrator for amendment by an order of the Q. B. D., dated 27th June, 1891, and the facts were so stated by the arbitrator as to raise the questions of law dealt with in the judgments.

On November 23, 1891, the motion came before the Court on the award as amended.

Sir R. Webster, A.-G., Bompas and Gore, for the company, contended that the company were not liable to the contractor for any damages sustained by him through any act or default of the chief engineer or resident engineer.

They cited *Stevenson* v. *Watson (a); Roberts* v. *Bury Commissioners (b).*

Littler, Q.C., and R. M. Bray, for the contractor, contended that the resident engineer was a mere clerk of the works and agent of the company, and had no power to stop the works as he had done, and that the company were responsible for delay caused by his unreasonable acts.

They cited *Stadhard* v. *Lee (c).*

The judgment of the Court was delivered by Mathew, J.

Mathew, J.: In this case, by an order of the Court, and by agreement between the parties, the evidence was stated by the arbitrator on the face of his award to enable us to deal with points of law which arose in course of the arbitration. The arbitration was held under a contract entered into between the Rio Janeiro Flour Mills Company and Mr. Snell, a contractor, on the 13th December, 1886.

The contract in many respects is in the ordinary form. The object was to erect at Rio Janeiro mills and granaries in which the company proposed to carry on the business of millers. The contractor was to receive for the work, when executed, a lump sum of 250,000*l.* From time to time he was to be paid by instalments upon the certificate of the chief engineer named in the contract, and upon the final completion of the works, and when they were handed over to the company, the contractor was to receive the balance of the money due to him. There was a further provision that there should be what was called a retention fund, that is, that a certain portion of the instalments should be kept back in order to secure the due execution of the works contracted to be done; and it was provided that the retention money, which was the amount of 20,000*l.*, should be invested in securities, to be selected by the contractor, and to be

(*a*) 4 C. P. D. 148.
(*b*) L. R. 5 C. P. 310.
(*c*) 3 B. & S. 364; 32 L. J. Q. B. 75.

1891
November 30.

Queen's
Bench
Division.

retained by the company until the final certificate of the chief engineer. There were also clauses, to which we must refer subsequently, directing the appointment of a resident engineer. The chief engineer was to remain in this country, and there was to be a resident engineer on the spot under whose supervision and superintendence the works were to be carried on. In one respect the contract differed from those with which we are familiar in similar cases, because it was provided that the certificates of the chief engineer should not be conclusive between the parties, but that if any disputes arose between them the same might be submitted to an independent arbitrator.

That was the outline of the contract entered into between the plaintiffs and the defendants. It was provided that the works were to be completed by the 30th November, 1888. What happened was this: plans in accordance with the terms of the contract were approved of by the chief engineer and resident engineer, and the works were commenced, and in the course of the works the resident engineer objected, in accordance with the powers which he conceived were conferred upon him by the contract, to certain materials proposed to be used, and to certain of the structures that were proposed to be erected. Upon those objections being made by the resident engineer, the works were suspended by the contractor, the difficulties that had arisen were referred to the chief engineer in this country, and he overruled the decision of the resident engineer.

After a considerable interval of time, an interval of five months according to the finding of the arbitrator, during which the works were suspended, the works were resumed, and that which the resident engineer had objected to was permitted to be done by the contractor. In consequence of this delay a claim was made by the contractor against the company, and when differences and disputes arose between the parties, and before the final certificate of the chief engineer was given, according to the terms of the contract, and after the works had been completed and handed over to the company, it was arranged that all those disputes should be submitted to arbitration, and it was upon the award in the course of that arbitration that the present questions of law have been argued.

Now the chief claim made by the contractor in respect of the delay is in consequence of the interference of the resident engineer, and it was argued before the arbitrator, and subsequently before us, that the company was responsible for the interference of the resident engineer. It was said that he was the agent of the company, and had interfered as the agent of the company, and that his acts were

1891
November 30.
───────
Queen's
Bench
Division.

the acts of the company, and inasmuch as it was argued that it was an implied condition of the contract that the contractor should not be prevented from carrying out the works, it was said that there had been a breach of that implied contract by the company, and that the contractor was entitled to damages. On the other hand it was argued for the company that the resident engineer was not in any sense their agent, that in making the objection that he did make he had acted in good faith, though he had been mistaken, and had made the difficulties which have arisen in discharge of what he considered to be, though it turned out erroneously, his duties as resident engineer, and that the company was no more responsible for the mistakes made by him than they would have been for mistakes made by the chief engineer.

Now it follows from that that the question discussed before the arbitrator, and discussed before us, as to what the functions of the resident engineer really were, depends upon the terms of the contract of December, 1886, and I propose, therefore, to refer to the leading provisions of the contract upon this subject.

[The provisions with reference to the functions of a resident engineer are contained in clauses 3, 12, 19, 25 and 26 of the contract, and clauses 1 and 19 of the specification. He read them and proceeded.]

Now, what was the law properly applicable to the case? It was not controverted seriously that if the mistake in question—what the arbitrator has found to be a mistake, and what he has found to be a mistake made in good faith, because it is not suggested that the resident engineer had acted in any way fraudulently or collusively—if such a mistake had been made by the chief engineer it was not, as I say, contended that the company would be, in any way, responsible for his default. The learned Attorney-General, in arguing the case for the company, referred to a series of authorities on the subject which were not questioned on the other side.

It appears abundantly from the case of *Clarke* v. *Watson* (a), where, as in this contract, it was provided that the certificate of an architect or an engineer shall be a condition of the liability of the company, the absence of the certificate will prevent the contractor from recovering, even though it should appear that the conduct of the chief engineer or architect had not been reasonable. So long as the company does not interfere; and so long as the architect or engineer, in a case of this sort, discharges his duty impartially with-

(a) 18 C. B. N. S. 278.

1891
November 30.

Queen's
Bench
Division.

out interference by either side, the conclusions to which he comes are binding upon the parties. His duties are quasi-judicial, and in the discharge of them neither party incur any liability for his default or mistakes.

Then comes the case of *Roberts* v. *The Bury Improvement Commissioners* (a). It was pointed out very clearly in what case one of the contracting parties will be made responsible, and that was where there had been an undue interference on the part of the person whose conduct was called in question, with the discharge of the duties of the architect or engineer, as the case might be. The implied undertaking is from each contracting party that he shall not interfere unduly or unfairly with the discharge of his quasi-judicial duties by the engineer, and as long as that course is adhered to there is no responsibility on either contracting party for the mistakes that may be made—honestly made in good faith—by the chief engineer. Again, in the case of *Stevenson* v. *Watson* (b), it was laid down that as long as the architect or engineer, in such a case as the present, discharged his duties without suspicion of fraud or bad faith, he could not be made responsible for errors of judgment committed by him in his work of superintendence.

So much for the position of the chief engineer. Do all those considerations and those principles apply to the case of the resident engineer under this contract? In my judgment they do. I think the resident engineer was placed here, under the sections to which I have referred, in the position of chief engineer. The chief engineer was in this country; the resident engineer was abroad. If the chief engineer had power in this country to see that the contractor completed his contract, the resident engineer, his subordinate, discharged the same duties abroad, and it seems to me the same principles of law apply to him as apply to the case of the chief engineer. But it was contended for the contractor that the resident engineer here was really not discharging any such duties as were imposed upon the chief engineer by the contract; that he was, in fact, the agent of the company, and that there he did interfere (this was a very subtle view of the matter put forward by Mr. Bray); he was not acting in his capacity as resident engineer, but as agent for the company, and therefore that the company was responsible for what he had done. I can only say, with reference to that, there is not a shadow of evidence that the company interfered in any way with the resident

(a) L. R. 4 C. P. 755; and on appeal in L. R. 5 C. P. 310.
(b) 4 C. P. D. 148.

1891
November
30.

Queen's
Bench
Division.

engineer; he acted upon his own responsibility and upon his own judgment of what was right. No doubt the company here was informed of what was being done, as the chief engineer was being informed of what was being done, but that afforded no evidence of any kind whatever of acts professed to be done on behalf of the company abroad, and they are not, it seems to me, responsible in any way for his acts as being their agent. The learned counsel for the contractor was so hard pushed that he had to refer to one clause of the contract which, he said, afforded evidence that this resident engineer was for all purposes the agent of the company, and that is clause 16. [The learned judge read the clause and proceeded.] That was the clause referred to to establish the agency for all purposes of the resident engineer. It is manifest that it has no such operation, and it is strictly confined by the terms to the consignments that were to be made on the application of the company abroad. It is necessary they should have some agent to receive the materials that were to be their property. If that is right, this clause is merely introduced to render the resident engineer their agent for that purpose, and not in any way to control the other operations of the company.

It appears to me that with reference to the claim, which was to a very large amount, 6,600*l.*, the contractor has no claim against the company, and the award of the arbitrator, who came to the conclusion that the company was liable, must be altered in that particular. The resident engineer was selected by the chief engineer because of his presumed skill and ability, and the company had no more independent voice in his selection than the contractor. Neither, under the circumstances, is responsible for the questions that might arise either way between the contractor and the company; neither is responsible for the defaults and mistakes that were made by the resident engineer in the course of his superintendence of the works. So much for the first point and the chief point in controversy between the parties—the largest in amount.

The next question that was raised is upon a claim advanced by the contractor for loss on the value of the securities in which the fund to which I have referred had been invested. It appears that the securities selected by the contractor were Argentine securities. Now the works were completed and handed over to the company in June, 1889. As I have said, the chief engineer did not think fit at that time to give his final certificate, and the securities were not handed over, and the securities remained in the possession of the company until the award made by the arbitrator in March, 1891. The arbitrator so decided, and his decision in that respect is not disputed, the works were handed over in June, 1889, and at that time the contractor was entitled to the final certificate of the chief engineer. The security remaining in the possession of the company, under the circumstances I have mentioned, there was a fall in the value of Argentine securities before the time came for handing them over to the contractor, and for that fall he sought to make the company responsible. The question is whether, under the terms of the contract, that claim can be maintained. Now the clause in the contract with reference to this subject, and with reference to the retention fund, is clause 11, subsect. C. [He read the clause and proceeded.] Now it was agreed that no final certificate had been given by the chief engineer. It turned out by the award of the arbitrator that he was wrong in withholding his certificate. The authorities to which I have referred establish, it appears to me, conclusively, that the company is not responsible in any way for that mistake made by the chief engineer, and it follows that in the terms of this submission this loss in the value of the securities cannot be cast upon the company.

Those are the two chief points discussed on behalf of the contractor. The rest of the argument referred to claims made by the company against him, with which I must now deal. The first of those was a claim by the company for a sum of 400*l.*, a month under clause 14 of the contract. [He read the clause.] There again the terms of the contract are perfectly clear, and, although I struggled, I confess, against the construction sought to be put upon them by the company, it seems to me, by the words of the contract, that it cannot be overcome. Therefore that 400*l.*, a month administration expenses must be paid up to the time when the works were handed over to the company.

The next claim is a claim that arose under clause 9 in the contract, with reference to 6 per cent. which the contractor bound himself to pay. To explain the clause, it appeared that, as was shown, it had been arranged between the company and the shareholders that 6 per cent. should be paid on the amount of their subscriptions up to the time when the works were commenced, and under those clauses, where cash was paid to the contractor, it appeared to have been intended that the responsibility should be put upon him. [He read the clause.] The arbitrator, by his award, limited the time for which that 6 per cent. was to be paid by the contractor, and I am clearly of opinion that he was wrong in imposing that limitation, and on the terms of the section it once more followed that up to the date when the works should be handed over to the company, that was July, 1889, this 6 per cent. was debited on this provision against the contractor,

Mr. Bray, who discussed the case very admirably for the con-

1891
November
30.

Queen's
Bench
Division.

1891
November
30.

Queen's
Bench
Division.

tractor, raised a point about this with reference to a further arrangement that had been entered into between the company and the contractor, and he said that clause contemplated the whole of the works remaining out of the possession of the company up to the time when they were handed over, but that under a supplemental contract it had been arranged that parts of the works might be taken possession of by the company, and therefore, he said, that clause was displaced and could no longer be decisive of the rights of the parties. That compelled us to have recourse to this supplemental contract which Mr. Bray says provided that the company should be at liberty to take possession of parts of the works. The contract is dated 17th May, 1888. Clause 11 of the supplemental contract provides: [He read the clause.] If the contract had stopped there, there would have been a good deal in the argument of Mr. Bray; but there follows a clause which decides the question against him in the plainest and clearest terms. The parties appear to have had in mind the very point Mr. Bray raises, namely, what was to occur with reference to this contract for the payment of the 6 per cent.; and by clause 11 it is expressly provided: "Nothing herein contained shall prejudice or release the contractor's obligations under the principal indenture in respect of final completion and guarantee of work, and payment of interest until completion"—terms perfectly clear and perfectly decisive of the question between the parties. That, it seems to me, disposes of all the questions raised between the parties. We have come to the conclusion that our judgment on the different points raised must be in favour of the company against the contractor. My Lord agrees with me in the conclusion to which I have come. For the terms in which the judgment is expressed I alone am responsible.

Lord COLERIDGE, L.C.J., concurred.

Award referred back to the arbitrator.

The contractors appealed.
Littler, Q.C., Rigby, Q.C., R. M. Bray and Macklin, for the contractors, argued as before, and also that the resident engineer had not acted honestly.
Sir R. Webster, A.-G., Bompas, Q.C., and Gore for the company.

Lord ESHER, M.R.: In this case there is a good substantial business dispute between the parties with regard to a large matter, and the Divisional Court has come to a decision upon every matter of law really in dispute, which cannot be challenged upon any one substantial point.

The dispute carried before the arbitrator was upon the contract and

1892
February 2.

Court of
Appeal.

upon its application to the facts, and it is clear that the award was made upon and involved the construction of the contract.

The first contested proposition was the main one with reference to the disapproval of materials by the resident engineer. Under clause 19 of the specification the resident engineer must inform the contractor if he disapproves of materials; and the contractor is bound forthwith, *i.e.*, immediately in ordinary business meaning, to remove the objectionable materials and bring other materials of which the resident engineer will approve. And where any part of the work, *in the judgment* of the engineer, is defective, the contractor must re-execute it in an approved manner.

It was argued that the resident engineer was a judge or arbitrator, and as such had misconducted himself in some way. He is not a judge, but simply a man put there to approve or disapprove, and has no judicial functions. He was not bound to hear the parties and then decide, but was there simply to look at the things and state whether he approved of them or not. And the contractor has contracted that if the resident engineer disapproves he will substitute approved materials and work for that disapproved of.

[He then discussed the finding of the arbitrator as to the acts of the resident engineer, and held that the finding that he had wrongfully disapproved simply meant "wrongly," and that there was no evidence or finding of any fraud on the part of the resident engineer; and continued.]

There being no fraud, it was the duty of the arbitrator to construe clause 19 and apply its legal construction to the facts. He found that the objection of the resident engineer to the work and materials was unreasonable and wrong, but inasmuch as the objection was honest, the contractor was bound to give effect to it or refer the matter to the chief engineer, and for the wrongful act of the resident engineer the company were, as pointed out by Mathew, J., not liable unless they interfered with him, of which there is not a tittle of evidence.

The next thing was this claim in respect of these securities. This is not one of the points upon which the parties thought more facts were wanted; that was a point which had been raised between them, but they did not want any more facts, the facts being before the arbitrator as clearly as possible. There again these securities were given upon a clause in the contract which has two specific dates in it, one referring to the date when they were to be given, the other to how long they were to be kept and when they were to be given up. Those were specified. They were not to be given up until the works

1892
February 2.

Court of
Appeal.

were handed over, and that fact was established on the certificate of the chief engineer. The date on which it was given was before the arbitrator. The date when the works were handed over was also before the arbitrator. It is obvious to my mind, on the face of his award, that he was applying the contract to those facts, but there he came to a view of the matter which is again contrary to the law. He came to a view that the chief engineer, although he had not given his certificate and did not give it at all, ought to have given it sooner, on a specified date, and it is obvious to my mind, on the face of the award, taking the date he mentions as the date on which the works were handed over, and finding that no certificate had been given, he says a certificate ought to be given at a particular time, and he puts it that at that time the company ought to have handed these things back to the contractors; that they went down in price after that, and therefore they must pay the difference. There again he was wrong in law, and obviously wrong in law. The company were not liable for the chief engineer withholding his certificate; they cannot be sued because he withheld his certificate; and he cannot be sued because he withheld his certificate; but these securities were not to be handed back until he gave his certificate. Neither party is liable for their not being handed back, for by the contract the time for handing these things back had not come. The arbitrator had decided this clearly and obviously upon an application of the contract and of the law of the contract to the facts of the case before him, and he was wrong in law, therefore again Mr. Justice Mathew is perfectly right.

Then when you come to the other matters, they really all depend on this view of the arbitrator, and a natural one for him to take, that the chief engineer ought to have given his certificate at a particular time; he never gave it at all, therefore I shall treat all these questions, on each part of the contract which refers to the certificate, as if the things ought to be done at the time when he ought to have given his certificate, although he did not give one at all. They all depend on that.

I think the law is that if people contract to pay only upon the certificate of another person, or to do anything only upon the certificate of another person, over whom they have no control with, respect to those matters, if that person does not do the things, the condition on which the others have to do something has not arisen, and they are not bound to do it. It used to be ordinary in building contracts that the building owner was not bound to pay the architect or the builder until he got a certificate from the architect, and then if

1892
February 2.

Court of
Appeal.

the architect wrongfully and wrongly refused to give his certificate, then the contractors, the builders, used immediately to sue the building owner for the payment of the money; but it was over and over again held in the Courts, you cannot sue the building owner for the money, although he has got the house, because he was not to pay until the architect gave his certificate. The architect has not given a certificate, therefore he is not bound to pay you. The builders then sued the architects, but unless the architect had done what he did fraudulently, they could not sue the architect either, for not giving the certificate. That law is very old law, and it was applicable to this case. The company were not liable to do any of these things which the arbitrator held they were bound to do; they were not bound to do them unless or until the certificate was given, therefore the contractors could not rely on the certificate not being given. There are claims made by them, therefore, on matters which clearly, according to law, had not arisen. All this was properly before the Queen's Bench, and the judgment is as clear and as plain a judgment as ever was read to the Court. I agree with every word of it, and all the reasons that are given in it, and I think that this appeal must be dismissed with costs.

FRY, L.J.: The main question in controversy in this case turns on the position and acts of the resident engineer under this contract. Now it appears to me that that is a question to be determined by reference to the contract itself; and that with regard to his disapproval of materials and to his requiring the removal of works which he judges to be imperfect, his duties are defined by the 19th section of the specification, which is itself made part of the contract. Now I can entertain no doubt at all that the true view of the position of the resident engineer was that which is expressed by the Divisional Court. I am clear that the resident engineer is not the servant of the company; that he stands in a position quite distinct from and different from that of a servant; that he is a person who has been selected by the chief engineer, and the chief engineer himself has been selected by the contracting parties, and in the event of any vacancy in the chief engineer's office it is to be filled up by consent, or by an independent appointment, and in the event of any vacancy in the resident engineer's appointment that is to be filled up by the chief engineer. So that the appointment of the resident engineer is not the appointment of the company, and he is not in any sense a servant of the company. He stands in a position of much greater independence. He is a person who owes duties alike to the company and to the contractor; he is a person who is bound to be independent alike of the one and the other; he is a person who is bound to act

1892
February 2.
_____
Court of
Appeal.

impartially between the two contracting parties; therefore there is an entire misapprehension of the true view of the position of the resident engineer in the view which was taken by the arbitrator.

The second point which was raised was this: it was a point upon the depreciation of the securities in which the retention fund was to be invested. Now the case raised by Mr. Rigby was that that point was not dealt with by the points of law tendered by the company, and therefore, he said, there were no findings of fact upon it by the arbitrator, and therefore, he said, it was not open to the Court to attempt to affect to deal with it.

The award contains a reference of course to the contract, and it contains also, as I have already observed, a reference to the contract for the purpose to be determined by the Court. The Court is required to look at the contract and specification and see how far they affect the powers of the resident engineer, therefore the award itself refers the Court to the contract and specification. The award sets out the claim made by the contractor. The first claim set out is in respect of this investment of the retention fund, and then the arbitrator finds this, that the chief engineer should have given his final certificate that the works were completed on the 30th day of June, 1889. Then he goes on to find that the company are responsible for the delay between that date and the date of the actual transfer of the security. Now that appears to me to be a finding of default on the part of the chief engineer in the performance of his duty. That is inconsistent with the idea that the real finding was one that the company were tampering with the engineer. It finds he might have done his duty but he did not do his duty. It is obvious, therefore, I think, that the award proceeds on this line of reasoning: the chief engineer ought to have given his certificate on a particular day; his not having done so is a thing for which the company are responsible; his not having done so led to delay in the transfer of the securities; therefore the company are responsible for the delay of the transfer of those securities. That, I think, is the fair inference from the face of the award. That is an inference erroneous in point of law. It proceeds from a misconception of the position of the engineer, analogous to the misconception that the arbitrator entertained with regard to the position of the resident engineer. He has not perceived the position which the chief engineer, as well as the resident engineer, may maintain. He is, in fact, not a servant of the company, but a person who has to do his duty between the two contracting parties. I think, therefore, the error does sufficiently appear on the face of the award, and that the objection, therefore, cannot prevail.

Appeal dismissed.

Solicitor for Morgan, Snell & Co.: T. Romer. Solicitors for the Rio Janeiro Mills Co.: Bompas, Bischoff, Dodgson & Co.

1892
February 2.

Court of
Appeal.

𝕳𝖎𝖌𝖍 𝕮𝖔𝖚𝖗𝖙 𝖔𝖋 𝕵𝖚𝖘𝖙𝖎𝖈𝖊 (𝕼𝖚𝖊𝖊𝖓'𝖘 𝕭𝖊𝖓𝖈𝖍 𝕯𝖎𝖇𝖎𝖘𝖎𝖔𝖓).

(MATHEW and SMITH, JJ.)

NUTTALL

v.

MAYOR AND CORPORATION OF MANCHESTER (*a*).

1892
April 27.

Queen's
Bench
Division.

Arbitration Clause—Engineering Contract—Arbitration Act, 1889—Motion to Stay Action—Alleged Bias of Engineer.

It is a good ground for refusing to stay an action under sect. 4 of the Arbitration Act, 1889, to show that the person named in the submission as arbitrator has, by reason of his relations to the parties or the nature of the issues involved in the litigation, a possible bias against or in favour of either party.

This was a summons taken out by the defendants under sect. 4 of the Arbitration Act, 1889, to stay an action commenced by the plaintiff to recover 71,472*l.*, alleged to be the balance due under two contracts to construct certain sewers for the defendant Corporation and for extras. The contract contained clauses referring all disputes to the City Surveyor, who was put in charge of the work. The summons was referred by the Judge at Chambers to the Divisional Court.

Moulton, Q.C., and Pankhurst, for the defendants, argued that the matters in dispute must necessarily go to arbitration, and that the City Surveyor, as the person named in the contract, was the proper arbitrator. They cited *Willesford* v. *Watson (b)*, *Hodgson* v. *Railway Passengers Accident Insurance Co. (c)*, *Adams* v. *Great North of Scotland Rail. Co. (d)*, and *Scott* v. *Carluke Local Board (e)*.

Gully, Q.C., and Yates, for the plaintiff, contended that the City Surveyor might have an interest or bias, as he might have to decide on his own negligent mistakes or want of skill in designing and supervising the work. They cited

---

(*a*) This case is reported shortly in 8 T. L. R. 513. As it has been discussed, and to some extent doubted, in the Court of Appeal in *Eckersley* v. *Mersey Docks and Harbour Board* (L. R. [1894] 2 Q. B. 667), it has been thought desirable to report it more fully, so that its exact effect may be more clearly appreciated.

(*b*) L. R. 8 Ch. App. 473.

(*c*) 9 Q. B. D. 118.

(*d*) L. R. [1891] App. Cas. 31.

(*e*) 6 Rettie (Sc.) 616.

1892
April 27.

Queen's
Bench
Division.

Lyon v. *Johnson (f)*, *Hughes* v. *Lancaster Mayor, &c. (g)*, and *Pickthall* v. *Merthyr Tydfil Local Board (h)*.

MATHEW, J.: This is a motion made under sect. 4 of the Arbitration Act, 1889, to stay proceedings in an action, on the ground of there being a submission to arbitration of the matters in dispute, and that there is no sufficient reason why the matters should not be referred in accordance with the submission.

The contract under which the disputes have arisen was a contract of an ordinary character between the plaintiff, the contractor, and the Corporation of Manchester, and no doubt the object of the contract appeared to be to place the contractor, in the case of any difference between him and the Corporation, under the jurisdiction of the City Surveyor. The City Surveyor had the ordinary power of supervising the execution of the work, and, in the event of any difference with reference to the execution of the work, clause 37 of the specifications provided that he, the City Surveyor, should determine the question between the parties.

There was a very large sum of money involved in the contract—some 80,000*l.* The contractor says he is entitled to the payment of nearly as much more in respect of the work that has been done, and an action has been brought by him against the Corporation to recover the amount. Upon that an application was made on the part of the Corporation to enforce this clause 37 of the specification, and to compel the contractor to submit to the Surveyor the question in dispute arising between him and the Corporation. In dealing with this matter it must be borne in mind that it is impossible for the Court to undertake the trial of the cause. We must deal with the case as it is put by the plaintiff, and give effect at the same time to the answer offered to the *primâ facie* case made by the plaintiff.

The plaintiff's main contention before us was that there was a previous mistake made by the City Surveyor, and our attention has been particularly called to one point where he says the City Surveyor is clearly wrong. It appears that in the construction of the sewer it had been necessary to use large quantities of timber. The contract provided that the contractor should only be paid for such timber as the City Surveyor authorised to be left. At a critical part of the work timber had been largely used, and the contractor proposed to leave the timber; he pointed out very clearly what the conse-

(f) 40 Ch. D. 579.
(g) Annual Practice (1892), 164.
(h) 2 T. L. R. 803.

1892
April 27.

Queen's
Bench
Division.

quence of removing the timber would be, but he was overruled by the City Surveyor, who ordered that the timber should be removed. In defence, evidence had been offered to show that the City Surveyor was right, and the Corporation sticks to that view of the matter, the view taken by the City Surveyor. It is agreed, however, that if there were any such mistake—I say it is agreed, but it must be conceded on the part of the Corporation that if any such mistake had been made it would have been a proper subject of a reference under the clause in the contract.

The question for us is whether we ought to apply that clause under such circumstances, and with reference to what dispute. Now, what is the position of the City Surveyor? If the plaintiff be right, he has made a great mistake. He has involved the contractor in a serious expense; he has caused by his decision extensive damage for which the contractor or the Corporation may be liable; therefore he would have the strongest possible motive to defend his judgment. He would be at once the chief witness for himself, and judge of his own cause; and without for a moment imputing to a highly respectable man that he would be guilty of improper conduct or dishonest conduct, it seems to me that we are bound, having regard to the decisions upon the subject, to treat him as not a proper person to refer that question to. We have no reason to hope that he will approach the question without being grievously fettered and grievously embarrassed by the fact that he has already decided, and that his professional character is involved in upholding the decision.

Other matters have been referred to. There is too much mystery about the case to deal with the other points to which our attention has been called. Speaking for myself, I do not consider myself sufficiently informed of the facts to be able to pronounce a decision upon them. I agree with what I understood to be the contention of Mr. Moulton with reference to the two other points that were referred to—that the matter had been decided by the arbitrator, and, therefore, there was nothing to refer. But that is not what my decision proceeds upon. My decision proceeds upon the fact that the arbitrator has the strongest interest in upholding a decision, to which he has already come, about the matter which ought, according to the contention of the defendants, to be submitted to arbitration under clause 37 of the specification.

SMITH, J.: This is an action brought by Mr. Nuttall, who is a contractor, against the Corporation of Manchester, for what he says he is entitled to receive from them for constructing a sewer or sewers in that city. He brings this action for a large sum of money.

1892
April 27.

Queen's
Bench
Division.

There is a lump sum in the contract somewhere about 80,000*l.*, and he brings his action for another large sum of money over and above that. My brother says it is nearly double. It is nearly double what the original contract was—not quite so much as double, but, at any rate, it is very considerably above.

The plaintiff issued his writ. The Corporation took out a summons under sect. 4 of the Arbitration Act, 1889, to stay the action, on the ground that the contract between the plaintiff and the Corporation contains an arbitration clause in the fullest terms, and that, therefore, this action should not be allowed to proceed but should be stayed, and that consequently the plaintiff, the contractor, should be driven to refer this matter to the arbitrator named in the contract, namely the City Surveyor.

I wish to say, emphatically, that in the observations I am now making I do not in any shape or way impugn the honesty, or the integrity, or the business capacity, of the City Surveyor, because that is not an issue which I have to decide to-day. The question is, it seems to me—of course I am only speaking for myself—whether or not under the Act of Parliament, under the provisions of which this summons to stay is taken out, there is sufficient reason for having this matter referred to the City Surveyor. It seems to me that under this statute I ought not to make the order and say that it should be referred, or rather that the action should be stayed.

Now, having had this case fully argued, I cannot shut my eyes to the fact that it appears from the letters and correspondence early in the progress of the works in July, 1890, that a controversy arose between the contractor and the City Surveyor as to what would be the effect of taking out the timber which had been put in during the progress of the construction of the sewer. On the one side—I am only stating it baldly now—the contractor said: "If you order me to take out those timbers there will be great mischief done to the gas and water pipes and the surrounding buildings." On the other hand there was the City Surveyor saying it would not hurt at all, and Mr. Clive, the gentleman under the City Surveyor, was echoing what the City Surveyor said. Meetings took place, and letters were written about this, and the result was—I am only summarising it—that some of these timbers were ordered to be taken out. These timbers were taken out because the City Surveyor would not pay for them, and the result was that a large amount of damage was done to the gas and water pipes and the surrounding neighbourhood. There was also a dispute which came about late in the day—I think Mr. Moulton is right there—about the deviation.

1892
April 27.

Queen's
Bench
Division.

There was also a dispute about the sand, which I will deal with in a moment. I want now to emphasize what I am saying about the removal of this timber. I cannot come to any other conclusion than that the City Surveyor was staking his professional knowledge against the contractor's professional knowledge, and that each of them called in an expert for their own aid. One said, "Go on without timber; withdraw it," and another said, "No, I cannot; damage will ensue." The result was that the timber was drawn out, and damage—although I do not know that it came therefrom—immediately afterwards ensued. The contractor at present has a large claim against the Corporation for being told to withdraw the timber, or for not being paid for the timber, and having it ordered to be left. It is immaterial under which head you put it, he has that large claim. This is the point upon which I wish to fix my judgment. No matter though the City Surveyor honestly believed and thought himself to be right, and no matter whether he may at the end of this case be found to be right and the contractor wrong, can it be said that that is the gentleman to whom this issue, involving many thousands of pounds, is to be referred? I cannot think so.

In my judgment that is quite sufficient in this case to cause me to say that there is sufficient reason why this should not be referred to the City Surveyor, who is the arbitrator named in the contract. I agree with the law laid down by Mr. Moulton where he cited Lord Selborne's judgment. He said that *primâ facie* it was the duty of this Court to carry out the contract. I agree to that; and I loyally follow that judgment. But it is this: We are to follow out the contract, and refer it to the party named in the contract unless sufficient reason be shown by the other side that that should not be done.

For the reasons given, I am of opinion that the City Surveyor is not the right person to whom these issues should be referred. I may also add this, and I add it simply because Mr. Moulton said that if judgment is given in this case against him they would never be able to refer to the City Surveyor or a gentleman in such like position hereafter. I deny that. There is also a peculiar fact in this case to which I wish to refer. It does seem to me that at a certain period of this work the City Surveyor and the contractor got into a special and peculiar friction. I am talking of the circumstances which led up to the supplemental agreement about the sand. In that supplemental agreement there is a passage which said—I am only paraphrasing it now—that the letters should be matters of oblivion and should not be brought up hereafter. I emphasize again that

1892
April 27.

Queen's
Bench
Division.

I do not impugn either the integrity, or good faith, or business capacity, of the City Surveyor; but it seems to me that he is too much of a judge of his own case here to be appointed the arbitrator to decide these matters between the parties, and, therefore, this application will be dismissed with costs.

Solicitors for plaintiffs: Rowcliffe, Rawle & Co., 1, Bedford Row, agents for T. Booth, Manchester. Solicitors for defendants: Austin & Austin, Coleman Street, agents for Talbot, Town Clerk, Manchester.

1892
February 24.

Queen's
Bench
Division.

𝕴𝖓 𝖙𝖍𝖊 𝕳𝖎𝖌𝖍 𝕮𝖔𝖚𝖗𝖙 𝖔𝖋 𝕵𝖚𝖘𝖙𝖎𝖈𝖊 (𝕼𝖚𝖊𝖊𝖓'𝖘 𝕭𝖊𝖓𝖈𝖍 𝕯𝖎𝖛𝖎𝖘𝖎𝖔𝖓).

(Mathew, J.)

1892
July 16.

Court of
Appeal.

𝕴𝖓 𝖙𝖍𝖊 𝕮𝖔𝖚𝖗𝖙 𝖔𝖋 𝕬𝖕𝖕𝖊𝖆𝖑.

(Lord Esher, M.R., Bowen and Kay, L.JJ.)

BOTTOMS

v.

LORD MAYOR, ETC. OF THE CITY OF YORK.

Sewerage Contract—Difficulties of Soil—Refusal to Vary Contract or Give Written Orders—Abandonment.

In the absence of any specific guarantee or definite representations as to the nature of the soil in which the works are to be executed, a contractor is not entitled to abandon the contract on discovery of the nature of the soil, nor because the engineer declines to give written orders entitling to extra payment in consequence of difficulties in executing the works which had not been foreseen by the contractor.

Action for damages for alleged breaches by the defendants of a contract under seal entered into with the plaintiff for the construction of sewerage works at York, and for an alleged wrongful seizure of the plaintiff's plant on the works.

Neither the plaintiff nor the defendants sank trial holes nor otherwise tested the soil before tenders for the sewerage system were invited, made, or accepted; and the soil turned out to be of a muddy and spongy character, so that the whole of each excavation had to be timbered, and the brick work, when put in, was crushed in several cases by the flow of the adjacent soil. The remaining facts sufficiently appear from the judgments.

The material portions of the contract are the following:—

YORK CORPORATION.

Sewerage Works, 1890.

General Stipulations and Conditions.

(1) In this specification the following words shall be understood as having the meanings herein assigned to them. . . . .

Interpretation.

Whenever any work is specified to be done to the satisfaction of the engineer, it is to be taken as including the resident engineer and the duly appointed inspectors.

(3) . . . .

Drawings.

. . . .

The engineer may issue such further or amended drawings as he sees fit, and all such drawings signed by him shall be held to be included in this contract.

(4) The descriptions of work required by the Corporation to be executed by the contractor are set forth in this specification and in the drawings, and the nearest approximations to the actual quantity of work required to be executed are set forth in the bill of quantities, but the engineer reserves the power to *vary, extend, or diminish the quantities of work, to alter* the line, level, or position of any work or part of any work, increase, change or decrease the size, quality, description, character or kind of any work, or to add to or take from the works included in the contract as he may think proper, without vitiating the contract; and the contractor *shall not have any claim* upon the Corporation for any such variation or extension, diminution, alteration, increase, change or decrease other than *for the work actually done,* calculated according to the prices of this contract.

Power to vary work.

(5) The contractor *shall, at his own cost and charges,* furnish all pipes, bricks, *timber,* ironwork, cement, lime, stone, gravel, sand, puddle, centering barrows, planks, carts, steam engines, pumps, and all other implements and materials, and also all steam, horse and manual labour necessary for the full and complete performance of his contract, including the construction, erection and maintenance of all necessary hoarding, dams, sumps, fences and bridgeways for traffic; and he shall in like manner furnish lights and watchmen and everything necessary for the safety of the public and for the protection of adjoining properties.

Materials, implements and labour provided by the contractor.

(6) The works will be set out by the resident engineer, who will give the proper lines, positions, levels, depths and particulars on the ground, the contractor providing, at his own cost, pegs, *sight rails,* labour in fixing, &c.

The contractor must check and satisfy himself of the accuracy of such setting out, and shall be responsible for *the finished* accuracy of the work in accordance with the contract.

Contractor responsible for finished accuracy of work.

(11) If the engineer uses the power reserved to *him under clause* 4 of this specification, or *if he orders the contractor to execute the works* or any part *thereof by day work, an order in writing signed by the engineer* or resident engineer *shall be given to the contractor to that effect,* and any works executed under such order shall be paid for at the rates set forth in the bill of quantities or schedule, where such rates, *in the opinion of the engineer,* apply, but if such rates do not so apply, a rate or price shall be agreed upon between the engineer or the resident engineer and the contractor in writing, and failing their agreement the contractor shall forthwith execute such order, *and the engineer shall determine*

Extra or varied works.

the rate or price at which the work shall be paid for. The contractor shall send in to the resident engineer, weekly, a written statement showing the quantity, nature and value OF ALL WORKS *executed, and if he fails so to do the engineer.* may use his discretion as to whether such works *shall be paid for or not.* The engineer shall also determine what, if any time is to be allowed for such works, in addition to or diminution of the time allowed for the completion of the contract, *Orders given verbally are to be regarded as instructions for the execution of the works included in the contract.*

Timber left in trenches.

(12) In any case in which the engineer or resident engineer may direct *that timbering shall be left in a trench, the price inserted in the bill of quantities will be paid for such timber, but if the necessity for leaving it in has,* in the opinion of the engineer or resident engineer, arisen from carelessness or *neglect on the part of the contractor,* the timber so ordered to be left in the *trench or trenches will not be paid for.*

No timber will be paid for unless it be ordered to be left in by the engineer or resident engineer in writing.

Defective work, delay, bankruptcy, &c.

(16) If the contractor does *not execute* the works in a sound and workmanlike manner, or with diligence, or with regularity, *or if he neglects to amend inaccurate work to the satisfaction of the engineer,* it shall be lawful for the Corporation to give the contractor notice in writing, signed by the engineer, requiring him forthwith to proceed with the due and proper execution of the works. *And in case the contractor shall delay, for the space of seven days after the service of such notice as aforesaid, to proceed with the due and proper execution of the works to the satisfaction of the engineer,* or if the contractor shall be declared bankrupt or petition any Court having jurisdiction in bankruptcy for the liquidation of his affairs by arrangement or composition, or for otherwise arranging or compounding with his creditors, it shall be lawful for the Corporation to take possession of all plant, implements and materials upon the works belonging to the contractor, and to employ any other contractor, builder, workman or other person by measure and value, day work or otherwise, to proceed with the said works and to complete the same; and on the expiration of the said notice, or on such bankruptcy, or petition, or arrangement; as the case may be, the contract shall, at the option of the Corporation, become void as to the contractor, but without prejudice to any right of action which the contractor may be subject unto for any neglect in not proceeding with the works in accordance with this specification, and any money due to the contractor for work executed shall be retained by the Corporation until the whole of the works are completed, and the Corporation may deduct from the sum due to the contractor the additional costs which the engineer may certify to have been incurred in consequence of the default of the contractor to execute the work, or if such additional costs exceed the sum due to the contractor the Corporation may recover the difference by action at law or otherwise.

Defective materials or plant.

(17) All the works shall be executed with the materials specified of the best of their respective kinds, with the best workmanship and in the best manner *to the satisfaction of the engineer.*

If, in the opinion of the engineer or resident engineer, any of the materials or plant brought on the ground for use on this contract are not of the quality or kind specified, or are unfit or insufficient for the works, either of them shall be at liberty to order the removal of the said materials or plant, and the contractor shall remove the same within twenty-four hours after notice has been given to him, and if he fails to remove them within that time, the Corporation may cause them to be removed and deposited anywhere off the site of the works at the risk of the contractor, and any costs incurred in so doing shall be deducted from the sum due to the contractor under the contract.

(22) The contractor shall maintain and keep the works in repair and good order for twelve months after the completion of the whole.

(27) When the contractor has executed finished work to the value, at the prices of the contract, of 2,000*l.* [two thousand pounds], and thereafter until the contractor has executed finished work to the value, at such prices, of 27,500*l.* [twenty-seven thousand five hundred pounds], payments will be made monthly, *on the certificate of the engineer,* equal to 80 per cent. of the estimated value of the work executed by the contractor [no allowance being made for plant or materials on the ground].

.   .   .   .

(32) It is to be distinctly understood that this specification is to receive its strict literal interpretation, and that the works are in all respects to be carried out in accordance with *it* and the drawings, TO THE SATISFACTION OF THE ENGINEER: but it is hereby provided that in case any dispute, question or difference arises as *to the value of any particular work not clearly stated in the* bill or schedules, *or with regard to any other matter or thing connected with the contract, such dispute, question or difference shall be decided by the engineer, whose decision and award shall be final and binding upon all parties.*   .

1892
February 24.

Queen's
Bench
Division.

Maintenance.
Payments.

Engineer's
decision to
be final.

Materials and Labour.

(33) .   .   .   .
The timber used for supporting the sides of the trenches must also be good, sound timber, approved of by the engineer; *walings, liners and runners* being of spruce, polings of spruce or elm, and stretchers of good, strong, square Swedish timber, or in narrow trenches of larch or other sound English timber, &c.

Excepting where specially stated to the contrary, parties tendering must calculate for getting out the trenches sufficiently wide at the top to admit of internal runners being started about the level of the top of the work and driven down as the ground is got out.

(54).   .   .   .   .
The summer level of the River Ouse is 16.75 feet above ordnance datum, floods of twenty to twenty-five feet above O.D. occur, and a flood of thirty feet above O.D. has been known, but the contractor is to take all risks of such floods or of greater ones.

The ordinary level of the water in the River Foss and in Wormwalds cut is shown on the drawings, but both are subject to floods.

(56) Subsoil pipes with open joints will be laid under the sewers with loose rubble or clean gravel on the top and sides, as shown on the drawings, in such places when, in the opinion of the engineer, the quantity of subsoil water requires them, and will be paid for at the contract rates, but if the ground is wet only in patches, and the contractor elects to make the subsoil pipe continuous to save sinking other sumps, he may, with the consent of the engineer, put in subsoil pipes at his own cost in the intervening parts.

(58) Tho brick sewers are to be built to proper templates, profiles and centres. The centering is not to be removed until the arch is set, and the filling *in is not to be proceeded with until the sewer is able to carry the load without settlement.* The

Timber

Syphons
and river
crossings.

Subsoil pipes.

Brick sewers.

1892
February 24.

Queen's
Bench
Division.
Trenches.

contractor is to keep the water below the brickwork by pumping until the work is set, in all cases, whether in brick, iron, concrete, or pipe sewers, and in manholes, &c.

(61) As a rule the ground must be got out in open trenches, tunnelling being allowed only by express permission of the engineer.

The sides must be supported by proper timbering, and the excavated material must be deposited neatly and compactly alongside the trench, so as to do as little damage and occasion as little inconvenience as possible.   .   .   .   .   .

No allowance will be made for excavation except that beyond line of sewer trench.

Webster, A.-G., and Bankes for the plaintiff. Lockwood, Q.O., and T. Willes Chitty for the defendants.

Mathew, J.: This is an action brought by the plaintiff against the Corporation of York for breach of a contract by the defendants, which had been entered into by them with the plaintiff for the construction of sewerage works at York, and also to recover damages for an alleged wrongful seizure of the plant of the plaintiff by the defendants.

The contract had been entered into in the month of March, 1891, for the construction of sewers in the City of York. The principal sewer was to run along the line of the Ouse, and was to extend over several miles of sewer to be constructed of brick. The Corporation had employed their engineer, a well-known gentleman, Mr. Mansergh, and he had prepared plans and specifications, and the bill of quantities upon which tenders were invited from contractors. The specification contained no description, and no undertaking in respect of the soil in which the sewer was to be constructed, and it was left to the contractor or those who tendered to ascertain for themselves what the nature of the soil was, and what difficulty it might present in the course of the construction of the sewers. The plans which were submitted to the examination of those who were prepared to tender contained two sections of the sewer, the one describing an ordinary brick sewer of certain dimensions, the other showing the same sewer with a footing of concrete. That was all the information the plans furnished on the subject. The specification was in what may be described as the usual form, although in some respects it was made more stringent as against the contractor than such documents ordinarily are. Quantities were set out at great length, and those who had to tender were to supply the prices at which the quantities mentioned in the bill of quantities were to be furnished.

Now the plaintiff was a man of humble beginnings. He had been a working man in the early part of his career, and by some thrift

1892
February 24.

Queen's
Bench
Division.

and industry, had managed to put together a few thousand pounds. It did not appear, although he had some contract work previously, that he had ever been engaged in any very large undertaking—no such undertaking as the one in question. He was attracted by the advertisement, no doubt, and, having examined the plans and specifications, he went down to York and walked over the ground, and took, what I fear was, a very superficial view of the nature of the soil in which the sewer was to be constructed, and he then made his tender. The prices worked out somewhere about 55,000*l*. Various other tenders had been made, and it appeared the plaintiff was far below—some 10,000*l*. below—the lowest of the other tenders.

The Corporation had had the opinion of Mr. Mansergh as to what the cost of the work would be, and his estimate was 5,000*l*. higher than the amount of the plaintiff's tender. The first step taken by the Corporation was to send a deputation to interview the plaintiff after his tender had been made, and the object appeared to be to ascertain his efficiency—whether or not he had means which would enable him to carry the work through. He had also some warnings given him by those who represented the Corporation; and he was told, although his recollection was not clear upon the subject—I have no doubt he was told—that his tender was 10,000*l*. below the lowest of the other tenders, and he was also told that the estimate of the engineer was higher than the amount for which he undertook to construct the works, and he was asked to look over his prices again. He did so, and came back. He was bent upon getting this contract, apparently, and he said he could then do the work for the money. He was not informed of what the Corporation knew from their own engineer, that he could only undertake the construction of the works for that amount at the certainty of a serious loss. I confess I regret the Corporation allowed themselves to be tempted to accept the tender from the plaintiff under the circumstances. I cannot help saying that I think the Corporation did, in its collective capacity, what no one of the highly-respectable gentlemen of whom the Corporation was composed would have done if the matter concerned himself only; but Corporations are popular institutions, because they are not afflicted with the qualms of conscience that sometimes disturb individuals of whom the Corporation is composed. They accepted his tender, and shortly after he had notice, under the terms of the specification, to go to work. The contract was duly executed, and the works were proceeded with under it.

Now, let us see in what position the contractor stood under the agreement into which he entered with the Corporation. The contract

1892
February 24.
Queen's
Bench
Division.

itself is in the ordinary form, and bound him to proceed with the works according to the instructions that might be furnished him by the engineer, in accordance with the plans and specification. The plans I have already referred to. The specification contained the following important clauses. [*Clauses 1, 3, and 4 were then read and referred to.*] Then came some other clauses which are not important.

The next important clause is clause 11 [*read*]. It is quite clear the effect of that was to deprive the contractor of any right to claim in respect of extra work upon the footing that the work had been varied under sect. 4, unless he had the written order of the resident engineer. It was entirely in the discretion of the resident engineer whether he would grant that written order or not.

Then clause 12 [*read*] is important with reference to the difficulties that arose subsequently, and it provides for the timbering to be left in trenches, again placing the contractor completely under the authority of the resident engineer.

Then clause 16 provides for defective work [*read*], and in case he fails, power is given to the Corporation to terminate the contract, and to take possession of the plant of the contractor. Clause 27 provides he was to have no certificate until he had finished the work, to the satisfaction of the engineer, to the amount of 2,000*l*. Sect. 32 provides for the engineer's decision: "It is to be distinctly understood that this specification is to receive its strict literal interpretation, and that the works are in all respects to be carried out in accordance with it and the drawings to the satisfaction of the engineer; but it is hereby provided that in case any dispute, question or difference arises as to the value of any particular work not clearly stated in the bill or schedules, or with regard to any other matter or thing connected with the contract, such dispute, question or difference shall be decided by the engineer, whose decision and award shall be final and binding upon all parties."

The last clause in the contract is probably the most significant of all. After directing that the contractor shall inform himself fully as to the specifications and drawings, it goes on: "Should any misunderstanding arise as to the meaning of this specification during the progress of the works, the decision of the engineer as to its true intent and meaning, and of any drawing, dimension, clause, word, sentence or sentences, shall be conclusive and binding."

That was the contract under which the plaintiff commenced to execute these works. It is right to say that before he signed the contract he had some further information from an officer of the

1892
February 24.

Queen's
Bench
Division.

Corporation, Mr. Creer, the civil engineer. Mr. Creer said he called at the office and warned him about the nature of the soil in which this sewer was to be constructed, and gave him a book or pamphlet prepared by a predecessor of his with reference to the soil of York and its suburbs generally. The plaintiff said he had not had time to look at it, and did not look at it. Mr. Creer said he had it in his possession for twenty minutes. Certainly it did not appear in any way to disturb the sanguine judgment the plaintiff had formed as to what he could do in the construction of these sewers. It did not appear that the pamphlet contained anything with reference to the particular locality in which the sewer was to be constructed, and it did not appear either that the Corporation had taken the precaution of ascertaining by trial holes, or in any other way, what the real nature of the soil was. At the same time the locality bordering upon the Ouse would be a sufficient indication to any reasonable man that he must expect considerable engineering difficulties in constructing a sewer in that locality. The soil was likely to be spongy and difficult to operate upon. The plaintiff, as it turns out, made an extremely foolish bargain. He cannot complain of that; it is no answer. The bargain was a foolish one, and those with whom he contracted knew that it was a foolish one. The difficulties were far greater than the contractor contemplated, and, I hope, far greater than the Corporation clearly foresaw.

Now, what was his position with reference to the engineer under this contract? There is no doubt about the law. The law was fully discussed in the case, very recently referred to in the course of the argument, of *De Morgan, Snell & Co.* v. *The Rio De Janeiro Flour Mills Company* (a). The engineer is not, with reference to any difficulties that arise under a contract of this sort, the agent of his employers. He was not the agent of his employers in this case. He occupied a position of quasi-arbitrator, and even if he honestly made mistakes in the course of the discharge of his duty, it is perfectly clear that neither party to the contract could complain of that. It was his duty to do his best to act fairly between the parties, and as long as he acted in good faith his decision, in a case of this sort, would be final, and for any blunder, if any blunders were proved, neither party could claim that he had done wrong or made the other contracting party responsible.

The plaintiff went to work, and from the first the difficulties were extremely great. He was compelled to timber the trench at great expense. I have photographs before me showing that it was neces-

(a) Reported *ante*, p. 185, and 8 T. L. R. 292, 470.

1892
February 24.

Queen's
Bench
Division.

sary to cover the whole of the surface of the excavation on each side with timber in order to keep the soil from tumbling in. It was muddy and spongy, and, no doubt, the expense of that portion of the operations was extremely great. The course that the plaintiff adopted was to use poling boards—short lengths of timber placed against the side of the trench, and strutted carefully with heavy timber, and when the trench had been excavated and timbered in this way, the next step taken was to put in a mould, which was described of the dimension of the sewer, to remove timbering at the bottom of the excavation, and there to put in concrete. When that concrete had settled, the mould was removed, and the sewer was constructed of bricks within the concrete on each side. Really, there is no question that this process was not always satisfactory. The concrete put in next to the soil (there was no other way of doing it) got crushed and never settled fully and satisfactorily, and then the brickwork, which was put in subsequently, was crushed from the pressure of the soil, and in that way reparation from time to time became necessary. It was said that this mode of timbering the sewer adopted by the contractor was injudicious. It was said for the defendants that he ought from the first to have employed runners, which are short piles driven into the earth; and they clearly afford far greater protection to the sides of an excavation of this sort than the poling boards used by the plaintiff. The plaintiff's excuse was that he had been for-bidden to use runners; that he had been informed by the resident engineer that if runners were used they must be taken out subsequently, but he would not be paid for them. That was denied.

There was hardly a step in this case which was not the subject of contradiction—conflicting evidence. That was denied on the part of the defendants, and the resident engineer said that he had called the attention of the plaintiff to the importance of using runners, but he told him that he would order the runners to be withdrawn subsequently if he could possibly do it; and, unquestionably, according to the terms of the contract, he was entitled to do that, that is to say, according to the clause I have read, the contractor was only to be paid for such timbering as was ordered to be left by the engineer when the works were completed. It does not, fortunately, matter, as it seems to me, which is right with reference to this part of the case, because if the engineer had prohibited the use of runners, or had said he did not prohibit them, but had said he would not pay for them under any circumstances, that would have been wrong; it was a mistake. But it is not a matter in respect to which, it seems to me, the defendants could be made responsible.

1892
February 24.

Queen's
Bench
Division.

On carefully considering the evidence on each side I prefer the statement of Mr. McKie's with reference to this point, to the recollection of the plaintiff. The plaintiff said that, having ascertained that he was not going to be paid for the runners, he thought it would be as well to use poling boards, and he continued to use the poling boards for a considerable time, certainly for more than a month; and, as I have said, the necessity of withdrawing the poling boards before the concrete was put in, it was agreed, was indispensable, and certainly had the effect of rendering it necessary that some portion of the work should be reconstructed. Now, the plaintiff has made the orders given him to reconstruct as the great reason for his withdrawal from this contract, and I have had to consider very anxiously the evidence offered upon that part of the case which was the subject of comment from the learned counsel on each side. Is the plaintiff right in the view presented by him that he was ordered to reconstruct time after time, and that the orders to reconstruct show that the plans originally furnished him were insufficient from an engineering point of view, and that he was practically called upon to carry out a contract substantially different from the contract he had entered into with the defendants? That was the position that he took. It is a remarkable thing that the plaintiff himself admits that when this reconstruction was directed he did not at the time ask for any written order. He now says he was clearly called upon to do something outside the contract. One would have expected, under such circumstances, that there would have been an immediate protest from the plaintiff, who was constantly upon the works; that a careful record would be kept of the extra material he was compelled to use and the extra labour required for his workmen. There was nothing of the sort, and he admitted himself, as I understood him, that it was not until towards the end of May that he ever made any requisition in respect of this extra work, and I come to the conclusion that an exaggerated view has been presented to me of the amount of reparation and reconstruction that was necessary.

It appears that Mr. McKie from time to time did direct the bricklayers to do again some work they had already done, and that they did so without a murmur; and it is not pretended that in the first instance, after considerable time, that anything in the nature of protest, or anything in the nature of demand for written orders in respect of that extra work, was made by the plaintiff on Mr. McKie. The work went on until about 136 feet of the sewer was completed, and that was towards the end of June. That work apparently passed the engineer, because directions were given that the sewer

1892
February 24.

Queen's
Bench
Division.

should be crowned, and I have had a strong body of evidence to show that the work so far was satisfactorily done, and has since stood, and has not been moved or disturbed in any way. When the plaintiff got to the 136 feet, far greater difficulties presented themselves than he had hitherto found before him. He got into what was called a slurry. He got to a place where there was nothing but mud all round; mud at the sides and mud at the bottom of the excavation —thick mud, and mud so deep that a rod could be driven into it for several feet, and no doubt the engineering difficulties in the plaintiff's way were very great. He appealed to Mr. McKie and he appealed to Mr. Strachan. Now, Mr. Strachan was the representative of Mr. Mansergh. Mr. Mansergh was away through illness, and Mr Strachan was at his office and occupying his place, and by the correspondence that passed between Mr. McKie and Mr. Strachan it was brought clearly to Mr. Strachan's attention that these unusual and apparently insuperable difficulties presented themselves.

Two orders were given for extras: one to enable the contractor to be paid for a platform which was allowed to be put at the bottom of the sewer to cover this muddy matter and to carry the sewer; the other an order for some reconstruction which had been rendered necessary owing to the yielding nature of the soil. But the difficulties grew greater, and those two orders were not enough for the contractor. He did not see his way to do it, and under the circumstances he communicated with Mr. Strachan, and Mr. Strachan came down to the works. The difficulties were obvious enough. Mr. Strachan did not attempt to deny that they were very great, although he did not consider them as serious as the plaintiff, and he gave a long account of the interview which took place on the 5th June between him and the contractor. The result of that was that the contractor told him that he could not go on; that he was losing money rapidly; that he had spent 3,000*l.* over the works; that he had not done work which would entitle him to a certificate for more than 500*l.* or 600*l.*, and he did not see his way to do it. It is remarkable at that interview (it is clearly made out, I think) that the contractor did not say one word about the portion of the extra work of reconstruction which he had been compelled to do in the previous month. That was not the ground upon which he put his complaint, not the ground upon which he intimated that he foresaw difficulties in continuing to carry the contract out. There was a subsequent interview on the 8th of June.

The plaintiff came up to town. At that time the slurry into which

1892
February 24.

Queen's
Bench
Division.

he had got was becoming more difficult and more troublesome to deal with, and he once more had an interview with Mr. Strachan upon the subject, and then for the first time, as Mr. Strachan pointed out to him, he complained that certificates had been previously with-held. He applied to Mr. McKie for them for the work he had to do, as he said, three or four times over, and Mr. McKie had refused to give him those certificates. Mr. Strachan, very naturally, called the attention of the plaintiff to this. When they were together upon the ground on the 5th June, and when the plaintiff might have pointed out to him what this reconstruction was, he had not done so.

Then Mr. Strachan went on to have a long conversation with him. Mr. Strachan, an exceedingly intelligent and clever engineer, dealing with this poor contractor, had very little difficulty in drawing him into a conversation about his real difficulty. There was a dispute as to what passed. Mr. Strachan said that the plaintiff had admitted to him that he had got to the end of his banker's balance, and he could not go on with the work; he was losing every day, and he saw nothing for it but to throw the contract up. Mr. Strachan expressed a willingness to assist the contractor in his difficulty, but with the saving clause that it could be only such assistance as the contract justified.

It is clear upon the evidence of both, the plaintiff said that would not do: that he could not possibly get over the difficulty presented by this pot-hole or slurry unless the Corporation agreed to treat the work as day work, as they were entitled to do under the contract in the discretion of the engineer; or consented to pay him for his work and materials, and something in addition for profit; and Mr. Strachan held out to him no hope that the engineer would decide any of those points in his favour, but he advised him to communicate with the Corporation; and the letter which was written by the contractor, on the 8th June, to the Corporation, states very clearly what position he then took. "I have been requested by the engineer to appeal to the Corporation *re* my position with the above. I have met with very bad ground, and I find that the six feet nine inches and four feet six inches brick sewer at Fulford will not stand during construction, which has necessitated my reconstructing the work, nearly the whole length, two, three and four times over."

As I have already said, in that respect, I consider that the contractor exaggerated what he had had to do previously. It was not true that during the construction he had been compelled to reconstruct the works nearly the whole length, two, three or four times over "This is causing me a very serious loss. I have appealed to the

1892
February 24.

Queen's
Bench
Division.

engineer *re* payment for same, and I have been directed by him to appeal to the Corporation. The work is costing me quite three times the amount I have for it"—I think that statement was correct; "and I wish the Corporation to relieve me of this section or devise some other method of carrying on the work, as it is impossible for me to continue under the present circumstances. The subsoil is really nothing but soft mud, and I find the present plan will not stand during construction, and I cannot be expected to do the work three or four times. I must also ask that the Corporation will pay me for the work I have constructed so many times." There is his statement that the work he had already done, which was the 136 feet, had been covered in and found not to be standing. In that respect I am compelled to come to the conclusion that this gentleman was inaccurate.

I had evidence before me that some portion of the work had given way after it had been completed by the contractor, and from that I was asked to infer that the whole plan for this sewer was a defective one. On the other hand, there has been strong evidence called on the part of the Corporation that from the month of June down to the present time the work, as completed by the contractor, has stood, and has not given way in any way. However, there is the letter. That was his request to the Corporation.

After that letter was received, an arrangement was made that there should be a meeting of the Corporation, which took place on the 12th of June, where the matter should be discussed. On the morning of the 9th, the day after this letter was written, the contractor dismissed his workmen. Now, his explanation of that was, that when he got to the works on the morning of the 9th, Mr. Beagley, clerk of the works, not the engineer, had suddenly ordered that a large portion of the completed section of the 136 feet should be taken down, reconstructed and under-pinned. Mr. Beagley stoutly denied he had said anything of the sort. Mr. Beagley, unfortunately for himself, kept a diary, and the diary certainly was inconsistent with his statement. I have no doubt something of that kind did take place as the contractor said, although perhaps the contractor's recollection was something more serious than what Mr. Beagley really did ask him to do. However, whether he is right or not about that, he had made up his mind at that time, I am quite satisfied, that unless the Corporation gave way and modified the contract he would not go on with the work. It may have been this interference by Beagley which was the last straw which induced him to dismiss his workmen and come to the resolution to do nothing more unless the Corporation came to new terms.

1892
February 24.

Queen's
Bench
Division.

Mr. McKie, it is said, must have known that that direction had taken place. Mr. McKie denied it positively, and there is no proof that he gave any such direction or intended to give any. But, again, suppose he did, the terms of this contract entitled him, so long as he acted honestly, to give a direction of that sort and require the work to be done, as it seems to me, and the plaintiff could not complain that the defendants were guilty of any breach of the contract because of this direction given by Mr. McKie. But there is no evidence at present that McKie did give any such instruction.

The meeting of the Corporation was held. The plaintiff was present. He stated his case. He repeated what he had said to Mr. Strachan, and asked that the indulgence of the Corporation might be granted him with regard to the work of the contract, that is, that they might allow the work to be done by day work, or make a modification in his favour. The position was made difficult for him. I am not satisfied (I have had no evidence before me) that the engineering difficulties could be overcome by any ordinary operation. I should have rather come to the conclusion that without pile-driving it would be impossible to carry those works out. In respect to that pile-driving it would have very much increased the cost of the execution of the works. The Corporation heard his application through their committee and refused to grant it, and they came to the resolution to give him notice, under the terms of the contract, to go on with the work. That notice was accordingly given. The plaintiff refused to go on with the work, and immediately afterwards, on the expiration of the notice, the Corporation seized the plant and took the work out of his hands.

I must confess I have struggled against the conclusion to which I find myself driven. I do not see any way of relieving the plaintiff from this contract into which he entered, and my judgment, therefore, must be in favour of the Corporation. At the same time, I think he has been hardly used, and I express my regret that the Corporation did not do what they were entitled to do, that is, refuse the lowest tender. I do not think that he and they were on a level or upon equal terms in coming to this bargain, and I think greater precaution should have been taken to inform him of the inevitable liability, of the inevitable loss, ruin, which was before him if he entered into the contract upon these terms.

The Corporation will have the satisfaction of informing the citizens of York that they have secured for them the amount of excellent work done by the contractor towards the construction of these sewers. The value of that work is 700*l*. 0or 800*l*. at the very least—at the

1892
February 24.
Queen's
Bench
Division.

lowest estimate. It cost the contractor a good deal. They have also got his plant. I give them judgment, but judgment without costs.

From this judgment the plaintiff appealed.

Webster, A.-G., and Bankes argued—

(1) That the contract did not authorise the engineer to direct the reconstruction of any part of the work, which had once been completed, except by written order, and as an extra.

(2) That the work contracted for was substantially different from that actually done, and that the contractor was entitled to treat the contract as off, and sue for work and labour done.

Lockwood, Q.C., and Newboult, for the defendants, were not called on.

1892
July 16.
Court of
Appeal.

Lord ESHER, M.R.: It seems to me we cannot disturb the judgment of Mr. Justice Mathew. We have heard the case most elaborately argued, and have heard everything said that could be said on the plaintiff's part, and we find ourselves unable to do other than the learned judge did, and to say that we are sorry that this hard-working man should have entered into such a bad contract. But having entered into it he was bound by it, and must stand by the consequences and by what he did.

The real question in this case is whether the findings of the judge upon the questions of fact are right or wrong. It seems to me that nobody can suggest for a moment but that it was the plaintiff who threw up the contract at a time when he had no right to throw it up, and for reasons which he had no right to act upon, and that the Corporation insisted upon his observing the contract and going on with it. But he resisted and refused to have anything more to do with it. If that be true, he had brought himself into a very difficult position, and was not able to enforce any payment whatever.

What other results may follow from what he has done we have at present nothing to do with. I take it that the real reason why he has come by this misfortune, indeed, is that he would go and tender when there was no guarantee given to him as to the kind of soil, and when there was no information given to him as to what the soil was—when there was no contract entered into by the people who asked him to tender as to what the nature of the soil was, and that he either too eagerly or too carelessly tendered and entered into the contract without any such guarantee or representation on their part at all, and without due examination and enquiry by himself. That is what has produced the difficulty. Still, you must deal with the difficulty when it arises. Now he had gone on and had done some

work. Before that work was accepted, and any order was given to
cover it, he had had orders from the people who, by the contract,
were entitled to give him orders, to vary and alter that work. They
might, as I understand it, have given him written orders; and, as I
understand the ruling of the judge, if they had done so, they might
have obliged themselves to pay for that extra work. But they were
not bound to give him a written order. They were entitled to give
him verbal orders, and if they gave him a verbal order to do anything within clause 4, then he was to do that and not be paid
for it.

Now section 4 of the contract entitled them, at all events, until they
had accepted a given part of the work as completed, to vary it and to
insist that it should be altered—and it is obvious that that would be a
stipulation on their part for such work as this. The work was to be
open to their superintendence. They were to be entitled to look at it,
and if they thought it required alteration they were entitled to insist
that he should alter it. That is what was done, and he did alter it.
Under the contract he had no right to be paid for that alteration. He
had no right to be paid for that alteration as for extra work. That
seems to me to be clear.

Then came a time when he, finding himself, as Mr. Justice Mathew
has demonstrated almost, that the soil was beating him—not that he
could not do the work that he had contracted to do, but that he could
not do it at a profit, he struck. He found, as he says, that he could get
no profit out of the concern, and by the end of the contract, if it went
on like that, he would be ruined. Well, what does he do? Here we
come to what is the true view of what he did. He first of all went to
Mr. Strachan, and asked him to alter the contract (that is what he
did), and to alter it in one of two ways, either to give up their option
as to whether they would have the work done by day work or not,
and to make a new arrangement with him that all the work which he
should do in the future should be by day work, or to alter the
contract in some other way. Either of these ways of it would be
altering the contract as he asked Mr. Strachan; and Mr. Strachan told
him that he could not do that, and he said, Go and ask the
Corporation.

He goes to the Corporation; and it is what passed between him
and the Corporation which is the determining point in this matter.
He went and saw them on the 9th of June, and unless those who
wrote the minute of the meeting were absolutely fraudulent, and
those who signed it were equally fraudulent, the judge would
naturally take that as the true account and act upon it; and the judge

1892
July 16.

Court of
Appeal.

who heard the witnesses has stated that that is a true account of what happened between him and the members of the Corporation who were there present. That is, that he came to them and said: "I have been asked to do this work over again; I cannot do it unless I am to be paid extra for it; I will not do it unless you agree that I shall be paid extra for it, and also that I be paid extra for the work that I have done." The terms are perfectly clear.

Mr. Bottoms informed the committee that he would throw up the contract, as he should be ruined by it; that is, that he should throw up the contract, to my mind clearly, unless those suggestions were to be applied to it—that the contract should be put on one side, and that he should carry on the work at a percentage, and find plant and tools, &c., and show his wages sheet to the engineer. That is an absolute alteration of the contract, and, therefore, the judge is justified in saying that he had made up his mind to throw up the contract, and not to go on with it unless they were to agree to alter the contract. They would not agree, and they were not bound to agree; and now it is stated that he went and acted upon what he had told them and dismissed his workmen, and refused from that time to go on.

Thereupon the Corporation, he having thrown up the contract in that way, give him formal notice that they insist upon holding him to the contract, so that they do not give up the contract. They would have been bound by the contract, whatever the true meaning of it was. They said to him, "Go on," of course subject to the term that they would be bound by the contract, whatever the true meaning of the contract was. He says, "No, I will not"; and he persists in saying, "No, I will not go on with the contract; you have done something which entitled me to throw the contract up, and I throw it up"; but he has failed to show that they had done anything which up to that time entitled him to throw the contract up, and therefore he threw it up wrongfully. He had not done any work which entitled him at that time to any payment, not upon what he refused to do as to some part of the work, but upon his refusal to go on with the contract at all. They were entitled then to put in force their powers, and to say, "Very well, we also now will put an end to the contract, but upon these terms, that we exercise our rights, which are not to pay you for that work which is unfinished which you have begun, and, further than that, we are entitled to take your plant and to keep that as satisfaction for the damages which we shall suffer by your breach of contract."

The judge's decision, it seems to me, was right in point of law, and

1892
July 16.

Court of
Appeal.

that his findings of fact were true in point of fact, and, under those circumstances, we are unable, as Mr. Justice Mathew was, to assist this plaintiff at all. He must take the consequences of having acted as he did, and accepted a hazardous and not very rational contract on his part. He was too eager to get a great contract, and, from his eagerness, that has befallen him which has befallen so many men of his class before, he has brought himself probably to bankruptcy, I should think. The appeal must be dismissed.

Bowen, L.J.: I am entirely of the same opinion. Mr. Justice Mathew seems to me to have found rightly on the facts, and certainly we should not differ from him on the materials before us, that the true ground upon which this plaintiff broke with the Corporation was that he found that he could not go on with the contract without ruining himself, and they would not alter it. At the beginning of June he saw the real difficulty before him. The ground, which he had not properly examined when he made the contract, turned out to be so seriously swampy as to make it impossible for him to go on with the contract. Now, by the contract, he also had a grievance pressing on his own mind, and it seemed to increase the difficulty of his position, that he had two or three times reconstructed portions of the work and he had not been paid for it.

With regard to the portion of the work which he had reconstructed already, as he had not obtained a written order before he did it, it is found, therefore, that he could not demand payment for that. Then he found that he was in all probability going to be ordered by the engineer, and an intimation to that effect had already been given by the clerk, to reconstruct another portion or some portion of the work on the morning of the 8th June. With regard to that latter grievance, whether or no he was entitled to refuse to do it without a written order, it was argued by the Attorney-General at great length and with great ability; but it is not necessary to decide that, because that was not the real ground that he took before the Corporation. He did not go to the Corporation and say, "I have been ordered to execute this, and I demand a written order, and I refuse to do it without a written order"—nothing of the sort; he was not in a position to do that, because he had received no directions from the engineer—he had not asked the engineer for a written order, and he had not been refused a written order. He had, however, these two grievances, and upon the last he might not have been right—it is not necessary to decide it; but the real difficulty staring him in the face was absolute ruin if he was kept to his contract.

1892
July 16.
_____
Court of
Appeal.

He tried to get the Corporation to alter the contract and they refused, and he withdrew his men, as he had no right to do. It is idle, to my mind, to say that the refusal to go on with the work was otherwise than wrongful.

If parties dispute about a contract and put different constructions upon it, the fact that one is putting a different construction from the other upon it does not justify the person who thinks he is wrong in doing so in throwing up the contract. It is only if the other side breaks or threatens to break it in a way that amounts to a repudiation of the contract or agreement which he has made in a particular which goes to the root of the whole transaction. But there is no such case here.

Throughout, the case was that he broke it on the ground which the judge mentioned, on a ground untenable in law, and the Corporation are within their strict rights. I am extremely sorry for the man—very sorry. It is undoubted that the judge did his best as the law allowed, for the man has done the work and it is hard that he should not be paid for it, but he has done the work under circumstances in which the law does not allow him to insist upon the right upon his part to be paid, and it seems to me, when the case is thrashed out, that it becomes perfectly clear that the plaintiff has no ground in law or equity for the relief which he asks.

KAY, L.J.: I am of the same opinion. I cannot help feeling the greatest possible sympathy for Mr. Bottoms in the position in which he is actually placed, and I have tried all along, as the argument was going on, to see whether there was any way of helping him and relieving him from the consequences of this decision of the learned judge of the Court below. The Attorney-General put his case very ingeniously indeed upon the refusal of the engineer to give him a written order for that last portion of the work which he had been directed to take down and rebuild. I confess that if that had been really the reason why he threw up the contract there might have been a great deal to be said for it. Perhaps I have given an opinion without very careful consideration as to whether he would have been right or not in requiring to have a written order which would entitle him to payment before he did that which had to be done and rebuilt it. I give no opinion whatever on that point, because I am quite satisfied that the learned judge was right, upon the evidence before him, in finding as he did find, that that was not the reason why he threw up the contract, but that he threw up the contract, in the words used by the learned judge in his judgment, because he had made up his mind that unless the Corporation gave way and modified the contract, he would not go on with the work. He had had a conversation with Mr. Strachan, of which Mr. Strachan took a note, and in that conversation it was proved, I think, satisfactorily, and the learned judge accepted that evidence, that he was requiring the Corporation to allow him to do the work in future by day work, or otherwise to modify the contract; that is, to pay him for his work and materials, and something in addition for profit; and he went to a meeting of the Corporation and discussed the matter with them; and from the evidence as to what took place at that meeting, and from the evidence as to what took place at Mr. Strachan's meeting, and from his own two letters on the 8th and 13th June, which have been read several times, so that I will not refer at length to them again, I think it is clearly proved that he had found that carrying on the contract in the way in which he had been doing up to that time, according to the terms of it, must result in loss, if not ruin, to himself.

He was requiring the Corporation to pay him for work which he had done, as he said himself, three or four times over upon verbal requests to do that work. As to that he was entirely in the wrong. His counsel both admit that he was foolish enough, if you like to say so, to do the work upon a verbal request two or three times over, and he could not then have any right upon this contract to be paid as though he had done it more than once. Therefore, to require payment for that work which he had done under verbal orders as though he was to be paid for it as having done it, according to his own statement, three or four times, was utterly wrong. He had no right to make any such demand under the contract. But that is not the most serious matter.

I think that besides making that request, which was a wrong request, he had completely determined that he would not go on with the contract, because it would ruin him if he did, unless he might either do it by day work or in the other way I have just mentioned, or unless some other modification of the contract were made. He did not throw up the contract because of the last order which was given, although, as the judge said, that might have been the last straw which induced him to do so; but he threw it up because he had come deliberately to the conclusion that, if he carried it out according to the terms of the contract, it would ruin him. Now it is impossible that he could be justified under the terms of the contract, and, therefore, when they required him to continue the work, which they did by written notice, they were acting entirely within their rights under the contract, and the result of his not complying with that notice was that they were entitled, under the terms of

1892
July 16.

Court of
Appeal.

the contract, to seize the plant, which they did, and which was to be treated as their property under the contract, and they were entitled to say, "You have not up to this time obtained any certificate; we have a counterclaim against you for damages, and we shall make you no payment at present." Therefore, I am sorry to say that I find myself quite unable to relieve this plaintiff from the result of the judgment in the Court below, and I think the appeal must be dismissed, with costs.

Appeal dismissed, with costs.

Solicitors for the plaintiff: Bird, Moore & Strode. Solicitors for the defendants: Sharpe, Parker & Co.

1892
October 31.

Queen's
Bench
Division.

1893
February 1.

Court of
Appeal.

In the High Court of Justice (Queen's Bench Division).

(Pollock, B., and Hawkins, J.)

In the Court of Appeal.

(Lord Esher, M.R., Bowen and Smith, L.JJ.)

McDONALD

v.

MAYOR AND CORPORATION OF WORKINGTON.

Engineering Contract—Difficulties of Soil—Abandonment—
Necessity of Certificate.

A contractor is not entitled to throw up a contract because the nature of the soil makes it difficult or impossible to construct the contract works in accordance with the specification. Where a certificate of the engineer is under the contract a condition precedent to the contractor's right to payment, the contractor, on abandoning the contract, is not entitled to payment for work done without producing a certificate of the engineer unless he can show that the certificate is collusively withheld.

The plaintiff entered into a contract in writing with the defendants, the Corporation of Workington, to construct a system of sewers for their district according to a specification and two deposited plans, and to such working and explanatory drawings and instructions as might from time to time be furnished by the defendants' surveyor. Part of the work, which involved certain tunnelling, turned out to be impracticable because of water in the soil, and the contractor suggested certain modifications, which were declined, and then threw up the contract and sued the Corporation for 7,000*l.* alleged to be due to him under the contract so far as proceeded with. No certificate had been given by the engineer for any part of the sum claimed.

1892
October 31.

Queen's
Bench
Division.

The statement of claims alleged —

(1) That before the contract was entered into, the defendants represented and guaranteed that the tunnelling should be through dry ground.

(2) That the defendants had refused and neglected to pay for the work done by the plaintiff except one sum of 500*l.*

(3) That the defendants refused to pay for deviations ordered by them and executed by the plaintiff.

(4) That the ground proved to be wet, and that it was impossible to carry on the tunnelling work in accordance with the plans and specifications, but the defendants refused to supply any sufficient further plans and specifications to enable the plaintiff to execute the work.

The action was referred to an Official Referee (Mr. Hemming, Q.C.), who gave judgment in favour of the defendants, holding that there had been no representation or warranty as to the character of the soil, and that *Thorne* v. *London Corporation* (*a*) applied.

The plaintiff moved before a Divisional Court (Pollock, B., and Hawkins, J.), to set aside this judgment and to enter judgment for the plaintiff or to refer the case back. The motion came before Pollock, B., and Hawkins, J., and was dismissed with costs.

The plaintiff appealed.

Gully, Q.C., and Henry for the plaintiff argued that the surveyor had been prevented from certifying by the Corporation, and that the abandonment did not constitute a breach of contract by the plaintiff.

Webster, Q.C., Young and Disturnal for the defendants.

Lord ESHER, M.R.: It seems to me that the more one looks into this case, the more clear it becomes. It seems to me to be the ordinary case in which a contractor has undertaken to do that which in the result he finds himself unable to do, so as to make a profit. If that is all, this action is wholly misconceived.

1893
February 1.

Court of
Appeal.

Now the relation between these parties was constituted by articles of agreement, and the rights of the parties depend entirely on what is the true construction of that agreement which was submitted to different contractors. I should suppose that they would tender for the work according to this draft agreement, and the plaintiff amongst others did tender and his tender was accepted. Then what is the construction of this provision that they shall do certain works which are mentioned in this agreement? How does the agreement mention the works that are to be done? It says—"works to be done according to this agreement"—that is, according to the specification and plan. Then, for the purpose of seeing what work is to be done, they

(*a*) (1875) 1 App. Cas. 170.

1893
February 1.

Court of
Appeal.

introduce a plan and specification into the agreement, and the agreement is to do such works as are described in this specification or shown on the plan. What are those works? There are other works which we need not trouble ourselves about which are part of one large scheme, but amongst other works which are shown on the plan and described in the specification are a brick sewer in certain land going down to the shore. Then the contract of course is to make that brick sewer as it is described in the specification, and as it is shown on the plan.

Then, there is in the contract a stipulation which is to take effect if any alterations or additions are to be made to the work which has to be done. There is nothing about saying, if the work becomes more difficult for the contractor to do, then he shall be paid for that difficulty. He is to be paid if there are alterations in the work which is described in the specification and shown upon the plan, and if there are other works to be done, additions to that, and the third clause says—"such alterations, omissions and additions as the contractor shall from time to time be required to make by order in writing sanctioned by the urban authority under the hand of their clerk, or their said surveyor, and no others shall be made by the contractor." Now, what is the meaning of that in this business contract? Of course it is that if you make inconvenient alterations or additions without having the order in writing sanctioned by the urban authority under the hand of their clerk or surveyor you are not to be paid for it. That is the true meaning of that.

Now, it is said that that makes the surveyor an arbitrator as to that clause. If it makes the surveyor an arbitrator it makes the clerk an arbitrator, not the particular clerk having the conduct of the works, but the clerk of the urban authority. It really is a farce to suppose that that is making him an arbitrator. They say that it is to be done by their order under the hand of their clerk or their surveyor. It requires, therefore, two things. First of all, that they should give the order or agree to the order, and then that that order should be made known to the contractor either by the clerk or by the surveyor, and the surveyor's duty in that part of it is only to make known to the contractor the order of the urban authority. I know that with regard to another part of the work, if the work is done according to the contract, and within the terms of the contract, the surveyor is to give a certificate.

Where a surveyor is put into that position to give a certificate I do not say that he is an arbitrator, but he is an independent person. His duty is to give the certificate according to his own conscience and

1893
February 1.

Court of
Appeal.

according to what he conceives to be the right and truth as to the work done, and for that purpose he has no right to obey any order or any suggestion by these people who are called his masters. For that purpose they are not his masters. He is to do that on his own conscience wholly independent of them, and to act fairly and honestly as between them and the contractor. Therefore, the surveyor has different positions in this respect. As to the additional works, he is to obey the instructions of the urban authority, and to make known to the contractor what he does not know already; but as regards the certificates he has an independent and further duty, which is a duty as between the contractor and the Corporation, and as regards that he ought not to take any suggestion except what he thinks right either from the contractor or from the urban authority.

That being so, the plaintiff here entered into a contract, and then going on with the works he comes to that part which he is bound to do—to make the sewer through a portion of ground which the specification and the plan showed—he is to make it according to the plan and specification; that is, he is to take the line shown on the plan, he is to make the sewer as described in the specification. It is not shown really that he cannot do that. It is being done now. Everything which he says it is impossible to do is being done, or has been done, but what he found was that he could not do it without taking some precautions—additional precautions which he had not anticipated. He found the ground wet when he thought it was going to be dry. He says that the specification indicated to him that it was going to be dry. What counsel have to urge is that that makes a difference. They have to urge it on behalf of their client, but it is a wholly wrong way of putting it. If a representation had been made that the ground as a fact was dry—if it was only a representation and no part of the contract, then it would not be a warranty. It would not be an undertaking binding them. It would be a statement which, if it was erroneous, would not bind them.

The truth is that the contractor ought to take the precautions necessary for the purpose of protecting himself, and he is not to be protected by the other contracting party unless they contract to do so. First of all, that statement in the specification does not seem to be a representation at all, and secondly, if it was, it is no part of the contract. They have not contracted that it shall be true, and therefore it is not a warranty, and is immaterial. This is just like some other cases that we have had where the ground is shown to the contractor. The plan shows him the ground, and before he contracts he ought to go to the ground itself and examine the ground, and see

1893
February 1.

Court of
Appeal.

whether he thinks he can do the work according to the plan, and whether he can do it on the terms of the specification. As we said in the *York case* (a) he ought to have gone into the grass meadows by the river and examined them, and if he found them to be a swamp, he ought not to have taken the contract until it was altered, and he ought not to go headlong at it, and then say, "Oh, I thought it was dry, and when I found it was wet I had a right to ask them to drain it, or to ask them to give me a cutting, in which I could make it independently, so as to enable me to do the work." He takes the risk of being swamped, and that is the case here, and therefore the contractor here had no right to throw up the work. He did throw it up, and in such a way as to entitle the Corporation to say, "You have thrown up the contract; we accept your throwing up of the contract subject to this, that we may be entitled to sue you for damages, otherwise we take it as a breach of the contract by you as entitling us to employ some one else in your place, which we do."

Then he says, "Supposing that is so, nevertheless I have done some work, and I ought to be paid for the work that I have done." The contract is express that if he has done work he is not to be paid unless he gets a certificate. Then there comes this: "However wrong the surveyor may be we admit that you cannot recover unless you have got his certificate, but we say that is altered if his wrongful act is done by collusion with us, because we should have been a party to preventing his giving a certificate which he ought to have given." It is not necessary to determine how that would be. I should say myself that if they wickedly by collusion with the surveyor prevented him giving the certificate which he ought to have given, I should treat the case as though he had given the certificate. But there is no shadow of evidence here to show that the Corporation did that wicked thing which was to instigate the surveyor and to agree with the surveyor that he should cheat the plaintiff by wrongfully refusing to give him a certificate. It is a suggestion made in the stress of the case. There is not a shadow of evidence for it, and there is no ground for it whatever.

Under these circumstances it seems to me that the plaintiff has clearly failed, and that this appeal must be dismissed, with costs.

As to the plant—the plaintiff has suggested that he has a cause of action because the Corporation have wrongfully kept his plant. I am inclined to think that they could not keep his plant of their own will, and that he would have a right to have that plant, but they

(a) *Bottoms* v. *York Corporation, ante,* p. 208.

1893
February 1.

Court of
Appeal.

have never assumed to keep it. They have never asserted that they could keep it. It has always been there for him to take, and he has never applied for it. Then, of course, you cannot maintain an action on the ground that they have wrongfully retained it, and they say now at this moment if he chooses to send for this timber he can have it. There is no ground for the action in that respect.

As regards the materials, it seems that under the fourth clause they were the defendants' materials and they have a right to keep them.

BOWEN, L.J.: I agree.

A. L. SMITH, L.J.: I agree. This is an action brought by a builder and contractor against the Corporation of Workington to recover over 7,000*l.*, and he brings his action for work and labour done and gives credit for 500*l.* which has been paid.

It is quite manifest that he cannot sue on his contract, for the best of all reasons, that he has not got the certificate, which is a condition precedent to his maintaining an action on the contract for work and labour done. Unless he can get rid of this condition precedent by showing that the Corporation and the architect, acting in collusion, have withheld the certificate—or I might go further and say—that the Corporation have themselves hindered and prevented the engineer from giving the certificate, the Corporation have a good answer to any claim on the contract—"Produce your certificate—we are not responsible on the contract." But then it is said on behalf of this contractor—"I am entitled to get rid of that and sue for a *quantum meruit* because you have broken your contract and prevented me completing my contract, and if not for a *quantum meruit* I am entitled to sue you for the damages I have sustained," and that brings me to the point whether the plaintiff has made out that the defendants have broken their contract. My Lord has said, and I agree with his statement of what the true meaning of this contract is. I do not think it right to recapitulate what he has said, but it seems to me that it is a mistake to argue that the works contemplated by the contract could not be carried out by the contractor, because in my judgment they could have been carried out, and can be carried out, and I believe are being carried out at the present moment.

The real thing is that they could not be carried out without some extra expense, and that is the whole history of this case, and they could not be carried out because water was found. A drain was required and a concrete bottom was required, and the point taken by the engineer to the Corporation was this—"The expense will fall on you and not on the Corporation." Says the builder, "Nothing

1893
February 1.

Court of
Appeal.

of the sort, unless you give me an order for what I will call the drain and the concrete, I will not go on at all," and the engineer says, "I will do nothing of the sort, because that is a liability which falls on you under the contract and not upon the Corporation." The question is, which is right on that? In my judgment the engineer was perfectly right. This contractor having undertaken to execute those works according to the plan and specification has not done so, and he has not done so because he would not put his hands into his pocket and execute some further works which were necessary (on account of the water that was found) to render the contract work capable of being carried out. Therefore I say that when he says that the Corporation have committed a breach of the contract so as to allow him to sue them for the breach of contract and for damages, he does not prove the breach, and he fails in that entirely.

I have nothing to add to what my Lord has said about the plant and materials, but I am clearly of opinion that this action wholly fails.

Appeal dismissed.

Solicitors for the plaintiff: Harrison & Powell, agents for McKeedy & Co., Carlisle. Solicitors for the defendants: Tatham & Procter.

1893
January 13.

Queen's
Bench
Division.

In the High Court of Justice (Queen's Bench Division).

(*Before* WILLS, J., without a Jury.)

D. CAMPBELL AND SON *v.* BLYTON.

*Quantity Surveyor—Memorandum of Charges on Bill of Quantities
—Tenders—Liability of Selected Builder to Quantity Surveyor
—Effect of Insolvency of Building Owner.*

The plaintiff, a quantity surveyor, was employed by the architect of a building owner to prepare a bill of quantities for tenders. The bill as prepared contained an item for the quantity surveyor's charges and a memorandum to the effect that they should be payable out of the first moneys received by the builder. Held, (1) that the builder whose tender on the quantities was accepted was liable to the quantity surveyor for the charges specified in the bill out of the first instalment received under the contract; (2) that the taking over by the builder of a mortgage on the building *bonâ fide* to protect his claim under the building contract was not such a receipt of moneys under the contract as to entitle the quantity surveyor to recover, nor such a prevention of his receipt of the instalment as to entitle the quantity surveyor to sue for his charges.

1893
January 13.

Queen's
Bench
Division.

The plaintiffs, who were quantity surveyors, sued the defendant, a builder, for 48*l.* 16*s.* 8*d.* commission calculated at the rate of 1½ per cent, upon the sum of 3,255*l*, the amount of a tender made by the defendant and accepted by one Henry Frederick Nash for the re-building of Nos. 285, 286, Strand, and for 36*l.* 10*s.* for expenses of lithography and for taking out quantities of credits of old materials and of an additional order for mosaic paving.

The plaintiffs took out the quantities on the instructions of Mr. Janson, the building owner's architect, before tenders were invited. The estimate in the bill of quantities, after summarizing the tender at 3,255*l.* 14*s.*, went on thus:—

| These two accounts to be the quantity surveyor's out of the first instalment received by the contractor. | Surveyor's charge for quantities, 1½ per cent. on the above amount .. | £48 16 0 |
| | Ditto for expenses of lithography, quantities of credits and separate amount, &c................. | £36 10 0 |

The defendant tendered upon the basis of this estimate, and his tender was accepted. He was unable to obtain payment of the first instalment, and took over a mortgage on the building to protect his interests under the building contract.

The plaintiffs rested their claim (1) on the memorandum annexed to the bill of quantities; (2) on the usage of the building trade.

The defendant resisted payment (1) on denial of the usage; (2) on an allegation that the building contract was rescinded; (3) that the payment of the charges for quantities was conditional on receipt of the first instalment, which had not been made.

The plaintiffs replied (1) that rescission was no answer to the claim; (2) that the defendant by taking the mortgage had either received the instalment or prevented its receipt, and was in either event liable for the fee.

Jelf and Herbert Jacobs for the plaintiffs.

They cited *North* v. *Bassett* (*a*), *Priestley* v. *Stone* (*b*), *Pilbrow* v. *Pilbrow* (*c*), *Scott* v. *Lord Ebury* (*d*), *Sunderland, &c. Co.* v. *Kearney* (*e*), and *Hancock* v. *Hodgson* (*f*).

Arthur Powell for the defendant.

WILLS, J.: This case is not free from difficulty, but seems to me to reduce itself to one very simple question. I have no doubt whatever what the contract is, and I cannot say that there is any question of custom arising here, or that it helps matters at all to talk about custom. Here is a quantity surveyor who takes out quantities, and

(*a*) [1892] 1 Q. B. 33.
(*b*) *Ante*, p. 134; 4 T. L. R. 730.
(*c*) 5 C. B. 440.
(*d*) L. R. 2 C. P. 255.
(*e*) 16 Q. B. 925.
(*f*) 4 Bing. 269.

he hands to the man who ultimately gets the contract the paper prepared by him which leaves two amounts in the margin (*vide supra*) which are to be paid to the surveyor for his charges, and paid to him undoubtedly by the person who gets the contract. In the margin are put these two amounts to be paid to the quantity surveyor out of the first instalment received by the contractor. Now, if that is not a good bargain between the quantity surveyor and the builder, quite apart from any question of custom or anything else, if that is not a good bargain on the evidence between these two persons that these two payments, amounting to about 84*l.* or 85*l.*, should be paid by the builder to the quantity surveyor out of the first instalment received by the contractor, and if it is not a good bargain by the quantity surveyor to take his payment out of that first instalment, I do not know what language means.

It does not seem to me that any of these questions as to whether it is a liability arising by reason of a custom or by reason of its being money had and received, or anything of that sort, makes the slightest difference. It is a contract between these two parties that the quantity surveyor should receive his charges out of the first instalment received by the contractor. Now, the first instalment was, under the circumstances which happened, 1,500*l.* If the contractor has received any portion of that 1,500*l.* sufficient to cover these charges, in my judgment he would be liable to hand it over—I will not say hand it over, but to pay money which he has contracted to pay out of the first instalment to the quantity surveyor, and if he has not received anything on behalf of the first instalment, it seems to me that he has not received the fund out of which the quantity surveyor was content to take and bound himself to take his remuneration. In this case he certainly has not received it, but he would be equally liable if he has done anything which prevents him from receiving it. Now, I am not at all impressed with the fact that he has altered the denomination of the liability from a liability to pay the only instalment, to a liability to pay the mortgage money. If there is any portion of the money which becomes due under the mortgage, which goes, or ought to go, in reduction of the liability of the building owner on this contract, that, it seems to me, would satisfy the description of the first instalment, and, under the circumstances, would be applicable to the payment of this sum.

Now, has he done anything to prevent himself from receiving that, or has he only taken the best steps which a prudent man would take, acting in the interests of the plaintiff, as well as of himself, to try and get that money? Nash, I cannot have any doubt, is impecunious, and would have been broken up. He, naturally, does not like to admit it in so many words: but I cannot have any doubt, upon the evidence before me, that if at the time that this mortgage arrangement was made between the defendant and Nash, if Nash had been pressed for this 1,500*l.* he would have been broken up, and probably no part of it would have been secured. But what does the defendant do under those circumstances?

He is liable himself to be turned out by the mortgagee and have the whole of his expenditure lost. He is threatened with that event by the mortgagee, and, of course, if that had been the case nobody can doubt that Magdalen College, the head landlord, would have interfered and would not have granted the leases, and the whole speculation would have ended in disaster, in which case nothing, certainly, would have been got out of Nash. He took, in order to avoid that, a transfer of the mortgage, and he was perfectly at liberty to do so, and having taken the transfer of the mortgage, as far as the 1,660*l.* is concerned, which is paid before the transfer, he becomes mortgagee in respect of that, and becomes properly and legitimately mortgagee, and that is a charge which will take priority of any other liability on the part of Nash to him. He also expends further money.

Now, if I thought that that had not been *bonâ fide* done for the purpose of getting anything out of the speculation and out of Nash, if it had been done for his own purposes and in order to create a debt which would swallow up everything that he could get from Nash to the detriment of the plaintiff, I should have felt very differently about it; but I think it was really money honestly expended in the nature of salvage and to prevent the whole concern, the whole speculation, from bursting up, in which case probably nobody would ever have got anything out of it at all. The result is that he, in that sense, has spent a large sum of money, and he has become entitled under those circumstances to a sum which brings Nash's liability to him under the contract up to 3,600*l.*

Now, if he had wilfully abstanied from receiving all that he could get out of Nash in order to keep the security going, and to get himself the advantage of a permanent investment instead of trying to get the 1,500*l.* paid, I should have said that that would not be right, and that if he had done anything of that kind he would have been disabling himself from receiving the money; but I am satisfied that he has *bonâ fide* endeavoured to get everything out of this that he could, and if he has been unable to get anything more than will

1893
January 13.

Queen's
Bench
Division.

cover the interest of the money that he cannot get paid, and which he is, against his own will, obliged to stand out of, then it seems to me that he has done nothing to disable himself from receiving the 1,500*l.* as soon as he can.

I think I am satisfied on the evidence that his conduct has been *bonâ fide*, and that there has been an effort on his part to get everything that he could out of Nash. It is said that he might have sold, but I do not see that he is bound to sell, and he is not bound to sell at a ruinous sacrifice in order to realise this particular sum to get paid off Nash's liability. I think that, under the circumstances which have taken place, he has received no money which is applicable to the reduction of this 1,500*l.* or the 3,600*l.*, that he will not matter which way you put it), and that his arrangements and dealings with Nash have been *bonâ fide* and with a genuine effort and desire to get out of him as much as he could, and to get his money paid and discharged as soon as he could. I am very clearly of opinion myself that if he ever does get anything which reduces that 1,500*l.*, whether he gets 100*l.*, or 1,000*l.*, or 1,500*l.*, that he will have got something out of that first instalment, as it ought to be looked at, as between him and the plaintiff, and that he will have to pay the money. But I think that, until he does do so, if he has not interfered or done something which a reasonable man ought not to do, which postpones that period, he is not liable, because I think that he has, in the natural course of things, and by no fault of his own, failed to receive the money which is necessary to constitute the fund out of which the payment is to be made. I think, therefore, that my judgment must be for the defendant with costs.

Solicitors for the plaintiff: Hubbard, Son, & Eve. Solicitors for the defendant: Dunkerton & Son.

𝕴𝖓 𝖙𝖍𝖊 𝕳𝖎𝖌𝖍 𝕮𝖔𝖚𝖗𝖙 𝖔𝖋 𝕵𝖚𝖘𝖙𝖎𝖈𝖊 (𝕼𝖚𝖊𝖊𝖓'𝖘 𝕭𝖊𝖓𝖈𝖍 𝕯𝖎𝖛𝖎𝖘𝖎𝖔𝖓).

1893
January 19.

Queen's
Bench
Division.

(DAY and COLLINS, JJ.)

IN THE MATTER OF AN ARBITRATION BETWEEN JOHN DONKIN AND THE COMPANY OF PROPRIETORS OF THE LEEDS AND LIVERPOOL CANAL.

Building Contract—Arbitration Clause—Delay due to Alteration in Plans—Alleged Partiality of the Engineer—Submission when Revocable—Arbitration Act, 1889 (52 & 53 Vict. c. 49), s. 4.

The High Court will not revoke a submission to arbitration contained in a building contract unless it is satisfied that the arbitrator cannot deal with the matter in dispute impartially or without adjudicating on his own neglects and defaults. The contractor is not entitled to have the submission revoked on the ground that he has claims in respect of the work done not within the arbitration clause with which it will be convenient to try disputes within that clause.

By a contract under seal, dated the 6th October, 1885, John Donkin agreed, for the sum of 48,989*l.*, to construct a reservoir at Winterburn in accordance with a tender and specification annexed to the contract and with other documents, drawings and writings signed by him or referred to on the tender and specification. It was stipulated that the work should be done to the entire satisfaction of the engineer for the time being of the company.

The 9th clause of the agreement was as follows:—

"And it is hereby declared and agreed that in case of any question or dispute arising between the parties hereto as to any matter connected with this contract, such question or dispute shall be settled by the engineer for the time being of the company, whose decision shall be final and binding on the said parties and without appeal."

The work was put under the superintendence of an assistant engineer, who was constantly on the spot. The consulting engineer was Mr. Henry Rolfe. During the progress of the works Mr. Rolfe made very extensive alterations from the works as originally designed and shown on the plans and specification. The contractor alleged that the alterations were unnecessary, and that their effect was that 18,800*l.* worth of the original work was executed, and that the altered and extra work amounted to 43,600*l.*, and that during the progress of the works continued delay occurred owing to change of design and failure to deliver the working plans and by the non-delivery of apparatus which the canal company had contracted to supply.

The works were completed on 18th August, 1891, some two years after the time fixed by the contract. After their completion the contractor sent in a claim for further payment, and was dissatisfied with the mode in which it was dealt with by the engineer. So in June, 1892, he formulated and sent in to the canal company a full statement of his claims for extras and for damage caused by delay, and repeating his complaints against the engineer, alleging that he

1893
January 19.

Queen
Bench
Division.

had refused to give any reasons for his disallowance of twelve items amounting to 5,000*l.* under the head of extras, and that he had, during the work, threatened to refuse certificates if the contractor disputed his decisions.

The company were of opinion that a number of claims included in the statement had not been adjudicated upon by the engineer, and they appointed the 20th December, 1892, to hold an arbitration under clause 9 as to the claims.

The contractor then moved to revoke the submission to arbitration on the grounds:

That the engineer was unfit to decide as arbitrator because of his conduct above stated, and because he would have to decide on the propriety or impropriety of his own acts, and to arbitrate upon his own negligence in estimating works at 43,000*l.* which had cost 63,000*l.* to complete, or, if the contractor's claims were allowed, 73,000*l.*

Sir R. Webster, Q.C., and R. M. Bray, in support of the motion, argued that claims for delay were not within the arbitration clause, and that the engineer was not a fit person to decide as to the extras. They cited *Lawson v. Wallasey Local Board (a)*, *Roberts v. Bury Commissioners (b)*, and *Jackson v. Barry Rail. Co. (c).*

Jelf, Q.C., and Gore, for the canal company, argued—

(1) That the claim for damages was within the arbitration clause.

(2) That no ground had been shown for revoking the submission.

(3) That the contractor had taken the chance of a decision in his favour as to part at least of the claim.

(4) That part of the claim had not been submitted to the engineer, and he had shown no bias with respect to it.

They cited *Ranger v. Great Western Rail. Co. (d)*, *Trowsdale v. Jopp (e)*, *Nuttall v. Mayor and Corporation of Manchester (f)*, *James v. James (g)*, and *Lyon v. Johnson (h).*

DAY, J.: I entertain no doubt that upon contracts of this description contractors are bound by the term which is ordinarily introduced, namely, that the engineer appointed under the contract shall be the arbitrator upon all questions concerning the contract or arising out of the contract. At the same time I am clearly of opinion that, unless some words such as I have never yet seen imported into these contracts are used, an engineer or architect, named in the contract as arbitrator, is not thereupon endowed with exclusive jurisdiction in case of claims made which involve the determination of whether the

(*a*) 11 Q. B. D. 229.
(*b*) L. R. 4 C. P. 755; L. R. 5 C. P. 310.
(*c*) [1893] 1 Ch. 238.
(*d*) 5 H. L. C. 72, 88.
(*e*) 2 Ct. of Sess. Cas. (3rd series) 1334.
(*f*) *Ante*, p. 203.
(*g*) 23 Q. B. D. 12.
(*h*) 40 Ch. D. 579, 583.

supposed arbitrator has or has not misconducted himself. I have never yet seen any contract the terms of which were such as to lead a Court to the inference that the parties had deliberately determined that the person whose conduct was impugned was to be the arbitrator to determine whether his conduct was justly impugned or not. It would be contrary certainly to the ordinary notions which one entertains of the administration of justice to provide that a person should be called upon to determine whether a third person had or had not a claim against an employer which involved the question of whether the arbitrator himself had brought that claim about by his own negligence or misconduct. Therefore it is clear to my mind that, upon a contract such as the present and which contained such words as these, the engineer is not entitled to arbitrate—has no jurisdiction to arbitrate upon any question involving his own misconduct; and that if any question involving his own misconduct is raised, the jurisdiction of such engineer is ousted, and the person is left to his ordinary remedy at law to secure redress.

1893
January 19.

Queen's
Bench
Division.

The present application is one to revoke the submission to arbitration, and we are asked to revoke the submission to this arbitration on the ground that some portion of the questions and the matters in dispute between the parties and which are to be submitted to arbitration, are questions involving misconduct on the part of the arbitrator; that is to say, misconduct in the sense of failure to deliver plans or to give instructions within reasonable times. The great bulk of the claim, or, at least, a large portion of the claim, is unconnected with any such alleged misconduct, but is matter which, ordinarily speaking, falls within the contract or arises out of the contract, quite irrespective of any alleged misconduct on the part of the engineer, and is matter which the parties have deliberately by their own contract elected to refer to the engineer, and matter which, therefore, the engineer has clear jurisdiction to try, and which the parties are entitled to have tried by the tribunal which they have selected by their contract for the purpose.

I should not have hesitated in the present case to hold that this submission should be revoked, if I had been satisfied that a substantial portion of this claim was in respect of some misconduct of the proposed arbitrator or of the engineer appointed by the contract. [The learned judge then went through the claims of the contractor in respect of alterations and delay, and continued.] But I am not satisfied that those are charges of delay other than such charges of delay as naturally will arise in the course of any extensive works of this description.

1893
January 19.

Queen's
Bench
Division.

I am not satisfied at all that they are charges of delay which had the character of charges of misconduct on the part of the company's servants, that is to say, charges' of negligence on the part of the company's servants to provide the necessary plans within a reasonable time;. but they may be taken to be, and they would seem *Primâ facie* to be, claims for delay in the ordinary course where change of plans takes place. Now, change of plans is necessarily contemplated in works of this more or less uncertain description where so much depends on the character of the ground when it comes to be disturbed, and where so much depends on the adaptation of means to ends which are constantly varying with the development of works of this character; the applicant has failed to satisfy me that he has a substantial claim against the company in respect of negligent discharge of duty on the part of the engineer who is appointed the arbitrator under the contract.

It seems to me that it would not be right, unless I were thoroughly satisfied that there was such a *bonâ fide* and substantial ground of complaint in respect of such matter, to revoke the submission merely upon the ground that an engineer in this position is disqualified from acting as arbitrator by reason of his having been employed on behalf of the employer to superintend the work of the contractor; to control the contractor; and to act in the interests of the employer towards the contractor. That is naturally the position which an engineer or architect under contracts of this description always occupies, and this provision is one which has been in force for a very great number of years. For a very long period that has been found satisfactory to contractors, on the one hand, and to employers, on the other, and is not likely lightly or idly to be interfered with or such submissions to be revoked, except upon grave and substantial grounds.

I do not mean to express any opinion, and I hope it will not be supposed that I entertain any opinion, for I certainly do entertain no opinion, as to whether the contractor in this case has or has not reasonably good and just grounds of complaint against the engineer. I myself always regret it when I find that employers insist upon the enforcement of conditions of this description. I think myself that it is eminently desirable, in the estimation of any just-minded man, that any dispute which he has with his fellow should be determined by some impartial person, and I think it is very undesirable that the decision of disputes of this sort by persons who may be even suspected of partiality should be insisted upon. These persons have made a contract under which they have left it to the engineer to determine these matters.

The engineer has acted in the interest of his employer. He is now called upon under this contract to act as arbitrator. The parties have made their contract and they must abide by their contract. I cannot interfere with the contract until I am satisfied that upon the evidence the person so appointed to act in the matter is a person who has become interested in the result by reason of some charge which is involved in the claim which is made and upon which he has to adjudicate. As I am not satisfied upon that subject I feel that I should not be justified in interfering at this stage with the submission which I am asked to decide should be revoked. I am of opinion that this application fails for the reasons which I have endeavoured to explain, but I hope it will not be understood that in any way I express any opinion whatever upon any of the facts which have been brought before us. Upon the facts all that I say is this, that I am not satisfied at present on these affidavits that the arbitrator has so conducted himself that the submission ought to be revoked. Under the present circumstances I am not satisfied that we ought to revoke this submission upon the ground that a substantial portion of the claim is a claim which involves a charge of misconduct, in the sense which I have endeavoured to explain, against the engineer.

COLLINS, J.: I am of the same opinion. The application is to revoke the submission. The applicant is a contractor who says he has a claim against the Company of Proprietors of the Leeds Canal to the extent of a sum of between 6,000*l.* and 7,000*l.* For work done under the contract; that is to say, for extras properly ordered by the person who is charged with the duty of ordering them, if he thought them necessary, namely, the engineer under the contract. He says also that he has another claim which he says is one outside the contract, for an independent wrong, namely, for the default of the defendants through their engineer in furnishing him with the necessary plans, whereby he was delayed in the performance of his work; and under those circumstances he asks the Court to revoke the submission.

He comes here, therefore, admitting that as to rather more than half the nominal amount of his claim there is unquestionably jurisdiction in the engineer to decide it: as to another part of his claim, he says that there is no jurisdiction, and the ground upon which he puts his application is, as to that part which is within the jurisdiction, that he has a right in one and the same action to embrace a claim for damage which is not within the submission, and a claim for money payable which is within the submission; and he says that

1893
January 19.

Queen's
Bench
Division.

1893
January 19.

Queen's
Bench
Division.

the two are so liked together that he ought to be at liberty to try them before one tribunal, and that therefore it is inconvenient to try them before the engineer on grounds he indicates, and that therefore he ought to be at liberty to revoke the submission which covers that part of the claim, as to which he admits that there is jurisdiction in the engineer to deal with it as arbitrator.

When one examines the contract and examines the grounds which are put forward by the applicant, I am of opinion that he has not made out his case. The contract gives very full powers indeed to the engineer; and the last clause of the contract provides that "in case of any question or dispute arising between the parties hereto as to any matter connected with this contract such question or dispute shall be settled by the engineer for the time being of the company, whose decision shall be final." And the 87th clause of the appended specification, which is also made part of the contract, provides further "that the engineer shall have full power to order any alterations in, additions to, or deductions from the works included in the contract that he may consider advisable, and the contractor shall be bound to execute any extra or other work which may be required by the engineer, or to leave unexecuted any work which the engineer shall require not to be done, or to alter any portions of the work in any manner that the engineer may require, &c., &c. [reading clause to the words], without extra charge." Clause 91 is also important. It says: "No alterations, additions, or deductions that may be made to or from the works shall in any way invalidate the contract," &c., &c. [reading to the words], "shall certify the same in writing."

Now, by the contract between the parties the engineer is placed in complete control over the contract. It is his duty to direct the contractor according to his judgment as to what he is to do. He has complete power to alter the contract and to order extras under the contract; and the contractor by virtue of this contract cannot complain, even though a very large amount of the original work contemplated by the contract is omitted, and a very large amount of work not contemplated by the contract is introduced. That is a matter as to which he has bound himself by the terms of his contract to leave himself in the hands of the engineer; and so far as any complaint of his is based on the fact that having expected to do works of a certain character embraced in the contract he has found himself compelled to do works of a different character not embraced in the terms of the contract, but still covered by the provision as to extras—so far as he grounds any complaints on these facts, he has no cause of claim whatever.

1893
January 19.

Queen's
Bench
Division.

Now, that being so, over and above the fact that a large amount of extras, which he had not thought he might have to deal with, have been ordered by the engineer to be done, and that delay has thereby been caused, he says that there has been also delay by the unreasonable withholding of the plans necessary to his purpose in order to execute the works ordered by the engineer. Now, I want to see how far these allegations carry him in the direction of saying that the engineer who is the person designated by this contract as the person to arbitrate between them is for any reason unfitted to arbitrate in this matter, and the applicant bases it on two grounds, as I understand, mainly.

First of all, he says it ought to be dealt with as though he had actually commenced an action and proceedings were taken by the defendants to stay the action under the provisions of sect. 4 of the Arbitration Act, 1889, and that it is to be decided on the same grounds, viz., that the judge, if satisfied that there is no sufficient reason why the matter should not be referred in accordance with the submission, and that the applicant was, at the time the proceedings were commenced, and still remains, willing to do all things necessary for the proper conduct of the arbitration, may direct a stay. Therefore, so far as he bases it on the 4th section, his point seems to be this, that he has a cause of action which could not be referred, that it is more convenient that that cause of action should be tried by the same tribunal that decides the cause of action which can be referred, and he submits by reason of the fact that there is a cause of action against the arbitrator which cannot be referred to him, that therefore the submission ought to be revoked.

Now, coming at this stage when he is *dominus litis* and can establish his claim as he chooses, and has a valid claim in his view for 6,000*l.*, as to which he has contracted to submit himself to arbitration, it does not appear to me that he is in any way bound to hamper that claim by introducing another claim for damages as to which he has not contracted himself to submit to arbitration; and he cannot come here and say, "I have elected to join this other claim, and therefore I claim to revoke the submission." There is nothing, as far as I can see at present, to prevent him, if he chooses—at all events, at this stage, he can consider his whole position—from saying he has a right to go to arbitration. He has an obligation to submit to arbitration as to 6,000*l.* of this claim: he is not bound to superadd the other claim. He might bring his action for the 6,000*l.* now if he liked, or for any damages he chose without in the slightest degree embarrassing and putting aside his claim for extras.

1893
January 19.

Queen's
Bench
Division.

On the one ground—the mere ground that he has a right of action which it would be inconvenient to try before the same tribunal as an arbitrator—he suggests that that in itself is a reason why it is not convenient that the matter should be referred, but it seems to me it would be very wrong to lay down as a principle that that position holds good, because one cannot help knowing that where the contractors have bound themselves to the onerous terms which are usual in these contracts when it comes to the point they constantly try to avoid going to the arbitrament of the engineer who necessarily has indicated an opinion on the matter. Well, if it were open to them, merely by bringing an action against the other party to the contract for something done independently of the contract and putting it in the same writ with the claim for extras, to relieve themselves from the obligation of going to arbitration by that simple expedient that there would be no use at all in introducing this clause as to arbitration to which they assent in these contracts. So that one has to scrutinize to see whether there is really any thoroughly substantial claim for some wrong outside that which it is contemplated by the contract shall be submitted to the arbitrament of the engineer. That is one ground.

The other ground that it is put upon by Sir Richard Webster is not merely this question of inconvenience being a sufficient reason and so on, going to discretion, but it is a ground which, if established, would show that the arbitrator was unfit for the post, that is to say, he suggests that there is such a bias on the part of the arbitrator as to unfit him for the quasi-judicial position of an arbitrator.

Now it comes back very much to the same point when we examine the allegations in the affidavits, because, though there are general allegations by the contractor that the engineer disallowed claims which he ought to have allowed, and behaved in such a way as in the opinion of the contractor to evince partiality, he does not descend to particulars in any way or point to any concrete instance which would afford evidence that the engineer was acting otherwise than *bonâ fide*. It is obvious that in a long contract of this kind there must be endless topics of complaint between the contractor and the engineer. There must be a great deal of friction, and no amount of friction of that kind would be a sufficient ground for relieving the contractor from his contract, which is to accept the arbitrament of the person who really is the master of the contract, and whose right it is to dictate to him how he is to do his work, what amount of work he is to omit doing, and what extra work he is to do. Mere friction will not do.

1893
January 19.

Queen's
Bench
Division.

On the other hand, it is equally clear, and although a contractor has bound himself to accept the arbitrament of an arbitrator who is necessarily not an unbiassed arbitrator, the engineer may so commit himself to an adverse opinion as to make it clear that he is not going to give a judicial or quasi-judicial mind to the consideration of a dispute arising upon the contract, and if that were made clear to the Court, the Court would of course refuse to allow him to act as arbitrator. The case of *Nuttall* v. *Corporation of Manchester (a)* has been cited as an authority for that proposition. The decision there I say nothing about. It has been suggested by Mr. Jelf that it is not consistent with another decision of the Lords Justices in another application of the same kind (*b*), but the principle laid down there no one can quarrel with.

The judges satisfied themselves in that case that there was conduct on the part of the engineer which showed that he could not and would not bring an unbiassed mind, or a mind in a quasi-unbiassed condition, to bear upon the questions submitted to him in the arbitration. He had indicated that he would not as an arbitrator consider it at all. He had committed himself to a particular course which in their view grounded the inference that he could not bring any judicial capacity to bear upon it at all, and if you arrive at that conclusion of course he could not be arbitrator. On the other hand the mere fact that he has been obliged to take an adverse line to the contractor on the point in question is no ground for relieving the contractor from going to arbitration before him, because that is the very thing that the contractor has contracted that the engineer shall do.

Now in this case, when one examines the grounds which the contractor puts forward, I find that in the forefront of his affidavit he puts the enormous amount of extras that has been introduced into the contract—the radical change which has been made in what he had to do from what he expected he would have to do. That is put in the forefront. So far as his case rested on that, as I have already pointed out, he has no case, because that was a matter which the engineer was entirely justified in ordering if he thought fit. But then he superadds to that that there was a delay in giving the plans. I have looked at his affidavit very carefully with a view to see whether he does do what in my judgment it is necessary that he should do in

(*a*) (1891), *ante*, p. 203.
(*b*) *Jackson* v. *Barry Rail. Co.*, (1893) 1 Ch. 238.

1893
January 19.

Queen's
Bench
Division.

order to succeed on that; that is, to show that there was delay in giving the plaintiff plans, other than the delay incidental to a radical alteration in the work to be done.

Now he has shown that the forefront of his complaint is a radical alteration in the contract. He then adds that there was delay in giving the plans. Undoubtedly there was delay. It is common ground that there must be delay, and, so far as that delay was reasonably incident to a change in the plans, that is no ground of independent action against the defendants at all. And I am not satisfied here—and I should require to be satisfied in the case of a person who was trying to get out of that which is a clear part of his obligation, namely, that of going to arbitration before this engineer—I should require to be satisfied by very clear evidence that he had a really substantial claim for some wrong done outside the contract and outside the terms of the submission before I yielded to the assertion that he had such a claim as a ground for relieving him from the obligation of going to arbitration.

Now, as has already been pointed out by my learned brother, not only is his case open to that observation made on his own affidavit which grounds his application here, but when one comes to look at what he did before this application was formulated, we find that in August, 1891, after all the work had been done under the contract, he sent in a most elaborate claim. He sent that claim in, accompanied by a letter going in the greatest possible detail into all his claims, and at the end of those claims he unquestionably did put in a claim which is in the nature of one for damages for delay as to some arrangement of valves which he says involved him in considerable delay, inasmuch as he was not placed in a position to do the work he was ordered to do; and in explaining his ground of complaint as to that delay in his letter he does not allude to the want of plans, though he must have had the matter in his mind and he must have had all the facts in his mind as to the delay caused by the want of plans. He never alludes to it at all, and he does put his delay, not as delay caused to him by the failure of the defendants to give him the materials for going on with the work, but he puts it as delay on the part of the defendants in withholding payment of money that was due to him after it was due, all these complaints which are formulated in the notice itself are of the same character. He says: "I make this claim in accordance with the notice given on the 18th November last. It is quite evident that the delay has been made for the benefit of the company, and surely you do not wish me to be a loser for their benefit, but whether the delay has been made for the purpose named or not, the claim must be paid, as it is beyond all reason that I should be expected to be at the expense of waiting here for twelve months after the works are completed, and that the company should hold 8,474*l.* of my money for the same period without any acknowledgment." The delay he is complaining of there, is substantially the delay, after the work had been done, in paying.

1893
January 19.

Queen's
Bench
Division.

Sir Richard Webster points out that it is a claim sent in by an unskilled person—sent in by the contractor without legal advice. I think that is against Sir Richard Webster's case, because an unskilled person would not divide, with the nicety which his legal adviser might, a claim under the contract for extras from a claim sounding in damages for some breach by the defendants outside the contract. It is obvious to my mind that he was then intending to formulate all his claim for all the money payable by the defendants to him, and he must have had in his mind at that time all the facts on which he now bases his claim for delay. I am of opinion that no case whatever has been made pointing to any misconduct or bias in the arbitrator, outside the mere fact that he may be liable to an action as suggested by the plaintiff, and I am not satisfied on the affidavits of the plaintiff that there is that solid substantial ground for believing that there is an independent right of action for some wrong outside the submission such as would justify us in saying that the two rights exist, that they ought to be tried by one tribunal, and that the designated tribunal, the engineer, is unfit to try them. On these grounds I think this application ought to be dismissed.

Motion dismissed with costs.

Solicitors for the plaintiff: Stewart & Son.
Solicitors for the defendants: W. J. Flower & Nussey, agents for Killick, Hutton & Vint, of Bradford.

1892
July 7.
October 28.

Queen's
Bench
Division.

1892
December 2.

Court of
Appeal.

1893
February 8.

Queen's
Bench
Division.

𝕴𝖓 𝖙𝖍𝖊 𝕳𝖎𝖌𝖍 𝕮𝖔𝖚𝖗𝖙 𝖔𝖋 𝕵𝖚𝖘𝖙𝖎𝖈𝖊 (𝕼𝖚𝖊𝖊𝖓'𝖘 𝕭𝖊𝖓𝖈𝖍 𝕯𝖎𝖛𝖎𝖘𝖎𝖔𝖓).

(MATHEW and BRUCE, JJ.)

(LORD COLERIDGE, L.C.J., and LOPES, L.J.)

𝕬𝖓𝖉 𝖎𝖓 𝖙𝖍𝖊 𝕮𝖔𝖚𝖗𝖙 𝖔𝖋 𝕬𝖕𝖕𝖊𝖆𝖑.

(LORD ESHER, M. R., and LOPES, L.J.)

CUNLIFFE *v.* HAMPTON WICK LOCAL BOARD.

Sewerage Contract—Construction—Certified Completion—Period of Maintenance—New Surveyor—Defects Clause.

> Where the surveyor who supervised the construction of sewerage works has certified completion, his successor, as surveyor for the time being, can act under the clause for maintenance or repair of defects.
>
> "Completion" held to mean "certified completion," and not completion in fact.
>
> With regard to the time of completion, held that "the several works" meant "the whole works," and not each section thereof.
>
> *Quære* whether the contractor is liable, under the defects clause, for defects consequent on the design, and not on its execution by him.
>
> Construction of word "appear" in a clause providing for defects appearing within a certain period.

1892
July 7.

Queen's
Bench
Division.

The plaintiff, a contractor, on the 14th August, 1889, entered into a contract, under seal, to execute for the defendants "the several works" therein specified or referred to, and forming a scheme of sewerage on the Shone Hydro-Pneumatic system, on the terms contained in the contract and the conditions annexed, and in a specification incorporated by reference, and under the superintendence, and to the entire satisfaction of the Hampton Wick Local Board, and of Mr. R. T. Elsam, their surveyor, or of such other surveyor as the Board should by resolution appoint.

The portions of the documents material for this report are as follows:—

(2) The contractor is to provide everything of every sort and kind which may be necessary and requisite for the due and proper execution of the several works included in the contract, according to the true intent and meaning of the *drawings and specifications taken together*, which are to be signed by Richard Thomas Elsam, the surveyor of the Hampton Wick Local Board, or the surveyor for the time being of the said Board (who are hereafter referred to as the surveyor)   .   .

(11) Any defects, shrinkage, and other faults, which may appear within three months from the completion of the several works, including any additional or extra works authorised by the surveyor under clause 6, and arising out of defective or

improper materials or workmanship, are, upon the direction of the surveyor, to be amended and made good by the contractor, at his own cost, unless the surveyor shall decide that he ought to be paid for the same; and in case of default the Local Board may recover from the contractor the cost of making good the works. The contractor shall maintain and keep in proper working order, during a period of three months from the completion of the same, the several works, including any additional or extra works which may be authorised by the surveyor under clause 6.

(14) The contractor is to complete the whole of the works within six calendar months after the commencement of the same, unless the works be delayed by reason of any inclement weather, or causes not under the contractor's control, or in the case of combination of workmen, or strikes, or lock-out, affecting any of the building trades, for which due allowance shall be made by the surveyor; and then the contractor is to complete the works within such time as the surveyor shall consider to be reasonable, and shall, from time to time, in writing, appoint; and in case of default, the contractor is to pay or allow to the Local Board, as and by way of liquidated and agreed damages, the sum of 50*l.* per week for every week during which he shall be so in default until the whole of the works (except as aforesaid) shall be so completed, provided that the surveyor shall, in writing, certify that the works could have been reasonably completed within the time appointed.

(16) When the value of the works executed, and not included in any former certificate, shall, from time to time, amount to the sum of 500*l.*, or otherwise, at the surveyor's reasonable discretion, the contractor is to be entitled to receive payment at the rate of 80 per cent. upon such value until the difference between the percentage and the value of the works executed shall amount to 10 per cent. upon the amount of the contract, after which time the contractor is to be entitled to receive payment of the full value of all works executed, and not included in any former payment, and the surveyor is to give to the contractor certificates accordingly; and the contractor is to be entitled to receive the balance of all moneys due or payable to him, under or by virtue of the contract, at the expiration of the period of maintenance of the works, namely, three months from the completion of the works. Provided always that no final or other certificate is to cover or relieve the contractor from his liability under the provisions of clause No. 11, whether or not the same be notified by the surveyor at the time or subsequently to granting any such certificate.

(17) A certificate of the surveyor, or an award of the referee, hereinafter referred to, as the case may be, showing the final balance due or payable to the contractor, is to be conclusive evidence of the work having been duly completed, and that the contractor is entitled to receive payment of the final balance, but without prejudice to the liability of the contractor under the provisions of clause No. 11.

(19) Provided always that in case any question, dispute or difference shall arise between the Local Board, or the surveyor on their behalf, and the contractor, as to what additions, if any, ought in fairness to be made to the amount of the contract by reason of the works being delayed through no fault of the contractor, or by reason or account of any directions or requisitions of the surveyor involving increased cost to the contractor beyond the cost properly attending the carrying out of the contract according to the true intent and meaning of the signed drawings and specification, or as to the works having been duly completed, or as to the construction of these presents, or as to any other matter or thing arising under or out of this contract, except as to matters left during the progress of the works to the sole decision or requisition of the surveyor under clauses Nos. 1, 9 and 10, or

in case the contractor shall be dissatisfied with any certificate of the surveyor under clause No. 7, or under the proviso in clause No. 14, or in case he shall withhold or not give any certificate to which he may be entitled, then such question, dispute, or difference, or such certificate, or the value or matter which should be certified, as the case may be, is to be, from time to time, referred to the arbitration and final decision of Isaac Shone, Esq., consulting engineer, or in the event of his death or unwillingness to act, then of F. Beesley, Esq., being a member of the Institute of Civil Engineers, or, in the event of his death or unwillingness to act, then of an engineer to be appointed, on the request of either party, by the President for the time being of such Institute; and the award of such referee is to be equivalent to a certificate of the surveyor, and to be final and binding on both parties, and the contractor is to be paid accordingly.

The specification (p. 11) contained the provisions following, which, as will be seen on comparison, to some extent overlap the provisions of the contract.

(A) The whole of the materials, workmanship, and mode of carrying out the contract to its completion must be to the entire satisfaction of the surveyor and of the consulting engineer.

(B) The whole of the works comprised in this contract must be entirely completed, to the satisfaction of the surveyor and the consulting engineer, within calendar months after the date of the order to commence, given in writing by the surveyor.

(C) For every month or part of a month beyond the before-mentioned period that the work remains uncertified as complete by the surveyor, the contractor shall be liable to a penalty of 50*l.*

(D) The contractor will have to maintain in thorough working order and repair the whole of the works herein described for a period of three months after the surveyor's final certificate that the works are completed to his satisfaction.

Some delay and difficulty arose in the execution of the works, but ultimately, on the 6th April, 1891, Mr. R. T. Elsam, the surveyor, who had supervised the works while in progress, gave his final certificate in favour of the plaintiff for 637*l.* 14*s.* 7*d.* Thereupon the defendants dismissed him and appointed another surveyor, Mr. Hope.

After the expiration of the period of maintenance the plaintiff sued for the certified amount.

The defendants at the outset disputed the certificate, and claimed a right to go to arbitration under clause 19 (*supra*, p. 251). But on appeal to the Divisional Court and the Court of Appeal, it was held by both Courts that clause 19 did not apply, and that the defendants were not entitled to stop an action on the certificate, which was not within clause 19, because they had made an affidavit that they had a counter-claim, which would, if disputed, be within the clause. The defendants could not counter-claim, because it would have been a step in the action which would have prevented them from referring.

The defendants by their defence set up, *inter alia*—

(1) That the surveyor had been dismissed, or was *functus officio*, at the time when he gave the certificate sued on.

(2) That he had included in the certificate items as to which he had no authority to certify.

(3) That, by the specification, the work must be done to the satisfaction of the consulting engineer (Mr. Shone) as well as of the surveyor; and that this condition had not been satisfied.

They also counter-claimed—

(1) For penalties for non-completion.

(2) For the cost of making good defects which, as they alleged, had appeared in the works within the three months specified in clause 11 (*supra*).

(3) For repayment of sums certified *ultra vires* by the surveyor.

The plaintiff, by his reply, traversed the allegations of fact on which the counter-claim was founded.

The action came on for trial before Lord Coleridge and a special jury, but was, at his suggestion, referred, by consent, to Mr. E. Ridley, Q.C., one of the Official Referees.

Lankester and Hudson for the plaintiff. McCall, Q.C., and Horace Avory for the defendants.

The Official Referee gave judgment for the plaintiff on claim and counter-claim, and found:—

(I.) That the work had been done to the satisfaction of the surveyor, and that the satisfaction of the consulting engineer was not also necessary.

(II.) With reference to the claim for penalties for delay in completion, he held that the defendants were precluded from recovering them, on the authority of *Laidlaw v. Hastings Pier Co., ante*, p. 13.

(III.) With reference to the words, "completion of the several works," in clause 11, he held that they referred, not to the certified completion of the whole works, but to the actual completion of the particular sections of the works.

He was of opinion that there were defects disclosed by the evidence in certain portions of the work, but that those defects before him did not appear within the time limited by the maintenance clause as above construed. He referred to *Bateman (Lord) v. Thompson, ante*, vol. ii., p. 36; *Goodyear* v. *Weymouth (Mayor, &c. of)*, 35 L. J. C. P. 12.

The defendants did not question the rulings of the Referee on heads I. and II., but applied to the Divisional Court to set aside the judgment on the counter-claim, on the ground that the Referee had misconstrued the expression "several works" (III.), and that completion meant "certified completion."

Finlay, Q.C., and Avory for the defendants. Tindal Atkinson, Q.C., Lankester, and Hudson for the plaintiff.

Mathew, J.: I think that the construction put on the contract by the learned Referee is incorrect. The action was brought to recover the price of work done by the plaintiff for the defendants. In the defendants' counter-claim it appears that under a clause of the contract with reference to maintenance, they counter-claim for a

1892
July 7.

Queen's
Bench
Division.

1892
October 28.

Queen's
Bench
Division.

1892
October 28.

Queen's
Bench
Division.

defect discovered within three months after the completion of the works. Now, that there was a defect must be assumed for the purpose of this judgment. The learned Referee came to the conclusion that the discovery of the defect had not been made in time, and that, according to the terms of the contract, the defect being in work which had been completed more than three months before the discovery, there was an end of the matter, and that his judgment on the counter-claim must be for the plaintiff. The scheme of contracts of this sort we are all familiar with. In the first place, it is vital to every contract of this sort that the surveyor should have an absolute control over the completion of the works, and to certify from time to time as to what the contractor is entitled to receive, and there is the usual clause that there shall be a reserve fund, and that a certain portion of the money which the contractor shall appear to have earned shall be held back for an additional period, during which the obligation is put on the contractor of maintaining the works.

When we turn to this contract we find it is a contract of the ordinary kind, and so it appears at the first glance. Every clause in it is consistent with the scheme which is the usual one in these cases, and one which usually works with perfect smoothness. But it was very ingeniously pointed out here to the learned Official Referee that there were certain expressions in this contract inconsistent with its general scheme, and that it would be taken that, on this extraordinary and novel form of contract so entered into—that within three months after the completion of any part of the work, whether it should be put into working order or not, if a defect turned up, the contractor must, nevertheless, be paid. The argument was this: that in the original contract it was stated that, in consideration of the sum of 5,523*l.*, the contractor agrees with the Local Board to do and execute *the several works* in and about the construction and completion of the main sewers and branch sewers; and then the several works are described—main sewers, branch sewers; and ventilating shafts, also for ejector chambers. The argument for the plaintiff was that the word "several" indicates "respective"; that it is to be construed as if the word were "respective." That word was used advisedly; it was used for the purpose of severing the different portions of the work—I do not know into what dimensions—into yards or otherwise; and it meant that the contractor should say: You have not discovered the particular defect which you complain of within three months after that particular portion of the work is done—that line of bricks was laid, or that portion of cement was made. To my mind that interpreta-

1892
October 28.

Queen's
Bench
Division.

tion is an impossible one. The word "several" must be construed "divers." It must be construed as a word comprehending all the works that were to be done, and not each portion of them.

Then attention was called to the use of the same expression in clause 11 (*a*). The contract goes on to provide that "the contractor shall maintain and keep in proper working order, during a period of three months from the completion of the same, the several works, including any additional or extra works which may be authorised by the surveyor under clause 6." The argument there was the same, that the word "several" was used advisedly; that it obviously means each portion. I should have thought it too clear for argument that the other was the proper meaning—that the word was a word of comprehension, and not a word distinguishing the different parts of the work.

Then, those two clauses being the clauses on which the argument has mainly rested, no attention whatever was paid in the first instance to a very significant and important clause contained in the specification; and the specification is part of the contract. It was suggested that it was to be rejected and treated as waste paper, and the contract considered apart from the specification. The specification is described to be part of the contract, and in that you find a clause which makes the whole thing work perfectly smoothly and easily: "The contractor will have to maintain in thorough working order and repair the whole of the works herein described for a period of three months after the surveyor's final certificate that the works are completed to his satisfaction." Can anything be plainer than that? But at once we are referred to other clauses which, it is said, ought to puzzle any person who has to interpret any document of this sort, and which introduces so much confusion that no one can make head or tail of what was intended to be done. The two clauses are clauses 16 and 17. It is perfectly plain, under the clause I have read, that what was meant was that there should be a certificate of the completion of the works, and that, for three months from the date of that certificate, the works should be kept in working order by the contractor.

Then our attention was called to sect. 16. I do not propose to go through it at all, but it provided, as I have said, in the ordinary way, for the payment of a certain sum down, and for the payment ultimately of the balance; and it provided that the contractor is to receive the balance of all the moneys due or payable to him, under or by virtue of the contract, at the expiration of the period of maintaining the works, namely, three months from the completion of the

(*a*) *Supra*, p. 250.

works. No reference is made there to the certificate, I agree. It is clear that the latter clause ought to have been incorporated to make it consistent, because of what follows, and which is printed in italics, and appears to have been considered a very material part of the clause: " Provided always that no final or other certificate is to relieve the contractor from his liability under the provisions of clause 11, whether the same is or not notified by the surveyor at the time or subsequent to granting any such certificate." The certificate was given to the contractor at the completion, and it does not relieve him in any way from the obligation of keeping the works in repair for three months. From what date? From the date when the certificate apparently was granted. Clause 11, when you turn to it, contains, on the face of it, this: " The contractor shall maintain and keep in proper working order, during a period of three months from the completion of the same, the several works, including any additional or extra works"; but that certificate is made subject to the clause which always preserves the liability of the contractor to maintain the works for three months, and three months apparently from the date when he receives the certificate of the surveyor that the works are completed. The same observation applies to clause 17. I have no doubt, therefore, as to the construction of this contract; and the learned Referee, who came to the conclusion that, a defect having been discovered in the work three months after that work had been executed, and that the contractor was relieved from liability, has come to a wrong conclusion, in my mind.

BRUCE, J., concurred.

The case was referred back to the Official Referee with a direction to re-hear the counter-claim on the footing that the date of completion was 6th April, 1891, the date of the final certificate.

The plaintiff appealed to the Court of Appeal.

Tindal Atkinson, Q.C., Lankester, and Hudson for the plaintiff. Finlay, Q.C., and Avory for the defendants.

Lord ESHER, M.R.: We must affirm the decision of the Divisional Court, and dismiss the appeal. The question is whether certain works ought to have been done by the contractor. The contract was to construct a system of sewerage. A certain portion was done before the whole was completed, and an interim certificate was given in respect of the part so done. The rest was not finished for some time, and then a certificate under clause 17 was given. A defect was then discovered in work which had been done long before the final certificate, and the question is whether the contractor is bound to rectify a defect discovered within three months after the final certificate. One

1892
December 2.

Court of
Appeal.

side says the defect was in a particular part of the system, and that the three months run from the actual completion of that part; the other side says that the liability to rectify every defect continues until three months after the final certificate.

Several clauses in the contract and in the specification are relied on; and the first question for us is whether the specification is part of the contract. That depends on the first condition in the contract. In my opinion, the fact that the specification is signed as a contract incorporates it with the contract; and the question is then to be decided whether the three months run from the completion of the several works, or of the whole contract. The first clause of the contract refers to " all the works," and the proper rule of construction is that "the works" should be taken as used in the same sense throughout the contract. Paragraph D of the specification is capable of being read as referring to the completion of the whole works, and must, therefore, follow the interpretation put upon it by the first clause of the contract. Paragraph B is capable of being read as referring to the completion of the whole works, and must, therefore, follow the interpretation I have put upon clause 1, and the words " completion of the same " refer to the completion of all the works. [The learned judge then referred to clauses 14 and 17, and continued.] I reckon the liability under the conditions to run for three months from actual completion. If the paragraph (D) in the specification is incorporated, then the maintenance runs from the certificate of the architect. The 17th clause of the conditions, in my opinion, makes the certificate of the architect evidence of completion, and I think it is to be the sole evidence of completion; and when the condition is read with the specification this becomes clear. The appeal must be dismissed.

LOPES, L.J.: I concur. The case is unarguable if the conditions in the specification are incorporated into the contract.

On the re-hearing before the Official Referee, he gave judgment for the defendants on the counter-claim for 900*l.*, on the grounds—

(1) That defects had appeared in one of the sewers within three months from the 6th April, 1891.

(2) That these defects were due not solely, if at all, to faults in the original plan of the sewer, nor to errors of the surveyor; but mainly, if not solely, to defective or improper materials or workmanship on the part of the contractor.

With respect to (1), it was proved that a stoppage occurred within the three months, but that the sewer was not opened up nor the cause of the stoppage

1892
December 2.

Court of
Appeal.

discovered within that period. But the Referee held the plaintiff liable under (2) for all breakages and defects discovered when the sewer was opened up in consequence of the stoppage.

The defendants applied to the Divisional Court to set aside these findings and the judgment.

1893
February 8.

Queen's
Bench
Division.

Lankester and Hudson for the plaintiff. Horace Avory for the defendants. It was argued for the plaintiff—

(i.) That the 11th condition only applied where the contractor had done bad work, overlooked by the surveyor, and the defects discovered arose from such bad work.

(ii.) That the new surveyor had altered the system to one more suitable for the district, and had charged the plaintiff with the extra cost.

(iii.) That the opinion of the surveyor when the work is done must be taken, and not that of a man subsequently appointed.

Avory, for the defendants, argued that the existence of the defect was discovered by a stoppage within the three months, and that the operation of taking up the sewer to discover the defects was continuous, and the defects opened up in July therefore fell within clause 11; and that there was a series of such defects due to bad workmanship, and not to the design of the sewers.

Lord COLERIDGE, C.J.: The Official Referee thought from the first that there were defects in the works: but on the first reference, on his view of the contract, the three months had elapsed. That view having been corrected by the Court, and the case sent back to him, he found that, to a great extent, the mischief arose from a faulty execution of the work. The proof of that was that there was a method by which the defects in the design might have been obviated; and in some few cases this method was directed by the surveyor and adopted by the contractor, and in those cases no mischief resulted. But in all other cases the method was not adopted, and the mischief resulted; the cause being that there was no proper and firm support of the pipes. It was argued that a large part of the sewer had been taken up and re-laid, and that it was unfair to charge the contractor with this, as the stoppage was only in one place. But the discovery of this leakage led to a further examination of the sewer, and a great many junctions were found broken, and were restored. The question on this part was for the surveyor, under the contract, to decide, under clause 11. It was objected that it was decided by the new surveyor (Mr. Hope); but the contract provides expressly that the contractor should follow the directions of any surveyor appointed by the Board. There is no ground for sending the case back to the Official Referee.

LOPES, L.J.: I agree on the construction of the contract; and there was evidence on which the Referee could find, as he has done, that the mischief arose from defects in the execution of the work by the plaintiff, and not from the design of the engineer or the directions of the surveyor.

Appeal dismissed.

Solicitors for the plaintiff: Wilson & Son. Solicitors for the defendant Board: Wilkinson, Howlett & Wilkinson.

1893
February 8.

Queen's
Bench
Division.

In the High Court of Justice (Queen's Bench Division).

(*Before* WILLS, J.)

BECK AND ANOTHER *v.* SMIRKE.

Surveyor and Valuer—Negligence.

1894
January 1.

Queen's
Bench
Division.

A surveyor who is employed to value property for the purposes of a mortgage is bound to use competent care and skill in inquiring as to the data upon which his valuation would be made, but is not bound to inquire into the financial position of the person seeking the advance nor into the nature of the title offered.

The plaintiffs, who were trustees under a marriage settlement in 1889, employed the defendant to survey and value an uncompleted house, No. 26, Strawberry Hill Road, Twickenham, upon which they were asked by the builder to make an advance out of the trust funds in their hands then available for investment. The defendant reported that the house was well built and worth 1,800*l.*, and was a good security for 1,000*l.*, the sum proposed to be advanced. On this report the plaintiffs advanced the 1,000*l.* The builder did not complete the house and fell into arrears with his interest. The plaintiffs were put to the cost of 400*l.* in foreclosure suit and in making repairs; and the house was ultimately sold by public auction for 810*l.* They then sued the defendant for negligence in his valuation and claimed as damages 588*l.*, *i.e.*, for the whole of the sum advanced plus the expenses, and less the amount realized on the sale.

Lawson Walton, Q.C., and Boyd for plaintiffs; T. W. Wheeler, Q.C., and A. T. Lawrence for defendant.

Evidence was given for the plaintiffs by Mr. Chancellor, estate agent, who had sold the house for the plaintiffs under their power of sale as mortgagees. He said that the sale was a fair one, the letting value being 80*l.* on a three years' agreement, the landlord doing the repairs, and 70*l.* upon repairing lease. It was worth fifteen years' purchase.

Defendant, Mr. Sydney Smirke, gave evidence that he went and visited the property on several occasions. He reported on April 18 that No. 26 would be finished in three weeks, and that it required papering. He had several interviews with Mr. Beck. He added to his report that he could not ascertain the

1894
January 1.

Queen's
Bench
Division.

rateable value; and that the property was worth 1,800*l.* He told Mr. Beck that
the house was unfinished and unlet. He communicated to Mr. Beck that it
would take 25*l.* to 30*l.* to finish the house. Mr. Beck said he thought it would
be safe to let the builder have the money, and he would deduct 30*l.* as
interest paid in advance. Mr. Beck told him that he had been informed that
Hart was not a speculative builder. In March, 1890, he heard that Hart was
bankrupt, and he went down to see the property and found it terribly
wrecked, without any caretaker. On April 25 he visited the premises again.
He thought it would take 120*l.* to make the house fit for letting. He visited the
house again in May. At that time the money ordered by the Court of Chancery
had not been expended.

Cross-examined: He arrived at the 1,800*l.* (1) upon rental value; (2) the cubical
contents; (3) by comparing it with other properties. He valued the building at
1,400*l.*, and the land at 400*l.* He took the 250*l.* as the value of the land before
development. He estimated the 400*l.* upon the basis of ground rent. He arrived at
the 1,400*l.* for the building upon an estimate upon the cost price of the building.
He did not ask Messrs. Egerton and Breach what they had certified for. It was
not the only way of arriving at the value of the house to ascertain what it would
let for. He thought the clear rental value was 90*l.* He told Egerton and Breach
that he was going to put the rent at 90*l.*, and Mr. Breach said that would do. He
did not ascertain what the other houses in the road were let for. He estimated
the value upon the basis of twenty-two and a-half years' purchase of 81. rental.

Two other surveyors were called for the defendant, who stated that they
estimated the value of the house upon the basis of twenty to twenty-two
years' purchase of the net rental, which they put at 80*l.* It was a sufficient
security for an advance of 1,000*l.*

Mr. W. H. Gibbs, of Messrs. Plews and Gibbs, builders, said he had
obtained advances of 1,000*l.* upon some of the houses in Strawberry Hill
Road built by them. The cost of the house would be about 1,900*l.*

Mr. Barella, the purchaser of the house, was called, and said the house was
now let at 75*l.* a year, the tenant doing repairs.

WILLS, J.: I have not a shadow of doubt as to the first question which
way my verdict should go. A surveyor who is employed to make a
report has to use competent care in making it. All the defendant
thought it necessary to do was to ask whether the house was worth
95*l.* a year. I can not see that there was any justification for the
statement of defendant that the houses were worth from 90*l.* to 120*l.*;
whereas it was stated that the rents averaged 80*l.* to 85*l.* The
defendant never took the trouble to ascertain whether the tenant or
the landlord was doing repairs. The defendant himself admitted that
in ascertaining the value it is necessary to get the net rental and
multiply it by the number of years' purchase. The valuation was made
in a most careless manner. Even after the person who wanted to
borrow said the house was worth 1,500*l.* the defendant brought it up
to 1,800*l.*, and when it was stated that 1,200*l.* had been spent on

1894
January 1.

Queen's
Bench
Division.

the house the defendant brought that figure up to 1,400*l*. Upon the evidence this value for the purpose of borrowing money ought not to have been put upon the house. With regard to Mr. Gibbs's evidence I am disposed to think that he has been financed by someone, and what that person lent on the houses said to be similar is no criterion in this case. The fair rental value of the house would be about 80*l*. Sixteen to eighteen years' purchase was much nearer the mark than twenty-two and a-half as stated. To say that such property as this is worth twenty-two and a-half years' purchase surprises me. The defendant knew he was advising trustees, and the margin of one-third was important, as it was meant to cover all sorts of contingencies, of which an auction sale was one. With regard to the damages, the great cause of the loss was that the money was advanced upon an uncompleted house. Upon the defendant was cast the responsibility of inquiring into the condition of the house, not into the financial position of the builder. It was quite plain that the plaintiffs were anxious to make the advance, because the defendant said it would be much better that they should hold back the money till the house was finished. The difficulties which led to a large portion of the loss were such as ought to present themselves to a lawyer, and not to a surveyor—namely, that the mortgagee could not do the repairs without a foreclosure suit. It would be unfair to put all the expenses of the foreclosure suit and the damage to the house upon the defendant. The advance and fair charges made up about 1,100*l*. He took 810*l*. as a fair sale price at the time, but he thought the house would have sold better if put earlier in the market, and he would give credit for a little more. He therefore thought if he gave judgment for 200*l*. he would be doing justice in the case.

Judgment for plaintiffs for 200*l*. with costs accordingly.

Note.—See *In re Soloman, Nore* v. *Meyer*, [1912] 1 Ch. 261.

1895
February 26.
April 9.

Court of
Appeal.

In the High Court of Justice (Court of Appeal).

(*Before* Lord Esher, M.R., and Loper and Rigby, L.JJ.)

LLOYD BROS. *v.* MILWARD.

Contract for building Houses—Construction of Arbitration and Certificate Clauses.

The construction to be placed on clauses similar to clauses 18 and 20 of the (former) conditions agreed to between the London Builders' Association and the Royal Institute of British Architects is that if disputes have arisen before the architect's certificate, under clause 18, is given, it is not final and conclusive; but otherwise it is.

This was an appeal by the defendant from the judgment of Lawrance, J., in favour of the plaintiffs, at the trial of the action without a jury, at Swansea.

The action was brought by the plaintiffs, who were builders, to recover from the defendant, the building owner, the balance of the price of work and materials alleged to be due under a contract dated January 9th, 1893, for rebuilding certain houses and premises at Swansea.

The agreement, which was based on the old form agreed to between the London Builders' Association and the Royal Institute of British Architects, contained the following clauses:—

(20) A certificate of the architect, or an award of the referee hereinafter referred to, as the case may be, showing the final balance due or payable to the contractor, is to be conclusive evidence of the works having been duly completed, and that the contractor is entitled to receive payment of the final balance, but without prejudice to the liability of the contractor under the provisions of clause No. 12.

(22) Provided always that in case any question, dispute, or difference shall arise between the proprietor, or the architect on his behalf, and the contractor as to what additions, if any, ought in fairness to be made to the amount of the contract by reason of the works being delayed through no fault of the contractor, or by reason or on account of any directions or requisitions of the architect involving increased cost to the contractor beyond the cost properly attending the carrying out of the contract according to the true intent and meaning of the signed drawings and specification, or as to the works having been duly completed, or as to the construction of these presents, or as to any other matter or thing arising under or out of this contract except as to matters left during the progress of the works to the sole decision or requisition of the architect under clauses Nos. 2, 10, and 11, or in case the contractor shall be dissatisfied with any certificate of the architect under clause No. 8, or under the proviso in clause No. 16, or in case he shall withhold or not give

any certificate to which the contractor may be entitled, then such question, dispute, or difference, or such certificate, or the value or matter which should be certified, as the case may be, is to be from time to time referred to the arbitration and final decision of   , architect, or in the event of his death or unwillingness to act, then of   , architect, and in the event of his death or unwillingness to act, then of an architect, being a fellow of the Royal Institute of British Architects, to be appointed on the request of either party by the President for the time being of such Institute, and the award of such referee is to be equivalent to a certificate of the architect, and the contractor is to be paid accordingly. Such award or certificate may be made a rule of Her Majesty's High Court of Justice or any Court of Record in England. The cost of the arbitration and award shall be in discretion of the arbitrator.

1895
February 26.

Court of
Appeal.

It appeared that the architect had, on June 14th, 1894, given a certificate showing the final balance due or payable to the contractor, but that prior to the signing of such certificate disputes had, to the knowledge of the architect and the parties, arisen between the plaintiffs and the defendant as to whether the works had been duly completed, and as to whether certain extras had been properly ordered and authorised, and properly charged for.

Lawrance, J., was of opinion that the certificate of the architect was final and conclusive as to the work having been duly completed, and that the plaintiffs were entitled to receive payment of the final balance, and gave judgment for the plaintiffs.

The defendant appealed.

A. Thomas, Q.C., and Benson, for the defendant, contended that clauses 20 and 22 of the agreement must be read together, and that upon the true construction of those clauses the architect had no power, when disputes had arisen beforehand, to give a certificate; that such certificate was null and void, and that the matter must be referred to the arbitrator under clause 22. They referred to *Clemence* v. *Clarke* (*a*), and pointed out that there no disputes had arisen beforehand.

Bowen Rowlands, Q.C., and Meager, for the plaintiffs, referred to "Hudson on Building Contracts," 1st ed. p. 517, sect. 3 (*b*), and *In re An Arbitration between Hohenzollern Actien Gesellschaft and City of London Contract Corporation* (*b*).

Judgment was reserved.

Lord ESHER, M.R.: In this case the action is brought by a firm of builders to recover from the building owner the balance of the price of certain works executed under a contract between them. The plaintiffs allege that they have duly executed the works, and obtained under clause 20 of the contract the architect's certificate, and they contend that such certificate is conclusive evidence of the work having been completed, and that they are entitled to receive payment of the final balance. It is obvious that, unless there is something to prevent

1895
April 9.

(*a*) (1879); *ante*, p. 54.
(*b*) (1886), *ante*, p. 100.

1895
April 9.

Court of
Appeal.

the application of clause 20, the plaintiffs are right, and are entitled to succeed in the action. But the defendant relies upon the provisions of clause 22 of the contract. He alleges that a dispute had arisen between him and the plaintiffs, and he contends that as soon as this dispute had arisen, and was known to both parties and to the architect, the power of the architect to give a certificate was gone by virtue of clause 22, and the dispute must be settled under the provisions of that clause by an arbitrator. I must say that at first I had a difficulty in reconciling the two clauses, but upon consideration I have come to the conclusion that they can be reconciled and read together, and that the contention of the defendant is right. I think that clause 22 is in the nature of a proviso upon clause 20, so that if the conditions contemplated by clause 22 arise before the architect has given his final certificate his power to give it is taken away. In my opinion the facts of the present case brought it within clause 22, and consequently the architect had no power to give the certificate upon which the plaintiffs rely. I think, therefore, that the appeal must be allowed and the judgment for the plaintiffs set aside.

Lopes, L.J.: For some time I thought that this case was governed by clause 20 of the agreement between the parties, but on consideration I have come to the conclusion that clauses 20 and 22 must be read together. It is important to bear in mind that here there were disputes in existence before the giving of the final certificate of the architect, which were known to him, and that he, knowing of those disputes, gave the certificate. It seems to me that the words in clause 20 "or an award of the referee hereinafter referred to" show that in certain circumstances an award of the referee may override or be substituted for the certificate of the architect. In my judgment, in certain cases, as where disputes have arisen, clause 22 overrides and controls what otherwise would be the effect of clause 20. The result is that the certificate of the architect is final, if there are no disputes; if there are, the award of the referee is to take its place and be substituted for it. In the latter case, the award of the referee is to be equivalent to the certificate of the architect.

Rigby, L.J.: I am of the same opinion. Upon the construction of clauses 20 and 22 it was, in my judgment, the intention of the parties that, with the exception of the cases particularly mentioned in clause 22, every dispute that might arise should be referred not to the architect but to the special referee mentioned in that clause. The excepted matters are described as "matters left during the progress of the works to the sole decision or requisition of the architect under clauses Nos. 2, 10 and 11." The architect has nothing to do with disputes on final completion of the works. In the present case disputes had arisen and were known to the architect and the opposite party, and therefore, in my judgment the jurisdiction of the architect to make a final certificate was thereby ousted, and the dispute fell to be determined by the special referee. In my judgment the final certificate actually given was, under the circumstances, *ultra vires*, and of no effect, and the judgment entered for the plaintiffs should be set aside.

Appeal allowed.

Solicitors for the plaintiffs: Field, Roscoe & Co.; for Collins & Wood, Swansea.

Solicitor for the defendant: W. Robinson Smith, Swansea.

[This report was made and kindly furnished to the author by Mr. G. Humphreys, barrister-at-law, Fountain Court, Temple.]

In the Court of Appeal.

(*Before* Lord, Esher, M.R., and A. L. Smith and Rigby, L.JJ.)

In the House of Lords.

In the Matter of an Arbitration between T. MEADOWS AND WILLIAM MEADOWS, carrying on Business as T. AND W. MEADOWS, AND GEORGE HENRY KENWORTHY.

Arbitration—"Unless provided for in the foregoing Clauses."

A building contract provided by clause 31, that disputes between the building owner or his architect, and the contractor, "unless provided for in the foregoing clauses," should be referred to arbitration. Clause 17 provided that extra work should be ordered in writing, that alterations of the works should not invalidate the contract, "but shall be measured and valued and certified for by the architect according to the annexed schedule of prices, or where the same shall not apply, at fair measure and value, and the amount thereof added to or deducted from the amount due under the contract." Certain extras were ordered in writing, but when the architect measured them up and valued them, the contractor was dissatisfied with his measurement and valuation, and sought to have the dispute settled by arbitration:— Held, that this dispute came within the exception in clause 31, as being provided for by clause 17.

1895
April 9.

Court of
Appeal.

1896
June 20.

Court of
Appeal.

1897
March 1.

House of
Lords.

1896
June 20.

Court of
Appeal.

On May 7th, 1892, Messrs. T. and W. Meadows contracted to construct certain works for Mr. G. H. Kenworthy for the sum of 13,651*l.* The contract contained (*inter alia*) the following clauses:—

(17) The architect may from time to time make any alterations, additions, or deductions from the works as set forth in the drawings and specified quantities, and in case any additional or extra work shall be done by the contractor in accordance with written orders from the architect, or in case of any deduction from the works contracted for, such alterations, additions, or deductions shall not invalidate the present contract, but shall be measured and valued, and certified for by the architect, according to the annexed schedule of prices, or when the same may not apply, at fair measure and value, and the amount thereof added to or deducted from the amount due under the contract.

(31) In case of a dispute or difference arising between the proprietor or his architect and the contractor touching any matter or thing arising under or out of the contract, unless provided for in the foregoing clauses, the dispute shall be settled and determined by the award of a referee to be jointly appointed in writing, and the award of the said referee, to be given within thirty days, shall be binding on all parties, and shall be made a rule of any division of the High Court of Justice, and the said referee shall have power to examine witnesses, including the parties in question, on oath, and to call for all documents and papers relating to all matters referred, and the costs and expenses attending and incidental to the said reference shall be borne and paid by the proprietor or contractor or both of them as the said referee may direct.

From time to time extras were ordered by the architect in writing, various sums were paid on account during the construction of the works, and when the works were completed the architect measured up the extras and gave his final certificate as follows:—

G. H. KENWORTHY, Esq.,
Instalments brought forward £11,025 0 0
                                                                            288 9 0
                                    Total £11,313 9 0
Instalment No. 16 and final certificate, October 5th, 1895.

I hereby certify that the sum of two hundred and eighty-eight pounds nine shillings (288*l.* 9*s.*) is due to Messrs. T. and W. Meadows in final settlement of all claims for work and materials supplied in connection with contract for shops and arcade, Ashton-under-Lyne, and including all extra works in connection with the said contract to this date.

288*l.* 9*s.*   JOHN BROOKE, *Architect.*

With this certificate the architect delivered a summary of additions and deductions to the contract showing—
                Additions amounting to £3,196 13 8
                And deductions amounting to 5,534 4 7
The contractors were dissatisfied with the final certificate, and alleged that the architect had blundered in the measuring and valuing of the additions and deductions, and wished to have the dispute referred to arbitration under

clause 31 of the contract; the building owner refused to refer, whereupon the contractors took out a summons under sect. 5 of the Arbitration Act, 1889, for the appointment of an arbitrator.

The summons was heard before Master Butler on March 12th, 1896, when the application was dismissed, with costs. The contractors appealed, and the summons was heard before Cave, J., on April 24th, 1896, and was again dismissed, with costs.

The contractors appealed to the Court of Appeal, where the case was argued on June 20th, 1896, before Lord Esher, M.R., and A. L. Smith and Rigby, L.JJ., when the appeal was dismissed with costs, Rigby, L.J., dissenting. The contractors then appealed to the House of Lords, where the case was heard on March 1st, 1897, and again dismissed, with costs.

The judgments in the Court of Appeal were as follows:—

A. L. SMITH, L.J.: I am about to read the judgment of the Master of the Rolls and myself.

This is an appeal by a contractor against a judgment of Mr. Justice Cave, who affirmed the Master, and who refused to appoint, at the instance of the contractor, an arbitrator under the provisions of sect. 5 of the Arbitration Act, 1889.

The application is made under the 31st clause of a building contract entered into between Mr. Meadows, the contractor, and Mr. Kenworthy, the building owner, who in the contract is called "the proprietor." By this clause it was agreed that in case of any dispute between the proprietor or his architect, and the contractor, touching any matter or thing arising under or out of the contract, "unless provided for in the foregoing clauses of the contract," the dispute should be settled by arbitration. In my judgment this clause, when expanded, reads thus: "Unless the matter out of which the dispute arises is provided for in the foregoing clauses of the contract, it shall be settled by arbitration." The question, therefore, is whether the matter out of which the dispute has arisen has been "provided for in the foregoing clauses of the contract."

The dispute is this. The contractor alleges that the architect when he made up his certificate of the final balance due to him, has blundered in the measurements he has made as regards the extras which he, the contractor, has executed under the orders of the architect. The architect asserts the contrary. There is no dispute as to what are or are not extras, or as to what extras the contractor has executed, or as to how the value of these extras is to be ascertained, nor is bad faith imputed to the architect.

The allegation of the contractor is that the architect's measurements of these extras are erroneous, and thus the balance certified for by the architect to be due to the contractor is too small.

1896
June 20.

Court of
Appeal.

Now, who by the contract is to make this certificate, and who is to make the measurements to ascertain what is to be certified for? If the architect is to do this, then, in my judgment, clause 31, as to arbitration, does not apply, for the matter out of which the dispute arises is "provided for in the foregoing clauses of the contract," and clause 31 is express that in such case the clause is not to apply. By clause 1 the whole of the works are to be executed to the entire satisfaction of the architect. By clause 5 payments are to be made to the contractor during the progress of the works at the architect's discretion upon certificates in writing under his hand at certain prescribed rates up to 95 per cent. of the works executed, and by clause 6 the balance of 5 per cent. is to be reserved for six months from the date of the certificate of completion, in order to ensure the execution of any works of reinstating or repairs that might be required by the architect, before the contractor should be entitled to receive the final certificate for the balance, and by clause 8 the architect's final certificate showing what is the final balance is to be conclusive evidence that the contractor was entitled to receive payment of that final balance.

There are, it will be seen, to be first of all certificates during the progress of the works, then a certificate of completion of the works, and then a certificate for the final balance. It appears to me that, in arriving at what is to be certified for, either as regards the certificates to be given during the progress of the works, or the certificate of the completion of the works, or the certificate for the final balance, the architect is the person to decide both when they are to be given and what such certificates are to contain, and no one else. That he is the person to measure and value the extras which may have been executed by the contractor is clear; for by clause 17 it is expressly provided that the architect might from time to time make any alteration, additions, or deductions from the work as set forth in the drawings and specified quantities, which should not invalidate the contract, "but that such should be measured and valued and certified for by the architect." This, in my judgment, means that any extra work ordered by the architect is to be measured and valued and then certified for by the architect, which would come either into the certificates under clause 5 or into the final certificate for the balance as the architect might determine. How, then, can it be said that the matter out of which the dispute arises is not "provided for by the foregoing clauses of the contract"?

It appears to me that it is, and consequently clause 31 as to arbitration does not apply to the matter in dispute, which has now

1896
June 20.

Court of
Appeal.

arisen. It was argued that this makes the architect sole judge as to measure and value of the extras, and that if this were intended it should have been so stated, as it is stated in clause 30 with reference to what is therein mentioned; but how does this show that the matter about which the dispute has now arisen was not provided for in the foregoing clauses of the contract? In my opinion it does not.

For these reasons I think that the Master and my brother Cave have arrived at a right conclusion when they refused to appoint an arbitrator to inquire into the measurement of the extras, and that this appeal must be dismissed, with costs.

RIGBY, L.J.: The question whether the dispute which has arisen in this case is one which ought to be referred to arbitration depends upon the construction of clause 31 of the General Conditions of Contract, attached to the tender of the firm of T. and W. Meadows, hereinafter called the contractor, the acceptance of which by the proprietor Kenworthy constituted a contract between them. The only submission to arbitration is contained in that clause, though clauses 30 and 32 regulate the manner in which references of disputes arising during the progress of the works are to be made under the submission. Clause 31 provides for the case of a dispute or difference, not only between the proprietor and the contractor, but between the proprietor's architect and the contractor, without providing for a dispute between the proprietor and his architect. This at once indicates an intention to treat the architect as to some extent identified with the proprietor, and not as acting in all matters as an arbitrator or final judge between the opposing parties, an intention which will more fully appear from an examination of the other clauses. The fact, that the parties contemplated that some disputes between the architect and the contractor were to be the subject of a reference, makes it, in my judgment, impossible to hold that the decision of the architect on every matter left to him by the contract was to be final, without express provision to that effect in the particular case.

It is not unimportant to observe that the architect is not named in the contract, though his clerk was an attesting witness to the signatures both of the contractor and the proprietor. The words of clause 31 that require to be construed are as follows: "In case of a dispute or difference arising between the proprietor or his architect and the contractor, touching any matter or thing arising under or out of the contract, unless provided for in the foregoing clauses, the dispute shall be determined by the award of a referee."

The only question that can arise is as to the meaning and effect of the phrase "unless provided for in the foregoing clauses." We are

1896
June 20.

Court of
Appeal.

not left without guidance in this matter. The same phrase re-occurs in a similar connection in condition 32 under the slightly varied form, "unless previously settled or provided for." There it operates as a limitation on the disputes to be referred, not on the subject-matter out of which the disputes may arise.

All disputes are to be matters of reference, unless previously settled or provided for. The words "previously settled" obviously refer to agreements subsequent to the arising of the dispute, and would include all such agreements.

The words "previously provided for" can add nothing, unless they refer, as in my opinion they obviously do, to something antecedent to the arising of the dispute, and that can only be something in the contract itself.

We thus have, by a reasonable if not necessary inference, the words "previously provided for " of clause 32 shown to be the same in meaning as the words "provided for in the foregoing clauses " of clause 31. When the foregoing clauses are looked to, there is found no express reference to any dispute or difference, but clause 32 proves that the parties considered disputes and differences to have been provided for, and if we notice that the phrase "provided for " is equivalent to "provided against " or "precluded," no doubt in my judgment remains as to its meaning either in clause 31 or in clause 32.

Clause 32 therefore shows that the words "unless provided for in the foregoing clauses" in clause 31, must refer to the dispute or difference supposed to have arisen, so that the effect of the whole sentence is that the dispute, unless provided for, is to be referred. This is the natural grammatical meaning of the clause taken as a whole. The words down to "unless" are introductory, only indicating the circumstances in which the operative words "unless provided for in the following clauses the dispute shall be settled, &c.," are to take effect. The only alternative is by what appears to me a somewhat strained construction to detach in meaning the words "unless provided for" from the words which follow, and to treat them as qualifying and limiting the preceding words, "any matter or thing arising under or out of the contract." One great difficulty in accepting this construction is that the qualification reduces to nothing the words which it is supposed to qualify, or at least confines them to matters not in any way dealt with by the contract. It is difficult to see how there can be any matter or anything arising under or out of the contract which is not provided for (either in express words or by construction) in the clauses of the contract.

1896
June 20.

Court of
Appeal.

This construction, if it were not negatived by the reasoning founded on clause 32, would be open to the fatal objection that it reduces the whole clause 31 to a nullity, or, to say the least, to something not thought worth providing for in the contract. It remains to determine what provision is made in the clause, preceding clause 31, against disputes or differences.

As above pointed out, the answer cannot be that whatever is by the foregoing clauses left to be done in the first instance by the architect, is thereby provided for within the meaning of clause 31, as that would make the architect the sole judge in everything left to him by the foregoing clauses, and there would be no dispute or difference between him and the contractor to be referred to arbitration.

But no real difficulty arises, if we find, in fact, that the foregoing clauses do in express terms make the decision of the architect in certain matters final, and the proper conclusion in my judgment is, that in those cases, and those alone, is the settlement of any dispute or difference between him and the contractor withdrawn from arbitration.

Under clause 5 payments during the progress of the works are to be made at the architect's discretion.

Under the same clause provision is made for payment of a further sum, making a total of 95 per cent. as near as can be estimated by the architect, on the architect's certificate that the contractor has completed the work to his satisfaction. This certificate, in clause 6 called the certificate of completion, is a different thing from the final certificate mentioned in the same clause and dealt with more particularly in clause 8, which last mentioned clause in favour of the contractor makes it conclusive evidence of the works having been duly completed, and that the contractor is entitled to receive payment of the final balance shown by it, thereby preventing the proprietor from going to arbitration on either of these points.

It is, however, very material to observe that neither in clause 8 nor anywhere else is it provided as against the contractor that the final certificate shall be conclusive as to the amount payable to him. This is a strong instance of a case in which the architect is treated as acting as the representative of the proprietor, and so binding him though not binding the contractor.

I think it equally impossible that the omission to bind the contractor should have been the result of an oversight, or that as a matter of construction it can be held, that in face of exact provision for the points upon which the certificate is to be conclusive evidence,

1896
June 20.

Court of
Appeal.

it should be held to be conclusive also as against the contractor claiming a larger balance than that certified for.

It may be, and probably is, the fact that no action for a larger sum could be maintained by the contractor against the proprietor, but the true inference seems to me to be that any claim for a larger sum would give rise, if resisted, to a dispute or difference between the contractor and both the proprietor and the architect not provided for by any other clause than clause 31, and therefore falling for reference to arbitration under that clause.

By clause 12 the architect is made the sole judge of the length of time and the sufficiency of notice for the removal of materials or workmanship of an inferior character.

Clauses 13 to 16 inclusive give powers of control to the architect during the progress of the works.

Clause 17 is that under which the question in the present case arises. It provides for additional or extra work done by the contractor in accordance with written orders from the architect being measured or valued and certified by the architect, but there is no provision that such measurement, valuation or certificate shall be final or conclusive, or that the architect shall be the sole judge with reference thereto.

A dispute or difference of a material nature has arisen between the proprietor and the architect on the one side and the contractor on the other, the contractor claiming about 1,850*l.* (the figures are not material), for which the architect certified at 285*l.* only.

The contractor has written orders for all the work in respect of which he claims, so that no question arises under clause 18.

Clause 19, which obliges the contractor to suspend and resume the works on notice from the architect, provides in express terms that any allowance for additional expenses incurred shall be at the architect's discretion. Clauses 20 to 29 inclusive provide in detail for the manner in which the works are to be carried on under the architect's control.

It will be seen that great care is taken to provide for the unquestioned control of the architect over the work to be done and the manner of doing it, and that wherever the architect is to have an uncontrolled discretion, express words are used to make it clear that he is to be the sole judge, or is to decide at his discretion. Clause 30 sums up by the provision that the architect shall be the sole judge during the progress of the works, and his decision final upon all matters arising out of the contract so far as relates to the quantities of materials and workmanship, the meaning of the specified quantities and plans, the rate of progress or the general management of the works.

The same clause makes special provision for the settlement of any question between the architect and contractor as to what is extra work. The reason for the special provision appears to be in the obligation imposed on the contractors to perform the work without written order and to give notice before performing the work of his intention to refer.

It is material, however, to observe that clause 30 does not provide that such question shall be submitted to arbitration, but that the contractor shall give notice that he will submit the question to reference or arbitration as thereinafter provided. This clearly takes it for granted that the question, though arising on a matter plainly left in the first place to the discretion of the architect by clause 17, is a case of dispute or difference between the architect and contractor within clause 31. It seems to me that, by parity of reasoning, a question as to measurement, valuation or certificate under clause 17, such as has actually arisen, though those matters are left in the first place to the architect, may equally give rise to a dispute or difference between him and the contractor, to be referred under clause 31.

The result would be that, as the proprietor refuses to concur in the appointment of a joint arbitrator, the Court ought to appoint an arbitrator under the Arbitration Act. Any other conclusion would amount in effect to striking out from the contract all words making the architect's decision in any case final.

I find nothing in any decided case to throw any difficulty in the way of such a conclusion as that above arrived at. Wherever a Court has held that the decision of a person occupying the position of the architect in this case is to be a condition precedent to payment to a contractor or a final determination as to his rights, it has been on the ground that the contractor has by plain language agreed to accept the decision as final and conclusive.

There is not anywhere, and there ought not to be, any leaning shown towards supplying such an agreement where it does not exist. That contractors should, without appeal, be subject as to important rights to the decision of a judge nominated by the opposing party, is not in itself, apart from express contract, a particularly desirable state of things, and often gives rise to much dissatisfaction. Here, it seems to me, the parties have very fairly striven to avoid the apparent injustice or hardship of such a one-sided bargain, and given a reference to a single arbitrator by way of appeal against any ruling

1896
June 20.
___
Court of
Appeal
___
1897
March 1.
___
House of
Lords.

of the architect where that could be safely done without impeding the progress of the work.

The contractors appealed from this decision to the House of Lords, where the case was heard on March 1st, 1897, when the appeal was dismissed with costs.

Solicitors for the appellants: Chester, Mayhew, Broome, Griffithes, agents for Sutton, Elliott & Turnbull.

Solicitors for the respondents: Pritchard, Englefield & Co.

1899
November
20.
___
Queen's
Bench
Division.

In the Queen's Bench Division (Commercial Court).

(*Before* BIGHAM, J.)

CROWSHAW *v.* PRITCHARD AND ANOTHER.

Estimate—Offer—Acceptance.

P. wrote to C. a letter in the following terms: "Estimate.—Our estimate to carry out the sundry alterations to the above premises, according to the drawings and specifications, amounts to 1,230*l.*" Held, that this was an "offer" to do the work for 1,230*l.*, that there was no custom that a letter in this form was not to be treated as an offer, and that if there were such a custom it was contrary to law.

This case came before Bigham, J., in the Commercial Court, on November 20th, 1899.

The action was brought by the plaintiff, the owner of freehold property, against the defendants, a firm of builders, to recover damages for breach of contract. The facts were shortly these:—

In August last the plaintiff, being desirous of having certain building work executed on his premises, caused the following letter to be written by his architect to the defendants. The letter was dated August 22nd, and ran as follows:—

"Our client, Mr. Crowshaw, of No. 116, Fenchurch Street, the freeholder of premises in the occupation of Messrs. Roberts, Adlard & Co., as above, is about to make additions to the property, and we should be glad to know whether you would be willing to give us a tender in competition for the work. No quantities will be supplied, and our client does not bind himself to accept the lowest or any tender."

The specification was sent to the defendants subsequently, and on September 14th the defendants wrote the following letter to the plaintiff, the letter being headed "Estimate":—

"Our estimate to carry out the sundry alterations to the above premises, according to the drawings and specification, amounts to the sum of 1,230*l.*"

On the following day the plaintiff wrote that he accepted the defendants'

1899
November
20.

Queen's
Bench
Division.

"offer to execute, for the sum of 1,230*l.*," the work in question. Later on the defendants wrote that they had made a mistake in their figures, and stating that under the circumstances they must withdraw their estimate. The plaintiff then had the work done by another builder, at a price higher than that given by the defendants, and brought the present action to recover the difference in price as damages for breach of contract, and the question to be determined was whether there was a complete contract binding on the defendants.

H. Reed, Q.C. (with him T. E. Scrutton), contended that on the acceptance by the plaintiff on September 15th there was a completed contract.

English Harrison, Q.C. (with him Acland), on behalf of the defendants, contended that the defendants' letter of September 14th was not a binding tender, and that the word "estimate" was advisedly used to avoid making a final and binding agreement, such as would have resulted from using such words as "we offer to execute the work," and called several builders to prove that this distinction was always observed in the trade.

BIGHAM, J.: I do not think there is any doubt at all about this case. The plaintiff, Mr. Crowshaw, wanted some repairs done to some premises at Bermondsey Wall; and, in the ordinary course of business, he instructed his architects to obtain tenders for the execution of the work. The architects accordingly communicated with a number of builders, amongst those builders being the defendants; and on the 22nd August, 1899, they wrote this letter to the defendants: "Our client, Mr. George Crowshaw, of No. 116, Fenchurch Street, the freeholder of premises in the occupation of Messrs. Roberts, Adlard & Co., as above, is about to make additions to the property, and we should be glad to know whether you would be willing to give us a tender in competition for the work. No quantities will be supplied, and our client does not bind himself to accept the lowest or any tender."

Now, that letter gave to the defendants notice of the man, the name of the man, and the address of the man for whom the work was to be done. It is suggested by Mr. English Harrison that there was no opportunity of inquiring into the financial position of the gentleman who was to make the contract. I do not think the observation has anything at all to do with the legal bearing of the questions in the case, but if it has there is the answer. They are told in the very first instance who the gentleman is for whom the work is to be done, and they are told his address; and, if they choose, they can make inquiries before they send in any tender at all. The next observation that is to be made on that letter is that it is an invitation to send a tender in competition for the work.

What is the plain meaning of that word "tender"? I think it means a statement of the price at which they are willing to contract

18 (2)

1899
November
20.

Queen's
Bench
Division.

to do the work. That is what they are asked, to send in, and, having been asked to send in that, they are told that they themselves will have to take out the quantities. It is a small job, and it is supposed, that the builders can themselves take out the quantities and they are told that they must do that. When this letter was sent they had not sufficient information to enable them to make any tender at all; and they did not get that information until about six days later—on the 28th August—when the plaintiff's architects wrote another letter in these terms: "We send you herewith the drawings and specification of the above work, and shall be glad to receive them back at your earliest convenience, and we will write you later on when your tender is to be delivered." The word is again used: "When your *tender* is to be delivered."

The defendants got the specification and the drawings. They know that there are no quantities to come, and they have therefore before them all the materials upon which they are intended to tender. Having the specification and the drawings and the invitation to tender, they send in the letter of the 14th September, headed "Estimate." "Our estimate to carry out the sundry alterations to the above premises, according to the drawings and specification prepared by Messrs. Barnes, Williams, Ford & Griffin, amounts to the sum of 1,230*l.*"

The real question that I have to determine is this. Is that letter of the 14th September an offer to do the work at that price? I am quite clearly of opinion that it is. It is alleged that there is some custom or well-known understanding in the trade by which such a letter is not to be treated as an offer at all. I do not believe that any such custom does exist, and I am quite sure if it does exist that it is contrary to law, because where a man offers to do a thing at a price, and another man accepts his offer, according to law that is a contract: and no custom in the trade can make it anything but a contract. Therefore, in my opinion, it is a contract. I believe, if it is necessary to say it, that both the plaintiff and the defendants intended that this document should constitute a contract; and I find the fact as the fact was found in the case to which I was referred of *Lewis* v. *Brass* (*a*), that the intention of the parties was that this document should constitute a contract.

That offer to do the work at that price having been sent in, on the next day this letter is written: "I accept your offer to execute, for the sum of 1,230*l.*, the work to the above-named premises, in accord-

(*a*) 3 Q. B. D. 667.

1899
November
20.

Queen's
Bench
Division.

ance with drawings and specification prepared by Messrs. Barnes, Williams, Ford and Griffin." It is said by Mr. Harrison, amongst other things, that that was not a contract, because the specification left blank the number of weeks in which the work was to be done. I do not think that fact affects the question as to whether there was a contract at all. If that clause in the specification is to be treated. as struck out, then the work is to be done in a reasonable time; but the real truth of the matter is this: that, in the ordinary course of things, there would have been an agreement subsequently as to the number of weeks in which the work was to be done. If they could not agree as to that, the fact that they could not agree did not set aside the contract already formed. There was a contract to do the work within a reasonable time, or if they choose afterwards to agree to some stated time in an agreement they might agree upon it. The contract, in my opinion, was complete.

Now, I want to see for a moment how the defendants treated the matter afterwards. It is said by Mr. Harrison that the custom in this building trade was such that the defendants must have known that they had made no contract at all. Did they take up that position? I see this. The day after the acceptance of the tender was sent the defendant firm wrote this letter: "We beg to acknowledge your letter of yesterday. Our Mr. Renwick, who has the above in hand, is out of town at present, and will not return until Wednesday next." There is no suggestion that the contract is not a complete contract. There is no suggestion that when the plaintiff wrote the words "I accept your offer" he had no business to write them, because no offer had been made, and there is no suggestion of the custom which is alleged to exist in this trade. Then, two days afterwards, on the 18th September, comes a letter from the defendants, in these terms: "We are much obliged by your letter, but since receiving same have looked into our figures and fear we have made an error." That is the real ground of the objection to carry out the work. They had made a mistake, and they wanted to get out of their bargain because they had made a mistake; not because there was not a bargain, but because they had made a mistake; "and we fear we have made an error. Under these circumstances, we must withdraw our estimate." It is too late to withdraw the estimate, which I regard as a complete offer to do the work, after it has been accepted and made the basis of a contract between the parties. Thereupon, on the same day, the plaintiff writes: "Upon the faith of your tender for the work which I accepted arrangements were made which cannot now be undone"; and on the 19th the defendant firm write

1899
November
20.

Queen's
Bench
Division.

again, not saying there is no contract because you had no right to accept what was never intended to be an offer, but they say: "In reply to your note *re* above, our Mr. Renwick, who had the entire matter in hand, is away in the north. Directly he returns, which we believe will be on Thursday, we will communicate with you." Then I see no further letter from them, but the plaintiff's solicitors then write to the defendants and they receive an answer from the defendants' solicitors; and not even in that letter is this supposed custom set up. "It is quite clear," say the solicitors for the defendants, "from the terms of their communication of the 14th, that there is no binding contract."

I understand that contention. That contention is that the document of the 14th is so worded that it does not amount to an offer. I do not agree with that contention, but I understand it. The point about that is, that it does not rest upon any supposed custom of the trade, but rests upon the wording of the document: "It is quite clear, from the terms of their communication of the 14th instant, that there is no binding contract to do the work at the sum of 1,230*l.*, and we have advised Messrs. Pritchard and Renwick to dispute any liability in this respect. The custom of the trade has not been observed by communicating to the builders the result of the various tenders, as was promised in Messrs. Barnes, Williams & Co.'s letter of the 13th instant." I have heard of no such custom. I have heard no evidence about it, and I do not know that any such custom exists. There is, no doubt, a letter upon which I made an observation earlier in the case, which seems to show that it was the intention of the plaintiffs to communicate to the different persons who had tendered the amount of the different tenders; and I was told, not by any evidence, but I was told by observations from counsel, that it was the practice to do this. The solicitors for the defendants take their stand upon the neglect to attend to that practice; they do not take their stand upon any custom of the character which some of the defendants' witnesses wished me to accept. They say: "The custom of the trade has not been observed by communicating to the builders the result of the various tenders"; and I want to point out this, that the defendants' solicitors themselves refer to these so-called estimates as tenders; they do not refer to them as anything but what I believe them to be—tenders to do the work "as was promised." Then they go on to say: "If you will favour us with this information, our clients will be prepared to reconsider the matter, and see whether they can give the usual undertaking to do the work at the price quoted."

In my opinion the case is abundantly plain. The defendants, no doubt, made a mistake. Well, they must stand by their mistake. It was not the plaintiff's mistake; it was their mistake, and they ought to have executed the work at the price that they had offered to execute it, and at the price at which the plaintiff said he was willing for them to execute it. In my opinion the plaintiff's case is unanswered, and there must be judgment for the plaintiff for 250*l.*

Mr. Herbert Reed: The difference is 287*l.*

Mr. Justice BIGHAM: I think if I give you 250*l.* that is enough.

1899
November 20.

Queen's
Bench
Division.

Solicitors for the plaintiff: Messrs. Parker, Barrett & Parker.

Solicitors for the defendants: Messrs. Mackrell & Co.

In the Queen's Bench Division.

(*Before* BRUCE and RIDLEY, JJ.)

In the Court of Appeal.

(*Before* A. L. SMITH, COLLINS, and VAUGHAN WILLIAMS, L.JJ.)

1899
February 18.

Queen's
Bench
Division.

1899
December 18.

Court of
Appeal.

IN THE MATTER OF AN ARBITRATION BETWEEN JAMES NUTTALL AND THE LYNTON AND BARNSTAPLE RAILWAY COMPANY.

Lump Sum Contract—Power to require Award to be stated in Form of Special Case—Excessive Quantities—Extras not ordered in Writing—"Earthworks"—"Soil."

N. contracted to construct a railway, including earthworks, for a lump sum. The contract provided that there were to be no extras, while the specification provided that no extras were to be paid for unless ordered in writing by the engineer at the time. The contract incorporated the specification. A bill of quantities was supplied by the railway to the contractor, which contained a note to this effect: "These quantities are not guaranteed as correct, and are furnished merely for the convenience of contractors."

By clause 12 of the specification, "the contractor was to satisfy himself of the nature of the soil . . . of the quantity of materials to be excavated from the cuttings . . . of all probable contingencies, and generally of all matters which could in any way influence the tender for the contract," and he was to take upon himself all the risk and responsibility of the due and careful execution of the works. Clause 57 of the specification defined "earthworks" as including "all

1899
February 18.

Queen's
Bench
Division.

excavations, embankments, and levelling of every description, whatever the materials may be."

When the works were completed N. claimed two items—(1) 30,000*l.* for blasting rock in the excavations, and (2) 6,000*l.* for excavations which were in excess of the quantities supplied to him.

The matter was referred to arbitration, and the arbitrator made his award in the form of a special case, in which he stated that, as to the first claim, the contractor contended that the word "earthworks" meant soil which could be excavated without blasting, and did not include rock which could only be excavated by that means, and that "whatever the materials may be" in clause 57 had reference to different kinds of soil as distinguished from rock; while the railway contended that the work in question was included in the term "earthworks."

As to the second point, the contractor contended that he was entitled under the contract to be paid for excess of quantities in the work done over and above the quantities contained in the bills of quantities and shown on the drawings; the railway contended that the bills of quantities were not incorporated in the contract, and that the company were not bound by them. The company also contended that they were entitled to require the arbitrator to make his award in the form of a special case.

The arbitrator asked the opinion of the Court on two questions—(1) whether the parties had a right to require the award to be stated in the form of a special case; (2) whether the contractor was entitled to be paid anything in respect of either of his items of claim. The arbitrator found, as a fact, as to the first item, that "soil" in an engineering sense did not include "rock" which had to be blasted; that the word "soil" in clause 12 was used in an engineering sense: that the contractor had been put to expense by reason of the stuff in the cuttings not being "soil" but "rock," and that the intention of the parties to the contract was that the stuff in the cuttings was "soil" in the ordinary sense of the term.

As to item 2, he found that the tender was based on the bill of quantities; that the parties to the contract intended the quantities of work to be done thereunder to be the quantities shown in the bills of quantities and the drawings, and that the contractor had done a large amount of work in excess of the quantities stated in the bill of quantities and drawings.

Held, (1) that the parties were entitled to require the award to be stated in the form of a special case; (2) that the contractor was not entitled to be paid under the contract anything in respect of the two items of claim.

Mr. Nuttall contracted with the Lynton and Barnstaple Railway Company, on March 6th, 1896, to construct about nineteen miles of railway. Mr. Frank W. Chanter was the engineer of the company. The contract stated, "It is hereby agreed that the contract is a lump sum contract, and no extras will be allowed." The contract also provided that, "(3) For the consideration aforesaid, the company do hereby covenant and agree that the company will pay to the contractor for the construction of the said railways and sidings, and other works connected therewith, referred to in the specification, the sum of 42,600*l.*, or such other sum of money as shall from time to time become and be certified to be due and payable to the contractor for and in respect of the said works aforesaid, according to the terms and conditions and stipulations aforesaid, and the true intent and meaning of these presents." The contract incorporated the specification. The material clauses of the specification were as follows:—

(1) The contract to which this specification refers includes the formation and

1899
February 18.

Queen's
Bench
Division.

construction . . . of so much of the railway as lies, . . . being a length of about nineteen miles, including all earthworks . . . and the entire consideration of which shall be a lump sum of money. . . . No work shall be considered as an extra work or paid for as such without and unless the engineer, previously to the commencement of such work, gives an order in writing and describes such as "extra work."

(12) The contractor must satisfy himself of the nature of the soil . . . of the quantity of materials to be excavated from the cuttings . . . and generally of all matters which can in any way influence his tender for this contract, and he must take upon himself all the risk and responsibility of the due and careful execution of the several works as specified or necessary for the formation of the railway, and generally of all the works included in the contract or which may become contingent thereupon, and no information on any such matters derived from the drawings or specification (excepting such as can be obtained only by reference to the drawings or specification and not by inspection or examination of the circumstances themselves), and no information obtained from the engineer, or from any agent of the engineer, or of the company, will relieve the contractor from any risks, or from the entire fulfilment of his contract, including all details and incidental works not particularly mentioned in the specification, but which, whether in the temporary or in the permanent works, must evidently be required by the nature of the works included in the contract.

(24) . . . In no case shall any dimensions be included in the measurement or any quantities be included in the accounts to be paid for which shall exceed the dimensions required by the contract or ordered as therein provided for as extra works, and if the dimensions of executed works exceed those marked upon the drawings the excess will not be allowed unless a written order, signed by the engineer, authorising payment for the same, is produced by the contractor.

(34) In the event of any dispute or question arising between the company and the contractor as to the intent and meaning of any part of the specification or of the drawings referred to therein, or of any further drawings to be prepared, or as to the intent and meaning of any part of the tender or schedule of prices, or of the application of the same to the accounts of the contractor, or as to the manner of executing the works or the quality or description of the materials, implements, or plant used or required to be used in the works, or as to the mode of measuring the works, or the computation of, or payments for, the same, or as to the interpretation, meaning, or effect of the clauses and conditions of the contract or of any of them, or as to any other matter or thing whatever connected with or arising out of the contract or incidental thereto, or not thereby provided for, such questions or disputes shall be referred to the consulting engineer, whose decision shall be conclusive and binding on both parties.

(57) Under the term "earthworks" shall be included excavations, embankment, and levelling of every description, whatever the materials may be, and for whatever the same may be required, and all other works contingent upon or relating to the excavations and embankments, as required by the nature of the contract.

(60) The contractor shall be responsible for the sufficiency of all the slopes of cuttings and embankments, notwithstanding the slopes shown upon the sections and cross sections; and no extra will be allowed for flatter slopes which may be considered necessary by the engineer, and which flatter slope shall be carried out by the contractor upon the order of the engineer or his assistant.

After the completion of the works, Mr. Nuttall, the contractor, made various claims for payment from the company beyond the lump sum fixed by the contract. These claims were, in pursuance of clause 34, referred to Sir

1899
February 18.

Queen's
Bench
Division.

J. W. Szlumper, the consulting engineer. The two items of claim to which the present case refers were:—

1. Blasting on contract 1	£27,747	3	6
In extra railway cutting	2,463	4	0
In foundations of contract bridges	115	1	0
	£30,325	8	6
2. Extra excavations in various parts of the works	6,092	12	0

As to item 1, the contractor contended that he was entitled, under the contract, to be paid the said sum of 30,325*l.* 8*s.* 6*d.*, inasmuch as the intent and meaning of the specification in reference to the word "earthworks" in paragraph 1 thereof was that the term meant and included excavations in soil only, as distinguished from rock, which could be removed only by blasting operations, and did not mean or include the blasting of solid rock, and that the words, "whatever the material may be," in paragraph 57 of the specification, had reference to different kinds of soil in the ordinary acceptation of that term, and as distinguished from solid rock, and should be read in reference to or connection with the word "soil" in paragraph 12 of the specification. The company contended that the contractor was not entitled to be paid any sum in respect of the said item for excessive cost in blasting rock, inasmuch as that work was included in the term "earthworks" in paragraph 1 of the specification, and was within the definition of that word in paragraph 57.

As to the second item, the contractor contended that, as the slopes varied from those shown on the specification and plans, he was entitled under the contract to be paid for excess of quantities in the work done by him over and above the quantities contained in the bills of quantities, and shown on the drawings, respectively, supplied to him by the company's engineer, and that was the intention and meaning of the parties and of the contract and specification. The company contended that the bills of quantities were not incorporated in the contract, and the company were not bound by them, and that the contractor could not recover for any excess.

The company also contended that they were entitled to have the award stated in the form of a special case.

On December 2nd, 1898, Sir James Szlumper stated his award in the form of a special case, asking the opinion of the Court on two questions:—

(1) Were the parties entitled to require the award to be stated in the form of a special case? If the Court should hold that the parties were not so entitled, he awarded 22,634*l.* 11*s.* to the contractor on the first item of claim and 4,735*l.* on the second item.

(2) If the Court should hold that the parties were entitled to require a case to be stated, was the contractor, upon the findings of fact hereinafter set forth, entitled to be paid anything in respect of either of the two items of claim in dispute?

The findings of fact in relation to the first item were as follows:—

(a) That the term "soil" in an engineering sense and when used in relation to engineering works does not include rock which can be removed only by blasting operations.

(b) That the term "soil" in paragraph 12 of the specification is there used in an engineering sense.

1899
February 18.

Queen's
Bench
Division.

(c) That the contractor has expended a very large additional sum of money in rock-blasting operations beyond what he has been paid, consequent upon these blasting operations having been necessary by reason of the stuff in the cuttings not being soil in the ordinary acceptation of that term.

(d) That the intention of the parties to the contract was that the stuff in the cuttings was "soil" in the ordinary acceptation of that term.

And as to the second item as follows:—

(a) The contractor's tender was based upon the bill of quantities supplied to the contractor by the company's engineer.

(b) Each of the parties to the contract intended the quantities of work to be done thereunder to be the quantities shown in the said bill of quantities and drawings respectively.

(c) The contractor has done a large quantity of work under the contract in excess of the quantities stated in the said bill of quantities and on the drawings.

The special case came on before Bruce and Ridley, JJ., on February 18, 1899.

Moulton, Q.C., and Loehnis, appeared for Mr. Nuttall.

Sir E. Clarke, Q.C., J. Walton, Q.C., and Duke appeared for the company.

The Court held, on the first point, that the parties were entitled to require the award to be stated in the form of a special case; and on the second point, that the contractor was not entitled to anything in respect of either of the items of claim.

Mr. Nuttall appealed, and the case came on before A. L. Smith, Collins, and Vaughan Williams, L.JJ., on December 18th, 1899.

Moulton, Q.C., Balfour Browne, Q.C., and Loehnis appeared for Mr. Nuttall, the appellant, and L. Walton, Q.C., and Duke, Q.C., for the company, the respondents.

The Court of Appeal dismissed the appeal with costs.

As to the first point, the decision of the Court of Appeal is reported 82 L. T. 17.

The following were the judgments in the Court of Appeal on the second point:—

SMITH, L.J.: This is an appeal from the judgment of the Queen's Bench Division, who gave judgment in favour of the defendants. Mr. Nuttall was the contractor. A strenuous effort was made, indeed, a whole day was spent in getting from us as to whether or not this was a case in which a special case ought to be stated. We came to the conclusion, at the end of a day and a quarter, that a special case ought to be stated. We have now to deal with the special case. It involves a large sum of money, some 42,000*l.*, which has reference to blasting, and the other point has reference to 4,000*l.*, which has reference to the bill of quantities, two large sums of money, no doubt.

Now, what is this case? It is governed by a contract dated in

March between Mr. Nuttall and the defendant company. The defendant company were desirous of having a short line of railway made between Barnstaple and Lynton, and it is stated in the contract that it was to be a railway nineteen miles in length, and they put this contract in writing. Now, first of all, what is this contract in writing? Is it a contract by Mr. Nuttall to construct this railway from Barnstaple to Lynton at a sum of 42,600*l.*, or is it not, in other words, a lump sum contract? Having heard both sides in this case, I have not myself the slightest doubt in the world that it was a lump sum contract to make this railway from Barnstaple to Lynton for the sum of 42,600*l.*

What does the contract say on this point? The contract of the 6th March refers to the specification and describes what works are to be executed by the contractor, and the works will be found set out in the first section, as I may call it, of the specification: "The contract to which this specification refers includes the formation and construction for a single line on a two feet gauge of so much" and so on, nineteen miles in length. That is the first thing. It is to construct a line of nineteen miles in length between the two termini and "including all earthworks, bridges, viaducts, tunnels, culverts, drains, road alterations and metalling thereof, river and stream diversions, providing all permanent way," and so on, "as shown upon the plans, sections, cross sections, or described in this specification, together with the complete fencing of the railway and works, and the entire consideration of which is to be a lump sum of money." That is the specification. If we stop there, is that a lump sum contract? There can be but one answer; but it does not stop there, because in the contract itself, in paragraph 3, it is thus stated: "For the consideration aforesaid the company do hereby covenant and agree with the contractor that the company will and shall pay to the contractor for the construction of the said railways and sidings"—that is, the nineteen miles of railway from Barnstaple to Lynton—"and other works connected therewith referred to in the said specification the sum of 42,600*l.* or such other sum of money as shall from time to time become and be certified to be due and payable to the contractor for and in respect of the said works, matters, things and premises aforesaid according to the terms and conditions and stipulations aforesaid and the true intent and meaning of these presents."

It is said that that clause which I have last read denotes that this is not a lump sum contract, and considerable argument was addressed to us on the point. I think Mr. Duke gave the right answer when he got up in the earlier part of his argument; he says that that refers

1899
December 18.

Court of
Appeal.

to paragraphs 35 and 36 of the specification. I will not read those clauses, it is sufficient for me to say that "or such other sum of money," and so on, does refer to the sum of money which will become payable to the contractor if and when under the terms of the contract the company were entitled to take the works out of the contractor's hands as done under the certificate of their engineer, they would have to pay the money for the work he had done up to the time the works were lawfully taken out of his hands. I do not think this clause "or such other sum of money as shall from time to time" cuts down the 42,600*l*. It does not rest here. "And it is hereby agreed that the contract is a lump sum contract, and no extras will be allowed." Oh, says Mr. Moulton, the man who drew that did not know what he was doing. That is a curious way of getting rid of a clause in a contract. I never heard of it before, that the man who signed it did not know what he was doing. This is a lump sum contract, and no extras are to be allowed. He says this is not a lump sum contract because there might be extras. That is misleading, it seems to me, because when you finish up with the words "and no extras shall be allowed," you finish with the work the contractor had to construct in this nineteen miles of railway according to the specification for 42,600*l*.

Now we come to another paragraph of this contract. What does the contractor do? He further agrees, that is a second agreement, he "further agrees with the company to execute, construct, and complete all such accommodation works and other works incidental to the contract whether specifically described," and so on, and making of "such accommodation works and other works incidental to the contract, whether specifically described or not, as shall be required by the company or their engineer in the manner and within the time, and subject to the terms, conditions, and stipulations set forth in the said specification," and now, "at the prices set forth in the schedule of prices affixed to the tender." That means as regards these other works, these accommodation works and incidental works, I will do them at the prices (if called upon to do them) which are set forth in the schedule of prices, and it seems to me that the meaning of this schedule of prices—it is headed, "Schedule of prices by which extra works are to be estimated"—coincides with the terms of this contract, that as regards the accommodation and incidental works which are over and above the contract, it is to be brought into play if any of those accommodation works and incidental works are ordered. I am of opinion without doubt that this is a lump sum contract.

1899
December 18.

Court of
Appeal.

What did he undertake to do for a lump sum? He undertook, it is said, to make this nineteen miles of railway from Barnstaple to Lynton, an absolute contract to do it. Now, it is said that he did not anticipate, and I have no doubt it is truth on either side, that in making this railway there would be granite or some other hard stone to be blasted. At one time I did state—I was in error, I did not know of the clause in this contract—that he took the contract for better and for worse, namely, if he got brick clay of great value he could appropriate that to his own use, and if rock came instead of soil that would be for the worse, and the other would be for the better; but it was pointed out by Mr. Moulton this morning that there is a clause in this schedule which shows that is not so as regards the materials excavated, they belong to the company and not to the contractor. He takes this for the worse and not for the better, but that does not settle this matter at all. I ask myself this question. This being for a lump sum to make this railway for 42,600*l.*, how does the contractor get out of it unless he can show that within the four corners of this contract it is not absolute in this way, that he was not bound to make that railway if rock got in the way? In other words, it was an absolute contract to make this railway except rock got in the way. I cannot see that.

It may be, and I believe it is the truth, that neither party antici- pated this rock getting in the way, but how that makes an exception out of the absolute contract to do this work for 42,600*l.* I cannot see. In my judgment it does nothing of the sort. Then it is said that the arbitrator was quite right (and the clause was referred to) in finding that the intention of the parties was that the subject of cutting was soil in the ordinary acceptation of the term. How about that finding in the face of a contract to do the work whatever the intentions of the parties were? On that point this special case was asked for and has been stated, namely, whether as a matter of law on this written contract, it is an absolute contract to do the work for the sum I have named, and secondly, whether he is excused from doing that work if rock gets in the way. I cannot find a trace of it in the contract. It seems to me, on the other hand, that the construction of this contract is otherwise, that it is an absolute contract; whether he found rock in a small degree, or whether he found rock in a large degree, the agreement made was to do the work for 42,600*l.*

Then we come to Sir James Szlumper's award to the contractor, 4,400*l.* over and above the lump sum of 42,600*l.* I need not say again on this point what I said about a lump sum contract. How is

1899
December 18.

Court of
Appeal.

he to get it? I cannot see. Certainly not by the contract, and what is more, there is an express clause in sect. 60 of this specification which deals with the liability there was in the original bill of quantities by reason of slopes being flattened to make them stand up. Therefore, in my opinion, and for the same reasons, I think this contract covered this.

There is only one other observation, and that is clause 12 of the specification is very much brought into play by the contractor, and the schedule word "soil" in that clause meant soil and not rock. Suppose it does; how does that get rid of the absolute contract to construct a railway from A. to B.? That clause in my judgment enures to the benefit of the company, and not to the benefit of the contractor at all; it only fortifies the contract; it was not necessary to have the clause, but being in it fortifies the company against any claim which the contractor might hereafter make against them over and above the 42,600*l.* plus the small matters I need not deal with. It entitles the company to say this: Did not I tell you by clause 12 of this contract that you were yourselves to go from A. to B. and see what the nature of your work was between those two points before you tendered, and that you took upon yourself the responsibility of there being any difference between the bills of quantities and the work you had to do? Right in the face of this it is now said that the contractor can turn round and say: Oh yes, I did not find out it was stone and rock, and therefore I can do away with my lump sum contract and get out of you the 6,000*l.* I had to spend in blasting and the amount I have had to spend in flattening these slopes. In my judgment the contractor cannot do this; it is in breach of his contract.

COLLINS, L. J.: I am of the same opinion. It is admitted now that this work was done under the contract. While being done under the contract it must be either part of the original primary obligations or extra work under the contract; it is not claimed as extra work, and it could not be claimed as extra work because no order in writing has been given for it. Therefore, the right of the contractor for payment must be tried on the footing that it is work done under the primary obligations in the contract—to make the railway of a given length between certain points, including all earthworks, &c., &c., which I need not recapitulate. On that hypothesis, which is the hypothesis we must adopt here in view of what has happened between the parties, the only question is: Does the contract provide for a lump sum for the payment of what is done under what I call the primary obligation,, or is it, as it was contended, a contract to pay such sum as shall be certified from time to time by the engineer as due to the contractor in

1899
December 18.

Court of
Appeal.

respect of the work done? It is quite obvious, when you come to look at this contract, that one central purpose of the parties to it was to make it a lump sum contract; they have certainly said it twice in terms—I am not sure that they have not said it oftener—and therefore it can only be contended that the price is something other than a lump sum, by showing that other stipulations in the contract are so inconsistent with this central obligation undertaken that we must clearly reject it.

That, of course, is a very very strong thing to ask us to do, to cut clean out of the contract that which the parties have twice deliberately stated in the obligation which they have accepted. "It is hereby agreed that the contract is a lump sum contract, and no extras will be allowed." That is in the contract itself, and is also in the specification. The whole of the argument that it is not a lump sum contract comes down when analysed to one short sentence in clause 3: "For the consideration aforesaid"—that is, for the execution of what I call the primary obligations—"the company do hereby covenant and agree that the company will pay to the contractor for the construction of the said railways and sidings and other works connected therewith referred to in the specification the sum of 42,600*l.*" Now come the words relied upon—"or such other sum of money as shall from time to time become and be certified to be due and payable to the contractor for and in respect of the said works, matters, things and premises aforesaid, according to the terms and conditions and stipulations aforesaid and the true intent and meaning of these presents." Now, one in looking at this contract is bound, if possible, to give effect to every part of it, and one is bound certainly, if possible to give effect to the twice-repeated undertaking that this should be a lump sum contract unless there is something to compel us to put a different construction upon it. Mr. Duke has pointed out at least one event in which this second passage that I have just referred to may come into operation, namely, that the payment made should be, not the whole lump sum, but something different from it on the certificate of the engineer. I think with him it was sufficient to point out one that would justify the presence of that clause to show that there was nothing in it which negatived the simple primary obligations undertaken in express terms by the parties. He has not shown one only; he has shown other circumstances which might explain the introduction of those clauses. It seems to me to be capable of covering the payments to be made from time to time by reference to measure and value; at all events, as a factor in the amount that is to be paid. There-fore, when one criticises that which is relied upon as cutting out

1899
December 18.

Court of
Appeal.

of the contract so clear and distinct an undertaking as that which between them here constitutes a lump sum contract, one finds that provision not only might be there, but ought to be there in order to give effect to, what was another intention of the parties to provide for, payment upon certificate in an event which might have ensued. That being so, it makes an end of that part of the case; it is a lump sum contract; the work by the admission of the parties is not an extra, and how is it to be paid? It is to be paid out of the lump sum.

There is another point on the contract to which my Lord has referred; it was not necessary to put it in, but it was a warning to the contractor. You undertake to make this railway between certain points for a lump sum, and you must distinctly understand that before you agree to a lump sum contract, you must, or you would be wise to look at the ground for yourself, and we tell you that the risk is with you. If the soil presents difficulty, that is your affair. We tell you distinctly that you must look at the ground yourself, and we guarantee nothing. But that is not necessary, because as my Lord pointed out, the undertaking to make the line on his part and under a lump sum contract put the burden upon him.

Accepting the finding of facts of the arbitrator, I am not sure I should have felt myself able to put the construction upon it which he has done; but, accepting that the primary obligation remains with the contractor, he has to make the line whether it is in stone or clay, and his only right to be paid for it is the lump sum contract. The second point is a corollary of the first. The contractor is warned that the company do not guarantee the slopes, and the particular work in respect of which he claims the larger sum—the work of making these cuttings—is again specifically dealt with by the 60th section of the specification, which says that "The contractor shall be responsible for the sufficiency of all the slopes, of cuttings and embankments, notwithstanding the slopes shown upon the sections and cross sections; and no extra will be allowed for flatter slopes," and so on. So that the very event contemplated by that 60th section, it seems to me, has arisen, and the necessary sloping of these embankments has involved a larger amount of work in excavation for the contractor than is shown in the contract. It is unfortunate for the contractor that that is so, but that was one of the contingencies which he had to take into mind when he was making an estimate which is an estimate to cover all risk, as well as to cover that which by measure and value he has to do. For these reasons I am of opinion that the judgment of the Court below was right.

1899
December 18.

Court of
Appeal.

VAUGHAN WILLIAMS, L.J.: I agree, but not without some reluctance. We have here to construe a contract, and we must construe the contract according to the true meaning of the words in the contract. None the less must we do so because I think that the case is a very hard case. If we do think so, we are bound to construe the contract according to the words that we find in it. But this is a contract which one would wish, if one could, to construe so as to avoid any hardship to the contractor; first, because the contract itself is not well worded—it is not a contract of which the meaning is very plain; and secondly, because this question is now raised in an arbitration to determine the final sum which has to be paid by the company to the contractor for the work that he has executed, and that has to be determined by the consulting engineer as arbitrator.

One cannot help thinking that the question of the construction of this contract may have frequently arisen in the course of the execution of the work for the decision of this same consulting engineer, and that he may, in the course of the construction of the works, have put upon it the construction in law which it is obvious by his award that he has thought to be the right construction, and which is not the construction which we are now putting upon this contract. But I do not see my way to put the construction on the contract which Mr. Moulton argued that we ought to put. The contract is that, "For the consideration aforesaid"—that is, the consideration of making this railway between these points—"the company shall pay to the contractor for the construction of the said railways and sidings, and other works connected therewith referred to in the said specification, the sum of 42,600l., or such other sum of money as shall from time to time become and be certified to be due and payable to the contractor for and in respect of the said works, matters, things and premises aforesaid according to the terms and conditions and stipulations aforesaid and the true intent and meaning of these presents, and it is hereby agreed that the contract is a lump sum contract, and no extras will be allowed."

Now, the words to which attention has already been called, "or such other sum of money as shall from time to time become and be certified to be due," are words which certainly would rather lead one to suppose that it was not intended that the lump sum mentioned should be absolutely final, but only that it cannot be final unless and until it was altered by reduction or increase by the certificate of the consulting engineer. But one cannot help thinking that to put such a construction upon the words would really make the contract cease to be a lump sum contract altogether, and, speaking for myself, I do

1899
December 18.

Court of
Appeal.

not think that the presence of that difficulty ought to compel us to alter the contract from a lump sum contract to a measure and value contract, even though one failed to find in the contract some matters to which these words, "such other sum of money as shall from time to time become and be certified to be due and payable," are applicable. I say that because I do not think that it is possible to explain those words by a reference to the provision in Article 35. Because Article 35 of the specification is an article which goes upon the basis that the full price, whatever it is, whether it is the 42,600*l.*, or whether it is some less sum, or whether it is a greater sum, will be within the words of that section to be ascertained by the engineer. I do not think that when once that is admitted it makes any difference that the engineer has to go on and certify the balance payable. The clause in the contract is not dealing with the balance payable. It is dealing with the contract price. The contractor, if he does not do the work, and leaves the contract an open contract, is not entitled to be paid the contract price, or any part of it; but if the even happens which is contemplated by sect. 35—that is, the building owner chooses to accept the work and go in and treat the whole work as being done under the contract—then what you have to find is this very contract price which is here spoken of as being 42,600*l.*, and you have to make a deduction from that and get a certificate. That being so, I do not think that you can possibly apply these words to the permission for granting the interim certificates. If one looks at the interim certificates, they are really certificates which are given merely for part payments; they do not in any way relate to the price which is to be paid for the work when done. They are, it is true, payments on account of it, but they have no relation to it whatsoever. "Or such other sum of money as shall from time to time become and be certified to be due" seems to me to relate to the ultimate payment. Subject to these observations, I quite assent that the construction put by the Divisional Court on this contract was the right construction.

Solicitors for the Railway Company: Mellor, Smith & May.

Solicitors for Mr. Nuttall: Rowcliffes, Rawle & Co., agents for J. Booth & Son, Manchester.

1900
February 20.

Court of
Appeal.

𝔍n the Queen's Bench Division.

(*Before* Wright, J.)

𝔍n the Court of Appeal.

(*Before* A. L. Smith, Collins, and Romer L.JJ.)

FREEMAN AND SON *v.* HENSLER (*a*).

Building Contract—Time—Delivery of Site to Builder.

Where a builder contracts to carry out works within a limited time, he is entitled within a reasonable time to possession of the whole site.

This was an action brought by builders against a building owner for damages for breach of a building contract in not giving possession of the site within a reasonable time. The plaintiffs, the builders, had agreed to pull down fifteen houses of the defendant at Greenwich, and erect upon the site twelve new houses within six months from the date of the contract. By agreement the commencement and the date of completion were postponed for a fortnight.

The defendant did not give the builders possession of the whole site until long after the fortnight had elapsed, and then he gave possession of the site piecemeal. The builders did not obtain possession of the last house until one month before the date fixed for completion. The material clauses of the agreement are sufficiently referred to in the judgments.

The action was tried before Wright, J., who held that the only implied covenant in the contract was to give possession within a reasonable time, and that in fact possession had been given within a reasonable time, and therefore he gave judgment for the defendant. From this judgment the plaintiffs appealed, and the case came on before the Court of Appeal on February 20th, 1900.

English Harrison, Q.C., and A. A. Hudson, for the plaintiffs: In this case the builders had to complete within a limited time. Time is stated to be of the essence of the contract, and if the builders failed to complete they were liable to penalties. The delay of the employer converted the contract from a summer into a winter contract. The building owner must always give possession within a reasonable time, and in these circumstances he was bound to give possession of the whole site (subject to the agreed postponement) immediately after the signing of the contract.

Crump, Q.C., and Lewis Thomas, for the defendant: The building owner must give possession within a reasonable time, but there is no evidence that the dates of giving possession here were unreasonable. The Court cannot read into the contract a fresh clause to the effect that the building owner must give possession forthwith.

(*a*) Also reported in 64 J. P. 260.

1900
February 20.

Court of
Appeal.

A. L. Smith, L.J.: What are the undisputed circumstances of this case? On the 4th July, 1896, the defendant, whom I will call the building owner, entered into a contract with the builders, that is the plaintiffs, Messrs. Freeman & Son, to build him twelve houses on a site where fifteen houses had stood before. These old fifteen houses faced the Woolwich Road, being bounded on the one side by Ratcliffe Road, and upon the other by Comerell Road. By the contract the builder was to pull down the old houses, and he was to erect twelve new houses instead of fifteen; the new houses being somewhat larger than the old ones. *Primâ facie*, before I go to the other parts of the contract, what is the meaning of that, supposing nothing more had been said? Says the defendant: "I will pay you 4,400*l.* if you will build me twelve houses on the site in question." The site does not belong to the builder; the site belongs to the building owner. First of all, if there was nothing more, what would be the implication which would arise from such a contract as that? I quite agree that implications are not to be brought into written contracts, unless it is necessary that they should be brought in, in order to carry out the obvious intentions of the parties to the contract. That is good sense and good law, and it has been laid down many times. But where the building owner contracts with the builder to pay him 4,400*l.* to build him twelve houses, the builder must have the right to enter and take possession of the land on which he is to erect those twelve houses. There must be something implied. The whole contract says nothing about the time when the builder is to come in, and it is perfectly obvious and necessary to imply something, otherwise he could not build the houses at all.

Now, let us come a little nearer to this case. There are one or two terms which are material in this contract. The first is that by clause 12, the contractor—that is the plaintiff—is, upon signing the contract (that is the document which he signed on the 4th July, 1896), to insure the whole of the buildings against loss or damage by fire. That looks as though the contractor was to start paying premiums in anticipation of the buildings being built up, and it seems to me to indicate strongly that he is to begin to build at once. I do not say in ten minutes, in half-an-hour, or in two or three days, but he is to start pulling down the old houses to put up new ones, and cover them in. That is the first indication in the contract.

I will now go on to another clause, which deals with the time within which the buildings were to be completed: "The contractor is to complete the whole of the work, except painting and such other work as the architect may desire to remain over, within six months

FREEMAN AND SON v. HENSLER.

1900
February 20.

Court of
Appeal.

of the date of the contract." That is the date contemplated; it is six months from 4th July, 1896, "unless the work should be delayed by reason of inclement weather, or causes not under the contractor's control, or in case of combination by workmen, or strike, or lock-out in the building trade, for which due allowance shall be made by the architect." If due allowance is made by the architect, the contractor is to complete the works within such time as the architect shall consider reasonable.

Then "time is to be considered as of the essence of the contract." I do not place any reliance on that here now, because a delay of a fortnight was agreed upon between the parties, and that would abrogate in my judgment the stipulation as to time being of the essence of the contract, for another time it was agreed upon at which the work was to commence. The contract provides that: "In case of default the contractor is to pay as and by way of liquidated damages the agreed sum of 10*l.* a week." I am not touching on penalties, because that has nothing to do with this case. But there is an indication that the contractor is to insure from the date of the contract: the next thing is that, excepting exceptions, he is to complete the buildings within six months. If he does not complete within six months he is to pay 10*l.* a week, and this is an important feature in the case. When is he to have the land to start building upon? There must be something implied in the contract as to the time when the land is to be given over to the builder.

Then there is another clause which is of some importance. There is a question about the bricklaying, and when one reads the clause about the bricklaying, in my judgment this bricklaying applies to the whole twelve houses which the plaintiff had undertaken to build. Now, what are the words? "The bricklaying is to be carried up simultaneously all round." Now, it is clear that the brickwork means the brickwork of the whole twelve houses. "The brickwork is to be carried up simultaneously all round: no portion to be more than five feet in advance of any other at any time." How could that be done, I ask myself, if the builder had not got possession of the land? He could not perform that part of the contract. Therefore, it seems to me perfectly clear, on reading this contract, that there is an implication in it that the building owner shall give the builder the site on which the builder is to erect the twelve houses, and in my opinion the implication is that they should be delivered over within a reasonable time.

Now, the action is brought by the plaintiff against the defendant, the builder alleging that he did not have the land within a reasonable

1900
February 20.

Court of
Appeal.

time. I care not whether it is called "forthwith" or "reasonable time"; or whether any other epithet is used. It is perfectly obvious to me that, upon the facts of the case, even if you take "reasonable time," that the building owner did not hand over the site, on which the plaintiff was to build the twelve houses, within a reasonable time or anything like it. It was handed over to the builder in driblets, and the last driblet was not handed over to the builder till the 14th December, 1896, under a contract which, as I have said, was made on the 4th July, 1896, five months before. In fact, this delay has driven what is called a summer contract into a winter contract, which, it is well known, is more expensive to the builder than a summer contract. It made no difference at all to the building owner, after he had made a contract with the plaintiffs to construct the twelve houses for 4,400*l.*, whether wages went up or down or delay occurred. It made no difference to him; he had only to pay 4,400*l.* when the whole twelve houses were built, but it made a difference to the builder whether he built in the summer or in the winter.

What ought to be done in this case? It is quite clear that judgment for the defendant cannot stand. What did my brother Wright find here? He deals with implications, and he says he cannot find any implications that the land is to be handed over forthwith. What does he say? "If anything had to be implied I think what ought to be implied is that possession should be given within a reasonable time, and no doubt that ought to be implied." I agree with him. "I should think it would be an implication in any contract that something which must be performed by the one party in order that the other party may have the benefit of it, should be performed within a reasonable time." I agree with that, although he gives judgment for the defendant. Then he says: "I see no evidence" (I cannot agree with him here) "that possession was not given within a reasonable time, except as regards one house possibly, and no such case was made by the plaintiff at the hearing of this action." The only different case made here is that Mr. English Harrison has used the words "reasonable time," and the word used before my brother Wright was "forthwith," and my brother Wright said that, under the circumstances, it was reasonable time. He says it has not been proved that the land should be handed over, in the case of a contract to be completed within six months, till five months have elapsed.

For these reasons I think that the judgment should be set aside and that there should be judgment for the plaintiffs. I think it should be taken that in this case a reasonable time had elapsed on

1900
February 20.
Court of
Appeal.

the 18th July, which was the day when, apparently by mutual consent, the land was to be handed over.

COLLINS, L.J.: I am of the same opinion. I think the contract clearly involves that the building owner shall be in a position to hand over the whole site to the builder immediately upon the making of the contract. I think that there is an implied undertaking on the part of the building owner, who has contracted for the buildings to be placed by the plaintiff on his land, that he will hand over the land for the purpose of allowing the plaintiff to do that which he has bound himself to do. The plaintiff is bound to complete the whole of the building within six months.

There are certain provisions in the contract which point to express agreement that the building shall be conducted as far as possible simultaneously over the whole of a given area, therefore it was essential to the plaintiff that the whole site should be handed over, and it seems to me, no date being expressed, but a limit of six months being fixed, and time being of the essence of the contract, that possession should have been handed over forthwith.

However, the parties appear to agree—that is rather putting it too high—the plaintiff appears to have waived his right of getting possession within the first fortnight. That takes out of the contract the covenant that time is to be of the essence of the contract, and substitutes a reasonable time for the earlier obligation which I think existed to hand over possession at once. I think we now are the judges of what is a reasonable time within which the plaintiff would be entitled to insist upon the site being handed over. I should say that the reasonable time cannot be extended beyond the fortnight during which the plaintiff was willing to acquiesce in not getting possession of the land. The reasonable time, in my judgment, ends at the expiration of that fortnight. I think the damage ought to be assessed on the footing that there was a breach in not handing over possession at that date.

My brother Wright has held that there was an obligation on the part of the defendant to hand over the land within a reasonable time. Somehow or other he has held that there being an obligation to hand over within a reasonable time in a contract in which time is described as of the essence of the contract, and which was made in the early part of July, 1896, and which was postponed by consent for a fortnight, he somehow or other arrived at the conclusion that to wait till 19th December, 1896, before the land was handed over was not to wait more than a reasonable time. I cannot help thinking that the learned judge has regarded "reasonable time" from a stand-

1900
February 20.

Court of
Appeal.

point which the law cannot accept—from the standpoint only of the person in whom the obligation was to hand over the land. He must have held that that was the true measure, and not the right of the person who had made his arrangements, and was entitled to make his arrangements, on the footing of getting possession at once. However, he arrived at it, I am sorry to say that I cannot agree with him. It is for us to decide what is a reasonable time. We are justified, in deciding within the limits I have named. Therefore my judgment must be for the plaintiff, with the right to have the damages assessed.

ROMER, L.J.: I agree. This, to my mind, is like the ordinary case of an owner of a site agreeing with the builder that a house shall be built on the site within a certain specified time, with penalties for not completing within that time. I say that this case is like that for this reason: that when you inquire into the case and see what were the houses to be erected in this case by the builder, you find that substantially it was one block—it was like one house—they were not detached houses, but one block of houses. The fact that they were to be built practically as one house is borne out by the provision as to the bricklaying, to which attention has been called by my Lord.

When an owner of a site contracts with the builder that the builder shall, within a limited time under threat of penalties, build a shop on the site for the owner, and there is nothing else in the contract as to an opposite view, in my opinion it is implied that the owner is in a position to allow the builder forthwith to commence his work; in other words, it is implied in that contract that the land shall be delivered up to the builder forthwith, so that he may be able to commence at once. That, in my opinion, is the true construction of the contract here. That is further borne out by the special provisions to which attention has been called.

As a matter of fact, the builder did give the land owner a fortnight's grace. What was the effect of that? In my opinion the effect was this: that he could no longer say that he had incurred damages because of that fortnight; it did leave it open to him to say that, in case, after that fortnight the land was not given up to him—and it should have been given up as a whole—there was a breach, for which he is entitled to recover damages.

Appeal allowed.

Solicitors for the plaintiffs: Bowerman & Forward.
Solicitor for the defendant: A. Syrett.

1900
April 4.

Queen's
Bench
Division.

In the Queen's Bench Division.

(*Before* PHILLIMORE, J., and a Special Jury.)

KELLETT *v.* NEW MILLS URBAN DISTRICT COUNCIL.

Contract—Performance to be certified by Engineers—Neglect of Engineers to Certify.

The plaintiff agreed to do work for the defendants to the satisfaction of an engineer, and the defendants agreed to pay the plaintiff upon the certificate of the engineer. The engineer never addressed himself to determine and certify, but wrongfully refused, or wrongfully and unreasonably delayed, so to determine and certify, and the defendants took advantage of his refusal and delayed payment. Fraud was not alleged. Held, that the plaintiff could recover from the defendants without a certificate.

Action by contractors for the balance of the price of work done under a contract, and for extras, tried at the Manchester Assizes on April 4, 1900.

It appeared by the writ, which was specially endorsed, that the plaintiff's claim was for the sum of 1,054*l.* 8*s.*, money due under an agreement made between the plaintiff and the defendants on April 28, 1897, for the execution of certain sewerage works, and for extras in connection with the said works.

The defendants, by their defence, pleaded (*inter alia*) that, by clause 39 of the agreement, payments were to be made on the recommendation of the engineer only, and so long as the works proceeded to his satisfaction, and at the rate of 75 per cent. of the value of the works executed by the contractor; an additional 15 per cent, on the certified completion of the works; and if the engineer should certify that the whole was in a good and substantial state of repair and delivered up to his entire satisfaction as executed in strict compliance with the contract, the balance at the expiration of twelve months; and in case the contractor should fail to complete the contract, that sum would be forfeited to the Council. That no final certificate for the contract had been made out, nor had the engineer certified that the whole was in a good and substantial state of repair or delivered up to his satisfaction as executed in compliance with the contract.

The reply contained the following paragraph:—

"The plaintiff, by way of equitable reply to the defence, further says as follows: The plaintiff has completed all the work agreed to be done by him under the contract in the defence mentioned.

"By the said contract the engineers therein mentioned were the servants or agents of the defendants for the purpose of certifying the date of completion of the works to be done by the plaintiff and the amounts payable by the defendants to the plaintiff upon such completion. The said engineers did not properly, in discharge of their duty as servants and agents of the defendants or at all, address themselves to determine and certify either what was the date of the completion of the said works by the plaintiff, or what was the

1900
April 4.

Queen's
Bench
Division.

amount due by the defendants to the plaintiff upon such completion, but the said engineers wilfully, arbitrarily and persistently refused to address themselves to determine and certify either the said date or the said amount, and thereby became and were discharged from their position as engineers under the contract.

"The defendants, knowing of such wrongful, wilful, arbitrary and persistent refusal by the said engineers as aforesaid, took advantage of such refusal of the engineers as aforesaid so as to prevent the plaintiff from receiving or recovering payment of the amount due to him for the works completed as aforesaid.

"The plaintiff does not suggest that the said conduct of the said engineers and the defendants arose from any fraudulent motive, but will submit that the said conduct was in equity a fraud upon the plaintiff's rights under his said contract and entitling him to the relief claimed."

The jury found that the works were completed in December, 1897, but that no certificate of completion had been given. They found that the engineers never addressed themselves to determine and certify that the works had been completed or what was the sum due to the plaintiff, but that they wrongfully refused or wrongfully and unreasonably delayed, so to determine and certify; and that the defendants were aware of such refusal or delay, and took advantage of it to refuse or unreasonably delay payment.

For the plaintiff: Pickford, Q.C. (Langdon with him). For the defendants: C. A. Russell, Q.C. (E. Sutton with him).

PHILLIMORE, J.: I have considered the argument of the learned counsel for the defendants, and I have considered all the cases which were cited to me.

I am of opinion that upon the answers to the questions put to the, jury it is my duty to direct an entry of a verdict for the plaintiff, and to give judgment for the plaintiff.

I am quite aware that this is a very important case; I think it is also true that in a sense it is a new case, and I should anticipate that it would go further; and, thinking that, I thought that at any rate one part of my duty would be to endeavour to get the facts ascertained, and the verdict of the jury upon the facts, so that the various Courts before which this case might go might deal with them.

On those findings I myself see no doubt. I think the language of Lord Chancellor Cottingham, though it may very well be *obiter*, in *Mackintosh* v. *The Great Western Railway Co.* (a), is language I should desire to adopt. I think that language, and the decisions in *Waring* v. *The Manchester, Sheffield and Lincolnshire Railway Co.* (b), and in *Pawley* v. *Turnbull* (c)—though I think that case may

(a) 19 L. J. Ch. 374.
(b) 18 L. J. Ch. 450.
(c) 3 Giff. 70.

1900
April 4.

Queen's
Bench
Division.

be open to some comment—and the language in *Botterill* v. *The Ware Guardians* (*a*), all support the plaintiff's contention, as does also the decision in *Clarke* v. *Westrope* (*b*) and *Clarke* v. *Watson* (*c*).

Mr. Russell has been driven to contend that where an engineer, or surveyor, or valuer, to the knowledge of the employer, without reason neglects to consider and/or determine what is due to the tradesman, the employer is entitled to take advantage of that known misconduct on the part of the surveyor, engineer, or valuer. He is driven further to say that supposing the engineer, surveyor, or valuer dies, or becomes insane, there would be difficulty even then in saying that the tradesman should have any remedy. He is driven to suggest that the only way in which a tradesman then could have a remedy would be because he would have no remedy against the engineer, surveyor, or valuer. How his remedy as against his employer can differ according as he has or has not a remedy against the engineer, surveyor, or valuer which may be useless, I fail to see. I am of opinion that the decisions are clear that where the employer colludes with the engineer, surveyor, or valuer, it is right to pass the engineer, surveyor, or valuer by, and to seek the determination of the Courts as in an ordinary contract; and I see no difference between the misconduct of the engineer, surveyor, or valuer being procured by the employer, and the employer knowingly taking advantage of the man's original misconduct.

I appreciate the force of the argument which Mr. Sutton has offered, that the proper remedy of the plaintiff here would have been to call upon the defendants to appoint another surveyor; and there is no doubt language *obiter* in *Clarke* v. *Watson* which supports that contention. In that case, however, the surveyor was to be appointed by the defendants themselves, and it was in the contemplation of the parties that he might be altered from time to time. Here it is admitted that no new surveyor could be appointed except by the joint consent of both; but be that as it may, though the point was taken in the pleadings it was not brought forcibly to our attention, and I was not asked to leave any question to the jury with regard to it, and I think it would have been well worth while if that point was insisted upon, that some question should have been asked the jury with regard to it. But I am quite prepared to take the case as it stands. It may well be that it would have been a reasonable

(*a*) 2 T. L. R. 621.
(*b*) 18 C. B. 765.
(*c*) 34 L. J. C. P. 148.

1900
April 4.

Queen's
Bench
Division.

course to suggest. Then I think the burden of doing that in this case lay upon the defendants; and I think that they knew here not merely that their man was not certifying, but that he was going through the process of pretended inquiry, which was almost worse than his refusing to inquire; and I think that they were bound in those circumstances to have taken some very decided action on their part. I may add that it does not at all follow that the plaintiff is as well off if they do appoint another surveyor, because he may get his money, but get it only after very much greater delay. One of the grounds of complaint is the delay. One of the great grounds is that he does not get his money when he ought to get it; and, at any rate, I think the verdict of the jury was right, and that the answers of the jury are right. I think upon their answers a verdict should properly be entered for the plaintiff, and judgment will follow.

Solicitors for the plaintiff: Lynde & Branthwaite.

Solicitor for the defendants: Rigby.

In the Queen's Bench Division.

1900
November 7.

Queen's
Bench
Division.

(*Before* Lord Alverstone, C.J., and Kennedy, J.)

LONDON STEAM STONE SAW MILLS *v.* LORDEN.

Lump Sum Contract, notwithstanding Quantities Part of Contract.

The S. Co. contracted to furnish stone to L. for certain works for a lump sum. The tender contained the following words: "The bill of quantities to form part of the contract, and all variations to be priced at the rate stated in the bill, and added to, or deducted from, the lump sum, as the case may be." There were variations from the quantities in the bill. L. contended that he was entitled to measure up the whole of the work and pay on that basis. Held, that the contract was one for a lump sum, and that the variations should be measured and valued, and the amount so arrived at added to, or deducted from, the lump sum, as the case might be.

This was an appeal from the decision of an Official Referee in a dispute on a building contract which had been referred to him.

The London Steam Stone Saw Mills, the plaintiffs in the action, entered into a contract to supply stone for a certain building in King Street, St. James',

1900
November 7.

Queen's
Bench
Division.

with Messrs. Lorden & Sons, the defendants. The documents which constituted the contract were the following:—

"Messrs. W. H. LORDEN & SONS.   "August 27th, 1897.
"DEAR SIRS,

"Re *Stonework, King Street.*

"We enclose our estimate for above, with the terms amended as agreed upon between us.

"If there is anything omitted which you consider necessary, will you let us know, and we will include it? Or if you prefer to have a different form of agreement drawn up, we will call and sign it.

"We called on the works yesterday, and your foreman sent us on to the architect to see the drawings. They are not quite ready yet, but Mr. Sawyer said we could come to his office and take off the sizes required at once. With your permission we will avail ourselves of the opportunity, as there is a large stone required to carry bay over angle corner which may be difficult to get.

"We shall require for our guidance a copy of the bill and of the specifications referring to our work.

"Yours truly,
"LONDON STEAM STONE SAW MILLS.
"A. FINDLAY,
"*Managing Director.*

"We return, with thanks, form of agreement lent us.—A. F."

Estimate sent to Messrs. W. H. Lorden & Sons on August 27th, 1897:—

"Messrs. W. H. LORDEN & SONS.

"DEAR SIRS,

"We agree to prepare, deliver, fix and clean down the whole of the stonework for new premises, King Street, St. James', all as per bill of quantities, and in accordance with contract drawings and specification, for the lump sum of three thousand and ninety-six pounds (3,096*l.*) nett, payments to be made to us fortnightly at the rate of 80 per cent. on the amount of work done. One half the retention money to be paid us when the work is cleaned down, and the remainder within three months afterwards.

"There is no carving nor any provisional amounts included in our price, and it is understood that you provide the necessary scaffolding, mortar, &c. as required for fixing the stonework, we finding our own hoisting and fixing tackle.

"We undertake to commence delivery within ten days after receiving order and sufficient drawings, and to deliver at the rate of not less than 500 cubic feet per week, and to complete the work to the reasonable satisfaction of the architect and yourselves.

"The bill of quantities to form part of the contract, and all variations to be priced out at the rate stated in the bill and added to, or deducted from, the lump sum, as the case may be.

"The acceptance of this estimate to constitute a binding agreement.

"Yours truly,
"LONDON STEAM STONE SAW MILLS, LTD.
"A. FINDLAY,
"*Managing Director.*"

"Trinity Road, Upper Tooting, S.W.

"August 27th, 1897.

"London Steam Stone Saw Mills.

"Dear Sir,

"King Street, St. James'.

1900
November 7.

Queen's
Bench
Division.

"We accept your price of three thousand and ninety-six pounds (3,096l.) for carrying out the Portland stone to the above job, you to be subject to the same conditions of contract that we have signed (copy of which you return). The only item we see that is not quite right is the retention is for six months, not three.

"We are glad you have again seen the drawings, but, when calling at the architect's office, please go as if you came from us.

"We are sending you copy of quantities and specifications by later post, as requested.

"Yours truly,

"W. H. Lorden & Sons."

The Official Referee found that the contract was one for a lump sum, and that variations from the contract should be calculated as additions to, or deductions from, the lump sum, as the case might be.

The defendants appealed from this decision, and the case came before the Divisional Court (Lord Alverstone, L.C.J., and Kennedy, J.) on November 7th, 1900.

C. C. Scott, for the defendants, contended that the defendants were entitled to measure up the whole of the work, and pay upon that basis, thus making the contract a measure and value contract and not a lump sum contract.

A. A. Hudson, for the plaintiffs, argued that the fact of the quantities having been made part of a contract for a lump sum did not entitle the parties to disregard the lump sum and ascertain the amount to be paid to the contractor on the basis of measurement of the work.

Lord Alverstone, L.C.J.: I do not think we can properly reverse the finding of the Official Referee in this case. The difficulty arises from the form of document which has been used (and I am afraid it is not uncommon for that difficulty to arise in the building trade), which really does not precisely explain what is the exact position of the parties. The early clause of the agreement provides that the plaintiffs were "to prepare, deliver, fix and clean down the whole of the stonework for new premises, King Street, St. James', all as per bill of quantities and in accordance with contract drawings and specifications for the lump sum of 3,096l." And then further on in the contract "The bill of quantities to form part of the contract, and all variations to be priced out at the rate stated in the bill and added to, or deducted from, the lump sum, as the case may be."

Now, when we look at the bill of quantities we find it contains specific general directions and particular directions as to what was to

1900
November 7.

Queen's
Bench
Division.

be the character of the stone, and as to the nature of the beds and joints, and certain directions as to the moulding and rubbing of the stone, and further, in various parts through the bill of quantities there are specific directions as regards each particular item. Then, the total quantity of stone, amounting to about 8,000 odd cubic feet, being specified and described in the earlier part, there are a large number of other items in the bill of quantities providing for different sorts of work, which, so to speak, may be required to be done or may not be required to be done, assuming the contract or the architect requires certain things to be carried out.

The specification also appears to contain some general directions and some particular directions with regard to the character of the stonework. It must be remembered that measure and value contracts are, of course, perfectly well known, and it is not uncommon for the employer to contract and require that all the work is to be measured up and priced in accordance with the schedule, and to that contract the word "lump sum" has no proper application. Mr. Scott's contention is that the effect of these two clauses together is to practically turn this into a measure and value contract; yet if there is no alteration of any sort or kind in the plans and drawings, directing that if the work as actually carried out should turn out to contain less or more stone than the bill of quantities, a deduction or addition must be made either against or for the plaintiffs in the matter. I think that is giving no effect at all to the expression "lump sum" in this contract, and I think it was intended to have some meaning.

Now, if it is not a purely measure and value contract, what is the true construction to be put on the contract? I think that the first clause did intend that the contractors, the London Steam Stone Saw Mills, should carry out the work which was indicated in all the three documents for the sum of 3,096*l.*, and I think the later clause did intend to say if there is a variation which affects items which are in any of the three documents, those variations shall be priced out, either additions or deductions, by the schedule which is affixed to the bill of quantities, and I think that the presence of the words "lump sum" in that last clause points to that being the true construction, because the variations are not to be merely carried in so that the total is priced according to measure or value, but they are something to be added to, or deducted from, something which the parties understand to be the lump sum.

Without in any way wishing to construe the contract by any other finding, I desire to point out that practically there would be great difficulty in working this contract on any other terms, because I

1900
November 7.

Queen's
Bench
Division.

understand that the work has been so carried out; in fact, that the method of executing and jointing the various stones renders the result of the contract, by reason of the quantities in the specification, or rather, to speak more correctly, the quantities in the bill of quantities and the quantities in the work as executed, not altogether trustworthy. Therefore, I think, that as this work has been executed the plaintiffs' claim, or the claim of the person claiming extras, is in respect of variations which have been made upon the work, necessitating opening up certain quantities in the bill of quantities, but not necessitating the whole of the quantities being opened up so as to make it a measure and value contract.

I think that the report of the quantity surveyors shows that they have estimated the extras and checked the extras which the London Steam Stone Saw Mills Company claim by reference to the items in the bill of quantities properly, but have pointed out that if they are to go further and inquire into the total quantity of stone, the particulars in the bill of quantities do not enable a proper re-adjustment to be made. I think, on the facts before him, that the learned Official Referee came to a right conclusion that he must allow the extra as an addition to, or deduction from the lump sum, as the case may be, but was not entitled to allow the other contracting party to open up all the quantities in the schedule and make it a measure and value contract. For these reasons I think, therefore, that the appeal must be dismissed.

Mr. Justice KENNEDY: I quite agree, and I add nothing to it.

Solicitors for the plaintiffs: Wetherfield, Son & Barnes.
Solicitors for the defendants: Badham & Williams.

1901
June 12.

King's Bench
Division.

In the King's Bench Division.

(*Before* BRUCE and PHILLIMORE, JJ.)

SATTIN *v.* POOLE.

*Delay caused by Owner or Architect—Extension of Time—
Liquidated Damages (a).*

S. contracted to build a house for P. The work was to be completed by a certain day. The work was to be completed by a certain day. The contract provided that, "If in the opinion of the architect the works be delayed . . . by reason of authorised extras or additions . . . or in consequence of the contractor not having received in due time necessary instructions from the architect, for which he shall have specifically applied in writing, the architect shall make a fair and reasonable extension of time." The contract also provided for 12*l.* per week as liquidated damages for delay. The work was delayed beyond the time fixed. S. then wrote to the architect asking him to grant or certify for an extension of time. The architect did not reply at once. S. then issued a writ claiming 681*l.*, which the architect had certified as due to S., subject to the question of penalties. The architect then wrote extending the time, but not to such a late date as that of completion, and certifying that 231*l.* was due to P. as liquidated damages for delay. S. wished to call evidence before the Official Referee to prove that the delay was caused by P. or his architect in ordering extras, in supplying material after the specified date, in delay in the selection of stone to be used, and in the alteration of the plans, and in other matters. The Official Referee refused to admit this evidence. Held, on appeal, that his decision was right, on the ground that the builder had applied to the architect for his decision as to an extension of time, and was bound by that decision, and, further, that the architect had jurisdiction under the contract to decide these particular questions of delay. (*Roberts* v. *Bury Commissioners (b)* discussed.)

In this case Messrs. Sattin and Evershed entered into a contract with Mr. Poole to pull down and rebuild St. James' Restaurant, at St. James' Street, Brighton. The contract was dated December 5th, 1898. The material parts of the conditions follow:—

(23) Possession of the site (or premises) shall be given to the contractor on or before the 5th day of December. He shall begin the works immediately after such possession, shall regularly proceed with them, and shall complete the same (except painting and papering or other decorative work which, in the opinion of the architect, it may be desirable to delay) by the 20th day of May, subject, nevertheless, to the provisions for extension of time hereinafter contained.

(24) If the contractor fail to complete the works by the date named in clause 23, or within any extended time allowed by the architect under these presents, and the architect shall certify in writing that the works could reasonably have been completed by the said date, or within the said extended time, the contractor shall pay to the employer the sum of 12*l.* sterling per week as liquidated and ascertained damages for every week beyond the said date or extended time, as the case may be, during which the works shall remain unfinished, except as provided by

(a) See *Wells* v. *Army and Navy Co-operative Society, post.*
(b) (1870), L. R. 4 C. P. 755; L. R. 5 C. P. 310.

clause 23, and such damages may be deducted by the employer from any moneys due to the contractor.

(25) If, in the opinion of the architect, the works be delayed by *force majeure*, or by reason of any exceptionally inclement weather, or by reason of instructions from the architect in consequence of proceedings taken or threatened by, or disputes with, adjoining or neighbouring owners, or by the works or delay of other contractors or tradesmen engaged by the employer or the architect and not referred to in the specification, or by reason of authorised extras or additions, or in consequence of any notice reasonably given by the contractor in pursuance of clause 12, or by reason of any local combination of workmen or strikes or lock-out affecting any of the building trades, or in consequence of the contractor not having received in due time necessary instructions from the architect, for which he shall have specifically applied in writing, the architect shall make a fair and reasonable extension of time for completion in respect thereof. In case of any such strike or lock-out the contractors shall, as soon as may be, give to the architect written notice thereof. But the contractor shall, nevertheless, use his best endeavours to prevent delay, and shall do all that may reasonably be required to the satisfaction of the architect to proceed with the works.

1901
June 12.

King's Bench
Division.

There was considerable delay in the completion of the works, but at last the architect (Mr. Clayton Botham, of Brighton) certified that 681*l.* was still due to the plaintiffs for work and labour done, subject to the question whether there should be a deduction for delay. The plaintiffs wrote to the architect asking him to extend the time under clause 25, and, not receiving a reply at once, issued a writ for the 681*l.* The architect soon afterwards wrote extending the time to September 20th, 1899, and certifying that the work could have been completed by that time, and, further, that 231*l.* was due to Mr. Poole as liquidated damages for delay. Mr. Poole paid 450*l.* into Court.

The action was then referred to Mr. Verey, the Official Referee.

F. Dodd appeared for the plaintiffs, and wished to call evidence to show that the delay was caused by the owner, or by his architect, in ordering extras, in supplying material after the specified date, in delay in the selection of stone to be used and in the alteration of plans.

Ashton Cross, for the defendant, objected to the admission of this evidence. The Official Referee upheld the objection, and found as a fact that the date of completion was delayed so long beyond September 20th, 1899, as that at least 231*l.* had become payable as liquidated damages.

The plaintiffs appealed, and the case came before a Divisional Court of the King's Bench Division, consisting of Bruce and Phillimore, JJ., on June 12th, 1901. F. Dodd appeared for the plaintiffs (the appellants), and Herbert Reed, K.C., and Kisch for the defendant (the respondent).

The Court dismissed the appeal.

PHILLIMORE, J.: In this case my brother has asked me to give the first judgment.

This is an application to set aside the award of one of the Official Referees, and the judgment directed by him to be entered upon the following grounds, which are chiefly on the ground that the learned Official Referee refused to admit evidence upon certain points which the builders, the plaintiffs, wished to bring before him. The points

1901
June 12.

King's Bench
Division.

stated are that he refused to hear evidence that the delays in completing the works were caused by the acts or defaults of the defendant; that he refused to hear evidence that those delays were caused by the acts or the defaults of the defendant's architect; that he held wrongly that the certificate of the defendant's architect was final and conclusive as to the terms of the agreement under which the building was carried on; that he refused to allow the plaintiffs to show that the date fixed by the architect was not a fair and reasonable time to allow the plaintiffs for completion of the works, having regard to the delays and hindrances alleged to be occasioned by the defendant and his architect; and that he was wrong in holding that the defendant and his architect had not waived their right to insist on penalties for delay by issuing progress certificates.

With regard to the last point, which I may deal with first, we were very early, both of us, of opinion that there was nothing in it. The progress certificates are expressly given, subject to revision, according to the common practice, in order to enable the builder to get money from time to time. They are not conclusive; at any rate, they are not conclusive as to the scheme upon which they are granted.

They may or may not be conclusive in the sense that no money so certified for can be recovered back, but they are not conclusive as to the scheme or theory upon which it is suggested they may be granted. They are only conclusive, if at all, on the fact that at some time or other the builder will be entitled to that sum at least, and the architect thinks it is reasonable that he shall have it now, and there is no waiver and no conclusion as to any matter when the progress certificate is made.

The other matters really all turn upon the construction of the agreement. By the agreement, which is an ordinary building agreement, the works were to be begun immediately upon possession of the site being given to the builders, and they were to be completed, except painting and papering, by the 20th day of May, 1900, by clause 23. Clause 25, which really logically comes next, enabled the architect to extend the time for completion in certain circumstances. I had better read the clause in full. (Clause read.)

Then follow certain other provisions not material. (Clause 24 read.)

The whole contest between the parties turns upon the question whether or not the employer is entitled to deduct a particular sum as damages by reason of delay in accordance with the provisions of clause 24. Apparently, shortly before the writ in this action was issued, the builders wrote to the architect and asked him, the time

1901
June 12.
King's Bench
Division.

being then long past, to grant or certify for an extension of time. The architect did not immediately answer, and without waiting further for his answer, they issued their writ claiming a balance which was unquestionably due to them, the architect having certified that a sum of 681*l*. was due to them for work and labour, subject only to the question whether there should be any deduction for delay. They issued their writ for this sum of 681*l*., and after the writ had been issued the architect answered their letter by certifying that in his opinion it was right that there should be an extension of time, but only to the 20th of September, and that as the works were, in his opinion, not completed till a much later date, there was a sum of 231*l*. due in respect of penalties which would be properly deducted from the sum of 681*l*., leaving only 450*l*. due. Upon that the defendant paid 450*l*. into Court. Then the matter was referred to the Official Referee, who has found in favour of the defendant; in other words, has declared that 231*l*. is a proper deduction, and that therefore the sum of 450*l*. paid into Court was sufficient, and that he was entitled to judgment and costs as against the plaintiffs.

The builders having invited an architect to decide the question, and the architect having, in fact, decided it, though since writ, it is a little strange at first to find the builders nevertheless contending that they are not bound by his decision; but in the very able and strenuous argument which was offered to us on behalf of the builders, reliance was placed, and no doubt rightly placed—the case required careful consideration—upon the authority of a decision of the Exchequer Chamber in the case of *Roberts* v. *The Bury Commissioners* (a).

In that case a clause something like clause 24 was in existence; the architect, however, was not required to certify by either side. He was not required to certify by the builders for extension of time under the parallel clause to clause 25 in this contract; and I forget whether there was any provision like clause 24, requiring the architect to fix the penalty as against the builders for the time of delay. In that case, in which, I have said, the clauses were something like these, it was finally held by the majority of the Court in the Exchequer Chamber, reversing the decision of the Court of Common Pleas, that a clause of this kind was or might, in certain circumstances, be so disadvantageous to the builder if construed in the sense in which the employer sought to construe it, that they must scan it narrowly, and, unless they found very express terms, they must hold that it did not bind the builder, and failing to find two matters upon which they placed

(a) (1870), L. R. 4 C. P. 755; L. R. 5 C. P. 310.

1901
June 12.

King's Bench
Division.

reliance, they decided that it did not bind the builder, though it might bind the architect.

The point taken there was this: There were delays, no doubt, but the delays were due either to the employer or to his architect, who is his agent, or to both, and the usual principles of contract law were applied, by which if A. contracts with B. to do a certain thing and does not do it, if he is prevented from doing it by the action of B., B. cannot rely upon A.'s breach which B. has, in point of fact, brought about himself. Therefore, they held on demurrer that if it should be proved, as the builders alleged, that in that particular case the delay was caused or contributed to or conduced by the action of the employers, the employers could not seek for penalties or to set off penalties in respect of the delay. No doubt that is quite true; if there were no such provision as clause 25 that would be past question, and the importance of the case of *Roberts* v. *The Bury Commissioners* (a) is not because they decided that point, which indeed was well established before, but because they decided that the particular power of certifying for a prolongation of time given to the architect in *Roberts* v. *The Bury Commissioners* by a clause something like clause 25 did not apply to the particular delay which was in question, or at any rate need not apply if, at the option of the builder, the builder preferred another remedy.

Now, they relied there upon two matters. In that case it was not provided that the architect should make fair and reasonable extension of time; it was provided that it should be lawful for him to make fair and reasonable extension of time, which they construed as meaning that he was not bound. There have been many cases, but at that time it was a very moot question whether the words "it shall be lawful" did not impose a duty. The matter was finally set at rest by the House of Lords in a much later case, but at any rate—and it is rather interesting to see—the Court in that case construed the words "it shall be lawful" as imposing no duty but only giving a power. They therefore said that the architect was not bound, and in fact he had not been applied to and had not granted any extension of time. That was the first point on which they laid stress. The second point was, that upon the various clauses of the contract construed together there did not appear to be any submission by the builder to accept the architect's ruling. He was to be entitled to rely upon the architect's ruling, and in fact the Court seemed to have looked upon the

---

(a) (1870), L. R. 4 C. P. 755; L. R. 5 C. P. 310.

1901
June 12.
King's Bench
Division.

architect's ruling as if it were a kind of admission by the architect or by his employer: "Well, I admit I cannot complain, and it is because it is my own fault," or a sort of adjudication by the employer's agent against the employer: "Well, my master cannot claim this, because I know perfectly well that it is either through my fault, or my doing, that this matter has been delayed."

Upon those two grounds the majority of the Court of Appeal—and taking the judges of the two Courts together there was an equal weight of judicial authority one way as the other—decided that the builder was not liable, and therefore that his common law remedy was open to him of insisting that it was the default of the employer which had prevented his carrying out his contract, and that therefore the employer could not rely upon the delay. No doubt for such a contract as that which was construed in *Roberts* v. *The Bury Commissioners*, *Roberts* v. *The Bury Commissioners* (a) is a binding authority, but this contract is different. Very possibly, if it is, as I suspect, mainly a common form contract, it has been altered in order to meet the decision in *Roberts* v. *The Bury Commissioners* (a), and we have to decide whether the difference takes this contract out of *Roberts* v. *The Bury Commissioners*.

I must say upon starting that it seems to me clear that to any plain man, looking at this matter plainly, it would be obvious that clause 25 intended to submit this matter to the decision of the architect and to make the decision of the architect binding. It would be a subtlety which would relieve the builder from the effect of this clause. No doubt, in certain cases, where very serious injury, apparently uncontemplated by one or other of the parties, would have ensued to one or other of the parties on a particular construction, it is open to the Courts to exercise very considerable subtlety in the construction of clauses; but I myself do not think that there is any very serious injury to the builder in leaving this matter to the decision of the architect; and, further, if I am to exercise subtlety, I do not see that by such exercise I can save the builder from the construction of clause 25.

It is no longer a case where the architect has power. He is bound to act. He is bound to make a fair and reasonable extension of time. He is bound to decide between the parties. That at once destroys one of the points taken in *Roberts* v. *The Bury Commissioners*, and it goes some way towards destroying the other. If he is bound to do it, it must be intended that his decision should be decisive. It is to be a fair and reasonable extension of time, that is, fair and reasonable

(a) (1870), L. R. 4 C. P. 755; L. R. 5 C. P. 310.

to both parties, and it would be a strange construction indeed if it were to be said that he was entitled and bound to come to a decision, and that that decision, if favourable to the builder, might be relied upon by him, and must be submitted to by the employer, but that if unfavourable to the builder it shall have no effect at all. Again, if we look at clause 23 there seems to be a sufficient explicit statement that the builder will be bound by the decision of the architect. By clause 23 the builder contracts to complete the works by the time specified, except painting and papering, that is, by the 20th May, subject nevertheless to the provisions for extension of time hereinafter contained. That seems to me to be an explicit contract. "I will complete by the 20th May unless the architect will give me an extension," or "except so far as the architect will give me an extension."

Then clause 24 comes in and says that if he fails to complete by that date or by the extended time, certain consequences follow. There, again, I see something in clause 24 which is of importance. It does not automatically follow that because the works are not completed by the date named or by the extended date, the builder is to suffer the loss of penalties by delay. The architect is to do an overt act; he is to certify that the works could reasonably have been completed by the date named or within the extended time. So that first of all the architect has power and a duty to consider the application of the builder upon any of the points raised, and granting, if any of those points are good, a fair and reasonable extension of time; and, secondly, if he were to fail in that, or even if he were to give a decision in that which would be unfavourable to the builder, that will not hurt him unless the architect again acting in, at any rate, a *quasi*-judicial manner, is prepared to certify that the works could reasonably have been completed by the time which he has fixed.

Upon those grounds it seems to me that on the general question the case of *Roberts v. The Bury Commissioners* (a) does not conclude this case, and that there is no reason why this clause 25 should have a unilateral effect only; and if it has a bi-lateral effect the decision of the Court in *Jones v. St. John's College, Oxford* (b), shows that it is the duty of all Courts to give effect to it even if there be, which I do not see that there is in this case, considerable hardship in consequence.

Then comes the minor contest. Counsel for the builders, the appellants, opened to us, and I think was rightly asked to open to us, the various heads of evidence he had proposed to give if the referee

(a) (1870), L. R. 4 C. P. 755; L. R. 5 C. P. 310.
(b) (1870), L. R. 6 Q. B. 115.

1901
June 12.

King's Bench
Division.

had allowed him, in order to show the default by the owner or the architect, or something which would estop the owner from relying upon the penalties. He put it under seven heads. The first was that the architect gave progress certificates after the date of September 20th without reserve; that is a matter with which we have already dealt. Secondly, that he ordered extras after the 20th September; that does not seem to me to affect this question at all. Thirdly, that he did not supply drawings for a cabinet till after September 20th. Fourthly, that he made other alterations in drawings in the month of November. Fifthly, that the building owner delayed in determining of what stone the house should be constructed. Sixthly, that the ornamental granite for facings was not received till May 25th, which he said he was prepared to show was a late date, and sufficiently late to make it unreasonable that the contract should be finished by the time suggested; and, seventhly, that a rolling way or lift, which was one of the articles provided for in the contract which had to be fitted and cased by the builder, was not ordered till September 18th, and did not arrive till January 13th, the extended date fixed having been the 20th September.

The learned counsel said, assuming that some of those matters are within clause 25, matters upon which the architect could have adjudicated and which therefore he must be deemed to have considered and adjudicated upon, others are not, and he especially relied upon the fact that the goods were not supplied in time— the stone, granite, and the rolling way. We discussed a good deal clause 25. Clause 25 requires the architect to give an extension of time in the case of *force majeure*, inclement weather, or delay in consequence of proceedings taken or threatened by, or disputes with adjoining or neighbouring owners, or by the works or delay of other contractors or tradesmen engaged or nominated by the employer or the architect and not referred to in the specification, or by reason of authorised extras or additions, or in consequence of any notice reasonably given by the contractor in pursuance of clause 12, or by reason of any local combination of workmen or strikes or lock-out affecting any of the building trades, or in consequence of the contractor not having received in due time necessary instructions from the architect for which he shall have specifically applied in writing.

Now, to deal with that last point, it is not suggested that there were any instructions delayed after specific application in writing. If they were delayed after specific application in writing, then they clearly come under this clause, and they are matters upon which the

1901
June 12.
_____
King's Bench
Division.

architect ought to adjudicate, and must be deemed to, have adjudicated. If the drawings for the cabinet were asked for and not supplied, if instructions as to the kind of stone were not given in time, either those instructions were asked for or they were not. If they were not applied for, then this clause applies. It was boldly contended by the learned counsel that if they were not applied for this clause did not apply, and then he was remitted to his only remedy. The answer is that the obvious construction of this clause shows that the parties did not intend to let it be held that there was any delay, unless the builder applied to the architect. The architect is to be entitled to suppose that the builder has got all he wants, having started with the original drawings and specifications, unless and until the builder applies to him, and if he does apply to him then this clause attaches.

With regard to the delay in supplying the granite, delay in supplying the rolling way, and possibly also the delay in fixing the stone—I am not so sure of that—they are covered by the earlier part of the clause, "works or delay of other contractors, or tradesmen engaged or nominated by the employer or the architect, and not referred to in the specification." Obviously that is to cover the delays under the now well-known head in building contracts of supply of provisions. These are all provisions: the granite is a provision; the rolling way is a provision; the cabinet is a provision; and if there were a delay in respect of supplying any of these, and in consequence the builder was further delayed, the architect ought to and must be deemed to have taken these matters into consideration. He has allowed the builders a very considerable prolongation of time, no doubt not so much as one side asked for, and we are bound to hold that he has considered these matters.

It may, and one knows constantly does, happen in building contracts of great complexity and magnitude, that the matter arranges itself in this way. First, the builder gets behind and vastly behind. Then some instruction which naturally is not given in detail, some order which naturally is not issued till the works have reached a certain stage, some supply of an article which would only be knocked about and injured if it were on the works before people are ready for it, is delayed. It is useless to give a builder an order for something till he has got a certain stage in his work. Probably the order has been kept back because until the building has reached a certain stage it is not quite certain what form that order had best take, certainly it is undesirable to send some delicate piece of work to lie about the works till it is really wanted.

1901
June 12.

King's Bench
Division.

Therefore it comes about that an architect actually does give very late, possibly after the original date of completion, an order for something which was in the original contract, but it would be perfectly inequitable for the builder to say: "I was bound to complete by the 30th May. You never sent me an order for the ornamental top of the chimney till the 30th June, and therefore I am entitled to say that all the provisions as to delay do not apply." The architect or employer could reply: "Yes, the proper time to give you that order was, say, one month before the completion of the works, but you were six months behind at that time; therefore it was only natural that I did not give you that order then." Those are exactly matters that do arise as we know constantly in contracts of this kind, and it is in order that the architect may be able to deal sensibly, as a business man dealing with business matters, that these matters are remitted to him.

Upon the whole, therefore, I come to the conclusion that the learned referee was perfectly right in refusing to hear this evidence, that the certificate of the architect was within his powers under the contract, and was by the contract in the absence of fraud, which is not alleged, final and conclusive, both as to the extension of time granted under clause 25 and as to the date when the works could reasonably have been completed under clause 24.

Therefore, there being apparently no question as to the date when the works were in fact completed, there was really nothing further for the referee to determine than that the sum of 231*l*. was rightly deducted from money otherwise due to the plaintiffs, and that therefore the sum of 450*l*. was a proper sum to pay to them.

BRUCE, J.: I am of the same opinion, and I have very few words to add.

I think the whole question turns upon the construction of the contract, and I do not doubt that in the proper construction of the contract in this case the parties have agreed that the architect should be the sole judge of the extension of time which should be given in the event of extra works being required, and he having given his determination, I think that the parties are bound by it. There is nothing inconsistent with that finding in any of the cases that have been referred to. The case of the St. John's College, Oxford, exactly bears that out, and shows that if parties enter into such a contract they are bound by it. The other case of *Roberts* v. *The Bury Commissioners* (*a*) shows that although the majority of the judges construed that contract in a way which showed that in their opinion

(*a*) (1870), L. R. 4 C. P. 755; L. R. 5 C. P. 310.

1901
June 12.

King's Bench
Division.

the architect was not bound to decide the question, and could not decide it so as to be binding upon the parties, yet all the judges agreed that if the parties had agreed that the architect should be sole judge, they would be bound by his decision.

Therefore I think that there is nothing in that case inconsistent with our decision in this. The motion must be dismissed with costs.

Solicitors for plaintiffs: Clarke & Catkin.
Solicitors for defendant: Lamb, Son & Prance.

1901
August 8.

King's Bench
Division.

𝔍𝔫 𝔱𝔥𝔢 𝔎𝔦𝔫𝔤'𝔰 𝔅𝔢𝔫𝔠𝔥 𝔇𝔦𝔟𝔦𝔰𝔦𝔬𝔫.

(*Before* CHANNELL, J.)

PAGE

v.

LLANDAFF AND DINAS POWIS RURAL DISTRICT COUNCIL.

Quasi-Arbitrator—Employer interfering

P. was employed by the L. Rural District Council to construct certain works. In the contract it was provided that "the decision of the surveyor with respect to the value, amount, state, and condition of any part of the works executed, or of any part thereof altered, omitted, or added, and also in respect to any and every question that may arise concerning the construction of this contract, or the said plans, drawings, specification, or bill of quantities, or schedule of prices, or the execution of the works hereby contracted for, or in anywise relating thereto, shall be final and without appeal." Disputes arose, and, after protracted negotiations, the surveyor gave his final certificate. P. brought an action against the Council, in which he alleged that the surveyor's final certificate "was not honestly made or given in the exercise of, or reliance upon, his own judgment, but was made and given by reason of the interference of, and in obedience to the directions and orders of, the Council." Held, that as the Council had interfered (though without any fraud on their part) with the surveyor in the exercise of his functions as *quasi*-arbitrator between the parties, the final certificate was not conclusive and binding on the contractor.

On August 31st, 1898, E. H. Page entered into a contract with the Llandaff and Dinas Powis Rural District Council, by which he undertook to erect and construct a sewage pumping station, tanks, sewers, and other works. The contract contained the following clause:—

(18) The decision of the surveyor with respect to the value, amount, state, and condition of any part of the works executed, or of any part thereof altered, omitted, or added, and also in respect to any and every question that may arise

concerning the construction of this contract, or the said plans, drawings, specification, or bill of quantities, or schedule of prices, or the execution of the works hereby contracted for, or in anywise relating thereto, shall be final and without appeal.

1901
August 8.

King's Bench
Division.

In the course of the construction of the works, disputes arose between Mr. Page and the Council, especially with regard to the amount of the payment to be made to him, which the parties tried to settle between themselves without the intervention of the surveyor. At last the surveyor made his final certificate by a document in the shape of a measured account, of fixed items, which was headed "Certificate No. 20 (Final)," and concluded in these terms:—

"I hereby certify that the above certificate is a correct sum due to the contractor in full and final settlement of work done on the above contract, less the amount of retention money referred to which is due to the contractor according to the contract agreement. "A.W. FRASER, A.M.I.C.E.
"*Engineer to the Council.*"

Mr. Page was dissatisfied with the amount thus certified for, viz., 479*l.* 6*s.* 1*d.*, and brought an action against the Council in which he claimed 11,465*l.* 18*s.* 9*d.*

Clause 17 of the contract contained the following provision:—

The sum payable to the contractor under the terms of this contract shall be paid by instalments . . . and the total amount to be paid to the contractor, subject to any addition thereto or deduction therefrom, under the terms of this contract shall be ascertained by an admeasurement or valuation of the actual work done, to be made by the surveyor upon the basis of, and at the respective prices contained in, the aforesaid bill of quantities or in the schedule of prices, as the case may be.

The statement of claim contained the following paragraphs:—

(10) The said surveyor did not at any time duly or properly, or at all, measure up or value the works in accordance with the terms of the said contract; but he neglected and refused so to do, although he was thereto required by the plaintiff.

(11) Alternatively, if the said surveyor purported to value the works, he did not value the same according to the schedule of prices or to the terms of the said contract; but he ignored the said schedule in cases where the same was applicable and should have been applied, and from time to time he altered the values he had before made, and he did so, not exercising or relying on his own judgment, but by reason of the interference, directions, and orders of the defendants.

(12) Further, alternatively, if the said surveyor purported to give a final certificate as to the value of the works, such certificate was not honestly made or given, or made or given in exercise of, or reliance upon, his own judgment, but was made or given by reason of the interference of, and in obedience to, the directions and orders of the defendants, and the surveyor informed the plaintiff, with reference to a certificate he was alleged to be making or to have made, that he could not help what he was doing, as he was forced by the defendants, but that he felt inclined to give an honest certificate and resign his position under the defendants; and if the surveyor made or gave any final certificate (which is denied), it is not in any way binding on the plaintiff.

1901
August 8.

King's Bench
Division.

(13) Further, the dispute as to the measurement and valuation of the works at the completion was not referred to or decided by the said surveyor, and he died before such dispute was referred to him, and the plaintiff had no opportunity of laying his case before the surveyor upon such dispute.

The defendants denied all these allegations, excepting that the surveyor was dead.

The case came on before Channell, J., at Swansea, on August 8th, 1901.

B. Francis-Williams, K.C., S. T. Evans, K.C., and St. John Francis-Williams appeared for the plaintiff.

Abel Thomas, K.C., and Sankey appeared for the defendant Council.

It was held that the final certificate could not stand, and that the matter must go to an arbitrator to ascertain the amount due to the plaintiff owing to the interference of the defendant Council.

CHANNELL, J.: I am of opinion—I do not say it is quite free from doubt—that there has been no final adjudication preventing Mr. Page, the plaintiff, from recovering whatever may be properly due to him according to the terms of the contract. I will first go through the reasons which make me say that I think there has been no binding decision in this case, fixing, as between the parties, the amount which is due upon this contract.

Now, the contract in many respects is a usual one; it has some peculiarities possibly, but, at any rate, it is a common form of contract; and one of the things that it does amongst other things is a thing which is extremely common in these contracts: it gives a particular person, the surveyor, the architect, or the engineer, or whatever he may be called (in this case it is the surveyor), a double position. So far as regards all the direction of the work, and saying what is or what is not to be done and so on, he is the servant and agent of one of the parties; but it has become the practice to make the person who is the servant and agent of one of the parties also perform a totally different duty: he is often authorised to act between the parties as an arbitrator or judge to settle matters between the parties. He has to act in a totally different way according as he is acting in one of those capacities or in the other. But the position is obviously one which is a difficult one. Even if the gentleman were a skilled lawyer, I think he might have some difficulties in performing those duties—of course he would as to one portion, namely, the engineering part, but I do not mean as to that—he would have a difficulty in separating his two duties, and a gentleman who possibly is extremely skilled in his profession is very likely to (at any rate, we lawyers see that they very often do) confuse the two portions of his duties; and, having to obey and follow the direction of one of the two parties in reference to the great proportion of what

1901
August 8.

King's Bench
Division.

he has to do throughout the business, he falls into the way of taking a certain amount of instructions from them with reference to either part of his duties. Now, I do not wish to say anything offensive to the memory of the late Mr. Fraser or to the members of this committee, but as I say, in my view the thing cannot stand.

Now, to go quite shortly through the contract in this case. It is a contract which, on the face of it, is for a lump sum. There are more than the usual indications in this contract that it was contemplated that there would be great and extensive variations in the work as it went on, and in point of substance it is a contract to pay the plaintiff according to certain prices for the work which he might happen to do, and what might be called for certain purposes the contract work is, so far as regards the amount that he is to be paid, of little importance. In this document, which is supposed to be the final certificate, it is to be observed that, although the contract sum happens to be mentioned as a sort of heading at the top of the document, it is never brought into the account at all right through the thing. That shows, therefore, that the contract was really what I say; namely, a contract for work to be done according to directions which might be given and to be paid for in a certain way. There is one provision of importance which I will come to when I come to consider the terms of the reference with regard to what was within the contract and what was not.

The contract goes on in reference to the payment, and the payment is to be "under the terms of the contract . . . . paid by the Council by instalments on account as the works proceed, at the rate of 80*l.* per cent. upon what, in the opinion of the surveyor (having regard to the measurement thereof), shall be the value of the work done and fixed in its place, and as certified in writing by the surveyor." This is where the final certificate comes in, I suppose, if at all— "and the total amount to be paid the contractor, subject to any addition thereto or deduction therefrom under the terms of this contract, shall be ascertained by an admeasurement or valuation of the actual work done, to be made by the surveyor upon the basis of and at the respective prices contained in the aforesaid bill of quantities or the schedule of prices, as the case may be."

Now, that gives the surveyor a limited authority as to the assessment of the amount that is to be payable under this contract, because he is only authorised to decide according to the prices in the bill of quantities or the schedule of prices: he is bound to proceed in that way: and either party to the contract is entitled to interfere then to this extent, that they are entitled to say to him: "Now, mind you go according to the terms of that contract; do not you exceed your

1901
August 8.

King's Bench
Division.

authority; please understand that we have not given you any authority in excess of that which the contract gives you;" and to that extent either of these parties—Mr. Page as well as the Board—is entitled to give directions, or dictate, if you please to use that word, to the arbitrator or surveyor what it is he is to do, but except by confining him to the duties which are given to him by the contract, they have no right to interfere with him at all.

They may each argue their case before him, and it would be perfectly right for the engineer to give opportunities to either of them by saying, "Now, my view is so and so: what have you to say to that?" provided he does it equally to the other person. There would be no objection whatever to his doing that, but he must, so far as regards the portions of his duty in which he is deciding between the parties, deal equally with both parties. If he gives opportunities to one, he must give the same opportunities to the other; and although he may listen to arguments which may be addressed to him, he is not to allow his judgment to be influenced by directions given him of the character which would properly be given to him if he were doing some other part of his work; namely, the part in which he is surveyor only, and directing the mode in which the work is to be done.

Now, what happened in this particular case? Long before any question of a certificate, or at any rate of a final certificate being given, had arisen, there were disputes more or less between the parties, and they do not say: "Well, if there are disputes between the parties, the surveyor is the appointed judge who must decide them," but they set to work to endeavour to settle the dispute. Some of the meetings appear to have been without prejudice, but we have had a good deal of evidence as to what took place at the meeting, and it is clear that there was an endeavour to come to an arrangement, and to come to an arrangement without a decision by the arbitrator. Now, in the course of that meeting, as appears either by the minute, or at any rate by the rough minute of the meeting, the committee direct Mr. Fraser, the surveyor, to prepare for them (as I understand it—and it is impossible to understand it in any other way upon the note of it), and for their guidance with a view to what they are doing then— namely, trying to settle the matter with the plaintiff—to prepare for them a statement of what he thinks fair and right.

They are not saying, and they do not pretend for a moment to say, "Now we have got to a stage in which we cannot settle. You, the surveyor, must do your duty as arbitrator, and decide this matter." They never say anything of the kind, but they ask to have a state- ment prepared for them. Then, whilst that is being done, there are

1901
August 8.

King's Bench
Division.

some communications between Mr. Page, the contractor, and Mr. Fraser, the surveyor; and Mr. Page deposes before me to those conversations, and they are conversations which indicate that Mr. Fraser (whether it had been intended by the committee or not) in fact feels that pressure is being put upon him.

Now, I agree that upon certain matters I do not think I can rely upon Mr. Page's recollection. I am convinced that he is wrong, for instance, about the red line being upon the contract, but then I thought at the time when he was speaking about it that it was a matter about which, in all probability, he would not be careful. Contractors are people who, beyond all others, are in the habit of signing documents without looking at them or reading them; it is a regular practice for them to do it, so far as I know. But in this particular case he was not really concerned in it, except for one small purpose, because the contract was that he was to be paid for whatever he did, and it was at that time of very small importance to him whether the average depth was to be fifteen feet, or fourteen, or twelve, or anything else. It is only that it turned out to be important, because water was found at certain depths, and for that reason only does it seem to me to be important.

But because he was wrong about that, it seems to me that I ought not to come to the conclusion that he is necessarily wrong upon this other matter. This other matter was a very important thing to him. If he is wrong upon it, he has not only sworn that which is not a mere matter of memory, but he must be intentionally deceiving us about it, because he must have written it into his diary, because it is there, and he must be a man therefore who is capable of making evidence to support his case. And the person who could have contradicted him is dead. It is a serious thing to assume against him.

But I will not say that I should have been inclined to assume that against him if there were nothing to support it except his own diary; but what I do find is a letter from him to Mr. Fraser, when Mr. Fraser was, of course, alive, which, to my mind, is a corroboration of it. It is not quite so strong, but it is something which cannot be accounted for, to my mind, unless something of the kind Mr. Page speaks of had happened. The letter I refer to is the letter of July 26th, which says: "The instructions that your committee have given you to make out your certificate for measurements and to ignore day work is, I think, wrong." Now, I agree, "is, I think, wrong," is not a strong way of putting something which he had entered in his diary as being dishonest; but it indicates that there had been a conversation in which Mr. Fraser had told him that he

1901
August 8.

King's Bench
Division.

had had instructions from his committee as to how he was to do the thing. Therefore it so far corroborates him. It corroborates him so far that it—I will not say satisfies me exactly—but it removes any doubt as to whether I ought or ought not to act upon his statement.

As to the exact terms of the statement, I think possibly there may have been a misunderstanding. He has not got it down in a very intelligible form in his diary. What he says is that "the measurements were to be made to suit." If that meant to say that Mr. Fraser was to invent things which were not in accordance with what is supposed to be the truth—to invent them altogether—it would be a very strong thing; but I do not think it did mean that. I think it was merely meant to be a statement in answer to the claim for day work. The day work is founded upon the ground that the thing could not be done by measurement, and I think this committee were saying: "We will not have day work upon any terms. If you have not got the measurements, and cannot get the measurements, why, estimate them to suit." That is to say, ascertain what the measurements must be that bring out the proper result; not necessarily to put things that do not exist—all wrong—not to put 100*l.*, when it was 50*l.*, but to estimate what it was, and to put, say, 75*l.*, if he thought that was the right amount, although he could not ascertain it for certain. That is, I think, what was meant.

Now, passing on, what does take place is this: that Mr. Fraser then makes out (and he certainly does not give Mr. Page information of what he is doing) an account, and he sends it for the purpose of having it considered. I do not know what that can mean except that it is with a view of seeing whether or not the parties approve of it. That is surrendering his judgment, and not necessarily in the events that happened, to theirs, because he had so cut down the amount that they did not object to it; but it is quite clear to my mind that if he had certified, for instance, about half of what the plaintiff's present claim is, or anything in excess of that—probably a very much less sum—the committee would have said: "We will not have anything to do with it; we will not stand your doing it at all." And they would not at all have understood that it was a decision already given against them by which they were bound, whether they liked it or not; and I do not think Mr. Fraser was meaning that it should be so at all. Then some items are added to it which are not very important.

It is unfortunate that we have not got the original document. It may be that there were alterations in it; one does not know; but nobody of their own memory can possibly say whether there were

1901
August 8.

King's Bench
Division.

or not. But Mr. Fraser then after that sends this certificate, or leaves it somehow or other, without any communication to Mr. Page. I never heard myself of a case of an arbitrator who was deciding a case between parties not giving information to both parties, and not writing. I should have thought that if Mr. Fraser really meant this to be final he would have written to Mr. Page, and said: "I have to-day made my certificate which you have been asking for so long," and so on. "I have made my certificate, and there the matter is at an end." He probably would have sent him a copy of it, but he might not. But, having done that, he would communicate the fact. But he did not do anything of the kind; it was never communicated at all. Then the action was brought.

My view is that this was not an adjudication between the parties which could possibly stand. Treating it as an award, I think it is very likely that, if application had been made to set it aside, instead of setting it aside simply and sending it to another arbitrator, I think it is probably one of that sort of cases in which the Court would have sent it back to Mr. Fraser himself, if he was still alive; in which case the Court would have said: "You have this gentleman to decide the disputes between you. There is a clause saying that he shall decide them, and we think Mr. Fraser ought to decide them." I think that is the view I should take myself. But he is not alive.

The consequence is that, in my view, there being no final assessment between the parties of what the amount is, it must go to some one to assess. That is my judgment upon the matter. Of course, I may be wrong; and if I am wrong, the parties will have the opportunity of setting my judgment aside.

Solicitors for plaintiff: Macintosh, Dixon & Co.
Solicitor for defendants: R. W. Williams.

1902
March 18.

Court of
Appeal.

𝔍n the 𝕶ing's 𝕭ench 𝕯ivision.

(*Before* KENNEDY and PHILLIMORE, JJ.)

𝔍n the Court of Appeal.

(*Before* COLLINS, M.R., and ROMER and MATHEW, L.JJ.)

IN RE FORD & CO. AND BEMROSE & SONS.

Lump Sum Contract—Errors in Quantities.

In supplying of Bills of quantities to a builder for the purpose of making his tender, there is no implied warranty or representation as to the accuracy thereof. There can be no usage which contradicts the terms of the contract.

This case came before the Court of Appeal on appeal from the judgment of a Divisional Court of the King's Bench Division, dated April 30, 1901, on a special case stated by Mr. Vigors, the arbitrator.

The material parts of the documents in the case were the following:—

AGREEMENT.

It is hereby agreed this 28th day of May, 1895, between Messrs. Bemrose & Sons, Limited, of the town of Derby, printers, &c., of the one part, and Messrs. Ford & Co., builders, of Talbot Street in the town of Derby, of the other part, that they the said Messrs. Ford & Co., for themselves, their executors, administrators and assigns, do hereby promise and agree with Messrs. Bemrose & Sons, Limited, to do and perform the whole of the works required in accordance with the plans and specification for the erection of the new works in Park Street, Canal Street, and Carrington Street, Derby, and provide all labour, plant, materials, &c., of whatever kind required at and for the sum of ten thousand, five hundred and fifty-nine pounds, and the said Messrs. Ford & Co. do hereby agree to abide by and be subject to the several clauses, conditions, and penalties herein-before mentioned and contained.

CONDITIONS OF CONTRACT

under which is to be carried out the erection and completion of new works in Park Street, Canal Street and Carrington Street, in the town of Derby, for Messrs. Bemrose & Sons, Limited, in accordance with plans and specifications prepared by Ernest R. Ridgeway, architect, Long Eaton, May, 1895.

The whole of the works included in the contract for the erection and completion of the works above mentioned must be executed in the best and most workmanlike manner, and with materials of the best quality, and in strict accordance with the requirements of the specification and drawings to the satisfaction of Messrs. Bemrose & Sons, Limited, or their architect. The drawings and specifications are to be considered as equally binding on the contractors who undertake the execution of the work, and if any part is omitted from the drawings and specifications which is usually noted or given or described in them, and which may reasonably be inferred from them as being necessary to properly carry out and complete the works, the same shall be equally binding on the contractor as if it had been specially shown or described.

1902
March 18.

Court of
Appeal.

Any alteration of the works contracted for which may be decided upon during their progress must be carried out at prices on which the contract is based, and the value of the alteration or deviation from the original plans after being so calculated by the contractor and the architect, shall be added to or deducted from the amount of the contract as the case may be, but in no case will any alteration or deviation from the original plans and specifications be allowed to invalidate the contract.

The decision of the architect on all matters connected with the carrying out of the contract shall be final and binding upon all parties concerned, unless either party shall within forty-eight hours after the architect shall have given his decision, object in writing to such decision, in which case the question in dispute shall be referred to arbitration under the provisions in that behalf hereinafter contained.

Specification and Quantities Referred to in the Agreement.

Specification and Bill of Quantities of Works required to be done, and materials to be supplied in the extension and completion of new works in Park Street and Canal Street, Derby, for Messrs. Bemrose & Sons, Limited, in accordance with plans prepared by Ernest R. Ridgeway, Mem. San. Inst., Architect, Long Eaton.

Generally.

The description in this bill of quantities must be taken as an abbreviated specification of the works and materials to which they apply, and such descriptions of any portion of the matters described herein may at any time be extended as the architect may consider necessary to further elucidate the requirements of the drawings and this specification and bill of quantities, but not in violation of them.

The measurements in this bill of quantities are taken nett, except in the slating, where an allowance of 12 in. is made for eaves.

The prices attached to the various items herein contained are to include all charges for materials, labour and fixing, including all carting, scaffolding and implements required for the due and proper carrying out of the work, and for leaving the whole of the works finished and complete, and perfect in every respect to the satisfaction of the architect.

*   *   *   *   *

The person whose tender is accepted must deposit with the architect within fourteen days of acceptance of tender a priced bill of quantities of all the works the same as on which his tender is based.

IN RE FORD AND CO. AND BEMROSE & SONS.

1902
March 18.

Court of
Appeal.

NOTE—The following extracts will more particularly illustrate the kind of descriptions in the above document:—

EXCAVATOR AND BRICKLAYER.

Yds.	ft.	in.			£	s.	d.
44	0	0	Cube.	Blue Staffordshire brick in cement to arcade piers, the cement to be used in the proportion of one of cement to two of clean-washed river sand, and every course to be fully grouted with semi-liquid grout.			

Yds.	ft.	in.			£	s.	d.
$96\frac{1}{3}$	0	0	Supr.	One brick reduced blue Staffordshire brick in cement to arcade piers.			
			No. 11	Extra for fixing and building into brick piers steel stancheons 20 ft. long, including cutting off brick-work to fit stancheons.			

PLUMBER AND GLAZIER.

Tons.	cwt.	qrs.		£	s.	d.
5	19	2	Milled lead and labour in laying in 6 lb. gutters and valleys, 5 lb. aprons, and 4 lb. soakers.			

PAINTER.

Provide the sum of One hundred and twenty pounds for painting to be done by a painter selected by the architect.

The following were the material parts of the special case:—

At some time prior to the date of the contract dated May, 1895, Messrs. Bemrose instructed Mr. Ernest Ridgeway, an architect, of Long Eaton, to prepare on their behalf plans for the erection of certain works in Park Street, Canal Street, and Carrington Street, Derby, and to invite tenders for the execution of such works. Mr. Ridgeway prepared the plans and invited tenders upon such plans and certain conditions of contract and a bill of quantities, and with such tender furnished a schedule of prices.

Such schedule of prices was for the purpose of determining the amount to be paid or allowed in respect of any alterations or deviations from the original plans which might be determined upon during the progress of the works, and the prices in the schedule were the prices referred to in the contract as the prices upon which the contract was based. Messrs. Ford's tender was accepted, and the contract in question entered into between Messrs. Bemrose and Messrs. Ford. The contract followed and incorporated and formed one document with a copy of the conditions of contract upon which Messrs. Ford tendered.

The arbitrator referred to the terms of the contract, the material parts of which are printed *ante*. The contract provided that all disputes should be referred to arbitration under the Arbitration Act, 1889, and contained a covenant by Messrs. Ford that they would "do and perform the whole of the works required in accordance with the plans and specifications for the

1902
March 18.

Court of
Appeal.

erection of the new works, and provide all labour, plant, and materials, &c., of whatsoever kind required, at and for the sum of 10,559*l.*"

Messrs. Ford completed the work included in the contract, and on April 1st, 1897, Mr. Ridgeway, by his final certificate, certified that there was a balance owing to Messrs. Ford of 1,530*l.* 13*s.* 5*d.*; but the latter being dissatisfied with it, and other disputes having arisen under the contract, recourse was had to the arbitration clause in the contract.

It was alleged before the arbitrator, and the arbitrator found as a fact, that the quantities set forth and stated in the bill of quantities upon which tenders were invited were in material and substantial respects insufficient, and that the actual quantities of the works required to be executed in carrying out the works in accordance with the plans exceeded those in the bill of quantities.

It was also alleged before the arbitrator, and found by him to be the fact, that it was a general usage in the building trade that where tenders are invited for the execution of works in accordance with plans, and a bill of quantities is furnished, a person making a tender is not expected to verify the quantities himself, but is expected to assume that the quantities are correct, and to tender upon that assumption; that if such quantities proved to be greater or less than the actual quantities, the price was to be reduced or increased by an amount ascertained and determined by the scale of prices given in the tender as the scale by which payment for extras was to be determined.

The arbitrator also found as a fact that Messrs. Ford did not verify the quantities, and tendered and entered into the agreement on the assumption that the quantities were correct.

He also found that various alterations of the works contracted for were decided upon during the progress of the works, and that the sum of 3,281*l.* was to be added to the contract price in respect of such alterations and deviations; that the total value of the work executed, at the prices upon which the contract was based, was 13,840*l.*; and that 8,750*l.* had been paid to Messrs. Ford by Messrs. Bemrose.

The questions left to the Court by the arbitrator to determine were:—

(1) Whether in ascertaining the amount to be paid by Messrs. Bemrose to Messrs. Ford regard was to be had to the aforesaid usage in the building trade.

(2) Whether Messrs. Ford were entitled only to be paid the sum of 10,559*l.* mentioned in the contract, with such deductions and additions as were by the contract provided to be made in respect of alterations or deviations from the original plans determined upon during the progress of the work, or

(3) Whether Messrs. Ford were entitled to be paid the value of all the works actually executed by them at the prices upon which the contract was based, and whether such value should be more or less than the sum of 10,559*l.* mentioned in the contract.

The arbitrator awarded that, if the Court answered question 1 in the affirmative, 5,090*l.* remained due to Messrs. Ford; question 2 in the affirmative, 2,303*l.* 10*s.* was due to Messrs. Ford; question 3 in the affirmative, 5,090*l.* was due to Messrs. Ford.

The Divisional Court (Kennedy and Phillimore, JJ.) answered the questions in favour of Messrs. Ford, the respondents, holding that the builders had a right to say that they had contracted upon the basis of the accuracy of the representations contained in the quantities forming part of the specifications. The Court held that there had been a breach of what the builders were entitled

1902
March 18.

Court of
Appeal.

to treat as a representation or warranty forming part of the contract, and to the extent to which the warranty was not fulfilled and the builders were damaged they were entitled to receive compensation. Judgment was accordingly entered for Messrs. Ford, the builders, for 5,090*l.*

Sir Edward CLARKE, K.C., and A. Lyttleton, K.C. (with them Coventry), argued on behalf of the appellants that the contract was for a lump sum, and that the quantities in the bill of quantities formed no part of the contract, and further that the respondents' only course was to sue on an express warranty, which they had not done. What the respondents did was to attempt to impose on Messrs. Bemrose a contract other than that which they had made, binding the appellants to go on with the work, and then to charge them one-third more than the lump sum which they had agreed to pay.

English Harrison, K.C., and Hudson, for the respondents, contended that the "specification and bill of quantities" really formed one document, which formed the contract. That there was an implied warranty that the quantities in the bill of quantities were correct. That the plans were insufficient to enable the builders to check the bill of quantities, and that that document being an abbreviated specification, the architect had express power to extend the works so far as he thought necessary, and that, therefore, Messrs. Bemrose were under an obligation to pay for the works so extended by the architect.

COLLINS, M.R.: In this case the question arises upon an arbitration arising out of a building contract. The builders entered into a contract with Messrs. Bemrose & Sons for the execution of certain works, and by the last clause in the conditions of the contract they undertook in these terms: "It is hereby agreed, and Messrs. Ford & Co. hereby promise and agree with Messrs. Bemrose & Sons, Limited, to do and perform the whole of the works required, in accordance with the plans and specifications, for the erection of the new works in Park Street," and so on, "and provide all labour, plant, and materials, &c., of whatsoever kind required, at and for the sum of 10,559*l.*" That is the substantive portion of the contract; by the earlier terms it is provided in the first of (they are called conditions of contract) "conditions of contract under which is to be carried out the erection and completion of new works" that the work is to be done in accordance with plans and specifications prepared by Ernest R. Ridgeway, architect. "The whole of the works included in the contract, for the erection and completion of the works mentioned, must be executed in the best and most workmanlike manner, and with materials of the best quality, and in strict accordance with the requirements of the specifications and drawings to the satisfaction of Messrs. Bemrose & Sons, Limited, or their architect. The drawings and specifications are to be considered as equally binding on the contractors who undertake the execution of the work, and if any part is omitted from the drawings and specifications, which is usually noted or given or described in them and which may be reasonably inferred from them as being necessary to properly carry out and complete the works, the same shall be equally binding on the contractors as if it had been specially shown or described. Any alteration of the works contracted for, which may be decided upon during their progress, must be carried out at prices on which the contract is based, and the value of the alteration or deviation from the original plans, after being so calculated by the contractors and the architect, shall be added to or deducted from the amount of the contract as the case may be, but in no case will any alteration or deviation from the original plans and specifications be allowed to invalidate the contract." Then there is a very wide arbitration clause, the terms of which I need not refer to at the moment.

1902
March 18.

Court of
Appeal.

In this case the ordinary practice was followed, that is to say, the building owner sent out for the purposes of tender, conditions of contract and specifications, and on the specification (it need not have been on that document, but as a matter of fact it was attached to the specification) were quantities set out, and on those materials tenders were invited. The builders, Messrs. Ford & Co., tendered. They had before them the specifications, they had plans, they had the conditions of the contract, and on the specifications, as I have already said, they had the quantities set out. By the terms of the contract I have just read, they undertook in the most emphatic manner to do all the work comprised in the plans and specifications for the lump sum I have named, and the plans and specifications are referred to, as I have pointed out, in more than one part of the contract as being the binding factors in the contract between the parties. There is no allusion whatever in the contract itself to anything beyond that the bills of quantities are not mentioned therein, but it is the fact that on the specification there were quantities set out.

Now disputes arose between the parties as to what sum was payable to these builders under the contract, and that dispute was referred to an arbitrator other than the architect. The point that arises for us is this: it turns out that in fact the quantities on the back of the specification were too small and to a considerable extent too small, that is to say, to do the work comprised in the plans and specifications would involve a larger amount of material and labour than was apparent from the quantities set out on the back of the specification. I emphasize that because it at once negatives and annuls the last argument addressed to us by the respondents in this case, that is to say, that there were in point of fact not materials before the builder at the time of his tender which would enable him to tender at all,

1902
March 18.

Court of
Appeal.

that is, that the thing was so indefinite that there was for all practical purposes no specification, but taking the specification and plans together the matter was at large.

That is really the logical result of the last point taken before us, but I point out that the special case before us is based on the fact that the plans and specification did disclose certain works, which as disclosed required a larger amount of quantities than was shown on the back of the specification, so that we have not the case where it may be treated as if there was no specification, and nothing to interpret the plans, and nothing to guide the builder, and accordingly he is at large to charge for measure and value.

Now, the question is, under these circumstances I have named, what is the effect of there being this mistake in the quantities, if there was a mistake? The builder contends here, and the Divisional Court have held that those quantities on the back of the specification constitute a binding part of the contract between the building owner and the contractor, and that, in point of fact, those quantities so set out on the back of the specification amount to a warranty by the building owner that those quantities are correct, and that, therefore, that representation contained in the quantities being a warranty, is the subject-matter of a cross-claim for damages to the extent of the extra cost which the builder has been put to by virtue of having been led to suppose that the works could be done merely at the expenditure of labour and material indicated by the quantities as distinct from what was indicated by the plans and specification. That point arises now not for the first time.

It seems to me that it is well ascertained practice (I think I am entitled to say so, because it has been so often the subject of discussion in these Courts) that a building owner does place before the builder the materials on which to make his tender. He gives him the plans, he gives him the specification, and he generally gives him also the quantities; but it has been well understood, and it has been settled in more than one case, that as to those documents, whether a bill of quantities is embraced and made part of one of the other documents, either in the specification or as a schedule to the contract, or whether it is a separate document altogether, it is not, and is not intended to be, a representation to be acted on in this sense—that it is to be deemed a warranty. It is an estimate, an estimate which a reasonable person such as a builder would probably act upon as being an honest representation made by a skilled person, but beyond that it does not go. The builder has the right to make his own estimate, and, in point of fact, in this particular contract, when you

1902
March 18.

Court of
Appeal.

come to look at one of the provisions of the specification which accompanied it, it is made a term that "the person whose tender is accepted must deposit with the architect, within fourteen days of acceptance of tender, a priced bill of quantities of all the works, the same as that on which his tender is based." So he accepts the obligation of himself furnishing a bill of quantities, and, of course, it is much easier for him and much shorter for him to put the prices on the specification that has been sent to him, and, if need be, adopt the quantities that have been sent to him, but it is part of his obligation to furnish one, and he is not relieved from that obligation because he chooses to take the quantities which are furnished him by the building owner. That he has done in this case. It is a perfectly reasonable thing to do, because there is no suggestion of anything but perfect honesty in this matter, and the builder would naturally rely on the honest estimate of a skilled person.

But that being the common sense and business aspect of the case, it cannot be pushed beyond that. It cannot turn an estimate made for the convenience of all parties into a contract, and whether it went by word of mouth or whether by writing, in order to turn a representation into a warranty you must find out from the whole together—from from the document if it be by document, or by word of mouth if it be by word of mouth—that it is intended to be something more than a mere representation, and has in fact become a contract of warranty.

There are many decisions on this matter, in all of which that is the governing line that this class of thing is not a warranty, but only a representation; but if we want distinct authority in point of fact that it takes no additional significance by reason of the fact that it is incorporated with one of the documents which is by one of the terms of the contract itself made a basis, I think we have distinct authority in the case which has been last cited of *Sharpe* v. *San Paulo Railway Company* (a), where you have a contract to do the work in accordance with plans and specifications, and in the contract itself, as one of the schedules to the contract, there was a specification with quantities. It turned out there (the quantities they were dealing with were very large figures) that the quantities were something like a half too little. They indicated certain work of excavation which was something like half what would actually have to be done; but there it was held that that did not give any remedy to the contractor; that he had had the opportunity of making his own estimate, and that if he had had the opportunity, but had chosen to accept that which was offered to him,

(a) L. R. 8 Ch. 597, 605, n.

1902
March 18.

Court of
Appeal.

and there being no *mala fides* in the matter, he must take the consequences. It is the same case we have to deal with here. But it does not stand there upon the authorities. If we go back to the older case of *Scrivener* v. *Pask* (a), in 1 Common Pleas, you find the same thing with this difference,—because there the building owner, through. his architect, sent in the bill of quantities—that it was a separate document, not appended to the specification, and not in that sense incorporated with it, and made the basis of the contract. But the principle is the same, because the principle at the bottom of it is that it is a representation and not a warranty. It is not intended to be anything more than an estimate, and it is not made part of the contract binding on the employer.

The next step taken is a very considerable one. We have it in the case I have referred to of *Sharpe* v. *San Paulo Railway Company* (b), where it was incorporated into the contract in this sense that it was made a schedule to the contract; but though it was part of the schedule to the contract it is only part of the representations put into writing in the schedule to the contract. So also the case in the House of Lords of *Thorn* v. *The Mayor of London* (c) seems to me to involve exactly the same principle. There, what was complained of was not a matter as to quantities, but there was a distinct statement in the specification. I think it was itself a distinct specification for caissons to be used in the erection of a bridge. The builder found it was impracticable to do the work with caissons, and the result was that not being able to do it with caissons he had to lose the labour and capital which he had expended in trying to do it with caissons, and he had to resort to other methods. He claimed there very much as the builder has done here for remuneration for the extra cost he had been put to in trying to carry out the work by means of caissons, and if there had been a warranty, as he set up, derivable from the fact that caissons were described in one of the documents which made the basis of the contract as the means by which the work was to be carried out,—if that involved a warranty—his case could have been relied on. It was not a warranty, but it was only the engineer's view; it was a suggestion to him as to the most convenient way of carrying out the work. It was only an estimate or suggestion and not a warranty, and for that reason the employer was held excused.

In the particular contract in that case there was this provision, the exact words of which I will read: "These plans are believed to be

(a) L. R. 1 C. P. 715.
(b) L. R. 8 Ch. 597, 605, n.
(c) 1 App. Cas. 120.

1902
March 18.

Court of
Appeal.

correct, but their accuracy is not guaranteed, and the contractor will not be entitled to charge any extra should the work to be removed prove more than indicated on these drawings." That qualification, though it related to the plans, does not appear to me to have any relation to the suggested methods of carrying out the plans as mentioned in the specification. It is a condition pointing to another matter, and therefore it seems to me that the question whether or not the representation as to the caissons was a warranty stands entirely outside the limitation or condition which was introduced for another purpose and did not qualify that particular part of the matter at all, and therefore it seems to stand broadly on the position that this statement in this specification indicates a way in which the work is to be carried out, and that it is not to be treated as a warranty, but only as what it purports to be—the best description that he can give of how he thinks the work ought to be done. That appears to make it quite clear in this case, the quantities not being a warranty and not being a representation other than a perfectly honest and *bonâ fide* one, that this mistake is not the subject-matter of a claim for work done thereunder. The work he has done he has done under the contract and nothing else, and having done it under the contract and nothing else he cannot claim on another contract which in point of fact never was made, when the matter is sifted.

Mr. English Harrison (who has said all that could be said, it seems to me, for his case) did not allude to the authorities on the question of warranty, but was obliged to fall back on this position. He said that, rightly understood, taking this contract together with this provision, the bill of quantities must be looked at as part of the contract, and that taking it altogether it amounts to this: that it is a contract to do all such work as is stated in the bill of quantities, and that if that should result in a sum larger than the 10,000*l.*, the contract price being expended, the difference must be made good; if, on the other hand, it should result in less than that amount, it ought to be excused to the builder. But that is to substitute a contract of measure and value for a contract for a lump sum. Mr. English Harrison does not seem to me to give the answer to that point that the lump sum ceased to have any significance in the discussion at all, if that is the true meaning of this contract. But it seems to me the cardinal point in this contract is that it is a contract for a lump sum, and therefore it seems to me that my learned brothers were wrong in the view they took of this contract.

No doubt they were captivated by the view that there was an apparent hardship on the contractor, who has found himself obliged

1902
March 18.

Court of
Appeal.

to expend more money than he calculated on because a mistake was made not by him but by the building owner; but it seems to me the answer to that and the justice of it is, it was perfectly competent for him to make his own estimate, and if he relied on what was done by the architect and chose to adopt it, he, just as much as the building owner, has backed his opinion of the architect's capacity, and must take his risk as much as the building owner takes his.

Under the circumstances I think the decision of the Divisional Court is wrong.

Upon the other point the Divisional Court, I think, agreed with the view I am taking, though they did not absolutely decide it; that is, as to the alleged custom found by the arbitrator in this case. He finds as a fact that there is a custom. "It was alleged before me, and I find it to be the fact that it is a general usage in the building trade, that where tenders are invited for the erection of works in accordance with plans, and a bill of quantities is furnished, a person making a tender is not expected to verify the quantities himself, but is expected and intended to assume the correctness of the quantities, and to tender upon that assumption, and that if such quantities in the event prove to be greater or less than the actual quantities, the price is to be reduced or increased by an amount ascertained and determined by the scale of prices given in the tender, as the scale by which payment for extras is to be determined." Then he submits the question whether regard may be had to that usage. It seems to me that is usage simply to contradict the contract and disregard the materials that are made part and parcel of the contract, the essential factors in the contract.

I do not think that such usage as that can be admitted, and I do not think that there I am differing from the opinion of the Divisional Court, though it is a question they did not answer. The arbitrator puts these three questions: first of all, "Whether, in ascertaining the amount to be paid by Messrs. Bemrose to Messrs. Ford, regard is to be had to the aforesaid usage in the building trade?" I think clearly not. Secondly, "Whether Messrs. Ford are entitled only to be paid the sum of 10,559*l*. mentioned in the said contract with such deductions and alterations as are by the said contract provided to be made in respect of alterations or deviations from the original plans determined upon during the progress of the work?" I certainly think they are. And third, and this is where I differ from the Divisional Court, "Whether Messrs. Ford are entitled to be paid the value of all the works actually executed by them for Messrs. Bemrose at the prices upon which the contract was based, whether such value should

1902
March 18.

Court of
Appeal.

be more or less than the sum of 10,559*l*., mentioned in the said contract?" As I understand, the Divisional Court have answered that question in the affirmative; there I think they were wrong. For these reasons I think this appeal must be allowed.

ROMER, L.J.: In my opinion when the documents in this case are looked at, it appears to me reasonably clear that the contract was one that I may call a lump sum contract, that is to say, the contract by the builder to build works as a whole for the building owner for a lump sum and not such a contract as the respondents in this case wished to make out; that is to say, a contract by the builder only to build or erect certain specified amounts of work, so many square yards of excavation, so many yards of brickwork, so many feet of carpenter's work, and so forth. It is clear to my mind that there was no such contract as that. It is not a case whereof if it turned out that the bill of quantities had been mis-stated, say, in favour of the builder, the building owner could have called on the builder to have made good any sum of money to him, because the builder had not expended quite so much labour as would appear by the bill of quantities he would have to expend, or, *vice versâ*, it is not a case where, if it turns out that the builder has to do more than appears on the bill of quantities, any compensation has to be paid to him by the building owner.

The fact is the bill of quantities in this case was no essential part of the contract at all. It was not really a part of the specification, but something to be deduced from the plans and specification, which really showed the work as a whole that had to be done by the builder. It was an estimate by a person who had taken out the quantities from the plans and specification, and which might just as well, for the purpose of this contract, have been contained in a separate document. It appears to me that, apart from other provisions of this contract, the true intent and effect of it are shown by the two first clauses of what are called the "Conditions of Contract." I need not read those two conditions of contract. They are contrasted one with another, and, stated shortly, what do they show? They show this: the first condition points out that the builder is really intended to do the work fairly as a whole, shown by the plans and specification, but that even if in some detail the specification may not have stated, or may even erroneously have stated some portion of the work, which on a fair construction of the work as a whole was intended to be done for a lump sum, that work will have to be done according to the true view of the work as a whole by the contractor, without his being paid for it. That is contrasted with the second

1902
March 18.
——————
Court of
Appeal.

condition, which points out when and under what circumstances moneys extra to the lump sum are to be paid. Moneys extra to the lump sum are to be paid only when there is extra work done by the builder in respect of alterations and deviations from the original plan. Contrast those two clauses, and they show clearly in themselves, apart from the rest of the contract (which also in my opinion is reasonably clear), that this contract is what I have stated it to be, a lump sum contract for the works as a whole.

That being so, the next point arises, What is the effect of the statement of the quantities in the margin of the specification? First, dealt with as a representation, what representation is it? Fairly looked at, as far as I can see, it is only a representation by the building owner that some qualified person has taken out the quantities in the usual way from the plans and specifications, and that that person's bill of quantities was, as stated, in the margin of the specification. That representation was perfectly true.

Then follows the question, Can it be inferred from the circumstances of this case that there was any warranty by the building owner that that person who had taken out the bills of quantities had taken them out correctly? It seems to me too late in the day to say that there was any such warranty, or even warranty to be implied. The cases alone settle that point, and I need not even refer to them after what my Lord has said. There is nothing, to my mind, in this contract, and in the circumstances connected with it, from which this Court ought to infer that there was any such guarantee or warranty as has been insisted upon on behalf of the respondents' case.

That really ends the case; if the construction of the contract be what I have said it is, and there is no warranty, there is no ground on which the respondents can base their claim before us.

With regard to the question of usage I have nothing to add beyond what my Lord has said. It is clear that such a usage cannot be imported here to practically contradict the meaning and effect of this contract. It appears to me, for these reasons, that the judgment of the Court below was erroneous, and ought to be reversed.

MATHEW, L.J.: In this contract the contract was to execute certain work according to the plans and specifications, and if the specification had been properly examined and dealt with, it seems clear that the work could only have been properly undertaken for one-third more than the price mentioned in the contract. The builder has to admit that. He says: I am exonerated from making

1902
March 18.

Court of
Appeal.

any such inquiry because you, the building owner, undertook the accuracy of the quantities and guaranteed them. It is said, on the other hand, that no such guarantee was made. There was no ground on which the builder could suppose that any such guarantee was intended.

To see what was meant by the parties we have to look at the course of business which has so frequently been brought to the attention of the Court. The building owner employs an architect to prepare specifications and plans and show the work to be done by the builder. That is all the building owner does in the first instance. In this particular case there is no proof that he knew anything about the practice of taking out quantities. It is said he should inform himself, and that he would be aware that quantities would be taken out. Under what circumstances are these quantities taken out? The architect who is desirous of carrying the matter through and finding a builder, who is not the servant of the building owner in any way, to facilitate the making of tenders, either himself or by a competent agent prepares an estimate of the quantities. That, it appears to me, is all he does. The utmost that could be imputed to the building owner in such a case is an undertaking that, before tenders are asked for, his architect, a competent man, on his own responsibility, and for the information of the builder, prepares a bill of quantities. That was done in this particular case.

As has been said, it is too late, after the authorities on the subject which we have had discussed, to assert that this bill of quantities enters into the contract and becomes part of or one of its terms. It would lead to the result which has been so forcibly pointed out by the learned counsel for the appellants: that the contract would not be the contract that the building owner had entered into, but something totally different. There is a contract, say, for 10,000*l.*, which turns out to be a contract for 15,000*l.*, by which he is to be bound. It would be a most impossible condition of things. The building owner, when asked about the quantities, would say: I know nothing about quantities; it is a matter for the architect and the builder, not for me. I do not take the responsibility for them.

Now the bill of quantities here, unfortunately, was not accurate. It was prepared, apparently, by a competent man, who made a mistake. It was quite open to the builder if he chose, after the tender had been accepted, or before the tender had been accepted, to verify them. He did not choose to do it. What is the meaning of that? The business meaning, it seems to me, is that he reposes confidence in the architect, and trusts him to have done what is

1902
March 18.

Court of
Appeal.

reasonably careful in the matter. Confidence is reposed by the builder in the architect in respect of other matters; he had authority given to him to deal with other questions that arise as to certificates and so on, subject to the somewhat unusual condition in these matters—the right to go to an independent referee. But such confidence is reposed in architects in such cases as leads one to infer that a builder would in this matter, as in all others, be guided by his judgment and by his skill.

The result here is, as has been stated before, that when the work is completed and measured according to measure and value, this large discrepancy appears and the building owner is called on to pay. He says: I never made that contract; the contract with me was for 10,000*l.*; you want me to pay 15,000*l.* It appears to me only necessary to state the proposition to make it clear that it cannot be what is suggested.

Then cases have been referred to. *Scrivener* v. *Pask*, fully reported in 18 Common Bench, New Series, with all the documents set out, is a case that approximates even as to its facts very closely to the present case. In the same way there there was a contract according to the plan and specification, and the bill of quantities was incorrect, and was held not to be binding on the building owner. The same principle was laid down in *Thorn* v. *The Corporation of London (a)*, and was still more clearly laid down in *Sharpe* v. *San Paulo Railway (b)*.

That being the business view, as it seems to me, of the matter, the argument for the respondents was that the form of the contract here was wholly different in character from the contract disclosed in those cases. Attention was called to the phraseology in the bill of quantities referred to in the contract. Does that show that the quantities have a different character in this contract from the character they would ordinarily have, and that a different obligation was intended to be taken by the building owner because of the phraseology as part of the specification? It appears to be scarcely arguable that if the bill of quantities had been on a different piece of paper, no one could contend that it was part of the specification. The contract being plain and specific, before it is entered into, the bill of quantities can be set aside, and is not binding upon the builder, because he can verify or discuss what is wrong, and tender on what he ascertains to be right. If he does not choose to do so, the bill of quantities does not lose its original character on that account. He merely indicates that he is trusting the architect in a particular case, and acting on his estimate.

(a) 1 App. Cas. 120.
(b) L. R. 8 Ch. 597, 605, n.

1902
March 18.

Court of
Appeal.

As far as custom is concerned, which was a final point taken on behalf of the respondents, it would be really a custom to alter a contract which people had entered into, which I have no hesitation in saying would be a bad custom. For these reasons I am of opinion that this appeal must be allowed.

COLLINS, M.R.: The order will be, "The Court being of opinion that Messrs. Ford are entitled to be paid only the said sum of 10,559*l.* with such deductions and additions as are by the said contract provided to be made in respect of alterations or deviations from the original plans determined upon during the progress of the work. Judgment for the sum of 2,303*l.* 10*s.* which by the award in this case is made payable by Messrs. Bemrose to Messrs. Ford. Then the balance in Court will have to be paid out."

Solicitors for the appellants: Messrs. Mackrell, Maton & Co.
Solicitor for the respondents: F. Stone.

𝕴𝖓 𝖙𝖍𝖊 𝕮𝖔𝖚𝖗𝖙 𝖔𝖋 𝕬𝖕𝖕𝖊𝖆𝖑.

1902
June 3.

Court of
Appeal.

(*Before* COLLINS, M.R., and MATHEW and COZENS-HARDY, L.JJ.)

CROSS *v.* LEEDS CORPORATION.

Arbitration—Bias—Disqualification of Arbitrator.

A named arbitrator, who was an official of the Leeds Corporation, wrote a letter in which he said that the claim of the contractors against the Corporation was outrageous. The contractors brought an action against the Corporation, which the Corporation applied to have stayed pending the arbitration; the contractors opposed this. Held, that the arbitrator was not disqualified.

This case came before the Court of Appeal, composed of the Master of the Rolls and Lords Justices Mathew and Cozens-Hardy, on the appeal of the defendants from an order of Mr. Justice Bucknill in chambers, affirming a decision of the master, and refusing to refer the question in dispute to arbitration. The action was brought under a contract between the plaintiff and the Leeds Corporation for the construction of works in connection with the extension of the Corporation markets. The defendants alleged excessive delay on the part of the contractor, but the plaintiff's answer to this was that there was delay on the part of the defendants themselves in delivering the plans. It appeared that there was a clause in the agreement providing that all disputes should be referred to the arbitration of Mr. Thomas Hewson, the city engineer. The plaintiff contended that Mr. Hewson had shown such bias that the dispute ought not to be referred to him. It appeared that Mr. Hewson had written a letter to the plaintiff containing the following passage: "After a careful perusal I do not admit any of your explanations or excuses, and have to refer you to the town clerk for the settlement of your account. Looking at the length of time this contract has been held over by you, and the loss that the Corporation and other contractors have suffered thereby, your claims seem to be simply outrageous, and likely to lead to claims on you from other contractors, as I must now write to each contractor to state, in writing, whether they have or have not a claim against you, but, however that may be, I shall only deal with you through the Corporation's solicitor."

Bucknill, J., in chambers refused to stay the action; the Corporation appealed to the Court of Appeal.

Lawson Walton, K.C., and Montague Shearman, for the Corporation, contended that Mr. Hewson had been guilty of no misconduct in his capacity of arbitrator, so as to disqualify him from acting.

Lawrance, K.C., and Willis, for the plaintiff, argued that Mr. Hewson had pre-judged the matters sought to be referred to him, and that the order of Bucknill, J., was right.

COLLINS, M.R.: This is an appeal from Mr. Justice Bucknill, who refused to stay proceedings under a provision in the Arbitration Act, which is analogous to the provisions under the old Procedure Act, on the ground that there was an agreement between the parties to refer matters to arbitration.

It is not disputed in this case that there is such an agreement, the defendants have set that out, and, of course, they cannot recede from that position. On the other hand, the plaintiff does not dispute that; and the whole question is whether the arbitrator who is appointed as such by the terms of the agreement has so acted in this matter as to show that he is unfit to be an arbitrator; and that therefore these defendants are not entitled to the relief which the section under which they applied gives.

I do not propose to repeat what has been often said, and I think now finally decided in this Court, as to the conditions under which an arbitrator appointed under one of these agreements may be removed from his office. But this is perfectly clear, that when the parties to a contract of this kind agree to an arbitration by a person who is appointed between the contractor and the building owner as the judge in the first instance of everything that has been done—a judge whose decision is final—when those are the stipulations of the contract, the parties are not entitled to come and say, "That person whom we appointed the judge between us in all these instances, and who as such has given an opinion, is incapacitated from becoming arbitrator because he has committed himself to a particular view." Their contract was that he should commit himself to a particular

1902
June 3.

Court of
Appeal.

view; and their contract was, that although he has committed himself to a particular view, he might nevertheless act as arbitrator, so that it is perfectly idle to come here and say that this man who we agreed should act as arbitrator has, as we agreed he should, given his opinion upon matters which are now suggested as matters of reference, and because he has given that opinion in accordance with our mandate to him to do so, we say that he is unfit to be an arbitrator.

That, obviously, cannot hold water; and the question has been repeatedly raised and discussed, and, I should think, decided now beyond all question, that unless you can find something more in the appointed person than that he has honestly, and it may be strenuously and vigorously, formed his opinions throughout the conduct of the contract, and acted upon them—unless you can find something more than that to impeach his impartiality, it is idle to make any application to re-arrange the whole dispute between the parties, and substitute for the biassed arbitrator which they contemplated, somebody who is a mere judge outside the discussion altogether, and coming into it without having had any previous opportunity of forming an opinion.

It is idle to discuss the matter on that basis. The parties have not agreed—that is the plain English of it—for an impartial arbitrator, because the person whom they have agreed upon as arbitrator is one who it may be pre-supposed may have formed to the best of his ability, and with all the information that was at hand, an adverse opinion to one of the parties on the points in dispute. You begin the discussion with that; but, nevertheless, because these contractors as well as employers know perfectly well what they are about, and assent to this clause for very good reasons, they cannot come afterwards and complain of the very thing which they have agreed to, namely, that the person who is now asked to act as arbitrator has expressed, and strongly expressed, an opinion as to a particular contention which they are now setting forth. It was a condition of the very existence of the matter that he was to be the person to whom the matter was to be referred; and that there would be nothing for them to raise an arbitration about unless he had given an adverse opinion to them.

That is the first step in the discussion. You have got to introduce something more than that; you have got to introduce something (it is very difficult to draw the line short of dishonesty), it may be something even short of dishonesty, as, for instance, if there is peverse conduct, and refusal to treat the matter at all, or where it is said, "I will not bring, as far as my human infirmities enable me to

1902
June 3.
———
Court of
Appeal.

do so, an impartial mind to bear on the matter which I have already decided," but unless you get something amounting to that you get nowhere at all.

When you look at this correspondence here it seems to me that undoubtedly the architect, or the engineer, did express a strong opinion upon one part of the case, in which the contractor differed from him. I do not pretend to give an opinion as to whether the engineer was right or wrong; but in dealing as arbitrator, I think that he had a perfect right to form a strong opinion. He did form a strong opinion; and though it might have been more delicate if he had not characterised the other view as outrageous, yet he was not doing any more than he was put there to do.

A strong man forming an opinion and acting upon it, and, if need be, expressing it, does not negative his right, for the reasons I have already pointed out, to act as arbitrator afterwards. You have got to get something more than a strong opinion strongly expressed before you have something equivalent to a refusal to consider the matter on its merits at all.

I find nothing of the sort on the correspondence; in fact, when you come later on, you find first of all a letter from the town clerk who is the person who finally acts for the Corporation in this matter, and on the 30th March, 1901, he says this: "Referring to our recent correspondence herein, I have now seen the city engineer, and he informs me that, having certified completion, he is waiting for the delivery of your account for any additions and deductions that there may have been in the smith's contract. So soon as this has been delivered he will go into the matter and put it on the same footing on which the iron founder's contract is. Thereafter I should be prepared to arrange an appointment with you and him to go into any questions which you may desire to raise on his certificate, and also to discuss the question of the amount of liquidated and other damages which the Corporation will require for the enormous delay in the completion of your work." That seems to me to suggest a very proper course.

On the 30th September, 1901, the engineer writes another letter which was relied upon by Mr. Willis: "In reply to your letter, dated the 26th instant, but which only came to hand this morning, I need not say that I hold as binding my decisions and awards of December 11th, 1900, and June 13th, 1901. As the six months period of maintenance has now expired I will go into that item and forward you certificate in due course."

Then we get on to a later period, in which, as has been pointed out by my brother, as late as April 2nd, 1902, after there has been a discussion in which the contractors have put forward their views very strenuously, the engineer writes thus: "Gentlemen,—In reply to your letter, I shall be prepared to see you at 2 o'clock on Friday next, to hear anything you may wish to lay before me in relation to the contracts between you and the Corporation, and to the certificate sent you on October 31st, 1901. I am now, and throughout have been, in the position given to me under the contracts under which my decision is binding on the parties, and the Corporation have never attempted in any way to bias or influence me in my judgment, but on the contrary insisted that I shall exercise it without any reference to them." That seems to me to be the assumption of a judicial attitude, and that he is a person who has formed an opinion, as he has stated before, but that he is prepared to hear the thing *de novo*, and, as far as he can, to do justice between the parties.

That is the very thing the parties have stipulated for; and they cannot come here now and say that because this person has already given an opinion, and expressed it in strong terms, we are outside our contract and are relieved from going before you to decide the case. It seems to me that this appeal must be allowed.

MATHEW, L.J.: I regret the necessity, which is so often imposed upon us, of repeating the reasons why builders cannot be allowed to escape from contracts of this sort which they have entered into. Every day, or very nearly every day, we sit here, and cases of this sort are presented to the Court; but for a great number of years the law on the subject has been well settled.

The engineer or architect under a contract of this sort is placed in two positions, and he is allowed to assume those two positions with the full knowledge of both contracting parties; and in the one position he is bound to do his best for his employer, and to look sharply after the builder whilst the work is going on, and it is his duty in that capacity to form an opinion as to what his employer is entitled to while the works are being executed. The contract, it seems to me, contemplates that differences are likely to arise between the builder and the architect or engineer, and that the time might come when the engineer should deal with them in a different capacity, and then he has to do his best as an honourable man to determine, judicially and finally, questions between the parties.

I can understand that many years ago it might have been urged that that position was an anomalous one, but now, fortunately, builders and building owners are treated as reasonable beings, and regarded as persons who best know how to deal with the con-

1902
June 3.

Court of
Appeal.

tract, and it is obvious that it is of the last importance, with reference to works of this sort, as to every portion of which there may be a dispute, that there should be a mode of determining them finally. This is a contract well known in its form, and well known in its construction which has been adopted in this case, and once more an attempt is made to escape from its terms, and to get rid of the engineer in his judicial capacity.

Now it is said that we ought to come to the conclusion that he was unfit to act judicially, because he anticipated the time when he would have to act judicially, without hearing or giving the opportunity of hearing the builder with regard to the matters in dispute; but if you look at the correspondence, it is a perfectly good-tempered correspondence from beginning to end, there is not in the course of it the smallest imputation upon the honour of the engineer, but he took the position when he was appealed to with reference to the matter, "I have given you your certificates and there they are, and I see no reason now for altering them."

Then an offer is made for compromising the matter, and an appeal is made to him on the part of the builders for consideration, negotiations proceed upon that footing and they fail, and then the time comes when something has to be done, and then it happens that the engineer is not satisfied with what has been done in the course of the execution of the work. Now, from the correspondence, it is perfectly clear that in 1901, and again in the year 1902, by the letter of April 2nd, the engineer with perfect goodwill states his real position, and was perfectly familiar with contracts of this character, and the answer to that, on the part of the builders, was a writ issued by the builders to determine the question judicially. Now it seems to me that the respondents are hopelessly wrong, and that the builders cannot possibly complain of the conduct of the engineer as showing any unfair feeling towards them, or as due to anything dishonourable or discreditable on the part of the engineer.

There is no reason why, in this case, as in every other case of the same class, the engineer should not undertake the duties, and discharge them to the best of his ability as an honourable man, with regard to the questions of difference between the parties.

Two minor points were dwelt upon which are supposed to indicate a strong feeling on the part of the engineer against the builders. The first one was that letters had been written to the contractors to ask them if they had any claims. It appeared, however, that before any such letters were written, there had been complaints by other

1902
June 3.

Court of
Appeal.

contractors that they had been delayed in the progress of the works by the slow way in which the builders had carried them out; but it was absolutely necessary that the engineer should know whether any claims were to be made against the Corporation by reason of the delay. That grievance really disappeared as soon as it was stated. The other point was that the engineers had allowed the claim for penalties upon the letter. It was said, "We have no other information upon the subject before us, but the builders promised to do their best to complete the contract within a certain time," the whole contract seems to have been definite with regard to the time, still the engineer had power to say within what time the work was to be done; and apparently, the right to penalties would accrue from the time when he issued notice, and the work was undertaken upon the footing of that notice. We do not know anything about the real facts as to this. We do not know anything beyond what appears from that letter.

It may be that there was a great deal more than appeared between the parties; but there is the further fact, namely, that it was said, and it appears from the documents in the case, that there had been additions and alterations to this contract. If it be so, the point arises at once whether any claims for penalties were not thereby blotted out from the contract. That is a matter for the arbitrator, and that is a matter upon which he is entitled to be informed as to the law.

I do not say in the least what his decision ought to be, but that is a matter for him. If, in the opinion of those who represent the builders, his decision should be wrong in point of law, there is a mode open to the builders of appealing from the decision of the arbitrator. It seems to me that there was no grievance whatever in this case, and no ground upon which the action should be allowed to proceed. I agree, therefore, that the appeal should be allowed.

COZENS-HARDY, L.J.: I am of the same opinion, and I do not think I can advance anything beyond what has been said by the Master of the Rolls and Lord Justice Mathew.

Solicitors for the plaintiff: Messrs. Burton, Yeates & Hart.
Solicitors for the defendants: Messrs. King, Wigg & Co.

1902
April 16.

King's Bench
Division.

1903
April 3.

Court of
Appeal.

𝔍n the 𝕳igh Court of 𝔍ustice.

(*Before* Wright, J.)

𝔍n the Court of Appeal.

(*Before* Vaughan Williams, Stirling, and Mathew, L.JJ.)

WELLS *v.* ARMY AND NAVY CO-OPERATIVE SOCIETY.

Penalties—Delay caused by Employer.

This case was a claim by a firm of builders for payment of the final instalments of 2,900*l.* of the contract price. The defendants claimed to set off against this payment an equal amount by way of penalties or liquidated damages. The facts will sufficiently appear from the pleadings and the material clauses of the contract which follow:—

Statement of Claim.

1902
April 16.

King's Bench
Division.

The plaintiff's claim is for 2,900*l.*, the agreed balance of account due to the plaintiff from the defendant company under a contract dated October 29th, 1897, and made between the defendant company, of the one part, and the plaintiff, of the other part.

Particulars.

	£	s.	d.
July 24th, 1900.—Final instalments certified by defendants' architect	3,793	3	2
August 16th, 1900.—Less cash received on account	893	3	2
	£2,900	0	0

The plaintiff also claims interest on the above sum of 2,900*l.*, at the rate of 4*l.* per cent. per annum from the date hereof to payment or judgment.

Defence.

(1) Subject to the matters hereinafter alleged by way of set-off and counter-claim, the defendants admit the plaintiff's claim herein.

Set-off and Counterclaim.

(2) The plaintiff is indebted to the defendants in the sum of 2,900*l.* as and by way of liquidated and agreed damages under a contract in writing made between the plaintiff, as contractor, and the defendant society, as employers, and dated October 29th, 1897 (which is the contract sued on herein), whereby the plaintiff agreed to complete the whole of the works within one year from the day of the date of the said contract, unless the said works should be delayed by reason of any alteration or addition in or to the works authorised as afore-said, or in the case of combination of workmen or strikes, or by the default of the sub-contractors whom the plaintiff was obliged to employ, or other

1902
April 16.

King's Bench
Division.

causes beyond the contractor's control; satisfactory proof of all which was, at the time of the occurrence, to be afforded to the Board of Directors of the defendant society, who were to adjudicate thereon and make due allowance therefor, if necessary, and whose decision was to be final; and then the plaintiff was to complete the works within such time as the said Board of Directors should consider to be reasonable, and in case of default the plaintiff was to pay or allow to the defendants, as and by way of liquidated and agreed damages, the sum of 10*l.* per day for every day during which the plaintiff should be so in default, until the whole of the said works be so completed.

(3) The plaintiff did not complete the said works until the 2nd day of January, 1900.

(4) According to the terms of the said contract, the Board of Directors of the defendant society, on May 25th, 1899, adjudicated on the various delays which had arisen in the execution of the said works, and having made due allowance therefor, decided that the plaintiff was entitled to an extension of three months, and no more, beyond the time fixed by the said contract for the completion of the said works.

(5) By reason of the premises the plaintiff became and was liable to pay to the defendants the sum of 10*l.* a day by way of agreed or liquidated damages from January 29th, 1899, until January 2nd, 1900.

The defendants claim, to set-off and counterclaim against the plaintiff's claim, 2,900*l.*

PARTICULARS.

290 days at 10*l.* a day = 2,900*l.*—A. G. McINTYRE.

REPLY AND DEFENCE TO COUNTERCLAIM.

(1) Except in so far as the defendants' defence contains admissions, the plaintiff joins issue thereon.

As TO THE SET-OFF AND COUNTERCLAIM.

(2) The plaintiff denies that he is indebted to the defendants in the sum of 2,900*l.*, or any sum as and by way of liquidated and agreed damages under a contract dated October 29th, 1897; and the plaintiff further denies that under the said contract he agreed to complete the whole of the works within one year from the day of the date of the said contract unless the said works should be delayed by reason of any alteration or addition, or otherwise, as in paragraph 2 of the set-off and counterclaim alleged. The plaintiff craves leave to refer to the said contract for the terms thereof.

(3) The plaintiff denies that he did not complete the said works until the 2nd January, 1900.

(4) The plaintiff denies that the Board of Directors of the defendant society on the 25th May, 1899, according to the terms of the said contract or at all, adjudicated on the various delays which had arisen in the execution of the said works, and he denies that they made due or any allowance therefor, and he denies that they decided that the plaintiff was entitled to an extension of three months and no more beyond the time fixed by the said contract for the completion of the said works.

(5) If the Board of Directors of the defendant society did adjudicate on

the said date (which is denied), such date of adjudication was subsequent to the date fixed by the contract for the completion of the works and (in the alternative) subsequent to the alleged extension of three months, and the said Board had no power then to adjudicate.

(6) Further, if the Board of Directors of the defendant society did adjudicate (which is denied), the plaintiff says that they had no power to adjudicate upon their own wrongful acts as in paragraph 10 mentioned.

(7) By such wrongful acts in paragraph 10 mentioned they were disqualified from adjudicating at all.

(8) If the Board did adjudicate or did extend the time (which is denied) subsequent to such alleged extended time, and (in the alternative) subsequent to such alleged adjudication the plaintiff was further prevented from completing the works by the acts of the defendants and their architect and delayed from various causes in the particulars mentioned, and the defendants further waived completion by any particular time.

(9) The plaintiff denies that by reason of the alleged premises or at all he became or was liable to pay the defendants the sum of 10*l.* a day by way of agreed or liquidated damages from the 29th January, 1899, or any other date until January 2nd, 1900, or any other day.

(10) The defendants, in breach of the said contract, prevented the plaintiff from completing the said works within the time named in the said contract, or (in the alternative) within three months beyond the time fixed by the said contract by failing to give the plaintiff possession of certain parts of the site of the premises on which the said works were to be executed, and by failing and delaying to give the plaintiff instructions for the execution of the said works, and in various other ways, and took possession of the said works during the progress thereof, and by reason of such breaches and of such taking possession delayed the completion of the said works, and also increased the burden of the plaintiff under the said contract, and disentitled themselves to claim the said liquidated damages, and waived completion of the said works within the periods above referred to.

(11) Further, the plaintiff was greatly delayed throughout the works by alterations and additions in or to the works, and by combination of workmen and strikes, and especially by the default of the sub-contractors whom the plaintiff was obliged to employ, as well as from other causes beyond the plaintiff's control; and had due allowance been made therefor by the Board of Directors of the defendant society, and had the said Board granted a reasonable extension of time, the plaintiff would have completed the whole within such extended time.

(12) By reason of the said breaches in paragraph 10 and the other circumstances set out in that paragraph, and in paragraphs 5, 6, 7, 8, 9, and 11, the time for completion named in the said contract was no longer the time within which the plaintiff was to complete the said works.

(13) In the alternative, the alleged adjudication of the Board of Directors of the defendant society, if it was made, was unreasonable and *ultra vires.*

Further particulars, exceeding three folios, are delivered herewith.

ALFRED A. HUDSON.

The material clauses of the contract were as follows:—

1902
April 16.

King's Bench
Division.

(7) Any authority or order given as aforesaid for any additions, omissions, or alterations in or to the works is to be binding on the contractors, and is not to vitiate the contract or the claim for penalties under clause 16, but all additions, omissions, or variations made in carrying out the works, for which a price may not have been previously agreed upon, are to be measured, and valued, and certified for by the architect, and added to or deducted from the amount of the contract, as the case may be, according to the bills of quantities signed by the contractor and deposited with the architect, or where the same may not apply, at fair measure and value, taking the bills of quantities as the basis of such valuation.

(16) The contractors are to complete the whole of the works within one year from the day of the date hereof unless the works be delayed by reason of any alteration or addition in or to the works authorised as aforesaid, or in case of combination of workmen or strikes, or by the default of the sub-contractors whom the contractors are obliged to employ, or other causes beyond the contractors' control, satisfactory proof of all which must, at the time of the occurrence, be at once afforded to the Board of Directors of the employers, who shall adjudicate thereon and make due allowance therefor, if necessary, and their decision shall be final, and then the contractors are to complete the works within such time as the said Board of Directors shall consider to be reasonable, and, in case of default, the contractors are to pay or allow to the employers as and by way of liquidated and agreed damages the sum of 10*l.* per day for every day during which they shall be so in default until the whole of the works shall be so completed.

(18) If the contractors shall become bankrupt or compound with or make any assignment for the benefit of their creditors, or shall suspend or delay the performance of their part of the contract (except on account of causes mentioned in clause 16, or on account of being restrained or hindered under any proceedings taken by parties interested in any neighbouring property, or in consequence of not having proper instructions, for which the contractors shall have duly applied), the employers, by the architect, may give to the contractors, or their assigns, or trustee, as the case may be, notice requiring the works to be proceeded with, and, in case of default on the part of the contractors and their assignee or trustee for a period of seven days, it shall be lawful for the employers by the architect to enter upon and take possession of the works, and to employ any other person or persons to carry on and complete the same, and to authorise him or them to use the plant, materials, and property of the contractors upon the works, and the costs and charges incurred in any way in carrying on and completing the said works are to be paid by the contractors to the employers, or may be set off by the employers against any moneys due or to become due to the contractors.

English Harrison, K.C., and A. A. Hudson (instructed by Mackrell, Maton, Godlee, and Quincey) appeared for the plaintiff, and Bray, K.C., and McIntyre (instructed by Tyrrell, Lewis, Lewis, and Broadbent) for the defendants.

WRIGHT, J.: This action is brought by a firm of builders to recover a balance admitted to be due under a building contract, dated 29th October, 1897. The defendants claim to set-off damages at the rate of 10*l.* per day for delay in completion of the buildings beyond the period of twelve months allowed by the contract.

The contract contained a provision of the ordinary kind for alterations, additions, or omissions to be made upon the orders of the

1902
April 16.

King's Bench
Division.

architect, and a special provision, in paragraph 7, that such orders should not "vitiate the contract or the claim for penalties under clause 16."

(Clause 16 of the contract was read.)

The completion of the works was delayed for nearly a year beyond the stipulated time. A principal cause of the delay was the defaults of sub-contractors, and an extension of the time by three months on this ground was allowed by the defendants' directors in accordance with clause 16. The plaintiffs claim to excuse the residue of the delay, firstly, on the ground of alterations and other matters, which are clearly within the scope of clause 16, and are, therefore, within the exclusive jurisdiction of the directors, and, secondly, on the ground that the defendants or their architect, by undue interference with the conduct of the works and by default in not giving possession of premises on which work was to be done, and in not providing plans and drawings in due time, so obstructed the works as to relieve the plaintiffs from their liability for the penalties.

The plaintiffs contend that the exclusive jurisdiction of the directors under clause 16 does not extend to questions of this second kind, and I think that their contention is well grounded. The clause might have been framed in general terms so as to include all delays, however caused; but it is not so framed. It enumerates specific causes of delay, and contains no general words except "other causes beyond the contractors' control." These words, in my opinion, ought to be construed with reference to the preceding specific causes of delay, and ought not to receive such an extension as would make the defendants judges in respect of their own defaults. As was said by Lord Esher, Master of the Rolls, in *Dodd v. Churton (a)*, "One rule of construction with regard to contracts is that when the terms of a contract are ambiguous and one construction would lead to an unreasonable result, the Court will be unwilling to adopt that construction." The construction which I have adopted is supported by clause 18 of the contract, which treats defaults by the architect in the giving of instructions as a matter not within the scope of clause 16. For these reasons I think that Mr. Bray's summary mode of disposing of the case must be rejected, and I must consider the evidence in relation to the alleged defaults and interferences on the part of the architect.

There are four matters to be particularly considered, viz.:—(1) Delay in giving possession of premises in which work was to be done; (2) delay in the supply of working plans and details generally; (3) a

---

(a) [1897] 1 Q. B. 562.

1902
April 16.

King's Bench
Division.

particular case of delay in relation to a water tower and tank; and (4) alleged interference by the architect with the relative order in which the different parts of the works should be proceeded with. The works comprised in the contract consisted of the erection of a new main building adjacent to the defendants' other premises and a lower wing building, and certain alterations of the older premises. The specification which was incorporated into the contract provided that possession of the site of the wing building should be given on the signing of the contract, and possession of the site of the new main building on the 10th January, 1898. Nothing was specified as to the date at which the plaintiffs should be allowed access to the older premises for the purpose of the work to be done there.

On the 9th June, 1898, the plaintiffs applied for permission to proceed with this work, as they were clearly entitled to do, but it was not until January or February, 1899, after the time for completion had expired, that they obtained access to the lower floors, and not until April, 1899, that they obtained access to the upper floors. There was evidence which satisfies me that it was a material detriment to the plaintiffs that they were prevented from carrying out the alterations of the old premises *pari passu* with the new building.

The defendants' excuses are that there was an express or tacit agreement for postponement, and that the plaintiffs were not until 1899 ready with certain iron doors by which it was intended to separate the old from the new premises. I am not satisfied that there was any such agreement for postponement as is suggested, and I find nothing in the contract or specification which required the plaintiffs to provide the iron doors before proceeding with the work. Their only obligation was to provide temporary screens. When they demanded possession in June, 1898, I think that they had done all that they were obliged to do in order to obtain possession, and that the defendants were in default in not giving possession until after the time for completion had expired.

The second head of default is perhaps more important. The contract and specification do not prescribe the times at which detailed drawings are to be supplied by the architect, and it seems to me that the plaintiffs were entitled to be supplied with them promptly upon request, because in the absence of them it would be impossible to make contracts for the provision and preparation of the materials. I find evidence of many and great delays in this respect on the part of the architect. For instance, details of ironwork ordered on the 16th January, 1898, were not supplied until April; details asked for on the 7th February, 1898, were not received until June; others urgently

1902
April 16.
King's Bench
Division.

required on the 11th March, 14th March, and 7th and 20th April were not received until June or July or even later, and in each of these instances the details required seem to have been necessary and important.

Remonstrances by the plaintiffs on the 11th March, 30th April, 8th July, 22nd July, indicate their importance. Some of the details were not even supplied until after the expiration of the time for completion. (See the letters 6th December and 19th December, 1898, and 21st, 22nd, 24th March, 1899.) The only answer given by the architect is that in his view the plaintiffs were not ready to go on with the works for which the details were asked. I think that this, even if proved, is not a sufficient answer. The plaintiffs must within reasonable limits be allowed to decide for themselves at what time they are to be supplied with details. It is very difficult to determine how far any particular defaults of this kind on the part of the defendants would entitle the plaintiffs to relief from penalties, especially when, as in this case, there were other and more important causes of delay which would not be grounds of relief in this action; but on the whole I think that the delays in giving details not merely contributed to the delay of completion, but were such as even in the absence of the other causes of delay would have prevented completion in due time, and in my view have to a great extent increased the delay of completion.

In the particular case of the water tower and tank, the architect on the 22nd December, 1897, informed the plaintiffs that the original plans would be altered. The plaintiffs immediately answered that some extension of time would be required. No details of alterations were supplied until 17th September, 1898. Here the delay did not make any difference in the result, because the plaintiffs were from other causes not ready; but I am satisfied that if they had been ready they could not, after the new details were supplied, have been reasonably expected to execute the work within the contract time, and it seems to me that when the defendants gave notice that the contract plans would be altered, it lay upon them to specify the alterations in sufficient time to make completion within the contract time reasonably possible.

It only remains to consider the complaint as to interference by the architect with the order of the works. On the 16th March, 1898, he directed the plaintiffs to proceed with the new main building in priority to the new wing building. It seems to me clear that subject to certain restrictions as to uniform height of walls, the plaintiffs were entitled to do the works in what order they pleased, and I am

1902
April 16.

King's Bench
Division.

satisfied that the change of order during the progress of the works was materially to the detriment of the plaintiffs, and must necessarily tend to delay completion. The architect says that the charge was made by arrangement with, and with the consent of, the plaintiffs' foreman, Sharpington. Sharpington is dead. The plaintiffs deny knowledge of any such arrangement, and I am not satisfied that there was any real consent. (See their letter of 24 June, 1898.) There was, undoubtedly, submission to the architect's order, but I do not believe that there was any agreement to preserve the obligation as to time.

On the whole, I think that the conclusion must be that the defaults of the defendants were such that in their cumulative effect they were inconsistent with their claim to insist on completion within the stipulated time. The defaults were, in my opinion, sufficiently substantial to cast upon the defendants the burden of showing that the defaults did not excuse the delay. It is true that, apart from their defaults, the plaintiffs had, by the default of sub-contractors, been delayed to an extent which might of itself have involved them in penalties, but in the absence of the further defaults by the defendants, it is impossible to say to what extent the liability to penalties might not have been reduced.

A difficulty in the way of the plaintiffs is that in their written and contemporaneous complaints they have insisted almost solely on the defaults of the sub-contractors as the cause of the delay and the ground for extension of time, so much so, that all the complaints on the ground of defaults by the defendants might seem to have been matters of afterthought. But this is, to a great extent, explained by the circumstances that the plaintiffs seem always to have expected that they would obtain all necessary extension on the ground of their sub-contractors' defaults. Nor can it be expected that ordinary builders should, in their daily communications with an architect whom they have strong reasons to conciliate, insist so strongly at the time on the matters in question as upon mature consideration during the progress of litigation it may appear that they ought to have done. The result is that there must be judgment for the plaintiffs, with costs.

The defendants appealed, and the case came on before the Court of Appeal April 3rd, 1903.

Reginald Bray, K.C., McIntyre, and Turner appeared for the appellants, and English Harrison, K.C., and A. A. Hudson for the respondents.

The Court of Appeal dismissed the defendants' appeal

1903
April 3.

Court of
Appeal.

Vaughan Williams, L.J.: This appeal fails. I agree in the conclusion of
Mr. Justice Wright in fact and in law. I do not consider it necessary in
this case to give a very long judgment, but I wish to say one or two
words of general application to this contract before I deal with the
specific points. It has been urged upon us, and properly urged, that,
never mind how hard or harsh the contract may seem to be, if the
contractor chooses to agree to those terms, those terms must be
enforced against him. In that I entirely agree, and in the judgment I
am going to deliver, I am not going in any way, either in words or in
substance, to relieve the builder from the obligations which he
voluntarily undertook.

But, when it comes to the construction of an ambiguous clause, I
think one ought to be careful to look at the whole of the contract, and
not to give a construction to any particular clause therein which will
defeat the object of the parties manifestly appearing upon the face of
the contract. I will deal with the specific clauses in a moment; but in
the contract one finds the time limited within which the builder is to
do this work. That means, not only that he is to do it within that time,
but it means also that he is to have that time within which to do it. It
seems to me that in the construction Mr. Bray wished us to put upon
clause 16 of this contract he was inviting us to put the construction
which would really put it in the power of the directors of this
company to deprive the builders altogether of the benefit of that
limitation of time. In my mind, that limitation of time is clearly
intended, not only as an obligation, but as a benefit to the builder.

Having said that, I will in a minute deal with the specific
allegations made by the builder here as to his having been delayed
by the building owners in the execution of these works; but before
doing so I want to say that, in substance, Mr. Bray had to admit that if
you take the findings in fact of the learned judge here, *primâ facie*
there was such delay as prevented the builder from executing these
works within the time limited, and also such conduct by the building
owners as prevented the builder from having the benefit of the time
clause. In my judgment, where you have a time clause and a penalty
clause, it is always implied in such clauses that the penalties are only
to apply if the builder has, as far as the building owner is concerned
and his conduct is concerned, that time accorded to him for the
execution of the works which the contract contemplates he should
have.

Mr. Bray having admitted really that, if you take the findings in
fact by the learned judge, the building owners had so delayed the
works as to prevent their execution within the time limited, and to

deprive the builder of the benefit of that time, meets the case by saying, "Oh, yes, that may be so; but the builder did not get on as fast as he might have got on, and I say, therefore, on behalf of the building owners, that you cannot say that the conduct of the building owners and the delay caused by them prevented the execution of this work within the time, because another contributory cause was the fact that the builder did not get on as fast as he might have done." It seems to me there are one or two answers to that—one an answer in fact, and the other an answer in law. The answer in fact is, that although there might have been some delay on the part of the builder, and I am including in the consideration of this the assumption that he was responsible under this contract for the delay in the delivery of the ironwork by Messrs. Lucy—even assuming that it was not in fact the delay of the builder or any delay by those for whom he was responsible which prevented the execution of this work within the contract time, in my judgment, whatever the builder might have done, the delay of the building owners and of their architect was such as to render the performance of the work within the contract time impossible. In law, I wholly deny the proposition Mr. Bray put forward, which was this really in effect: "Never mind how much delay there may be caused by the conduct of the building owner, the builder will not be relieved from penalties if he too has been guilty of delay in the execution of the works." I do not accept that proposition in law.

Having said this, I will deal shortly with the various matters that appear here. One of the main clauses one has to read is clause 7: "Any authority or order given as aforesaid for any additions, omissions, or alterations in or to the works is to be binding on the contractors, and is not to vitiate the contract or the claim for penalties under clause 16, but all additions, omissions, or variations made in carrying out the works for which a price may not have been previously agreed upon are to be measured, and valued, and certified for by the architect, and added to or deducted from the amount of the contract as the case may be." I wish to say, in passing, in regard to that particular clause, that the inclusion there of the words "is not to vitiate the contract or the claim for penalties" is obviously introduced in order to get rid of the effect of the decision in *Dodd v. Churton* (a), in which it was held that the mere presence of words with reference to the execution of alterations and additions and that orders for such works were not to vitiate the contract, did not amount to a contract to do all the works, including any extras that might

(a) [1897] 1 Q. B. 562.

be ordered, within the specified time for performance of the original work, and I have no doubt that it was hoped by the draughtsman of this contract that by introducing those words "or the claim for penalties" the inference in law would have to be drawn that such a clause would have the result, in case of orders being given for additions or alterations to a contract, that everything which had to be done, whether under the original contract or under the orders for extras and additions, would have to be done within the time specified for the original works, and that the penalty clause remained in operation.

The other clause one has to read is clause 16: "The contractors are to complete the whole of the works within one year from the day of the date hereof unless the works be delayed by reason of any alteration or addition in or to the works authorised as aforesaid, or in case of combination of workmen, or strikes, or by the default of the sub-contractors the contractors are obliged to employ, or other cause beyond the contractors' control, satisfactory proof of all which must at the time of occurrence be at once afforded to the board of directors of the employers, who shall adjudicate thereon and make due allowance therefore if necessary, and their decision shall be final, and then the contractors are to complete the works within such time as the said board of directors shall consider to be reasonable, and in case of default the contractors are to pay or allow to the employers as and by way of liquidated and agreed damages the sum of 10*l.* per day for every day during which they shall be so in default until the whole of the works shall be so completed." The materiality of that clause to that argument which has been addressed to us is this: the Army and Navy Stores say, "it may be that these delays did take place by reason of the causes stated by Mr. Justice Wright," but the whole of those causes are causes which are included within the words of this clause 16, and, if by reason of any such causes there was a delay, clause 16 provides that the contractors shall come and apply for an extension of time and that the directors shall perform, what I should say is a very unpleasant duty to any men of proper feeling, that of judging in their own cause, and shall determine whether or not there ought to be an extension of time and the terms of such extension.

It is said, inasmuch as the contractors did not get the board of directors to extend the time, the result is that, by the very terms of the contract, the builder is not to be entitled to take advantage of these delays, either as entitling him to disregard the time fixed by the contract for the completion of the works or to relieve him

1903
April 3.

Court of
Appeal.

in any way of the penalties. The first answer I have to give to that is this: when one comes to look at the causes of the delay, which are set forth here by Mr. Justice Wright, it is quite clear that some of them do not come, if indeed any of them do, within the ambit of clause 16. By way of illustration, take the postponement of giving possession. It is quite clear that postponement of giving possession does not come within the words of this clause. It is sought to say that, although such postponement does not come within the particular words of this clause, yet postponement does come within the wide words "or other causes beyond the contractors' control." In my judgment those general words do not admit of such a construction as to include postponement of the works, or of anything else by the building owners themselves. In my judgment those words "other causes beyond the contractors' control" mean other causes *ejusdem generis* with those which are particularised before. For that reason I think the argument on behalf of the Army and Navy Stores based upon clause 16 fails.

Now let me deal with the matters which are considered by Mr. Justice Wright:—First, delay in giving possession of the premises in which the work was to be done; secondly, delay in supplying working plans and details generally; thirdly, the particular cause of delay in relation to the water-tower and tank; and, fourthly, the alleged interference of the architect with the manner in which the different parts of the works were to be proceeded with. In my judgment it is perfectly manifest that there was in fact delay in giving possession of the premises in which the work was to be done. It is quite true, as was urged by Mr. Bray, that there is no time specified for giving possession of the old premises which had to be dealt with in the carrying out of this contract; but it is obvious that this contract contemplated possession of such old premises being given within a reasonable time, and in my judgment it is plain that the Army and Navy Stores being desirous—quite properly desirous—that their trade should be as little interfered with as might be, did, in a way which was wholly inconsistent in regard to the time within which the builder was to execute these works, delay the handing over of possession of the premises to the builder. When one really looks at the correspondence and sees the letter putting forward the excuse about the fireproof doors, it is very difficult to avoid the conclusion that the architect was really inventing an ingenious excuse in order to suit the trade convenience of his employers.

The next one is the delay in the supply of working plans and details generally. I can only say in regard to that, that in my judgment there was most substantial and material delay. In the case of joinery, which I only take as an instance, it is not in fact for a moment denied by the architect, but what he says is: "The works were not so advanced that it was necessary to erect or put in the joinery," and he gave the working details in plenty of time for the putting up of the joinery. The answer is that we have only to look at the 157th clause of the specification to see that the contract recognised, and the architect recognised, that which common sense would tell anyone that, if you have a big job of this sort to carry out, the contractor will start his shops almost immediately, including his joinery shop, and if the joinery is to be properly executed with seasoned stuff, it is idle to suggest that he is not to begin his joinery work until the time when his building, his plastering, and all the rest of it has been done. In my judgment the view of Mr. Justice Wright as to this delay is perfectly right.

With regard to the next item, the water-tower and tank, again I do not know any better word to describe the view of the architect than to describe it as an ingenious view in the interest of those who employed him. They first gave a very embarrassing notice at the end of the year 1897, from which possibly one might draw the inference that they meant to omit the water-tower altogether, and possibly to substitute some other arrangement, but at all events, the orders given by the builder for the necessary materials were either to be countermanded or withheld. As to how far this was to affect the building generally, there is no intimation. This state of things goes on until September in the next year, the contract having to be completed on the 29th October, in that year, and then, in September, the architect, or rather the Army and Navy Stores through their architect, gave details and an order for the necessary tanks, and gave that order at a time when admittedly even the tanks could not be completed within the year limited for the execution of these works. Having done that, they say two things: First, that what they did at the end of the year 1897 was an omission, and therefore came within the ambit of clause 16, but, being an omission, it did not justify an application for extension of time. Then they come to September, and say that the re-ordering of the water-tower was an addition or an alteration, and for that reason it could only be dealt with by an extension of time, which was not asked for, or, if asked for, was not granted. The answer to all these ingenious suggestions is, that in substance and in fact there can be no doubt that all that was done by the building owners with regard to the water-tower and

1903
April 3.

Court of
Appeal.

the tank was a postponement of the work, and does not come within clause 16.

The last point is the alleged interference by the architect with the relative order in which the different parts of the works should be proceeded with. That delay relates mainly to a postponement of the wing while the main building in the contract works was being got on with. It is justified on the ground of an alleged agreement between the architect and Mr. Sharpington, the foreman or representative of the contractors, that this should be done. I agree with Mr. Justice Wright that the onus of proving such an agreement was clearly on the Army and Navy Stores. I am not going to say that the correspondence does not afford a certain amount of evidence of that; but, unfortunately, Mr. Sharpington is dead, and undoubtedly the letters written by the contractors at the time—I think it was at the end of July or the beginning of August—while these matters were really being done, give an immediate denial of the existence of any such agreement. But even assuming that Mr. Sharpington did make such an agreement, it is not suggested either by the evidence of Mr. Bull, the architect, or by the correspondence, that such an agreement for the transposition, I think it is called, of the work, included an agreement that the work should be done within the original time, and that the penalties should be enforced.

Under these circumstances, I think, as Mr. Justice Wright said, that these matters of delay, Nos. 1, 2, 3 and 4, were such as to prevent the work being carried out within the original time, and I further think that to apply the time clause or the penalties to the state of things which eventuated here would be something which would be altogether out of the contemplation of either of the parties on which this contract was executed.

In my judgment this appeal ought to be dismissed, and dismissed with costs.

STIRLING, J.: I entirely agree, and I concur in the reasons given by Mr. Justice Wright and my Lord. I should only like to add this, that the greater part of the argument in support of the appeal is ultimately based on the language of clause 16 of the contract, and it is urged that a wide meaning, in fact, the widest possible meaning ought to be put upon the general words "other causes beyond the contractors' control," which are found in that clause after the enumeration of certain specific matters which are to bring the clause into operation. Now, I entirely agree with what has been said by my Lord, that in construing a clause of this kind, having regard to the peculiar powers which are to be given to the directors of the

1903
April 3.

Court of
Appeal.

defendant company, who in this case were the building owners, we ought to be very careful not to expand it beyond what we find therein expressed. The words "other causes beyond the contractors' control," may be read as wide words, or they may be read as referring to matters of a similar kind to those mentioned before, and it is always a matter of some nicety to decide which of these views ought to be taken as the meaning of the words. I should say even upon the clause itself, as my Lord has already said, that the narrow meaning ought to be applied, but I do think in this particular case that the matter is made almost clear by the subsequent clause 18, which is a clause which gives, in the case of delay on the part of the contractors in performing their part of the contract, power to the building owners to enter and complete the works, and from that is excepted first of all, delay on account of causes mentioned in clause 16, and then it goes on, "or in consequence of not having proper instructions for which the contractors shall have duly applied. Now, if the wide meaning which is contended for on the part of the building owners is to be given to these words, "other causes beyond the contractors' control," it would include not having proper instructions for which they had duly applied, and it seems to me that the language of clause 18 shows that that event was not meant to be included amongst the causes mentioned in clause 16, which immediately precedes it.

I therefore agree that the appeal ought to be dismissed.

MATHEW, J.: I am of the same opinion. I think there was abundant evidence here to justify the conclusion that the defaults of the defendants were such that they were inconsistent with their claim to insist upon completion within the stipulated time. That was the judgment of my brother Wright. I do not propose to go in detail through the evidence; but he had abundant evidence before him to justify the conclusion that the defaults of the defendants consisted, in the first place, in their not giving possession of the works as was contemplated by the contract, and in such time as would enable the contractor to complete within the year; secondly, that in the course of the works to the water-tower proper instructions were not furnished, that is, instructions contemplated by clause 18 to enable the contractor to go on in ordinary course with the work; and lastly, that the order in which the work was to be done was altered so as to delay the contractor. On all those grounds there is ample evidence in support of them, and I entirely concur in Mr. Justice Wright's conclusions on the question of fact. "But," says Mr. Bray, "it is all very well, and it would be an artful answer under other circumstances

1903
April 3.

Court of
Appeal.

than these to claim for penalties, but this is a contract in a peculiar form, and there was power here to do all that had been done by the defendants and their architect, without affecting their right to claim for penalties."

In the first place reliance is placed upon the language of clause 7, and that runs: "Any authority or order given by the architect for any additions, omissions, or alterations in or to the works, is to be binding on the contractors, and is not to vitiate the contract or the claim for penalties under clause 16." Mr. Bray said there was a postponement of the works, and there was a power to postpone for any time the defendants liked—it may be for a year or two years—and that would be an addition, omission, or alteration in or to the works within the meaning of clause 7. Really that is flying in the face of the language used, and in utter defiance of it. It is plain that what is meant by that clause is, not to provide for any alteration in point of time, but any alteration in the mode of carrying the works out. It is consistent, as I have said, with clause 18, and consistent with the specification.

Now, we turn to clause 16, which says: "The contractors are to complete the whole of the works within one year from the day of the date hereof, unless the works be delayed by reason of any alteration or addition in or to the works authorised as aforesaid." You cannot have plainer language as to what was contemplated—any alteration of the ordinary kind and the mode of carrying the works out. Then the clause goes on with reference to causes beyond the contractors' control. It appears to me to be those which are embraced by the subsequent part of that clause. There is no foundation whatever in the language of the contract for the suggestion that there was this unlimited power to alter the terms of the contract, and alter the time of its execution, which Mr. Bray is claiming. The penalties are intended to secure the performance of a contract according to its terms, and when a departure from the terms takes place by one of the contracting parties, in this case by the building owner, the claim by that building owner for penalties disappears as a matter of course, and as a matter of common sense.

Under those circumstances I entirely agree that the judgment of Mr. Justice Wright must be affirmed.

Solicitors for plaintiff: Mackrell, Maton, Godlee & Quincey.
Solicitors for defendants: Tyrrell, Lewis, Lewis & Broadbent.

1903
April 6.

King's Bench
Division.

1903
November 3.

Court of
Appeal.

𝔍𝔫 𝔱𝔥𝔢 𝕶𝔦𝔫𝔤'𝔰 𝕭𝔢𝔫𝔠𝔥 𝔇𝔦𝔟𝔦𝔰𝔦𝔬𝔫.

(*Before* RIDLEY, J.)

𝔍𝔫 𝔱𝔥𝔢 ℭ𝔬𝔲𝔯𝔱 𝔬𝔣 𝔄𝔭𝔭𝔢𝔞𝔩.

(*Before* COLLINS, M. R., MATHEW and COZENS-HARDY, L.JJ.)

WALLACE

v.

BRANDON AND BYSHOTTLES URBAN DISTRICT COUNCIL.

Building Contract—Payment—Certificate Condition Precedent.

A building contract provided "(1) The works shall be *completed* in all respects . . . . on or before the 16th day of December, 1901, to the *satisfaction of the surveyor* . . . . to be testified by a certificate under his hand, and in default of such completion the contractor shall forfeit and pay to the District Council the sum of one pound for each day during which the works shall be incomplete after the said time . . . . as and for liquidated damages. (4) . . . . the contractor shall be paid by the Council at the rate of eighty per cent. of the value of the work done in each month, and the balance one month after completion of the contract. Provided that the District Council shall not be required to pay to the contractor any sum exceeding the value as valued by the said surveyor or other officer of so much of the works as shall have been executed by the contractor during the preceding month." Held, that a certificate by the surveyor that the work has been *completed* to his satisfaction was a condition precedent to the payment of the retention money.

1903
April 6.

King's Bench
Division.

W. T. Wallace contracted, on September' 2nd, 1901, with the Brandon and Byshottles Urban District Council to construct an asphalte footpath. The contract contained the following clauses:—

(1) The works shall be completed in all respects and cleared of all implements, tackle, impediments, and rubbish on or before the 16th day of December, One thousand nine hundred and one, to the satisfaction of the surveyor or other officer of the District Council duly appointed in that behalf, to be testified by a certificate under his hand, and in default of such completion the contractor shall forfeit and pay to the District Council the sum of one pound for each day during which the works shall be incomplete after the said time, and the sums so forfeited may be recovered by the District Council from the contractor for and as liquidated damages.

(4) The price or consideration aforesaid to be paid to the contractor by the District Council shall be as follows:—[*here follow schedule prices*] and the contractor shall be paid by the Council at the rate of eighty per cent. of the value of the work done in each month, and the balance one month after completion of the contract. Provided that the District Council shall not be required to pay to the contractor any sum exceeding the value, as valued by the surveyor or other officer, of so much of the works as shall have been executed by the contractor during the preceding month, *and shall have been certified under the hand of such surveyor or other officer to the District Council to have been completed to his satisfaction.*

Mr. Wallace brought an action against the Council for 215*l.* 7*s.* 3*d.*, the balance of the contract price, which, he alleged, amounted to 1,105*l.* 7*s.* 3*d.*, 890*l.* having been paid on account. The Council set up that a certificate from the surveyor that the work had been completed to his satisfaction was a condition precedent to Mr. Wallace's right to bring an action.

The case came on before Ridley, J., and a common jury at Durham Assizes, and was adjourned, after a verdict for the plaintiff, for further consideration on the point of law whether a certificate of the surveyor's approval was or was not a condition precedent to the right to sue.

On April 6th, 1903, Ridley, J., gave his judgment, and held that clauses 1 and 4 of the contract did not make the certificate that the work was completed a condition precedent to the right to payment.

Macaskie, K.C., and E. Shortt appeared for the plaintiff.

Manisty, K.C., and A. Roche appeared for the defendants.

The defendants appealed to the Court of Appeal, in which Court the case was heard on November 3rd, 1903.

Robson, K.C., and E. Shortt appeared for the plaintiff (respondent).

Manisty, K.C., and A. Roche appeared for the defendants (appellants).

The Court of Appeal allowed the appeal, with costs.

COLLINS, M.R.: This case turns on the construction of a contract for work done. I think it was making a footpath for the local authority. The defence is that by the contract it was made a condition precedent to the liability of the defendants that there should be a certificate from the surveyor of the completion of the work. Mr. Justice Ridley has construed the document, and has come to the conclusion that there is no such condition precedent, and at the trial he overruled that defence and arrived at the conclusion that, owing to another clause in the contract certain certificates—interim certificates—that had been given by the surveyor were conclusive on the point, and that therefore no evidence was admissible to show, as the defendants contend, that the work in point of fact had not been done. The point is very small in itself, and it depends on the construction of the contract, which appears to me to be simple.

The agreement is dated the 2nd September, 1901, and it is between the plaintiff, Mr. Wallace, and the local authority. It goes on, "Whereas the contractor has agreed to execute the works hereinafter mentioned"—which are set out in the specification. "Now, therefore, the contractor for the consideration of the sums hereinafter named to be paid to the contractor by the District Council in the manner hereinafter stated, does hereby for himself contract and agree with the District Council and their successors that the said contractor will in a good, substantial and workmanlike manner, and with materials sufficient and proper of their several kinds, execute and complete all and singular the works and things mentioned or described in the

1903
April 6.
King's Bench
Division.

1903
November 3.
Court of
Appeal.

1903
November 3.

Court of
Appeal.

specification hereto annexed (hereinafter called the works) according to the said specification within the time hereinafter limited and subject to the conditions and stipulations following, that is to say"— then comes the first and most important—" The works shall be completed in all respects and cleared of all implements, tackle, impediments, and rubbish on or before the 16th day of December, one thousand nine hundred and one, to the satisfaction of the surveyor or other officer of the District Council duly appointed in that behalf, to be testified by a certificate under his hand, and in default of such completion the contractor shall forfeit and pay to the District Council the sum of one pound," and so on. That is a condition imposed upon the right of the contractor to payment on completion—that the whole of the works are by a given date to be completed to the satisfaction of the surveyor or officer, to be testified by a certificate under his hand.

It seems to me that that clause in itself makes the certificate under the hand of the surveyor a condition precedent to the contractor's right to demand payment upon the completion of the work. A few paragraphs further down we come to a special provision for interim payments: "The price or consideration aforesaid to be paid by the District Council to the contractor shall be as follows." Then come the provisions as to the freestone, gravel, asphalte, and so on, and the rates at which they are to be paid for; and then comes this clause which is relied upon by the defendants: "And the contractor shall be paid by the Council at the rate of 80 per cent. of the value of the work done in each month, and the balance one month after completion of the contract, provided that the District Council shall not be required to pay to the contractor any sum exceeding the value as valued by the said surveyor or other officer of so much of the works as shall have been executed by the contractor during the preceding month and shall have been certified under the hand of such surveyor or other officer to the District Council to have been completed to his satisfaction."

From time to time as the work went on a number of accounts were sent in by the contractor for work done, and those accounts were initialed by the surveyor, and payments were made of 80 per cent., 20 per cent. being retained as retention money. The time came when the contractor demanded the payment to him of the retention money— the 20 per cent. which had been withheld—and if he could have shown and produced the evidence which by the contract was made a condition precedent to his right to get it, if he could have shown that the work was now completed, evidenced by a certificate from the surveyor to that effect, of the entire completion of the work

1903
November 3.

Court of
Appeal.

to his satisfaction, he would have been in a position to sue. He comes without that certificate, and the point is taken directly on the pleadings, and it is pleaded as a condition precedent that he should produce a certificate of the surveyor's satisfaction, not with the work, but with the completion of the work. He comes, and there is no certificate that the work has been completed. He has a number of vouchers from the surveyor of the work done, but that is entirely consistent with the fact that there is a great deal more work to be done.

One cannot tell on those certificates whether or not the whole work has been completed to the satisfaction of the surveyor, and there is certainly not produced that which by the terms of the contract, in clause 1, is made distinctly a condition of his being entitled to sue for the retention money. That being so, how is that got over? In the pleadings it is simply traversed, that is to say, it is set out that there is no such condition, and that it was not a condition precedent, and that it would be open for him to say that, being a condition precedent, he has fulfilled it. But when it comes to the point, he admits there is no such certificate, and he does not give any excuse for not getting it. We have had some things suggested, but on the facts there is no evidence and there is no other issue raised than this: that being a condition for the benefit of the employer, it should somehow be dispensed with so that he would be entitled to sue. Nothing of the kind is contended for or suggested, but the construction of the contract is relied upon as showing that, though it comes in the forefront of the contract and seems *primâ facie* to be the most salient provision in it, it is not in point of fact a provision which has any relevance at all, because it is over-ridden by a subsequent clause which must be taken to be substituted for that which has been specifically provided in the first clause. The effect of the subsequent clause as to the interim payments has been to wipe clean out of the contract that which *primâ facie* appeared to be the most prominent. That is the construction which the learned judge has put upon it. I cannot myself agree with that construction. I think that the two series of certificates are not in the slightest degree inconsistent with the view which was expressed in *Morgan* v. *Birnie* (a), where the interim certificates give as complete an assertion, not merely that the work is done, but that it has been done to the satisfaction of the architect, as in this case.

The learned judge in that case said: "It appears to me that the effect of the certificate would be altogether different, applying to the manner in which the work has been done, while the checking of the

(a) 9 Bing. 672; 3 Moo. & Sc. 76.

1903
November 3.

Court of
Appeal.

accounts applies only to the propriety of the charges," and the same observation applies to this case. It is perfectly compatible with all those interim certificates being properly given, and according to the facts, as the initials would seem to authenticate, that the work was not completed to the satisfaction of the surveyor. The evidence to the contrary is wanting in this case, and therefore it seems to me that there must be judgment for the defendants.

MATHEW, L.J.: I am of the same opinion. It is quite clear from the earlier part of the contract that the work to be done was work specified in that document. The work according to the specification was to be done in a certain time, and payment was to be made on the certificate of the surveyor that the work had been done to his satisfaction. It appears that the work must have gone on, the surveyor had to be satisfied and payment was to be made, but there was a provision in the later part of the contract for payment by instalments. It seems to me that the contract is absolute and beyond question. Eighty per cent. is to be paid each month on the value of the work done; "at least one month after the completion of the contract," means completion of the contract, it appears to me, as certified by the surveyor. Then the contract goes on: "Provided that the District Council shall not be required to pay the contractor any sum exceeding the value, as valued by the said surveyor or other officer, of so much of the works as shall have been executed by the contractor during the preceding month, and shall have been certified under the hand of such surveyor or other officer to the District Council to have been completed to his satisfaction."

Throughout the course of the contract instalments had to be paid and the same condition attached, on the reasonable construction to be put upon this clause. In each case the surveyor had to certify. What happened subsequently was this—the work was done, and done from time to time, and the accounts were sent in initialed by the surveyor. The Council appeared to have been satisfied, and payments were made accordingly. I cannot regard those accounts signed in that way as any compliance with the contract terms. We now know that the work was not executed in accordance with the specification, and I cannot help thinking that if Mr. Gardner had been called upon to certify that the works had been done in accordance with this specification, he would have declined to do so. Therefore, I do not regard the certificates as amounting to anything approaching a certificate within the meaning of the contract. The Council were most precise in requiring that the approval of the surveyor should be established in one way, and in one way only, and that is by the production of a document

1903
November 3

Court of
Appeal.

under his hand and certified by him. Of course, the object of that is perfectly obvious. It is a common clause in all contracts of this sort, and the object is to prevent any controversy on a question of fact whether or not the surveyor has approved. "I must have the certificate. It must be established by the production of evidence." I should have thought it clear that these documents were not certificates within the meaning of the contract. But it is argued that no certificate was necessary. "Granted that the certificates are not granted in the form that is required by the contract, they are unnecessary." I am unable to accept that argument. If anything is clear in this contract it is that there should be a certificate, otherwise this extraordinary result will follow. The contractor sending in his account at the end of the month would be entitled to sue for eighty per cent. of it, and the District Council would not be protected in any way against the demand.

Then it was said that there was evidence that Mr. Gardner had modified the contract, and on that ground it was said: "Assume that, and then you may treat these different receipts as certificates, and then the plaintiff may arrive at his result."

The evidence is conclusive. Mr. Gardner had no authority to go beyond the terms of his specification, because there was that interview of October, where there was a slight deviation. The matter was gone into, and it was overlooked by the Council whom he was representing at the time, but imperative instructions were given that there should be no such departure in the future. What was done was an entire departure from the terms of the contract. It is said that there was some difficulty. The District Council called in Mr. Gregson to make an examination of the work, and to tell them whether or not the contract had been fulfilled. He did report, it is quite clear, that there had been very considerable departure from the contract, and evidence was given as to what that departure really involved, because as I understand, the plaintiff had the offer of an account taken on the principle of measure and value, and he declined it. It shows that the real value of the work done is far short of the amount according to the contract. In those circumstances I see no ground whatever for the decision of the learned judge. I am quite clear that the appeal must be allowed, and that the judgment of the learned judge was wrong.

COZENS-HARDY, L.J.: I agree.

Appeal allowed.

Charles Rogers, agent for Criddle & Criddle, solicitors for the plaintiff.

Cunliffes & Davenport, agents for J. G. Wilson, Ornsby & Cadle, solicitors for the defendants.

1904
May 13.

King's Bench
Division.

In the High Court of Justice (King's Bench Division).

PATMAN AND FOTHERINGHAM, LIMITED

v.

PILDITCH.

Bills of Quantities, part of Contract.

Where a building contract provides that the work is to be done for a lump sum "according to the plans, invitation to tender, specification and bills of quantities," the quantities are to be regarded as defining the amount of work included in the price, and if the contractor is required, in order to complete the work, to do more work than is in the quantities, he is entitled to be paid therefor an addition to the contract sum.

Trial before Channell, J., without a jury.

By a contract in writing, dated the 13th July, 1900, and made between the plaintiffs, contractors, and the defendant, who was an architect, the plaintiffs agreed to erect and complete fit for occupation a block of flats in South-ampton Row, Bloomsbury, in a good, sound, lasting and workmanlike manner, according to the plans, invitation to tender, specification and bills of quantities signed by the contractors, and within the time specified in and subject to the conditions thereto annexed, which said plans, specifications, invitation to tender and conditions had been prepared by the defendant, who was both architect and employer. The defendant had also taken out the quantities.

The material conditions were as follows:—

(1) The contractors shall supply everything of every sort and kind which may be necessary and requisite for the due and proper execution of the several works included in the contract, according to the true intent and meaning of the drawings, specification and quantities taken together, which are to be signed by the architect and the contractors, whether the same may or may not be particularly described in the specification and shown in the drawings, provided that the same are obviously or reasonably to be inferred therefrom without being actually expressed, and in the case of any discrepancy between the plans or drawings and the specification, the architect is to decide which shall be followed.

(3) . . . . The contractors to provide all plant, labour and materials which may be necessary and requisite for the works, all materials and workmanship being the best of their respective kinds, and the contractors to leave the works in all respects clean and perfect at the completion thereof.

(6) The contractors not to vary or deviate from the drawings or specification or execute any extra work or day work of any kind whatsoever, unless upon the written authority of the architect, to be sufficiently shown by an order in writing upon his printed order form, and such order shall state the extension of time (if any) which is to be granted by reason thereof.

(7) Any authority given by the architect for any alteration or addition in or to the works is not to vitiate the contract, but all additions, omissions or

1904
May 13.

King's Bench
Division.

variations made in carrying out the works for which a price may not have been previously agreed upon are to be measured and valued and certified for by the architect, and added to or deducted from the amount of the contract, as the case may be, according to the prices in the detailed bills of quantities upon which the tender was based, or where the same may not apply at fair measure and value, and the contractors for the above purpose to give into the hands of the architect a copy of their bills of quantities and prices in detail upon which the estimate was based, before signing the contract, and the arbitrator's decision in respect of the above shall be binding and final on both parties in event of any disagreement. No additions, omissions, or variations to be made, or will be allowed for, except such as have been authorised by the architect on one of his printed order forms.

(18) The contractors to complete the whole of the works and buildings complete and fit for occupation within fifty-two weeks from the date of the contract. . . .

The plaintiffs' claim was for the balance due to them pursuant to the contract, and the item in dispute was a sum of 1,669*l.* 19*s.* 10*d.* in respect of errors in the quantities, whereby their tender was less by that amount than it would have been (at the same prices) had the quantities correctly represented the work in the plans and specification.

The defendant denied liability for the errors in the quantities, which were assumed, for the purpose of the argument, to exist, though their existence was denied in the pleadings.

A. T. Lawrence, K.C., and Arthur H. Poyser, for the plaintiffs. The quantities define the *quantum* of work included in the contract price, and whatever is required beyond this must be paid for. *Williams* v. *Fitzmaurice* (*a*).

H. E. Duke, K.C., and A. Beddall, for the defendant. Whatever is necessary to complete the works as a whole must be done for the contract price quoted. *Ford* v. *Bemrose* (*b*), *Scrivener* v. *Pask* (*c*), *Sharpe* v. *San Paulo Railway* (*d*), and *Thorn* v. *Mayor of London* (*e*).

CHANNELL, J.: This matter is of course one of considerable doubt upon the construction of this contract. The bills of quantities are incorporated into the contract in an unusual manner. I have been referred to a statement of the Master of the Rolls (*f*), in which he said, dealing, I think, with the ordinary case of bills of quantities, that it was well understood, and that it had been settled in more than one case, that this document, the bill of quantities, whether it was embraced in and made part of one of the other documents, whether by being in the specification or by being scheduled to the contract,

(*a*) (1858), 3 H. & N. 844.
(*b*) Hudson on Building Contracts, Vol. II. 4th ed. p. 324.
(*c*) (1866), L. R. 1 C. P. 715.
(*d*) (1873), L. R. 8 Ch. 597.
(*e*) (1876), 1 App. Cas. 120.
(*f*) In *Ford* v. *Bemrose*, at p. 330.

1904
May 13.

King's Bench
Division.

or was a separate document altogether, was not, and was not intended to be, a report to be acted on in the sense of being a warranty. Now as regards all the instances which the Master of the Rolls gives, except as to being introduced into the contract, that of course is all perfectly clear, but he speaks in general words of it being introduced by, amongst other things, a schedule to the contract. He does not say in the contract itself; and if it is introduced into the contract it seems to me to be perfectly obvious that the operation of it depends upon the mode in which it happens to be introduced into the contract, because it is perfectly possible, although the thing is a bill of quantities, and has been prepared as a bill of quantities, for the ordinary use of a bill of quantities, still if the people like to incorporate that into their contract as a description of what the work is that is contracted to be done, they can do it, and therefore if you find it in the contract, you have to construe the contract simply, and say what it means, and in this case, as in almost any other case, if one has to deal with the way in which the Courts have construed other and different contracts from the one in question, it does not afford very much help.

I suppose every one understands by this time what a bill of quantities is, and how it comes into operation. It is prepared as a rule by some independent person, who, under a special arrangement that is made in such matters, takes the place of the builder's clerk, and if there were no such thing as the making out of a bill of quantities, when the plans were submitted to tender, each builder would have to do it himself, and have to pay his own clerk for doing it, but for general convenience it is done in a different way, and that man whose services, rendered before he, the builder, knows anything about it, are adopted by the builder in each particular case, stands very much in the same position, in fact in quite the same position, as if he had been originally employed by the builder to take out the quantities for himself, although he has been employed in fact by somebody totally different.

Now we have to see what is the true meaning of this contract so far as regards what is the contract work, which there is a contract to do for 17,000*l.* As a general rule, of course the contract work is described in plans and specifications. The bill of quantities is the estimate made by some outside person as to the quantity of work which those plans and specifications show, and, assuming that it is properly done, the work described in the bill of quantities and the works described in the plans and specifications would be identical. In this case the suggestion is—and for the purposes of argument,

1904
May 13.
———
King's Bench
Division.

and for the purposes of argument only, it has been admitted that they are not identical, and that there were very large discrepancies between the bills of quantities which were in point of fact made out, and what ought to have been the true bills of quantities upon the contract, plans, and specification.

Those being the facts the contract is entered into in this shape: "The contractor will substantially complete, &c., for the sum of 17,OOOZ.. the several works required to be done in the erection of a block of buildings on a site." If it had been left there it would have been of course absolutely and entirely indefinite. The next sentence is: " In a good, sound, lasting and workmanlike manner." That is the manner, and we have not yet got the particular description turning the indefinite block into some definite amount of contract work. Then there is: "According to the plans, invitation to tender, specification, and bills of quantities signed by the contractors." Now " signed by the contractors" grammatically, and in fact in this case, no doubt applies to all the thing, although I do not suppose the invitation was signed by the contractors. It may have been. But the plans were signed by the contractors ; the specification was signed by the contractors; the original bill of quantities was not signed by the contractors, but the priced bill of quantities which they gave in was. I think therefore that those bills of quantities signed by the contractors meant the priced bills of quantities. So far I think at any rate Mr. Duke is right.

Now the question is that following those words: " According to the plans, invitation to tender, specification, and bills of quantities," that is, following upon an indefinite description of the work to be done, you must find the description of the work that is to be done, the thing that turns a block of buildings indefinite into some definite block of buildings. You must find that somewhere or another in these words that follow: " The plans, invitation to tender, specification, and bills of quantities." But also we have in these four documents to find the mode of doing the work, because that has come just before in "a sound, lasting and workmanlike manner according to these documents." So that you would expect these four documents would do two things: (1) define what the work that is to be done is, and turn the indefinite "a block of buildings" into the definite block of buildings, and (2) would also contain the instructions as to the mode in which the work is to be done. You would expect to find both of those somewhere or another in the four documents. Now, are you to say that some are to be looked at for some matters and some for others, or are all of them to be looked at for both purposes? I think

1904
May 13.

King's Bench
Division.

if there is anything material in any one of them for either of the two purposes you must look at it for that purpose as well as for the other, that is to say, you must look at both. So far as they have got anything material to both purposes you must look at them for both purposes—to define the work and also to show the mode in which it is to be done. Now, for which purposes are you to look at the bill of quantities? The bill of quantities is the document which specially says, when you have got it incorporated like this, what the quantity of the work is to be.

Mr. Lawrence's argument is that I must deal with it in the same way as any contract or anything else we have to construe—that is to say, you deal with the specific things as overriding the general things and governing them, just as, even I think without a clause to that effect, in a contract you would say that figured dimensions override mere dimensions arrived at by taking the scale. It is usually provided for, and it is an instance of what you would do. Now, I think that there is great doubt about the way in which one should look at it, but on the whole I cannot help feeling that Mr. Lawrence is right in saying that if it was merely wanted to introduce bills of quantities for the purpose of showing the way in which the extras were to be priced, that was already sufficiently done by clause 7, and that it was unnecessary to introduce the words " bills of quantities " in the way in which it has been unless it was intended to make that, as the other documents with which it is coupled are, a part of the description of what the contract work was, and turning the indefinite block of buildings into some definite amount of work.

I confess that it is not the first time one has had experience of these building contracts, and I have always taken the view that when the bills of quantities were introduced (and I have seen one or two of that sort) in this particular way and made part of the contract it is for the express purpose of varying the usual effect of these bills of quantities and making them part of the contract, instead of a mere estimate of what it is. My view, therefore, not arrived at by any means without doubt, is that here so far as the bills of quantities and the plans can be put together and looked at as a thing in accordance generally with the plans and with the quantity of work shown in the quantities, so far as that is possible (and I take it that it is in these matters)—my view is that then the quantities provide the amount of the work, and if in the course of doing the work the contractor is directed to exceed that amount of work for the purpose of making it accord with what it is desired to have in regard to the building, I think that then that is an extra, subject of course to the further things in the contract as

1904
May 13.

King's Bench
Division.

to the mode in which it is to be done, and so on. I think therefore, on the whole, that it is incorporated into this contract as a part of the description of the contract work, and that therefore apart from any question of negligence which might possibly be, and which would have to be dealt with in a different shape, as I have said before, if the facts for that purpose only are admitted, the plaintiff is necessarily entitled to something beyond what he has been allowed. I say, therefore, that my judgment, subject of course to the reference, will be on the construction of the contract for the plaintiff.

Mr. DUKE: That would be a declaratory judgment, and I take it that the plaintiffs are entitled to recover as against the defendant for work included in the plans and specifications, but not comprised in the bills of quantities mentioned in the pleadings.

CHANNELL, J.: I am not sure whether that expresses quite exactly my view. My view is that the whole of the quantities are introduced into this contract as part of the description of the contract work, and that therefore if he is required, in order to complete the work, to do more work than is in the quantities he is entitled to have that as extra. That is nearly the same thing.

Mr. DUKE: The plaintiffs are entitled to have the work comprised in the plans and specifications, but not comprised in the quantities.

CHANNELL, J.: I think that must be so. But about the word "comprised" my view is that the plans do not go to quantity. I should not like myself to deal with all the cases in a general form like that. I am not by any means sure that there might not be cases of accidental omissions from the quantities: for instance, of a thing that might not be clearly specified in the plans and might not be part of the contract work, like the flooring in the case you cited. I do not mean to put it like that. I mean to say that where there is a quantity specified which may be a quantity of brickwork, for instance, that is the quantity to be done, and if in order to do a thing that makes the building in accordance with the scale of the plans you want to do more you are to be paid for it, otherwise it will be regarded as an extra. But I should have to deal specifically with the cases of things that everybody must understand are to be done, but which happen to be omitted in the quantities. I think the case (*a*) in Hurlstone and Norman would cover that.

CHANNELL, J.: If you and Mr. Lawrence can settle the form of the judgment between you I shall be glad, and if you cannot you will mention it presently.

(*a*) *Williams* v. *Fitzmaurice, supra.*

1904
May 13.

King's Bench
Division.

CHANNELL, J.: Upon the construction of the contract I decide that the bills of quantities are part of the description of the contract work, and that the whole of the documents must be construed together upon that footing.

The minute of the judgment was agreed. It declared that the bills of quantities were, and should be construed as forming part of, the description of the work contracted to be done, and as defining more accurately the amount thereof, and that the plaintiffs were entitled to be paid by the defendant, in addition to the sum of 12,338*l.* mentioned in the contract, for all such work done by them in carrying out the said contract as should have been omitted or understated in the bills of quantities.

There was no appeal, and the case was afterwards settled.

Solicitors for plaintiffs: Ford, Lloyd, Bartlett and Michelmore.
Solicitors for defendant: Booth & Smee, agents for FitzHugh, Woolley, Baines and Woolley, Brighton.

1905
January 30.

Court of
Appeal.

In the Court of Appeal.

(*Before* MATHEW and COZENS-HARDY, L.JJ.)

STRACHAN *v.* CAMBRIAN RAILWAYS.

Arbitrator declining to Act—Refusal to appoint Arbitrator—Power of Court to appoint Arbitrator—Stay.

By the general conditions of a contract, disputes were to be referred to the engineer for the time being of the company. A dispute was so referred, but after the first day's hearing, C., the arbitrator, declined to proceed with the arbitration, on the ground that he had resigned his post as engineer to the company, and was shortly to relinquish his duties. The contractor gave the company notice to appoint an arbitrator under sect. 5 of the Arbitration Act, 1889. The company declined to do so, contending that the new engineer was the proper arbitrator, he being the engineer for the time being. Held, that the power of the Court to appoint a fresh arbitrator arose at the moment when C. declined to act, and that the company was not entitled to a stay and reference to the new engineer.

In this case Mr. Strachan, who had contracted with the Cambrian Railways Company for the construction of a light railway in Wales, after the completion of the works, sent in a claim to the defendant company for various extras and other works, and not being able to come to any settlement with Mr. A. J. Collin, the engineer of the defendants, he, on April 18th, 1904, made a formal request to Mr. Collin, as engineer for the time being of the company, to arbitrate on the dispute under the arbitration clause in the contract, which ran as follows:—

"Any dispute which may arise under this contract shall, on the completion of the works and not before, be referred to Alfred Jones Collin, or other the engineer for the time being of the Cambrian Railways Company, and his decision shall be final and conclusive."

The engineer fixed a day for the hearing, and on that day partially heard the contractor's contentions. When, however, the contractor applied to the engineer as arbitrator to fix another day, Mr. Collin wrote on May 6th, 1904, saying that he could not continue the arbitration, and on the same day the company, through their general manager, informed the contractor that Mr. Collin had tendered his resignation as engineer of the company, and that Mr. G. C. Macdonald had been appointed to succeed him, and that that gentleman would take charge of the department as and from Monday next, May 9th. On the same day (May 6th), the solicitor for the contractor gave the company notice to concur in the appointment of an arbitrator under sect. 5 of the Arbitration Act, 1889, and suggested three names as arbitrators. On May 7th, the defendant company replied, saying (*inter alia*), that under the general conditions of contract Mr. Macdonald, as engineer for the time being of the company, would in the ordinary course become the arbitrator, and therefore they did not appoint any of the gentlemen named by the contractor.

On this a writ was issued by the contractor claiming, *inter alia*, the balance due under the contract, whereupon the company took out a summons to stay the action. The case came before Bray, J., in chambers, who refused to stay. The defendants appealed to the Court of Appeal (Mathew and Cozens-Hardy, L.JJ.), and the appeal was heard and dismissed on January 30th, 1905.

McCall, K.C., and J. R. Atkin appeared for the appellants (defendants).

Duke, K.C., and A. A. Hudson appeared for the respondent (plaintiff).

MATHEW, L.J.: I am of opinion that this appeal must be dismissed, on the broad ground that I do not think the clause is applicable to the circumstances which have arisen. The words of the clause are: "Any disputes which may arise under this contract shall, on the completion of the works and not before, be referred to Alfred Jones Collin, or other the engineer for the time being." When disputes arose as to either contract, those disputes were to be referred to Mr. Collin, or other the engineer for the time being. Mr. Collin was first designated, but Mr. Collin declined to act. Then what is to happen? Mr. Macdonald would have been the person to act if he had been the person designated. Mr. Collin had gone, and the next person, as I say, if he had been designated, would have been Mr. Macdonald. Certainly, when Mr. Collin declined to act, there was no arbitrator who could deal with the disputes arising in the arbitration under the contract. Having regard to the circumstances,

1905
January 30.

Court of
Appeal.

it seems to me that the reasonable and correct view is that the present engineer, Mr. Macdonald, was not substituted, and that there was no arrangement that he should act in lieu of the former engineer who declined to act because he said that he was interested in one of these light railways, and I assume he thought the common arrangement between the parties would involve the appointment of another engineer who was competent to deal with these matters of business.

The appeal must be dismissed with costs.

Cozens-Hardy, L.J.: I agree for the same reasons.

The appeal was accordingly dismissed with costs, and an order was made by consent referring all matters in dispute between the parties to an engineer as arbitrator.

Solicitors for plaintiff: Messrs. Batten, Proffitt & Scott.
Solicitors for defendants: Messrs. Le Brasseur & Oakley.

1905.
March 3.

King's Bench
Division.

In the King's Bench Division.

(*Before* Channell, J.)

In the Matter of an Arbitration between the URBAN DISTRICT COUNCIL OF WALTON-ON-THE-NAZE and THOMAS JOHN MORAN (trading as J. Moran & Son).

Building Contract on a Schedule of Prices—Discrepancy in Plans— Unpriced Work.

A contract was made for the construction of works, including "cast iron outlet pipe to low water," "as described in the specification and conditions and set forth on the drawings." The contractors also agreed to deliver a copy of the priced bill of quantities on which the tender was based. The general plan of the works showed the outlet pipe extending to low-water mark, but the section showed it as extending 279 feet further into the sea. The length of pipe in the bill of quantities corresponded with the length of pipe shown in the section, but there was no price fixed in the bill of quantities for under-water works. The contractor executed the work according to the section extending to about 279 feet beyond low-water mark, and claimed to be paid for the work beyond low-water mark at fair and reasonable prices for such work. Held, that the work done beyond low-water mark was not covered by any price in the contract, and that the contractor was entitled to be paid the price he claimed, the liability and not the amount being disputed.

1905
March 3.

King's Bench
Division.

The Walton-on-the-Naze Urban District Council invited tenders for certain sewerage works, to be constructed as described in the specification and conditions and set forth in the drawings signed by the engineers.

The specification was entitled, "Specification of works and conditions of contract for the construction of (*inter alia*) cast-iron outlet pipe *to low water.*" It contained the following material provisions:—

SEWERAGE.

(1) List of drawings:
No. 1. General plan.
No. 2. Sections of sewers.

(2) The sewers and works hereinafter described are to be of the lengths, to run in the directions, and to be of the inclinations, sizes, and constructions specified and shown on the general plan and sections for the general work, and such other drawings and detail drawings as may be supplied from time to time, and the several drawings are to be taken as referred to, whether or not specially mentioned in connection with any work or part thereof throughout the whole of the specification.

CAST IRON PIPES.

(27) The cast iron pipes from the outlet *at low water* to the esplanade are to have flanged joints . . . . .

BRICKWORK.

(49) The circular manhole on line of outlet pipes *to low water* is to have cast iron invert and cover plate (as per detail), with all necessary bolt holes, bolts, nuts, and washers.

SECURING OUTFALL PIPES.

(63) The levels of the outlet and tides are supposed to be correct, but the contractor is to verify these particulars if he thinks fit, as he will be responsible for all sea risk, and for any alteration in the surface level owing to the shifting of the sand or beach, as no extra price will be allowed for these contingencies.

(96). . . . Any increase or diminution in the quantity of work or materials herein specified or provided shall be added to or deducted from the amount of the contract agreeably to the rates specified in the schedule of prices for regulating such extra or diminished works, or as otherwise specified.

GENERAL CONDITIONS UPON WHICH THE WORKS HEREINBEFORE DESCRIBED ARE TO BE PERFORMED.

(1). . . . The term "works" [shall mean] any works shown on the plans, sections, or drawings, or referred to in this specification, together with any additional works which may be found necessary.

(9) In the event of this specification and the plans not agreeing, and any dispute arising therefrom, the engineer's decision with reference thereto shall be final and binding on all parties concerned.

(13) The contractor shall deliver to the engineers a true-priced copy of the schedule of quantities, which quantities shall be similar to those on which the estimate is based. It must be distinctly understood that the prices so given are to provide for every contingency that may be met with.

(16) The plans, sections, drawings, specifications, and quantities are to be considered as explanatory of each other, and should anything appear in the plans, sections, and drawings which is inconsistent or not described in the specification and quantities, no advantage shall be taken of any such omission, and the contractor is so to consider in submitting his estimate.

1905
March 3.

King's Bench
Division.

(17) Should any discrepancies appear, or should any misunderstanding arise as to the meaning or import of the said specification, the plans, sections, or drawings, or about the quality or dimensions of the materials, in the due and proper execution of the works, or as to the workmanship under this contract, or as to the extras thereon or deductions therefrom, the same shall be explained by the engineers, and their explanation shall be final and binding upon all parties, and the contractor is to execute the work in accordance with such explanation.

The material part of the schedule of quantities was as follows:—

CAST IRON PIPE OUTLET TO LOW WATER.

Reference to Letters on Plan.	Road, Street, or Field.	Size of Pipes.	Average Depth.		Lineal Yards.	Price per Yard.			Total Cost.		
			ft.	in.		£	s.	d.	£	s.	d.
A to B	Beach to Esplanade.	18	4	0	160	2	12	6	420	0	0
„	„ „	18	15	0	79	3	0	0	237	0	0
„	Fields	18	18	6	152	2	16	6	429	8	0
„	„	18	12	0	210	2	9	6	519	15	0
Item:	Allow for 15 tons specials(provisional).	. .	. .		. .	16	0	0	240	0	0

The general plan of the works showed the cast-iron outfall pipe extending to a point at low-water mark, while the section showed the pipe extending 279 feet further under the sea. The length of 160 yards mentioned in the schedule of quantities coincided with the length shown on the section. The engineers insisted upon the contractor constructing the outfall pipe to a point 279 feet beyond the point marked on the general plan.

Before executing any substantial amount of the works below low-water mark the contractor gave notice of his intention to submit his claim that this work was "extra" or "additional" to arbitration under the general conditions. On this the engineers gave the contractor formal notice under clause 17 of the general conditions. They explained the discrepancy between the plan and the section, in the sense that the 279 feet was within the contract, and included in the tender and contract price.

The contractor completed the work under protest, and then claimed 1,664*l*. 16*s*. 3*d*. for the alleged cost of carrying the outfall from the point shown on the plan to the point shown on the section.

The dispute was referred to arbitration, and the arbitrator stated his award in the form of a special case as follows:—

(a) If the Court be of opinion on the facts stated in the schedule hereto that on the legal construction of the contract I am bound to treat the carrying of the cast-iron pipe outlet seaward of the said point as work for which a rate is contained in the schedule of quantities and prices, then I award and declare that no sum is due from the Council to the contractor in respect of his claim.

(b) If the Court be of opinion on the facts aforesaid that I am entitled to treat the carrying of the cast-iron pipe outlet seaward of the said point as work for which no rate is contained in the schedule of quantities and prices, then I award that the sum of 1,664*l.* 16*s.* 3*d.* be paid by the Council, to the contractor within two months from the date of such opinion being given, with interest at the rate of 4 per cent. per annum from July 1st, 1902.

1905
March 3.

King's Bench
Division.

The special case was argued before Channell, J., on March 3rd, 1905.

Robson, K.C., and Ernest Pollock, for the Council, contended that the work in question was covered by the contract, and was work for which a rate was contained in the schedule of quantities and prices.

C. A. Russell, K.C., and A. A. Hudson, for Messrs. Moran and Son, argued that this being a schedule contract (as was conceded before the arbitrator) the only question for decision was the price at which the contractor ought to be paid for the work seawards of low water. Further, that the engineers had decided that he was under an obligation to execute the work seawards of low water, and the case for the respondents was the same, and therefore it followed that as there was no price in the schedule for such work the amount was at large, and the arbitrator had decided the amount, and that amount was what was due to the contractor. They also argued that if it had been a lump sum contract, and the contractor had omitted to insert a price in his estimate for work seawards of low water, the case would have been different, but the contract being a schedule one, the extent of the work to be done under the contract was immaterial for the purpose of this case, as the contractor had to be paid for the actual amount of work he did. If there was no price fixed in the schedule for any part of the work which he was bound to do, a price had to be fixed by the engineers. The Council, however, were willing that the arbitrator should fix, and he had fixed, the sum in his award accordingly.

CHANNELL, J.: I hardly like to say that this is entirely unarguable, because Mr. Robson and Mr. Pollock have succeeded in arguing it with an ingenuity which is very admirable, but really it is as plain a case as ever was possible to be conceived. There are difficulties in it, or, rather, there might have been difficulties in it. If only it were possible to find a schedule of prices for under-water work, then there would have been great difficulty. One would be met with the fact that the contract is described in every place in which it is described at all as a contract for the construction of sewers and a cast-iron pipe outlet to low water. Therefore it is a contract as to work on land, but, as to part of it, under water at certain times of the tides. That is work which I have heard described, and I think it is well described, as "tide work." It means work that, at some time of the tides, you can always get to without going under water—at some times of the tide—but work which will be covered at other times of the tide. This contract includes work of that character, and it includes work upon land. It is described in every place in which it is described at all as "to low water," and the operation of that obviously is that there is no point included in the contract which will not be uncovered

1905
March 3.

King's Bench
Division.

at some time of the tide. It is unnecessary to consider whether it means mean neap tides or whether it means spring tides or anything else; it is unnecessary to consider that in this case. All those would have created difficulties under certain circumstances, but it does not signify, as it seems to me, here.

Then there is undoubtedly a discrepancy between the section and the other documents, and there is in this contract that which one finds in most contracts nowadays—that the person who has prepared documents of that sort is to be the person to explain any discrepancy which may exist, and say which is to override—the one or the other. In this case, I think that, subject to the condition that he must not explain the discrepancy so as to entirely alter the whole character of the contract, which would have made a difficulty—subject to that, it seems to me that this discrepancy is a thing which the engineer could explain, and that, therefore, he could, in all probability, subject to that one difficulty about the entire contract apparently being for above-water work, explain it, and he could have put it into the contractor's contract. Then, when it got into the contractor's contract, if it had been a lump sum contract, he would have to do it for his contract price, and then there would have been difficulties and very considerable litigation undoubtedly, inasmuch as he would have been placed in a very awkward position by that.

But that does not arise in the present case for this reason, as it seems to me: The contract, when looked at, is clearly a schedule of prices contract merely, and the work that is in the contract has to be done at the prices specified in the schedule of prices, and according to the amount that may ultimately be required—more or less, according as he is required to do more or less, but at a schedule of prices rate only. Extras are to be also done, and to be done at the schedule of prices rate. Consequently, it is absolutely immaterial, in reference to any particular piece of work that he has got to do, whether he does it as contract work or as extra work, because in either case he has to be paid at the same rate—at valuation if no price is specified in the schedule of prices, and at schedule of prices if the price is specified Therefore it is quite immaterial whether it is in the contract or not, and all the difficulties which, otherwise, one might have had to deal with do not arise if there is in fact no price mentioned in the schedule of prices for under-water work. I think it is as clear as anything possibly can be that there is no price. The schedule of prices is not the contractor's schedule. The prices are the contractor's prices, but the schedule of what he is asked to specify prices for is the engineer's and the local body's, who are asking for a tender upon those terms.

1905
March 3.

King's Bench
Division.

They put what is in front in the document before me, the things which they require him to specify prices for, and, leaving out the things that are clearly and admittedly immaterial, the only portion of it which is material is, "Cast-iron pipe outlet to low water." That is in big letters at the top of a certain series of prices "to low water." Then "A to B, beach to esplanade, average depth four feet"—that is, at an average depth below the surface of the earth, not the surface of the water—"160 yards; and ditto, average depth below the surface 15 feet, 97 yards." That is all put as work that is above low-water mark, and, having regard to the fact that everybody cannot help knowing that prices must be entirely different for work that is to be under water at all times of the tide, it is absolutely impossible, even if there had not been this clause in it, about the dimensions not being as important—even if there had not been that clause there—it would have been impossible to say that that meant 160 lineal yards, a part of which is under low water. It could not be such a thing as that.

The result is that, supposing this contractor was a careful person, and supposing he did look at that section, and supposing that he did see that that section differed from all the other documents, and that it purported to put the outlet of this pipe some distance under low-water mark—supposing he saw that, he might have thought: "Dear me; I must go and ask the engineer about this. What am I to do?" And then, if he looked further at the contract, he would say: "It does not signify a bit, because I am not asked to specify for work of that kind. I am only asked to specify for land work; therefore I need not trouble myself about it." And I should think it is not at all improbable that that is what really, in fact, happened. I do not know whether this discrepancy is so very apparent on the section. If he looked at it at all, it is very difficult to say that he would not have noticed it; but if he did notice it, he would come to that conclusion: "Well, I am not asked to specify for under low-water work, and therefore I will not put my price for that, and if they want me to do it—I do not know whether they will—of course they will have to pay me for it, because there is no schedule of prices there for it."

The whole point really in this case is, Can you treat the 160 yards as overriding the express statement that it is only to low water? I am quite clearly of opinion that you cannot, and I do not think you could have done it if there had been no such clause as, in fact, there is, namely, that 160 yards is only the estimated dimension, which does not matter a bit. The one thing which you have to recollect is that it is an average depth of four feet, and that there will be about

1905
March 3.

King's Bench
Division.

160 yards. The 160 yards is only important to enable the contractor to see what price he will put upon a four-feet excavation for it. Of course, it makes a difference if you are only going down fifteen feet for a space of a foot or two; what you do a foot or two of that sewer for or what you do a substantial amount for, and it is only for the purpose of enabling him to put the price on that the 160 yards is material. It is a little material for that. It is not material when he is only to be paid for the amount that is done. I am quite clearly of opinion that there is no price mentioned in the schedule of prices.

That being so, it is entirely unnecessary to go into the other questions, which are questions of some difficulty. I assumed them rather in favour of Mr. Robson. I did not call upon him to argue them or to go into them. I accepted his argument for the purpose of the case, because he was unable to satisfy me that there was any price in the schedule of prices for the under low-water work. That being so, the award stands for the amount that the arbitrator has found.

Mr. Russell: With the costs of the special case?

Mr. Justice CHANNELL: Yes.

Solicitors for the contractors: Morris & Bristowe.

Solicitors for the Urban District Council: Gribble, Oddie, Sinclair & Johnson.

1905
March 28.

King's Bench
Division.

In the King's Bench Division

1906
May 10.

Court of
Appeal.

(*Before* KENNEDY, J.)

In the Court of Appeal.

(*Before* VAUGHAN WILLIAMS, STIRLING, and FLETCHER MOULTON, L.JJ.)

GEARY, WALKER & CO., LTD. *v.* W. LAWRENCE & SON.

Sub-contractor—Sub-contract subject to Main Contract—Retention Money.

L. contracted to construct a council chamber, &c. for the E. Urban District Council. G. was employed by L. as sub-contractor to do certain part of the work. The sub-contract provided (*inter alia*) that "the terms of payment for the work in question shall be exactly the same as those set forth in clause 30 of the said conditions of contract." Clause 30 of the conditions of contract was as follows:— "The contractor shall be entitled under the certificates to be issued by the architect to the contractor . . . . to be paid at the rate of 80 per cent. of the value of the work so executed in the building until the balance retained in hand amounts to the sum of 2,000*l.*, after which time the instalments shall be up to the full value of the work subsequently executed." When the works were practically completed and so certified by the architect 1,500 was to become due, 300*l.* more at the expiration of three months, and 200*l.* at the expiration of twelve months from completion. The whole cost of the work was about 35,000*l.*, and the amount of G.'s sub-contract was about 1,050*l.* After the completion of the work, K., the surveyor employed by the architect, wrote as follows:—"Mr. G. S. (the architect) desires me to say that he has been through your accounts in this case, and allowed the repairs to the terrazo in full, although he very much doubts the propriety of the charge, but that he entirely declines to allow the charge of repairs to woodblock flooring, which he says was badly laid in many places, and was continually complained of." L. retained part of the money payable to G. G. thereupon brought an action for the balance before the architect gave his certificate that the work was completed to his satisfaction. L. set up (*inter alia*) that clause 30 of the contract entitled him to do so, and that there was no certificate of the architect that the work was completed to his satisfaction. Held, that L. was justified in retaining a part of G.'s contract price proportionate to that retained from his by the council.

Lawrence & Son were employed on 23rd January, 1902, by the Edmonton Urban District Council to construct swimming baths, a council chamber, council offices, a postmortem room and a mortuary, in accordance with a specification and plans prepared by Mr. Gilbee Scott, F.R.I.B.A. There was a "schedule of conditions of contract," clause 30 of which was as follows:—

"30. The contractor shall be entitled, under the certificates to be issued by the architect to the contractor, and within fourteen days of the date of each certificate, to payment by the employer from time to time by instalments, when in the opinion of the architect work to the value of 500*l.* (or less at the reasonable discretion of the architect) has been executed in accordance with the contract, at the rate of 80 per cent. of the work so executed in the building, until the balance retained in hand amounts to the sum of 2,000*l.*, after which time the instalments shall be up to the whole value of the work subsequently executed. The contractor shall be entitled, under the certificate to be issued by the architect, to receive payment of 1,500*l.*, being a part of the said sum of 2,000*l.*, when the works are practically completed, and in like manner to a payment of 300*l.* within a further period of three months, or as soon after the expiration of three months as the works shall have been finally completed, and in like manner to payment of the balance of 200*l.* within a period of twelve months from final completion, and after all defects are made good according to the true intent and meaning hereof. The architect shall issue his certificates in accordance with this clause. . . . ."

On March 16, 1903, Messrs. Geary, Walker & Co., Limited, agreed with Walter Lawrence & Son to carry out all mosaic and other work . . . . "to the architect's entire satisfaction, orders for which have been or will be sent to us from time to time by the said Walter Lawrence & Son . . . . and the terms of payment for the work in question shall be exactly the same as those set forth in clause 30 of the said conditions of contract above referred to; and in fact we are willing and hereby agree to be bound in every respect

1905
March 28.
King's Bench
Division.

by the whole of the terms, clauses, and conditions as set forth in the contract dated 23rd January, 1902, aforesaid."

On the same date, 16th March, 1903, Geary, Walker & Co. wrote to Lawrence & Son a letter containing the following words: "We enclose agreement signed herewith. It is understood that we may obtain the balance of our contract in two months from completion of same, on certificate of satisfactory completion from the architect." Orders were from time to time given to Geary, Walker & Co., which they executed. The amount of these orders came to something over 1,000*l.* The amount of Messrs. W. Lawrence & Son's contract was 28,245*l.*, but extra works increased the cost of the work to about 35,090*l.*, of which 33,090*l.* was paid to them by instalments. Messrs. Lawrence & Son paid Geary, Walker & Co. 850*l.* by instalments, and retained the balance. On 12th May, 1904, Messrs. Geary, Walker & Co. issued a writ for 106*l.* 2*s.* 11*d.*, made up as follows:—

Credit—to work		£1,058	6	11
By payment on account	£850 0 0			
10 per cent. allowance (to contractor) as agreed..................	102 4 0			
		952	4	0
Balance due		£106	2	11

On 23rd September, 1904, Mr. Gilbee Scott gave his final certificate, which included work done by Messrs. Geary, Walker & Co. amounting to 1,045*l.* 12*s.* 11*d.* On this certain negotiations took place between the parties, and Messrs. Lawrence, by their solicitors, offered to pay Messrs. Geary, Walker & Co. 88*l.* 19*s.*, each side to pay their own costs. This offer was declined. By the Rules of the Supreme Court it was too late for Messrs. Lawrence & Son to pay the 88*l.* 19*s.* into Court.

The case was heard before Kennedy, J., without a jury, on 28th March, 1905.

Lewis Thomas appeared for the plaintiffs.

G. A. Scott appeared for the defendants.

Kennedy, J., held that clause 30 of the contract was practically incapable of being applied to the sub-contract, and gave the plaintiffs judgment for 88 19*s.* The defendants appealed, and their appeal came on for hearing before Vaughan Williams, Stirling, and Fletcher Moulton, L.JJ., on 10th May, 1906.

Eldon Bankes, K.C., and Lewis Thomas appeared for the plaintiffs (respondents).

J. A. Scott appeared for the defendants (appellants).

The judgment of Kennedy, J., was reversed, and judgment entered for the defendants, on the ground that the 88*l.* 19*s.* was not due and payable when action brought, because Lawrence & Son were entitled, by the operation of clause 30 of the contract as applied to the sub-contract, to retention money from Geary, Walker & Co. proportionate to that which the Urban District Council were entitled to retain under the contract.

1906
May 10.
Court of
Appeal.

VAUGHAN WILLIAMS, L.J.: I am so far glad that the outcome of this little discussion enables us to give judgment at once. If the

1906
May 10.

Court of
Appeal.

outcome had been different, and Mr. Lewis Thomas had contended that there was here a document which satisfied the final clause of the letter of March 16th, as being a certificate of the satisfactory completion from the architect, which certificate was given before writ issued, that is to say, before this action had been begun, I should have thought myself that he might have put himself in a position to say that the condition precedent had been performed, and that therefore this action was rightfully brought. But it is never any good to make a point in favour of litigants, which point the litigants themselves do not accept and really elect not to rely upon. Therefore, under those circumstances, we must treat this letter of March 16th, 1903, in the way Mr. Justice Kennedy treated it; that is to say, as not having qualified the contract in any way, being in no part a document which can be referred to for the purpose of the construction of the contract.

The state of things then is this: We have to look merely to the contract of the 16th March. That contract runs: "We, the undersigned, Messrs. Geary, Walker & Co., Limited, hereby agree and undertake to carry out all mosaic and other work at the town hall, baths, and council chamber buildings, Lower Edmonton, for Walter Lawrence & Son, of Canal Works, Waltham Cross, and to the architect's entire satisfaction; orders for which have been, or will be sent us from time to time, by the said Walter Lawrence & Son: the work to be carried out as and when required by them." For the present I will read no further in that contract, but it is manifest under the words of that contract, that the satisfaction of the architect expressed before the bringing of the action is not requisite; it is not a condition precedent to the bringing of the action, and under those circumstances one has to ascertain whether the plaintiffs here, looking at this contract by itself, have performed that which was necessary for them to perform. The contract goes on: "W further agree that no claim shall be made by us for any extras of any kind, unless the same has been ordered in writing by the said Walter Lawrence & Son, and that we will maintain in proper working order the whole of the work executed by us, until the expiration of the term for which the said Walter Lawrence & Son are bound by their employers under their contract dated 23rd January, 1902, and we will also indemnify them against any loss upon any question that may arise under clause 20 of the conditions of contract above mentioned, and the terms of payment for the work in question shall be exactly the same as those set forth in clause 30 of the said conditions of contract above referred to: and in fact we are willing, and hereby agree to be bound in every

1906
May 10.

Court of
Appeal.

respect by the whole of the terms, clauses, and conditions as set forth in the contract dated 23rd January, 1902, aforesaid."

With regard to that latter part of the contract, if the contract had been controlled by the letter of March 16th, I should have been disposed to say that clause 30 would have to have been read subject to this qualification that nothing in the contract should prevent the sub-contractors being entitled to obtain the balance of their contract in two months from completion of same on certificate of satisfactory completion from the architect.

Now, Mr. Justice Kennedy is of opinion that really it is impossible practically to apply at all events so much of this contract as incorporates clause 30 of the original contract to this case at all. I should hesitate very much to come to this conclusion, and under those circumstances it seems to me the proper way to apply this clause is to read this contract as applying *mutatis mutandis* clauses 20 and 30 of the contract as between the contractor and the sub-contractor. Clause 30 I have already called sufficient attention to. Clause 20 is of no very great importance, but it deals with the question of the employment of sub-contractors so far as between the building owner and the main contractors; and as far as it goes, the inclusion of that clause must mean that every part of this contract, including clause 20, is, as far as possible, to be applied as between the contractor and the sub-contractor. Under those circumstances I am not at present prepared, if this letter of the 16th March had been excluded, to say that the retention clause may not be applied as between the contractor and the sub-contractor in due proportions.

That disposes really of the case, because if the retention clause does apply then it is plain that so far as suing for the whole is concerned there was no right of action for the whole amount at the moment when this action was brought, which, if I remember rightly, was on the 12th May.

That leaves the question to be determined as to whether there has been work done in fact to the satisfaction of the architect. It is said, and I think rightly said, that if the satisfaction of the architect is not a condition precedent, then the plaintiffs may prove at any time up to the issue of the writ that the state of things was such that the work was really work done to the satisfaction of the architect, although he had not expressed that satisfaction. Great reliance was placed upon a letter of December 11th. I think myself that that letter ought to be taken as having been written by the desire, as it is expressed in the letter to have been, of Mr. Gilbee Scott, but I do not think it at all concludes the question as to whether the work had been done to his satisfaction. In my opinion at that moment it had not been. Under these circumstances I have to look elsewhere to try and see whether the work was done to the satisfaction of the architect at the moment when the writ was issued. One must bear in mind that the subsequent correspondence and documents really do show that the state of things was such as not to satisfy him.

Under these circumstances it seems to me, although it is not a condition precedent, yet if you read in these clauses in the contract, and I decline to say that they cannot be read in, the plaintiffs ought not to have the judgment which has been given in their favour.

Lord Justice STIRLING: I always regret to find myself differing from Mr. Justice Kennedy, but I have come to the conclusion that on this occasion his judgment cannot be upheld.

In the first place I agree with what has been said by my Lord, that *primâ facie* the covering letter of the 16th March, 1903, ought to be treated as introducing a new term into the contract which was accepted by the defendants by their making no objection; but as neither side desires in any way to rely upon the letter, it is far better, I think, that our judgment should not rest upon that, and I am quite content to proceed upon the formal contract of the 16th March, 1903. I need not read that again as it has already been read in full, but the question turns upon these words: "and the terms of payment for the work in question shall be exactly the same as those set forth in clause 30 of the said conditions of contract above referred to." It has been said that it is impossible to give effect to that stipulation. I am not persuaded of that. What are the terms of payment as they appear from clause 30 of the contract? First that the contractor, meaning there the main contractor, was to be entitled under the certificates to be issued by the architect to him, to payment by the employer by instalments (reading the material parts of it) at the rate of 80 per cent. of the value of work so executed in the building until the balance retained in hand amounted to 2,000*l.*, after which time the instalments were to be up to the full value of the work subsequently executed.

Now the contract, of which clause 30 is a part, was a contract to erect buildings at a cost of, speaking in round figures, 28,000*l.*, and 2,000*l.* was to be the fund which was to be kept in hand by the employer by means of deductions from the amount which appeared by the architect's certificate to be due. The sub-contract with which we have to deal was, in comparison, a very small contract. The whole sum which was to be received in payment was somewhere about 1,000*l.*, and obviously, therefore, literally the 2,000*l.* (if that is

1906
May 10.
Court of
Appeal.

read as being part of the contract) would make it impossible to work; but what the document of the 16th March, 1903, says, is not that clause 30 is to be read in its very language into that document, but that the terms of payment for the work are to be exactly the same as in that document.

Now one of the terms of clause 30 was that a sum of 2,000*l.* of 28,000*l.* was to be retained. It seems to me that the exactly similar term would be that a similar proportion of the 1,000*l.* should be kept in hand, and that the sub-contractor should from time to time receive from the main contractor 80 per cent. up to the time when the sum bearing the same proportion as the 2,000*l.* bears to the 28,000*l.* had been accumulated, and after that full payment.

Then that being the term as to the payment of the instalments the clause contains a provision as to how the 2,000*l.*, which was to be kept in hand, is to be dealt with. It provides that the contractor shall be entitled under the certificate to be issued by the architect to receive a payment of 1,500*l.*, being a part of the 2,000*l.*, when the works are practically completed, and in like manner to payments of a further sum of 300*l.* within a further period of three months, or as soon after the expiration of such period of three months as the works had been finally completed, and in like manner to payment of the balance of 200*l.* within the period of twelve months from final completion, and all defects were made good according to the true intent and meaning thereof. Having got over the difficulty as to the 2,000*l.*, it seems to me that there is no difficulty in saying that the stipulation that the term for the payment of the retention money should be dealt with in a similar manner; that the fund kept in hand should be divided into three parts, one of which bore the same proportion to the total retention money as the 1,500*l.* did to the 2,000*l.* Then the second part which would be dealt with would be a sum which bore the same proportion to the total amount of the retention money under the sub-contract as 300*l.* to the 2,000*l.*; and then there would be the ultimate balance ascertained. So far, it seems to me, that effect can be given to the contract; but then there follows this stipulation, which has created a considerable amount of difficulty to me, because there is a positive stipulation that the architect will issue his certificate in accordance with this clause.

Now, prior to this contract of the 16th March, 1903, the architect had positively declined to issue certificates to any sub-contractor under the main contract; and it does seem to me a difficulty which has to be met as to what the effect of that was on the stipulation. I think that both parties must have been aware of the course of business.

1906
May 10.

Court of
Appeal.

In fact Mr. Walker, who was called, really admits that, although he does not admit that he knew the details as to the distribution of the retention money. It seems to me that the proper way to read the clause in that case is to treat them as being satisfied to deal with the certificates, in accordance with which payments were to be made, as being those which were to be issued by the architect to the main contractor, and not to treat this clause as introducing a separate bargain for separate certificates between the main contractor and the sub-contractor.

That being so, if that is the true construction of the clause, it seems to me that the plaintiff failed to make out that he was entitled at the time when he brought this action to succeed in recovering the balance. This appears to me to be borne out by the whole course of dealing between the parties subsequently. The sub-contractor never made any objection to the deductions in fact being made at the time. They did not amount, it was true, excepting in the first place, to 20 per cent.; but 10 per cent. was always retained. Both parties were perfectly satisfied with that, and, of course, it was competent for the main contractor to waive his strict rights. No difficulty arose until the final application was made for the payment of the balance, the delay in which was caused, as it seems to me, by the delay on the part of the architect in giving to the main contractor a certificate which entitled him to any proportion of the 2,000*l*. which was outstanding.

I think it is plain, therefore, that the plaintiff fails to make out his case that he was entitled to payment of this balance at the time he brought this action, and on these grounds I think this judgment ought to be reversed.

Lord Justice FLETCHER MOULTON: I am of the same opinion. To obtain judgment for any sum of money on the ground that it is money owing to him, the plaintiff must show that it is due and payable at the date of the writ. In my opinion, in this case, the plaintiff failed to fulfil that onus which lay upon him.

The case arises from a course of business not at all uncommon. In almost all building contracts of considerable importance sub-contractors have to be employed by the main contractor, and it is usual, though not universal, to make the main contractor responsible for the whole of the work that they do, the architect keeping some control over the choice of sub-contractors who are to be employed. But the architect and building owner regard only the main contractor, and, unless he takes special precautions in his contracts with the sub-contractors, he finds himself often in the position that the architect's

1906
May 10.

Court of
Appeal.

certificate is absolutely conclusive both as to the date of payment
and the amount of payment, whereas his contracts with his sub-
contractors may leave him under the obligation to pay them before
he receives the money for the work that they have done. Accordingly,
it is not at all uncommon for the main contractor to make the sub-
contractor accept, in some form or other, obligations similar to those
which exist between him and the building owner. That does not
make the sub-contractor in any sense a party to the contract with the
building owner, but it makes the obligations towards the sub-
contractor more in harmony with those obligations which he has
taken towards the building owner.

In the present case the sub-contractor was fixed upon, part of the
work was ordered, even part of it was done, and a certain proportion of
the price was fixed upon, before the thorny question was settled as to
the extent to which the sub-contractor was to accept the conditions in
the principal contract. It seems that the architect was called in to
exercise his influence with the sub-contractor; at all events, on March
16th the parties met, and a memorandum of terms was drawn up which
the sub-contractor was willing to accept. These were reduced to writing
by the main contractor, and sent by him to the sub-contractor. The sub-
contractor signed them, and sent them back with a covering letter
introducing an additional term, which either had been omitted *per
incuriam*, or which had not been fully understood at the time between
the parties. The covering letter, and the memorandum of terms, was
accepted by the main contractor, and, if it were necessary to decide it in
the present case, I should have no hesitation in saying that that added
term was a term binding on both parties, but, whether we introduce it or
not, when we look at the terms which were drawn up, it is clear that they
do not make a complete contract in writing. For instance, there is no
stipulation as to price, although the contract contemplates work to be
yet ordered being executed under it. So one feels a good deal freer to
draw inferences from the conduct of the parties as to what was the
meaning of the contract, certain terms of which were reduced to writing.

For my own part, I have no difficulty in arriving at what the parties
meant by the written terms of March 16th. I agree that the terms in
that memorandum give considerable room for argument and discussion, but they would give very much less difficulty to a business man
than they would to a lawyer. One of the most important parts of a
building contract is the stipulation with regard to payments on
account. The amount of those payments and the extent of the balance
which is to be kept in the building owner's hands are things of vital
importance to contractors who, of course, are engaged, if they are in

1906
May 10.

Court of
Appeal.

a large way of business, on works many times the value of the amount of capital which even the richest contractor can hope to possess. Accordingly, these terms stipulate that the sub-contractor accepts terms of payment for the work in question exactly the same as those set forth in clause 30 of the conditions of contract. Clause 30 is the one clause which fixes the terms of payment, the interim payments, the amount of retentions, and the dates on which those retentions are to be paid. So that, as between business men, it meant that the sub-contractor was to be satisfied by payment from the main contractor just in the same way as the main contractor was to receive payment from the building owner.

If you look at the terms of clause 30 they do give rise to difficult questions, such as have been remarked upon by the President of the Court, and by Lord Justice Stirling, but, broadly speaking, those terms of payment are as follows: You start with deducting, for the purpose of retention, 20 per cent, from the value of the work executed, but you do not pursue that to the end of the contract, contenting yourself with letting it amount to something which is rather less than 10 per cent, of the total amount of the work; and that you consider sufficient to hold to the end of the work. I am satisfied that the parties meant that, broadly speaking, those terms of payment should be adhered to; and I am strengthened in this by an examination of the statements made out by the plaintiffs themselves as to the money due to them from the main contractor as this work proceeded. The earlier statement begins by a deduction of 20 per cent., but, if you go on, you find that the deduction in future is 10 per cent., so that the amount which is outstanding is something less than 10 per cent. of the total amount of the work; that is to say, just about the same proportion as would, at the end of the work, be outstanding between the building owner and the main contractor. So that it is evident that the conduct of the parties showed that they intended the system of payment to be substantially that which they carried out, and that the balance was to be in the position of the retention money under the principal contract.

Though I do not propose to decide this case by incorporating the added term to be found in the letter of March 16th, 1903, I may say that the added term strongly confirms my view that this is the proper interpretation of the contract, because it is a term insisted upon by the plaintiffs as one which they consider to be more in their favour than the terms of the contract of March 16th; and when you examine that added clause you see that it recognizes that there will be a balance unpaid at the end of the work, and that it stipulates that that

1906
May 10.

Court of
Appeal.

shall be paid within two months from the certificate of the architect, when the work has been satisfactorily finished. It therefore contemplated a balance existing at the completion of the work which was not to be paid immediately on the completion, but was to be paid two months after a certificate from the architect of satisfactory completion That absolutely negatives any suggestion that there is any implication of immediate payment. In my opinion the plaintiff was bound to show, either under clause 30, or under this added clause, if he accepted it and claimed that it should be added to the terms, that the period for the payment of this balance, which both parties agree was outstanding at the completion of the work, had then arrived.

Now, if we examine what passed at the trial, we find that the plaintiff made no attempt to prove anything of the kind. He treated it just as an ordinary case where there is an implication of immediate payment. He did not show that the balance was overdue, what proportion it bore to the original, whether or not it was in compliance with clause 30, nor did he attempt to show that there was any certificate of satisfactory completion by the architect made two months before he brought his action. In other words he did not produce any proof that the date for payment of the balance unpaid at the completion of the work, and which it was contemplated by both parties would remain unpaid at that date, had arrived. Therefore, he had not made out his case, and in my opinion the defendant was entitled to succeed.

Lord Justice Vaughan Williams: I want to say one word with regard to the letter of December 11th, because I am not quite sure that I said clearly what I meant to say, and therefore I have written it down shortly. I meant by what I said about the letter of December 11th to say that I did not think that it was such an expression pression of satisfaction as to dispense with the obligations of clause 30 as to payment on account by instalments and retention moneys.

The appeal was allowed with costs.

Solicitor for plaintiffs: G. Munro Miller.
Solicitors for defendants: Mackrell, Maton, Godlee, & Quincey.

𝕴𝕟 𝕿𝖍𝖊 𝕳𝖎𝖌𝖍 𝕮𝖔𝖚𝖗𝖙 𝖔𝖋 𝕵𝖚𝖘𝖙𝖎𝖈𝖊.

(*Before* BIGHAM, J.)

𝕴𝕟 𝕿𝖍𝖊 𝕮𝖔𝖚𝖗𝖙 𝖔𝖋 𝕬𝖕𝖕𝖊𝖆𝖑.

(*Before* COLLINS, M.R., COZENS-HARDY and FARWELL, L.JJ.)

1905
November
15.

King's Bench
Division.

1906
December 11.

Court of
Appeal.

BYWATERS & SONS *v.* CURNICK & CO.

Contract—Bonus—Prevention—Damages.

B. tendered, on January 29th, 1903, to do certain alterations to C.'s restaurant for the sum of 12,395*l.* At an interview, on February 4th, between B. and C. the tender was accepted. Simultaneously it was agreed as follows:—"That in consideration of B. undertaking to give possession of the basement and ground floor within nine weeks from the commencement, C. would pay to B. the sum of 360?. as a bonus." This agreement was confirmed by B. by letter of February 4th. B. began to work on February 11th, 1903, but was at once stopped, as C. had not made arrangements with the occupier of the adjoining house as to interfering with a party wall. B. was unable to resume working until March 3rd, when a party wall award was made. Possession of the ground floor was given on May 16th. C. paid the 12,395*l.*, but refused to pay the 360*l.* Held, that there was such a prevention by C. of B. earning the 360*l.* as to entitle B. to damages, and that, as no attempt had been made at the trial to quantify the damages, a judgment giving to B. 360*l.* as damages must be upheld.

Curnick & Co. and Mr. Oddenino, being desirous of having certain alterations made in a restaurant known as the Imperial Restaurant, Messrs, Bywater and Sons, on January 29, 1903, tendered to do the work for the sum of 12,395*l.* On February 4, 1903, an interview took place, at which were present Mr. Oddenino, Mr. Robinson, his architect, and Mr. Gregory, who was Messrs. Bywaters' estimating clerk and surveyor. Mr. Oddenino said: "I don't care when the whole is completed, but I must have the ground floor and basement in nine weeks."

Mr. Gregory consented to this on behalf of Messrs. Bywaters, and wrote the following letter at Mr. Robinson's dictation: "Referring to our conversation with Mr. Oddenino this day, we understand that, in consideration of our undertaking to give him possession of the basement and ground floor within nine weeks from date of commencement, he agrees to allow us 40*l.* per week for the whole of this period as a bonus, or a total of 360*l.*"

Messrs. Bywaters began to work on February 11th, 1903, but on the next day, February 12th, it appeared that the employers had not obtained an award under the London Building Act, so as to entitle Messrs. Bywaters to deal with a party wall. In consequence of this Messrs. Bywaters had practically to stop working until March 3rd, 1903, when the award was obtained.

Messrs. Bywaters gave possession of the ground floor on May 16th, 1903.

1905
November
15.

King's Bench
Division.

The remainder of the works were subsequently completed, and the employers paid to Messrs. Bywaters what was due under the contract, with the exception of the 360*l*.

On December 27th, 1904, Messrs. Bywaters issued a writ against Messrs. Curnick & Co. and Mr. Oddenino, claiming the 360*l*. The material parts of the statement of claim were as follows:—

1. On or about the 4th day of February, 1903, the defendants requested the plaintiffs to execute certain work described in a tender of the plaintiffs dated the 29th day of January, 1903.

2. The said work was to be done for the sum of 12,755*l*., and expedition was to be used so that possession of the basement and ground floor should be given by the plaintiffs within nine weeks of the work being started.

3. The plaintiffs duly started the said work, as far as they were allowed by the defendants so to do, on or about the 11th day of February, 1903, and used great expedition; but owing to delays and interferences caused by the defendants they were unable to give possession of the basement and ground floors until the 16th May, 1903. Particulars of delay and interference are delivered herewith.

4. The plaintiffs have been paid the sum due to them in respect of the work in paragraph 1 mentioned, except the sum of 360*l*., which the defendants refuse to pay.

5. (*This paragraph was not in the result material.*)   A. A. Hudson.

Particulars of delay and interference were also delivered.

DEFENCE.

1. The defendants admit that the plaintiffs did do work for them in the year 1903, but say that the amount agreed to be paid the plaintiffs for such work was 12,395*l*., and not 12,755*l*. as alleged in the statement of claim. The said amount of 12,395*l*. is specified in the tender of the plaintiffs, dated January 29th, 1903, and which tender was sent to the defendants by the plaintiffs, as showing the price at which they would do the said work.

2. The plaintiffs have been duly paid by the defendants all the sums which have been certified for by Mr. Robinson, the architect superintending the said work, as being due and owing from the defendants to the plaintiffs, and there is now no sum whatsoever due from the defendants to the plaintiffs in respect of the work alleged in the statement of claim to have been done by the plaintiffs for the defendants.

3. The defendants do not admit that any contract was made between the plaintiffs and the defendants whereby the defendants were to pay to the plaintiffs 12,755*l*.?, or that the defendants were to pay any sum for expedition, or that the plaintiffs used special expedition in reference to the works so executed, or that the plaintiffs did extra work or rendered extra services to the value of 360*l*., as alleged in paragraphs 2, 4 and 5 of the statement of claim.

4. The defendants do not admit that they requested the plaintiffs to use more expedition than under the tender of the plaintiffs, dated January 29, 1903, the plaintiffs were bound to use in the execution of the works which they were doing for the defendants.

5. The plaintiffs did not complete the work in reference to the said ground

floor and basement, and give complete possession of the said floors to the defendants, until May 16th, 1903, and the plaintiffs did not do the said work within nine weeks of the said work being started.

6. The defendants do not admit that there were delays and interferences caused by the defendants which prevented the plaintiffs giving possession until May 16th, 1903, as alleged in the statement of claim. The defendants do not admit that any of the delays or interferences set out in the particulars to paragraph 3 ever occurred, or that they interfered with or delayed the work being done by the plaintiffs on the basement and ground floors.

7. Except as hereinbefore admitted, the defendants deny each and every of the allegations alleged in the statement of claim.

MORTON W. SMITH.

The case was tried on November 15th, 1905, before Bigham, J., who gave judgment for the plaintiffs for 360*l.* with costs.

Mr. A. A. Hudson appeared for the plaintiffs.

Mr. Morton W. Smith appeared for the defendants.

The defendants appealed, and their appeal was heard before Collins, M.R., and Cozens-Hardy and Farwell, L.JJ., on December 11, 1906.

C. A. Russell, K.C., and A. A. Hudson, appeared for the plaintiffs.

C. Montague Lush, K.C., and Morton Smith, appeared for the defendants.

The appeal was dismissed with costs.

*1905
November
15.*

*King's Bench
Division.*

*1906
December 11.*

*Court of
Appeal.*

Judgment.

COLLINS, M.R.: This is an appeal from a decision of Mr. Justice Bigham upon a question as to the rights between certain parties to a building contract. The plaintiff here is a builder, and he made a contract with the defendants for certain alterations in their premises. The defendants were very anxious that these alterations should be made as soon as possible. Accordingly, after the main contract had been made, a collateral arrangement was made between the parties, which was expressed in a letter of the 4th February written by the plaintiffs to the defendants:—"Dear Sir,—Referring to our conversation with Mr. Oddenino"—that is one of the defendants—"this day, we understand that, in consideration of our undertaking to give you possession of the basement and ground floor within nine weeks from the date of commencement, he agrees to allow us 40*l.* a week for the whole of this period as a bonus, or a total of 360*l.*" That letter is treated as expressing the bargain between the parties, and upon it the action is brought.

The builder claims that the defendants interfered with his work in this way: they did not give him an opportunity of beginning

1906
December 11.
Court of
Appeal.

and going on with the work so as to make it possible for him to earn this extra sum by completing the work within a period of nine weeks, and his case is that it was due to their delay that he was disabled from completing it, and therefore he claims what is technically a claim for damages, but which he measures at the full amount of the 360*l.*, and I do not see that any attempt was made at the trial to quantify the damages or to reduce them in any way, if damages were recoverable. It was strenuously contended by the defendants that they were not in any sense responsible for the failure of the plaintiffs to complete within the time, so that the question as to whether there was any other measure of damages than the whole sum does not seem to have been raised by the defendants or fought out at the trial.

The relevant facts are these:—Possession was given by the building owners to the builder on, I think, the 10th or 11th February. That is a common factor between the parties, and it was admitted at the trial in terms, but on the very day after, when the builder did take possession and began to do the work, it was found that there was a difficulty about a party wall which had to be dealt with in the building operations, and as to which the necessary proceedings had not been taken; at all events, they had not resulted in an arrangement which enabled the builder to deal with the property, and therefore his work, which had been begun, was suspended during the time that the proceedings were going on under the statute as to the arrangement about the party wall which resulted in an award. Those proceedings occupied until the 3rd March, with the result that it became quite impossible for the builder to complete the work within the nine weeks stipulated, and that delay was due to the default of the building owners, who had not put it in the power of the builder to carry out his contract.

Under those circumstances, the plaintiff claims that he is entitled to damages by reason of being prevented from earning his money by the acts for which the defendants were responsible, and that was the main point discussed at the trial; and the learned judge came to the conclusion—indeed, I do not think there has been any dispute about the facts in the matter—that the plaintiff was right in saying that the reason why he had not handed over this building completed within the time was because he was prevented by the failure on the part of the defendants to put him in a position to carry on the work. The learned judge adopted that view, but he was then invited to go into an alternative view, I think chiefly at the instance of the defendants, who contended very strenuously that the true date at

1906
December 11.

Court of
Appeal.

which the contract rights ought to be ascertained was not the 10th or 11th February, but a later date in March.

Even upon that alternative, and treating the 4th March, I think it was, as the date on which the rights of the parties had to be ascertained, the learned judge came to the conclusion, even on that hypothesis, that the defendants had after that date intervened or interfered with the carrying on of the work by the plaintiff in such a way as to again prevent him, even from that date, completing the work within the nine weeks. An argument has been raised upon that question before us to-day. It seems to me that there is rather more difficulty upon that part of the case. I am not at all prepared to say that Mr. Justice Bigham was not right on that part of it also, but it is enough for me to say that it is unnecessary for us to consider the rights of the parties on that hypothetical case, that is, that the rights are to be measured on the footing that the obligations under the contract did not begin until the 3rd or 4th March. It seems to me unnecessary to deal with that, because, in my opinion, the learned judge, upon the first part of the case, was perfectly right: there was a default on the part of the defendants which prevented the plaintiff from earning his money.

I agree, strictly speaking, that that is an action for damages; it seems to have been treated rather as an action for a specific sum of money, but I see no reason myself to suppose that the true measure of damages was not in this case the whole sum which the plaintiff says he lost by reason of the failure of the defendants to enable him to earn his money. As I say, no point was really fought at the trial to attempt to quantify or limit the damages to something else.

Under these circumstances, it seems to me that we cannot interfere with the decision of the learned judge, and that this appeal must be dismissed.

Cozens-Hardy, L.J.: I agree.

Farwell, L.J.: I agree.

Mr. C. A. Russell: The appeal will be dismissed with costs?

Collins, M.R.: Yes.

Solicitors for the plaintiffs: Tyrrell, Lewis, Lewis & Broadbent.
Solicitors for the defendants: Allen & Son.

1905
May 29.

King's Bench
Division.

1906
July 10.

Court of
Appeal.

𝔍𝔫 𝔱𝔥𝔢 𝕶𝔦𝔫𝔤'𝔰 𝕭𝔢𝔫𝔠𝔥 𝕯𝔦𝔳𝔦𝔰𝔦𝔬𝔫.

(*Before* DARLING, J., without a Jury.)

𝔍𝔫 𝔱𝔥𝔢 ℭ𝔬𝔲𝔯𝔱 𝔬𝔣 𝔄𝔭𝔭𝔢𝔞𝔩.

(*Before* LORD ALVERSTONE, L.C.J., GORELL BARNES, President, and
FARWELL, L.J.)

FELTON *v.* WHARRIE.

Building Contract—Forfeiture—Delay—Liquidated Damages.

F. contracted to pull down certain houses for W. within fortytwo working days from
the time when he should be admitted on the site. He was to be paid 75*l.* for the work,
and was to be entitled to have for his own use all materials pulled down. In the event of
the work being delayed, F. was to pay to W. 1*l.* for every working day the work was
delayed. The work was in fact delayed, and some time after the expiration of the time
limited by the contract for completion of the work W. complained of F.'s delay, when
F. said that he could not tell if the work would be completed in four months. A
fortnight after this interview W. forcibly took possession of the site, and employed
another contractor to complete the work. F. had paid a deposit of 100*l.* to W. for the
due fulfilment of the contract. F. brought an action to recover the 100*l.* deposit, and for
damages for breach of contract. Held, that W. had no right to determine the contract,
and that F. was entitled to the return of the deposit, the contract price, and damages
for lost profit on the unfinished balance of the contract. Held, also, that W. was not
entitled to liquidated damages accruing after the date of his taking possession.

1905
May 29.

King's Bench
Division.

On June 15th, 1904, Alfred William Felton agreed with Thomas Wharrie to
pull down all the houses and buildings on a site in Great Portland Street in
consideration of a sum of 75*l.* and the materials pulled down. The contract
further provided that the contractor should erect a sufficient hoarding, which
was to become the property of the employer on the completion of the work.
Clauses 10 and 11 of the contract ran as follows:—

(10) The contractor hereby also agrees that he will, within fortytwo working days
from the time he is admitted on to the site or ground for the purpose of such pulling
down, completely clear and remove all materials and rubbish from off the said site
unless prevented by accident, weather, strikes of workmen, or other reasonable cause,
in which case the surveyors of the employer shall have power to extend the time.

(11) And also will, in case the said works shall not be completed on or before the last
day of the abovementioned period of fortytwo working days, save as aforesaid, pay to
the employer as and for liquidated and ascertained damages incurred by such default,
the sum of 1*l.* per working day for every subsequent working day until the said work
shall be completely finished.

The contractor was admitted on the site about June 16th or 20th, and did
about threequarters of the work. On August 16th he had an interview

1905
May 29.

King's Bench
Division.

with Mr. Wharrie's solicitors, who complained of the delay, and said,"Will it take one month, two months, three months, four months ?" The contractor replied, "I cannot say." On August 29th Mr. Wharrie forcibly took possession and put in another contractor to complete the work.

Mr. Felton brought an action against Mr. Wharrie, claiming the return of his deposit and damages for breach of contract. The defendant alleged that the plaintiff had said, on August 16th, that he could not complete the work for four months, and thereby refused to carry out his contract; and that consequently he had employed another contractor, who charged 300*l.* to do the work; and counterclaimed 125*l.*, being the 300*l.* less 75*l.*, the contract price of the work, and 100*l.* deposit, and also damages for delay. The plaintiff replied, alleging that the delay was caused by the defendant, and denying the defendant's right to terminate the contract.

The case came before Darling, J., on May 29th, 1905.

Cababe appeared for the plaintiff, and Lord Coleridge, K.C., and McLeod for the defendant.

DARLING, J.: I have come to this conclusion: I find that the plaintiff did not go on reasonably with the work. I concede that there was a little delay on the defendant's part, but I find that the plaintiff was in no way hindered after the 22nd June. He ought, therefore, to have finished by the 12th August. The plaintiff told the defendant that he could not finish in less than four months. This was so unreasonable, and such a nonperformance of the contract, as entitled the defendant to determine it and to employ another contractor. The work was finished on the 22nd September; calculating the delay for which the plaintiff owes 1*l.* a day, from the 12th August, he would owe the defendant, deducting Sundays, 36*l.* So much for the facts. Now I hold that the defendant is entitled to judgment on the claim, because the contract was broken, and the plaintiff cannot recover, therefore, the 75*l.*; I hold further that the defendant is entitled to damages for breach of contract, because the contract was broken. I fix those damages at 36*l.*, which is the same amount as would be due for delay if the contract had not been determined but had been completed by the 22nd September. I do not give them as liquidated damages, because liquidated damages contemplate that the contract continues, but that the 1*l.* a day becomes payable for each day over and above the fortytwo days. As the contract was broken by the plaintiff, I hold that the defendant is entitled to keep the deposit of 100*l.*, for the reason that the contract was broken, and that the 100*l.* is deposited as a guarantee or security for the performance of the contract. Therefore there will be judgment for the defendant on the claim, and on the counterclaim there will be judgment for 36*l.* It is not necessary to say anything about the 100*l.* in the judgment.

1906
July 10.

Court of
Appeal.

The plaintiff appealed, and the case came before the Court of Appeal, consisting of Lord Alverstone, L.C.J., Gorell Barnes, Pres. P. D. and A. Div., and Farwell, L.J., on 10th July, 1906.

Cababe appeared for the appellant (plaintiff); and Lord Coleridge, K.C., and McLeod for the respondent (defendant).

The Court allowed the appeal; the judgments were as follows:—

Lord Aleverstone, L.C.J.: There really is no dispute at all to my mind about the principle of law applicable to this case. The deposit has been paid, and I quite agree, that if the circumstances justify the defendant saying that the plaintiff repudiated the contract, the money would remain in the defendant's hands.

It seems to me, with great deference to the learned Judge of the Court below, that there really is no evidence at all to justify the defendant in assuming that the plaintiff would not, or could not, carry out the contract. Now the delay was contemplated as a possibility. Nobody denies that, nor could they, because there is a penalty clause which applies if the work is not done within fortytwo days. What happened was this: It was a bad job, apparently, and there was delay up to the 16th of August, and there was a remonstrance by the defendant to the plaintiff. I should think, in all probability (knowing the class of man we are dealing with), that the statement which the plaintiff made to the defendant was not as wise as it might have been—at any rate, it was not a sufficiently candid statement as to when the work would be completed. The defendant let him go on, according to the evidence (I am only speaking of that), without a word of warning to him; he allowed him to continue the work from the 16th of August to the 29th, a period of two weeks. Then, without any further notice, he came and took it away altogether, and refused to allow him to continue. It seems to me impossible to suggest that he was justified in doing that under any clause in the contract. If he were going to act upon the plaintiff's conduct as being evidence of his not going on, he ought to have told him of it, and to have said, "I treat that as a refusal," and the man would know of it; but the fact of allowing him to go on cannot be any evidence of justification of re-entry on the 29th.

I think, taking the rule most strongly against the plaintiff, the defendant failed to give any evidence that the plaintiff had so conducted himself as to show that he would not complete his contract. That being so, I think the turning out was wrong. That would entitle the plaintiff to 75*l.*, and to the 100*l.* deposit. As regards the unfinished balance of the contract, there would be some profit, and I am going to take 50*l.* for the amount of that. That would make altogether a

1906
July 10.

Court of
Appeal.

sum of 225*l*. I think it is quite plain that the defendant would not be entitled to have any penalty, or damages in the nature of a penalty, after the 29th of August. I am not quite clear, in my own mind, that he may not be entitled to have some claim in respect of the delay up to that time, but that is a very small matter. We think that if a sum of 210*l*. were & paid to the plaintiff it would be a proper judgment between the parties.

The PRESIDENT: I agree. I think there is no evidence in this case of any renunciation on the part of the plaintiff which would operate as a rescission of the contract so that the other party might adopt the renunciation and put an end to the contract. That being so, I think the position of the parties is that which has been indicated by my Lord.

Lord Justice FARWELL: I agree. I have nothing to add.

Solicitor for plaintiff: W. R. J. Hickman.
Solicitors for defendant: McMillan and Mott.

𝔍n the Court of Appeal.

1909
July 29.

Court of
Appeal.

ROBERT W. BLACKWELL & CO., LTD. *v.* THE MAYOR, ALDERMEN AND BURGESSES OF THE BOROUGH OF DERBY.

Arbitration Act, 1889, s. 4—Summons to stay—Questions to be tried—Conduct of Arbitrator as to such Questions.

In cases where, subsequent to the signing of a contract in which the engineer is arbitrator, there are allegations of continued *unreasonableness* on the part of such arbitrator, and that is the real dispute between the parties, there is sufficient reason (under sect. 4 of the Arbitration Act) why the matter should not be referred to him.

Appeal by R. W. Blackwell & Co., Ltd., from an order of the judge in chambers ordering the action to be stayed under a submission to arbitration contained in a contract between the parties.

By a contract in writing, dated the 15th of February, 1907, the company agreed to lay certain tramways for the Derby corporation. During the course of the work there was much friction between the company and the borough surveyor who was arbitrator under clause 43 of the contract, which was as follows:—

43. That in case of any doubts, disputes, or differences arising or happening, touching or concerning the said works or any of them, or relating to the

quantities, qualities, description or manner of work done and executed, or to be done and executed, by the contractor, or to the quantity or quality of the materials to be employed therein, or in respect of any additions, enlargements, deductions, alterations, substitutions, or deviations made in, to, or from the said works or any part of them, or the value thereof, or touching or concerning the meaning or intention of this specification, or of any part thereof, or of the contract entered into by and between the corporation and the contractor, or of any plans, drawings, instructions or directions referred to in this specification or the contract, or which may be furnished or given during the progress of the works, or touching or concerning any certificate, recommendation, order or award which may have been made by the engineer, or in anywise whatsoever relating to the interests of the corporation or of the contractor in the premises, *such doubts, disputes, or differences shall from time to time be referred to and be settled and decided by the engineer, who shall be competent to enter upon the subjectmatter of such doubts, disputes, or differences with or without formal reference or notice to the parties to the contract, or either of them, and who shall judge, decide, order, and determine thereon,* and that whether the contract be then existing, completed, or determined; and who shall have full power and authority to correct or amend any clerical or verbal inaccuracy in such contract, or in any certificate, recommendation, order, or award made by him in relation thereto, and if and when necessary to supply the deficiency of any valuation, certificate, recommendation, order, award, extension of time, or other document whatever which might or ought to have been made at any previous period, and to antedate the same accordingly, and any agreements, admissions, withdrawals, or arrangements made or come to between the parties or their respective agents or counsel during the pendency of any reference to the engineer shall, if the same be duly announced to him in writing signed by the parties, or if the same be verbally stated at any formal hearing held before him, be valid and effectual, anything in this specification to the contrary notwithstanding; and in the latter case the notes of the engineer shall be admitted by both parties as evidence of such verbal agreements, admissions, withdrawals, or arrangements respectively. And to the engineer shall also be referred the settlement of the said contract, and the determination of the sum or sums, or balance of money to be paid to or received from the contractor by the corporation; and (subject as aforesaid) the directions, decisions, admeasurements, valuations, certificates, recommendations, orders, and awards of the engineer (which said directions, decisions, admeasurements, valuations, certificates, recommendations, orders and awards respectively, may be made from time to time) shall be final and binding upon the corporation and the contractor respectively, and the contractor shall not commence any action at law, nor institute any proceeding at law or in equity, or otherwise against, nor make any claim upon the corporation in respect of any matter or matters in relation to which the directions, decisions, admeasurements, valuations, certificates, recommendations, orders and awards, or any or either of them, is or are to be given or made by the engineer, until such directions, decisions, admeasurements, valuations, certificates, recommendations, orders and awards, or any or either of them, as the case may require, shall have been given or made by him, and in case the engineer shall be put to any costs, trouble, loss of time, or expenses by or in consequence of any such directions, decisions, admeasurements, valuations, certificates, recommendations, orders, or awards, or by or in consequence of any suit, claim, or proceeding, and whether as a party thereto or otherwise, and shall make any claim or demand in respect thereof, the reasonable amount of such claim or demand shall be paid and satisfied with full costs (if any) as between solicitor and client, jointly by the corporation and the contractor as expenses mutually incurred in carrying into effect and winding up the contract entered into by and between the corporation and the contractor; and it shall be competent for the engineer to recover the same by action at law or otherwise from either of the parties to the contract, and for either of the parties to the contract to pay for and on behalf of, and recover a moiety of such claim or demand so paid and satisfied from the other, and neither the contractor nor the corporation shall, or shall have any power or authority to revoke, annul, or interfere with the power and authority of the engineer; and if either party shall, in the opinion of the engineer, attempt so to do, or to hinder or delay the engineer from making any certificate, order, or award, it shall be lawful for the engineer, if and when he shall see fit so to do, to proceed *ex parte*, and any certificate, order, or award which may be made by him thereafter shall be final, binding, and conclusive on the parties, notwithstanding the determination of the contract or any attempted revocation by either of them or otherwise. And it shall also be competent for the engineer, for the better determination of any doubt, dispute, or difference, if and whenever he shall so think fit, or at the instance and request of either of the parties to the contract, to call to his assistance and, if needful, to act as his assessor or assessors, any barrister, solicitor, or other disinterested person or persons; and the fees and charges of any and every such barrister, solicitor, or other such disinterested person or persons, shall be deemed to be part of the costs and charges in the reference. And it is lastly stipulÁted that in the event of any submission to reference being had, other than that above mentioned, effect shall be given to all such of the foregoing conditions of this section so far as the same are capable of being applied to the subjectmatter of the doubts, disputes, and differences so submitted, except, and except only, so far as the same shall be expressly varied by such submission.

The nature of the disputes which arose was indicated by a letter from the solicitors to the company, dated the 10th August, 1908, and addressed to the town clerk.

The material part of the letter was as follows:—

"Several months ago we were consulted by our clients, Messrs. R. Blackwell & Co., Ltd., with regard to the treatment meted out to them in relation to the construction by them of tramways in Derby, and particularly the deduction of 1,500*l.* from the contract price on the ground of delay by our clients in completing the work. We regret that we have been unable to write you at an earlier date, but we delayed doing so at first because we understood that the borough surveyor was on the point of leaving to recruit his health, and latterly because of the state of the writer's health. Our clients feel, in regard to this contract, that the treatment they have received at the hands of the corporation and its officials has not been that which they were entitled to expect, nor indeed has it been the treatment which the corporation and officials have seen fit to mete out in regard to other tramway contractors doing work for them in the borough.

"It is of course quite impossible within the compass of one letter to deal in any measure exhaustively with the merits of a difference of this kind, but we feel sure that were the members of the corporation to possess themselves of a knowledge of all the facts relating to our clients' contract, the request of our clients for payment of the balance of the contract price would at once be complied with. The date fixed for completion of the contract was originally July 22nd, 1907, but the time for completion was extended by the borough surveyor to the 24th October, 1907, as even he had to admit the justice of the claim of our clients to a considerable extension of time. The contract was signed in February, and our clients had the right to expect that they would have been able at once to bring their materials upon the ground and to commence work within three or four weeks of that date, and then be allowed to proceed uninterruptedly without undue hindrance.

"In the matter of the execution of the contract our clients were largely in the hands of the borough surveyor, and they had on many occasions to protest against the hampering conditions which were placed upon them by this gentleman. He insisted upon a method of working that caused the greatest possible delay and expense to our clients, and this when considered in conjunction with the alterations and changes made in regard to the work to be done, entirely accounts for the delay in the completion of the work.

"Without in any way exhausting the circumstances we may mention the following facts:—

"(1) A few days after the contract was signed the specification was altered and amended drawings were required for lateral instead of equilateral turnouts (an entirely different article altogether).

"(2) There was constant change of plans necessitating rearrangement and delay; for instance, towards the end of May, 1907, an arrangement was made for a second lateral turnout in Uttoxeter Road, only to be cancelled a few days later.

"(3) The anchor joints were not delivered until the end of May. (This was the fault of the makers, for which our clients were not in any way responsible.)

"(4) The interlacing lines were not decided upon by the corporation engineer under the Great Northern Bridge and in the Wardwick until the end of May.

"(5) Even then, however, there was indecision in regard to the wood pavement.

"(6) Our clients did not receive the tracings for the interlacing lines from the corporation's surveyor until well into June"—that is shortly before the date of completion—"and even then our clients were informed that the area to be paved was to be settled later on.

"(7) On the 19th June the class of paving in the Ashbourne Road was altered, although our clients pointed out to your council that a delay would result, the extent of which our clients had obviously no means of controlling. Even then no information could be obtained from the borough surveyor as to what Jarrah blocks were required, or where they were required. This led to an absolute stoppage of work on that road.

"(8) The method of working upon which the surveyor insisted was an even greater cause of expense and delay than the changes on the work to which we have alluded. Instead of adopting the manner of progress intended to be followed when the contract was signed, the places at which work was allowed to be carried on were altered after our clients had ordered their material, with the inevitable result that hundreds of tons of material lay idle which otherwise would have been put into the work in proper order and time as delivered. The course of progress intended to be followed by our clients when the contract was signed, and which had been agreed to by the borough engineer, was to commence with one gang of men at the end of the Ashbourne line, and after the labourers employed at Derby had got thoroughly conversant with their work, form a second gang who would commence at the end of the Uttoxeter Road. Both these roads would then be finished to their junction at about the same time, and the two gangs would be available for driving quickly through the remaining and most important portion of the work in the centre of the town, causing an absolute minimum of inconvenience and delay. On the basis of this arrangement the materials were ordered forward. Instead of being allowed to follow this reasonable and proper course, our clients were only allowed to proceed a portion of the way along Ashbourne Road, and were absolutely stopped before coming to the railway bridge for want of levels, which the borough engineer could not supply, and special work which was not forthcoming because of the delay in deciding upon what was required and getting it constructed. Instead of allowing our clients to commence at the end of the contract line in Uttoxeter Road, the borough engineer insisted upon their commencing at the end of the extension (a piece of line which was an extra not contemplated in the main contract, not included in our clients' tender, and intended at first to be constructed last). Apart from other considerations the effect of this was disastrous and farreaching. The materials for the Uttoxeter Road line were ready to come through to Derby, and much of them had come through. But our clients were prohibited from opening up that road and constructing that line until the extension was finished. And the extension required a different kind of sett paving. Therefore, this particular kind of sett had to be obtained hurriedly, and the delivery of all the other materials suffered. The setts already ordered had either been delivered at Derby (and there was, we believe, at one time approximately 800 tons of setts in the town which our clients were not allowed to lay) or were manufactured and were ready at the quarries to come through, and it became necessary either to accept delivery of material which could not be used because the work was not allowed to proceed as intended, or to refuse such delivery. Our clients suggested that the corporation should give credit for the materials brought upon the ground so as to allow of that material being accepted by our clients and stocked. The corporation refused to do this, giving only a payment for some wood blocks, but allowing nothing for setts. There was therefore in reason no course to follow but to refuse delivery of any material but that which was at the time being required. One result of this was that when the materials of the kind once available were required there was inevitable delay and difficulty, as the

1909
July 29.

Court of
Appeal.

stock had to be replenished by new materials, the former having gone to other purchasers.

"The conditions under which instructions were given as to the wood paving also caused a wholly unnecessary amount of trouble, annoyance, expense, and delay. Our clients could obtain no certain knowledge as to whether in some and what parts the engineer required hard wood blocks or creosoted deal blocks, or partly one kind and partly the other, thus prohibiting the placing of definite orders.

"Our clients also had to complain of the utterly unworkmanlike manner in which they were allowed to proceed, and the utterly capricious way in which they were required to leave portions of the roads untouched, and move men and plant from place to place unnecessarily. In the narrow part of the Ashbourne Road, for instance, obviously the course to have followed was the one our clients wished to adopt, namely, to take up and complete onehalf the road, going back over the other half afterwards. The course insisted upon by the engineer, namely, laying both tracks and one breastwork at the same time, thus causing our clients' carts to be constantly mixed up with and interrupting the traffic, was fatal to expedition and seriously hampered our clients in the construction.

"Another fruitful source of annoyance and delay was the refusal to allow our clients to place a reasonable amount of material ahead of the work or on the footpath. The facilities afforded to the constructor of the other tramways were refused to our clients, and even the ordinary and usual facilities which are invariably granted and which our clients had the right to expect were either absolutely denied or only grudgingly conceded after great delays and much pressure. Our clients have constructed tramways in all parts, and never, until they came to Derby, have they experienced such treatment as they received regarding the putting materials on the road in advance of the work. It was utterly unreasonable.

"The method of filling in and floating the concrete and the delay insisted upon by the engineer before the road could be used after construction seems to have been chosen for the purpose of causing the maximum amount of annoyance and delay. In ordinary cases the contractors are allowed to pave the day following that on which the concrete is floated, and traffic is allowed upon the pavement the day after it is completed. In Derby the engineer insisted upon several days' delay in these respects. We think we are right in saying that there are instances of as much as four days being insisted upon for the concrete to set, and as long as ten days after the pavement was laid before it was opened for traffic.

"There were complaints of delay which were not justified, and suggestions that night work should be done. Then when extra time or night work was in fact resorted to, another complaint would be forthcoming that the men were tired and could not do their work properly, and this was used as a pretext for condemnation on the ground of indifferent work.

"Furthermore, some letters were written and complaints made because of delay on the footing that proper sand was not provided by our clients. This is really a matter which the corporation ought to look into. The surveyor refused to pass any sand but that obtainable from Mr. Tomlinson. It was well known that during the course of our clients' contracts another contract for the construction of tramways had been let to that gentleman's son, and the sand available from his sand pits not being sufficient for both contracts, preference was naturally and doubtless very properly given to the other contractor. Our clients therefore obtained an adequate supply of proper sand elsewhere, but the surveyor would not accept it. We are within the mark when we state that more than twenty samples of proper sand were submitted, and, on one pretext or another, rejected. When one or two samples were accepted and truck loads of that particular sand were obtained, the truck loads of that sand (which were exactly the same as the sample) when they arrived were rejected. Our clients were then instructed by the borough engineer to get sand from Whatstandwell. Our clients obtained it. The borough engineer then rejected it. Even the sand which was used in large quantities in the construction of the tramways included in the other tramway contract just referred to was rejected when our clients proposed to use it. A mixture of sand which was eventually allowed to be used by our clients had been rejected a month earlier. On enquiry we think it will be found that in regard to another sand which it was suggested should be obtained from Nottingham, and truck loads of which were ordered (which sand was used by your corporation for other purposes), the supply to the other contractor in the construction of the other tramways was allowed to take precedence of the supply of the same sand to your corporation for other purposes, although that precedence was not extended to the supply of the same sand to our clients.

"Owing to the difficulties put in our clients' way they were never allowed to get two full gangs of men working at Derby, and long delays were in the circumstances inevitable. In short, the whole cause of the delay was owing to the frequent changes of mind on the part of the corporation or its officials; their indecision at important junctures and the arbitrary and unreasonable attitude frequently adopted by persons whom they put in control. We must therefore ask you to be good enough to bring this matter before the corporation without any delay, together with an urgent request for the immediate payment of the balance of the contract price due to our clients. Our clients will be loth to institute proceedings, but if these must be resorted to we shall be glad to know whether you will accept service of process."

On the 12th December, 1908, the company issued a writ for the balance of amount due for work done and materials supplied under the contract, and on the 27th January the judge in chambers made the order appealed from.

The statements of fact in the above letter had been embodied in an affidavit.

Atkin, K.C. (R. M. Montgomery with him), for the appellants, the contractors: It is a question whether the discretion of the Court ought to be exercised in favour of the plaintiff, because the questions that arise in the action are questions that involve from the start to the finish the conduct of the engineer, who is to be the arbitrator. The plaintiffs have had a certificate for the full amount of the work, but the corporation have under a clause in the contract deducted a large sum because of delay. The sole dispute is as to this deduction; we say that the delay was occasioned entirely by the conduct of the corporation through their engineer in not allowing us proper facilities for proceeding with the work.

DANCKWERTS, K.C. (ETHERINGTON SMITH with him), for the Derby Corporation: The disputes which have arisen in this case are those which arise in every similar case, and are the very matters for which the arbitration clause is inserted in these contracts.

The Court it is true has a discretion, but in exercising it certain principles must be followed. One of those principles is that where the parties have necessarily contemplated the very event which has happened then the Court will not interfere, unless there is some consideration of an outside character which comes in, as for example, if the arbitrator has been bribed. He referred to *Ives and Barker* v. *Willans* (a), *Cross* v. *Leeds Corporation* (b). No reply was called for.

FLETCHER MOULTON, L.J.: I do not think that there is any doubt as to the law which is to be applied in this case. Of old, an agreement to submit disputes under a contract to a domestic tribunal for arbitration was not enforceable at all, but the legislature recognised that an undertaking to refer disputes under a contract to arbitration was part of the contract, and that it was not fair, giving rights to each party under that contract, if it did not give attention to, and, to some extent, enforce, that clause. In my opinion, it very wisely took this course—it left it impossible for parties to a contract to go to arbitration in such a way that the jurisdiction of the Courts was ousted, so that a man could still have the right to come to the Court; but, if a person who, under a contract, has undertaken that the disputes under that contract should be referred to arbitration brought an action on the contract, the other party had a right to come to the Court and ask that that action should be stayed. He had to prove first that he was, and always had been, ready and willing on his part to go to arbitration, and then the Court had the power, under sect. 4 of the Arbitration Act, to stay the action if it saw no good reason why the matter should not be decided in the way the parties had originally intended. The meaning of that provision is so plain that I do not think it is necessary to go in detail through it.

Each case must be decided on the facts of the case, and in my opinion, where the nature of the dispute arising from facts which were subsequent to the contract is such that we are of opinion that the tribunal is not likely to be able impartially to deal with the dispute, it is open to us, and it would usually be the duty of the Court, to refuse to enforce the arbitration clause. It has been suggested that this would make us tear up all arbitration clauses, but in my experience a Court is quite capable of judging what is the substance

(a) (1894) 2 Ch. 478.
(b) Hudson on Building Contracts, 4th ed. Vol. II. 339.

1909
July 29.

Court of
Appeal.

of the dispute, and it will not be so easily misled by mere allegations.

But in the present case I am satisfied that the dispute is in substance as to whether the engineer has not, from the first, acted unreasonably towards a contractor, viewed from the point of view of the contract. Corporations are, in my opinion, often too fond of putting officers of theirs in the position of engineers under a contract, and they forget that, as they are performing other duties to the corporation, there may arise a conflict between their duties in these other offices, and their duties as engineers under the contract, which may give rise to unfair treatment to the contractor by reason of the zeal with which the officers perform their other duties. Of course, if you have exalted an officer of that kind as the arbitrator under the contract, you cannot say merely, because he is an officer, that therefore he is an unfit judge; but if facts subsequent to the signing of the contract have given rise to a substantial dispute, in which there are allegations of continued unreasonableness on his part, and that is the real dispute between the parties, I think we should not be acting in the spirit of the law if we shut the doors of the Court to such a dispute, and forced it to be referred to arbitration.

I do not want to say any more about the facts of the case excepting this, that I am satisfied that there is a substantial dispute of this kind, and I do not think that we ought to force it to be tried by the engineer whose conduct is practically the sole point of dispute.

I therefore think this appeal ought to be allowed, and allowed with costs. The costs here and below will be the plaintiffs' in any event.

Buckley, L.J.: An agreement to refer to arbitration does not oust the jurisdiction of the Court. A covenant not to sue does not oust the jurisdiction of the Court. The Court still has jurisdiction, but, of course, in determining whether it will exercise it or not, it will be influenced by the existence of the agreement to refer to arbitration, or the covenant not to sue. If it be a case of agreement to refer to arbitration, the matter is governed by sect. 4 of the Arbitration Act, which provides that where an application is made to stay proceedings, the Court or judge, if satisfied that there is no sufficient reason why the matter should not be referred, may make an order staying proceedings. That, of course, is pregnant in two ways as showing that the Court has a discretion; in the first place its being satisfied that there is no sufficient reason, and then, when you get to the end of the sentence, it is not "shall" make, but "may" make an order staying the proceedings.

1909
July 29.
―――――
Court of
Appeal.

Now, as to all this, Mr. Danckwerts does not raise any question at all. There undoubtedly is a judicial discretion. Although there may be an agreement to refer to arbitration, or an agreement not to sue, there is a judicial discretion as to whether the action should be allowed to go on. Mr. Danckwerts has cited to us cases, the cases which are always cited on these occasions—*Ives & Barker* v. *Willans* (a) and *Cross* v. *The Leeds Corporation* (b)—which may be summarised, I think, thus: that in these cases very frequently the one party has agreed to refer the matter which arises in dispute to the engineer of the other party, and it is a part of his contract that he shall not have an impartial arbitrator: he has, with his eyes open, accepted as referee a person who was acting for the other side, and whom he knew would be, or might be (not in any improper sense), but in point of fact, a biassed person. It is not a ground for refusing to allow an arbitration to go on, but, if it does go on, the referee will be the person whom he thus accepted, being, as he knew, not an impartial partial person. That, I think, is the whole result of these authorities.

That being so, here the fact that the referee was the officer of the corporation was not sufficient ground, but the point here is that the contractors' case—whether true or not is a matter to be determined—is this: I could not complete my contract in time, and the reason why I could not complete it in time was that you, the contractual referee, were an unreasonable person; you hindered me in every conceivable way; you would not let me deposit my material in such a way as it is usual to allow me to deposit my material—in advance of my work—you placed all sorts of impediments in my way. Now, the worst possible referee on the question of unreasonable conduct is the person who is accused of being unreasonable. How could you expect him to say, if a person of any character at all, that the acts which he did were unreasonable acts? It is not human nature to suppose that he can properly determine that he himself is an unreasonable person. That is the subjectmatter of the dispute, and really all we have to consider here is whether we are satisfied that there is no sufficient reason why the matter should not be referred. I think that there is sufficient reason why the matter should not be referred, being such as this is, to this particular gentleman.

Therefore, without reflecting in any way upon him, all I say is that in this particular matter he is not the person who ought to determine the dispute.

(a) (1894) 2 Ch. 478.
(b) Hudson on Building Contracts, 4th cd. Vol. II. 339.

On that ground I think that the order ought to be that this appeal be allowed.

    Appeal allowed.

Solicitors for the appellants: Lloyd George, Roberts & Co.

Solicitors for the respondents: Sharpe, Pritchard & Co., agents for Town Clerk, Derby.

𝕴𝖓 𝖙𝖍𝖊 𝕮𝖔𝖚𝖗𝖙 𝖔𝖋 𝕬𝖕𝖕𝖊𝖆𝖑.

WILLIAM KENNEDY, LTD. *v.* THE MAYOR, ALDERMEN AND BURGESSES OF BOROUGH OF BARROW-IN-FURNESS.

Arbitration Act, 1889, s. 4—Summons to stay—What is an Arbitration Clause?

Where from the context of the clause it appears that the duties of the engineer are administrative and not judicial, such clause is not an arbitration clause.

Appeal by William Kennedy, Ltd., from an order of the judge in chambers staying the action under a clause in a contract between the parties, on the ground that such clause was a submission to arbitration.

By a contract under seal dated the 23rd May, 1904, the company agreed to execute a masonry concrete dam at Seathwaite Tarn and other works for the BarrowinFurness Corporation.

Clauses 3 and 33 of the conditions of contract were as follows:—

(3) The whole of the work included in the contract shall be under the control, direction and supervision of the engineer, and shall be carried out to his satisfaction. He shall have full power to alter, vary, extend, enlarge or diminish any of the works included in the contract. He shall be the exclusive *judge* upon all matters whatsoever relating to the construction, incidents and consequences of these presents, and of the tender, specifications, schedule and drawings of the contract, and in regard to the execution of the works or otherwise arising out of or in connection with the contract, and also as regards all matters of account, including the final balance payable to the contractor, and the certificate of the engineer for the time being given under his hand shall be binding and conclusive on both parties.

(33) The contractor shall be entitled to be paid monthly on the certificate of the engineer, at the rate of 90 per cent. of the value of the work done, the remaining 10 per cent. to be retained by the corporation, until two months after the expiration of the period during which the contractor is required to maintain and keep the works in repair, when, provided all the conditions of the contract have been fulfilled, but not otherwise, the

1909
July 14.

Court of
Appeal.

corporation will, upon the certificate of the engineer, pay to the contractor the balance in their hands, after making the deductions, if any, hereinafter provided for.

The engineer may from time to time, by any subsequent certificate, correct any preceding certificate or certificates.

The certificate of the engineer shall have the force and effect of an award, and may be made a rule of his Majesty's High Court of Justice, or any Division thereof, at the instance of either party hereto.

The company claimed to have completed the said contract, and on the 24th September issued a writ against the corporation for work and labour done and goods sold and delivered.

The corporation applied to stay the action under sect. 4 of the Arbitration Act, 1889.

Radcliffe, K.C., and Otter Barry for the company, and W. J. Jeeves for the corporation.

The arguments sufficiently appear from the judgments.

VAUGHAN WILLIAMS, L.J.: In my opinion this appeal should be allowed. I am going to give my decision, basing it upon the fact that there is no arbitration clause whatsoever in the contract, and that under those circumstances there is no submission to arbitration, and no ground for bringing into operation sect. 4 of the Arbitration Act, and staying this action.

We have discussed at considerable length the clauses which were relied upon as going to show that there was an arbitration provided for in this contract. Clause 3 was the first clause relied upon, and the next clause relied upon was Clause 33. I do not know that I need read Clause 3 at length again, but I wish it to be taken that I read it as part of my judgment. If one looks at that clause it is plain that a great part of the functions which the arbitrator, as he is called, the engineer, had to exercise under Clause 3 were functions which any architect or engineer would have to exercise, or to do if there was no arbitration clause, and no pretence for saying that the contract contained a submission to arbitration. Then when one looks at the third clause it says that the whole of the work shall be under the control, direction and supervision of the engineer, and shall be carried out to his satisfaction. Then it gives him power to "alter, vary, extend, enlarge or diminish any of the works included in the contract."

There I would like to say that not only are those functions to be exercised where there is no pretence for saying that the engineer is named as arbitrator, but they are functions which come exactly within the distinction which I read just now, as having been acted upon in the cases of *Re Hammond*, 62 L. T. 808; *Re Carus-*

1909
July 14.

Court of
Appeal.

Wilson 18 Q. B. D. 7; and *In re Dawdy*, 15 Q. B. D. 426. It is said that, "the distinction between an arbitration and a valuation still holds good. The former is to settle a difference which has arisen between the parties; the latter is agreed upon to prevent any difference arising." It seems to me that those words to which I am now referring are words which are intended to prevent any difference arising. Then the clause goes on to say: "He shall be the exclusive judge upon all matters whatsoever relating to the construction," and so on.

It is said that the use of the word "judge" there and the subjectmatter upon which he is to judge, that is, the construction, incidents and consequences of these presents, are matters which necessarily constitute this clause a submission to arbitration. I can only say that I do not agree, and it seems to me that those words, although they are not wide enough to include the functions of an arbitrator, are also narrow enough to include the functions of an engineer not intended to be an arbitrator. Then the clause goes on and deals with the tender, specification, schedule and drawings of the contract, and in regard to the construction of the works, or otherwise arising out of or in connection with the contract; then it deals with matters of account; and then it says that the certificate of the engineer for the time being, given under his hand, shall be binding and conclusive on both parties. One has only to look at any of the books which contain precedents of building contracts to find, again and again, those words: "The certificate of the engineer for the time being, given under his hand, shall be binding and conclusive on both parties." It would be impossible to contend that he was intended to be an arbitrator.

Then when one comes to Clause 33 there is a form of words suggesting that the certificate of the engineer is not of itself an award. The words are "the certificate of the engineer shall have the force and effect of an award, and may be made a rule of his Majesty's High Court of Justice or any division thereof, at the instance of either party hereto." The very fact that those words are thought necessary to be introduced into the contract goes far to show that the parties feel that without the introduction of those words the certificate of the engineer could not have the effect of an award. Why not? Because it was not an award. I do not know that there is any need for me to say any more, because the subject is not a particularly pleasant one to deal with, or one that one ought to deal with unless it is necessary to do so. I mean that the subjectmatter is one with regard to which some misunderstanding might

1909
July 14.
Court of
Appeal.

arise in some way or other, and therefore I wish to avoid saying anything on the subject. I can only say, as I have already said in the course of the argument, that I never intended to make any imputation upon the engineer, Mr. Strongitharm. It is true that I thought it was quite possible that having made an affidavit which was in direct conflict with statements in the affidavit of the contractors, he might be anxious, if he could, to avoid being placed in the position of an arbitrator, and I have no reason to suppose now that if Mr. Strongitharm was left to exercise his own judgment in the matter, he would not wish to act as arbitrator on this question. He apparently thinks that towards the corporation, having regard to the view he takes of the meaning of this contract, his duty will not affect his position as arbitrator however unpleasant and difficult it might be. There is no imputation upon him at all. Most of the cases have been cited to us, and it is perfectly manifest that there is a great and material difference in cases where you object to the arbitrator, because he never ought to have been selected, and the cases where you object to an arbitrator because circumstances have occurred since the dispute which make it undesirable that he should act as arbitrator.

All I will add is to declare emphatically that in my opinion the making, or refusing to make, an order staying an action is a matter for the discretion of the Court or the judge, as the case may be, and that there is no limitation as to the cases in which a judge may exercise his discretion by refusing to stay. I do not deny at all that there is a number of cases which show, and show in the strongest manner, that a judge or Court, *primâ facie*, ought to assume that the right thing to do is to stay the action, and allow conventional arbitration to go on. As I say, although that is so, it is open to the judge or the Court, and it is the duty of the judge or the Court, if they see good reason to suppose that justice will not be done in the arbitration, having regard to the events which have occurred since the making of the contract which contains the submission to arbitration, to say that the action should not be stayed, and it is open to them to exercise their discretion.

FLETCHER MOULTON, L.J.: I have also come to the conclusion that this appeal ought to be allowed.

The action is framed in a peculiar way, obviously by counsel who are well aware of the difficulties in dealing with a contract of the present kind, and as it stands, the statement of claim is based upon two allegations: one upon a repudiation on the part of the defendants of the contract accepted by the plaintiffs, and another that through their behaviour there has been such a change of circumstances that

1909
July 14.

Court of
Appeal.

the conditions of the contract, including all the conditions of the contract, are inapplicable, and the parties are driven to a *quantum meruit.* I am not going to say a word as to the substantiality of either of those methods of framing the claim. As to the question of there being any ground for saying, in the course of the argument, that the contract has been repudiated, I am not going to make that part of my judgment.

Now it cannot be denied that neither of those claims are such that we should be entitled to stay the action. If the contract has, by the repudiation of the defendants, ceased to exist, it is clear that neither party can rely on the arbitration clause. I think it also true that if it could be shown that subsequent events have made the whole of these conditions inapplicable, so that practically the work was done under such conditions that both parties ought to have realised that the contract did not apply, it is possible (I do not say more than that) that some claim might be made on a *quantum meruit.* But there, again, if the conditions did not apply there would be no ground for a stay. So that strictly speaking, the plaintiffs, I think, have a right to say: "Our cause of action is for damages, whether we can make it good at the trial or not," and certainly as that is the only cause of action put forward it is beyond our jurisdiction to stay the action.

When we come to look at the contract there seems to me to be a more fundamental objection to our staying the action. The contract is drawn up with very great care, and there is an absence of a formal arbitration clause. Mr. Scrutton has only been able to point to condition 3, and to the latter part of condition 33, as being equivalent to an arbitration clause. Condition 3, no doubt, gives the engineer power to decide questions arising between the parties, and questions arising during the course of the works, and questions arising at the end of the works, but I think that clause 3 was drawn up with the intention of avoiding the use of the word "arbitration." If clause 3 is carefully looked at it will be found to refer to matters which the engineer has to decide, *de die in diem,* during the progress of the works—whether certain work has been done properly, or must be done over again, or whether the materials are such that they should be accepted by him or not. It is also made wide enough to include a vast number of other questions. Now the words on which Mr. Scrutton relies to make this equivalent to an arbitration clause, namely, the words "exclusive judge," apply to the whole of these powers of the engineer, and we cannot say that he is in the position

1909
July 14.

Court of
Appeal.

of arbitrator with regard to one unless he is also in the position of arbitrator with regard to all.

I am satisfied with regard to the bulk of these questions, which in all probability would be most numerous, that the engineer was not intended to be an arbitrator, in the strict sense of the word, and was not tied to any particular, or even to any legal procedure in determining the questions which came before him. He was an administrative officer whose word was law; and, feeling that, I am not disposed to regard this carefully drawn up clause as an arbitration clause. I do not believe it was meant to be relied upon as an arbitration clause. I do not think that the engineer was intended to be put in the position of an arbitrator regulated by the legal principles which the Courts have laid down applicable to arbitrators with regard to any or all questions.

The corporation could make him administratively decide these questions fairly, of course, but still administratively, and they did not intend, in my opinion, to make him an arbitrator in the strict sense of the word. Now I do not feel at all justified in using the power of the Court for the purpose of staying an appeal to the Courts of the realm by reason of the presence of a clause which is so doubtful as an arbitration clause. In my opinion it was not intended as an arbitration clause, and it is not expressed in the proper phraseology to carry that out. Therefore I think that this is a case where we ought not to stay the action. The parties will go before the law courts with undiminished rights; they each of them have the rights given to them by these conditions under this contract, if the contract is still in existence, and if it is not in existence, then they have the rights which they can make out from the facts of the case. As I have said, I think that defendants have, by taking this step to get the case referred, in no way abandoned their right, if they can show that the contract is still in force, to claim the benefit in part of clause 3 and of every part of clause 33.

BUCKLEY, L.J.: I shall only deal with one of the points which have been argued in this case; for if, as I think, this contract contains no submission to refer to arbitration, it is clear that the order under appeal cannot be sustained. The jurisdiction of the Court exists, of course, apart from contract, and, notwithstanding the contract, in a civil cause the parties may agree not to appeal to the jurisdiction, but to substitute a domestic Court. The result is not that the Court has not jurisdiction, but that the Court will not exercise its jurisdiction, and may, under the Arbitration Act, decline to exercise

1909
July 14.

Court of
Appeal.

it, and it ought, upon principles now clearly established by authority, to decline to exercise it if a domestic forum has been agreed.

In order to show how I arrive at the conclusion that there is no arbitration clause I ought to look at the contract. Mr. Scrutton quoted one authority, *Chambers v. Goldthorpe* (a); but I prefer to look at the contract first, and I will say a word as to the authority after.

Now the only relevant clause of the contract is clause 3, with the addition of the last words of clause 33. Looking at clause 3, the first sentence provides that the engineer is to control the work, and the work is to be done to his satisfaction. In doing those acts he is representing the corporation for whom the work was to be done. He was put there as the person who was to control the work done for them and to see that it was done to his satisfaction. The next sentence is a sentence which gives him power to enlarge or diminish the scope of the work, acting, of course, for the corporation. He can direct the contractor to do something further, or he can say that the contractor shall do something less, and, of course, in considering what orders he gives to the contractors who are employed by the corporation, he has to have regard to the interests of the corporation. Those are the first two sentences.

Then comes the sentence on which the question arises, and I take, first, certain words out of that, and those words are: "The engineer shall be the exclusive judge" upon all matters whatsoever in regard to the execution of the works. Now I think that those words are similar to the words which precede it, and mean that it shall rest with the engineer alone to determine any matter which arises on the execution of the works. He may say: "Do it in this way," or "Do it in that way," and in so directing he is, I think, not acting judicially at all. He is the person whose determination is required by the parties. It is not a judicial act, but it is an administrative act in the interests of the corporation who is going to pay, and he is to be the judge, or a kind of arbitrator, or a person whose decision is to be final in the matter of the execution of the works. I do not think that means that he is an arbitrator, or acting in a judicial capacity at all. If these words are equivalent to these other words, which no doubt are of wider import, as, for instance, that he is to be "the exclusive judge upon all matters whatsoever relating to the construction, incidents and consequences of these presents," that

(a) (1901) 1 K. B. 624.

1909
July 14.

Court of
Appeal.

rather shows that it is an administrative act and not a judicial act. I agree.

But in this sentence the words, "he shall be the exclusive judge," must have the same meaning that all the subheads ought to have; and if he is not a judge, that is to say, acting judicially with regard to any of them, he cannot, it appears to me, be acting judicially with regard to others of them. It is quite true that he is to be an impartial person, no doubt; he is to determine the construction of the contract, and he must not seek to construe it in favour of the corporation as distinguished from in favour of the contractors; he must act fairly as between the parties. Therefore he owes a duty to the contractors as well as a duty to the corporation, but he, I think, does not hold any judicial duty to one or to the other. Then if you add to that the last words of section 33, all that you find there is that his certificate as to the work done, the money to be paid and so on, "shall have the force and effect of an award, and may be made a rule of his Majesty's High Court of Justice, or any division thereof, at the instance of either party hereto." I do not think that adds anything to it. It is not that this certificate is an award, but it is to be treated as something which it is not, and it is treated as if it were an award. That is the conclusion I come to upon the construction of that clause.

Now the case which was referred to, of *Chambers* v. *Goldthorpe*, which is reported in 1901, 1 K. B. D., at p. 624, is not, I think, an authority which supports Mr. Scrutton's argument, but, as I read it, it is an authority against him. What was in question there was, whether an architect who had to determine certain things could be sued for negligence. The contract in question contained an arbitration clause, and under the arbitration clause the architect was not the arbitrator. There was an arbitration clause, but the architect was not the arbitrator. What the Court said was this: that notwithstanding that the architect was not arbitrator, he was, for certain purposes, entitled to the same immunity as if he had been that which he was not. He was a person to determine fairly between the parties in that sense what was right as regards a certain matter, and in that respect he was entitled to the same immunity as if he stood in the position of an arbitrator, which, in point of fact, he was not.

I come to the conclusion upon this contract that the engineer here, although no doubt he owed duties to the contractors as well as to the corporation, was not to be the arbitrator; and that here there is no submission to arbitration, with the result, of course, that sect. 4 of the Arbitration Act does not apply, and therefore I think the appeal from the order must be allowed.

1909
July 14.

Court of
Appeal.

Solicitors for the plaintiffs: Radcliffe, Cator & Hood, agents for Hill, Brown & Co., Glasgow.

Solicitors for the defendants: King, Wigg & Co., agents for Town Clerk, Barrow-in-Furness.

𝕴𝖓 𝖙𝖍𝖊 𝕶𝖎𝖓𝖌'𝖘 𝕭𝖊𝖓𝖈𝖍 𝕯𝖎𝖛𝖎𝖘𝖎𝖔𝖓.

1911
January 25.

King's Bench
Division.

(*Before* CHANNELL, J.)

LEICESTER BOARD OF. GUARDIANS *v.* TROLLOPE.

Building Contract—Work not according to Contract—Architect's Negligence—Misconduct of Clerk of Works.

An architect, under contract to supervise work, is entitled to leave details to the clerk of the works, but is personally responsible for seeing that his design is carried out. Where, therefore, the clerk of the works fraudulently permitted a floor to be laid, otherwise than in the way, and without the precautions against damp, provided for in the specification, and the supervising architect failed to see that this part of his design was adhered to, such architect was held personally responsible for the consequences resulting from dry rot in such floor.

The defendant was the sole surviving partner in a firm of architects. In November, 1900, this firm entered into a contract in writing with the plaintiffs to prepare surveys, levels, plans, specifications, &c. for an infirmary and other buildings, and to superintend the carrying out of the work. Contractors were selected and the work went forward under the supervision of the defendant's firm.

In pursuance of the contract between the parties, the plaintiffs appointed a clerk of the works for the job. This clerk of the works, wrongfully and for corrupt purposes of his own, permitted the contractors to lay the ground floor without the specified precautions against damp, and so to deviate from the design. These deviations the defendant's firm failed to discover, and a certificate of completion was granted to the contractors. Two years after this certificate, dry rot was found to have set in on the ground floor, and these deviations were discovered. The defendant then, without admitting liability, wrote a letter to the plaintiffs' solicitors offering to rectify the mischief. In view of this letter, the plaintiffs did not take proceedings against him as they would otherwise have done. The defendant did rectify part of the mischief, but, in 1909, refused to proceed further therewith.

The plaintiffs claimed damages for breach of the contract to superintend the work and for breach of the subsequent agreement to rectify the mischief.

1911
January 25.

King's Bench
Division.

The defendant pleaded that the plaintiffs had appointed an unfit and improper clerk of the works, denied negligence on the part of his firm, and contended that, if the contract was broken, it was so broken by reason of the negligence and fraud of the clerk of the works, who was, he contended, the servant of the plaintiffs. He further pleaded that his offer to rectify the mischief was a purely voluntary undertaking. And by way of counterclaim he claimed that, if he was liable to the plaintiffs, they were liable to him in the same amount for breach of their undertaking to appoint a fit and proper clerk of the works, or, alternatively, for damages for the false and fraudulent representations and concealment of their servant.

The action was ordered to be heard before a judge, without a jury, and, in the first instance, upon the question of liability alone, leaving that of amount to be tried as the judge at the trial should direct.

Hugo Young, K.C., and Alec Neilson appeared for the plaintiffs.

E. Pollock, K.C., and C. B. Marriott appeared for the defendant.

Mr. Justice CHANNELL: In this case I am sorry to find that the defendant is under a serious liability, in respect of a matter, in which, undoubtedly, he personally is not greatly, if at all, in default. The plaintiffs have gone out of their way to say that they make no imputations at all upon his good faith or anything of that kind. If I may add to that, I was much impressed by the candid way in which he gave his evidence in the witness box. One is sorry to give judgment against him; but I think the facts are extremely clear.

Here is a building contract of very much the usual character. I do not find anything in it which differs very much from an ordinary building contract. It contemplates the appointment of a clerk of the works, and it mentions a clerk of the works as a perfectly well known person, holding an office which is well understood. It does not go out of its way to define him; it mentions certain things that he may do, but it treats a clerk of the works as it treats an architect, as a perfectly well known person with known functions and duties. Then there is an agreement between the plaintiffs and the defendant and his then partner, who, unfortunately, has since died, and that is the usual agreement. The only important thing that is special in it is that the architects agreed to take substantially less than the usual rate of remuneration.

Under these circumstances the building was built, and then some three or four years after it was completed it was discovered that all the lower floor timber was very badly affected with dry rot. Investigation took place, and it was discovered that the design—that was intended to prevent the occurrence of dry rot—had not been complied with. Somebody was undoubtedly to blame. The builder was to blame: he certainly had not performed his contract; he had got no authority from the architect to deviate from it, and that authority was the only thing that would have justified him in deviating from it. Therefore, the builder was undoubtedly to blame. But there was this difficulty in the way of suing him, that he had got the architect's certificate of completion, and that the contract practically said that if he had got the architect's certificate of completion, and if a period of nine months had then elapsed, during which he was to be responsible, he was not to be responsible afterwards. Therefore, there was that difficulty in the way of suing the builder.

1911
January 25.

King's Bench
Division.

It is not my business to say, and I suppose that I ought to avoid saying, anything that will prejudice any claim that anybody may hereafter think fit to bring against the builder, but, as part of the history of this case one cannot help saying that, if it is the fact, as appears to be the case, and as is contended by Mr. Pollock, that there was a fraud and that there was collusion between the clerk of works and the builder, it seems to me that the builder would not have been entitled to rely upon that certificate, and that, therefore, he might, in all probability, have been sued. There was, however, that difficulty in the way of suing the builder.

Then the Board of Guardians, perhaps not unnaturally, said to the architects: "You ought to have seen to this, and we make a claim against you personally." They made that claim most positively, and the present defendant took the view that although he repudiated all liability, for his own credit, and that nobody should have any sort of complaint against him with reference to an important work of this kind, he would make the matter good.

Upon that, the Board of Guardians omitted to take the proceedings which they were threatening. I cannot entertain the slightest doubt that that was a binding agreement. It has all the elements of it. There was the forbearance. It is true, I think, that mere forbearance not at the request of the other party would not be a consideration; but here there was forbearance at the request of the other party. The letters that passed are quite clearly a request not to take proceedings. They are written in reference to that very matter, and I cannot, therefore, entertain any doubt as to that being a binding agreement, subject only to the question of seal, which I will deal with in a very few words now.

In the course of the negotiations, after, possibly, an agreement had been come to, a further term was proposed by the solicitor for the defendants, "Although we do this, if we mean to claim over against the builders, of course you will give us every assistance to do that." The Board of Guardians very properly said that they

1911
January 25.

King's Bench
Division.

would. That is part of the agreement on their part. It may be that the agreement was concluded before, and it may be they might have said if they had liked: "We have not promised to do all that, and we are not going to reopen the matter, because it is already concluded," but when an agreement is just made, and has arrived, possibly, at the stage at which they might say it was concluded, if parties consent to reopen the matter and to add a further term it seems to me that they do reopen the matter, and that the agreement is the agreement which they make when they have added those terms to it, and that they cannot then go back and say: "Before we agreed to that there was already a concluded agreement."

It is all one agreement, and they assented to it as one agreement. The result is that it contains a term which has not yet been completely executed because the time has not yet arrived. Therefore one cannot get out of the difficulty about a seal on the ground that it is an executed contract on one side, which I think is held now to bo sufficient in most cases. One cannot quite get out of it on that ground. Therefore it gave me a difficulty.

I was prepared yesterday to decide this case upon the question that that agreement was sufficient. Amongst other things I may say that I thought it was a very clear ground, and that I desired to decide it on that ground rather than on the ground that this gentleman had neglected a duty, and therefore was chargeable with negligence. I thought that it was better for him that it should go through, on the ground that he had voluntarily agreed to pay the money, especially as I saw that it was almost inevitable that I should have to decide the other question, if I did decide it at all, against him. However, this point about the seal was put forward, and it did create some difficulty in my mind.

Therefore I thought that in view of the possibility of the case going to the Court of Appeal on that, I ought to hear and decide the whole question. Now on that matter as well Mr. Hugo Young has now quoted cases which I think appear to me, as far as I can see, to remove the difficulty. I think, therefore, that the decision might go against the defendant upon the ground of that agreement, but I have had to hear the whole case, and I must give my judgment upon it.

Now the defence is that this was the fault of the clerk of the works. In one sense, no doubt, it was the fault of the clerk of the works. Whatever the duty of the defendant and his late partner was it was clearly the duty of the clerk of the works to call attention to this. Not only did he not do so, however, but he seems to have connived at it, and concealed it, so that there is no doubt that it was the fault of the clerk of the works. But does that relieve the defendant?

1911
January 25.

King's Bench
Division.

I think there is no difficulty in seeing what are the respective functions and duties of an architect, and of a clerk of the works. I had a very clear idea of it myself, and the witnesses who have been called for the defendant, two gentlemen of position in the profession, and the defendant himself, who is a gentleman of position in the profession, all practically agree. They all agree that the clerk of the works has to see to matters of detail, and that the architect is not expected—in this case we know that he was not expected—to do so. I do not lay any stress on the conversation that he was expected to be there once a month or something of that sort—that is only a little conversation as to matters which are going to take place—that does not alter the duties of the parties.

Everybody knows that an architect cannot be there all the time, and everybody knows that the clerk of the works is appointed to protect the interests of the employer against the builder, mainly because the architect cannot be there. The same gentlemen who tell us that tell us also that the architect is responsible to see that his design is carried out. That fairly indicates what the respective duties of each are, but it leaves one in each case to say whether the matter complained of is a matter of detail or a matter of seeing whether the design is complied with.

The matter in this case is a very important matter in reference to the building. It is not exactly the foundations of the main building, but is the concrete under the floors. And I suppose that when you put floors on damp earth, any man—even one not very much skilled in such matters—must know that you have to make protection against the damp. Here a protection was devised, and it was an essential part of the design. Now the architect admitted that they took no steps to find out whether that was carried out, or whether it was not. It is not a case in which they inquired even of the clerk of the works, in which they pointed out to the clerk of the works: "This is a very important matter; we hope that you will see that this is done properly," or anything of that kind. Nothing of the kind took place. It is a very large area of building, and although in some parts it was better done than in others, over the greater part of it this concrete was all wrong.

If in this case the architect had taken steps to see that the first block of buildings was done all right, and then in the next block of buildings he had left it to the clerk of the works with instructions to see that it was done in the second block in the same way as it

1911
January 25.

King's Bench
Division.

was done in the first, I should then have had some doubt whether he would have been liable if the clerk of the works had neglected that, and allowed it to be done in a different way in the other part. But here there was nothing done at all to see that the design was complied with, and it was not in fact complied with.

It does not seem to me that it excuses the architect from seeing that his design is complied with, that he thought that the clerk of the works would be sure to see that it was all right, and it seems to me that this is not a matter of detail which it was justifiable to leave to the clerk of the works. It may be that it was rather natural that he should do it, and therefore it is not one of the cases where one puts very serious blame and says: "Here is a gentleman who was incompetent in his profession," or anything of that sort. There is no ground for thinking anything of that kind here. But in my judgment there was an oversight, an omission to do that which it was his duty to do, namely, to see that this design in this important particular was in fact carried out, and nothing more.

Now it is said that the clerk of the works is the servant of the plaintiffs, and therefore that the defendant is excused. If a party to a contract prevents the other party from performing his contract, of course that is an answer; but it cannot possibly be put that this conduct of the clerk of the works, even assuming him to be, as for certain purposes he undoubtedly was, the servant of the plaintiffs, amounts to the plaintiffs, through their servant, preventing the defendants from performing their contract, and if they did not do that their conduct is not an answer to the action. And is it a ground of counterclaim? I must say that I think it is not, on the ground I put just now. An employer is not liable for the fraud and misconduct of his servant if the servant does it in his own interest, and not in the supposed interest of his employer. If he commits a fraud in the course of the execution of his duties, and within the scope of his duties, and does it in the supposed interest of the employer, although it is not in fact in his interest, then the employer is liable. But if the servant does it on his own account, and for his own purposes, the employer is not liable. In this case it is impossible to state that the clerk of the works did it in the supposed interest of the employer (*a*). Consequently it is not a ground of counterclaim.

Without going further into the matter, it does seem to me that this is not a matter of detail, that is, is a matter of an essential part of the design of the building which the defendant omitted to see com-

(*a*) As to this passage, see now the decision of the House of Lords in *Lloyd* v. *Grace Smith & Co.*, [1912] A. C. 716.

plied with; and therefore I think that upon the main question I must hold him responsible.

1911
January 25.

King's Bench
Division.

I think, as I have said before, that even if he had not been responsible on that he would have been responsible on the special contract. In either case, therefore, the defendant is liable.

I have said that I am sorry that it is so because it is undoubtedly a serious liability, and he has really behaved extremely well in the matter, with the possible doubt that, having most handsomely agreed to do the whole work, he, finding that it was more than he anticipated, tried to back out of the agreement. With that single exception, merely succumbing to a natural temptation, he has behaved as well as anybody could do in the matter, and he has given his evidence in such a way as to command my respect. Nevertheless, I think he is liable in law on this claim, and I must give judgment against him, with costs.

Solicitors for the plaintiffs: Crowders, Vizard, Oldham & Co., agents for Owston, Dickinson, Simpson & Bigg, Leicester.

Solicitors for the defendant: Clowes, Hickley & Steward.

[The history of the publication of the report in the following case will not be without interest. The case was decided in 1911, and the author had prepared a report of the case for the purpose of his practice as well as for publication in this edition of this work, because, though important to the highest degree, it had not apparently been thought worthy of report by any of the regular law reporters. In the course of an arbitration, in which the author was engaged, however, he had occasion, while the report was still in manuscript, to cite it in the course of argument, and in that way it became known.

Later, the manuscript was borrowed from the author by the Court of Appeal for use during the case of *Aird* v. *Bristol Corporation*, and the author was then requested to publish it, which he did in a supplement to the third edition of this work.

In that form it was used in the case before referred to in the House of Lords.

After that judgment of the House of Lords had been delivered, a report of *Roberts* v. *Hickman* appeared in the Law Reports, [1913] A. C. 229.

The author has, however, thought it well to preserve the original report in this edition, as it is the only report, so far as he is aware, which contains the judgments in the Divisional Court and in the Court of Appeal.

The report has been supplemented, as it now appears, by copies of the material portions of the correspondence.]

1909
Nov. 2.

King's Bench
Division.

In the King's Bench Division.

(HAMILTON, J.)

In the Court of Appeal.

(VAUGHAN WILLIAMS, FLETCHER MOULTON, and FARWELL, L.JJ.)

In the House of Lords.

(LORDS LOREBURN, L.C., ASHBOURNE, ALVERSTONE, L.C.J.,
ATKINSON, and SHAW.)

ROBERTS *v.* HICKMAN & CO.

Architect's Duties and Conduct as Certifier—Conclusiveness of
Final Certificate—Certificate dispensed with.

Where an architect in a quasijudicial position, e.g., a certifier, does not preserve that attitude of judicial independence needed and required of him to discharge his duties (though he may not be guilty of fraud or collusion) he is no longer fit to be a judge, and in the event of his acting in the interests of the building owner or by his direction, the building owner cannot in such circumstances rely upon the architect's certificate as a condition precedent to payment, or as an adjudication binding upon the builder.

In this case the plaintiff, Charles Philip Roberts (the respondent in the House of Lords), sued Messrs. Hickman & Co., the defendants (appellants in the House of Lords), for work and labour done and materials supplied under a building contract dated the 31st December, 1906, and for extras. The writ was specially indorsed.

Particulars.

	£	s.	d.
Amount due under contract	2,750	0	0
Amount due for extras ordered by the defendants' architect	753	14	11
	3,503	14	11
Credits —			
By omissions, &c.			
„ cash on account	2,949	12	6
Balance due to plaintiff	£554	2	5

The writ was issued on the 15th July, 1908. After action brought, the defendants' architect gave a final certificate for 339*l.* 9*s.* 4*d.*

The defence set up that under the said contract it was provided that payment was only to be made upon the certificate of the defendants' architect; that all amounts so certified prior to the date of the issue of the writ had been paid. That under the said contract the decision of the said architect as to the value of any of the work done or materials supplied to the plaintiff was final, and that on the 21st August, 1908 (after action brought), the said architect gave his final certificate, and assessed the value of the work done by the plaintiff at 3,039*l.* 9*s.* 4*d.* The defendants further said that all that was due to the plaintiff, after crediting payments on account, was 339*l.* 9*s.* 4*d.*, which had been paid to the plaintiff under the order of the Master.

The plaintiff replied that the defendants were not entitled to rely upon the absence of a certificate nor upon the certificate given by the said architect after action brought, and they alleged collusion between the said architect (Robert W. Hobden) and the defendants.

The plaintiff under the particulars of such collusion alleged that the defendants interfered with the exercise by the said architect of his quasijudicial functions as to giving any further certificate to the plaintiff and as to deciding the prices to be paid for extra work and in respect of delay; and they further alleged that the said architect, under the directions and influence of the defendants, withheld certificates to which, in his independent judgment, he thought the plaintiff was entitled, and which but for his desire to consult the wishes and convenience of the defendants he would have given to the plaintiff. The alleged interference appeared in certain correspondence between the said architect and the defendants.

By way of rejoinder, the defendants set up that if there was any interference with the said architect it did not amount to collusion. The defendants further set up that the plaintiff was aware of all the matters given in the reply by way of particulars, and that he waived and lost any rights that he might have had in respect of such alleged interference by accepting on the 16th June, 1908, with full knowledge of such alleged interference, a certificate from the said architect, and sued for and obtained payment of the same.

The contract contained the following clause:—

17. The decision of the architect relating to any matters or thing or the goodness or sufficiency of any work, or the extent or value of any extra or omitted work, shall be final, conclusive and binding on all parties.

There was also an arbitration clause providing that—

In the event of any question arising between the architect and the employer and the parties to the contract as to the meaning of any clause in this specification, of any portion of the signed drawings, or on any other point in connection herewith, and of which the decision of the architect does not meet with the approval of the contractor, he (the contractor) can have such matters in dispute referred to the arbitration of any other architect—to be appointed, &c. . . . .

Nothing turned upon the existence of this clause, and no reference was made to it in the judgments, although in those in the House of Lords the term "arbitrator" is constantly used in reference to Mr. Hobden.

1909
Nov. 2.

King's Bench
Division.

Clause 29 was as follows:—

Payment will be made to the contractor as the work proceeds on the certificate of the architect at the rate of 80 per cent. of the work actually done in sums of not less than 400*l.*, a further 10 per cent. to be paid on the practical completion of the work, and the balance on the completion of the contractor's term of maintenance. By clause 22 the period of maintenance was fixed at three months from certified completion.

The correspondence contained the following letters:—

"34, Finsbury Square, E.C.
"March 9th, 1907.

"Messrs. Hickman & Co.

"Dear Sirs,

"Re 16, *Christopher Street.*

"Please note that I have had an application from Mr. C. P. Roberts, the contractor for this work, for a payment of 500*l.* upon the above works next week. I shall be giving him a certificate on Wednesday next, if he is entitled to same, unless I hear from you in the meantime.

"Yours faithfully,
"Robt. W. Hobden."

"3, Rutland Place, E.C.
"March 11th, 1907.

"R. W. Hobden, Esq.,
"34, Finsbury Square, E.C.

"Dear Sir,

"16, *Christopher Street.*

"We are in receipt of your letter of the 9th inst. conveying notice from Mr. Roberts that he will require a payment of 500*l.* We have sent your letter on to Mr. Hickman, and as soon as we get his reply we will telephone you to issue the certificate.

"Yours truly,
"Mark Bromet.
"per W. H."

"34, Finsbury Square, E.C.
"November 8th, 1907.

"Messrs. Hickman & Co.

"Dear Sirs,

"Re 16, *Christopher Street.*

"We have now received from Mr. Roberts his claim for matters in connection with the 21 weeks' delay, which amounts to 235*l.* 12*s.* 6*d.*, made up principally by 42*l.* foreman's time, and 150*l.* for hire of scaffolding and plant. This claim is accompanied by full details, which are all more or less in order. I have also his account for making the alteration to the building, which amounts to 255*l.* 5*s.* 3*d.* Of course both of these claims will want very careful investigation, with the view to considerably reducing the amounts. There is, however, no reason why Mr. Roberts should not be ordered to proceed with the work without prejudice to his claim, because the contract provides that the value of all alterations, additions, &c. are to be left in my hands for valuation.

"I have, therefore, written Mr. Roberts to that effect.

"Yours faithfully,
"Robt. W. Hobden."

"3, Rutland Place, E.C.
"Nov. 12th, 1907.

"R. W. Hobden, Esq.,
"34, Finsbury Square, E.C.
"Dear Sir,

"16, *Christopher Street.*

"I am in receipt of your letter of the 8th inst., and am somewhat amazed with Roberts's claim, and I quite agree with you it will want very careful investigation. Of course, the question is, how does our contract read? If you will remember, I took some objection at the time to certain conditions he put in, and no doubt, I suppose, this is the result, therefore I trust to you to get this claim reduced as much as possible. In the meantime, we should like to see the details. Of course it is as well to explain to Mr. Roberts that if he wants to do any more work for us he must be reasonable, and not take advantage of our unfortunate position. I quite agree with you that there is no reason whatever why Mr. Roberts should not proceed with the work without prejudice, and I shall be glad, therefore, if you will instruct him to do so at once, as the quicker we get our building finished the less loss we shall make. I am afraid this job is going to be a very unremunerative one through the fearful difficulties which have been raised all round.

"Yours truly,
"Mark Bromet.
"per W. H."

"138, St. Paul's Road,
"Highbury, London.
"March 27, 1908.

"R. W. Hobden, Esq.,
"34, Finsbury Square, E.C.
"Dear Sir,

"Re 16, *Christopher Street, E.C.*

"We beg to inform you that we shall require a further payment on account of work at the above, and shall be obliged if you will kindly let us have your certificate for 750*l.* as early as possible, as we should very much like to have a cheque during next week. Our last application for a certificate was on the 29th January. The works are now practically completed, and we expect to finish early next week.

"Yours faithfully,
"C. P. Roberts & Co."

"34, Finsbury Square, E.C.
"March 28, 1908.

"Messrs. Hickman & Co.
"Dear Sirs,

"I enclose copy of a letter from Messrs. Roberts, re 16 Christopher Street. . . . . I will make a survey of the building early next week and let you know with regard to the certificate. The amount of Messrs. Roberts' contract is 2,750*l.*, and there are some extra matters on top of that. They have already had 2,300*l.* on account. They are probably entitled to something, but I cannot see that it is so much as they state.

"Yours faithfully,
"Robt. W. Hobden."

"3, Rutland Place, E.C.
"March 31st, 1908.

"R. W. Hobden, Esq.,
"34, Finsbury Square, E.C.
"Dear Sir,

"16, *Christopher Street.*

"We are in receipt of your letter of the 28th inst., enclosing copy of letter from Mr. Roberts. . . . .

"With reference to the certificate, I should say on no account should you issue this until we have got Roberts' a/c for the extras, as we believe you said these would have to be gone into very carefully indeed, as you thought he is making charges he has no right to make. You must also bear in mind that there is a lot of work in the contract which has not been done and which has been substituted for other work; but I have no doubt you will be able to check it all. However, if you will get the account and send it on I will then show it to Mr. Hickman; but I think you will be unwise in issuing the certificate until we have the accounts.

"Yours truly,
"Mark Bromet.
"per W. H."

"34, Finsbury Square, E.C.
"April 14, 1908.

"Messrs. Hickman, Ltd.
"Dear Sirs,

'Re 16, *Christopher Street.*

"Unless I hear from you to the contrary I shall be giving Mr. Roberts a certificate for 600*l.* in the course of Wednesday. You will remember I have written you several letters in this matter to which you have not given me any reply, and as Mr. Roberts is entitled under the contract to a certificate I must, of course, give it to him.

"Yours faithfully,
"Robt. W. Hobden."

"3, Rutland Place, E.C.
"15th April, 1908.

"R. W. Hobden, Esq.,
"34, Finsbury Square, E.C.
"Dear Sir,

"With reference to Mr. Roberts' request for a certificate, and referring to your letter of 28th November last, at that time I communicated with Mr. Hickman, and his reply was that we were not to pay any more money until we had the account. He further said, as one who understands building, this should have been sent in at once, as it was no use asking him to see the job when the account had not been delivered, as he said he had a similar experience in Red Lion Street, and he does not want it to occur again; therefore, any account Roberts has should be dealt with at once. You will please understand it is no use issuing a certificate as I am sure Mr. Hickman will not sign a cheque, so that it is best to get the account at once and have it properly checked, and so get the whole matter cleared up. I am sure if we pay Roberts a cheque on a/c it will cause delay and perhaps a deal of expense. I shall, therefore, be glad if you will carry out the wishes of Mr. Hickman and myself, and I am sure Mr. Roberts cannot object to this.

"Yours truly,
"Mark Bromet.
"per W. H."

"34, Finsbury Square, E.C.
"April 16, 1908.

"Messrs. Roberts & Co.
"Dear Sirs,
"I regret I cannot enclose certificate, my clients' instructions being that the certificate I next give you is to be a final one, including for a complete settlement of the work done, into which I shall be prepared, to go after Easter.

"Yours faithfully,
"Robt. W. Hobden.
"pp. A. G. P."

"34, Finsbury Square, E.C.
"April 16, 1908.

"Messrs. Hickman & Co.
"Dear Sirs,
"Re 16, *Christopher Street.*
"In reference to yours of the 15th, I cannot see how my letter of the 28th November last bears on the matter, because in advising you as to the amount of the certificate I proposed issuing I had taken this into account. However, I have written Messrs. Roberts that you have instructed me not to issue another certificate until the account has been issued and agreed. At the same time, I must express my opinion that I think you are wrong in not agreeing to the certificate I proposed to give, viz., 500*l.*

"Yours faithfully,
"Robt. W. Hobden."

"34, Finsbury Square, E.C.
"April 24th, 1908.

"Messrs. C. P. Roberts & Co.
"Dear Sirs,
"Re 16, *Christopher Street.*
"In reply to yours of the 22nd, had you not better call and see my clients, because in the face of their instructions to me I cannot issue a certificate, whatever may be my own private opinion in the matter.

"Yours faithfully,
"Robt. W. Hobden.
"pp. A. G. P."

"34, Finsbury Square, E.C.
"May 9th, 1908.

"Messrs. Hickman & Co.
"Dear Sirs,
"Re *Christopher Street.*
"I enclose copy of letter I have received from Messrs. Roberts' solicitors. Please let me know what I am to do in the matter.

"Yours faithfully,
"Robt. W. Hobden."

1909
Nov. 2.

King's Bench
Division.

"34, Finsbury Square, E.C.
"May 19th, 1908.

"Messrs WHITELOCK & STORR.
"DEAR SIRS,

"Re 16, *Christopher Street.*

". . . . I have no objection whatever to giving your clients a certificate, but you can understand my position if you will refer to my letter to Messrs. Roberts on the matter, wherein I explain that my clients wish to have the whole matter settled and one certificate for the balance.

"Yours faithfully,
"ROBT. W. HOBDEN."

"3, Rutland Place, E.C.
"May 27, 1908.

"R. W. HOBDEN, Esq.
"34, Finsbury Square, E.C.
"DEAR SIR,

"16, *Christopher Street. Roberts & Co.*

"I have received another letter from the solicitors, and as we want to avoid expense, I shall be glad if you will kindly let me have the account with any remarks you have to make, as Mr. Hickman would like to see it. I need not say you must reduce the account as much as possible on account of the heavy expenses we have already had in the matter.

"Yours truly,
"MARK BROMET.
"per W. H."

The other facts of the case sufficiently appear from the judgments.

To his affidavit, in opposition to a summons for summary judgment under Ord. XIV., Hobden exhibited a final certificate of the same date, showing a sum of 339*l.* 9*s.* 4*d.* as due to Roberts. The Master ordered this to be paid over to Roberts forthwith, but gave Hickman & Co. leave to defend as to the balance of the claim.

C. F. Vachell, K. C., and Boydell Houghton for the plaintiff.

Hugo Young, K. C., and Macpherson for the defendants.

HAMILTON, J.: This is an action brought for the balance of work and labour done and materials used under a building contract, and for extras, by Charles Philip Roberts, who is now deceased, the action being continued by his executors, against Messrs. Hickman & Co., who, under the contract with the freeholder for the building of 16, Christopher Street in the City, had to pull down some premises there and to erect new ones, and who had made therefore a contract with Messrs. Roberts, dated the 31st December (which incorporates a quantity of general conditions of contract), and is for a sum of 2,750*l.*

Under the terms of this latter contract, which I need not go into in any detail, because they are common ground between the parties, Mr. Hobden, the architect, occupied the usual position of being

1909
Nov. 2.

King's Bench
Division.

the person who had to issue certificates for instalments of the moneys payable to the builder, and whose certificates had to be obtained before the builder would be entitled to receive the money, and who, in the case of extras or other claims by the builder, would, as between the parties, have to settle and determine those claims. The clause that is perhaps of most importance is clause 29, under which the provisional or interim certificates were to be at the rate of 80 per cent. of the work actually done, in sums of not less than 400*l.*, a further 10 per cent. to be paid on the practical completion of the work, and the balance on the completion of the contractors' term of maintenance, which it is agreed, though not stated in the clause, was three months. Some time in August, 1907, owing to difficulties with adjoining properties, the work was, at the instance of the defendants, brought to a standstill; it was not resumed until November, 1907. It is agreed that the suspension of the work was, as between the parties in this case, at the instance of the defendants and to the prejudice of the plaintiff, and under such circumstances as would make the defendants liable to compensate Mr. Roberts in respect of it, subject to Mr. Hobden, the architect, dealing with the amounts to be allowed. Some correspondence took place in the month of November, 1907, Mr. Roberts then sending in claims which he put at the amount of 238*l.* 12*s.* 6*d.* for the stoppage, and being asked to estimate for some other work which would be required to be done. He was induced to continue the work without these claims being immediately settled, but the letters did not amount to an agreement that the claims for stoppage should stand over until any particular time. As a matter of fact, the work was, according to Mr. Roberts, "practically complete," in the words of section 29, on or by the 2nd April. In the language of Mr. Hobden, the architect, the building was finished, and a certificate of practical completion was due as early as the 10th April; and as a matter of fact the keys were handed over to Mr. Hobden on, I think, the 1st May. Consequently it appears to me that under clause 29 the three months during which the retention money was to be withheld would run until somewhere between the 2nd and 10th July. That point is of some importance in connection with the interview of the 17th June.

At the beginning of April Mr. Roberts was pressing Mr. Hobden to give him a considerable certificate on account. Correspondence occurred which I must come back to. No certificate was given, and by the latter part of May the plaintiff was consulting his solicitors, and on the 23rd May his solicitors sent detailed accounts of his claims both to the architect and to the defendants. What those accounts

1909
Nov. 2.
―――――――
King's Bench
Division.

are it does not very much matter. The stoppage claim was the old claim made in the previous November. The work having been done, the variations could be measured up by the architect upon the spot; but at any rate those accounts are the materials upon which ultimately the architect gave the certificates. Prompt attention was promised to these accounts by Mr. Hobden on the 25th May, but until the 15th June nothing practically had been done. The correspondence, and the inferences to be drawn from it, I will deal with subsequently.

On the 15th and 16th June Mr. Davey, the estimator on behalf of the plaintiff, met Mr. Porri, the manager for Mr. Hobden, and all items were agreed except the stoppage account and some minor items for work in addition to the stoppage claim which these two gentlemen could not settle, and which therefore were outstanding when they had finished their meetings.

On the 17th June an appointment was arranged at which Mr. Bromet was to attend, and, although Mr. Bromet, a member of the defendants' firm, came late, eventually Mr. Hobden gave to Mr. Roberts a certificate for 400*l.* It was not until a writ had been issued against Messrs. Hickman & Co. upon that certificate that the 400*l.* was paid with some costs, but eventually it was paid, and then, owing to continued disputes, the writ in the present action was issued on the 15th July.

I think it is important to observe that down to the 17th June (assuming matters to stand as they stand now, after Mr. Hobden has given his certificate, as he did, for 339*l.* 9*s.* 4*d.*, being a final certificate on the 21st August, 1908, pending this action) Mr. Roberts was not entitled to quite so much as 400*l.*, because, assuming that the right to retention money was not waived by the building owner, the 400*l.* to some extent, which it is not necessary for me to investigate, overpaid Mr. Roberts up to that time, and the right to the 10 per cent. which was being retained, would not accrue to him until some date in the first part of July.

The issues raised in the case are, first of all those which go to the entire defence, and secondly, some substantial ones of detail, which it was agreed that it would not be necessary to go into if the defence to the whole claim succeeded. The questions therefore which turn upon the true position of the parties with regard to the architect and his certificate have been gone into in the first instance. The defendants say: You cannot sue for your balance, however much it be in amount at the date of the writ, for you have no certificate from the architect, because there is a condition precedent unfulfilled

1909
Nov. 2.

King's Bench
Division.

to your right to sue at all. The plaintiff replies: I do not require that certificate, because the architect has so misconducted himself that he can no longer be impartial between the parties, and therefore I am not bound by any certificate he may make. The defendants say, he has, pending the action, certified for 339*l.* 9*s.* 4*d.* Instead of insisting that a fresh action should be brought for that, we pay that money under Order made in Chambers, and rely upon the fact, if that certificate is good, that the same certificate which puts you in a position to sue puts you out of Court, because we have paid you all that you are entitled to get. Two questions arise: First of all, the smaller question, whether the plaintiff was in a position to sue at all at the beginning of this action on the 15th July, 1908; and secondly, whether the certificate made by the architect does conclude him or not.

Now, that involves looking into the facts a little more closely. The plaintiff says: I will show by the conduct of Mr. Hobden, the architect, that prior to the commencement of this action he had ceased to be impartial between the parties, that that was furthermore at the instance of the defendants who procured him to refuse certificates which he felt and admitted to be due, and to constrain the plaintiff to wait for his money, with the object of enabling the defendants to have the advantage of having all the matters in dispute settled up in one settlement before any further money was paid after the completion of the buildings. As to that, I do not think that anything serious appears in the correspondence until the work is completed.

Attention is drawn to the fact that the architect regularly wrote to what he called "his clients," the defendants, when the plaintiff asked for a certificate, and said he wanted more money; but I am unable to see in that or in the replies that were made by the defendants anything inconsistent with the duty of the architect. Matters only begin to be worthy of close attention after the commencement of April and when the work is practically finished. One finds, then, that Mr. Hobden, on the 28th March, wrote to Messrs. Hickman saying that the plaintiffs wanted a certificate, that they were probably entitled to something, and that he personally could not see that the amount was as great as that demanded. Upon the 31st March Mr. Bromet wrote back and said that the account for extras would have to be very carefully gone into; that there was a lot of work which had been omitted for which other work had been substituted, and that he thought it would be unwise to issue the certificate until the accounts from Mr. Roberts had come in. I may say here, as regards the

1909
Nov. 2.

King's Bench
Division.

desire of Messrs. Hickman to have all accounts settled at once, to have the stoppage account and the claim for stoppage, and the claim for extras sent in and disposed of at the end of the building as promptly as possible and to produce a prompt settlement by not having any further payments on account, seems to me to have been in itself a sensible business desire. I do not regard their desire as indicative of any improper conduct on their part, but it does not at all follow that Mr. Hobden was entitled to pay any attention to it.

On the 2nd April Mr. Roberts is pressing for a certificate, and saying that he trusts that the building owners will not insist upon any retention money. Mr. Hobden then writes a number of letters, which I need not read in detail, but which are certainly rather remarkable. They run from the 8th April to the 25th April. Mr. Hobden in these letters eventually arrives at this conclusion, that he tells the defendant, whom he calls his client, that the plaintiffs are in his opinion entitled to a considerable certificate, and yet he refuses to issue any certificate at all. He was asked for a certificate for 600*l.* He wrote on the 10th April to the defendants: "There is no doubt they are entitled to their certificate of practical completion as the building is now finished and Roberts are giving up possession. I must hear from you at once as I shall have to give Roberts a certificate early next week for 500*l.* or 600*l.*"

On the 14th April he writes in the same sense: "and as Mr. Roberts is entitled under the contract to a certificate I must, of course, give it to him." He then on the 15th April gets a letter from Mr. Bromet saying: "I am sure if we pay Roberts a cheque on account it will cause delay and perhaps a deal of expense. I shall therefore be glad if you will carry out the wishes of Mr. Hickman and myself, and I am sure Mr. Roberts cannot object to this." Mr. Hobden in fact did carry out the wishes of Mr. Hickman and Mr. Bromet, but unfortunately Mr. Roberts did object to it strongly. Mr. Hobden wrote to Messrs. Hickman to say that he was not issuing any other certificate "until the account has been issued and agreed. At the same time I must express my opinion that I think you are wrong in not agreeing to the certificate I proposed to give, namely 500*l.*" At the same time he wrote to Messrs. Roberts: "I regret I cannot enclose certificate, my clients' instructions being that the certificate I next give you is to be a final one including for a complete settlement of the work done, into which I shall be prepared to go after Easter." He also wrote on the 24th April: "Had you not better call and see my clients, because in the face of their in-

1909
Nov. 2.

King's Bench
Division.

structions to me I cannot issue a certificate, whatever may be my own private opinion in the matter."

I am unable to understand Mr. Hobden's explanation of that correspondence. It appears to me to be perfectly plain that the defendants endeavoured to interfere between the architect and the builder and themselves with regard to the giving of one of the certificates which it was the architect's duty to give under the contract. It appears to me to be quite clear that Mr. Hobden, instead of remaining adamantine to that pressure, yielded to it at once, and called it what I think it was, "instructions from his clients." It appears to me that in doing that he was quite well aware that he was disregarding what he would have done if left to himself, and setting aside what he calls "my own private opinion." He has given an explanation today which is this: I saw Mr. Bromet, and I suggested to him what indeed Mr. Roberts had suggested to me, that having regard to the delay in the previous year, it would be a graceful act to waive any claim to retention money; I could not get Mr. Bromet to make up his mind one way or the other, and therefore I kept writing to Mr. Bromet to say, if you do not say something I shall have to give this man a certificate for 500*l.* or 600*l.*, knowing in my own mind that 400*l.* was about all he was entitled to, but with the object of getting Mr. Bromet to decide favourably to Mr. Roberts something which I myself as the architect had no power under the contract to do. And therefore he said in terms—he used these words to me himself— that it was out of his sympathy with Mr. Roberts that he took this course with Mr. Bromet. I do not think that was his real motive at the time, and I do not think that it is an explanation which will hold water.

No doubt Mr. Hobden desired, as far as he conveniently could, to keep well with both sides. In that I think he was right. His business is one which requires a good deal of tact, and an endeavour not only to be just to both sides but to let each side believe that he has been just. But I cannot believe that he really thought that the way to get any practical sympathy expressed by Mr. Bromet towards Mr. Roberts was to withhold all certificates and leave Mr. Roberts to go and see Mr. Bromet and try to get his rights direct. There are, however, two important facts to be observed about this. The first is to my thinking, that he told Mr. Roberts exactly what the position was; he told him in plain terms: "I cannot enclose certificate, my clients' instructions being that the certificate I next give you is to be a final one, including for a complete settlement of the work done." It is quite true that he did not in letters at that time add: and my

1909
Nov. 2.
King's Bench
Division.

opinion is that 500*l.* or 600*l.* is the sum you ought to have. But then I do not think that 500*l.* or 600*l.* was the sum which Mr. Hobden then thought he ought to have. I think 400*l.* or 450*l.* was the sum which, if left to himself, Mr. Hobden would most probably have certified for, after making a fuller enquiry into the actual figures. Therefore, I think that the whole substance of what Mr. Hobden had done wrong was at once communicated to Mr. Roberts.

In my opinion Mr. Hobden was disregarding his obligations to the two parties, because under the contract it was clear that the building owner could not insist as a condition of a certificate being given that it should be a final certificate. At that moment, under clause 29 of the conditions, the builder was entitled to an interim certificate, and Mr. Hobden, in yielding to the wishes of Messrs. Hickman, was doing that which he was not entitled to do as the architect between the parties; but then, as he told the plaintiffs exactly what he was doing, except for the amount of money, and the very amount of money that he was prepared to give was subsequently told to Mr. Roberts, namely upon the 17th June, it appears to me that Mr. Roberts was put in possession of all the grounds that he then had for complaining against Mr. Hobden.

I ought to say, although I do not think the account given today by Mr. Hobden of his motives in 1908 is one that I can accept, that I see no ground for thinking that this was done corruptly. The expression "collusion" is one which does not fit the circumstances of the case. As soon as you take note that Mr. Hobden told Messrs. Roberts that he was receiving and acting upon instructions, and although under the contract Mr. Hobden was not doing his duty, there was no turpitude about what he was doing, and therefore there is nothing in what he did on that occasion which would make him from the point of view of abstract justice an unfit person to be allowed to settle any further disputes between the parties at all.

My view is that upon the knowledge coming to Mr. Roberts' mind of the way in which Mr. Hobden had been acting, he would have been entitled to say: You have departed from your quasijudicial duty as architect once, and I am no longer bound to submit to you and your decisions; and he might have elected, if he had chosen, to decline any longer to be bound by the certificates of the architect, but if he elected to continue to treat the architect as the person to decide these matters and to seek his decisions, it appears to me that he cannot any longer, at any rate in a case where the architect's conduct has been contrary to the contract only, but not contrary to good

1909
Nov. 2.

King's Bench
Division.

faith or honesty, thereafter say that when a certificate has been given by that person he will decline to be bound by it.

The proposition advanced on behalf of the plaintiff was that his conduct had dethroned him, and the word "waiver," which is relied upon by the defendants, was deprecated as not being the correct legal description of what the plaintiff did. I do not use either term, accordingly, but I think all that happened was that the plaintiff was given the right to refuse any longer to be bound by the decisions of Mr. Hobden, who had failed in this particular to conform to his duty under the contract, but, although he had the right to do so, if he chose to exercise it, he could, if he liked, further submit to the decisions of that authority, and if he did so he would have to be bound by them. This therefore makes it material to consider what the subsequent conduct of the parties was.

Mr. Roberts, although he complained of the unusual and unfair way in which the defendants were acting, says expressly on the 25th April that he thanks Mr. Hobden for the trouble he has taken in the matter, and felt sure he would only wish to do what he considered fair. It is therefore obvious that Mr. Roberts was not struck at the time, nor at any subsequent time, I think, with any feeling that Mr. Hobden was not behaving honestly, and I am not at all sure that Mr. Roberts did not perfectly appreciate the motive with which Messrs. Hickman desired to have the question of extras disposed of once and for all. There was probably as much advantage to be gained by Messrs. Roberts in getting a large interim certificate at this stage as there would have been advantage to Messrs. Hickman in getting all certificates withheld until Messrs. Roberts' claims were all made and settled, and could be disposed of at once.

The correspondence goes on during the month of May, and I think the only thing to be observed upon it is that the letters that passed during May confirm the conclusion that I have arrived at on the April correspondence. I think there is no doubt that Mr. Hobden was dilatory in dealing with these accounts. It appears to me that neither at this, nor at any later stage, could delay on the part of the architect of itself give the plaintiff the right to refuse any longer to be bound by those certificates, unless he was in a position to show, which in regard to delay I think he cannot show, that there was such deliberate and calculated delay as in itself to amount to a misconduct and a disregard of his duty as architect. But whether it was that he had other fish to fry, or that he did not think Mr. Roberts was a very important person, I think there is no doubt that Mr. Hobden took his time with considerable leisure with regard to the claims of Mr. Roberts.

1909
Nov. 2.

King's Bench
Division.

When Mr. Roberts first went to his solicitors, they wrote on the 8th May, 1908, to Mr. Hobden complaining of a refusal to give a certificate on the ground that he had received instructions from Messrs. Hickman not to do so, and therefore Mr. Roberts had been advised on the precise facts of what it was that Mr. Hobden had been doing. They asked whether Mr. Hobden "has any reason for not granting the certificate asked for, other than the reason that Messrs. Hickman & Co. have requested you not to do so." In Mr. Hobden's absence his manager passed that on to the defendants, and asked what he was to do in the matter. Mr. Hobden himself replied to the solicitors: "I have no objection whatever to giving your clients a certificate, but you can understand my position if you will refer to my letter to Messrs. Roberts on the matter, wherein I explain that my clients wish to have the whole matter settled and one certificate given for the balance." There would have been Mr. Hobden's opportunity to have said: "My conduct has been prompted by my sympathy with your client and a desire to put you in a position to do more for yourself than I can do for you." But he did not take that opportunity; he stated what I think was the fact, that his position was taken up because his clients wished to have the whole matter settled and one certificate given. The full detailed accounts were then sent in, and litigation was threatened.

There is a letter on the 27th May from Mr. Bromet to Mr. Hobden, in which he says, having asked to see the accounts: "I need not say you must reduce the account as much as possible on account of the heavy expenses we have already had in the matter." The fact that Mr. Hobden makes no reply to that, in his own language that he ignored what he admits to be an irregularity, although he will not call it an impertinence, is the only evidence that I can find against him of having been influenced in regard to the amount to be allowed, as distinguished from the date at which a certificate should be issued. I come to the conclusion on the whole of the evidence that insofar as Mr. Hobden has dealt with the amount to be allowed to the plaintiff, he has done so independently, applying his mind in the ordinary way, using the services of a deputy, as he was entitled to do, and not in any way cutting down the allowances to the plaintiffs in order to accommodate the defendants. If I thought that he had done that I should not have been able to exonerate him from the suggestion of corrupt conduct, as on the evidence I do.

The accounts were looked into, in the way I have stated, in June. On the 4th June, Messrs. Whitelock and Storr, the plaintiff's solicitors, are pressing Mr. Hobden for his certificate, and threatening him with an action if he does not issue it. They are not saying:

1909
Nov. 2.

King's Bench
Division.

You have misconducted yourself, and therefore on behalf of our clients we will have no more to do with you or your certificates; on the contrary, they are saying: In spite of what has happened, we want your certificate, because we want to bring an action upon it, to assert our claim relying upon it. They say the same thing on the 6th June: Our client is entitled to an interim certificate, and it is this certificate which we require. On the 9th June that letter was sent by Mr. Hobden to Messrs. Hickman, saying: Messrs. Roberts are no doubt entitled to a certificate under the contract, without waiting for the account to be settled; and on the same 9th June, Mr. Hobden writes to the plaintiff: "I have now been through your account, and as I cannot agree some of the dimensions I shall be glad if you will make an appointment for your surveyor to go into these items with me at your early convenience." It was as a result of that letter that Mr. Davey met Mr. Porri, and they settled most of the items, excluding the big stoppage item. On the 17th June, at this interview, my opinion of the evidence is that Mr. Hobden made it quite clear to Mr. Roberts that he was still acting upon the instructions of Mr. Bromet as regards giving an interim certificate.

Mr. Hobden gave no explanation that I could understand of what he said was the fact, that he said to the plaintiff who attended this appointment before Mr. Bromet had come, he being late for the appointment: This is an important appointment; I want to wait till the last moment before I give a certificate for 400l., so that Mr. Bromet may be here. When Mr. Bromet did come, Mr. Hobden had to go, so Mr. Hobden signed the certificate and left it on the desk, and as a result of the certificate being there, somehow or other, I suppose with Mr. Bromet's assent—certainly without his interference—the certificate reached Mr. Roberts, who took it away with him. It seems to me to be quite clear that Mr. Roberts was then told what I think was the state of Mr. Hobden's mind: "Under the contract you ought to have 400l. on account; I would give you the certificate for it at once if I was not attending to Mr. Bromet's instructions, but I do not want to do it without his instructions, and he will be here in a few minutes." When he came, something or other passed which was equivalent to Mr. Bromet's instructions or assent being given to its being handed over. I think the importance of that is that again Mr. Roberts had it brought home to his mind, if he paid attention to it, that Mr. Hobden was in this particular matter not acting as a free agent, and therefore he was in a position to have said: No, Mr. Hobden, I am entitled to a great deal more than 400l., and as you are no longer acting independently between

1909
Nov. 2.
—————
King's Bench
Division.

us, I will have no more to do with you or your certificate. Instead of that, he took the certificate like a wise man and endeavoured successfully to enforce payment of it.

It is also important to notice that if you assume that the certificate for 339*l.* 9*s.* 4*d.* of the 21st August decided the matter between the parties, that 400*l.* was at that moment, and pending the next three weeks or so, an overpayment to some extent, because, had the retention money clause been fully insisted upon, not so much as 400*l.* was to be paid. The figures were gone into between counsel; I was satisfied upon them, and I think both parties agreed that upon strict calculation that was so. The strategy—because I think there was a great deal of strategy on both sides here—became complicated. Messrs. Hickman would not produce a cheque for the 400*l.* certificate; that was no fault of Mr. Hobden's, and I think no affair of his; but Mr. Hobden did say to me, that although he was not concerned with the solicitors' proceedings, he had forborne to give a certificate earlier than the 17th June upon the instructions of what he calls "our solicitors," which meant the defendants' solicitors, and that he did not issue the final certificate, pending the suit, in August, until the defendants' solicitors instructed him to do so; but that is only a continuation of the other conduct of which it seems to me that Messrs. Roberts have had the fullest notice.

Now, you find that down to the second week in August Mr. Roberts and his solicitors were pressing for this certificate. They were pressing for appointments, in order that the outstanding claims might be gone into, with a view to a final certificate; and it appears to me they were taking every step that they could to make Mr. Hobden, who was still the tribunal they had to go to, perform what they conceived to be his duty of giving a decision without further delay. I think Mr. Hobden was taking his time, and after the beginning of the action, on his own admission, he waited for instructions before he gave the final certificate; and the time when it became necessary to give him those instructions was the time when something had to be sworn to under Order XIV., and therefore it was a convenient thing to get a final certificate and append that to an affidavit and pay that money over under the Order of the Master, which was what was done; but still, on the 27th June the plaintiff's solicitors are writing to Mr. Hobden: "We understand from our clients that you have now agreed with them upon the matters relating to the contract for the building of the above premises, with the exception of two items, and although an appointment has been promised to settle the two outstanding questions, up to today such appointment has not been made, and we are

1909
Nov. 2.

King's Bench
Division.

afraid we must ask you to at once give us an appointment to settle the matter." That was correct.

The evidence of Mr. Roberts was that on the 17th June, the stoppage question, as to which he was then claiming a sum of 238*l.*, stood over for Mr. Hobden to investigate and decide it; and the other matters stood over for some further measurements to be taken. "We must ask you to at once give us an appointment to settle the matter," say Messrs. Whitelock & Storr. "As there has been considerable correspondence with reference to your certificate, we must ask you to accept this letter as final." Then on the 28th July, Messrs. Greenwell & Co., the defendants' solicitors, wrote to the plaintiff's solicitors, after paying the 400*l.* cheque for which the first action was brought: "As regards your client's claim of 538*l.* 9*s.* 11*d.*, in respect of which we understood no certificate has been granted, we have written our clients as arranged with you, that your client should meet Mr. Hobden and take up his final certificate." The plaintiff's solicitors then consulted Mr. Roberts upon that, and replied on the 31st July: "We have now seen our client, who instructs us that he is prepared to meet Mr. Hobden on Monday, the 10th prox., at 12 noon here for the purpose of endeavouring to agree upon the outstanding item in respect of their account, and pending such interview you may take it, subject to the costs of the first action being paid immediately upon the Taxing Master's certificate being taken, we will not move in the action"—that is, in the present action. Accordingly, the costs in the first action were paid.

On the 10th August there is again a letter from Mr. Hobden offering Messrs. Roberts an appointment, and complaining that appointments have not been kept, and saying that as soon as these matters have been settled he can give a final certificate. Then the summons came on under Order XIV.: the final certificate of the 21st August was made, and it was attached and exhibited to the affidavit, and, as I understand, an Order was made by the Master without any point being taken that a fresh action ought to have been brought. The cheque for 339*l.* 9*s.* 4*d.*, the amount of that certificate, was paid, and has been finally acknowledged by the plaintiff's solicitors.

Now it seems to me to be clear that up to the moment when the final certificate was given, the plaintiffs were soliciting it, and soliciting Mr. Hobden to act as the person between the parties who would have to give that final certificate. There is no evidence at all to show that the defendants interfered, or that Mr. Hobden yielded to any interference instead of making up his mind how much should be

ROBERTS v. *HICKMAN & CO.*

1909
Nov. 2.

King's Bench
Division.

allowed upon it; and it appears to me that I must accept, and do accept, that as being his honest determination of the amount which was due. It was truly pointed out to me by Mr. Boydell Houghton that the certificate was never delivered to the plaintiffs. It was asked for, but it was only delivered to them in the shape of an exhibit to an affidavit, but I do not think it becomes either invalid or fails to be binding because there has been no formal delivery of it to the plaintiffs prior to its being used in the proceedings. It was pointed out, also truly, that payment of the amount was not received as payment of the certificate, but as payment ordered by the Master consequent upon an admission by the defendants that that much at least they must pay. Again, I do not think its binding effect depends upon the money having been accepted under it, but upon the fact that the person who makes the certificate was by contract the person whose decision bound the plaintiff, and the plaintiff having had, in my opinion, full knowledge in substance of what there was to say against Mr. Hobden's conduct, had elected not to rely upon that, but had elected to continue to treat Mr. Hobden as the person by whose decision he was bound.

It seems to me, therefore, unnecessary to discuss whether that should be technically called a waiver or not. The analogy that was presented to me by Mr. Vachell, that I should treat it as though it was adultery and objectionable conduct which had been once condoned, but is revived by subsequent misconduct, appears to me to be one that is not applicable to this class of case. The result is that the defence to the action is complete; the action is prematurely brought. When it was brought there was no final certificate. As regards the amount outstanding to be dealt with, the final certificate has determined that that amount is the amount which alone the plaintiff can recover, and the result is that the action from the inception has been brought under a misapprehension, and that the plaintiff wholly fails. There is therefore no necessity for going into any questions of details, and my judgment is for the defendants, with costs.

1910
April 21.

Court of
Appeal.

IN THE COURT OF APPEAL.

(*Before* Vaughan Williams, L.J., Fletcher Moulton, L.J., and Farwell, L.J.)

Vaughan Williams, L.J.: I may as well, so as not to go into the same matter twice over, say at once that we are going to allow this appeal, and that the order, so far as the costs are concerned, will take the form which I have just mentioned—that is to say, that the defendants will have to bear the costs from the date of the notice of trial down to the conclusion of the trial, except in so far as any of those costs relate to the question of *quantum* solely. Having said that, I will now deal with this case.

The judgment of Mr. Justice Hamilton is a judgment which leaves one very little to comment on. I agree with the conclusion of Mr. Justice Hamilton up to a certain point; that is to say, I agree in the general conclusions which he seems to have arrived at, that the conduct of the architect in this matter and the performance of his duties in collusion with and by the instructions of the defendants, whose mouthpiece in this matter was one of their partners, Mr. Bromet, was such as to render it impossible for the plaintiff to get the certificate of the architect. I agree that on this contract the certificate of the architect was a condition precedent to suing for the amounts due for this work on this building. The plaintiff has done the work, and he sues, as appears on the Statement of Claim—the writ being specially endorsed—for work and labour done and material supplied under a building contract and for extras amounting to 534*l.* 2*s.* 5*d.*

Now, the defendant sets up by his defence really that the giving of the certificate of the architect was under the contract a condition precedent to the recovery of this money. I think it was, but I say, in my opinion, that it became impossible for the plaintiff to obtain this certificate, because the collusive acts of the architect and the building owner together were such as to incapacitate the architect from giving in this matter the certificate between the two parties to the contract. In my judgment their collusive conduct was such as to incapacitate the architect. As I understand, Mr. Justice Hamilton takes the same view. He seems to take the view that but for what has been called the waiver—Mr. Justice Hamilton does not use the proper term quite—that but for certain conduct of the plaintiff this conduct of the defendants and the architect—I do not wish to use harsh words, but it approaches fraud really—this fraudulent conduct between the defendant and the architect disqualified the architect from acting in this matter. I think Mr. Justice Hamilton, although he would not have used the word which I have just used, "fraudulent," agrees that fraudulent or not the conduct was such as would have disqualified the architect, but for the subsequent conduct of the plaintiff, who acquiesced in the architect going on after he, the plaintiff, was aware of this misconduct; and Mr. Justice Hamilton treats him as having, with full knowledge of all these facts going to disqualify

1910
April 21.

Court of
Appeal.

the architect, taken advantage of the position of the architect to induce him to give certificates upon which the plaintiff intended to act, and which he intended to make use of.

Mr. Justice Hamilton says that the plaintiff with knowledge and disclosure of all these facts elected to treat the architect as a person fit and competent to perform these duties, and did so for the purpose of getting the architect's certificate and acting upon it. If the plaintiff had acted in this way and made this election with full knowledge of all the circumstances—I have not got to decide it, but I am prepared to say that that would not have inured to make the plea of the nondelivery of this certificate, or the nonperformance of the conditions precedent, a good plea. But, in my opinion, it is perfectly clear when you look at the correspondence that the plaintiff in the course of this matter up to the bringing of the action, which he had to bring, had not full disclosure of the improper relations of the defendant and the architect.

I think it would be a waste of time to go through all the letters in respect of which there was not a complete disclosure. I will take only one example. There was a letter, the date of which I need not trouble to look for now, in which there was information conveyed by the architect to Mr. Bromet as to the amount which he considered was really due to the builder, which was never communicated to the plaintiff at all. I have only spoken of matters at present up to the bringing of the action. I say generally that up to the bringing of the action the fact that the architect was constantly referring to the building owner to ask him to determine what answer he should give to the plaintiff's, the builder's, claim to a certificate for money—the fact that the architect was constantly asking and receiving these instructions was not communicated to the plaintiff.

Now, when we come to the time of the bringing of the action, not only after action brought do these relations between the defendant, or between Mr. Bromet and the architect continue, but actually the architect receives instructions and acts upon them; from whom? Why, from the defendants' solicitors in the action. It seems to me under those circumstances that it is impossible to say that there was any election made with full knowledge of the true relations between the defendant and the architect.

I wish to take a different view from Mr. Justice Hamilton as to the proper way of characterising this conduct of the architect. I will read the portion in which I say that I do not agree with him. He says: "The expression 'collusion' is one which does not fit the circumstances of the case." I think it does. "As soon as you take

1910
April 21.

Court of
Appeal.

note that Mr. Hobden told Messrs. Roberts that he was receiving and
acting upon instructions and although under the contract Mr. Hobden
was not doing his duty, there was no turpitude about what he was
doing." I think there was about what he was doing, and I think that
that which was told Messrs. Roberts was far from the truth. "And
therefore there is nothing in what he did on that occasion which
would make him from the point of view of abstract justice an unfit
person to be allowed to settle any further disputes between the
parties at all." I cannot agree. I think that the relations as disclosed
by these letters between the defendants and the architect were such
as to render the architect an unfit person to be allowed to settle
disputes as between the parties at all.

Then Mr. Justice Hamilton says: "My view is that upon the
knowledge coming to Mr. Roberts' mind of the way in which Mr.
Hobden had been acting, he would have been entitled to say: You
have departed from your quasijudicial duty as architect once, and I
am no longer bound to submit to you and your decisions"—there I
agree that he was entitled to say that, that is my view—and not
having had full disclosures of the relations he is still entitled to say
that—"and he might have elected, if he had chosen, to decline any
longer to be bound by the certificates of the architect"—I think that
when this action was brought it was pleaded that he still wanted that
knowledge—"but if he had elected to continue to treat the architect
as the person to decide these matters and to seek his decisions, it
appears to me that he cannot any longer, at any rate in a case where
the architect's conduct has been contrary to the contract only, but
not contrary to good faith and honesty"—I do not agree there; I think
it was much more than that, I think it was contrary to good faith and
honesty—"thereafter say that when a certificate has been given by
that person he will decline to be bound by it."

In my judgment the plaintiff here had never made the election after
full disclosure of the facts and with full knowledge of all the facts as
to the relations between the defendant and the architect, and I think
that under these circumstances the judgment of Mr. Justice Hamilton
was wrong and ought to be set aside.

I have already said what I have to say on the question of costs so
far as the trial is concerned. I have only to say that the defendants
will have to pay the costs of this appeal.

FLETCHER MOULTON, L. J.: I am of the same opinion, and I adopt the
judgment which has just been delivered by the President. Lord
Justice Vaughan Williams has gone so fully into the question of the

1910
April 21.

Court of
Appeal.

disqualification of the architect that I do not intend to add any words upon that.

I only wish to notice the argument of Mr. Hugo Young, in which he tried to draw a distinction between an architect's forgetfulness of his duties with regard to the granting of the certificate, and the unfitness of the architect or arbitrator to decide on a matter of *quantum*. I want to point out that the misconduct on the part of an architect in allowing himself to receive instructions from one of the parties, and to act in that party's interest, goes to the status of the architect. It makes him incapacitated to act as judge, and it is obvious that that affects his decisions on every point, and not only on the point on which you can show that he has taken a direction from either side. He is no longer fit to be a judge because he has been acting in the interests of one of the parties, and by their direction. That taints the whole of his acts and makes them invalid to whatever subsequent matter his decision is directed.

FARWELL, L.J.: I am of the same opinion. I entirely adopt the judgment the President has given, and I only desire to make one observation on the argument of Mr. Hugo Young. In my view an architect whose duty it is to give certificates, on which alone the builder can get payment, is bound to act fairly between the builder and the building owner. It is quite true, as Mr. Hugo Young said, that the architect as such is retained to advise the building owner, and to act for him as an architect, but in his capacity of giving certificates for the amounts, he is acting as an umpire or an arbitrator between the owner and the builder, and it is not the true view that he is entitled if he pleases to take into consideration the convenience of the owner and say:—"It will hamper him if I give a certificate at present; I will let it stand over for three or four months," or "It is inconvenient to him to pay so much; I will make him pay less." He is bound to act fairly between the two. In the present case if you once segregate the position of the architect as arbitrator from his position as architect pure and simple, it is perfectly obvious, to my mind, that it is improper for him to consult behind the back of one of the two parties with the other one as to how much the one should be allowed to receive or when he should be allowed to receive it.

It is perfectly clear on perusing this correspondence, as indeed the learned judge has found, that the architect did not consider himself a free agent. He considered himself bound to obey the directions of the building owner, and the fact that he says: "I think you ought to have a certificate, but I cannot give it to you because the owner objects," shows that he misapprehended his position. One of the worst letters which I have seen in the correspondence is the one of the 27th May, when the building owner writes to the architect and says: "I need not say you must reduce the amount as much as possible"—not for any reason of bad work, or anything of that kind, but "on account of the heavy expenses we have already had in the matter." A more improper letter from the building owner to the architect I can hardly imagine. It is rather significant that the architect makes no answer, and although he seems to have said that he was not influenced by it, it is very difficult to say how far you can accept that, when you see the mode in which the architect has acted and obeyed the orders of the building owner. I think he has entirely misapprehended his position, and I confess I think there is the clearest evidence of the misconduct of the architect and collusion with the building owner.

1910
April 21.

Court of
Appeal.

IN THE HOUSE OF LORDS.

1911
May 9.

House of
Lords.

(*Before* Lords Loreburn, L.C., Ashbourne, Alverstone, L.C.J., Atkinson and Shaw of Dunfermline.)

The Lord Chancellor: My Lords, in this case I do not think that any of your Lordships are in doubt that we ought to affirm the judgment of the Court of Appeal. I will not enter upon the story at all, but will merely put my reasons for concurring with the Court of Appeal. I think the defendants cannot rely upon this certificate, either as a condition precedent or as an adjudication binding upon the other party. The architect, Mr. Hobden, did, I think, place himself in a position which deprived his certificate of the value which otherwise it would have had. Moulton, L.J., after referring to what he had done, says: "He is no longer fit to be a judge, because he had been acting in the interests of one of the parties, and by their direction. That taints the whole of his acts and makes them invalid, whatever subsequent matter his decision is directed to." I agree with that, but I should like to say this: it is not in my opinion a case to which the terms "turpitude" or "fraud" are apt. I think the real error of Mr. Hobden was that he mistook his position, that he meant to act as a mediator; that he had not the firmness to recognise that his true position was that of an arbitrator, and repel unworthy communications made to him by the defendants. It is undoubted

1911
May 9.
_____
House of
Lords.

that the defendants, Messrs. Hickman, tried in this respect to lead him astray in their own interests.

It is argued by Mr. Young that, knowing the attitude taken up by Mr. Hobden, the plaintiffs really waived his irregularity with a full disclosure of the facts. I will not enter upon it, but I do not think there was full disclosure of the facts. I think that if these letters had been shown to Messrs. Roberts they would then have instantly taken a stronger line than they did.

I also think that the unexplained delay after the 17th of June in doing what was his duty as regards his certificate was due to the mistaken view he had taken of his being required to procure the assent of the defendants before he discharged his duties under the contract.

My Lords, as to Messrs. Hickman, I will only say that they seem to have been trifling with a just claim for a long time, and that they would be properly punished by having to pay the costs of this action, as well as whatever may hereafter be adjudged to be due from them.

Lord Ashbourne: My Lords, I quite concur. I am of opinion that the arbitrator here, Mr. Hobden, did not preserve that attitude of judicial independence which was needed and required of him in the discharge of his responsible and possibly difficult duties; but I do not think it necessary to go so far as to adopt the words which may be noticed in the reading of the case to have been used, the words "turpitude" and "fraud." I think that he had not present to his mind, and did not act upon, that need for judicial independence that is requisite for anyone in his position, and I entirely agree with the conclusion upon that subject expressed in the judgment of the Court of Appeal.

Lord Alverstone: My Lords, this case has such general importance that I will detain your Lordships a few moments in concurring, as I do, with the motion which my noble and learned friend the Lord Chancellor has made. My Lords, it has been pointed out in several cases in the Court of Appeal, and particularly by Lord Bowen in *Jackson* v. *The Barry Railway Co.* (a), that the position of these arbitrators is a very important one, and that the system could not have been allowed to exist for so long, or to have been relied upon commercially, had it not been that it has been found that persons in the position of engineers or architects are able to maintain, and do

(a) [1893] 1 Ch. 283; 9 T. L. R. 90; 68 L. T. 472.

maintain, a fair and judicial view with regard to the rights of the parties. My Lords, it has to be remembered that in the great majority of cases they are the agents of the employers. It has also to be remembered that they not infrequently have to adjudicate upon matters for which they themselves are partly responsible. Both these matters have been pointed out, as I have said, by the late Lord Collins and the late Lord Bowen, and therefore it is very important that it should be understood that when a builder or a contractor puts himself in the hands of an engineer or architect as arbitrator there is a very high duty upon that architect or that engineer to maintain his judicial position.

My Lords, the only ground upon which Mr. Justice Hamilton decided against these plaintiffs was that, with full knowledge as to what had happened prior to the giving of the final certificate, or I ought to say prior to the 17th June, they went on and allowed the architect to adjudicate upon matters between them. I desire to say that had I thought that the view taken by my brother Hamilton of the facts was correct I should have concurred in that view; but it seems to me, for reasons that I will very briefly explain to your Lordships, that as the facts strike me, that view cannot be taken. It has been a little overlooked in the argument of Mr. Hugo Young at the Bar that there are two questions here. The first question is whether the action could be brought without there being a certificate. A decision in his favour upon that point would only affect the question of the costs of the action, but the real fight and battle here is not only as to whether or not the action could be brought without a certificate, but whether the certificate of the 21st August is a binding certificate, because under the procedure, and the very reasonable procedure adopted in the case, assuming it was a binding certificate, that money in the course of the action was paid over to the plaintiffs, and they have no further claim in the matter. Therefore, we have not merely to consider whether or not an action could be brought without any certificate, but whether this certificate when given is binding so as to preclude the plaintiffs from recovering any further amounts before the Official Referee.

My Lords, I desire most respectfully to adopt the language of the Lord Chancellor, and to say that I do not propose to use any hard or strong language, but to say that it seems to me that it is quite clear upon the correspondence that this architect had forgotten his duty to act strictly judicially through the whole course of the proceedings, and that it cannot be said that the plaintiffs had such knowledge of his conduct or of what had passed between him and Messrs. Hickman

29 (2)

1911
May 9.

House of
Lords.

as to prevent them now raising that point. My Lords, I do not propose to go through the correspondence, but there are four letters to which attention should be called as illustrating the point that I make.

In Mr. Hobden's own letter of the 8th November, 1907, to the defendants, when he first writes with regard to a claim made for the delay and the extra works, he says: "Of course, both of these claims will want very careful investigation with the view to considerably reducing the amounts." I quite agree, if I may say so, with the argument of the learned counsel at the Bar that that of itself would not amount to very much, although it does not seem altogether a strictly judicial expression, because his duty was not to consider reducing the amounts but to say what was fair between the parties. But, my Lords, what was much more important is the letter that was written to him by the defendants on the 12th November, 1907, in reply. I desire to point out to your Lordships with regard to this letter, as well as with regard to two others to which I shall have to call attention, that an architect or an engineer acting as arbitrator and recognising his judicial position ought at once to have repudiated any such letter when written to him. Messrs. Hickman, as my noble and learned friend the Lord Chancellor said a few moments ago, certainly were not themselves maintaining the judicial position of Mr. Hobden, for they write then to him: "Of course it is as well to explain to Mr. Roberts that if he wants to do any more work for us he must be reasonable, and not take advantage of our unfortunate position." That, to my mind, was referring to a matter which ought to have had no influence whatever—the prospect of further work—when Mr. Hobden was performing his judicial duties. Mr. Bromet (a member of defendants' firm), on March 31, 1908, writes again: "I should say on no account should you issue this until we have got Roberts' account for the extras, as we believe you said this would have to be gone into very carefully indeed, as you thought he was making charges he has no right to make. You must also bear in mind that there is a lot of work in the contract which has not been done, and which has been substituted for other work." That, to my mind, is an indication that Messrs. Hickman were not leaving Mr. Hobden alone, but were indicating to him matters in their favour with regard to the claim that was being made.

Then, if I may for one moment refer to the letters which were referred to in the Court of Appeal, it seems to me that they show conclusively that throughout the whole of this time Mr. Hobden was not properly recognising or appreciating what his position was. Mr. Hobden had sent on to Messrs, Hickman Messrs, Roberts' letter

1911
May 9.

House of
Lords.

pressing for a certificate, and then they reply at once, on April 15th, 1908: "He (Mr. Hickman) further said, as one who understands building, this should have been sent in at once, as it was no use asking him to see the job when the account had not been delivered, as he said he had a similar experience in Red Lion Street, and he does not want it to occur again, therefore any account Roberts has should be dealt with at once. You will please understand it is no use issuing a certificate as I am sure Mr. Hickman will not sign a cheque, so that it is best to get the account at once and have it properly checked, and so get the whole matter cleared up."

My Lords, we know what had happened. It is only necessary to consider what happened in two sentences to see that these letters may have had, and probably did have, some effect upon Mr. Hobden's position. We know that with regard to the issue of an interim certificate he did, without justification and against his own opinion, abstain from issuing it from the month of April down to the 17th June, and we further know that he did not issue his final certificate till he was directed by the solicitors for Messrs. Hickman to do so. My Lords, I now ask myself this question: Had Mr. Roberts known of this correspondence, of these communications between their arbitrator architect or architect arbitrator and the employers, would he have consented to have gone on? The Court of Appeal obviously thought he would not, and it seems to me, my Lords, under those circumstances that it is quite impossible to say that the judicial finding of a certain amount against Mr. Roberts, made when he was in ignorance of that which had passed between Messrs. Hickman and Mr. Hobden, the architect, ought to be binding upon him.

One notices, and it is important to notice it, that, as was elicited by Mr. Vachell, Mr. Hobden was an intimate friend of Messrs. Hickman, and a gentleman who had done as much as 100,000*l.* worth of work for them. These are the very conditions as pointed out in the judgment to which I have referred, as showing the confidence that is entertained by builders and by contractors in referring their disputes, and allowing them to be referred, to the engineer, who is the agent of the employers. But, my Lords, the consequence of that practice is that persons who act in that judicial position must maintain that judicial position throughout, and I think that it would be contrary to justice if it were held (which is the important matter in this case) that this adjudication which Mr. Hobden has made against, or at all events upon, the interests of Messrs. Roberts was binding upon them.

1911
May 9.

House of
Lords.

My Lords, I humbly concur in the motion that the Lord Chancellor has made that this appeal be dismissed.

Lord Atkinson: My Lords, I concur, and I shortly base my judgement upon three conclusions at which I have arrived. First, I think it is clearly established upon the evidence that this arbitrator had ceased to be a free agent, that he had forfeited his independence as an arbitrator, and had allowed himself to be under the control or under the influence of the building owners. I think it is not satisfactorily proved that he ever recovered his independence, but that on the contrary the fair presumption from the entirely unexplained delay in giving his final certificate is that he was still under the influence of the building owners. So far as the point is concerned about adopting him with all the defects and weaknesses he has shown, in order that that should be effective there ought, in my view, to have been a full and ample disclosure of every communication that had passed between him and the building owners. That did not take place, and therefore, in my opinion, the argument which has been addressed to the House cannot be sustained. At the same time, my Lords, I quite concur with what has fallen from my noble and learned friend upon the woolsack that the conduct of the architect in this case has probably been too severely censured. He was led astray. He was induced to forfeit his independence, and to be influenced by the requirements, or an anxiety to promote the interests, of the building owners, but I think it is quite possible that that may have been done without any intention on his part to do what was wrong, or possibly without even the knowledge that he was doing what was wrong. Therefore, as regards the use of the words "collusion," "corruption," or "fraud," those terms are rather extravagant terms to apply to the conduct that has been established against him. I do not refer to the correspondence to which my noble and learned friend who has preceded me has already referred. For these reasons I think the appeal should be dismissed.

Lord Shaw of Dunfermline: My Lords, the position of an architect in a building contract is one of great delicacy. He is placed in that position to act judicially, when, to the knowledge of both parties, the person who is his master and his paymaster is one of the parties to the contract. It has been affirmed by Courts of law, however, that that being the case his judicial position must be accepted, and it follows from that that in the peculiarly delicate situation in which such a man stands the Courts of law must be very particular to see that his judicial attitude is maintained.

1911
May 9.

House of
Lords.

With regard to Mr. Hobden, I desire to say that I do not think anything has occurred in this case to suggest for one moment that when the ultimate accounting between owners and the contractor took place Mr. Hobden's certificate would have overstated by a single penny or understated by a single penny the amount that in his judgment was due between these parties. It is right and just to Mr. Hobden that I should say so; but upon the other hand, my Lords, I look to his judicial position, which, as I say, was one of delicacy—delicacy which ought to be aided by judgments of Courts of law—and I find that it is conclusively established in my judgment that he did not act with sufficient firmness to enable him to decide questions according to his own opinion, those questions affecting the issue of certificates and the interim amounts thereof. Instead of doing so, my Lords, he accepted the instructions or orders of the owners and their solicitors upon that topic.

My Lords, I need go no further than Mr. Hobden's own letter of the 24th April, 1908, in which he says in these broad terms, speaking not to both the parties, but to one party to the contract: "Had you not better call and see my clients, because"—he then adds "in the face of their instructions to me I cannot issue a certificate, whatever be my own private opinion upon the matter." My Lords, that seems to me to be an open and a frank avowment that this judicial actor on this stage was not acting except under instructions and orders from one party in the cause. My Lords, that happened on the 24th April. I do not see any evidence in this case that Mr. Hobden's position was ever changed from one of external control to judicial independence, but, on the contrary, I find that so late as the month of August he swears in his evidence that he never issued his final certificate till the solicitors instructed him to do so. My Lords, in these circumstances I ask myself what was the situation of the parties when the 15th July was reached and this action was brought? The state of matters there can be summed up in three propositions: first, that the entire contract work was done; secondly, that the three months' period of maintenance after the doing of the contract work had expired, and thirdly, that a certificate was wrongly withheld on account of the submission of the arbitrator's judgment to the judgment of the proprietors, the latter preventing the issue of that document. In those circumstances, my Lords, the reasons given were improper, and it was on account of that control exercised over him by the appellants and their solicitors that the certificate was delayed. The grant of a certificate cannot, my Lords, in my judgment, be a condition precedent to a right to recover if the

1911
May 9.

House of
Lords.

architect's conduct and judgment are controlled as stated. That being so, I think the action was properly raised, and, having been raised, my Lords, the *litis contestatio* was entered into between these two parties, and it was too late for the architect whose conduct had brought about the raising of this action, to issue such a certificate as one party can found upon now, and in my judgment the Court of Appeal has adopted a correct course in sending this to an independent referee.

Order of the Court of Appeal affirmed, and appeal dismissed with costs.

Solicitors for plaintiff: Whitelock & Storr.
Solicitors for defendants: Greenwell, Higham & Co.

1911
July 7 and 8.

Court of
Appeal.

In the Court of Appeal.

(*Before* Vaughan Williams and Buckley, L.JJ.)

PETHICK BROTHERS *v.* THE METROPOLITAN WATER BOARD.

Summons to Stay—Arbitration Clause—Jurisdiction of Arbitrator to determine fact on existence of which his jurisdiction depends.

Where the right to go to arbitration depends upon the happening of an event, the arbitrator cannot adjudicate as to whether the event has happened or not.

This was an action brought by the plaintiffs, who were contractors, against the defendants for damages for having interfered with the plaintiffs in the performance of a contract made between the parties, and for wrongfully determining the said contract.

The defendants took out a summons to stay the action under sect. 4 of the Arbitration Act, 1889, and this was an appeal from the order of the judge in chambers staying the action.

The material clauses of the contract were as follows:—

34. If the contractor during the continuance of this contract shall become bankrupt, &c. . . . . (*here follow different events*) . . . . or shall not in the judgment of the engineer (and his judgment shall be final and conclusive), to be certified in writing to the Board or some committee thereof, have proceeded or be proceeding with the execution of the contract with such diligence as has ensured or will ensure the complete execution thereof within the time limited by clause 30 of this contract, or any extension thereof granted under that clause, then the Board may, by a notice in

writing under the hand of the clerk of the Board, given or sent through the post in a registered letter addressed to the contractor, or his legal personal representative, at the contractor's usual or last known place of abode or business, determine this contract. . . . . And all the powers of the engineer with respect to the determination of any doubts, disputes, and differences, and with respect to the settlement of the contract, and the determination of the sum or sums or balance of money to be paid to or received from the contractor, and otherwise in respect of this contract shall be and continue in force with respect to the same as though such contract had not been determined.

35. In case this contract shall be so determined as aforesaid, the Board may relet the undertaking of the contractor, or any part thereof, and under such conditions as the Board may think fit . . . . (*various powers here referred to*) . . . . and any doubts, disputes, or differences arising or happening with respect to the determination of the contract, or in consequence thereof, shall be settled and decided as herein prescribed with respect to any other doubts, disputes, or differences arising or happening under the contract.

50. Lastly, if at any time *before* completion of the works any question, dispute or difference shall arise between the Board, or the engineer on their behalf, and the contractor as to the construction of this contract, or as to any other matter or thing arising under or out of this contract, then such question, dispute or difference (unless it relate to matters and things which are under the terms of this contract left to the final decision, requisition, certificate or order of the engineer) shall be referred to the determination of the engineer, whose decision shall be abided by until the completion of the works, when such question, difference and dispute may, as hereinafter provided for, be referred to the decision of the arbitrator.

If on completion of the works there shall remain any question, difference or dispute upon any of the matters or things referred to or specified in the first part of this clause, or as to payments to be made to the contractor, the same shall be referred to the award and decision of some person to be mutually agreed upon, or, failing agreement, of some engineer to be appointed by the President for the time being of the Institution of Civil Engineers, whose decision shall be final and conclusive between the parties. The provisions of the Arbitration Act, 1889, shall apply to any arbitration under this clause.

The engineer certified under clause 34 that the contractors were not proceeding with such diligence as would ensure the complete execution of the contract within the time limited by clause 30, and the defendants gave notice in writing to the contractors determining the contract.

The substantial question between the parties was whether the action of the defendants in determining the contract, partly depending on the engineer's certificate and partly on the time when the notice was given, was justified or not. The contract had not been completed at the date of the issue of the summons to stay.

Clavell Salter, K.C., and A. A. Hudson for the plaintiffs: The question here is as to the certificate of the engineer. That certificate is, by the terms of clause 34, made final and conclusive, and is, therefore, expressly excluded from arbitration by clause 50. Further, the substantial dispute

1911
July 7 and 8.

Court of
Appeal.

being as to the conduct of the engineer, the Court will in the exercise of its discretion refuse to stay the action. The engineer cannot decide whether or not the determination is wrongful upon which the right to arbitration depends. As to the second part of the clause, completion has not taken place.

ELDON BANKES, K.C., and SHAW for the defendants: Under clause 35 any disputes with respect to the determination of the contract are to be decided as in the contract prescribed with respect to any other disputes or differences, *i.e.*, by arbitration.

BUCKLEY, L.J.: You do not get to a determination at all unless there is a certificate of the engineer; therefore the last words of clause 35 do not take effect unless there is a certificate of the engineer. This certificate is final and conclusive; therefore these words cannot refer to that.

Mr. ELDON BANKES: Under clause 34 I agree that it is said that the certificate is to be final and conclusive, but when we come to clause 35 there is a distinct provision that "any doubts, disputes, or differences arising or happening with respect to the determination of the contract" shall be settled and decided as in the contract provided as to other disputes.

BUCKLEY, L.J.: Those words take effect "in case the contract shall be determined as aforesaid." That is a condition precedent, but in that condition precedent is involved the certificate of the engineer.

Mr. ELDON BANKES: The contractor and the building owner have a dispute as to whether the contract was properly determined or not.

BUCKLEY, L.J.: I cannot understand how you can say that if the occurrence of an event is the hypothesis upon which an arbitration clause is to arise, the arbitration arises as to the occurrence of the event.

VAUGHAN WILLIAMS, L.J.: This is an appeal against the order of the learned judge, Mr. Justice Scrutton, staying the action in law, and in my opinion it must succeed. I will state as shortly as possible the grounds on which I come to this decision. I am of opinion, looking at this contract which I have in my hands, that there is no clause in it which sends the main question in this action to arbitration, and under those circumstances, if there is no arbitration clause which covers this cause of action, there is no right or jurisdiction to stay the action at law or to say that the jurisdiction of the court is ousted. In my opinion it is not.

1911
July 7 and 8.

Court of
Appeal.

That is the ground of my decision, but we have gone into a very long argument to see whether this particular subjectmatter is one of the subjectmatters referred to arbitration. I will call it the subjectmatter for short, as Mr. Bankes called it when he was giving the summary of section 35, when he said that section 35 covered the question whether the giving of the certificate was right or wrong, and I say that this action is brought to ascertain whether the giving of the certificate was right or wrong, and to get damages in case it was wrong.

In my judgment, when you look at section 35, you find that the giving of the certificate and the consequent determination of the contract is a condition precedent to the application of section 35. Section 35 uses these words: "Shall be settled and decided as herein prescribed." We have to find out how it is "herein prescribed," and when one looks at section 50 one sees how it is "herein prescribed." When one looks at the description there the words are: "Lastly, if at any time before completion of the works, any question, dispute or difference shall arise between the board or the engineer on their behalf, and the contractor as to the construction of this contract, or as to any matter or thing arising under or out of this contract, then such question, dispute or difference (unless it relate to matters and things which are under the terms of this contract left to the final decision, requisition, certificate or order of the engineer) shall be referred to the determination of the engineer, whose decision shall be abided by until the completion of the works, when such questions, differences and disputes may as hereinafter provided for be referred to the decision of the arbitrator."

It is agreed in this case, really, that at the time of the taking out of this summons and the hearing of the summons the works had not in fact or in law been completed, and under such circumstances it seems to me that the words in brackets exclude from arbitration the matters which are really sought to be dealt with in the action which has been stayed.

I do not know that there is any need for me to say any more in the matter. At all events, as to this part of the matter, I hesitated whether I should say it at all, because Lord Justice Buckley has expressed the same point in such vigorous logic during the course of the argument that I feel I can have added nothing to the point by my paraphrase of his argument, but I do wish to say further that if this matter was not as clear as it seems to me to be, I think, if the matter was doubtful, that it would be a fair question for a master or a judge or this court whether in the exercise of their

1911
July 7 and 8.
Court of
Appeal.

discretion the question raised by this summons might come before it. and that they could not say that they would stay the action. I think there are ample reasons, without falling back upon the exercise of the discretion. I only mention it because I think that the discretion might be exercised.

I think that this appeal must be allowed with costs here and below.

BUCKLEY, L.J.: Clause 50 consists of two parts; the first part is limited, in point of time, to any time before the completion of the works, and it is limited in respect of subjectmatter in that it excludes matters and things which are, under the terms of the contract, left to the "final decision, requisition, certificate or order of the engineer." The second part relates to another point of time, namely, on the completion of the works; that means, of course, on or after the completion of the works. Then there is a reference to someone, not the engineer. At the date when the summons was issued the works had not been completed, and I have, therefore, only to do with the first part of clause 50. I may say that my own impression is that the works at the date when the summons was issued had not been completed.

Now, that being clause 50, I will first consider the matter apart from clause 35, upon which Mr. Bankes has mainly relied. The relevant clauses for this purpose are 34 and 50. Inasmuch as the determination of the contract is by clause 34, that arises only, in the event which we have to do with here, if in the judgment of the engineer the contractors have not proceeded with due diligence, and inasmuch as clause 34 provides that the judgment of the engineer in that matter shall be final and conclusive, it is plain that that subject matter is excluded from the first paragraph of clause 50. So far, therefore, there is no arbitration clause relating to the matter, for this action is brought for damages for preventing the performance of and determining the contract to execute the works. So far, therefore, there would be no arbitration clause that is relevant to the matter, but Mr. Bankes says that clause 35 makes a difference. Now, the relevant words of clause 35 are these: "In case this contract shall be so determined as aforesaid . . . any doubts, disputes or differences arising or happening with respect to the determination of the contract, or in consequence thereof, shall be settled and decided as herein prescribed with respect to any other doubts, disputes or differences arising or happening under the contract."

This is a clause, therefore, which introduces a contractual right to arbitration in an event, and that event is "in case this contract

1911
July 7 and 8.

Court of
Appeal.

shall be so determined as aforesaid," and Mr. Bankes argues that the arbitration clause which follows, extends to the determination of whether or not the event has happened upon whose happening the arbitration clause is to come into existence. I confess that that is an argument which does not commend itself to my judgment. It seems to me that if you have an event defined upon which there is to be a right to arbitration, the arbitration cannot extend to ascertain whether the event has happened or not. However, he says that you ought to read the clause as if it were "in case this contract shall purport to be determined as aforesaid, then any dispute as to whether it has been determined or not shall be referred." It seems to me that then the same result would ensue. I think that that is not the true construction, but if it were, it seems to me that then the same result would ensue.

Then we have got this, that the question whether the contract has been properly determined or not, is to be settled and decided as "herein prescribed." Now, we find that what is "herein prescribed" is that only certain matters that might arise as to the determination of the contract shall go to arbitration, namely, matters to the exclusion of that which is left to the final decision of the engineer, and one of the matters, namely, as to whether the contractors have proceeded with the work with due diligence, is left to the final decision of the engineer. That leaves plenty for the clause to act upon, and, supposing that this decision is to be final in that respect, it might be contended that, notwithstanding that, the contract was not properly determined because consequent upon the engineer's certificate the Board had not taken the proper steps by giving notice within the proper time, or some such matter as that.

In this event, it seems to me, that even if Mr. Bankes' construction of clause 35 was right (and I think it is wrong), again there would be no arbitration clause addressed to the matter. The result of that is, that the plaintiffs are entitled to proceed by action, that the order to stay was, I think, wrong, and that the appeal must be allowed.

Solicitors for appellants: Law & Worsam, agents for Bond & Pearce, Plymouth.

Solicitor for respondents: Walter Moon, clerk to the respondents.

1912
May 1.

Court of
Appeal.

𝕴𝖓 𝖙𝖍𝖊 𝕶𝖎𝖓𝖌'𝖘 𝕭𝖊𝖓𝖈𝖍 𝕯𝖎𝖛𝖎𝖘𝖎𝖔𝖓.

(*Before* COLERIDGE, J.)

𝕴𝖓 𝖙𝖍𝖊 𝕮𝖔𝖚𝖗𝖙 𝖔𝖋 𝕬𝖕𝖕𝖊𝖆𝖑.

(*Before* VAUGHAN WILLIAMS, FLETCHER MOULTON and FARWELL, L.JJ.)

ASHWELL AND NESBIT, LTD. *v.* ALLEN & CO.

*Building Contract—Sub-Contract—Certificate of Architect—Power
to order Variations in Sub-Contract.*

Where, by the terms of a sub-contract, the sub-contractors are to be paid upon the certificates of the architect, and there is no power in the sub-contract to vary the work to be done by the sub-contractors, the only certificate that will entitle the sub-contractors to payment is a certificate relating to the work they have contracted to perform. If they vary the work on the architect's instructions no valid certificate for he final balance due under their contract can be given to them, although other work, equivalent in value to that specified in their contract, has been performed by them.

The defendants contracted with L. & A. to erect certain premises in Regent Street. The specification, which was part of this contract, provided for the supply of 180 radiators and 50 hydrants. This work was not intended to be done by the defendants, but both parties contemplated that it would form the subject of a sub-contract. A sub-contract was entered into in respect of it with the plaintiffs, and this sub-contract provided (*inter alia*) that the plaintiffs should be paid *upon the certificates of the architect.*

The plaintiffs varied the work upon the architect's instructions, and did other work equivalent in value to that contemplated by the sub-contract.

The architect issued a final certificate in respect of the work, but the defendants refused to pay, and the plaintiffs sued upon the certificate.

The defendants pleaded that the work under the contract had not been done, and that the certificate was bad as including work which had not been done, as the architect well knew, and as giving credit for work outside the contract between the parties for which he had no authority to certify.

On 28th November, 1911, Coleridge, J., decided that although the work contracted for had not been completely performed, work equivalent to it in value had been done, and that the certificate was fair under the circumstances and was binding. Judgment was accordingly entered for the plaintiffs. From this the defendants appealed.

For the plaintiffs there appeared Mr. J. B. Matthews.

For the defendants there appeared Mr. A. A. Hudson and Mr. Arnold Inman.

1912
May 1.

Court of
Appeal.

Mr. HUDSON: If your lordships please: this is an appeal from the judgment of Mr. Justice Coleridge, which was given upon a certificate in favour of a sub-contractor as against a contractor. I think the sole point for your lordships' decision is whether the certificate is valid or not.

The architect ordered the plaintiffs to omit some of the work contracted for and to do certain other work of an equivalent value. He said that he had a perfect right to give orders to Messrs. Ashwell & Nesbit without consulting us in any way, and to vary the contract which we had entered into with Messrs. Ashwell & Nesbit behind our backs, and without consulting us, and then, as he admitted to the learned judge, to certify as against us for variations.

The plaintiffs indicated that what their case would be, would be that certain radiators had been omitted, but that other work of a different nature had been added, or substituted to make up for the difference, and that therefore we ought to pay the amount certified, although the contract had been altered, and altered by him without our knowledge.

FLETCHER MOULTON, L.J.: The letter of the 17th May contains none of those powers.

Mr. HUDSON: My Lord, that is my point: it contains no such powers. Therefore I say that the certificate was bad. The architect said: "I have varied it because I have the right to vary it, and I act for my employers, Messrs. Lewis & Allenby." I say it is bad, because they never did perform their contract. They took orders from the architect which they had no right to take.

FLETCHER MOULTON, L.J.: It is common ground that the certificate was not good in respect of the work under the letter of the 17th May. Then that certificate has no effect at all.

VAUGHAN WILLIAMS, L.J.: It says: "I hereby certify the sum of 377l. is due from Messrs. Ashwell & Nesbit, the balance of their contract amount, for heating and hot water services. It purports to be all in respect of the contract amount.

Mr. HUDSON: Yes, it does, my Lord, but it, in fact, was not.

FLETCHER MOULTON, L.J.: Everything turns on the interpretation of the letter of the 17th May.

Mr. HUDSON: That is my submission. The only explanation given was that the architect had power, and had, in fact, substituted other work to make up an equivalent.

VAUGHAN WILLIAMS, L.J.: I propose to ask Mr. Matthews what he has to say.

1912
May 1.

Court of
Appeal.

Mr. J. B. MATTHEWS: My simple case was, it being admitted that there was no fraud and no collusion, that is out of the case. By the letter of the 17th May I was to do certain things enumerated in the specification to the satisfaction of the architect. I read my letter of the 17th May, and I put in the architect's certificate; and I am entitled to rely upon the certificate of the architect as final and conclusive upon it in the absence of fraud.

VAUGHAN WILLIAMS, L.J.: The certificate of the architect can only be given in respect of the contract work, and if there was something outside the contract which was not included you cannot take advantage of it.

Mr. J. B. MATTHEWS: My proposition was that in the absence of fraud or collusion the certificate of the architect under a contract in these terms is conclusive not only of the quality of the work, but as to whether the work contracted for had, in fact, been done. That was my case.

FLETCHER MOULTON, L.J.: Now if these certificates had to be given in respect of the work under the letter of the 17th May, and they were given in respect of something else, they clearly are not the certificates referred to in that letter of the 17th May. There is the certificate referred to in the letter of the 17th May, but the certificate in question is not that certificate: it is a certificate given in respect of other matters.

VAUGHAN WILLIAMS, L.J.: Out of the mouth of your own witnesses it was shown that the work which was certified for in this certificate was not work of the character at all, or done by the people who were contemplated by this contract of the 17th May.

Mr. J. B. MATTHEWS: I will tell your Lordship what the undisputed evidence was with regard to this matter. I was under obligation to put in 115 radiators. I put in 112 of the radiators of the contract size. I put in a double size, one to equalise two more, and for the odd 7*l.* worth I did some extra work which has to be treated as the equivalent of the missing radiator.

VAUGHAN WILLIAMS, L.J.: It simply was not work done under this contract.

Mr. J. B. MATTHEWS: My two propositions are that in the absence of fraud or collusion the certificate given in my favour was decisive not only as to the quality of the work, but that the work contracted for had, in fact, been done. That is the first and main proposition. Failing that, then I fall back upon this, which is my second pro-

1912
May 1.

Court of
Appeal.

position: Though true it is that the contract between Messrs. Allen & Co. and Messrs. Lewis & Allenby is not in terms incorporated into my contract, yet inasmuch as this was a sub-contract for the doing of a portion of that which was comprised in the larger contract, that the general authority conferred upon the architect to make variations in the larger contract must be treated as conferring upon him the authority to make variations in my sub-contract.

Nobody disputes that the variations were in fact made with the authority of Mr. Verity, and he boldly claimed that he had that authority, and he put it on the ground that under the main contract the architect has the widest possible powers to order any variations.

No witness was called on the part of the defendants to say that they did not know of these small variations, to challenge the fact that the architect had authority to order the small variations, and I say, therefore, that the position of things necessarily was that the architect was obliged to have, although not expressed in our contract, authority to direct, for instance, that the one larger radiator should take the place of two small ones. On one or other of those propositions I submit I must succeed.

This was a portion of the work governed by the general contract; that under the general contract the architect had undoubted authority as between Allen & Son and himself to order any sort of variations; that that authority must in fact have been subsisting with regard to this contract. Your Lordship sees I am not bound in any way to incorporate in terms in my sub-contract the terms of the general contract to the extent of the authority of an architect as agent for Allens.

FLETCHER MOULTON, L.J.: Yes, but under the May 17th letter you bound yourself to take payments on the certificates, and the certificate you produce was not in respect of that work. If you show that that certificate was given in respect of other matters it is no certificate at all. You chose to do by arrangement with other parties other work. The certificate given in respect of the other work is absolutely strange to this matter. Your rights are, and only are, under the May 17th letter, and even if Mr. Hudson's clients had abandoned the whole of their claim or sold it for 5*l*. it would not affect your rights. The only question is the certificate given in respect of the matter. Supposing you had had some works at Bow and some at Poplar, and the certificate ran in the same words, and you had a certificate which was conclusive because your Poplar work had to be paid, and it was proved that this certificate referred to work at Bow. Do you suppose that that could bind you?

1912
May 1.

Court of
Appeal.

Mr. J. B. MATTHEWS: No. If it was wholly different work, of course, that would be so.

FLETCHER MOULTON, L.J.: There is no distinction. The only point we have before us is whether the certificate is an estoppel under the May 17th letter.

Mr. J. B. MATTHEWS: I take it that there must be a new trial, because what happened was that there was an alternative claim on quantum.

FARWELL, L.J.: It is obvious there must be a new trial.

Solicitors for the plaintiffs: C. S. Oxenburgh & Son, for Tutin, Marshall & Co., Nottingham.

Solicitors for the defendants: Laytons.

1912
May 14.

Chancery
Division
(Ireland).

𝔍𝔫 𝔱𝔥𝔢 𝕳𝔦𝔤𝔥 𝕮𝔬𝔲𝔯𝔱 𝔬𝔣 𝔍𝔲𝔰𝔱𝔦𝔠𝔢 (𝔍𝔯𝔢𝔩𝔞𝔫𝔡) (𝕮𝔥𝔞𝔫𝔠𝔢𝔯𝔭 𝕯𝔦𝔳𝔦𝔰𝔦𝔬𝔫).

(*Before* RT. HON. R. E. MEREDITH, M.R.)

M'KEE AND M'NALLY v. MAYOR AND CORPORATION OF DUBLIN & O'SULLIVAN.

Building Contract—Arbitrator Prejudging—Injunction to Restrain Arbitration—Interest.

S. was the engineer under a contract between the plaintiffs and the defendant corporation for the construction of waterworks. The scheme proved unsatisfactory and variations were necessary. The plaintiffs refused to carry out the altered works as an "extra" to the original contract, at a valuation by S. They contended that S. had estimated the cost of the works at 7,000*l.*, and that they would cost three times as much as that, and that S. was precluded from acting as arbitrator by prejudging the case, or by reason of having made statements which rendered it impossible for him to decide the issue fairly, or by reason of the fact that his conduct was the real question in the case, and that he was the real defendant. Held, that he had done nothing to render himself unfit to judge between the parties. *Jackson* v. *Barry Rly. Co.*, [1893] 1 Ch. 238; *Eckersley* v. *Mersey Docks & Harbour Board*, [1894] 2 Q. B. 667; *Freeman & Sons* v. *Chester Rural District Council*, [1911] 1 K. B. 783, quoted and approved.

A contract was entered into between the Dublin Corporation and one Kinlan on 19th March, 1908, for the construction of waterworks in County Wicklow for a sum of 86,000*l.* odd. In April, 1909, Kinlan assigned his interest to the plaintiffs. The work included the construction of a dam or embankment about half a mile in length. The embankment as designed was to be stonefaced, and behind and underneath it was to run a puddle trench. This puddle trench was to be about five feet below rock level, but the foundation was found unsatisfactory, and the trench was made wider and sunk in places to as much as 36 feet below rock level. At one point there was to be a shoe of concrete for the purpose of affording a grip to the puddle. The contractors complained of great delay by reason of the non-supply of working plans for these changes, and that excessive pumping had been necessary.

In November, 1911, independent engineers inspected the works for the corporation, and reported that the original scheme was unworkable, and that the whole trench must be filled with concrete. O'Sullivan, the city engineer, and one of the defendants, estimated that this would cost 7,000*l.*, but the plaintiffs estimated the cost as likely to be 21,000*l.* The plaintiffs refused to execute the work as an extra to the contract to be paid for upon the engineer's valuation, but desired a fresh contract for it.

The corporation gave notice to refer the dispute to O'Sullivan as arbitrator under the contract.

The plaintiffs contended that O'Sullivan had rendered himself unfit to arbitrate, on the ground that he had prejudged the matter, and precluded himself by his statements from being able to decide the question fairly, and because his actions were in question and were the real issue between the parties, and they applied for an order restraining the defendants, pending the hearing of the action, from proceeding with or attempting to proceed with the arbitration. They also contended that O'Sullivan was not the arbitrator within the clause in the contract, which appears in the judgment.

Henry, K.O., M'Sweeney, K.C., and Patton appeared for the plaintiffs.

The Solicitor-General, Ronan, K.O., and White appeared for the corporation.

O'Connor, K.O., and M'Grath appeared for O'Sullivan.

Rt. Hon. R. E. MEREDITH, M.R.: My friend, Mr. M'Sweeney, at the conclusion of one of the ablest arguments I have ever heard at the Irish Bar, summarised the contention on which his clients rely. They contend, in the first place, that Mr. O'Sullivan is not an arbitrator within the meaning of the clause in the deed and the conditions under which this contract is being carried out; secondly, they say that Mr. O'Sullivan has precluded himself from acting as arbitrator by hopelessly prejudging the case; thirdly, that he has precluded himself, not perhaps by hopelessly prejudging the case, but by a series of statements which render it impossible for him to decide fairly and justly the issues arising for determination between himself and the Corporation of Dublin and the contractors; and fourthly, on the ground that he is the real defendant in the case, and that the question of his conduct in reference to the construction of the works and the orders given from time to time to the contractors is the real question to be determined in the case. I have, I think, fully and fairly stated the views embodied throughout the

1912
May 14.

Chancery
Division
(Ireland).

arguments, and expressed in the able summary of Mr. M'Sweeney, and I do not intend to shirk any one of these four questions.

As to the first, I wish to say at once that I have no hesitation whatever in deciding or determining that on the question of whether Mr. O'Sullivan is the arbitrator or not within the meaning of the arbitration clause in the deed, I am entirely and absolutely against Mr. M'Sweeney. Mr. Henry added the weight—and necessarily it was great weight—of his view to the argument of Mr. M'Sweeney; but in my opinion it is impossible to hold, on the construction of the contract, that the Borough Engineer for the time being, unless displaced by a definite order in writing by the Corporation, is not the "engineer" within the meaning of the contract. The terms of the interpretation clause are—"Engineer shall mean the Borough Engineer, Mr. Spencer Harty, or other the engineer for the time being, or from time to time duly authorised and appointed in writing by the Corporation to act as Engineer in the construction of the said works."

Let me now turn to the clause upon which further reliance is placed. "Clause 81—In case of disputes or differences arising touching the works or the construction of the contract, or measurements, or materials, or concerning any certificate, order, or award which may be made by the engineer, such disputes or differences shall be referred to and decided by the engineer, it being expressly understood that such decision of the engineer shall be final and without appeal." Read in connection with the interpretation clause, I can find no outlet, no escape from the decision that the Engineer, as defined, is to be the person selected by both parties to the contract who is to determine and decide all disputes and differences, either touching the works or "the construction of the contract, or measurements, or materials, or matters of any character whatever, or concerning any certificates, order, or award which may be made by the Engineer, ... it being expressly understood that such decision of the Engineer shall be final and without appeal."

There is, indeed, in this clause 81, what I may call a peroration. In no contract that has ever come before me, either at the Bar or on the Bench, have I ever found these words which are embodied in this clause, but they are essential terms of the contract, and I see no reason why any court should hold that, as between two parties standing on equal terms, they should not be competent to enter into such a provision as that contained in the words I am about to read— "Moreover, it shall not be competent to the contractor or the corporation, at law or in equity, to take exception to any hearing before

1912
May 14.

Chancery
Division
(Ireland).

or determination of the engineer in such disputes or differences." It is a strong clause. I do not think it has ever come before any of the courts who have had to consider these contracts from time to time, but it seems to me merely to emphasise and enforce what the law was prior to the entering into of this contract between the corporation and the predecessors in title of Messrs. M'Kee and M'Nally.

Personally I may have my own view—and I daresay I shall always be regarded as one having individual views in reference to matters somewhat similar to these matters—that it is almost impossible for any human being to separate and differentiate between his views expressed in the ordinary course of business as an engineer and his views as an arbitrator called upon to decide between his views as an engineer and the views of the contracting parties on either side. But perhaps I take too narrow and too pessimistic a view of human nature. And the law undoubtedly is laid down in clear and unmistakeable language, that a man may in his capacity of engineer, or representative of an employer, express views, direct works to be executed, nay more, may express the view that such works are within the conditions of the contract under which he is acting as engineer, and yet be wholly competent to decide as an arbitrator, unbiassed, free from all prejudice of any sort, whether his views as an engineer are to prevail as between his employers and the other parties.

Now, the foundation, as I understand it, of the law with reference to the unfitness of the arbitrator or the right of the court to grant an injunction in a case in which any injunction may be granted, is to be found in the case of *Jackson* v. *Barry Railway Co.* ([1893] 1 Ch. 238). The judgment of Lindley, L.J., in that case is, as Mr. M'Sweeney has so ably argued, one based upon the facts of the particular case. The question of fact before the mind of the learned judge was "whether Mr. Barry, who was then about to enter upon his duties as arbitrator, had not left his mind open, but had, before hearing the case, and before being advised by his legal assessor, so tied himself down by this letter (that is a particular letter referred to) as not to leave it reasonably open to him to depart from the view which he had previously taken and previously expressed." I can only characterise the words of this letter in the terms used by the Solicitor-General as being a stiff letter—I should say a very stiff letter indeed. But the learned Lord Justice goes on— "Unquestionably if I drew the same inference from this letter I should agree in the consequence, but I am unable to draw that inference. It appears to me, when you look at this letter carefully, that it well admits of this construction, that Mr. Barry merely repeats what he had

1912
May 14.

Chancery
Division
Ireland).

said scores of times before, that in his opinion the contract entitled the company to have stone without paying extra for it." Can any mortal mind conceive any stronger expression of opinion on the part of a person who is to be arbitrator than the declaration thus referred to, that in his opinion the contract entitled the company to have the stone without paying extra for it, followed up by a letter in which he reiterates that statement, which he made scores of times before? "I do not," says the Lord Justice, "understand this letter as expressing or implying or insinuating 'I have made up my mind, and whatever I may hear or my assessor may advise me, I shall stick to my opinion.' I think it would be a strained interpretation to come to that conclusion. Unless that is so, unless we can draw the inference that the engineer has precluded himself by this letter from keeping his mind open and from deciding according to the evidence and according to the advice which might be given him, we ought not, in my opinion, to stop this arbitration, and I say that the more readily because under the 19th section of the Arbitration Act, 1899, there is a method by which the contractor can, if he feels aggrieved, obtain the opinion of the court upon the true construction of the contract. Under that section, the engineer can, and if directed by the court he must, state a case for the opinion of the court upon any question of law arising in the course of the reference, and I would infer from this letter that Mr. Barry was not in the least reluctant to exercise that power, even without the direction of the court."

Well, that judgment of Lindley, L.J., has been commented upon as being somewhat weak. There is no weakness in the judgment of Bowen, L.J. I say this—and if I am wrong I can be corrected in a very short time elsewhere—that in my opinion the judgment pronounced by Bowen, L.J., in this case, has formed the real ground and material for all decisions in applications like the one now before the court, and that there has been no whittling away of that principal judgment, except in cases which amount to fraud, misconduct, or, as I may say, absolutely proved probability of the arbitrator going wrong. "It was," said Bowen, L.J., "an essential feature in the contract between the plaintiff and the Railway Company that a dispute such as that which has arisen between the plaintiff and the Company's engineer should be finally decided, not by a stranger or by a wholly unbiassed person, but by the Company's engineer himself. Technically, the controversy is one between the plaintiff and the Railway Company, but virtually the engineer, on such an occasion, must be the judge, so to speak, in his own quarrel." I call the attention of everyone who has to deal with this case hereafter,

1912
May 14.

Chancery
Division
(Ireland).

to these words of the learned Lord Justice, because, in my opinion, if the law is to be altered, it must be altered by the legislature, and not by the courts. "Virtually the engineer, on such an occasion, must be the judge, so to speak, in his own quarrel," and so it is, and the maxim, "No man can be judge in his own cause," can have no application, in its ordinary or man-in-the-street sense, to a case in which two parties, entering into a contract, knowing that the engineer of the employers on the one side is to be the dominant and governing mind in respect of the contract, is to direct and control the operations, elect and determine for themselves that in the last resort, in the absence of agreement, in the absence of compromise, that the same person whom Bowen, L.J., has declared to be "virtually . . . . the judge, so to speak, in his own quarrel," is to be the judge to decide whether he or the contractor was right or wrong. It may be that from a higher plane we might consider that that is not an entirely fair course, but so long as two parties, according to the law of England, enter into a contract with their eyes open, and with a knowledge of all that may result from the plain meaning of the English language before them, so long as they enter into that contract they must be bound by it. Bowen, L.J., continues—"Employers find it necessary in their own interests, it seems, to impose such terms on the contractors whose tenders they accept, and the contractors are willing, in order that their tenders should be accepted, to be bound by such terms. It is no part of our duty to approach such curiously-coloured contracts with a desire to upset them, or to emancipate the contractor from the burden of a stipulation which, however onerous, it was worth his while to agree to bear." Those who read that language will do well to bear in mind that the contractor is not only a willing contractor, but that he believes in his heart and soul that it is worth his while to bear his burden. Was there ever a case in which these words were more applicable than the present case? This is no case of an ordinary employer who might employ a casual engineer to decide between him and his contractor; it is the case of the great Corporation of the City of Dublin, who, according to my view of their contract, make their Borough Engineer their arbitrator. And could it be conceived that any contractors entering into a contract with the Corporation of the City of Dublin could for one moment doubt that their Borough Engineer would be a man who would be a man of honour, integrity, judgment, and discretion?

There is, of course, the alternative I have already pointed out in the opening of my judgment, that it would have been open to the

1912
May 14.

Chancery
Division
(Ireland).

Corporation to appoint some other engineer. I think that is the true construction of the contract, and if they thought that their Borough Engineer was not available for the purpose of this particular work, they might have appointed some other engineer.

But the result appears to me to be exactly the same. The position of the employers, the position of the Dublin Corporation, was such as, in my judgment, rendered it absolutely futile, absolutely absurd, that they would degrade their high offices and their high powers by appointing some person who would not be competent to fill the duties under the contract of engineer and arbitrator.

I have, perhaps unwisely, interpolated these words of my own between the words of the learned Lord Justice. But I resume—"To do so would be attempt to dictate to the commercial world the conditions under which it should carry on its business. To an adjudication in such a peculiar reference the engineer cannot be expected, nor was it intended, that he should come with a mind free from the human weakness of a preconceived opinion." And can any contractor in the world, under such a contract as this, come to me and tell me that it is possible for any human being to come to an arbitration free from that weakness? The whole point of this commercial contract and this morality rests upon the basis of the inward conscience and true sense of justice of honourable and highly-placed, men; and contractors, who are the most shrewd of business people, know well, and by entering into these contracts, in my opinion, show that they know well, that there is in human nature a depth of honourable feeling, of justice, and of right which can overcome the *primâ facie* preconceived opinion and the *primâ facie* weakness of a preconceived opinion. "The perfectly open judgment," the Lord Justice points out, "the absence of a previously formed or pronounced view, whcih in an ordinary arbitrator is natural and to be looked for, neither party to the contract proposed to exact from the arbitrator of their choice. They knew well that he possibly, or probably, must be committed to a prior view of his own, and that he might not be impartial in the ordinary sense of the word. What they relied on was his professional honour, his position, his intelligence; and the contractor had a right to demand that whatever views the engineer might have formed, he would be ready to listen to argument, and, at the last moment, to determine as fairly as he could, after all had been said and heard. And I say, having listened to the arguments, not one of them one sentence too long, having listened to the cases which have been cited on both sides, that that

1912
May 14.

Chancery
Division
(Ireland).

judgment of Bowen, L.J., holds the ground, and that no one has dissented from the views that he there laid down, and that they are as applicable to the contrÁct which is before me to-day as they were applicable to the contract with which he dealt in 1892.

I am asked to say that there have been cases in which the judgment of Bowen, L.J., has been commented upon; I am asked to say that there are cases in which his view has been held not applicable to special facts. I entirely agree. There are cases, and there will be cases, in which the principles that I have thus read and endeavoured in my own feeble language to illustrate, in which these views must be held not applicable, having regard to the special and particular facts of the case; but there is no case in which the wise words of the learned Lord Justice, having regard to the existing state of the law, have, in my opinion, been regarded with disapprobation or dissent. He goes on to say—"The one question in the present appeal is, whether the engineer of the company has done anything to unfit himself to act, or render himself incapable of acting, not as arbitrator without previously formed, or even strong views, but as an honest judge of this very special and exceptional kind." The word "but" is a word to which the strongest significance must be given in that sentence. In all the cases to which I have been referred, it seems to me that the same prevailing note is there, and that whether you take a case like that of *Eckersley* v. *Mersey Docks and Harbour Board* ([1894] 2 Q. B. D.), and refer to the judgment of Lord Esher, M.R., or any of the other cases that have been referred to, the predominant, vital vital principle in reference to these cases laid down by Bowen, L.J., holds good and inviolate. I will take one passage from the judgment of Lord Esher at page 671—"If it was not for the agreement of the pÁrties—if the rule applicable to judges were to be applied—it is obvious that it would be impossible to say that the engineer, under whose superintendence the work was to be done, could act as arbitrator, because some persons would suspect him of being biassed in favour of the parties whose servant he was[a] But that cannot be the case here, because both parties have agreed that the engineer, though he might be suspected, shall be arbitrator. A stronger case than that must therefore be shown; it must, in my opinion, be shown, if not that he would be biassed, that at least there is a possibility that he would be biassed. That seems to me distinctly to have been decided in *Jackson* v. *Barry Railway Company*. The case relied upon by the plaintiff is *Nuttall* v. *Mayor of Manchester* (8 Times L. R. 513). That decision has been discussed"—and I shall leave the case once and for all with the comment made by Lord

1912
May 14.

Chancery
Division
(Ireland).

Esher, to which I can add no words that would be of any weight whatever—"That decision has been discussed, and, as I understand, it may be explained on the grounds that there was an unseemly personal dispute raising a vindictive feeling between the engineer and contractor, and also that the engineer had expressed an opinion on the matter he had to decide so strongly as to amount to a prejudgment. If these were the grounds of the decision, the case is to be supported entirely; but it is not in point in the case before us, because the facts are quite different[a] If, however, the case decides that the mere fact that the arbitrator will have to decide upon his own conduct is sufficient of itself to satisfy the Court that there is a good reason why the matter should not be referred to him, I think we ought not to agree with it."

Let me now refer to *Freeman & Sons* v. *Chester Rural District Council* ([1911] 1 K. B. 783). The decision of the present esteemed Master of the Rolls in England is relied on, and properly relied on, with great force by Mr. M'Sweeney. I read from the decision of the Court of Appeal in England, and from the judgment of one of the most learned judges who ever sat on the Bench in that court. Buckley, L.J., says—"I so entirely agree with the robust good sense of Bowen, L.J.'s language in *Jackson* v. *Barry Railway Company*, that if this matter had been for my judgment alone. I should have been of opinion that this appeal ought not to be allowed, and an order made to stay proceedings. I cannot find Mr. Priest 'has done anything to unfit himself to act, or render himself incapable of acting, not as arbitrator without previously formed or even strong views, but as an honest judge of this very special and exceptional kind.=' " That was his view. "To succeed," he says, "the contractors must, in the language of Lindley, L.J., in *Ives and Barker* v. *Williams* ([1894] 2 Ch. 478), 'attack the character of the engineers to such an extent and in such a manner as to show that the engineers will probably be guilty of some misconduct in the matter of the arbitration, that they will not act fairly.' " In my humble judgment, the view of the learned Lord Justice in that case was that the words of Lindley, L.J., in *Ives and Barker* v. *Williams*, were synonymous with the words used by Bowen, L.J., in *Jackson* v. *Barry Railway Company*, and in that particular case the court held that the action ought to be stayed, for the reason that the Judge of the court below had in a matter of that description expressed his opinion, and that one of the judges of the Court of Appeal agreed with him. I do not think that is the practice, because if the mere ruling of a judge of first instance and one judge of the Court of Appeal agreeing with

1912
May 14.

Chancery
Division
(Ireland).

him is a reason for the two judges of the Court of Appeal agreeing with the court below, then certainly many cases in the Irish Courts have been wrongly decided.

What I rely on in that case is this, that so far as Buckley, L.J., could lend weight and authority to the decision of Bowen, L.J., he agreed with "the robust good sense" of the language used, and he decided that unless the contractors could, in the language of Lindley, L.J., "attack the character of the engineers to such extent and in such a manner as to show that the engineers will probably be guilty of some misconduct in the matter of the arbitration, that they will not act fairly," they could not succeed.

I have been pressed with cases under the arbitration clauses of the Common Law Procedure Acts. In my opinion all those cases decided under those Acts rest upon a different basis to actions like this. In those cases every judge has to consider for himself whether, under all the circumstances of the case, the action is one which ought to be referred to arbitration, and he is not bound, is not restricted in any way, by the settled law applicable to this species of contract, in which the plaintiff and the defendant have named their arbitrator, have agreed, knowing that he may have human feelings, human instincts, may prefer possibly his own view of matters to the view of another person, have nevertheless said, "We rely on the integrity and honour and sense of justice of the individual we have named (or not named) as a judge between ourselves (the contractors) and the employers; we rely on the sense of his integrity, honour, and justice as a judge, and to him we are willing to submit all the questions that may arise in reference to what comes within this contract, what prices should be paid in respect of the work done, and the hundred other similar matters that may arise during the course of the completion, of the works."

I now have, I think, the entire evidence before me—at least all the evidence that could be of any weight in enabling a judge to decide this question, all the evidence as to what happened between Mr. O'Sullivan and Messrs. M'Kee and M'Nally—and I say that the plaintiffs have wholly failed to establish in my mind that Mr. O'Sullivan, notwithstanding all that has passed, will not be a just judge, a competent arbitrator within the meaning of the terms of the contract, and within the meaning of the authorities. The furthest the plaintiffs can put it is, as Lord Esher says, "It must, in my opinion, be shown, if not that he would be biassed, that at least there is a probability that he would be biassed." That must be read in con-

1912
May 14.

Chancery
Division
(Ireland).

nection with and in conjunction with all the other authorities in the case. I am not going to repeat myself as to what Bowen, L.J., said. You must take him as the engineer in charge of the works; you must know that he has had experience in connection with the very matters on which he is to arbitrate; you know very well, as contractors entering into a contract of this description, that he will know more about it than anybody outside. But you must take him with all his faults; you bargained for him, and you have got to take him as he is. When Lord Esher uses the word "probability," and when the word "probability" is used in other cases, to my mind the word means much more than "possible." It means that the judge, having heard all that was to be said, and read all the letters and correspondence in the case, has come to the conclusion that the man is a man who would go wrong for his employers, and would not hold the scales of justice evenly between the parties.

In my opinion, from first to last, there is no evidence on which I could not say, as a judicial and impartial judge, that Mr. O'Sullivan had ever in this case shown anything except perhaps excessive zeal to have the works carried out according to his views—excessive in the sense that in the course of his duty to his employers he considered that it was a matter of great moment that the works should be carried out in the speediest manner possible. And he would not be worth his salt, in my opinion, if he had not shown that zeal in the discharge of his duties. But I shall be very much mistaken indeed if any court or judge would hold, from any letter from first to last, from any act from first to last of Mr. O'Sullivan, proved or to be inferred from his conduct throughout these proceedings since he succeeded Mr. Spencer Harty, that he is unwilling or unable to bring to bear upon the determination of the difficult questions that arise in this case an open and impartial and unbiassed mind. I am not going to shelter myself upon the suggestion that if I decided the other way I should cast a slur upon Mr. O'Sullivan which would be difficult to remove. If my mind was impressed with the view that he had written anything in his capacity as arbitrator, or in relation to his capacity as an arbitrator, that would render it possible or probable that he would decide in favour of himself as against the contention of Messrs. M'Kee and M'Nally, averse as I would be to damn the character of any man in his position, I should not hesitate to say it.

On all these grounds—perhaps not presented in the same precise form as if I had delayed my decision for a longer time—I hold that the application for an injunction to restrain Mr. O'Sullivan fails.

1912
May 14.

Chancery
Division
(Ireland).

I hold that I have power to deal with the writ as I find it. The writ claims that Mr. O'Sullivan "is not the person designated to act in the determination of disputes and differences between the plaintiffs and the defendants touching the contract between them, dated 19th March, 1908." I hold on the true construction of the document, that he absolutely is the person. I cannot conceive myself reversing myself on any further or better consideration of that point. I may be wrong, but I hold that he is the arbitrator.

On the second point raised against Mr. O'Sullivan, that he has precluded himself from acting as arbitrator by already prejudging the case, I hold that he has not.

On the third subsidiary point, I hold he has not precluded himself by a series of orders, of what I might term pinpricks, from dealing fairly with the matter.

I hold that he is not the real defendant in the arbitration, and that the question of his conduct is not the question to be tried.

I hold that he is the person whom the plaintiffs, or the persons through whom they derive title, with full knowledge of all the consequences, knew would be the person to decide, in certain events, upon the question whether the engineer's orders were followed or not, accepted him as the arbitrator and the judge, and that the decisions in the cases I have cited prevent the plaintiffs relying upon that ground.

As regards the questions proposed or suggested in the argument of the learned Solicitor-General, that in some way I am not competent to interfere with a case in which the question is whether a work is inside or outside the clause of arbitration, it seems to me wholly immaterial, from what I have said, that I should decide that point one way or the other. The Solicitor-General says I am bound, whether the matter is out of or within the contract, to let it go to arbitration, but I think Mr. Henry has clearly pointed out, and the writ appears to sustain him, that what the plaintiffs ask is that the matters in dispute under the contract should be determined by the court, and should not be referred to arbitration. I do not think that it is therefore necessary for me to give a considered judgment upon the question raised by that case of the *North London Railway* v. *Great Northern Railway* (11 Q. B. D. 30). It is a very large and difficult point. According to my present view I should be entirely in favour of the argument of the Solicitor-General and Mr. Ronan, but I must let the matter take its course.

1912
May 14.
───────
Chancery
Division
(Ireland).

What I have said seems to me to cover the whole ground, and therefore the order I shall make is, to refuse the application to restrain the arbitration, and reserve for the trial of the action the question of costs.

Solicitor for the plaintiffs: John Hoey.
Solicitor for the corporation: Ignatius J. Rice.
Solicitors for O'Sullivan: Messrs. J. J. O'Meara & Co.

───────────────